DISCOURSES:
CONVERSATIONS IN POSTMODERN ART AND CULTURE

In Memory of William Olander, 1950–1989

DISCOURSES:
CONVERSATIONS IN POSTMODERN ART AND CULTURE

EDITED BY
RUSSELL FERGUSON, WILLIAM OLANDER, MARCIA TUCKER,
AND **KAREN FISS**

FOREWORD BY
MARCIA TUCKER

A PHOTOGRAPHIC SKETCHBOOK BY
JOHN BALDESSARI

THE NEW MUSEUM OF CONTEMPORARY ART, NEW YORK
THE MIT PRESS, CAMBRIDGE, MASSACHUSETTS; LONDON, ENGLAND

THE NEW MUSEUM OF CONTEMPORARY ART, NEW YORK
DOCUMENTARY SOURCES IN CONTEMPORARY ART
SERIES EDITOR: MARCIA TUCKER

VOLUME 1.   **ART AFTER MODERNISM**: RETHINKING REPRESENTATION
             EDITED BY BRIAN WALLIS
VOLUME 2.   **BLASTED ALLEGORIES**:
             AN ANTHOLOGY OF WRITINGS BY CONTEMPORARY ARTISTS
             EDITED BY BRIAN WALLIS
VOLUME 3.   **DISCOURSES**: CONVERSATIONS IN POSTMODERN ART AND CULTURE
             EDITED BY RUSSELL FERGUSON, WILLIAM OLANDER, MARCIA TUCKER,
             AND KAREN FISS

THIS VOLUME IS MADE POSSIBLE THROUGH A GENEROUS GRANT FROM THE
HENRY LUCE FUND FOR SCHOLARSHIP IN AMERICAN ART.

PHOTOGRAPHS: *A SKETCHBOOK FOR TENTATIVE WORKS* BY **JOHN BALDESSARI**

DESIGNED BY **KIM SPURLOCK**, *ART & LANGUAGE*
PRODUCTION COORDINATION AND COPYEDITING BY **JACK BANKOWSKY**

PRINTED BY **HALLIDAY LITHOGRAPH CORP**., WEST HANOVER, MASS.
PRINTED AND BOUND IN THE UNITED STATES OF AMERICA

LIBRARY OF CONGRESS CATALOGING-IN-PUBLICATION DATA

DISCOURSES: CONVERSATIONS IN POSTMODERN ART AND CULTURE / EDITED BY RUSSELL FERGUSON... (ET AL.).
P. XXX CM.—(DOCUMENTARY SOURCES IN CONTEMPORARY ART: V. 3)
ISBN 0-262-06125-2 (HB), 0-262-56063-1 (PB)
1. POSTMODERNISM
2. ARTS AND SOCIETY.
3. POPULAR CULTURE.
I. FERGUSON, RUSSELL . II. SERIES.
NX456.5.P66D57   1990
700' .9' 048—DC20
90-5561 CIP

FIRST MIT PRESS PAPERBACK EDITION, 1992

Contents

FOREWORD
Marcia Tucker

"Discourses are perhaps best understood as practices that systematically form the objects of which they speak." [1] —Madan Sarup

This third volume in The New Museum of Contemporary Art's series, *Documentary Sources in Contemporary Art,* follows a first book of critical and theoretical essays from the 1980s and a second anthology of writings by a broad spectrum of contemporary artists. Here we have presented a heterogeneous collection of voices. The selections included range from a feminist theorist's internal dialogue with the criticisms of an anonymous reader of her book *Reading Lacan,* to a symposium of some half-dozen participants addressing the impact of homosexuality on questions of taste.

Our editorial team chose to focus on conversational modes—monologues, dialogues, interviews, panels, and symposia—because of the relative informality of these forms. Despite the complexity of some of the topics the speakers address, these conversations are frequently more accessible than is generally the case with theoretical texts.

The term "discourse," occasionally maligned as an unnecessarily esoteric form of the words "conversation," or "dialogue," is used here in Michel Foucault's sense as a "great surface"[2] of mediation rather than "an ideal, timeless form."[3]

> We must conceive discourse as a series of discontinuous segments whose tactical function is neither uniform nor stable. To be more precise, we must not imagine a world of discourse divided between accepted discourse and excluded discourse, or between the dominant discourse and the dominated one; but as a multiplicity of discursive elements that can come into play in various strategies...because of its inherent multiplicity, no discourse is all-encompassing nor finite, none ultimately "correct."[4]

The discussions are divided into five loosely-knit arenas of current critical concern. Because this series focuses primarily on theory and criticism in America (with occasional incursions into Western European practice), our scope is necessarily limited. Within these parameters, however, we have considered the heterogeneous nature of American culture, and tried to present a multiplicity of voices—those of different races, classes, genders, and sexual preferences. In many cases, a particular discussion might be appropriate to several different sections, creating multiple cross-references between the issues highlighted in separate chapters. This flexibility reflects the fluid nature of ideas and discussions in process, not fixed or finite agendas.

We chose not to limit the discussions presented in this volume to the visual arts, but to acknowledge that art and art issues are implicated in a broader spectrum of social concerns. In the same spirit, the term "art" is used in the broadest sense, to encompass its many forms, including those of film, photography, performance, music, writing, and architecture. Larger questions—of feminism, colonialism, history, representation, power, and control—are addressed in the understanding that works of art, and the artists who make them, do not exist in isolation from the world at large.

Our editorial team brought to this anthology a range of interests, experiences, and points of view. That we were able to agree on the texts included here is to some extent a measure of our homogeneity; the volume's contradictions and inconsistencies are equally a measure of our differences.

We would like to thank the many organizations and individuals who made this volume possible. First and foremost, our gratitude to the Henry Luce Fund for Scholarship in American Art, who supported the previous two volumes in the series. Without the generosity of the Luce Foundation, the Museum's horizons could not have expanded to include much-needed critical and theoretical publications. We are delighted to be able to work once again with MIT Press, and thank Roger Conover for his enthusiastic endorsement of the project.

We are especially grateful to Brian Wallis, whose early work on this volume contributed substantively to its present form; and to Jack Bankowsky, Production Coordinator and Copy Editor, who pulled the volume together and made it happen.

Our gratitude also to John Baldessari, for illustrating the book—or perhaps it would be more accurate to say "illuminating" it—with his own work and thus creating a visual "text" that parallels the discursive one. Kim Spurlock, our designer, used his considerable skill to bring together an enormous amount of material in a coherent fashion, for which we are most grateful.

Jennifer Montgomery, our proofreader, undertook a difficult job and performed it brilliantly. Tim Yohn provided invaluable last minute editorial assistance with the introductory material. Janice Woo compiled an index in record time, and Susan Rosenberg tracked down the publication permissions for a collection culled from unusually various sources.

Our thanks also to Angelika Festa and Clare Micuda for accurate and insightful transcriptions, to Gillane Seaborne for diligently retyping manuscript revisions, and to Ellen Holtzman, Sowon Kwon, Barbara Niblock, and The New Museum staff generally for their help with innumerable details of the project.

Finally, and most importantly, our thanks to the many contributors who have changed the ways in which we think about art and culture in the larger order of things.

1. Madan Sarup, *Post-Structuralism and Postmodernism* (Athens: University of Georgia Press, 1989), p.70.
2. Michel Foucault, *The Archaeology of Knowledge & The Discourse on Language* (New York: Harper Torchbooks, 1972), p.79.
3. *Ibid.*, p.117.
4. Michel Foucault, *The History of Sexuality, Vol. I: An Introduction* (New York: Vintage Books, 1980), p.100.

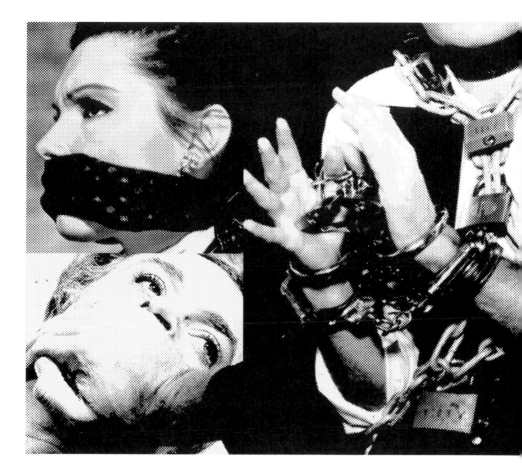

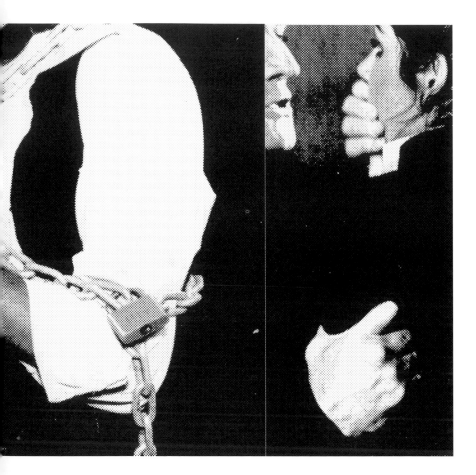

A BOX OF TOOLS: THEORY AND PRACTICE

Russell Ferguson

The role of any theory is to explain. But as recent critical debate has taught us, systems of discourse are themselves implicated in real social and political relationships of power. Explanations inevitably privilege one set of interests over others, and today few of those engaged in critical work would claim to speak from a neutral or objective place. Theoreticians now aspire less to the erection of alternative global systems and more to the questioning and challenging of existing patterns of cultural power. In the current climate, any smooth and unambiguous unity of theory is likely to arouse suspicion. The most insidious explanations are the ones which see no need to explain themselves.

In conversation with Gilles Deleuze, Michel Foucault emphasizes the functional relationship between systems of discourse and practical social activity. Foucault rejects the model of an intellectual sphere detached from the day-to-day exercise of power. For him, changes in consciousness are inseparable from the struggles of the powerless, and intellectual activity should take its place as part of such political struggles.

For Deleuze, theory and practice are linked pieces in a kaleidoscopic relationship of power and struggle. He does not consider practice as simply the expression of an existing theoretical approach, but neither does he see theory growing entirely out of practical experience. Theory and practice interact in a constantly shifting dynamic.

Key to the arguments put forward by Foucault and Deleuze is the awareness that any presumption to speak on behalf of others is itself a form of repression. By renouncing the traditional role of the intellectual as "spokesman" for the masses, a role which implicitly renders dumb those who are spoken for, they further problematize the relationship between theory and practice.

Film has been one of the primary sites of theoretical analysis, yet the filmmakers whose discussions are presented here almost all express ambivalence about the relationship of theory to their filmmaking practices. Analysis of the connections between discourse and power has led to a questioning of the concept of the avant-garde, which depends on a vision of the artist at the head of a common herd which must follow along behind. It is no longer self-evident that this is where an innovative artist should be positioned. The trademarks of avant-garde film—non-narrative structure, violent jump cuts, dislocation, the hand-held camera, etc.—have been, on the one hand, recuperated as the signifiers of "hip" advertising, and, on the other, marginalized as elitist and hopelessly self-referential.

Trinh T. Minh-ha, Laleen Jayamanne, and Leslie Thornton see their films in a different context. They choose to work from a self-consciously ambiguous position which resists any strict classification or definition. Theirs is a position which moves, often tentatively, between an uncertain center and margins which are themselves constantly redefined. Rather than claim vanguard status for their own directorial voices, they seek to make films in which many voices are heard, not necessarily in unison.

John Akomfrah makes a similar point: "Ultimately one needs to challenge the assumption that you can tell it like it is." *Handsworth Songs,* directed by Akomfrah, was attacked by Salman Rushdie[1] precisely on the grounds that it didn't "tell it like it is." Rushdie's challenge implies that Akomfrah's film should have countered the media presentation of the riots in Handsworth by presenting a completely separate, "authentic" version of these events. The notion, however, that one can simply replace an unsatisfactory popular image with the "real story" is rejected by Akomfrah. As he puts it in the film, "There are no stories in the riots, only the ghosts of other stories." Dominant images cannot simply be ignored, but they can be recontexualized and thrown into doubt.

The members of Black Audio Film Collective and Sankofa challenge what Martina Attille calls the "asexual, classless, raceless" voice of film theory by introducing all the specificities associated with sex, class, and race. As soon as these suppressed interests force their way into the picture, the neat, rigid theories begin to fall apart. No one in these conversations expresses any desire to draw up a new set. They don't want to tell anyone how it is.

Griselda Pollock, in her conversation with Laura Mulvey, Dee Dee Glass, and Judith Williamson, makes the important point that the feminist movement has produced a number of films which effectively call into question not just the language of film but the broader meanings of visual pleasure generally. The work of feminist filmmakers, artists, and writers has been vitally important in opening up alternative systems of identification and representation. Pollock, however, does not posit the feminist cinema as "merely oppositional, a negation" of established practice; rather, she argues for a practice which operates in the spaces between "mainstream" culture and the alternative viewpoints which exist, simultaneously, outside it and in its midst.

In her interview with Julia Kristeva, Alice Jardine begins by accepting that "there is no longer an independent place from which one can advance a practice of liberation in the classical sense of the term." Kristeva's comments, however, reveal a certain ambivalence on this score. On the one hand she argues that the "role of the intellectual is on the cutting edge." On the other, she claims that "I don't place myself in a contemporary perspective with regard to AIDS and Star Wars.... My work is a bit historic in that sense." Kristeva's remarks sum up the traditional position of the theoretician, simultaneously ahead of and outside the rest of society, yet she acknowledges that it is no longer very useful to offer any sweeping system of explanations. Ultimately she rejects the formulation of problematics in global terms as an archaic and totalizing approach to history.

The artists represented here have drawn extensively on critical theory in the development of their work. They recognize, however, that "theoretical" formulations that initially fulfilled a liberating function can harden into oppressive doctrine, which can inhibit the production of their work. They don't want to consult theoretical texts like instruction manuals, or rulebooks. Instead, as Deleuze puts it,

> A theory is exactly like a box of tools.... It must be useful.... It is strange that it was Proust, an author thought to be a pure intellectual, who said it so clearly: treat my book as a pair of glasses directed to the outside; if they don't suit you, find another pair.

While recognizing that recent critical theory has provided the tools to challenge totalizing systems of thought, these filmmakers also feel the need, quite consciously, to step back from theory for a moment in order to create an open space for their work into which images and stories can flow, and from which a critique can re-emerge. There is a sense in which theory itself can be treated as a narrative like any other—as a kind of story, or myth, from which they can draw as they need to.

There are many stories available, and the ghosts of many stories. Each of us can find the most useful tool for our purpose. As Foucault puts it, "All those on whom power is exercised to their detriment...can begin the struggle on their own terrain."

1.   Rushdie, "Songs doesn't know the score," *The Guardian* (January 12, 1987): 10.

INTELLECTUALS & POWER
Michel Foucault & Gilles Deleueze

MICHEL FOUCAULT: A Maoist once said to me: "I can easily understand Sartre's purpose in siding with us; I can understand his goals and his involvement in politics; I can partially understand your position, since you have always been concerned with the problem of confinement. But Deleuze is an enigma." I was shocked by this statement because your position has always seemed particularly clear to me.

GILLES DELEUZE: Possibly we're in the process of experiencing a new relationship between theory and practice. At one time, practice was considered an application of theory, a consequence; at other times, it had an opposite sense and it was thought to inspire theory, to be indispensable for the creation of future theoretical forms. In any event, their relationship was understood in terms of a process of totalization. For us, however, the question is seen in a different light. The relationships between theory and practice are far more partial and fragmentary. On one side, a theory is always local and related to a limited field, and it is applied in another sphere, more or less distant from it. The relationship which holds in the application of a theory is never one of resemblance. Moreover, from the moment a theory moves into its proper domain, it begins to encounter obstacles, walls, and blockages which require its relay by another type of discourse (it is through this other discourse that it eventually passes to a different domain). Practice is a set of relays from one theoretical point to another, and theory is a relay from one practice to another. No theory can develop without eventually encountering a wall, and practice is necessary for piercing this wall. For example, your work began in the theoretical analysis of the context of confinement, specifically with respect to the psychiatric asylum within a capitalist society in the nineteenth century. Then you became aware of the necessity for confined individuals to speak for themselves, to create a relay (it's possible, on the contrary, that your function was already that of a relay in relation to them); and this group is found in prisons—these individuals are imprisoned. It was on this basis that you organized the information group for prisons (G.I.P.),[1] the object being to create conditions that permit the prisoners themselves to speak. It would be absolutely false to say, as the Maoist implied, that in moving to this practice you were applying your theories. This was not an application; nor was it a project for initiating reforms or an enquiry in the traditional sense. The emphasis was altogether different: a system of relays within a larger sphere, within a multiplicity of parts that are both theoretical and practical. A theorizing intellectual, for us, is no longer a subject, a representing or representative consciousness. Those who act and struggle are no longer represented, either by a group or a union that appropriates the right to stand as their conscience. Who speaks and acts? It is always a multiplicity, even within the person who speaks and acts. All of us are "groupuscules."[2] Representation no longer exists; there's only action—theoretical action and practical action which serve as relays and form networks.

FOUCAULT: It seems to me that the political involvement of the intellectual was traditionally the product of two different aspects of his activity: his position as an intellectual in bourgeois society, in the system of capitalist production and within the ideology it produces or imposes (his exploitation, poverty, rejection, persecution, the accusations of subversive activity, immorality, etc.); and his proper discourse to the extent that it revealed a particular truth, that it disclosed political relationships where they were unsuspected. These two forms of politicization did not exclude each other, but, being of a different order, neither did they coincide. Some were classed as "outcasts" and others as "socialists." During moments of violent reaction on the part of the authorities, these two positions were readily fused: after 1848, after the Commune, after 1940. The intellectual was rejected and persecuted at the precise moment when the facts became incontrovertible, when it was forbidden to say that the emperor had no clothes. The intellectual spoke the truth to those who had yet to see it, in the name of those who were forbidden to speak the truth: he was conscience, consciousness, and eloquence.

In the most recent upheaval,[3] the intellectual discovered that the masses no longer need him to gain knowledge: they *know* perfectly well, without illusion; they know far better than he and they are certainly capable of expressing themselves. But there exists a system of power which blocks, prohibits, and invalidates this discourse and this knowledge, a power not only found in the manifest authority of censorship, but one that profoundly and subtly penetrates an entire societal network. Intellectuals are themselves agents of this system of power—the idea of their responsibility for "consciousness" and discourse forms part of the system. The intellectual's role is no longer to place himself "somewhat ahead and to the side" in order to express the stifled truth of the collectivity; rather, it is to struggle against the forms of power that transform him into its object and instrument in the sphere of "knowledge," "truth," "consciousness," and "discourse."[4]

In this sense theory does not express, translate, or serve to apply practice: it is practice. But it is local and regional, as you said, and not totalizing. This is a struggle against power, a struggle aimed at revealing and undermining power where it is most invisible and insidious. It is not to "awaken consciousness" that we struggle (the masses have been aware for some time that consciousness is a form of knowledge; and consciousness as the basis of subjectivity is a prerogative of the bourgeoisie), but to sap power, to take power; it is an activity conducted alongside those who struggle for power, and not their illumination from a safe distance. A "theory" is the regional system of this struggle.

DELEUZE: Precisely. A theory is exactly like a box of tools. It has nothing to do with the signifier. It must be useful. It must function. And not for itself. If no one uses it, beginning with the theoretician himself (who then ceases to be a theoretician), then the theory is worthless or the moment is inappropriate. We don't revise a theory, but construct new ones; we have no choice but to make others. It is strange that it was Proust, an author thought to be a pure intellectual, who said it so clearly: treat my book as a pair of glasses directed to the outside; if they don't suit you, find another pair; I leave it to you to find your own instrument, which is necessarily an instrument for combat. A theory does not totalize; it is an instrument for multiplication and it also multiplies itself. It is in the nature of power to totalize and it is your position, and one I fully agree with, that theory is by nature opposed to power. As soon as a theory is enmeshed in a particular point, we realize that it will never possess the slightest practical importance unless it can erupt in a totally different area. This is why the notion of reform is so stupid and hypocritical. Either reforms are designed by people who claim to be representative, who make a profession of speaking for others, and they lead to a division of power, to a distribution of this new power which is consequently increased by a double repression; or they arise from the complaints and demands of those concerned. This latter instance is no longer a reform but revolutionary action that questions (expressing the full force of its partiality) the totality of power and the hierarchy that maintains it. This is surely evident in prisons: the smallest and most insignificant of the prisoners' demands can puncture Pleven's pseudoreform.[5] If the protests of children were heard in kindergarten, if their questions were attended to, it would be enough to explode the entire educational system. There is no denying that our social system *is totally without tolerance;* this accounts for its extreme fragility in all its aspects and also its need for a global form of repression. In my opinion, you were the first—in your books and in the practical sphere—to teach us something absolutely fundamental: the indignity of speaking for others. We ridiculed representation and said it was finished, but we failed to draw the consequences of this "theoretical" conversion—to appreciate the theoretical fact that only those directly concerned can speak in a practical way on their own behalf.

FOUCAULT: And when the prisoners began to speak, they possessed an individual theory of prisons, the penal system, and justice. It is this form of discourse which ultimately matters, a discourse against power, the counter-discourse of prisoners and those we call delinquents—and not a theory *about* delinquency. The problem of prisons is local and marginal: not more than 100,000 people pass through prisons in a year. In France at present, between 300,000 and 400,000 have been to prison. Yet this marginal problem seems to disturb everyone. I was surprised that so many who had not been to prison could become interested in its problems, surprised that all those who had never heard the discourse of inmates could so easily understand them. How do we explain this? Isn't it because, in a general way, the penal system is the form in which power is most obviously seen as power? To place someone in prison, to confine him there, to deprive him of food and heat, to prevent him from leaving, from making love, etc.—this is certainly the most frenzied manifestation of power imaginable. The other day I was speaking to a woman who had been in prison and she was saying, "Imagine, that at the age of forty, I was punished one day with a meal of dry bread." What is striking about this story is not the childishness of the exercise of power but the cynicism with which power is exercised as power, in the most archaic, puerile, infantile manner. As children we learn what it means to be reduced to bread and water. Prison is the only place where power is manifested in its naked state, in its most excessive form, and where it is justified as moral force: "I am within my rights to punish you because you know that it is criminal to rob and kill." What is fascinating about prisons is that, for once, power doesn't hide or mask itself; it reveals itself as tyranny pursued into the tiniest details; it is cynical and at the same time pure and entirely "justified," because its practice can be totally formulated within the framework of morality. Its brutal tyranny consequently appears as the serene domination of Good over Evil, of order over disorder.

DELEUZE: Yes, and the reverse is equally true. Not only are prisoners treated like children, but children are treated like prisoners. Children are submitted to an infantilization which is alien to them. On this basis, it is undeniable that schools resemble prisons and that factories are its closest approximation. Look at the entrance to a Renault plant, or anywhere else for that matter: three tickets to get into the washroom during the day. You found an eighteenth-century text by Jeremy Bentham proposing prison reforms; in the name of this exalted reform, he establishes a circular system where the renovated prison serves as a model and where the individual passes imperceptibly from school to the factory, from the factory to prison, and vice versa. This is the essence of the reforming impulse, of reformed representation. On the contrary, when people begin to speak and act on their own behalf, they do not oppose their representation (even as its reversal) to another; they do not oppose a new representativity to this false representativity of power. For example, I remember your saying that there is no popular justice against justice; the reckoning takes place at another level.

FOUCAULT: I think that it is not simply the idea of better and more equitable forms of justice that underlies the people's hatred of the judicial system, of judges, courts, and prisons, but—aside from this and before anything else—the singular perception that power is always exercised at the expense of the people. The antijudicial struggle is a struggle against power and I don't think that it is a struggle against injustice, against the injustice of the judicial system, or a struggle for improving the efficiency of its institutions. It is particularly striking that in outbreaks of rioting and revolt or in seditious movements the judicial system has been as compelling a target as the financial structure, the army, and other forms of power. My hypothesis—but it is merely an hypothesis—is that popular courts, such as those found in the Revolution, were a means for the lower middle class, who were allied with the masses, to salvage and recapture the initiative in the struggle against the judicial system. To achieve this, they proposed a court system based on the possibility of equitable justice, where a judge might render a just verdict. The identifiable form of the court of law belongs to the bourgeois ideology of justice.

DELEUZE: On the basis of our actual situation, power emphatically develops a total or global vision. That is, all the current forms of repression (the racist repression of immigrant workers, repression in the factories, in the educational system, and the general repression of youth) are easily totalized from the point of view of power. We should not only seek the unity of these forms in the reaction to May '68, but more appropriately, in the concerted preparation and organization of the near future. French capitalism now relies on a "margin" of unemployment and has abandoned the liberal and paternal mask that promised full employment. In this perspective, we begin to see the unity of the forms of repression: restrictions on immigration, once it is acknowledged that the most difficult and thankless jobs go to immigrant workers—repression in the factories, because the French must reacquire the "taste" for increasingly harder work; the struggle against youth and the repression of the educational system, because police repression is more active when there is less need for young people in the work force. A wide range of professionals (teachers, psychiatrists, educators of all kinds, etc.) will be called upon to exercise functions that have traditionally belonged to the police. This is something you predicted long ago, and it was thought impossible at the time: the reinforcement of all the structures of confinement. Against this global policy of power, we initiate localized counter-responses, skirmishes, active and occasionally preventive defenses. We have no need to totalize that which is invariably totalized on the side of power; if we were to move in this direction, it would mean restoring the representative forms of centralism and a hierarchical structure. We must set up lateral affiliations and an entire system of networks and popular bases; and this is especially difficult. In any case, we no longer define reality as a continuation of politics in the traditional sense of competition and the distribution of power, through the so-called representative agencies of the Communist Party or the General Workers Union.[6] Reality is what actually happens in factories, in schools, in barracks, in prisons, in police stations. And this action carries a type of information which is altogether different from that found in newspapers (this explains the kind of information carried by the *Agence de Press Libération*).[7]

FOUCAULT: Isn't this difficulty of finding adequate forms of struggle a result of the fact that we continue to ignore the problem of power? After all, we had to wait until the nineteenth century before we began to understand the nature of exploitation, and to this day, we have yet to fully comprehend the nature of power. It may be that Marx and Freud cannot satisfy our desire for understanding this enigmatic thing which we call power, which is at once visible and invisible, present and hidden, ubiquitous. Theories of government and the traditional analyses of their mechanisms certainly don't exhaust the field where power is exercised and where it functions. The question of power remains a total enigma. Who exercises power? And in what sphere? We now know with reasonable certainty who exploits others, who receives the profits, which people are involved, and we know how these funds are reinvested. But as for power.... We know that it is not in the hands of those who govern. But, of course, the idea of the "ruling class" has never received an adequate formulation, and neither have other terms, such as "to dominate," "to rule," "to govern," etc. These notions are far too fluid and require analysis. We should also investigate the limits imposed on the exercise of power—the relays through which it operates and the extent of its influence on the often insignificant aspects of the hierarchy and the forms of control, surveillance, prohibition, and constraint. Everywhere that power exists, it is being exercised. No one, strictly speaking, has an official right to power; and yet it is always exerted in a particular direction, with some people on one side and some on the other. It is often difficult to say who holds power in a precise sense, but it is easy to see who lacks power. If the reading of your books (from *Nietzsche* to what I anticipate in *Capitalism and Schizophrenia*)[8] has been essential for me, it is because they seem to go very far in exploring this problem: under the ancient theme of meaning, of the signifier and the signified, etc., you have developed the question of power, of the inequality of powers and their struggles. Each struggle develops around a particular source of power (any of the countless, tiny sources—a small-time boss, the manager of "H.L.M.,"[9] a prison warden, a judge, a union representative, the editor-in-chief of a newspaper). And if pointing out these sources—denouncing and speaking out—is to be a part of the struggle, it is not because they were previously unknown. Rather, it is because to speak on this subject, to force the institutionalized networks of information to listen, to produce names, to point the finger of accusation, to find targets, is the first step in the reversal of power and the initiation of new struggles against existing forms of power. If the discourse of inmates or prison doctors constitutes a form of struggle, it is because they confiscate, at least temporarily, the power to speak on prison conditions—at present, the exclusive property of prison administrators and their cronies in reform groups. The discourse of struggle is not opposed to the unconscious, but to the secretive. It may not seem like much; but what if it turned out to be more than we expected? A whole series of misunderstandings relates to things that are "hidden," "repressed," and "unsaid"; and they permit the cheap "psychoanalysis" of the proper objects of struggle. It is perhaps more difficult to unearth a secret than the unconscious. The two themes frequently encountered in the recent past, that "writing gives rise to repressed elements" and that "writing is necessarily a subversive activity," seem to betray a number of operations that deserved to be severely denounced.

DELEUZE: With respect to the problem you posed: it is clear who exploits, who profits, and who governs, but power nevertheless remains something more diffuse. I would venture the following hypothesis: the thrust of Marxism was to define the problem essentially in terms of interests (power is held by a ruling class defined by its interests). The question immediately arises: how is it that people whose interests are not being served can strictly support the existing power structure by demanding a piece of the action? Perhaps, this is because in terms of *investments*, whether economic or unconscious, interest is not the final answer; there are investments of desire that function in a more profound and diffuse manner than our interests dictate. But of course, we never desire against our interests, because interest always follows and finds itself where desire has placed it. We cannot shut out the scream of Reich: the masses were not deceived; at a particular time, they actually wanted a fascist regime! There are investments of desire that mold and distribute power, that make it the property of the policeman as much as of the prime minister; in this context, there is no qualitative difference between the power wielded by the policeman and the prime minister. The nature of these investments of desire in a social group explains why political parties or unions, which might have or should have revolutionary investments in the name of class interests, are so often reform oriented or absolutely reactionary on the level of desire.

FOUCAULT: As you say, the relationships between desire, power, and interest are more complex than we ordinarily think, and it is not necessarily those who exercise power who have an interest in its execution; nor is it always possible for those with vested interests to exercise power. Moreover, the desire for power establishes a singular relationship between power and interest. It may happen that the masses, during fascist periods, desire that certain people assume power, people with whom they are unable to identify since these individuals exert power against the masses and at their expense, to the extreme of their death, their sacrifice, their massacre. Nevertheless, they desire this particular power; they want it to be exercised. This play of desire, power, and interest has received very little attention. It was a long time before we began to understand exploitation; and desire has had and continues to have a long history. It is possible that the struggles now taking place and the local, regional, and discontinuous theories that derive from these struggles and that are indisociable from them stand at the threshold of our discovery of the manner in which power is exercised.

DELEUZE: In this context, I must return to the question: the present revolutionary movement has created multiple centers, and not as the result of weakness or insufficiency, since a certain kind of totalization pertains to power and the forces of reaction. (Vietnam, for instance, is an impressive example of localized counter-tactics.) But how are we to define the networks, the transversal links between these active and discontinuous points, from one country to another or within a single country?

FOUCAULT: The question of geographical discontinuity which you raise might mean the following: as soon as we struggle against exploitation, the proletariat not only leads the struggle but also defines its targets, its methods, and the places and instruments for confrontation; and to ally oneself with the proletariat is to accept its positions, its ideology, and its motives for combat. This means total identification. But if the fight is directed against power, then all those on whom power is exercised to their detriment, all who find it intolerable, can begin the struggle on their own terrain and on the basis of their proper activity (or passivity). In engaging in a struggle that concerns their own interests, whose objectives they clearly understand and whose methods only they can determine, they enter into a revolutionary process. They naturally enter as allies of the proletariat, because power is exercised the way it is in order to maintain capitalist exploitation. They genuinely serve the cause of the proletariat by fighting in those places where they find themselves oppressed. Women, prisoners, conscripted soldiers, hospital patients, and homosexuals have now begun a specific struggle against the particularized power, the constraints and controls, that are exerted over them. Such struggles are actually involved in the revolutionary movement to the degree that they are radical, uncompromising and nonreformist, and refuse any attempt at arriving at a new disposition of the same power with, at best, a change of masters. And these movements are linked to the revolutionary movement of the proletariat to the extent that they fight against the controls and constraints which serve the same system of power.

In this sense, the overall picture presented by the struggle is certainly not that of the totalization you mentioned earlier, this theoretical totalization under the guise of "truth." The generality of the struggle specifically derives from the system of power itself, from all the forms in which power is exercised and applied.

DELEUZE: And which we are unable to approach in any of its applications without revealing its diffuse character, so that we are necessarily led—on the basis of the most insignificant demand—to the desire to blow it up completely. Every revolutionary attack or defense, however partial, is linked in this way to the workers' struggle.

—March 4, 1972

1. "Groupe d'information de prisons": Foucault's publications *I*, *Pierre Rivière* and *Discipline and Punish* result from this association.
2. Cf. *Theatrum Philosophicum*, p. 185.
3. May 1968, popularly known as the "events of May."
4. Cf. *The Order of Things*, pp. 47-53.
5. René Pleven was the prime minister of France in the early 1950s.
6. *"Confédération Générale de Travailleurs."*
7. Liberation News Agency.
8. *Nietzsche and Philosophy* (N.Y.: Columbia University Press, 1983) and *Anti-Oedipus*, in collaboration with Félix Guattari (Minneapolis: University of Minnesota Press, 1983).
9. *"Habitations à loyer modéré"*: moderate rental housing.

ORIGINALLY PUBLISHED IN *L'ARC*, NO. 49. REPRINTED FROM MICHEL FOUCAULT, *LANGUAGE, COUNTER-MEMORY, PRACTICE: SELECTED ESSAYS AND INTERVIEWS*, EDITED BY DONALD F. BOUCHARD, TRANSLATED BY DONALD F. BOUCHARD AND SHERRY SIMON (ITHACA: CORNELL UNIVERSITY PRESS, 1977), PP. 205-217.

Sankofa Film/Video Collective and Black Audio Film Collective are the most celebrated and controversial Black media groups to emerge from the British workshop movement of the 1980s. They are members of the first generation to experience and reflect on the dilemma, a state of dual consciousness, of being Black and British, of identifying with a culture in diaspora, while at the same time participating in the transformation of British national identity. Their first major works—Sankofa's *Passion of Remembrance* and Black Audio's *Handsworth Songs*—set off polemical debates in Britain's mainstream and Black press, as well as in film theory circles, on the legitimacy and viability of formal experimentation in Black cinema. The contributions of these collectives have brought the analysis of postcolonial discourse and institutionalized racism to bear on British film culture. Formulating an implicit critique of the cultural nationalist tendencies in Black activism, and of that nationalism's alliance with realist documentary traditions, Sankofa and Black Audio have sought to reframe the terms of Black cultural politics in Britain in order to explore how radical politics and aesthetics might converge in the present.

SANKOFA: MARTINA ATTILLE & ISAAC JULIEN

COCO FUSCO: What was happening in the independent film sector when you formed as a group? What made you come together to form a workshop?

ISAAC JULIEN: We wanted to challenge the fairly Eurocentric positions of white independents making films about Black people. In 1984 we organized a discussion series called "Power and Control." One of the issues in the series concerned the power to appropriate. What was being asked at the time, and what continues to be asked, is whether Third Cinema[1] can be produced by white filmmakers. The kind of questions that we tried to propose had to do with power, i.e., Black people's relationship to the media technology and where they were placed in it.

FUSCO: What was different about your situation, comparing it to that of the first generation of Black filmmakers in Britain?

JULIEN: There's a gap between the first Black films that were made in the 1960s by Lionel Ngakane and Lloyd Reckord[2] and our work. There had not been a full development of Black film culture until the development of the workshops. Other filmmakers appeared, such as Menelik Shabazz and Horace Ove, but they were working as individuals. There was no Black film organization making institutional demands. It was precisely because we went to university, and because of the 1981 riots, that we could then pull together and make an intervention into the media. The Workshop Declaration was designed without our participation but we saw it as a very important space where we could develop several things at once.

MARTINA ATTILLE: The programs of study we chose at university were critical of cultural forms and their production. When we began to work as filmmakers we were compelled not only to make films but also to make an intervention into film theory and critique it. We did not only want to address mass communications but also education—everything that threatens to take away the autonomy that we have to define ourselves. For Black people there are very few spaces where you can actually define your own activity and define and control the quality of your life.

Film became available to us because Channel 4 came on the scene. That was a moment in which we had an entry point into media. There have been other Black people in television, but they were on the periphery, working on short term contracts, trying to negotiate membership into the union. The workshop movement offered a certain amount of security just to develop ideas, to make interventions that were broader than just television or just cinema or individual programs. The workshops were built around the idea of continuity of work. That's what we wanted.

FUSCO: What prompted you to make *Territories* (1985) at the time that you did and in the way that you did?

JULIEN: In retrospect, I was tired of the realist debate, the populism versus modernism debate, which was focused on fairly conventional documentaries. In looking at several of those documentaries in the very limited Black film history that existed in Britain at that time I noted that there were several films about carnival, because it was the biggest event. At the same moment I was reading "The Other Question" by Homi Bhabha which appeared in *Screen³* in 1983. In a way, those two things synthesized. I saw many films about Blacks made by Black and white filmmakers which didn't really grapple with the question of exotica in that representation. There wasn't a politics of representation in those documentaries.

Territories was a film about the politics of representation which included the Black subject. Within the arena that included the Black subject carnival was a very pivotal point. (I wasn't familiar with the writing of Mikhail Bakhtin⁴ at the time, but in retrospect I can see the way they are directly related.) Carnival was the space where, for a day, disorder was allowed. That is what is so interesting about carnival: there were so many different eruptions around sexuality, around smoking "ganja," around the way that area was policed. Those different tensions were all placed in that space.

FUSCO: What were the cultural questions that were relevant for you to deal with in *Territories?*

JULIEN: Questions of the diaspora, questions of policing. The significance of the sound systems in the carnival. In other words, what does Blackness mean to a Black culture? That was the main question. What does it mean for us? There are many films about racism and anti-racism, but what do these signs mean for us? In the second part of the film there are montages of the two Black men dancing with each other, which you see a lot in carnival, but you wouldn't necessarily interpret it as something that would be called a homosexual relationship. I wanted to explore those questions, anchor the debates in that space, in a Black space. I can look back on it now and I can see how I was trying to break with the realist debate and do something else. I can see now how the format I chose also had its limitations, but it was important for me at the time to try to do something like that. I saw *Territories* as a film essay around civil disorder and semiological questions for Black people.

FUSCO: Do any of those issues carry over to *Passion of Remembrance* (1986)?

ATTILLE: *Passion of Remembrance* started as a project called "Systems of Control." The reality of the way Black communities are policed is still very much a part of our experience and it is part of our concern. When we started doing the research, however, we looked away from the traditional areas—such as metropolitan policing—focusing instead on the ways in which policing takes on more intimate forms within our communities and relationships.

FUSCO: Why was policing an issue?

ATTILLE: Because control is an issue. If you're engaged with a medium like film, you're trying to communicate ideas to people. And those ideas inevitably come from your experience of the world. We as filmmakers had control over the images we created. But there was a sense of accountability imposed on us by our community to produce certain types of images. In a way we anticipated that. We had had screenings and discussions called "Power and Control," and we heard audiences ask for positive images. There needed then to be a critique around what positive images were.

JULIEN: At the same time we were sick of seeing images of Black people involved in civil disorder, because of the riots.

ATTILLE: The cliché of Black person as victim of police brutality was a quite sensational way of looking at Black experience. I think there are many more subtleties to it than that.
      With *Passion* we took things to point zero: the family, the man, and the woman.

Those were metaphors we used to talk about our experience in Britain at the time. We quite deliberately chose to look at the intimacies of our relationships to each other. And we also wanted to open up certain ways—we're not only talking about Black people, we're talking about British society as well. When you set up a company like Sankofa it is important to have a profile, to gather interest in your work. So we chose to work on a feature length fiction, rather than documentary, in part as an attempt to expand our potential audience. Working within that medium we wanted to create a narrative rich in imagery. Some people say it was quite literary.

JULIEN: Or eclectic.

ATTILLE: We quite deliberately used two geographic spaces. One is the urban landscape, the cityscape with the Baptiste family placed in it. Maggie Baptiste is looking at England. She's looking at archive footage, looking to history for some sense of what has gone on before and what's going to come in the future. She's looking at English streets cast with long shadows of previous struggles and protest. At the same time she and her friends look for release of the tension on those same streets, in the cheap glitter of their clothes and the cheap glitter of the West End. The urban landscape, that claustrophobic landscape, that was our experience. There is no time to sit down and explain to people how you're feeling or what's going on in your mind, or that you're worried about the future. It's jobs or no jobs. You dance, kiss, and run.

With the open landscape, on the other hand, we wanted to evoke a dreamscape. A place of deliverance, of redemption. A place where there's nothing to get in the way of intimate contact. The man and the woman in the landscape don't touch each other because there is so much between them that hasn't been resolved. There is so much bitterness and frustration. They can't even come close to each other in the end, and instead look away from each other.

FUSCO: What were the most important agendas?

ATTILLE: The legacy of the sixties is important. The Black movement has a particular style which historically has been male-dominated. As the woman in the landscape says, you can't hide behind the fist forever. Although the fist was a crucially important rallying symbol we must look behind the sign to see what it stands for.

JULIEN: It has to stand for much more now. Its agenda has to broaden. Other men have found the Black fist to be something that doesn't include them. Nor did the symbol originally include questions of sexuality and gender. Those questions informed *Passion* to a great extent. Many Black male directors continue to make films about policing and racism because those are the areas in which they feel most directly affected.

ATTILLE: We're not just making films to entertain, to get people to relax. We're trying to make some intervention, or take up and respond to our environment. If we sit down as three Black women and a Black man, whose parents come from the West Indies, or whatever, we do so with certain cultural and political positions and priorities. *Passion* is a fiction film but it is very much a document of the time we came together as four young Black people. It embodied that coming together as a relatively young media organization on the media scene. The media scene here is extremely competitive—not just among Black people, but as a whole. So *Passion* represents all the tensions of those things. The man and the woman in the landscape could easily be the old guard versus the new guard; the static old guard man, and the young, volatile woman with a new sense of politics, full of resentment and frustration. *Passion* comes out of a time when there didn't seem to be that much dialogue between different sections of our community. The leaders weren't as obvious as they had been in the past and *Passion* was suggesting that it was about time that we talked.

JULIEN: I don't think *Passion* was only about the politics of us coming together though. It was also about what had come before. Extensive research was done on Black political organizations in the sixties and the seventies. We did an enormous amount of research on policing. Altogether this work informed the characters. They were archetypes.

FUSCO: Can we discuss the way in which the legacy of Black American radicalism from the sixties and seventies informed the film. What is your relationship to this? Why turn to it, as opposed to, let's say, African nationalist revolutionary texts from the fifties and sixties? Obviously, we're not talking about a film history informing your films, we're talking about a political history and a written history informing your films.

JULIEN: There was a Black Power movement in Britain that borrowed many of its signs and symbols from America. We do borrow from other cultures within the diaspora, but we are specifically talking about a Black British experience—and we have to be very careful not to substitute an American experience for a Black British experience.

ATTILLE: The similarities between the American and British experience are in the politics of the diaspora really. It's not like an African nationalism directed back to the homeland, back to the source. We wanted to follow the journey back in stages. The experience of migration, of coming to England, and of people being taken to America—of having to assert your identity within a foreign environment—was quite important. In some parts of Africa we're still talking about colonial relationships, about the involvement of outside forces occupying those territories. People have migrated here following the resources, following their own resources. And then they have to assert their right to be part of society in the same way that Black Americans had to do. There are differences between our and their experiences, different experiences within the economy—slavery in that country—whereas the West Indian experience was one of colonialism and coming over here—leaving, to some extent voluntarily, though in reality people didn't always have the choice.

JULIEN: In relation to your question of borrowing or talking about influences from the Black American experience—in borrowing those things, we were also prioritizing issues such as British national identity. We did not naïvely try to transplant a Black American experience onto the Black British experience. It was very important to us to talk about our experience in the diaspora, and the specificity of that Black experience.

We always thought that *Passion* would be very interesting for American audiences. Not very many people had recognized Britain as being either Black, or mixed-race, or Asian. They didn't recognize all those other identities in Britishness.

ATTILLE: In the male speaker there's the popular rhetoric of that movement that echoed out into other territories. But at the same time there's the character Maggie who is our vehicle for looking specifically at England. Our eye through the Baptiste family is very firmly on the British experience. Whereas the landscape represents a more international concern, something that is transatlantic, something more universal.

FUSCO: We've talked about philosophical, theoretical and literary influences. What about visual? Much of the criticism concerning your work claims that the arguments are Black and the film style is Euro-American, i.e. white avant-garde. I don't believe that that is really the issue, nor is it the way that your approach need be characterized. What are the dynamics that you seek to evoke on a visual plane?

JULIEN: The white avant-garde can't help but try to seize upon *Passion* and claim it as borrowing from The Grammar, from their film grammars. I've never seen, for example, *Riddles of the Sphinx*.[5] I've never seen many of these films. As much as I like Laura Mulvey and her essay "Visual Pleasure and Narrative Cinema,"[6] which is very important, her pleasure is not the same as the kind of pleasure that we're talking about and articulating. There's a difference. And I think that in a sense, when you talk about the avant-garde as it were, it's very easy to try to compare the way *Passion* is made with white avant-garde filmmakers. That's not to say there aren't influences.

There are some avant-garde filmmakers, such as Ken McMullen and Sally Potter, whose work I am interested in. But if I were going to cite direct influences, I would look to Haile Gerima and Charles Burnett.

ATTILLE: And Med Hondo's work.

JULIEN: There is still to be developed a vocabulary of Black film criticism that can start to talk about our work.

FUSCO: Some Black cultural critics have argued that "authentic" Black cultural tradition is found in preaching and other oral, performative discourses. In thinking about culture and colonization, it has historically been the case that visual culture is the first to be dominated, and is extremely difficult to develop as a sphere of resistance. How do you relate these issues to your own situation as, in a sense, visual artists?

JULIEN: *Territories* was an attempt to deal with the question of what Black representation means for Black people. That was its first question. As far as I'm concerned the avant-garde is dead. *Territories* and *Passion of Remembrance* are not about the things that were going on in the white avant-garde. We're not interested in just breaking rules and conventions. Which is not to say that there isn't a cultural and political world that informs the white avant-garde of the seventies, because there is. But I think that it's too easy to reduce cultural endeavor to a formal exercise.

FUSCO: How do you respond to the argument that these issues were hashed out in the seventies, because in a sense, sexism, racism, and colonialism are the same problematic being recast over and over again on different terms?

ATTILLE: Each of these moments—the prioritizing of race, of sexuality, etc. has almost been like an academic exercise, an intellectual exercise in which we explore in more depth what the crisis in each of those areas is. But I don't think that it really happens like that in real life. One's experiences of these states is more relational, shifting in relation to who you are talking to, where you're standing, what country you're in. The frustration I feel with the way our work is put into established categories is that although we were educated with those theories, we also resisted them. We had no choice but to resist because there wasn't really a place for us. We hadn't actually shaped that theory. We had to study Eurocentric traditions in our own absence. One of the reasons that Sankofa formed was to explore the gaps in the theory and also the gaps in the visual representation. We as Black media producers have self-conscious political priorities which we bring to that. Our work isn't just informed by established traditions that existed before us. We also sought to transform the established theories. The work that is being produced by groups like Sankofa is a few steps ahead of the language of critique that could actually make sense of the work.

FUSCO: Could you say more about the problem of a lag in critical language?

ATTILLE: A workshop movement develops in England, and then an established white film critic can say something to the effect that Black groups came along on the tail end of that movement. Now, we came into the movement knowing what the inadequacies were, realizing the ways in which Black film was marginalized. Nonetheless, the workshops offered the chance to have some autonomy over what we created. In addition to this, there were certain experiences—certain histories that hadn't really been talked about in the British context which we could begin to talk about.

In forming as Black groups, we identified our specificity in terms of race and other issues of interest such as gender and sexuality. On the other hand, in terms of critics and film theory—the voice of authority—the subjectivity of the voice is never clearly identified. It's asexual, classless, raceless. Until you can get to the point where the theory can identify its own cultural and political priorities then it's going to be out of step with the work, which is very self-conscious, very specific about what it's trying to do.

JULIEN: The Black cultural theories that are being developed at this particular moment are largely limited to the historical traditions which Black people have been participating in and developing and shaping. These traditions have influenced the twentieth century to such an extent that one has to talk about vernacular culture and the relationship between those cultural practices and the Black intellectual.

On the other hand, when we talk about the visual we must address the psychoanalytic, which also has its limitations. It's only very recently that any work has begun which tries to look at Frantz Fanon's writings and derive a theory of Black representation, and which confronts the pleasure of the visual. Psychoanalytic discourse has been the most successful intervention in developing a critique of the visual dimension of cinema in its attention to fantasy and memory, to spectatorship, gender and sexuality. What we are now developing is a discourse about the Black subject and the visual plane.

ATTILLE: Once we had the responsibility of Black representation or Black images, we found out that there's no space for fiction allowed. Even if you say that you're making a fiction film, people still want to know who those characters are. They want them to add some sort of credibility to their own lives. There still exists a desire for identification among Black audiences. As a filmmaker you try to create a fiction in which there is enough distance for you to read what the film is saying as a whole. Still, the grip of realism remains very tight in terms of a Black audience.

JULIEN: One of the phenomena you can trace in the diaspora is that Black subjects are never really in the visual plane. We want to explore what happens to Black subjectivity when it sees white images. We know that forty percent of American film audiences are Black, and they see many kinds of films. There don't have to be Black images all the time, but then we know from the psychoanalytical work done on Black subjectivity that in our psyches there is a massive dilemma taking place. It affects you in every moment as a Black person. You don't see yourself.

ATTILLE: You think you're white.

JULIEN: How do you start to grapple with these sorts of questions? Well, these are questions that we are starting to grapple with. We do need psychoanalysis.

FUSCO:　Is it psychoanalysis precisely or a more reflexive position towards representation?

JULIEN:　You must realize that linguistic, literary, and in some cases theoretical arenas of representation, are not talking about representation, as it were, in the visual text. We must develop a contestation as we theorize how our work functions visually. Filmmakers such as Haile Gerima have compared their work to experimentation in jazz and bebop. You can look to Langston Hughes' poems, like "Montage of a Dream Deferred."[7] He uses the word montage, which is very interesting to me, in order to talk about Black urban experiences. I would say that *Passion* is a montage. In *Passion* we're asking questions about the state of British culture. There are no whites in the film—but why shouldn't white people go to see films about Black culture and Black people the same way that Black people go to see films about white culture and white subjects?

The crisis around race is not just a theoretical one, it's a crisis at all levels. It's very obvious what informs it in the age of Reaganism and Thatcherism. When you walk in New York streets and you see the number of Black people on the streets begging something tells you that there is something wrong about the system. If you go to the Dia Art Foundation for a lecture on issues relating to colonialism and there are no Black people in that room, but there's one Black person giving the lecture, you think to yourself, well there's something wrong. In London this hasn't happened as much. I was really surprised by the cultural apartheid in New York. Issues such as Nicaragua, first world involvement in the third world, and the invasion of Grenada—these are questions that we cannot not talk about. And these are key sites of representation. And this is precisely what is being signalled when people like Jean Baudrillard[8] talk about the end. It's about certain kinds of worlds coming to an end. We can see that one of the biggest problems in the discourse of postmodernism is that it doesn't talk about the Black subject. Nor does it address colonial discourse.

FUSCO:　There is some discussion in third world cultural debates about postmodernism in that context as a kind of appropriation or reinterpretation of the strategies that are associated with postmodernism in the first world. The formal relativism implied by postmodernist discourse might have specific resonances for those who have been in a situation of subjugation, in terms of a visual vocabulary. It has been argued that this can have a kind of emancipatory potential, because it makes anything available without any guilt attached. It can be seen as the theoretical recognition of a situation in which the cultural producer is constantly bombarded by images coming from all over the place all the time. There is an extremely problematic history to be dealt with here. Historically speaking, when third world artists borrow from the first world it has been called colonialism, but when the modernists borrowed from Africa, for example, it was an enrichment of the vocabulary of the fine arts.

JULIEN:　Can there be a return to an enrichment of the white avant-garde in its

Eurocentric vein, or is it truly dead? At moments of crisis it does turn to other things to revitalize it. There are positions from which we can debate these arguments. This time the old arguments are not going to work. Our entry into postmodernism is predicated on being used as an alibi for the West, for white critical discourse. And I think that that is very important in relation to all the different struggles that are being waged at this time, by other Black peoples. Theorizing our own experiences around modernity is very important.

ATTILLE: If anything, Black representation must confront modernity, and question whether our understanding of modernity embraces Black experiences. Black people's experience of capitalism hasn't really been dealt with enough. For us to leap to the postmodern would be to overlook the unfinished business of modernity: the way that Black people have travelled, in search of resources, in search of better lives; how they shaped new societies, new cultures, new vocabularies, and new accents within the modern world. There are great gaps in documenting that experience from a Black perspective.

We must be sure that when we talk about race, the white subject doesn't slip out the back door, and leave the Blacks to sort this out among themselves. It's as if whiteness doesn't find a place within the discourse around race until you actually get white subjectivity to declare its interest, to actually explore its colonialist past, its fascination and its fetishes.

JULIEN: Its fears and desires and pleasures.

ATTILLE: Unless you get people to discuss race in terms of what is invested in Blackness, and what is invested in whiteness, what is denied by both, then you're always going to get the subject of race being the subject of Blackness.

FUSCO: You just talked about how the race question is not just a Black question. How can you relate that to the question of whether or not there is a Black aesthetic?

ATTILLE: I think that if your aesthetic is determined by your relationship to power, then yes, there is a difference. It results in a difference in one's perception of the world. But we are part of an environment which is Black and white. It seems to me that to construct a notion of a Black aesthetic allows you to leave another aesthetic untouched, unchallenged. It's never clearly labelled as such, but it's a white aesthetic. We have to adjust ourselves in relation to that aesthetic. When people talk about Black aesthetics and go on a search for one, I see a kind of reductionism in the assumption that we the Black people must be doing something else outside and separate from our total environment. There are many aesthetics, not just one. There are many experiences, many economies to work with. I resist actually trying to form a Black aesthetic that doesn't take into account the diversity and range of our experience.

JULIEN: Because of modernity, I think our interception there can be called upon to make things more interesting. Where does Black experience fit in? In a sense *Passion* and Black Audio's *Handsworth Songs* are trying to grapple with these issues. To talk about diasporic culture is to talk about the process of modernity and your relationship to it as a Black subject. In a sense, I am not a postcolonial subject, I'm sorry.

ATTILLE: If I am a postcolonial subject, then so are the white people. This is the aftermath. We're still reaching for things. Our colonial history isn't that far away. We're still going through that process. Colonialist attitudes are still quite strong in our society.

JULIEN: Especially when you start talking about the nation. People talk about multiracial culture, but what about multiracial nations?

FUSCO: Can we talk about *Dreaming Rivers* a bit?

ATTILLE: *Dreaming Rivers* (1988) started off as a project about representation of Black women, following a discussion series we had organized called "Black Women and Representation." I wanted to talk about images of Black women in film. And what audiences were meant to see or read from images of Black women. In researching it and talking to artists such as Sonia Boyce, Simone Alexander, and Marlene Smith—I began to feel that the original conception was to talk about the images, but that the moment would be best used by trying to make an image, to tell a story through the images, to express a mood, a feeling. Discussions with Sonia Boyce (who became the film's set designer) were quite crucial—her practice as a visual artist for me captures some of the intimacies of Black life in this country without being apologetic, without relying on theory. Her point of view, her family, the textures, and even the smells and tastes of that experience. I wanted to capture something as unapologetic and as there and as real as those pictures, those paintings. And so, with *Dreaming Rivers*, although the issues were there—in those images—they are less dependent on the spoken word, and more dependent on the knowledge of the recent history of visual representation produced by Black women artists in the U.K. The film is therefore about continuity and transformation.

Dreaming Rivers is about Miss T., a Black, dark-skinned woman from the Caribbean. A colonial subject relocated physically, but psychically connected to that past homeland. She is caught between both directions really, leaving the Caribbean to come to England—for dreams, for hope, for love. And then not realizing some of those ambitions, she is caught in the stormy sea, in the Atlantic, on the way back to a place of security, past happiness of youth. Miss T. is a subject in the process of migration, in the midst of the journey. And the imagery for that is like death, which promises new life. The journey hasn't ended—it's represented by her children, who have to lay her down. They represent differences—one person split into three—which fractures into even more again. I wanted to deal with the postcolonial situation and the experience of migration. I would date one point of our modernity from the stage of migration, and the complex processes by which we constantly interact with and change our environment with our histories.

Sankofa: mythical bird which signifies the act of looking into the past to prepare for the future.

1. Third Cinema is a cinematic term originally proposed by Argentine filmmakers Fernando Solanas and Octavio Getino in their 1969 essay, "Towards A Third Cinema." In contrast to the commercially-oriented "first cinema" of Hollywood, and auteurist endeavors—which fall into their "second cinema" category—they posited a third cinema of liberation, a politically engaged, militant cinematic practice integral to decolonization, and unassimilatable to any dominant political system.

2. Lionel Ngakane made *Jemimah and Johnny* in 1963, and Lloyd Reckord made *Ten Bob in Winter* in 1959.

3. Homi K. Bhabha, "The Other Question—The Stereotype and Colonial Discourse," *Screen 24*, no. 6 (November-December 1983): 18-36.

4. Mikhail Bakhtin, Soviet literary theorist of the early revolutionary period, is the author of *The Dialogic Imagination*. His studies of the novel present notions of literature and language in modernity as stratified, fragmented subunits of constant flux and in constant conflict with one another.

5. *Riddles of the Sphinx* is a film by Peter Wollen and Laura Mulvey.

6. Laura Mulvey, "Visual Pleasure and Narrative Cinema," *Screen 16*, no. 3 (Autumn 1975): 6-18.

7. "Montage of a Dream Deferred" is an extended work, divided into 87 sections, depicting Black urban experiences. Formally, the structure of the work is influenced by bebop and jazz. The poem can be found in *Selected Poems of Langston Hughes* (London: Pluto Press Limited, 1959), pp. 221-272.

8. French philosopher Jean Baudrillard's books include *The Mirror of Production, The System of Objects, For A Critique of the Political Economy of the Sign, On Seduction,* and *Simulacras and Simulation.*

BLACK AUDIO FILM COLLECTIVE:
JOHN AKOMFRAH, REECE AUGUISTE, LINA GOPAUL, & AVRIL JOHNSON

COCO FUSCO: Rather than asking you when the riots took place and when you came together, I would like to get a sense of what ideas, what arguments were being debated at the time that you all began to work.

LINA GOPAUL: I'll just open by saying that there was always a sense of the lines we didn't want to pursue, lines which were more didactic. That the riots, for example, happened because of x y z, and that these are the reasons and these are the solutions for it—regardless of whether they were being thrown out by the Left, be it the white or the Black Left. I think our coming together at that time was an expression of not wanting to take up one of those particular positions. And by choosing not to we threw ourselves into a field that was very grey. We then tried to pull out certain themes that we agreed with—what Stuart Hall[1] might have been saying at that time, or what Paul Gilroy[2] might have been saying. They weren't as didactic.

JOHN AKOMFRAH: But you're not just talking about making *Handsworth Songs* (1986) are you?

FUSCO: I'd like to go back further, prior to *Handsworth*.

GOPAUL: Even before that our position was not one of which you could actually say that it takes its meaning from this or that.

FUSCO: It seems that there was a strong cultural nationalist position that was generated by the Black activist community—and to some extent, the more conventionally-oriented Black media sectors. But speaking in terms of ideas, in terms of theorizing race and nationality, such activity was not coming out of those sectors.

REECE AUGUISTE: They were the residues of the 1970s, of the Black Power movements that existed here, which did have a very strong nationalist slant. What motivated us was not wanting to rearticulate past political positions but rather to engage with broader theoretical issues which had not yet been addressed, or at least not in the way that we wanted to address them.
     There were many discussions in the seventies and early eighties about the post-pan-Africanist vision, or the pan-Africanist vision. And a lot of that was, in many respects, undertheorized. So what we did was to combine, very critically, elements of those debates, drawing also on our own theoretical background which we had developed at colleges. We are in many respects a kind of hybrid: we are able to draw

from Foucauldian discourse, psychoanalysis, Afro-Caribbean discourse, and colonial and neocolonial narratives. I was going to signpost Jacques Lacan, but in many respects I think that Frantz Fanon[3] would be closer to what I am communicating. *Expeditions* (1983), which was our first cultural project, was a way of testing those ideas and trying to extend the power of the images and debates around the colonial and postcolonial moment. In order to do that we had to articulate a particular language and vision of that moment. We felt we could only do so by drawing on those European, theoretical discourses.

AKOMFRAH: If you look at the moment of becoming for the Black film and video sector in this country, there are a number of words which were key. One of them obviously was representation. The other was more a category than a term: colonial discourse. The minute you begin to work out the political etymology of those terms themselves you are effectively charting the histories and trajectories of those individuals and collectivities.

The notion of representation has been jettisoned into the forefront by a number of discussions in post-Althusserian[4] circles. Different political currents in this country had interest in it for different reasons. What was being debated was the value of a Left political culture and how one represents that culture in discourse theory. Gramscians[5] had an interest in it because they had come to the conclusion that political power and cultural symbolic power were organized around consent. In terms of a Black interest—on one level a number of collectivities, including ourselves, were familiar with the semiologic activities of Parisian intellectuals who were interested in fashion and so on.

FUSCO: You make them sound so trivial. The English talk about politics, and the French talk about fashion.

AKOMFRAH: The interesting thing was when they stopped talking about fashion and started talking about spaghetti.

So all those currents inform how the collective was set up. Four years ago in England you couldn't sit through a discussion, a film meeting, without representation coming up about fifteen million times.

FUSCO: What was meant by that?

GOPAUL: It goes a bit further than that. Before the issue of representation comes about, we were involved in doing work with *Expeditions* in an attempt to put another phrase or category on the political agenda—colonial discourse. It wasn't being discussed everywhere, mostly in discussions in particular academic circles. And what we wanted to do was to address those debates, those theories, and to bring that onto a visual landscape.

AKOMFRAH: People used the term representation for a number of reasons. The different uses give you a sense of the complexity of the trajectories involved. At one level people used it to simply talk about questions of figuration. How one places the Black in the scene of writing, the imagination and so on. Others saw it in more juridic terms. How one is enfranchised, if you like, how one buys into the social contract. What is England and what constitutes English social life? Some interests were broadly academic, but we were focussing on how to turn our concerns into a problematic, to use an Althusserian term, in the cultural field. We were interested in representation because it seemed to be partly a way of prying open a negative/positive dichotomy. It seemed to be a way of being able to bypass certain binaries.

FUSCO: Are you referring now to the negative and positive image debates?

AKOMFRAH: Yes, and its specifically English variant—which is obsessed with stereotypes, with grounding every discussion around figuration and the existence—presence and absence in cinema in terms of stereotyping. It was a way of going beyond the discussions which would start at the level of stereotype, then move on to images, and then split images into negative and positive, and so on. We wanted to find a way to bypass this, without confronting it head on. I think that the lobbies which were really interested in debates around stereotyping were too strong, to be honest. And we were too small to take them head on. In a sense the negative/positive image lobby represented all that was acceptable about anti-racism, multiculturalism, etc. It's the only thing that united everybody who claimed they were against racism.

Everybody was talking about a non-pathology of racism. The Labor party activists would talk about it. So would the Liberals. For the anti-apartheid groups it was the limit-text, if you like. We sensed that it had political inadequacies, and cultural constraints, and that the theoretical consequences of it hadn't been thought through. But we didn't know exactly how to replace it. We did not want to try to set ourselves up as another interest group to combat the multiculturalists or the anti-racists.

FUSCO: Can we discuss *Expeditions* more specifically than in terms of mapping out a political etymology?

AUGUISTE: The positive/negative image discourse had become the organizing principle of what representation was supposed to have been about, what representation was. *Expeditions* was an attempt to critique that discourse on positive and negative images. We wanted to go beyond purely descriptive categories and try to forge another kind of analytical strain, which could then open up that space in which we could begin to articulate our own ideas about representation by problematizing representation itself.

When *Expeditions* was first completed we had a number of theoretical, political, and cultural battles with those who had very defined ideas about what representation was. The first point that was made was that it was inaccessible, because we were using language which was grounded in Foucauldian ideas, and Fanonian ideas, and so on. Second, there was the issue of the kind of images we used, which had not been used before. The way, for example, in which we would actually appropriate from English national fictions—like the Albert and Victoria Memorial—going back and really engaging with the archive of colonial memory. We were not only constructing a colonial narrative, but also critiquing what was seen as the colonial moment—critiquing what was seen as the discourse around empire.

AKOMFRAH: When we were making *Expeditions*, a number of tentative voices were beginning to challenge what was effectively an orthodoxy in English cultural debate, which was the notion that colonial history and the colonial narrative was past—that it was the instrument of a past English glory which has now foundered. Before there was colonial history, after there's postcolonial history. And we wanted to problematize that very obvious splitting of memory into past and present. It seemed that the only way we could do that was to pay less attention to what historiographers and political commentators said about past and present, and look at what the iconography of those moments signified now. We weren't really interested in whether the Victoria and Albert was built in 1898. Nor did we believe that was the only moment that it meant anything, because it is still here and it is still in the middle of London. And ten thousand tourists see it every day. We felt then that the politics of signification was alive.

AVRIL JOHNSON: What was also happening around this time was the Falklands war, which had begun the year before. Margaret Thatcher called upon a notion of British identity in which, supposedly, all true Englishmen could identify.

GOPAUL: And there were many who argued that the fact that we were chronologically in a postwar era made everything different—that we were postwar theoreticians engaged in a postwar agenda.

FUSCO: I have a clear sense from what you are saying about how this relates to the politics of social life in contemporary England, but I wanted to ask some more aesthetically-oriented questions. Many of the images of empire you use are ones that had already been displaced from classical civilization. The recycling of images that you were playing with for political reasons taps into an aesthetic discourse of neoclassicism that connects you to postmodernism and the transavant-garde.

AKOMFRAH: Two things were happening at the time. On the one hand, formalist photographers and artists—such as the constituency around *Block*[6] were becoming much more interested in the expressive qualities of the remnants of the English national past. They were using these remnants in a very formalist sense, as a kind of backdrop against which one mapped out one's anxieties of difference onto the past. You could see that people were drawing on the neoexpressive qualities of those statues and icons, without necessarily thinking about questions of desire.

FUSCO: One of the desires of postmodernism in its most Eurocentric form is to sever the tie between the political implication and the formal manifestation. In *Expeditions* you use similar strategies of appropriation with a different motor. Do you see these as two postmodernisms hitting off one another? Were you misread because of this?

AKOMFRAH: Our enterprise emerged before the category of postmodernity meant anything in English aesthetic debates. At the time not even Victor Burgin[7] or any of the high priests of avant-garde theories and debates in this country were using it.

AUGUISTE: One of the problems of the discourse of postmodernity lies in what it excludes. The crisis that the postmodern is supposed to address is seen as something internal to the logic and the rationale of Western Classical Civilization. In philosophical discourse there is the crisis around reason. Then there is a crisis around form, as manifested in architecture. What interests me most about these debates is the exclusion of the so-called neocolonial world. To me the crisis doesn't have so much to do with what's happening to the West, to the internal discourse of the West, as it does with what the non-European world is doing to the West. The crisis now is in Lebanon, in South Africa.

AKOMFRAH: In terms of the beginning of making *Expeditions*, it's important to say that there are two convergences there. On the one hand, we realized that there was a kind of reappropriation, which we now understand to be postmodernist reappropriation of the past, taking place in very formalist circles, such as the kind of work that Victor Burgin and others were doing in photography. What we decided to do—which again, with hindsight, we now realize places us firmly in that camp—was to appropriate classical or neoclassical images. But we appropriated them using methods of avant-garde photography which effectively begin with Alexander Rodchenko—extremely angular kinds of framing, etc. That was the key difference. If you look at the formalist work on the other hand, the methods of composition were extremely straightforward. Henri Cartier-Bresson[8] could have done it. What people found unnerving about what we were doing was that the play of postmodernism wasn't there. *This* parody and pastiche was underpinned by biblical sounding tones concerning colonial narratives and expeditions and so on. We wanted to say that it was an expedition, that on the one hand you went through these exhibitions—you pack your bag from different aesthetic fields, from neoclassical architecture, from Russian formalist photography. But the interest was in colonial narrative. The interest was not, in the end, in play.

FUSCO: Let's move on to *Handsworth Songs*. I am interested in the symptomatic qualities of the responses to it. I do think that the fact *Handsworth Songs* has been the subject of controversy has to do with something larger than the film. It has to do with a desire to damage the kind of position you represent. Salman Rushdie's frequently mentioned review in *The Guardian* [9] doesn't really address the film—he demonstrates no relationship to the filmic aspects of the work. He juxtaposes the notion of an authentic voice to image manipulation.

GOPAUL: I think this goes back to what we were saying about where we located ourselves in relation to the political and theoretical positions that prevailed prior to our existence as a collective. When we emerged people tried to didactically map out the cultural and visual terrain for us to slot into.

If they are not actually addressing the film, well then what is it that they are addressing? Transgression, basically. Why is it such a strong response not to the film, but our existence? To what you represent? Those who criticized us most vehemently were prioritizing a line about community and people in the streets. There was no other way of representing yourself other than the way they put forward. That's what I think is largely behind the sometimes almost violent responses to us.

AKOMFRAH: The question of paternity and transgression was very important. One of the things which people would always say to us was, isn't *Handsworth Songs* too avant-garde? Quite simply, the problems we faced in making *Handsworth* were very practical ones—to do with melodrama—orchestrating means of identification, rather than distancing people and dazzling them with techniques. The editing might be considered unconventional, but the techniques are very straightforward. So it's not avant-garde in that sense. My mistake was in assuming people wouldn't see it as a transgressive text.

In terms of the established boundaries of discussion—aesthetic interventions around race—there were questions of paternity at stake. In other words, who was the holder of the law—the law of enunciation? Who had the right to speak, who had the right to map out and broaden the field that everybody had to speak in? It was in that sense that the film was received as a transgressive text, because it clearly didn't fall into line with the established concordat concerning the Black intelligentsia and their discussion of race. That then makes the film an avant-garde text. Those who were willing to live with a more mixed economy of dialogue around figuration and race accepted it, and those who didn't, didn't accept it.

That was one symptom, but the morbidity also has to do with the inability of cultural workers to make any meaningful sense of that moment. One has the sense that people were trapped in their own rhetoric, claiming that the 1981 riots occurred because of unemployment, etc. having to signpost all the social reasons why Black people take to the streets. The minute we began to speak and give the impression that somehow one was going to reopen the questions rather than repeat the answers, people got very nervous.

JOHNSON: Those people who felt trapped had benefitted from what happened in 1981. They don't want to recognize that the problem still exists.

GOPAUL: It was also a move away from the specificity of location. After 1981, there was a generalized understanding of the riots, whereas in 1985 it was different. How can we begin to understand this situation, people would ask, in Birmingham, which didn't riot in 1981? Birmingham has a very specific Black political history. It's one of the central spots for Black political development and for anti-racist development. It has a number of institutions, like the Center for Contemporary Cultural Studies, which are based within those communities. There is something quite specific happening there.

AKOMFRAH: We have to be careful not to overestimate the transgressive potential of certain kinds of aesthetic intervention. At a certain point, the nightmares which weigh on the brain are not necessarily historical ones—they are very conjunctural ones. The fact of the matter is that a number of things were collapsing at a certain point. And the film in many ways mirrors that collapse. It's not an avant-gardist intervention, in the sense that it doesn't frame a series of devices that would get us out of the crisis. It mirrors those forms collapsing, and it says what a shame.

FUSCO: How did people respond to that sort of mirror?

AKOMFRAH: When people saw the film they saw all the fractures, all the unevenness—which are quite deliberate. Part of the problem that we have has to do with the question of whether Black people should be involved in visual arts, in creating aesthetically challenging visual work. The assumption when we foreground avant-garde technique is either that we don't know anything else, and have stumbled across it by accident, or that we are imitating other forms.

GOPAUL: Or that we have no foundation in the Black communities, that we've left that behind too.

AKOMFRAH: The idea of prefacing the film with a phrase—"There are no stories in the riots, only the ghosts of other stories"—and then to work on it in terms of splits and unevennesses and so on without trying to center it was what alarmed many people. The triumphalist vision of race and community operates on the assumption that there is essentially a core of affect that is structured around oratory, around song—giving it an irreducible unity—which wasn't present in the film. It plays with it, at some stages discards it, it takes it on board, then it says it's probably not possible, do not work with it, but there you are, and so on. But the film doesn't fix its sentiments around it. That is what was frightening. It then leads to the discussion of whether avant-garde techniques, or disruptive techniques, profilmic techniques, are in safe hands when they are given to Blacks. Both certain Black theorists and the white theorists would say that; they would want to know whether authorship is really safe with us.

If the notion of diaspora has any credibility, it has to be understood as a formation which exists both on the margins at certain points, and at the center of English social life.

And if it plays those dual functions, then it's bound to be negotiated into a series of practices, visual or otherwise, which exist in this country. So that even if a visual history wasn't present in our "history," the very fact of communality at the center of the metropolis makes it impossible to ignore, to put it crudely, that every little Black kid in this country, at one stage or another, will have the chance to go to an art college, or to take part in art classes at school.

FUSCO: And they live in a world that is absolutely inundated with images, although the vast majority of them do not include Black people. Would you want to venture into theorizing around what this absence does to the psyche, and the question of representation and race?

AKOMFRAH: In terms of reproduction in the very classical sense, Marxian or otherwise, of social relations in this country, I know that the Black independent sector, which has organized itself around questions of representation and collective practice, represents the new wave of English filmmaking. I also know that in terms of the kinds of questions raised by filmmaking practice in this country, which took its cue from Jean-Luc Godard, from Chris Marker, the Nouvelle Vague, political cinema in Russia and so on—this new wave comes to it with a certain kind of agnosticism and skepticism around its transgressive potential as we hit the 1990s. And I also know that our interest in filmmaking as a new wave possibly gives English independent film practice a chance to breach what has been an impossible gap between the mainstream and independents. We are obviously aided by the existence of television—nevertheless, we are the fortunate inheritors of that confusion, that growth, that progression. And I don't think it is possible to be that closely associated with all those things without having some very deeply entrenched familiarity with the visual landscape in this country. That's what I know. What I don't know is how we then proceed. What I don't know is what to say to people who say, well how can Black people be in that position.

One of the problems that the independent sector always faced in this country is this crisis of identity around collective security—it never really understood its strategic power. It never truly understood where it stood in relation to mainstream audiovisual culture in this country. People always assumed that the very act of doing something is transgressive. In a culture where the transgressive is in fact the cutting edge of advertising, that makes your identity very unstable.

FUSCO: How do you respond to the claim that while you get attacked for the forms you operate within, the fact that you choose to work within those forms makes it easier for your work to be aired on television, whereas a more straightforward, monological documentary on a politically controversial issue, like *The People's Account*,[10] cannot.

AKOMFRAH: On one level, we've had people who've "told it like it is" in their documentaries. That has to be said with a certain element of skepticism, because ultimately one needs to challenge the assumption that you can tell it like it is.

Can we talk about where aesthetics used to belong in classical philosophy? The term "aesthetic" was coined by Baumgarten, who was an ally of Herder, who was working with Kant. Black filmmaking has been and will probably continue to be straddled with what Kant calls the categorical imperative. People assume that there are certain transcendental duties that Black filmmaking has to perform. They assume that and because of that Black filmmaking has to work with the understanding that it's in a state of emergence. And because it is in a state of emergence its means always have to be guerilla means, war means, signposts of urgency. When that begins to inhibit questions of reflection—doubt, skepticism, intimacy and so on—then the categorical imperative does exactly what it is supposed to do—it imprisons.

FUSCO: It is precisely the arguments around urgency that foreclose entry into aesthetic practice, or any discussion of aesthetics as the property of a Black artist. How can you start to talk about a term that exists within aesthetics, when you're supposedly not engaged in aesthetics?

AKOMFRAH: Because the transcendental duties are always *a priori,* because they are always there before you start. Everything else is only given contingent license. Aesthetics, efficacy, are each given tentative license. Their only use is the extent to which they take you closer to your transcendental mission, which is to announce that we are here and we can't take it anymore. If the situation of war is an apt metaphor, and in many ways it probably is, then I would say that our position of dissidence is that one resolutely refuses to be turned into cannon fodder. We would like to take our bread and hit the mountain because it is safer to be a guerilla. The struggles we've engaged in have had some moderate successes. We've argued that we don't just live beneath our navel.

FUSCO: In what sense do you deal with sexuality and gender in your films?

AKOMFRAH: We've decided to deal with these questions in different ways. It's a very complicated question for us. On the one hand we try to deal with it by working with Pratibha Parmar on her videotape *Emergence* (1987), trying to make an input into an area which is already defined as one of sexuality. On the other hand, we try to make sure that it gels into the mesh of concern that we have for the Black subject in our own work.

When Isaac Julien's *Territories* (1985) appeared it was obvious that we were beginning to swap one set of transcendental clothes for another. Once you stop being angry you had to be another other, and adopt another transgressive tone. And we began to think of ways to slip past that. If there is a voice of dissidence that echoes and strains in our work, it's an attempt to find a position from which to speak certain questions—which beguiles expectations and is genuinely uncanny in many ways. It was obvious that once *Territories* appeared, with the kind of reception that it got in this country—it was then supposed to be the beginning of a convention. Regardless of what one's interest in the politics were. I don't think, in the end, that we don't deal with sexuality. But we try to find a much more complicated dialogue with the issues than was expected of us once *Territories* appeared.

JOHNSON: The other thing is that we are not making sexuality a cornerstone. We are making it something that is mediated, not necessarily the central process. It's informed by a number of different things.

GOPAUL: There are times when people prioritize sexuality as a singular issue, which is what tends to happen in moments of struggle or crisis. But after that—how do you then bring it back into an everyday part of your life, and then into a filmic practice? I find that far more difficult than addressing it head on. People don't live like that.

AKOMFRAH: We are also in a position to take a number of things for granted. The search for intimacy, the reflective quality of *Handsworth Songs*, does not simply have to do with a realignment of Black discourses. They have to do with our sensitivity to questions which are raised in other sorts of politics, not necessarily racial ones. Obviously, Black women talk about questions of femininity. We try to make sure that the text you operate with is open enough to allow for those kinds of interventions.

Two articles appeared in the *London Review of Books* a while back—I didn't realize how informative they were until much later. It was a debate between Richard Sennett[12] and Michel Foucault. And it's also a kind of debate that has taken place since then in the gay community.

FUSCO: What were their positions?

AKOMFRAH: They had to do with whether or not when one forged a politics around identity, placing it in the public arena—whether doing that was simply allowing oneself to become inserted in a well-policed arrangement of things. What does calling yourself a Black collective entail, or imply? Is it possible to work through identity politics without having to announce the name of your identity? I was left with a deep sense of skepticism around identifying identity and championing it in a very triumphalist way.

Blacks are expected to be transgressive in English cultural life. To me this is just as wearying, just as draining as the old "you must be the conscience of the nation" approach. Either one of them requires a certain act of a kind of emancipatory front—for the nation. We don't have the strength or the energy. So there may be reticence around these questions on our part.

FUSCO: Africa has an extremely important symbolic function in the history of Black film and Black images—and in the Black consciousness movement—as the promised land, the age of innocence. With your new film, *Testament* (1988), which was shot in

Africa, you seem to have walked into a rather overloaded symbolic minefield.

AKOMFRAH: It is loaded. In many ways, Africa is one of the key primal scenes, one of the primal moments in diasporic culture. I suspect that what we are going to do with that understanding isn't going to please everybody, but there you are. That is the way of the world.

AUGUISTE: Specific histories of subjectivities are not the issue. The issue is that within the Black community there is a lot of innocence and naïveté about the continent Africa. There is a certain kind of romantic engagement with Africa, which is one of the residues of the neonationalist moment. On one level, Africa should be celebrated; on another level, people in the diaspora should critically engage with the continent. And in particular they should engage with those historical figures who have supposedly enunciated Africa, or the pan-Africanist movement. All those Africanist leaders are still held in a frame of innocence. What that has done is to project a certain kind of retardation in thought. It's feeling and not thinking.

What we are saying now is that after twenty to twenty-five years of independence, no one can argue that the problem in Africa is something outside—that it's the West, always the West. There are real problems that are internal, that are specific to the continent. In order to break away from this romantic engagement one has to recognize and smash that innocence and rip it up and see what is really taking place. Otherwise we are engaged in transcendental thinking about the continent, which doesn't get those out here in the West thinking about the continent very far.

AKOMFRAH: Let's speak about it also in terms of the aesthetics of that primal moment. If the dichotomy in Black art is between protest and redemption, or protest and affirmation, and if Africa as the primal scene functions significantly in the affirmation moment, as the moment of liberation, of catharsis, what if—and this is an aesthetic question we pose in the film—what if you have a character for whom that redemption is a problem? What if you have a character who can't live with that primal moment? One of the things that the character says in the film is that perhaps I am a new kind of animal for whom the very thought of peace is a burden. We have a number of alternatives—we can debunk the lore, with reference to sociology, or we can take the rhetoric of the primal scene seriously and say that it does exist, and that it has real effects on people's lives. There are people whose lives have been made much more complicated, destroyed almost, by these sorts of assumptions around Africa. That seems to me to be a starting point. We must go there and find a character for whom Africa is not a place of redemption, precisely because Africa thinks of itself that way. We have to come out with a character like that. That is the aim of the film. Once you decide that the primal scene is that borderline, which people cross in different ways—once you have defined it in those terms you get stuck on one side or the other. What I am not exactly sure about—it doesn't worry me or anybody else here—what we are not sure about is whether that person actually comes back or gets swallowed up by the border.

FUSCO: Perhaps we should also talk about the U.S. as a place of redemption. Black American culture carries a tremendous amount of weight here in England. You touch on it in the film with references to Malcolm X and the dialogues and questions that are raised about a legacy of radicalism.

JOHNSON: It has to do with what you hear on the news—that what happened in America ten years ago happens in Britain today. And I think that is because Black people have been there in much larger numbers much longer—and in a sense people still look to what Black Americans are doing. And it is also easier not to look at what is happening here.

AKOMFRAH: The connection goes back a long way. At each moment of Black radical life in this country there has been an interface with concerns around race in America. You can go back to the discussions around emancipation here. Black people who lived in this country at that time, their concerns with slavery here and in the Americas were always interlocked. The founding of the pan-Africanist conference was always only possible when in many ways the anticolonial fighters began to take W.E.B. Du Bois[12] seriously and work with him in some ways. Marcus Garvey went to America and then came here. There has always been a sense of exchange, if you like, between the two spaces. And there was that famous conference in this country in 1967 called 'The Dialectics of Liberation," where people were first exposed to the personages of Black Power—Stokely Carmichael turned up and made his famous speech in which he said that the only place for a woman is prone. This first symbolic contact with Black Power left a very contradictory legacy in this country.

Nineteen-sixty-eight itself—the founding of the New Left in this country—was deeply implicated in a kind of dialogue and exchange with Black American culture.

Now if we are talking about our own fascination with America I suspect that it is split in very different ways—there is a kind of aura around American life in its different manifestations, which you find in different spaces. For Black women's politics in this country, Black American women writers have almost canonical significance.

GOPAUL: There is a sense that they had all done it before we had done it.

AKOMFRAH: There is a sense that Black American culture throws down a certain gauntlet which people then have to pick up and live through and with.

FUSCO: What about in film?

AKOMFRAH: In film I don't think the connection is there that much.

JOHNSON: It also has to do with the Caribbean. Most of us come from the Caribbean, where America is it.

AKOMFRAH: Wim Wenders said that Americans have colonized our unconscious. In many ways he is right. Anywhere in the world—in the darkest part of Manchester even—you find counter-culture which premises American life in some form, be it hip hop, or whatever. And it is in that very generalized sense that America has been useful. But I don't think I ever really seriously thought that Black American independent filmmaking was something to take a cue from.

AUGUISTE: I think we have been more interested in the New Latin American Cinema, the so-called Third Cinema.

1.   Originally from Kingston, Jamaica, Stuart Hall is one of the founders of Black cultural studies in Britain and one of the leading spokesmen of the New Left. He was the first editor of *New Left Review* and assisted in organizing the Center for Contemporary Cultural Studies (CCS) at the University of Birmingham. He is currently professor of Sociology at Open University. He is coeditor of many CCS volumes, such as *Culture, Media, Language*, and coauthor of *Policing the Crisis: Mugging, the State and Law and Order*.

2.   Paul Gilroy is Senior Lecturer in Sociology at the Polytechnic of the South Bank. He has also worked as a musician, disc jockey and journalist. He is coeditor of *The Empire Strikes Back: Race and Racism in '70s Britain*, and the author of *There Ain't No Black in the Union Jack: The Cultural Politics of Race and Nation*.

3.   Frantz Fanon was born in Martinique, studied psychiatry in France and worked in Algeria during the Franco-Algerian War. He is the author of *Black Skin, White Masks, The Wretched of the Earth*, and *A Dying Colonialism*.

4.   One of the leading Marxist philosophers of the 1960s in France, Louis Althusser is the author of *For Marx* and *Reading Capital*. Known for having emphasized the implications of Marxism for philosophy and aesthetics, Althusser developed a concept of ideology as a "lived" relation between human beings and their world. He saw this as different from science in its giving more weight to the social and practical modes of understanding, rather than theoretical forms of knowledge. He employed Freudian terms such as condensation, displacement, and overdetermination to explain how contradiction—the dialectical process of historical development—can be understood in relation to its time and place in history.

5   Antonio Gramsci, the most important Italian Marxist theorist of the early twentieth century, is the author of *The Prison Notebooks*. He is best known in England for his theory of hegemony and the concept of national-popular politics, which provides the groundwork for understanding cultural and ideological production and reception and for analyzing the politics of the modern nation-state as effective through consent, rather than force. Like Althusser, Gramsci also employed categories from Freudian psychoanalysis.

6.   *Block* is a British art magazine.

7.   Victor Burgin is a British photographer and theorist and the editor of *Thinking Photography* (London: MacMillan, 1982).

8.   Henri Cartier-Bresson, the French photographer and photojournalist.

9.   The following is Salman Rushdie's article, "*Songs* doesn't know the score," from *The Guardian* (London), January 12, 1987, p. 10.

    In *The Heart of a Woman*, volume four of her famous autobiography, Maya Angelou describes a meeting of the Harlem Writers' Guild, at which she had read some of her work and had it torn to pieces by the group.
    It taught her a tough lesson: "If I wanted to write, I had to be willing to develop a kind of concentration found mostly in people awaiting execution. I had to learn technique and surrender my ignorance."
    It just isn't enough to be Black and blue, [or] even Black and angry, the message is plain enough in Angelou's self-portrait, in Louise Meriwether's marvellous *Daddy Was A Numbers Runner*, in Toni Morrison and Paule Marshall; if you want to tell the untold stories, if you want to give voice to the voiceless, you've got to find a language. Which goes for film as well as prose, for documentary as well as autobiography. Use the wrong language, and you're dumb and blind.

Down at the Metro cinema in Soho, there's a new documentary starting a three-week run, *Handsworth Songs*, made by Black Audio Film Collective. The "buzz" about the picture is good. *New Socialist* likes it, *City Limits* likes it, people are calling it multi-layered, original, imaginative, its makers talk of speaking in metaphors, its director John Akomfrah is getting mentioned around town as a talent to watch. Unfortunately, it's no good, and the trouble does seem to be one of language.

Let me put it this way. If I say "Handsworth," what do you see? Most Britons would see fire, riots, looted shops, young Rastas and helmeted cops by night. A big story; front page. Maybe a West Side Story: Officer Krupke, armed to the teeth, versus the kids with the social disease.

There's a line that *Handsworth Song[s]* wants us to learn. "There are no stories in the riots, it repeats, only the ghosts of other stories." The trouble is, we aren't told the other stories. What we get is what we know from TV. Blacks as trouble; Blacks as victims. Here is a Rasta dodging the police; here are the old news-clips of the folks in the fifties getting off the boat, singing calypsos about "darling London."

Little did they know, eh? But we don't hear about their lives, or the lives of their born-British children. We don't hear Handsworth's songs.

Why not? The film's handouts provide a clue. The film attempts to excavate hidden ruptures/agonies of "Race." "It looks at the riots as a political field colored by the trajectories of industrial decline and structural crisis." Oh dear. The sad thing is that while the filmmakers are trying to excavate ruptures and work out how trajectories can color fields, they let us hear so little of the much richer language of their subjects.

When Home Secretary Hurd visits Handsworth looking bemused, just after the riots, a Black voice is heard to say: "The higher monkey climb the more he will expose." If only more of this sort of wit and freshness could have found its way into the film. But the makers are too busy "repositioning the convergence of 'Race' and 'Criminality,'" describing a living world in the dead language of race industry professionals. I don't know Handsworth very well, but I do know it's bursting with tales worth telling. Take a look at John Bishton and Derek Reardor's 1984 photo-and-text essay, *Home Front*. There are Vietnamese boat people in Handsworth, where Father Peter Diem, a refugee himself, runs a pastoral center to which they come for comfort.

Here are two old British soldiers. One, name of Shri Dalip Singh, sits stiffly in his army tunic, sporting his Africa Star with pride; the other, a certain Jagat Singh, is a broken old gent who has been arrested for drunkenness on these streets over three hundred times. Some nights they catch him trying to direct the traffic.

It's a religious place, Handsworth. What was once a Methodist chapel is now one of many Sikh *gurdwaras*. Here is the Good News Asian Church, and there you can see Rasta groundations, a mosque, Pentecostal halls, and Hindu Jain and Buddhist places of worship. Many of Handsworth's songs are hymns of praise. But there's reggae too, there are Punjabi *ghazals* and Two Tone bands.

These days the kids in Handsworth like to dance the Wobble. And some of its denizens dream of distant "liberations," nurturing, for example, the dark fantasy of Khalistan.

It's important, I believe, to tell such stories: to say, this is England: Allahu Akbar from the minaret of a Birmingham mosque, the Ethiopian World Federation which helps Handsworth Rastas "return" to the land of Rastafari. These are English scenes now, English songs.

You won't find them, or anything like them, in *Handsworth Songs*, though for some reason, you will see plenty of footage about troubles in Tottenham and Brixton, which is just the sort of blurring you know the Harlem writers would have jumped on, no matter how right-on it looked.

It isn't easy for Black voices to be heard. It isn't easy to get it said that the state attacks us, that the police are militarized. It isn't easy to fight back against media stereotypes. As a result, whenever somebody says what we all know, even if they say it clumsily and in jargon, there's a strong desire to cheer, just because they managed to get something said, they managed to get through.

I don't think that's much help, myself. That kind of celebration makes us lazy.

Next time, let's start telling those ghost-stories. If we know why the caged bird sings, let's listen to her song.

10 *The Peoples Account* (1986), by the Workshop Ceddo, commissioned by Channel 4, but not shown.

11. Richard Sennett is the author of *The Fall of Public Man and Authority*.

12. Poet and essayist W.E.B. Du Bois is one of the greatest and most influential Black American writers of the late nineteenth and early twentieth century. He is the author of *The Souls of Black Folk* (1903).

REPRINTED FROM COCO FUSCO, *YOUNG, BRITISH AND BLACK: THE WORK OF SANKOFA AND BLACK AUDIO FILM COLLECTIVE* (BUFFALO: HALLWALLS/CONTEMPORARY ARTS CENTER, 1988), PP. 23–60.

IF UPON LEAVING WHAT WE HAVE TO SAY WE SPEAK: A CONVERSATION PIECE

Laleen Jayamanne, Leslie Thornton, and Trinh T. Minh-ha

TRINH T. MINH-HA: One way of discussing your film work is to talk about avant-garde filmmaking in the late eighties. How do you see the changes taking place?

LESLIE THORNTON: I think there is an avant-garde practice within cinema, but that it is dispersed, or rather, not constituted as a coherent movement. It depends on how we define "avant-garde"; for myself it means work that actively challenges accepted forms and the divisions between forms. I see this work as having a difficult relation with the established exhibition circuit, though the New York/San Francisco-based circuit has a particular history and focus. I think work that stretches the form is often hybrid in genre, crossing the traditional categories of narrative, documentary, and experimental film. My own interest is in the outer edge of narrative, where we are at the beginning of something else.

TRINH: Before we discuss your interest in questions of narrative, let's come back for a minute to your affirmation that avant-garde film practices continue to thrive mostly outside the more visible experimental film circuits. You are aware of Fred Camper's essay in the twentieth anniversary issue of the *Millennium Film Journal* on "The End of Avant-Garde Film," in which he specified what a "great film" is for him and also addressed the question of how the viewer individuation in avant-garde film can constitute a social challenge to the mass culture conformity of the postwar decades. The insights he offers on the historical avant-garde, and the social dimension he incorporates in the notion of "personal" work are very useful in explaining the cultural impact it had during the years 1946-66, which he terms "the individual period" of American avant-garde filmmaking.

THIS CONVERSATION PIECE IS COMPOSED OF TWO DIALOGUES PRESENTED HERE IN JUXTAPOSITION. IT WAS ORIGINALLY CONCEIVED AS A SINGLE TALK GATHERING LESLIE, LALEEN, AND MYSELF. BUT DUE TO THE FACT THAT SHE HAD RECENTLY BECOME A MOTHER, LALEEN, WHO LIVES IN AUSTRALIA, WAS UNABLE TO COME TO NEW YORK WHEN HER FILM *A SONG OF CEYLON* WAS SHOWN AT THE COLLECTIVE FOR LIVING CINEMA IN MAY 1988. WE HAVE THEREFORE DECIDED TO CARRY ON A CONVERSATIONAL EXCHANGE BY CORRESPONDENCE, HENCE THE (WRITTEN-IN-THE-INTERLOCUTOR'S-ABSENCE) NATURE OF SOME OF THE QUESTIONS, WHICH I HAVE KEPT. —TM

TRINH T. MINH-HA: Your film *A Song of Ceylon* and your writings situate your work at the intersection of postmodernism, poststructuralism, and feminism. Do you agree with this? If not, why? If yes, how would you describe this intersection?

LALEEN JAYAMANNE: Situating *A Song of Ceylon* (1985, Australia) at this intersection now would validate it in a way that is not very useful. Such a maneuver leaves no room at all to examine what doesn't work in the film, which is the only thing about it that still interests me. Constantly referring to the theoretical discursive apparatuses that make certain films possible or readable, has also become a way of blocking *critical* engagement with "x" number of "independent radical films." When I introduced the film at a Sydney screening in 1985, I half-jokingly called it a postcolonial dance film. On other occasions I have called it an ethnographic film of the body.

Since the *Standard Oxford English Dictionary* defines "conversation piece" as "a kind of genre painting representing a group of figures," I am reminded of another intersection—that museum relic of a film, Godard and Gorin's *Wind from the East,* which has the charm of an intensity or passion spent and utterly dated. The scene I am thinking of is the one in which the late Brazilian film director Glauber Rocha stands at an intersection with his hands extended in a Christ-like gesture. A pregnant woman with a camera approaches him, asking "which way to political cinema?" Rocha gestures in one direction speaking of a marvellous Third World cinema, but the pregnant woman strolls off in another direction—(I may be embellishing this as it has been at least five years since I last saw the film and used that scene and dialogue in a live performance).

My writing now is distracted by an identification with that pregnant woman with a camera articulating differences between Western and Third World cinema. I like the way the woman negotiates that intersection via a simultaneous gesture of engagement and deflection. The urbane relaxed felicity implied in the term "conversation" is made difficult by that state of distraction called "motherhood."

Of importance to me is his rejection of a reductive and isolationist over-emphasis of the "personal" found in recent experimental films. Camper also analyzes the teaching of avant-garde film technique within institutional structures as "a recipe for the end of avant-garde film." This is certainly a challenge, on the one hand, to filmmakers eager to rank themselves among the avant-gardes by simply working with the established vocabulary of the movement; and on the other hand, to those of us who teach in order to continue to make films, even if we count ourselves among the teachers who play a tight game with academism and provide students "with a whole system both to learn and rebel against."

Yet, as Camper recognized himself at the end of his essay, his concept of great film can be, and has been considered the very source of his problem with newer work. Numerous other notions he advanced such as "originality," "authentic expression," the artist's visionary role in society; the need to "find a new artistic mode to work in," or to reinvent cinema; and the idea of opposing "a state of decadence" to "a genuinely avant-garde movement," are central objects of the postmodern attack. These notions may be said to partake in this vertically imposed form of individualization whose ideology of separation ultimately helps to maintain the status quo. The problem of our time, as Michel Foucault would say, is not to liberate the individual from the state and its institutions, but from both the state and the type of individualization inscribed in its power structures. What is your view on these issues?

THORNTON: As a filmmaker it is odd to read so many commentaries bemoaning the demise of experimental cinema. A lot of this is misleading, because what is really happening is that people are speaking in a generational way, and are feeling a passage. They see the passing, and also the diminishing, through derivative work, of what they trust and found expansive.

I think there is also an element of sexism at work here. Experimental film of the fifties and sixties was a male-dominated practice and involved considerable grandstanding. Jonathan Rosenbaum made himself unpopular when he said as much in his book *Film: The Frontline*. Now when much of the most interesting recent work is made by women, it is amazing to me that so little attention has been paid to this development, even among feminist writers.[1] The development marks not only a shift in sexes, but also in the kinds of work being done. In my own case, I have been accused of working in a manner that is "feminized." Perhaps this is because the work doesn't announce its agenda, it is not confrontational in the usual sense, and it does not take an overt position in relation to power as it is currently constituted.

I do agree with some of the reservations about an academic/experimental film link. It's difficult when teaching not to be put in a position of authority, even if everything you do is intended to counter such a position. This and other factors endemic to academia can lead to a kind of reinforcement of a status quo. Despite everything though, I think academic institutions provide at least one kind of meeting ground, which becomes more interesting when it cuts across generations and disciplines.

CONTEMPLATING DISTRACTION—"MOTHER & ~~CHILD~~ DAUGHTER"

PHOTO: RANEE GUNASEKERA

We know that the "maternal" and the "feminine" are not isomorphic with mothers and women, just as we have been told not to confuse the "phallus" with the penis. After Barthes refused to show us his mother's image some men engaged in theoretical work in the anglophone world have initiated an autobiographical discourse about the maternal/the mother, the function of which in their respective discourses may be worth thinking about, but in my state of distraction I can't sustain that interest and want, instead, to talk about the ritual in *A Song of Ceylon* which is governed by two mythical avatars of the maternal found in South Asian religious imagery. One is Pattini, the good mother and the other Kali, the evil mother; both are figured very differently from the beautiful spaced-out virgins of western Christian imagery. The film yokes these two contradictory figures, whereas in the ritual of spirit possession and cure the reigning figure is Kali. The disturbed biological familial relationships are restored at the end of the ritual under the auspices of the priest dressed in drag as Kali. The maternal as the space of primary narcissism is an atemporal, eternal concept of that dual dynamic, and if women want to bring the maternal into the flux of time, then different operations are required, though what these might be is a matter for film to explore.

I suppose I'm rambling on about the feminist thematics of the film. *Song of Ceylon* attempted to work through an impasse in an aspect of feminist film

TRINH: Perhaps you can say something about the avant-garde energy that continues to stimulate you, and try to describe the situation in which, as you put it, we are "at the beginning of something else" and straight anti-positions no longer appeal to a feminist sensitivity.

THORNTON: That is a huge question. One thing I see happening in work which is vital is that the focus is shifting from film as an art *form,* to film as a vehicle to approach problems or issues—to tell or untell stories. The lessons of a more formal investigation have been absorbed and have become part of a working language; the parameters are greatly expanded, maybe they are dirtier around the edges, in a positive way. An avant-garde cinema cannot understand itself in the simple oppositional terms which were originally used to mark off the field. Rather, there is a positioning of an avant-garde within a range of possibilities in cinema and media. I don't see this as a capitulation, but as a potentially subversive deepening—a maturing. When boundaries begin to break down between the political and the personal, the popular and the obscure, truth and fiction, some interesting elements begin to slip through cracks. We have to look again at what we mean by these categories.

TRINH: Yes, one way in which what is named "postmodernism" distinguishes itself from (a certain concept of) modernism is with respect to the question of novelty. As some have said, we live in an era of the decline of the new. While the modernist project is promoted through a claim to create from zero and to make tabula rasa of traditional values, no such conception of language could be confidently relied upon in today's context of critical thinking without appearing naïve. Postmodernism, in a way, has always existed; it does not merely come *after* modernism, but exists before, with, and after it. This is what Jean-Francois Lyotard is probably pointing to when he affirms that a work can only be modern when it is first postmodern. These two qualifying terms do not stand in opposition to each other and postmodernism is here defined as modernism in its nascent stage—one that is always recurring. As in all "ism" histories, however, the urge to circumscribe and unify the situation is unavoidable, hence the tendency to turn the postmodern condition into "another version of that historical amnesia characteristic of American culture—the tyranny of the New," as Stuart Hall puts it. One can never situate oneself outside mainstream values. In challenging them, one has to go constantly back and forth between the center and the margins.

THORNTON: It is important when considering the possibility of an avant-garde to draw a distinction between newness, or novelty, and change. We do suffer from a certain "tyranny of the new" in our culture, but what has somehow become lost in all of this is the possibility of change, which I see as a more fundamental process, not always visible or comfortable in its moment. My reservations about postmodernist theory relate to a lack of distinction on this count, and to its resignation with respect to present and ongoing political, social, aesthetic forces. In the arts, for instance, I believe theory overdetermined by what I call protestant feminism. But the film's impulse was not purely reactive. The possessed woman interested us because her body was not one—in fact, here was an example of the infamous poststructuralist "decentered, heterogeneous, subject-in-process" displaying the very processes of subject formation and displacement in extremis. We loved this possessed body which could say to the priest and audience and the gods, "Do you know who this woman is? This woman is Somawathi. Do you know me well? Do you think I am a woman? Ha! Do you? Do you?" We loved her verbal and bodily dexterity, even as she enunciated the cultural text of a body in extremis. The problem then was how to stage this dynamic without presenting THE MAD WOMAN. So we thought we'd spread the contagion of possession democratically across gender boundaries, across many bodies so that the difficult pleasures of masochism, narcissism, and hysteria could be viewed and voiced with the cinematic means. And here the most interesting question to keep in mind is the one Homi Bhabha asked me at an Edinburgh film festival forum: "What was it that resisted the theoretical discourses you were working with (at the time of making the film) even as you used them?" This question is vital if one wants cinema to do something other than simply mirror theoretical discourses.

As for my writing, I wish to comment on the use of my late mother's name, Anna Rodrigo, as the interviewer in the fictional interviews I did for *Discourse* and *Fade to Black*. The maternal as the space of primary narcissism for the son is part of the history of the Western genre of painting called "Mother and child." For me, the interest in working with the maternal is not an autobiographical one. To converse with the maternal in an unsticky tone, where there is space for tonal shifts and distancing, I find very appealing. Is this a way of writing a poststructuralist feminist biography?

TRINH: In an interview with Geeta Kapur and Yvonne Rainer for *Art & Text*, you asked whether the notion of postmodernism has any relevance to contemporary Indian art. I would like to rethink the connotations of this question. For me, to affirm (like some of us Third World members) that postmodernism is mainly a phenomenon of American culture, or to assume (like some First World members) that the avant-garde is spurred and controlled by the West, is in a way to concede "history" to the West all over again. In other words, it is to assent to the West's cultural hegemony. This does not mean, however, that postmodernism as promoted by Western theorists and artists is not context-specific. What is designated as postmodernist on the New York scene, for example, does not really indicate what is happening in other parts of it is essential to imagine a marginality, to perceive an edge from which to work. One can be entirely cynical and say that this edge is illusory, that it is already absorbed, but then it becomes impossible to work. So I think one has to combine any cynicism with a (cynically) constructed dream—a space for yourself.

Another reservation I have concerns our culture's voracious appetite for naming. In some cases the deployment of Theory, as a prescriptive or legitimizing device, becomes just another mode of commodification. This has been especially true in the arts. I first encountered the term postmodernism when I was finishing the film *Adynata*, a kind of pastiche of images of Orientalism, meant as a condemnation of a certain Western or colonial gaze. Yet the film, the making of it, the discovery of it, happened in muteness. I don't mean to naïvely suggest that the film came out of nowhere. In fact Edward Said's *Orientalism* helped trigger the project. The strategies employed, however, and the film's refusal to situate itself within a recuperable political discourse, while remaining somehow political, this was born of muteness.

Then one day you sit down over coffee and read about postmodernism and it is like a recipe book for what you just had such difficulty locating. The problem is not that the theory reduces a precious experience, but that it is partial, comfortable, and taming. I feel that in *Adynata*, I was attempting to tap a certain "unspeakable," and that it was important for the audience to have this experience as unspeakable. However, a difficulty arises when, under the name of postmodernism, a descriptive reading of the work's attributes precludes an in-depth reading and compromises its political thrust. What I'm addressing here is really an ambivalent relationship to theory; the irony in this is that I see my work as somehow "theoretical," or at least as converging with related trends.

This brings me back again to the idea of an avant-garde, which I do not see as a well-considered reworking of established codes, but as an improvisational act, drifting back and forth between reason and the unfamiliar.

TRINH: Instead of engaging in a discussion about the specific relationship between theory and practice (which is another endless topic; so is the question of the role of criticism in the making and exhibiting of a work as well as in the building of an audience), I would rather try to talk around this place from which you make films. It's not that we need to identify it to fortify the presence of the artist as the one who fully controls the creative process. I am more curious to understand what I see in your work as a certain uneasiness with regard to the avant-garde scene, or perhaps I should call it the *arrière-garde* scene. Your films are identified as avant-garde, exhibited mainly within avant-garde milieus, but they remain marginal even within their own category. I guess this is also a way of saying that by their marginality, they contribute to keeping the notion of the "experimental" alive, hence to resisting modernist closures often implied in the very label of "avant-garde."

THORNTON: I see my own work as a kind of "minor literature"—in the sense that Deleuze and Guattari talk about this, "like a dog digging a hole, a rat digging its the country or the world. One cannot overlook the heterogeneous nature of the histories of all socio-aesthetic movements. The "failure" of modernism, as Lyotard viewed it, is due to the resistance of the multiplicity of the worlds of names (a resistance which your answer to my first question exemplifies so well) and to the irreducible diversity of cultures. Postmodernism depends upon a rereading of culture, and this rereading is a "transversal" struggle not limited to any single country or context. As Third World subjects, we run the constant risk either of falling into the Master's hands by making his preoccupations central to ours, or of giving up our parts in the struggles by denying our very contributions to the process of questioning modernist ideals—of bringing forth new forms of subjectivities (hence of socialities)—by rethinking the self in relation to the political.

JAYAMANNE: The historical avant-garde is after all a Western phenomenon. The valorization of the new and the denigration of the old (i.e. tradition) is a Western avant-garde attitude made necessary by the historical exigencies that the various movements faced in their particular cultures. I don't think the notion of an advanced garde is very useful in the context of late capitalism and the mass culture it produces. As for postmodernism being mainly a phenomenon of American culture—that is true in a restricted sense as it defines art work that circulates in galleries and journals where pastiche is a defining feature of signification. As Geeta Kapur said in the *Art & Text* interview you mentioned, Indian art is not postmodernist in this sense, it is rather eclectic, because of the differences between cultures of surfeit and those of scarcity.

But, if postmodernism is defined in Fredric Jameson's sense, as the cultural logic of late capitalism, then in so far as the world is American, as a Sri Lankan (and here the distinction is from Indian culture which has strong regional traditions) I am interested in the effects the project of modernization has on visual culture in the postcolonial era—the era *after* the introduction of indigenous film production in 1947 and the electronic media (both T.V. and video in the early eighties). I think the latter marks the postmodern moment in our culture, along with major economic policy changes. Due to a complex number of factors involved, the statement about the "irreducible diversity of cultures" needs to be tested in particular contexts rather than simply asserted like a mantra. I know ethnographic views on the matter are sharply divided and maybe one has to repeat the slogan like a mantra even as "diversity" is homogenized in an international media culture. This is where filmmakers can intervene; the conditions for the rapid transformation of the culture are there, and can be deployed in the service of either an extreme traditionalist reaction burrow," working through that language which is given to us, in this case, that of dominant cinema and the historical avant-garde. They speak about being nomads, immigrants, Gypsies, in relation to one's own language.

I do think that when you work this way you are carving out for yourself—no place, at least in any immediate, practical sense. Working this way produces a dis-ease, and what is surprising, a resistance from even those factions that claim to support the advancement of film as an artform.

It is a rather discouraging time to be involved in a marginalized activity within an already marginal network. Financial pressures and general burnout make this a conservative period, a time of getting by. But that doesn't mean that challenging work does not continue; it is there; and when there is an adequate summoning of energy, changes in the support system will follow. Unfortunately, today the inverse is often the case—works are being produced to meet the funding and exhibition priorities which are already in place, institutionalized, commodifiable. I think it is up to the artists and writers and scholars who are feeling the limits of their systems to provoke change. Otherwise we doom ourselves.

TRINH: It's necessary to point out that we do not operate outside the exhibition network, but that we play an active part in its making, even when we think our actions can only remain passively circular within a delimiting system. I would, however, like to persist in another facet of my question concerning the work itself, or rather the filmic text that is being produced. If your work meets with difficulty circulating within the established network, and even within the already recognized alternative exhibition venues, it is perhaps because it addresses its own ambiguous relationship with the established, predominantly male tradition of avant-garde filmmaking. It has not crossed the borderlines separating works that concern themselves with paradigms of modernist artistic practice and those that grow with contemporary theoretical practices. *Adynata, There Was an Unseen Cloud Moving,* and the series on *Peggy and Fred* deal with the discourse of feminist film theory, but only to impulsively "cross" it or to instantly disperse and undermine its authority. (This is not far from Teresa de Lauretis' notion of feminist *deaesthetics.*) Perhaps the dis-ease you mentioned has to do with the concept of the "personal" we discussed earlier. I would relate it here to the deconstruction of the opposition between the private and the public implicit in feminist activities and the emphasis these activities have consistently laid on the political personal. What is implied here is a critical stance that resists the collapsing and the convenient separatism of the two notions, and offers insights into the direct relationship between institutions and individuals, sociality and subjectivity, language and consciousness. Where does language start. Where does it end? In a way, no political reflection can dispense with reflection on language. The working with language and with the process of producing meaning is precisely a concern with which purist avant-gardists have problems. Visualism and its tendency to reject the verbal image (or sound) as elements of pollution in the safeguarding of the purity of the vision, partake in this ideology of the visible or a joyously indiscriminate acceptance of all that is foreign. Real women are now emulating an image of femininity made popular by the Sinhalese cinema that has been invoked in a call for cultural purity. The phenomenon suggests that work can be done in other directions too.

TRINH: With the growing awareness of different ways of thinking about knowledge and reality (Third world, feminist, and so-called philosophical "antihumanist"), it has become more and more difficult today to turn a blind eye to power relations and to take the referential status of one's images and meaning for granted. One way of understanding the current deconstructive thrust in the arts and the humanities is to inquire about the ways the "real" is dealt with within the representational limit of a specific work or medium. How do you deal with this question in your films? In other words, how is the filmic text construed?

JAYAMANNE: In an era of simulation in which the image precedes and determines the real, can one really make images or does one need to maintain that as a fiction in order to work?

TRINH: Among the many textual strategies in vogue such as simulation and pastiche which you mentioned, those of appropriation and parody, or of bricolage, dissemination, suspension, quotation, grafting, spacing, and mapping, which, if any, come closest to speaking the displacements effected in your film on the cinematic body as spectacle? Also, since the script of *A Song of Ceylon* is adapted from an anthropological text, its title reappropriated from Basil Wright's *The Song of Ceylon,* and its visuals formed by five main sequences composed around a "possessed" body as related to film stills from Godard's films, *Passion, A Married Woman, Pierrot le Fou,* and Hitchcock's *Vertigo,* do you think that, in order to understand your film, the viewer has to be knowledgeable with regard to these references? Can one refer to tradition as a store of styles and symbols to expropriate without questioning this tradition's status as tradition, or challenging the accepted notion of tradition itself?

JAYAMANNE: Even if one has to maintain the fiction of making images, sooner or later one becomes aware of how one's images echo previous ones. But what is essential is to try to rework and rethink the material one is using. Quotation is perhaps the main device used in structuring the images in my film but I hope that the quotations do not rely upon the erudition that a knowledge of the original material would entail. Visual culture today is so much a collage which links the purist avant-gardist's discourse to the one that dominates the film industry.

THORNTON: I agree with much of what you are saying, including your last point, but where we may differ is in the value of delineating contrasts between an avant-garde practice then and now. As in the notion of post-feminism, I would prefer to say we are in a different place, a developing place; the kinds of priorities that are emerging within a marginalized practice in cinema—a focus on language and subjectivity, for instance, or a rediscovering of narrative—this is where we can invest our energies.

What is more interesting to me is the way in which a commerce can develop across works—the way a visualist practice can be taken up, the way a feminist practice can be taken up—not as a prescriptive strategy, but as one of many traces, in a mesh of traces. The danger is in any totalizing agenda, any "master discourse." Even feminism is susceptible to this kind of reification.

The point you make about the relationship between the public and the private is an important one. Maybe the "Self" is not that interesting, I don't think it is, but what flows through it can be.

TRINH: In the film series *Peggy and Fred* for example, by pointing to something very close, very familiar to American culture, you allow those who, like yourself, are part of it, to look at it differently. You make this culture "other" (an other among others). It is here that I feel what is very personal becomes a site for cultural resistance. Can you talk about some of the displacements effected in *Peggy and Fred?*

THORNTON: Yes, *Peggy and Fred in Hell* is a science-fiction-like chronicle of two small children making their way through a post-apocalyptic landscape. It uses mundane everyday images and concepts to construct a kind of devious phantasmagoria. It creates an unstable picture, in terms of character, plot, set, language, and time. Signs are stacked up arbitrarily, madly, one on top of another. Because they are decontexualized, moved just slightly, there is an estrangement which occurs, a disturbance; the mundane becomes exotic. The project looks for the structures we rely upon to make sure "reality" flows by us invisibly, that we flow within its stream. It achieves this in part by working with children, because children are not quite us and not quite other. They are becoming us, or they are becoming other. They are at a dangerous point.

TRINH: In listening to your description of the process in *Peggy and Fred*, I hear a difference. The stacking up of signs of a culture in order to understand it is an activity common to cultural analysts, but more often than not, they are stacked up in order to make something coherent out of them. Although every making is a way of playing with order, the urge to generalize, interpret, and clearly communicate is usually not dealt with as an element in the making process, so that the analyst usually comes out on top of his stack, in a position of power above the work. With such an attitude, what you have on that my preference in using quotation is not simply to take a bit from somewhere and stick it in my piece, but to try to rework what is derived from tradition in some way. For example, in the section borrowed from *A Married Woman* (which is in black and white) we alternate (more or less) between fragmenting the male body and the female body and hopefully at some point it is not clear if it is male or female but just a nice piece of ass. In Godard's film of course, it is the woman whose body is viewed tenderly by the man. In the scenes derived from *Vertigo* and *Jeanne Eagles* the role of Kim Novak is played by Juan Davila, a voluptuous man. So the burden of embodying the classical (Hollywood) lineaments of the feminine is borne by a man. By making the human bodies of the performers more like still sculptural forms, the idea was to foreground affective (possessed) gestures which seize the body, but without getting involved in character because the voice-over enactment of the ritual of cure carries the narrative.

TRINH: One type of reality that continues to be widely discussed and challenged in Third World contexts is the one characterized by a transition between tradition and modernism. What is at stake, on the one hand, is the recycling of these concepts within the framework of dualistic thinking and vertical ranking (East/West; North/South; Developed/Underdeveloped; Regress/Progress; Instinct/Reason; Nature/Culture; Heart/Mind; Woman (guardian of Tradition)/Man (advocate of Modernity)—hence the impasse that results from such perceptual stagnation; on the other hand, the denial of, or blindness to the collapse of the modern project and our confidence in its enlightening and emancipatory potential. In other words, Tradition as the Past is a modernist idea. It is in such a context that the urge to break with tradition and to install a better and entirely new way of living and of thinking is made an indispensable goal. It is also in this context that the reactive impulse to retrieve tradition in its authenticity becomes a need. Postmodernism therefore does not come *after*, but *with* modernism; it does not work so much against modernism (hence the modernist character of any anti-position) as it sets into relief its fissures and its blind fields. Since you are working now on a feature film in Sri Lanka, I assume that you must be confronting these problems.

JAYAMANNE: Yes, women have functioned as the killjoy guardians of tradition, resistant to change. What is very interesting now is the way in which "Woman/women and modernity" has become a topic of investigation both in theoretical work and filmic work. The coupling of the terms is a relatively recent development which seems to me to hold a great deal of hope for the one hand is the claim of transparency of representation and immediacy of experience, and on the other, the sovereignty of the personal/meaning subject or decoder. A film like Chris Marker's *Sans Soleil,* for example, may stay away from objectivist modes of textual production by offering the viewer a subjective layered interpretation of the cultures presented, but in spite of its impressive ability to weave images from disparate places, liberal comments and insightful analyses, it is still caught up in the process of filiation and it leaves the speaking/making subject in position as master and decoder. The difference in your work is that you do not really separate yourself from this process, not even to offer a subjective position; so that the stacking of signs is experienced mainly as an activity of production, the reading of which requires that the viewer in a sense recreate the filmic text.

THORNTON: Yes, the effort is to displace any authoritative discourse. The viewer is then put on the spot to invent, along with the film, a way of reading.

Will you indulge me for a moment? I will try to point to an aspect of my own "dream space for working." Two virtues in my book are what I'll call "stupidity" and slowness. I see stupidity as a strategy of resistance to authoritative discourses and to fashion. It offers another path to thought. I have a reference which helps me tease this through. In certain of the Gnostic texts, "thinking" is broken into various stages —Forethought, a present-thinking, and Afterthought. In other words, thinking doesn't happen in one place, in Language, for instance. Furthermore, forethought doesn't always proceed to thought, and more complex, afterthought may come first. I see the thinking in *Peggy and Fred* as happening in a "fore" and "after" space, and not so much in the middle. For example, to some extent it is true, and to some extent I affect a certain blindness to conventional narrative codes in cinema. This resistance is visible in *Peggy and Fred.* It is as if Story is being discovered. In some ways hopefully, this describes the viewer's experience as well. It is as if this were early cinema—a proto-cinema—in which Story has taken a different turn.

And slowness—you give yourself, and your work and your audience time. This project has gone on for six years now, and it is taking that long to fully understand its potential. Nothing in our culture is organized around slowness—another site for resistance?

TRINH: What accompanies the discovery of "Story" is a process of reversal in which the self is displaced. The self becomes foreign. It becomes self-other; it does not negate itself nor assimilate the other.

THORNTON: Right. It is in the interplay of difference and recognition that otherness is revealed. By working closely with our traditions, our stories, *Peggy and Fred* destabilizes the familiar. It points to an otherness within. To recognize an otherness within is to see ourselves.

opening up certain impasses within feminist work. In fact, in the new film I am researching now, *Image in the Heart,* I hope I will not make the opposition Heart/Mind. The heart of the film is the paradox of the very first star of the Sinhalese language cinema who is an ethnic Tamil but has never been perceived as such by the predominantly Sinhalese audience. As the star was both a singer and an actress, I have the chance to explore in a fairly complicated way the processes of modernization (i.e., the introduction of indigenous film to Ceylon, as it was then called) via the image and voice of a woman who galvanized audiences for several decades. It will not be a biography but a ruse to explore strategies for addressing new kinds of questions vis-à-vis women and modernization, including the issue of the "feminization of labor" in the hi-tech division of the international labor economy. So we will have a contemporary film director—a woman in her sixties—and an actress in her late thirties researching and rehearsing the film about the dead star. It will employ a film within a film structure which will permit the space/time needed to pose certain questions about the contradictory and conflicting temporalities that women are brought into through the processes of modernization. Woman as figure of modernity in torsion is something that the cinema can explore very well.

TRINH: Another, not unrelated question, concerns the very negative reactions of a large number of feminists to the term postfeminism. Why see postfeminism mainly as a term that declares feminism outmoded or as a form of going beyond feminism? Why not understand it in the sense of postmodernism, both as a disengagement of the feminist liberating project, and as a resistance to Woman and to monolithic Feminism? In other words, as a different form of subjectivity that does not come "after" feminism so much as "with" feminism, remaining alert to the movement's political closures, and keeping it from reproducing the centered, unitary, masculine subject of representation? Is the difficult work of differentiation effected between modernism and postmodernism already always effective in feminism, rendering the prefix "post" unnecessary and even destructive because of the risk it incurs in deepening the fissures that already exist in the women's movements, or are the rejections of the notion of postfeminism equivalent to modernist claims on behalf of the authority and autonomy of the signifier and its reification in a legitimation of power?

JAYAMANNE: Just putting "post" in front of feminism will not make the problems that Feminism foregrounded go away, but feminism itself has

TRINH: You have just provided me with a link between what I've said earlier on the prevailing type of individualization in the system and the myth of filiation in producing works. Actually, when you insist that works have to interact among themselves, this reminds me of the by now familiar differentiation proposed by Roland Barthes, between the notion of work and that of text. One can say very broadly that the notion of work implies a finished product, "a fragment of substance" that closes on a signified, whereas that of text brings to the fore the question of relations, the interaction among texts.

The text has a generative quality that allows it to always defer the signified. This notion, while it does not exhaust what is seen, is quite useful when one wants to talk about, for example, your video *There Was an Unseen Cloud Moving*. Perhaps, however, you could return to *Peggy and Fred* and discuss its structure?

THORNTON: The project is being produced and released as an ongoing series of 16mm films and videotapes. Though they are intended to be screened in chronological order, they can be shown individually. In an ideal screening situation, both mediums would be used—film screen in front, and TVs off to the side and in the audience. Each medium would retain its own kind of presence—cinema its epic and ethereal quality, and the television its intrusive intimacy. The seriality allows for an open-endedness in the narrative and means that new issues, strategies, and styles, can continually emerge. At this point I see the series continuing indefinitely.

Now, this brings up something we talked about earlier, which is funding and distribution. The sprawl of *Peggy and Fred* makes it questionable as a commodity. Funding agencies require a specific agenda, if not a script, then at least a confined product. In setting up shows, programmers ask when the project is going to be finished. I respond that it is happening, that I would like to show it as it develops. But I have encountered skepticism about showing something that is incomplete, a "work-in-progress." Yet its tentativeness is one of its most essential qualities. So it is important, though sometimes frustrating, to stick close by the necessities of the work, rather than succumb to the demands of the marketplace.

TRINH: Two points arise from your statements. First, I would take up again what you said earlier regarding our active participation in the process of creating exhibition possibilities, and suggest that perhaps in the case of a work like this, you may have to change the way you present it to programmers and audiences.

It seems to me that the term "work-in-progress" which has been used in relation to *Peggy and Fred* has to be redefined or used differently. As long as you retain the term "work-in-progress" in an unqualified way people will adopt habitual attitudes towards what they consider to be an unfinished work—a work awaiting a "better," more finished version. For me, every book or film I've made is a work-in-progress. So, what you have is what you get. The step you take is the finished step. But every finished step is still a step, a work-in-progress.

produced its own problems, so your definition of postfeminism as a way of remaining alive to the political and aesthetic closures of feminism is a good move. I think it is necessary to question and shake up feminist smugness and legitimation when certain discursive operations are exhausted. As Baudrillard said in Sydney, the unconscious may disappear but psychoanalysis will certainly go on regardless, and I sometimes feel when reading work that comes from the U.S. in Feminist Film Theory, that due to the powerful academic industry there, some of the work tends to repeat a certain limited number of propositions, even when terms are changed. This is connected with what I said earlier about not having much space to consider film X a bad film, it "deconstructs patriarchal modes of perception and the sound and image are montaged, etc...." But by now these strategies can amount to a too-familiar rhetoric of validation.

TRINH: Postmodernism, isolated as a *fin-de-siècle* phenomenon, can also be seen in conjunction with what is often called today the death of man/the author/the subject and the end of the real/the political/ philosophy. Thus the overall sense of impotence if not of doom, attributed to this postindividualist experience. As Baudrillard puts it, in this "social void" and "system of deterrence," no distinction can be made between active and passive, between resistance and hyperconformity. As for me, rather than talking about death, I would prefer to talk about threshold, frontier, limit, exhaustion, and suspension; about void as the very space for an infinite number of possibilities; about the work effected on one side and the other of the limit, refusing to settle on any reductive position outside or inside, and instead making possible the undoing, redoing and modifying of this very limit. The work is brought to the borderlines, to a certain exhaustion of meaning, thereby suspending its closure, this seems quite different from either escaping or annihilating meaning. Where do you draw the fine line between "anything goes" and "anything may go" (when nothing basic is taken for granted)?

JAYAMANNE: It is an exhilarating moment to be in when "nothing basic can be taken for granted," and this also goes for feminism.

THORNTON: I agree.[2]

TRINH: The second point concerns a certain notion of the actor that is implied in the way you work with the children and conceive the series, which continues to be formed as the protagonists grow (in life as well as in their acting) and as the audience feeds the process with their expectations. This notion reminds me of Godard's concept of the actor-medium, in which the actor is capable of seeing and showing at the same time, rather than just acting.

THORNTON: Yes, I've come to understand the presence of the actors in this way. It was Bill Krohn, who writes for *Cahiers du Cinema* who first pointed this out to me. He felt that I was making quite literal the documentary recording of the actors acting, in both *Peggy and Fred* and in *There Was an Unseen Cloud Moving*—the simultaneity of what is "acted" in the presence of the "actor." I think it creates a real tension in viewing. The actors leap out of the same fictional space they are constructing.

TRINH: Yes, talking about the simultaneity of the act in the presence of the figure, the text is precisely a notion that foregrounds the density of experience. In other words, instead of having a meaningful narrative line representing an experience, one would present an experience in its thickness or density.

THORNTON: Exactly. Even cinema-verité does not have this "thickness," because it too is usually organized around a storyline, so that "real life" gets naturalized into a stable narrative figure. The tension occurs in the combination of fiction and document. Both are rendered volatile.

I can give a specific example. In *Unseen Cloud,* I worked with four different women playing the lead role of Isabelle Eberhardt, the Victorian traveler and adventuress. None of these women were actors. At times they were basically being themselves, at times, they were asked to do or say specific things. In one section, one of the Isabelles describes "paradise." What she recites is actually an interpretation of the Islamic conception of paradise, as interpreted by a nineteenth-century Englishman. It appears as a footnote in what was incidentally the first English translation of the Koran. So this is already a derivative reading, a Western reading of an Islamic image. I wanted her reading to have about it a kind of absence, to mark this distance. I recorded the text and then, through a hidden earphone, she heard it for the first time as she spoke it. She describes an exotic lushness, ("and there is a tree so large that it would take over a hundred years to ride from one end of it to the other," etc.) in a manner that is both haunting and absent.

TRINH: The idea is very close to Godard's way of working with actors, but your text has a very different effect.

THORNTON: I later heard that Godard uses the same earphone technique. One of the qualities of the work which is disturbing to people is that they are uncertain of how to position the individuals involved—where they are and what their role is.

TRINH: It seems to me that there is currently a renewed interest in the science fiction genre among filmmakers who have long worked with the limits of the documentary and fictional modes. They usually find fiction unsatisfactory, and documentary too limiting. *Peggy and Fred* has been referred to as a science fiction; would you talk about this aspect of the film series?

THORNTON: When you make the effort to construct a different kind of story, another framework for time, space, social intercourse, language, etc., you might also imagine that this is possible, some time, some place, in the future. The future becomes a richly imaginative site for speculation, for an otherness, which puts you in the realm of "science fiction." However, I am cautious about using the term as an apology for certain interventions—"Oh well, that strangeness in time—that's just science fiction time." I prefer a position which is less clear—maybe science fiction, maybe not.

What is more interesting to me is the process through which we may come to recognize alternatives, to the kinds of stories we tell ourselves about ourselves. One way I think this can happen is through encounters with difference, across cultures, or across times. Last night I had a strong experience of this in the film we saw together, *Sambizanga*, by Sarah Maldoror. Apart from the film's ostensible subject matter, what I could not stop watching was the time, time as ongoing, and the time involved in looking at an event or situation. It was different from what I experience in Western cinema. Even though all of the familiar codes were there—the shots and angles, the continuity—there was something which completely exceeded the accepted form. It must reside in a cultural difference.

TRINH: The factors of time and of difference you point to are also strong experiences and very inspiring elements for me in *Sambizanga*. Although I would agree with you that the difference is a cultural one, I do think it is also more than culturally specific. Indeed, Sarah Maldoror said herself that through the rhythm of the film, she was trying to recreate "the slow pace which characterizes African life." And when one looks at films like Safi Faye's *Kaddu beykat*, Haile Gerima's *Harvest: 3000 Years* (which remains a fabulous film for me, in its different mode of storytelling as well as sense of time), or even my film *Naked Spaces–Living is Round*, one can easily say at first sight that it's "African time." But if one goes a bit further one may realize that it is not just a question of African time versus Western time, but also a question of the relations between the viewer and the context of viewing. In other words, this is not a mere case of cultural difference which people can easily dismiss ("Oh well, it's cultural..." or "You see, I'm not from your culture...."). This element of time which stands out so strongly for both of us in a Western viewing context, would probably not strike me the same way if I were sitting in an African audience. I think that it retains our attention because it is situated in the context of a dominant mode of action-cinema. To work with the notion of time in such a context to resist that very notion of time that is synonymous with action. As this latter conception is common, it is hardly surprising that most people simply understand time only in the sense that it derives from the editing of the film and constitutes its overall length. The time in *Sambizanga*, like the time in the films of Chantal Akerman and Marguerite Duras, is not merely the synthetic time of the film, it is constantly at work within the image without being subordinated to actions and camera movements.

Julia Kristeva, for example, wrote about extrasubjective and cosmic time—a form of *jouissance* she attributes to female subjectivity. This "time" inserts itself in history even as it refuses the limitations of history's time—linear time. Working *with* time means therefore working differently with the image. Gilles Deleuze classifies the body of cinematic works according to two categories: those primarily characterized by movement, and those in which time is the dominant factor, hence his two volumes on *The Movement-Image* and *The Time-Image*. There is a reversal process involved in which time is not made the measure of movement; through movement a perspective on time is made visible. The film takes on this pensive quality which Barthes considered subversive, not because it frightens, repels, or strikes, but because it *thinks*. The filmic image becomes a thinking image. This different relationship to time is the result of a mutation in the way one works with the image—a way not submitted to the "perception-action-affection" system.

THORNTON: Yes, to respond to your first point about *Sambizanga,* it is always a question of context. Yet it was in that combination of difference and recognition that time became salient. How different is this from Orientalism? On the other hand, how different is this from learning from a friend? It depends on how and why it is done, how it is used. I think that is where we must make the distinctions.

Regarding the idea of a "time-image," if I can digress for a moment, I think one of the more interesting aspects of much of the earlier avant-garde cinema was its address of time (curiously, this was seldom a focus of its criticism). Ernie Gehr's work, Peter Gidal's, Hollis Frampton's, Andy Warhol's, each produced what we might call an excruciating "time-image." This accounts in part for its affect of pensiveness.

TRINH: Talking about Deleuze's theories in relation to your films, I have another question. Deleuze sees two things happening simultaneously in the time-image. On the one hand, the image tends to become cliché; this civilization of image, as he wrote, is in fact a civilization of clichés whose powers work at hiding from us (certain things of) the image. On the other hand, the image endlessly attempts to perforate the cliché and free itself from it. This need to extract a real image from the clichés comes from the difficult knowledge that an optical or a sound image are not in themselves clichés, unless images are re-used as formulas. But to overcome clichés, it is not enough to parody them, to try to empty them, or to disturb the sensory-motor links. One has to bring to the image forces that belong neither to a simply intellectual conscience nor a social one, but to "a profoundly vital intuition," as he puts it. This way of looking at what could strongly disturb the system of action-perception-affection-image seems to me precisely what you have been working on in your films. Would you like to expand on this?

THORNTON: Let me do this with an example. When collecting material for a new episode of *Peggy and Fred in Hell*, I had copied all of the music, large stretches of silence, and occasional dialogue from Polanski's *The Tenant*, thinking I might surreptitiously weave some small trace of it into my film. Upon listening to the recording later, I realized this is it, this is the sound track for the next film, as is—grand larceny. My work had incorporated found material before, but never such a complete and unadulterated quotation.

The music is eerie and suspenseful, as are the silences. The dialogue is fleeting and provocative. Through working an image back into this sound—mostly nature images, a flock of ducks, rushing water, trees shuddering in the wind, and eventually the children, climbing out of a hole in the earth—a strange kind of horror developed, one both invisible and pervasive. There is a schism between what we see and hear, an impossibility, and in this dislocation the horror becomes unmotivated, random, and hence more threatening. It is not *The Tenant*, although it is haunted by *The Tenant*. It is not the children's story, but they are its victims.

Perhaps this is a kind of thinking through film not unrelated to what Deleuze talks about, again, through an intrusion into the familiar.

TRINH: Is it necessary for viewers to be knowledgeable about the sources of appropriation to understand the appropriation?

THORNTON: Yes and no. With knowledge it works one way, without it works differently. If you happen to have watched *The Tenant* that morning, it would have another kind of resonance. In all cases, one experiences a borrowed narrative space, superimposed.

TRINH: I see. I asked that question because I've always found very questionable the tendency in certain postmodern works to merely plunder a number of historical styles without suggesting a different reading of history. The historical status of the material from which these styles are extracted is taken for granted. So is the notion of history itself.

THORNTON: Yes, what are the ethics of appropriation? As a device or strategy it quickly exhausts itself. At its best it is a matter of problematizing judgments, at its worst, it simply defers judgments.

TRINH: Where appropriation is deployed unproblematically, the old opposition between form and content prevails, with form maintaining its decorative function. The work becomes a mere vehicle for the transmission of knowledge. It becomes a closure: you wrap up a story—some information, an analysis for the viewer—instead of keeping filmmaking alive as a mode of knowing. Working always involves a desire to modify one's consciousness or the limits of one's thinking, and to shift, not from one place to a better one, but rather intransitively. One is quickly bored with one's work where this generative quality is absent.

THORNTON: Right. I have been reading *Nomadology* (Deleuze and Guattari) and I feel very drawn to their notion of becoming, and the commerce they describe between a "royal science" and a "nomadic science." There is a wonderful metaphor they use, and that is in the building of the first Gothic cathedrals. The possibility of such height and grandeur in architectural space is something that happened originally and literally from the ground up. The stones were carved one by one to fit onto the preceding level, with an active role in the part of the maker (stone-cutter/engineer), who would see how far this possibility could extend. And what is wonderful is that sometimes the buildings actually fell down. There was that kind of risk involved. Soon, other parties in the Church and State became aware of and concerned about a certain anarchic side to this practice. It became necessary, instead of just building, to first submit plans, which would be approved and then stored some place. This brought about a whole different kind of practice and maker.

In general, the codified practice of royal science would lay a groundwork for the next intervention or layering brought about through a nomadic practice. This distinction may also be useful in considering the arts, and actually touches on many of the issues we have been talking about today.

1.   One notable exception is the work of Berenice Reynaud. See her *Film: The Frontline*, an annual publication from Arden Press.
2.   There have been recent promising developments in this direction, including a series of presentations organized by Mark McElhatten for the Collective for Living Cinema.

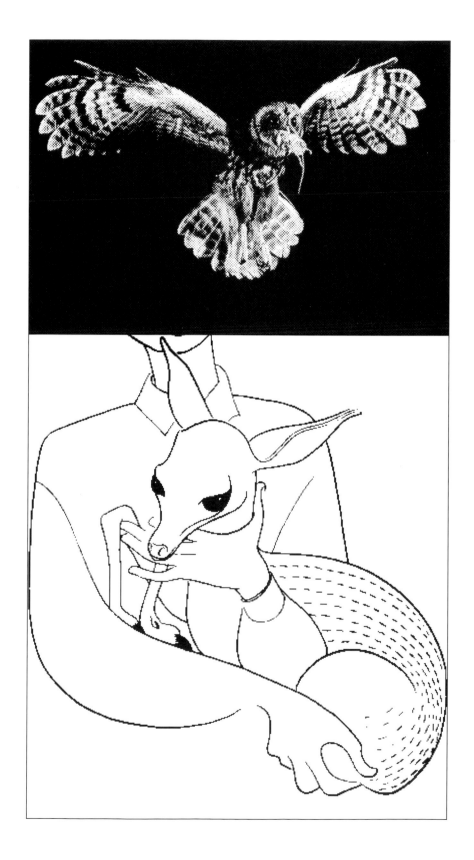

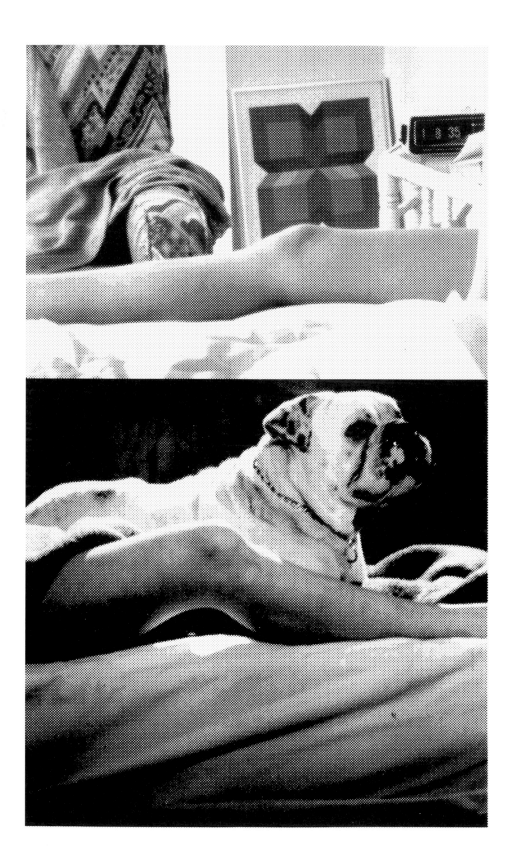

FEMINIST FILM PRACTICE & PLEASURE
Dee Dee Glass, Laura Mulvey, Judith Williamson, & Griselda Pollock

THE PLEASURE OF ACTIVITY

Women as producers, makers of meaning, filmmakers—these are fundamental new pleasures for women who have been largely excluded from the production processes of mainstream capitalist cinema. In the past decade, the impetus of the women's movement and the new opportunities afforded by technical changes—the availability of 16mm and 8mm film, for example—have encouraged women's intervention within filmmaking. Their experiences are contradictory. On the one hand, there may be the pleasure of agency and directorship, but the institutional conditions of production, in both film and television—tight budgets and limited time schedules, all-male film crews, and so forth—create conflict and constraint.

FEMINISM, PLEASURE, & THE AUDIENCE

Several years ago I went to see Chantal Akerman's *Les Rendez-vous d'Anna* at a Regional Film Theatre. The usual audience was swelled by a large number of women who had been alerted to this showing of a "feminist" film by a laudatory article on Akerman in *Spare Rib*. Much of this audience was angry and disappointed at the end—"So much for that as a feminist film!" I suspect that the laconic, highly formalized yet superbly timed progress of Akerman's film about filmmaker Anna's travels and encounters in Europe as she takes her film from regional showing to regional showing failed to provide the expected pleasure of feminist identification with a narrative about women or with a heroic female character. Most of the feminist audience was probably unfamiliar with the particular traditions of filmmaking from which and on which Akerman works. Rather than the theoretically informed stylization of *Les Rendez-vous d'Anna*, the audience had anticipated a feminist experience couched in the familiar and pleasurably reassuring conventions of realism. The question raised here is this: what do feminists expect from films? What sort of films offer them what sort of pleasure?

A different approach to these questions has been developed within feminist film theory, both in teaching and in journals like *Camera Obscura* and *Screen*. Here the emphasis has been on what feminist *readings* can discover in explicitly nonfeminist films—the pleasures of knowledge, analysis, and deconstruction. Are the pleasures of traditional film forms and feminism incompatible—or are they there to be reworked?

FEMINISM, THEORY, & PLEASURE

How do we transform the disappointment of a feminist audience anticipating the traditional narcissistic pleasures of cinema—ego-ideal identification, the search for maternal plenitude, the bisexual fantasy of the "active" phase—yet confronted with feminist interventions precisely in and against those ideologically potent structures of visual pleasure? Feminist theoretical work in photography as much as film confronts this problem. A "theory vs. practice" hostility expresses not only a fear of excessive intellectualism but also a suspicion about the alienating effect of theoretical work for a feminist audience. Yet as Laura Mulvey herself argued in 1975, the deconstruction of the pleasures of narrative cinema (identification, narcissism, and imaginary release) is a vital political project:

> The magic of the Hollywood style at its best (and of all the cinema which fell within its sphere of influence) arose, not exclusively, but in one important aspect, from its skilled and satisfying manipulation of visual pleasure. Unchallenged, mainstream film coded the erotic into the language of the dominant patriarchal order. In the highly developed Hollywood cinema it was only through these codes that the alienated subject, torn in its imaginary memory by a sense of loss, by the terror of potential lack in fantasy, came near to finding a glimpse of satisfaction: through its formal beauty and its play on his own formative obsessions. This article will discuss the interweaving of that erotic pleasure in film, its meaning, and in particular the central place of the image of woman. It is said that analyzing pleasure, or beauty, destroys it. That is the intention of this article. The satisfaction and reinforcement of the ego that represent the high point of film history hitherto must be attacked. Not in favor of a reconstructed new pleasure, which cannot exist in the abstract, nor of intellectualized unpleasure, but to make for a total negation of the ease and plenitude of the narrative fiction film. The alternative is the thrill that comes from leaving the past behind without rejecting it, transcending outworn or oppressive forms, or daring to break with normal pleasurable expectations in order to conceive a new language of desire.[1]

Much subsequent writing about the question of pleasure has been influenced by Laura Mulvey's argument in "Visual Pleasure and Narrative Cinema." But the article, partly because of its author's simultaneous engagements in filmmaking, also belongs in a network of practices beyond the purely theoretical and critical. Film strategies were developing which already called into question the normative processes of visual pleasure in film—Jean-Luc Godard's severance of the semiotic codes by separating image and sound is but one example[2]—and these found an echo in the separation of the visual and the textual in art discourses. Since 1975, photographic and film practice generated within feminism and associated political perspectives have produced a variety of work which can be recognized as components of a new language of desire, productive of new order, new visual pleasures.[3] What are these? How do they function? How are viewers to *read* them?

—Griselda Pollock

DEE DEE GLASS: I do think there is some kind of common women's culture. So addressing women is fairly easy because if I adopt an attitude and show certain images around it, I feel other women are going to be able to identify with that attitude. But then, it's easier for me to say that because, in terms of film language, the documentaries I work in are much more conventional than, say, the language Laura works in.

JUDITH WILLIAMSON: So one important pleasure for you would be that identification in the sense of getting across to your audience?

GRISELDA POLLOCK: But identification is not something which happens spontaneously in the viewer—it's a result of processes actively putting you in the position that you think you're identifying with spontaneously. Often when talking about feminist film culture there is a kind of idealism—the idea that you the filmmaker are just evoking something that's already there. It's almost like the romantic theory of art as a bridge between the person who makes the film and her audience. And while I'm interested in the question of evoking a hidden sense of a public, I think that feminist film might have to consider the question of how identifications are actually constituted.

LAURA MULVEY: I was struck, Dee Dee, by what you were saying about women's culture and women's experience being something separate—that you appeal to it in turning the private and the personalized into a visual experience. There you were talking about a popular experience the dominant culture hadn't bothered to take into account. You seem to be trying to find areas of life which dominant mass culture hasn't explored and exploited. One can see that search for the uncolonized in quite a lot of alternative work, and in feminist work as well. It was also one of the impulses behind *Riddles of the Sphinx*—taking the question of motherhood and the mother-child relationship as an area that patriarchy has relegated to the nursery. So one can see various gestures towards discovering and exploring things in these "other" areas: the fact that they're small and "not important" makes them of greater importance.

WILLIAMSON: That's actually what my film was about, from a different angle. The brief was very general—it was supposed to be about advertising, based on my book.[4] I didn't want to do it that way, because it's now six years since I wrote *Decoding Advertisements* and I have become much more interested in the debate raised by your film. At that point I was trying to work out whether there really are uncolonized areas—which I think is fairly dubious. What I've brought to the topic of advertising on this occasion is work I've been doing about the way that not feminism but capitalism constantly attempts to find uncolonized areas.

MULVEY: What do you mean?

WILLIAMSON: That there is a desperate search which feeds off the desire which Dee Dee is describing. It's a real desire to find new areas, but it's also an economic one. We are using "colonization" as a metaphor. Our way of life is based on the rise of industrialism, and that was made possible in this country by going outside the domestic cultural sphere to colonize "wild," untouched areas. Today, the equivalent search seems to be for uncolonized areas *within* society—geographically, we cannot go outside anymore. There's a really good chapter in *Woman's Consciousness, Man's World,*[5] where Sheila Rowbotham talks about the boom in products for women's personal use and in health products—the move into fringe areas, into the body, into private areas, in fact.

MULVEY: I'm sure you can consider that movement as having two directions—the turn to nature and then a move inwards to the private, the body.

WILLIAMSON: Images of the wild and the natural have now been overtaken by images of the woman. And because they seem to be uncolonized, they're like a diversion. They are the other side of what is acceptable in modern life. It reminds me of insurance adverts—slave away and pour your money into things so that over here, you can have your wife and family, your home. The areas that justify everything else are the personal ones.

GLASS: I think the significant issue here is capitalism's relentless search for areas within a culture that can be colonized. Take the absorption of the Black Power movement and the women's movement in America. You have Afro sprays and all that, and you have the Virginia Slims cigarette campaign ("You've come a long way, Baby") which uses the image of the successful woman. You take whatever the women's movement has accomplished and you colonize it, you sanitize it, and you make it safe. In purely capitalist terms, it's extremely successful. But what I really wanted to ask you goes back to the question of audience. Do you think that by making what I think are feminist films and putting them on television, I am allowing them to be colonized? Television is like an enormous sandwich, so you may see *Mind Your Language* before my film goes on and then some appalling Sussex vicar talking about God and family life after it. Is that somehow colonizing my films?

WILLIAMSON: Not necessarily. I also think that women who aren't consciously feminist see things on television which affect them. I remember seeing a program in my teens about premenstrual tension. It was an ordinary documentary, but the fact that it was on television, that it was public, was very powerful. I remember feeling identification and a kind of triumph that this should be regarded as a subject for a documentary in fairly prime time. Although one can go into all the things behind that, the way that television seems to validate certain things, you can't just push it aside and say that if you work in the mainstream everything you do is colonized.

GLASS: Well, it's very difficult to work that one out. For example, I made a film about anorexia for Southern Television in which I used half a dozen clips from the Disney *Sleeping Beauty* and *Snow White* cartoons—images of the witch giving Snow White the apple, the Sleeping Beauty being awoken by the prince, the slaying of the dragon, and all that. Even though they only made up a total of perhaps ten minutes, it was actually very difficult to prevent them taking over the film—because they are such powerful images from our collective childhoods.

WILLIAMSON: I had the same problem using advertisements in my film. My strategy—which I don't think was very successful—was to mix archive and contemporary adverts with very plain, slow tracks. No quick cutting or zippy camera movements, everything square, a very ex-RCA[6] puritanical style very recognizable to me now. So there was a contrast between what I had shot and then, suddenly, these fast, exciting adverts. Although there are some shots that I still like, especially pans and camera movements where there was something else happening in the frame, this plain section now seems a bit pedantic. That problem of the pleasure of the advertising material leads into a more general argument about pleasure in film—the debates that Laura's work started off. Although I accept that a lot of the pleasure in mainstream films is gender based—the pleasure of looking at women and so on—I know that I still get another kind of pleasure from watching films which comes from particular combinations of camera movements, from other movements, from music, and things like that. So the question of whether to produce pleasure or combat it becomes broader—a question of style and how you make films. When I was at film school you were regarded as reactionary, you were virtually fascist if you did anything in your film that produced a kind of cinematic pleasure. There was a closed-in feeling, based on a critique of mainstream films, that you mustn't do any of these little exciting things.

MULVEY: But do you think that's a kind of functionalism, like the rejection of Victorian style by the Bauhaus—a rejection on an aesthetic level?

WILLIAMSON: I think it was a rejection of a style *and* a rejection of pleasure. It ties in with something deeper—with a puritanical attitude which feminism has only recently become really aware of and started to tackle. At first, I think, a lot of the feminist movement had a very ambiguous relationship to puritanism, as opposed to pleasure—in the debates about pornography, for example, which I'm certainly not very clear about. In combatting traditional forms of pleasure, how far are you combatting all pleasure? And in that case, what kind can you retain in your own filmmaking?

THEORY & PRACTICE

GLASS: As you both started making films after you had worked on them theoretically, do you feel that your attitudes about the pleasure they give you and also your theoretical attitudes have shifted at all?

MULVEY: Do I see films differently?

GLASS: Yes—and how do you see films differently? I mean, I can read an essay about John Ford and know from the inaccuracies and the technical mistakes that the author has never been near a film set. Decisions about how to shoot and how to put shots into a film, which I assume you picked up from working, are often nontheoretical. In other words, you see this wonderful wide shot in which Ford has the sun setting behind John Wayne, and you can write fifty pages about the meaning of life, the lone man in the desert, and all the rest of it. Then it actually turns out that the shot was like that because the studio said this was the last day of filming, the light was going, and so there was only time to shoot that one shot. So the reason wasn't to do with the meaning of life—it was actually to do with practical considerations.

MULVEY: That's difficult to answer because I don't think my way of looking at films has been much affected by my own way of making films—which is so different from a Hollywood set in the studio system, it's almost like chalk and cheese. I don't think I have learnt much that I could apply backwards, though I do feel I constantly learn from the body of cinema and try to think that through even though the conditions of production are so different.

Where I have learnt most is probably through teaching and looking at films in great detail. Obviously one teaches films that seem aesthetically successful, but actually I think rather the opposite to you. What astonishes me is how much more was thought out than one might have imagined. That sense of intense detail of construction is one of the fantastic pleasures of Hollywood cinema. I think it's something that comes from that very, very controlled way of working in the studio and on the set, where very little happened by accident. It's very different from the location-based Hollywood of the sixties and seventies, which is much speedier.

WILLIAMSON: In making my film, I was working in a very straight set-up, mostly on a set, with an ordinary crew, all of them were men—I was the director. That's what I really couldn't cope with. When you've only got ten minutes left before everyone is on triple overtime and the fuse has gone on the video thing, so you can't do the shot you planned and so you've got to rewrite something very quickly—in those situations you're still forced into making definite choices, even if you're not consciously thinking theoretically. So I disagree with Dee Dee's point that practical, working decisions aren't theoretical—the idea of "theory" may be a red herring, because it sounds deliberate, but your decisions are still based on how you want the film to look, what you want it to mean, and how you want it to give an impression to people. And those things *are* precisely what "theoretical" criticism looks at. In fact I think that often it's when you're under greatest pressure, like making snap decisions, that your underlying *assumptions* about film get put into practice, whether deliberately or not. If the light's going and you can only do one shot, what that one shot is will say an awful lot about the meaning you want it to achieve. Anyway, in answer to your question, when I see films by other people, I feel tremendous admiration and jealousy that they have managed to make things happen the way they wanted, that they've got a grip on these details.

FEMINISM, PLEASURE, & FILMMAKING

POLLOCK: Even if all production is more or less materially determined, I don't think that can be reduced to the question of practical constraints. Although the technical area hasn't been adequately incorporated into theoretical explanations of film, I don't think a theory/practice opposition will get us anywhere. In terms of feminist film practice, the theory/practice contrast just doesn't work—on two levels. First of all, if you use the argument about material determination, there wouldn't be any feminist film. We actually have to go out in the first instance and create the conditions for financing, to get together the collectors or companies to provide backing, to exploit the independent circuits. To make feminist films requires quite an active policy.

GLASS: That only applies if you don't believe in subversion.

POLLOCK: But you do have to construct spaces as part of a much broader movement actually to create the possibility of an alternative independent film culture. And secondly, you have to think about what kinds of films feminists should be making and what kinds of jobs they are going to be doing. Whether you call it theory or you don't call it theory, it means trying to understand the nature of the film culture into which you may be intruding.

GLASS: I think it's less a debate between theory and practice than a debate about where you start from. I'd be very unhappy if I had to sit down and decide how feminist films ought to be constructed.

POLLOCK: No, I'm not saying we should decide how feminist films *ought* to be constructed, but that any feminist making a film makes decisions which are informed by a sense of what a film is. You make decisions, that's essential. Now those decisions can either be programmatically conjured out of your back issues of *Screen* or Noël Burch's *Theory of Film Practice* [7]—identify every law of film and break it. That's an easy way to an alternative film culture. Or, in the sense we're talking about, those decisions depend on the ways that feminist film can mobilize features we've come to understand, appreciate, or be amazed at in cinema—recognizing the ideological significance of certain moves and realizing how feminist film can avoid being merely oppositional, a negation, but go into those spaces. That requires an informed knowledge about the film tradition we've gone back to.

WILLIAMSON: But to an extent we're already in those spaces, in two distinct ways. In studying and teaching Hollywood films—films that weren't consciously made as feminist—it's possible to draw out a feminist dimension that can be discussed. Secondly, there are feminists already in structures like television. So it's not just a question of feminists wondering, how shall I make a film? What's really important is where these things tie up—having found elements in mainstream films and other kinds of filmmaking that not just feminists or women can use or enjoy. So the question isn't just, does being a feminist mean you make a feminist film? There are all these different possibilities—you get women and feminists, you get feminist films made by women who aren't setting out to be feminists. In a way my film isn't deliberately feminist. I'm a feminist, I'm making a film about advertising, but it wasn't specifically to do with advertising and women. It reminds me of an argument at the Co-Op[8] once about a simplistic version of Laura's idea that the male view is the basis of "the look" in traditional cinema. Some people were arguing that there had to be a camerawoman shooting, otherwise the look would be a male look—having a camera*man* was absolutely out. I think it's difficult having a cameraman on your crew if you're a woman making a film for other reasons.

GLASS: I don't think anyone would argue with you on that point!

WILLIAMSON: There are all these questions about what makes a feminist film. What you were saying implied that a feminist would sit down and think, well, how do I make a feminist film?

POLLOCK: I don't see why not. We don't have to get into the problems of categorizing. We agreed that there are ways that feminists discover and make use of critical, subversive elements in films that don't ostensibly claim to promote the cause of women. But if you ask yourself what constitutes a feminist practice, then what sort of things are you concerned to do?

MULVEY: I think that takes us back to the question of pleasure. You can only make a film in a way that actually pleases you. I think it's really significant that I feel I can learn a lot from Hollywood movies and you don't feel you can, Dee Dee, because the kind of movies we make and our approaches to film are very different. It's essential to realize that I couldn't make films like you do because I just couldn't! I could enjoy your films and learn a lot from them, but I couldn't make them. A problem one sometimes faces in talking about a film after you present it is that people ask you, why did you do that? Wouldn't something else have been better? People often seem to want to re-make your film for you. It's difficult to answer, because often you've done it that way because that's the way it pleases you.

WILLIAMSON: Having that confidence in your ideas, in what you want to see and how you want to make it look and the things you want to do seems quite feminist in itself, given the difficulties facing a woman making a film. It's like women in the movement reclaiming the way they feel or their right to do things. Rather than asking what is a feminist film practice, I'd ask what is *my* feminist film practice. I probably wouldn't even put "feminist" in because I know I'm a feminist and I wouldn't need to say it to myself when I was at my desk.

POLLOCK: This seems to me the classic fetishism of the artist. Granted, there are special difficulties in mobilizing the resources, finances, and machinery needed to get a film made. But why is your practice as a filmmaker different, for instance, from my practice as a writer about cultural artifacts and history? I wouldn't just say, I'm a feminist and that inevitably comes through. I ask myself, what is it to do feminist history or feminist art history? What have other feminists done? Where does that end them up? How did they produce cultural myths about artists and notions about the aesthetic which are ideologically regressive? It seems to me that the project of feminism has to include not just a pluralistic individualism, but a questioning of ourselves and what we do. That's not a moral imperative or a unitarily imposed program—"This is what a feminist film is." But you ask yourself that question because you know that everything you carry with you—from what turns you on in the cinema to what happy memories you have—are both potentially progressive *and* positively regressive. They have to be negotiated with some care.

WILLIAMSON: One reason I feel so vehemently about this is because I now think that parts of my film suffered because I felt pressurized to stick to certain ideas about radical filmmaking. They were bound up with my particular situation, the women around me, the group I was in, being at the RCA—ideas that this was a radical thing to do, this was a feminist thing to do, you must have a woman doing this or that. There were various things I felt I ought to do as a feminist and as a Marxist, and that was very restrictive. I still think the most successful parts of the film—which are no less Marxist or feminist—are those where I did follow through an idea I had or something I wanted to do. It sounds like your classic artist!

POLLOCK: The point I was making is that the myth is there for us to fall into. Putting it crudely, there are so many traps which have to be negotiated by nourishing a constantly evolving political consciousness.

MULVEY: Yes, but talking in terms of pleasure, Griselda, the point was that there should be a pleasure in what you're producing even if the work is a minimal one and may not appear pleasurable to the people consuming it. It may seem like an ultimate demand on the spectator to work, but for the person who is making the film, there must be some kind of pleasure involved in producing it. Even from the point of view of seeing yourself as a woman filmmaker, as Judith described herself, or as a feminist filmmaker, which is more as Dee Dee describes herself, you can see how utterly diverse these instances of pleasure are. That can take you back to the actual psychoanalytic individual—which I think is possibly the right theoretical approach. Rather than dismissing this as a romanticism of the individual artist, you can see that—even while we've all been part of a struggle to create a feminist culture and an alternative, feminist way of looking—at the same time our own psychoanalytic stances are valid. And that produces very varied practices.

POLLOCK: There's a point underlying that which really intrigues me—it only dawned on me recently when writing about women artists. Women artists are up against the notion that the artist in the most general sense of our culture is the most self-fulfilling and privileged form of creative actor.

MULVEY: Oh, now I know what you are talking about. It's like that discussion at the ICA[9]—there was total misunderstanding between two sides of the room....

POLLOCK: Yes, and it led me onto this. The problem is that on the one hand, women have been denied cultural creativity both in terms of recognition and in terms of practice. And on the other hand, think of the place women occupy in the work scene—the antithesis of self-fulfilling creative work, not just alienated labor but repetitive drudgery. They are the replaceable secretary, nurse, clerical worker, housewife.

What interested me is the way that women involved in making either art or film are demanding a creative individuality (or at least recognition of their own creative individuality within a profession where it is denied them) on behalf of *all* women—who have generally been seen as noncreative. Yet at the same time there is a reasonable criticism of the mythology, the romanticism of the creative individual.

MULVEY: The film community, if one can roughly call it that, appears to have rather different problems from the visual arts. I was really surprised that afternoon to see how strong the desire to be an artist was among the women there. They felt that was a position denied them, but they wanted to get at it by delving into a particular sensitivity that was in itself feminine. Out of that they would produce feminine art or feminist art.

The film community is quite different in various ways. I don't know if the others would agree, but I think one thing that has marked many of us is the historical moment. Alternative practices in cinema, the availability of 16mm equipment and stock, and so on, came on the scene at a crucial moment. It coincided, on the one hand, with the development of alternative politics in the U.S.—the antiwar movements and women's movements—and quickly became a political instrument. You can see a first wave of alternative films that were specifically politicized, made by people who didn't see themselves as artists and used the film as a weapon of agitation. Then on the other hand, on the aesthetic front, you can also see film being adopted by people in the art community who were questioning the place of the artist—photography became important to some artists around the same time. So that kind of experimental film is also marked by a questioning of traditional views of art. What's interesting about independent avant-garde films is the way these two tendencies have cross-fertilized at various points whilst staying apart.

At the same time, here we are sitting around talking in a way I don't think would be possible about any other medium at the moment. It's our background in film *and* in the women's movement which has made this kind of thing possible, whereas in the visual arts there hasn't been that kind of traumatic history.

GLASS: On your initial question about what gives us pleasure, I keep coming back to the word collectivity—the collectivity of filmmaking or of making television programs. Judith was saying she felt ill-equipped for directing a film with a bunch of men around because it was a role we as women are not trained to do. When I was first directing television, there were no other women film directors in that company and no other women in my office except for secretaries, who refused to treat me as anything but a director. So it took a long time before I had anything like an equal relationship to them, on top of which I had to use staff crews on the first two films I made. What happened was that without noticing it, I became a "man." I went home after my first film and my husband was chopping the veg or something for dinner. I just walked into the kitchen and said, "Look, why don't you put the potatoes on before you do the carrots." And he turned round to me and said: "Just sit down and stop directing this dinner. I'm doing the dinner, you're going to eat the dinner, pull yourself together." It was extremely important that people were saying things like that to me because that happens to most women who produce and direct television programs, and actually to women who enter any kind of power structure.

Eventually two other women started work as researchers in my office and we formed a sort of united front against the world. But one can also prevent the process by becoming involved in collective organizations either around one's work or completely outside it. There are groups of women in which one is supported not because one makes £500 a week and can control a budget of £60,000, but through a process of collective questioning which is both challenging and supportive.

POLLOCK: That theme around the actual conditions of production has come up a couple of times. What do you think are the priorities for change in the organizational base for feminist film? Ages ago, Judith, we were talking about how difficult it had been to make your film and you mentioned the contrast with the way Sally Potter made *Thriller* [10]—how it might be more possible to achieve the "feminist look" within a collective because other members of the crew share your concerns and premises. I'm interested in the question of how the formal problems we can discuss in relation to different types of feminist film are related to the way the films are actually made.

WILLIAMSON: I remember that conversation. I wasn't really contrasting my own position with the way Sally Potter was working in a collective. What I was saying was that there wasn't a great division of labor. I remember going to the Co-Op and finding her working on *Thriller*. The film was in black and white, and she had done just about every single thing herself. She was alone in the little cutting room. It was very peaceful and she had plenty of time. There wasn't someone saying, I've got to have this in three weeks time, will you have completed it by then? The Co-Op has the facilities for developing your own film, so you don't have to rush up and down hassling the people at the labs. So that's what I was talking about—this feeling of her working in her own time, in her own way, controlling every part of the process.

GLASS: But Sally Potter is allowed to do that and Laura is allowed to do what she does on her films because they're outside the power structure. Once you're filming on 35mm or if the film's going to be transmitted on television, then you're going to come closer to various problems, like how you are going to deal with the ACTT.[11]

MULVEY: Basically we work with union people.

GLASS: But the real problem we haven't addressed is that I think many people who make independent films have decided, consciously or unconsciously, that what's important is the *process* rather than the product or what happens to the product. That's to say, a few hundred people are going to see the film and they're all going to know what you're doing anyhow—so to a great extent it's going to act as a reinforcement. Now I've made the crude political decision that because films are so expensive and because I want most people to see my films, I am willing to fight within television to get them made. How do you reconcile these two approaches? If all feminist filmmakers are independent filmmakers, then they would have to answer the question, "Are you doing the same thing as an artist painting squares and circles or wrapping polythene around the west coast of Scotland? Are you doing it just for your own pleasure?"

WILLIAMSON: It would be awful if there were no feminist interventions in television—both things have to be going on side by side. You can't abandon television but, because of the women's movement and the work of women teaching, there are other contexts than film societies in which to show films like Laura's. If my film was finished, it would mainly be shown in colleges, perhaps to sixth formers in schools and also to women's groups. People often want to use a film in a meeting or discussion—so the audience for independent films isn't really so select.

GLASS: One of the basic tenets of feminism is reaching out to other women. If, like me, you believe that there are things which all women have in common and it's vitally important to analyze these things, then feminism has urgent reasons for getting feminist films seen by as many people as possible.

MULVEY: Whereas when Peter Wollen and I made *Riddles of the Sphinx,* we wouldn't have thought it could really benefit the film or anyone to have it shown on television. Partly that's because of the way it was shot—it's very much a *film* film rather than a television film—but it's also because at that stage we were really trying to experiment with film. We see those films not as final products but as part of what's generally called "ongoing discussion"—they come out of that and so have to appear within it. If they were just plonked on television they wouldn't have the same meaning. They weren't made with a wide audience in mind but with the intention of changing particular people's attitudes to film—on the one hand, women interested in questions of representation and, on the other hand, people involved in film and interested in film and politics. I think there is a place for that kind of work and for research and experimentation in film. This isn't to say that there wasn't an aesthetic drive and pleasure at the same time for me in making the films, but I don't see them having a place outside an area of discussion. As the area of discussion changes, it expands and the context changes.

WILLIAMSON: It's also interesting the other way around. When I was working on *Time Out*, I remember typing out the programs for a season of Women's Films at the Institute of Contemporary Arts. They mixed together independent films made at the Co-Op with straight half-hour television programs about an aspect of women's lives. There was much more interaction between the two fields than had been possible before—it would have been unthinkable a while ago for the ICA to show this mixture of early films made by women in 1916, contemporary independent feminist films, and also the television films. By putting them alongside each other as women's films, it showed how feminism has broadened interest in women's issues and in women's filmmaking. I think all of that is really important and it has been broadened by the women's movement.

1. Laura Mulvey, "Visual Pleasure and Narrative Cinema," *Screen*, vol.16, no. 3 (1975): 87.

2. See Colin MacCabe, *Godard: Images, Sounds, Politics* (London: BFI/Macmillan, 1980).

3. See for example, Victor Burgin, "Seeing Sense," *Artforum* (February 1980); Angela Martin, "Chantal Akerman's Films: A Dossier," *Feminist Review*, no. 3 (1979); Yvonne Rainer, "Looking Myself in the Mouth," *October*, no. 17 (1981); Ann Sargent-Wooster, "Yvonne Rainer's *Journeys From Berlin*, 1971-1980," *Drama Review*, no. 2 (1980); Gillian Swanson and Lucy Moy-Thomas, "An Interview with Sally Potter," *Undercut*, no. 1 (1981).

4. Judith Williamson, *Decoding Advertisements* (London: Marion Boyars Publishers Ltd., 1978).

5. Sheila Rowbotham, *Woman's Consciousness, Man's World* (Harmondsworth: Penguin, 1973).

6. Royal College of Art, London.

7. Noël Burch, *Theory of Film Practice* (London: Secker and Warburg, 1973).

8. The London Film-makers Co-op.

9. The reference here is to a discussion at a conference held at the Institute of Contemporary Arts, London, in association with the exhibition *Issue: Social Strategies by Women Artists*, selected by Lucy R. Lippard, November 14–December 21, 1980.

10. *Thriller* directed by Sally Potter, 1979. See Sally Potter, "On *Thriller*," and Jane Weinstock, "She Who Laughs First Laughs Last," *Camera Obscura*, no. 5 (Spring 1980).

11. The Association of Cinematograph, Television, and Allied Technicians.

REPRINTED FROM FORMATIONS EDITORIAL COLLECTIVE, EDS., *FORMATIONS OF PLEASURE* (LONDON: ROUTLEDGE & KEGAN PAUL, 1983), PP. 156-170.

JULIA KRISTEVA
Alice Jardine

ALICE JARDINE: Let me present our work a bit first, since to take up the subject of this end of the century may not be an altogether obvious thing to do. As I have told you, © is a new journal founded by myself and some friends and students around the question: "What's left to be done?"

JULIA KRISTEVA: Everything!

JARDINE: This quotation-question returns today as a result of the innovations as well as of the dead ends, the impasses, in contemporary theory and practice, and for some of us, one might say postmodern theory and practice. For us, it has become more and more evident that there is no longer an independent place from which one can advance a practice of liberation in the classical sense of the term. So we began asking ourselves a whole series of questions: in a world where events and effects have become more or less interchangeable; in a "hyperreal" world, as Baudrillard would say; in this world where the systems by which we reproduce more and more repetitively and homogeneously our social conditions, our knowledge, our desires, and ourselves; in a world where these systems have achieved in my opinion a flexibility which can absorb any challenge presented in any form by anyone.... In this world where there seems to be nothing new, where there is a kind of boredom catching up with everyone.... *Is it possible*—this is the question with which we began—is it possible to escape the code anyway? To imagine new forms of personal and political liberation? Or to produce "something new," as you might say? So we decided to begin asking these questions in the first issue of ©, an issue of reflections around our end of the century. That's the title, a re-iteration, with great irony; an end of the century which is also an end of the millennium, of course. And in attempting to distinguish the principal questions, we the strong-willed, who are still somehow engagé, or at least insist on remaining engagé in a struggle for the radical change of our society....

Well, perhaps we can begin by evoking the exhibition which has just ended at the Pompidou Center on Vienna, that other *fin de siècle,* an end which has been presented as the place and time of the birth of our modernity—from Freud to technology. Many have celebrated the "newness" of that moment—with all of the good and bad consequences we know about. Do you think one can speak in a parallel manner today about an analogous phenomenon, a birth of a postmodernity, or is it instead necessary to speak of a regression towards a premodernity, or perhaps both at once? And, with this in mind, is there a place, is there a Vienna today, where all these things occur more than anywhere else?

KRISTEVA: I think the phenomenon of Vienna is overvalued because of the fact that we are in the process of assessing the catastrophe which Europe and the world experienced during the nineteenth century, at the end of the nineteenth, and at the beginning of the twentieth, and that there is an insistently present melancholic spirit that constantly wants to reexamine this catastrophe; it does not recognize that we are no longer there, that something else is happening now. It is a kind of addiction to pain, like to a drug, which is an important part of human psychology—as an analyst, I'm in a good position to know this—but which in the social arena consists in believing that the Second World War did not happen, and that the free world did not triumph, that France, America, and England did not conquer fascism, and that the after-effects of the war—existentialism, the *nouveau roman,* etc. were still the phenomena of injury and consequences of this immense catastrophe—are not dying out. So there is this melancholic addiction. There is also the fact that what is happening now is still difficult to perceive, as with all new phenomena, and that due to this incapacity to distinguish what is new, there is the tendency to hypostasize what happened before, and thus to discover things which have endured, but which were important a long time ago. As Hegel always said, history is like...the historian and the philosophers are like owls who awake at dawn after everything has happened; they come in the morning to say, there it is, it happened, but *it happened.* So what is really happening today? I do think, actually, that we are in a postmodern effect which is attempting to recapture phenomena previous to the nineteenth century: possibilities of pleasure, desire, and *jouissance,* phenomena which are profoundly inscribed in the French eighteenth century. And what is trying to take shape from this point of view, in the sense of an anti-Vienna or a post-Vienna (because it is not a question of burying these phenomena—they happened, it is necessary to meditate on that—but one must not stop there) is a resurgence of French "taste," of the eighteenth-century spirit from Diderot to Crébillon, the libertine side, of *joie de vivre,* pleasure of the text, etc. I am always very disturbed when my students, while studying Barthes, for example (which is a recent phenomenon—this year a number of new books on Barthes have appeared) place him beside Blanchot or Duras. It is true that Barthes, in fact, did record a kind of modern upheaval. His was an evaluation of values in a post-Nietzschean, in effect, marginal spirit. But he also placed taste, distinction, jouissance, and pleasure of the text above this enormous wound. And this is what is happening now. There is currently an enormous upsurge in France among the very young, the generation after Barthes, *Tel Quel, L'Infini,* etc., young writers who I see as formulating a demand for a "national identity" that I perceive as a potential antidote to Le Pen—especially insofar as there does seem to be this sort of wound that French citizens sustain in seeing themselves invaded by foreigners. There are a lot of people who are not necessarily fascists and Nazis, and who react to this in various ways and which explains this phenomenon.... But at the intellectual level this reaction clearly undergoes a metamorphosis: there is an attempt to emphasize and promote tradition, the tradition of the eighteenth century. And how does this manifest itself? In terms of an anti-Vienna reaction: against morbidity, against melancholy, against this ideology of the loss of meaning, which is the ideology of the modern—and yet without repressing it either. One will not create a literature of naïve optimism, but one can attempt to trace above this volcano new possibilities for pleasure, for joy, for ways of living which one knows are ephemeral, but which nevertheless may remain options. This is an affirmation of the positive.

JARDINE: And you find this optimistic? Do you find this promising?

KRISTEVA: It is a form of subtle optimism, I would say, because it is not the optimism of someone who has not been disturbed by the phenomena, the losses of meaning, of which we speak, but I see here the promise of another aesthetic. And if something is going to emerge, it is in this direction, otherwise one is condemned to repeat ad infinitum the sort of collapse of Europe which took place in central Europe, Nazi Germany. But for me, that moment is already over; the very existence of the Pompidou exhibit shows that we are getting some distance. There will always be people who do not know about it, and who will take their university and high school classes through an exhibit like this one, so it is useful. But one should not take this as a horizon, because one must see the other events taking place around us now, fed by an impatience with this morbid spirit. They are trying to exceed it without ignoring it, starting from a tradition which once manifested the vital force of European culture. And after all, the war, we were the ones who won it, not Vienna, not Hitler, nor the painters exhibited there. I think the current vitality is a cultural phenomenon responding to forms that we associate with the United States, and that find perhaps a more popular, mass culture in the interest of young people for Reaganism, long-live-America, let's be the victors, let's be the conquerors. This can be seen as extremely regressive and thick-headed, but it also corresponds to a desire to go beyond an intellectual ideology of negativity, of nihilism. So it is necessary to take into account such phenomena, to attempt to propose a culture which acknowledges the decline of values yet offers a possibility for living. And not the permanent fascination in the face of death.

JARDINE: I wonder how, though.... In the U.S., a little less here perhaps, but in the U.S., it is at times very difficult to discern or distinguish between the young people for Reagan, who speak without knowing, without having experienced this melancholy or this crisis, and those who are attempting to create something new. All of this tends to get confused.

KRISTEVA: Yes. But one role of the intellectual is to be on the cutting edge of these two current worlds, and to try to give them a new content other than the one being asked for, and not, as is often the case with American intellectuals, to be the epigones of European movements of ten years ago.

JARDINE: Do you think there is a most urgent question or problematic for our end of the century, for our era?

KRISTEVA: In my present state of mind, I think that all *global* problematics are archaic; that one should not formulate global problematics because that is part of a totalitarian and totalizing conception of history. One cannot say, "This is the problematic." Such an approach is due to the development of the sciences, the development of the media, and to the atomization of individuals. So I think one must try to find regions, localized problematics which are having a vital impact. And this is in a way what a certain number of people of my generation did, for example, when they abandoned, or began to abandon, the great philosophical preoccupations in favor of textual analysis, or psychoanalysis, or anthropological projects, or very precise linguistic work. I think that one should, from the region where one is located, pose these vital problematics. One must ask different specialists how they see the approaches.... Because if one continues to posit large problematics, what is the solution? There is no solution, there is no global solution, because one is caught in globality. There is no globality. The universe, contrary to what appears on television—namely, the idea that everyone reads in the same way—this totality, this unification of the universe is false. Where are things actually happening? In specific regions in our intimate lives, or in different fragmentations of knowledge through very specific research.

JARDINE: Given what you have just said, I do not really want to return to *global* problematics. But our group has attempted to localize a few very *general* problematics for the end of this century: there is the question of the State and the problem of how to govern; religion; technology; sexual difference; art, etc. For example, we worked for a long while on questions around the State. For the young, in particular, there seems to be a lack of models in a Western world which is more and more mediatized. They feel caught between totalitarian systems, where there is a gap between what one calls reality and the information one has about it, and a so-called free and democratic system, in which one is saturated with information. But this is an information which has itself become the real at a certain level, or where the image and its information precedes the real in a certain way. So for them, the inevitable question becomes: are there any other possibilities? One feels caught between two extremes. How is it possible to govern? How can we rethink this ancient concept of the State today? And can we even ask this question, or should we perhaps erase the word and begin elsewhere?

KRISTEVA: I am not a specialist in this field, and what I will say is thus something based on neither knowledge nor statistics: it is the point of view of a citizen. I have a feeling that after having lived according to religion, transcendental religion, the religion of God, we have lived under the regime of political religion. We believed that these are political relations, and consequently, that it is the State which finally represents them, which can resolve the great difficulties of the human condition. And then we realized as we lived through developments in the forms of the State, that both of these two states, as you said, finally undergo a dogmatization and, at that moment, they can resolve nothing, but rather they oppress individuals, or they turn into a haze of technocratic dust. It is my impression that, for example, currently with the French State (which is one of the most evolved forms of State)—because from this perspective we must not forget that there are evolutions in the forms of State—we are witnessing a devalorization of the notion of government itself. It becomes management, a technocratic management; the people in it are only asked to manage affairs as one might manage a firm on an economic level: profitability, economic well-being, social and welfare benefits, no unemployment, in essence a kind of optimization of productivity. But the ideological value which the State could represent, i.e., as transmitter of a certain number of a society's values, this function no longer exists. In my opinion, so much the better. That way we will perhaps reach a point where these values, which are moral values, ethical values, will be resolved in smaller and smaller groups, and from there will move closer and closer to the individual. At that moment it may be the individual discourses which will acquire greater importance...but I think that this devaluation of the notion of the State, this technocratization, is a good thing, because it liberates us from the religion of the State.

JARDINE: About religion. We wondered in our work group whether today the modern confrontation between the most ancient religions is a question of a return of religion or, on the other hand, a sort of fight to the death, in other words, a "last breath"?

KRISTEVA: I believe it's both. I believe that in a certain part of the world—because we live in very different historical times—one has the impression that the Hegelian idea of universal history really doesn't hold up. There are different historical strata: those in Iran do not necessarily live in the same time as those in New York or those in Israel. So, in certain types of societies there is a return to the religious and an importance placed on religion either as a force of repression, or as a force of liberation. For example, in Eastern countries, the recourse to Catholicism is a liberation, because liberation is based on the values of the individual against a general leveling out. But then I have a very particular reading (which I hope to work out) on the development of monotheistic religions. It is my impression that, if one goes to the end of Catholicism, one runs into atheism. Moreover when one reads the theologians, one wonders whether what they see as a logical development of the comprehension of religious spirit does not lead to a "beyonding" of transcendence and to a conception of the "transcendental" functioning as the logic of psychological functioning itself. From there, it is a question of trying to understand better how the human being functions. The idea of God, in that case, is capable of being replaced by the symbolic moment, which for us is language. So it seems to me that there is today, at least at certain levels of Western society, an interest in Christian religion, particularly Catholic religion; an indication of having passed through it, of its expenditure, as Bataille said, and of its inversion, but one which does not lead to a form of mechanical atheism, but rather to an attempt to rethink the logic which once took refuge in religions, and which was the logic of subjectivity. All the voyages of man toward God, of the soul into hell, of the soul toward God, these are extremely subtle spaces of interior experience which we must rethink and recapture, because otherwise modern man becomes a man-machine.

JARDINE: But, precisely, with regard to the machine...there are people, especially in the U.S. today, who think that technology is the key to our future for better or for worse. Do you think that technology occupies this position, or is this even further globalizing the problem?

KRISTEVA: It is in any case an important problem. I think that the big problem is to know what meaning one gives to machines. When one says machine, one is also including all the exploits which one can accomplish. One can reproduce people with machines. This is the technological, biochemical problem. But the big question is to know why: what is the effect of all this? If one can create pregnant men, and embryos in machines: why? For whom? And it is at this point that the large religious questions return. Furthermore, the problem which always presents itself is the notorious problem of the ethics of science. Recently, I read an article about the possibilities of biological eugenics, that is, the different interventions into genetic inheritance, etc. And initially the scientists were very certain about what they were saying: they can do all sorts of things which have not yet been done but which are technically possible. Then they were joking, saying that these were absurd ideas, that only perverts would.... "We should not do that, but if someone asks us to, why not?; in any case we do not take responsibility for it." So one sees very clearly that the space where the question of the meaning of these things must be asked is empty. It cannot necessarily be asked in courts of law, because the law does not know where to begin, there is no foundation for the intervention of the law in such matters. One does not know from what place one should proscribe or not proscribe. Hence, before asking questions concerning prohibition, one must ask questions about what this means for whom and why, and at that point the whole dimension of the psychological, of desire, returns.

JARDINE: This brings us most definitely to the question of sexual difference. One wonders sometimes whether this question of the difference between the sexes will continue simply to be added to these other problems, or whether people will continue to try and show how this question of sexual difference is an ontological problem intimately connected to, and even at times at the root of, these other problems. Do you think that we are in a period where one is more and more aware of how important sexual difference is and how it is connected to these other issues, or is the question becoming a tired one, brushed aside?

KRISTEVA: I think that one is not really aware...that is, one does of course realize it among subtle minds, among people who are asking questions seriously...but in the media and in public opinion, what is encouraged is perversion, and the idea that sexual difference does not exist, that anything is possible. It's a difficult situation.

JARDINE: You have often argued in favor of art as a place of possible and radical transformation. Do you think there will be a place for art in the twenty-first century, or with all of these other problems, are we in the process of putting a lid on it?

KRISTEVA: This is a big question, because actually one does have the impression that not only in the twenty-first century, but right now, art is generally considered as something insignificant. It's not serious.... What are these things?... This isn't really what's important. Perhaps this always has been the case, but now it is even more so with these larger problems of biology, of the State, of religion, of all these large, increasingly urgent issues around. But I think that it is an extremely important problematic, an extremely important practice, and I think that if humanity does not succeed in conserving this practice, it will condemn itself to a sort of psychological death. Just now we were speaking of biological problems: a big question which seems extremely important right now is to figure out what the exact status of psychical representations is. That is, on the one hand, there is the somatic, the cells; and on the other hand the human being is someone who operates with psychical representatives [*représentants*] which we now know can have a retroactive effect on the cells of the brain and thus, as a result, on the body. What is the exact status of these psychical representatives? In other words, what is the possible biological anchoring of symbolicity? This is a big question to which we must find an answer someday. Further, it is evident that certain psychical representatives have great impact on physical life: even the psychical representatives as varied, as flexible, one might even say as regressive, as sophisticated, as the psychical representatives which concern art, those which are connected to and provoke in us pleasures, desires, and pain. This type of language, which provokes in us pleasures, desires, and pain, has an immense power to modify the totality of the human personality. These are cathartic modules, modules that regulate psychic and physical life, modules of survival itself, which society has always used without knowing what it was doing. So, in one sense, we are moving toward a better understanding of why the fact of speaking of pleasure, of reading pleasure, of experiencing pleasure from painting and music can have a feedback on my general state—on my developing cancer, for instance, eventually even blocking it. Thus, we will begin to know more about all of this, and in another sense, we may become aware of the necessity to be in contact with these artistic phenomena through practice itself, not only as knowledge, but as a practical regulator of states of crisis.

JARDINE: At the beginning of the twentieth century, the surrealists conducted a survey, actually many surveys, but there was one in particular on the question of love and suicide. Our work-group found these *fin de siècle* surveys intriguing, but we have found ourselves concentrating not on love, but on work (love and work being the fundamental activities according to Freud). And not on suicide (with all its attendant moral questions), but squarely on death.

KRISTEVA: Work and death...aha.

JARDINE: Your work. Abjection, love, melancholy.... It seems that you are establishing, or that you are trying to establish, a sort of "symptomologic" of our *fin de sièle*. How has this work been generated by our era?

KRISTEVA: I don't know. I hope that it will be recognized as corresponding to our time. I am part of what I observe around me, of what patients, friends, or students bring to me, and then, as is always the case in such situations, one speaks of something intense: I think this has a great deal to do with introspection; that is, with phenomena proper to the theoretician, produced from a kind of permanent self-analysis. I think that insofar as this work encounters an echo, and that my choices are confirmed not only by my own observations, but by the reactions I receive, these are then definitely problems of our *fin de siècle,* especially to the extent that they are related to situations of crisis.

JARDINE: For many, the whole question of how to work today, how to find a voice, how to proceed, is at this moment a very difficult one. For many of them, your work is very important because it is tuned into our time....

KRISTEVA: One can only ask: what interests me? What preoccupies me right now? Particularly in the field of the humanities, one still has the opportunity there to ask questions which can be "personal" questions. Of course, given that the literary and sociological fields in general ask all the questions.... One must find a direction. It is all so rich that a direction must be chosen. You wonder which direction to take...but you must take the direction which preoccupies you today and now. Something which seems untenable to you, and which someone indicated to you as the most important question, something which itself is considered vital. One is then sure to find these questions in the work right under one's eyes. From there one has something perhaps interesting to say, otherwise one is obliged to repeat, and that is not work.

JARDINE: That is not work, no. So. Finally. The end of the ends: death. This at times feels like quite an apocalyptic era. Terrorism, the nuclear situation and its radioactive clouds, new diseases like AIDS.... The end has taken on quite a global scale, Star Wars, etc. Sometimes it seems—we were talking about melancholy—that our "progress" has surrounded us increasingly with forces of death which are not only uncontrollable, but invisible. Does death occupy a place in your thinking, and how does it do so, very briefly, with regard to this *fin de siècle?*

KRISTEVA: On a level which in the end is fairly metamorphosed: most obviously through my research on melancholy, where I ask myself questions about the importance of death in the history of the thinking which has preceded us, the history of the creations which have preceded us. I don't place myself in a contemporary perspective with regard to AIDS and Star Wars.... My work is a bit historic in that sense. But what really preoccupies me is to show this permanence of our preoccupation with death, which is heightened today because much more significant means of destruction are at our disposal. This preoccupation is counter-balanced by an immense power to go beyond and cross over this destructive moment. What has interested me was to show how the human being, through the strength of her/his connections and the power to create them, through the strength of idealization which s/he possesses, is capable of fighting with death. This doubled fascination with death is after all our condition—regardless of the excesses towards which technology is driving us. I wanted to show this. I wanted to show that this fascination with death, this kind of hole in life (both lived and psychic life) which the thought of death introduces, is counter-balanced, actually thwarted by our powerful capacities to move against death and to create something new from that very place.

—May 8, 1986

Translated by Heidi Gilpin.

REPRINTED FROM *COPYRIGHT*, NO. 1 (FALL 1987): 22-29

Marcia Tucker

The problem of identity—personal, cultural, social, sexual, and racial—is one of the most vexing critical issues of our time. The mythical notion that there is a single identity discoverable "within" a particular individual or group has been replaced in recent years by the growing understanding that fixed identities are the product of the far from disinterested ways in which we are represented to ourselves and to others. The critics and writers included in this chapter challenge such myths of coherence by demonstrating how identities are constituted and whose interests these fabrications serve.

Edward Said, in conversation with Phil Mariani and Jonathan Crary, addresses the issue of Western representation of colonized peoples, pointing to the violence implicit in the process of representation itself, which inevitably decontextualizes and reduces the subject portrayed. Focusing on the Orientalist distortions that continue to determine the way in which the Israeli-Palestinian conflict is represented in Western mass media, Said points out that advances in the electronic transfer of images have exacerbated circumstances rather than corrected them. Dominated cultures have become increasingly reliant upon First World representations, even for information about their own situation. As a result, Third World elites have begun to internalize reactionary representations of themselves.

The discussion between Jacques Derrida and a group of students from Brown University centers around the implications of the institutionalization of "Women's Studies" within American academia. Though the university programs provide a centralized locus for feminist discourse, Derrida cautions that because Women's Studies as a discipline reproduces a phallocentric model, its ability to dismantle the "law" it purports to critique is in some measure undermined. Derrida concedes, however, that the risk is worth taking.

Crucial to Derrida's position is his observation that so-called universal terms, such as "man," are in fact not neuter or neutral, but masculine. Like the other writers whose voices are heard here, Derrida attempts to posit identity not in terms of binary oppositions such as man/woman, black/white, heterosexual/homosexual, but as "difference," which is infinite in its variety.

Walter Adamson's interview with Gayatri Spivak, who has described herself elsewhere as a "Deconstructivist Marxist Post-Colonialist Feminist," raises the question of identity within the practice of critical discourse itself. Spivak faults reader response theory for "assuming a community of readers," and for essentializing the material under consideration as a "continuous configuration" which can be controlled by the writer acting as a "universalizing knowing subject." If critics are to open up their texts to others outside academia without speaking for them, they will have to "unlearn" the privilege of their own vocation by taking into account their position as part of a social, political, economic, and psychosexual order.

The final piece in this section is the edited transcript of a symposium held at The New Museum in connection with the 1982 exhibition entitled *Extended Sensibilities: Homosexual Presence in Contemporary Art*. The discussion predates the widespread realization of the extent and seriousness of the AIDS epidemic, and reflects the mood of exhilaration that characterized the period following successes in the New York gay liberation movement, as increasing numbers of lesbians and gay men came out and openly asserted their identities. Though several panelists localize similar elements of gay (male) style or sensibility—exaggeration, ornamentation, fantasy, and theatricality—Jeff Weinstein points to a more unanimous perception when he quips, "there is no gay sensibility and it has a tremendous amount of influence." From the long history of codified homosexual expression in popular art forms, to the expressive manipulation of fashion represented by the "clone" style of gay male dress, to the mannerist posturing that informs camp taste, what emerges as an element linking the various manifestations of gay sensibility is the experience of having to assert one's identity in the face of constant pressure to deny it.

Our attempts to understand and define ourselves are necessarily made in conjunction with attempts to understand and define those who are different, or "other" than we are. Examining the extent to which we assert our own experience as the norm, and the degree to which we exoticize, mythologize, and/or marginalize the experience of those of other cultures, races, ages, genders, or belief systems is a crucial step towards understanding identity as a powerful ideological tool that can be as easily used to serve repressive interests as to promote the sense of group unity crucial in struggling against oppression. Positing identity as a mutable fabrication rather than a stable "truth" is one way to resist the coercive agendas these representations can come to perpetuate.

JONATHAN CRARY/PHIL MARIANI: As a way of raising a number of questions, we wanted initially to go back to the early sixties. In 1961 two books were published by authors whose work has certain affiliations with your own: Fanon's *Wretched of the Earth* and Foucault's *Madness and Civilization*. We have then the production of two texts, one from within France and the other from one of its colonies, that describe, in very different ways, related mechanisms of exclusion that were embedded in European institutions since the Renaissance. What were some of the forces that might have generated this coincidence of texts?

EDWARD SAID: I don't really know much about the circumstances that produced Foucault's book, although I could speculate on what they might have been. But obviously Fanon's text—the more significant of the two in my opinion—came out of an ongoing political struggle, the Algerian revolution. It is important that Fanon's book was the result of a *collective* struggle, as opposed to Foucault's work, which evolved out of a different tradition, that of the individual scholar-researcher acquiring a reputation for learning, brilliance, and so on. Apart from their different origins, both were certainly oppositional books. They dealt with not only systems of exclusion, but systems of confinement. Fanon's most powerful image in the book is of the colonial city: the native *casbah* surrounded by the cleanliness, the well-lighted streets of the colonialist town, a European town, violently implanted in a native society. And above all, the common motif in both was that whatever was done in the way of violence to the subject was justified in the name of reason or rationality—civilization. But, I still think that it's important to note that Fanon's book is the more powerful because it is rooted in, you might say, the dialectics of struggle.

CRARY/MARIANI: Rather than because it comes out of a certain practice of historiography.

SAID: Yes, precisely, but more importantly, what is present in Fanon's work and absent in the early Foucault is the sense of active commitment. Ten years after *Madness and Civilization,* in Amsterdam in 1972, Foucault was involved in a television debate with Noam Chomsky. While Chomsky spoke about his own libertarian ideals, notions about justice, and so forth, Foucault backed away and essentially admitted that he believed in no positive truths, ideas, or ideals. And this was not true of Fanon, whose commitments to revolutionary change, solidarity, and liberation were very powerful and appealing to such as myself. Foucault's work was rather a matter of a quite remarkable ingenuity and acuity of philosophical perception. I would also say that the political force of Foucault's work did not become fully apparent until much later, after he had produced more books—*The Order of Things,* for example—and not before the work of several others as well (Jacques Donzelot, for instance). Fanon's work is really the last in a series written by him throughout the fifties, while Foucault's was the beginning of his series.

CRARY/MARIANI: Let's return for the moment to violence, the subject, and civilization. In *Orientalism*, you delineate a broad alliance between Western academic scholarship and the colonialist project, applying concepts of representation in a critique of instrumentalized knowledge. Specifically, how do you define representation and its political economy?

SAID: I'm not sure I could define it economically, or neatly for that matter, but certainly representation, or more particularly the *act* of representing (and hence reducing) others, almost always involves violence of some sort to the *subject* of the representation, as well as a contrast between the violence of the act of representing something and the calm exterior of the representation itself, the *image*—verbal, visual, or otherwise—of the subject. Whether you call it a spectacular image, or an exotic image, or a scholarly representation, there is always this paradoxical contrast between the surface, which seems to be in control, and the process which produces it, which inevitably involves some degree of violence, decontextualization, miniaturization, etc. The action or process of representing implies control, it implies accumulation, it implies confinement, it implies a certain kind of estrangement or disorientation on the part of the one representing. We could take as an example a linguistic treatise, Ernest Renan's work on Semitic languages: what is in Renan's mind as he catalogues his material is the display case in a museum, and when you display something, you wrench it out of the context of living life and put it before an (in this case, European) audience. Because, above all, representation involves consumption: representations are put to use in the domestic economy of an imperial society. In the case of *Orientalism*, I was speaking of an economy whereby the manipulation and control of colonies could be sustained. Now, obviously, there are many other kinds of representations, but these that are produced by and for a dominant imperial culture are the ones that interest me because of the circumstances of my own life, where I was subjected to their authority. I was sent to colonial schools—quite willingly by my parents, there was no force involved—where, by the time I became an adolescent, I knew a great deal about English history, and nothing about my own history, Arab history. What I was being taught was that the only representations that counted were the representations of English history and culture that I was acceding to by virtue of an education. I was also taught to regard myself as somebody whose worth in that economy was considerably less than that of the English, who were, in fact, ruling. And out of that context, I couldn't help but come to understand representation as a discursive system involving political choices and political force, authority in one form or another.

CRARY/MARIANI: So, as you've demonstrated in your writing, there is a direct and active relationship between domination—political, socio-economic, cultural—and systems of representation: one produces/sustains the other, and vice versa. In terms of affecting change in structures of domination, is the ultimate goal to transform representations or to eliminate those systems altogether? In either case, what would prevent the establishment of another, equally exclusive, discursive practice?

SAID: Representations are a form of human economy, in a way, and necessary to life in society and, in a sense, between societies. So I don't think there is any way of getting away from them—they are as basic as language. What we must eliminate are systems of representation that carry with them the kind of authority which, to my mind, has been repressive because it doesn't permit or make room for interventions on the part of those represented. This is one of the unresolvable problems of anthropology, which is constituted essentially as the discourse of representation of an Other *epistemologically defined as radically inferior* (whether labeled primitive, or backward, or simply Other): the whole science or discourse of anthropology depends upon the silence of this Other. The alternative would be a representational system that was participatory and collaborative, noncoercive, rather than imposed, but as you know, this is not a simple matter. We have no immediate access to the means of producing alternative systems. Perhaps it would be possible through other, less exploitative fields of knowledge. But first we must identify those social-cultural-political formations which would allow for a reduction of authority and increased participation in the production of representations, and proceed from there.

CRARY/MARIANI: You've dealt with this problem of constructing alternative systems in relation to the exclusionary mechanisms of the Western media in *Covering Islam*. Do you think that the implementation of a new kind of instantaneous, global electronics network that produces and disseminates news could fundamentally change the set-up within which people in the West consume representations of what is defined as the non-West? Or is power becoming even more consolidated?

SAID: If anything, the crisis is deepening, for several reasons. First, with the advances in the electronic transfer of images, there is a great deal more concentration of the means of production in so-called metropolitan societies by the great transnational conglomerates. And secondly, so much so that dependent societies—the peripheral societies in the Third World and those just outside the central metropolitan zones—are to an extraordinary degree reliant upon this system for information about themselves. We're talking now about *self*-knowledge, not only knowledge about other societies.

CRARY/MARIANI: So that the only categories through which these "dependent" societies arrive at self-knowledge are immanent within that system?

SAID: Immanent, precisely. They are insidious because they're presented as natural and real in a way that is virtually unassailable. We have not yet devised the means to deal with a television or film or even a script image, and to criticize the framework in which that image is presented, because it is *given* as reality, mediated so powerfully, and accepted almost subliminally. Finally, and perhaps most important, the response to this growing media dominance, and the solutions offered by the Socialist and Third World countries to combat the situation, are so primitive and crude that they don't stand a chance of dealing with the challenge. For instance, limiting the means of production, government censorship and intervention, and so forth, are more likely to extend the hegemony these measures are intended to combat than to limit it. What the proponents of a New Information Order are saying is essentially that either the West allows them to control their own news production and the entrance of its work into theirs, or they will simply remove themselves from the system and cut the West out. Then what do they offer their citizens as a result? A kind of illiteracy and parochial isolation that simply makes them more, rather than less, vulnerable to the blandishments and consumerist ideology of the prevailing technology and its metropolitan origins.

CRARY/MARIANI: Then what we are seeing now is an increasing geopolitical stratification, based on access to data networks and to scientific/technological information?

SAID: Yes, absolutely, and such complete dependency on these data bases as to breed a whole psychological mindset that will carry forward into generations.

CRARY/MARIANI: Earlier on you explained that you came to understand that the production of representations always involved political choices made in the interest of exerting and maintaining authority. In this case, there is nothing neutral about the way, for instance, sociological information is programmed into a data base.

SAID: No, of course there never is anything neutral about it: the entire process represents choice and selectivity, exclusions and inclusions, and things of that sort that are highly sophisticated. But what is truly ominous about this monopolization of information production is not so much the problem of access to the information itself, but rather access to the means of *criticizing* the information. In other words, what can we do outside of this system that enables us to treat it as a productive, rather than a natural process? Through what apparatus? The myth of coherence and inevitability about the whole process overrides any consideration of entry at the source, so to speak. There seem to be no options or alternatives and, as a result, resistance is becoming more and more difficult and increasingly the responsibility of metropolitan intellectuals.

CRARY/MARIANI: Resistance in the form of critical activity.

SAID: I think so. It has to be: potentially, you can only do this kind of work in the context of a place like New York where these images and representations are generated, available, and concentrated. I don't see any other way, and I certainly don't think we can rely on rigorous oppositional work from governments—Western, Third World, Socialist, or otherwise.

Interestingly, my experience at a convention of the American-Arab Anti-Discrimination Committee in Washington in a way exemplifies the complexity of the issue, since it demonstrated quite clearly how those who operate within the media system view the problem. The conference was organized specifically to combat the stereotyping of Arabs in the media, the last ethnic or national group that can be represented in caricature form with impunity. Ted Koppel was invited to "dialogue" with me about the problems of representation in the media. Now, Koppel is a very smart man, he runs *Nightline* which has tried to be fair, and so on. But the fact is that Koppel is a creature of the media, and a star to boot. He's a celebrity, which means, in effect, that for him representation as a philosophical issue cannot, indeed must not, enter into the discussion. Rather, what is assumed to be the central issue, and the solution as well, is simply getting more time on the media. In other words, he views us as potential guests, stories, issues to be let in on his show; as for us, in this context, we seem to be asking him to let us into the system by giving us air time, exposure, etc. And Koppel's response is that, because he has taken notice of us, *we are in*, the reportage is balanced, and so forth. So the crucial issue—*how* we are represented—is displaced by the essentially technical and commercial problem of who gets on and for how long. On the one hand, Koppel wants to appear independent; on the other hand, he's part of a system, ABC, which is part of a bigger system, the network organization. And on a third, strangely enough, he also represents the interests of the government. All of these journalists, particularly those on a national level—Brokaw, Jennings, Koppel, Rather—do not only give us the *news*, they also (usually unconsciously) represent what's happening from the standpoint of U.S. interests. Journalists internalize governmental norms to a degree that is quite frightening. If the problem were censorship, or even self-censorship, it could be dealt with and pointed at, but what we have here is a process of incorporation and introjection via an efficient ideology of inclusion, so that everything can be and is objectively itemized, framed, formed: the news media can therefore take in *anything*, and incorporate any point of view. For instance, in a radio discussion with some NBC media people, I was asked what I thought of the coverage given to the crisis in Lebanon over the last few months. Naturally, I brought up the fact that they hadn't dealt with the political aspects of the situation at all but, instead, concentrated on the Marine presence near the Beirut airport, which is, after all, a tiny corner of the Lebanese crisis. Well, then, I was told: we did a special on January 4, and identified the Druze, the Shi'ites, every party involved. In other words, they could say with quite literal justification that they had *covered* everything. What in fact occurs is, as Raymond Williams says, a process of setting limits and exerting pressures, so that the focus ultimately becomes: what *our* boys are doing in Lebanon. Everything else simply fades off into nothingness, as the nightly story revolves around the two-hundred-and-fifty Marines killed, or the two thousand Marines at the airport, and so forth.

CRARY/MARIANI: By highlighting the more emotional points of a story, it would seem that journalists are actually making a concerted effort to obscure other aspects.

SAID: But the stories are not always emotional, they *become* emotional by virtue of the fact that journalists focus on them. They are not in and of themselves emotional, and could be treated as neutrally as anything else. If you see the Marines at the airport on French or British television, they are only, after all, Marines at the airport.

CRARY/MARIANI: But newscasters know that Americans will identify with their boys. So it would seem that to concentrate on these aspects of a particular event represents a more programmatic effort to elide the facts.

SAID: I don't think it is programmatic, but as I said, a matter of internalized norms. Journalists *assume* that the interests of Americans will of course be the fate of other Americans. There are two points to be made here. First of all, none of these American journalists has, as a citizen, ever been involved in a continuing war-invasion process, unlike an Asian or European, for example. For them, the war is something to be visited—the standpoint of spectacle is very much inscribed in this process. Everything is viewed from the perspective of Washington and New York, as well. Second, the process involves fragmentation: nothing is seen for any length of time, there is no assumed collective memory, and little carry-over from day to day. There is no background, but only a moving foreground. There is no accumulation of history in any of the nightly broadcasts, except when they deal with domestic issues. But in terms of the rest of the world, they give you simply: we were there yesterday, we'll go back tomorrow, so you don't have to worry about what happens between then and now because we'll be giving it to you in a thirty-second slot tomorrow, should the crisis continue. In a strange way, the whole process is antinomian: extremely primitive in terms of its assumptions, but tremendously sophisticated at the same time from a technical standpoint. Bringing you the news requires satellite transmission, the expense of a bureau *out there*, and so on. Not a simple process, but the concept is primitively simple, and self-perpetuating. And, as I said, the most striking feature of the whole operation in my opinion is that every news reporter thinks that he or she is a Secretary of State. They immediately ask: what U.S. interests are at stake out there? From a professional point of view, they are not there to report U.S. interests, but a news story in another society, another country, not U.S. interests in that country or society. That is the explicit ideology. Most of the time, however, the interests of those involved are never acknowledged, but always elided, as you say, or assumed in the story. So, as you know, *we* lost Iran, *we* lost Nicaragua, *we* lost Lebanon, and so forth.

CRARY/MARIANI: A recent article about Israel in *The New York Times Magazine* [March 25, 1984] demonstrates that the convention of reportage from the standpoint of our own interests applies as well to media treatment of Israel. The title of the article is revealing: "Israel after Lebanon"—likewise, "The U.S. after Vietnam." In both cases, the emphasis is placed on our/Israel's moral trauma, our/Israel's potential for reconstruction, completely overlooking the fact that Israel and the U.S. were the aggressors, the invaders, and denying the existence of a victim. This kind of coverage implies an affinity between the two countries that goes well beyond the usual (at worst) polite treatment accorded other U.S. client states—El Salvador, for example.

SAID: Total, a more or less total identification. Moshe Arens is a perfect example: he's an American engineer. In that same article, the writer reports that Congress voted Arens $200 million more for weapons because, in a private telephone call with Arens at three in the morning, George Schultz *understood* Moshe's emotions about territorial security. The identification with Israel operates on many levels, and it becomes more and more clear that these are two societies that, in a certain sense, have totally obliterated their own history. In the discursive play of current American society, there is very little room for the Native American Indian, and in Israel, for Palestinians—they don't belong.

CRARY/MARIANI: One could point to Israel's military and political links with countries like South Africa and Argentina which, like the United States, have formative nineteenth-century experiences involving the dispossession and extermination of an indigenous population, impelled in part by a notion of societal homogenization.

SAID: Homogenization, yes, but also the continued effacement of the native, who becomes a mere cipher in the landscape. Look at the images from Zionist films of the thirties: the land is always displayed as empty. Insofar as Arabs are present, they are acknowledged only as camels and keepers walking across the screen at one moment or another, to supply a kind of exotic local color: This is *not* a field in the Ukraine, this is the exotic East. A camel and a Bedouin pass by—what Barthes calls "the effect of the real"—this comes across, that's enough. But the rest of the landscape is empty. And the same idea occurs in America: the pioneering spirit, errand into the wilderness, the obliteration of another society, and the continual sense of enterprise, that enterprise is good for its own sake, especially because a Book says so. It doesn't matter that enterprise means killing people, bombing apartment houses, emptying villages. But it's enterprise of a particular kind, the kind associated with a new settler society. And with it goes a tremendous hostility to traditional societies, which are posited as backward, primitive, reactionary, and so on: Islam, for example.

CRARY/MARIANI: So this process of extermination basically becomes a series of technical problems.

SAID: Absolutely. On one level, a series of technical problems, and it is carried forth into the media. I think that it is unique in history, this case of a whole society such as Israel delivered, as it were, on the American political and intellectual scene by a massive apparatus for concealing the reality. People would be horrified beyond description if they knew what goes on in Israel and the occupied territories—Chomsky talks about this in his recent book, *The Fateful Triangle*. But it's systematically pushed out, and when Americans do see it, as they did in the summer of 1982, with the invasion of Beirut and the massacres in the Sabra-Shatila camps, after awhile it is simply forgotten because it's got no place to go. And always, there are the choruses of praise for Israel's moral superiority, its nobility, the democracy, and civilization, etc. One of the things that disappointed me in the reviews of *Orientalism*, was that a lot of the reviews published by Jewish or Zionist journals missed the point that I was trying to make: that the roots of European anti-Semitism and Orientalism were really the same. Ernest Renan, for example, was a tremendous anti-Semite and anti-Muslim, and his view of both was essentially the same: that the Semites, whether Muslim or Jew, were not Christians and not Europeans, and therefore had to be excoriated and confined. What then occurred is that the Zionists took on the view of the Orientalists *vis-à-vis* the Palestinians; in other words, the Palestinians became the subject for the Israeli Orientalist, just as the Muslim and others have been the subject for the colonial or imperial Orientalists. Dani Rubenstein, an Israeli journalist, acknowledges this in a recent article where he cites the influence of Orientalism on the administration of the West Bank: there, the colonial administrators have all been Orientalists, Islamic scholars educated at the Islamic Studies Department of Hebrew University. Menachem Milson, former civilian governor of the West Bank, wrote a book on Arabic literature, for example.

CRARY/MARIANI: You mentioned the core-periphery relationship. Do you see this opposition undergoing a transformation, for example in the fact that the major Western cities encompass increasingly large non-Western populations, what Paul Virilio calls "infra-urbanisms," so that the very heart of what was the imperial core is attracting to it elements of the periphery? Is it at all possible that these population flows, brought about by the ongoing relocation of global production processes, could modify the collective sense of homogeneity, of difference among Western peoples?

SAID: Historically, that has not been the case. In fact, I think what occurs, as in England, is an intensification of racial feeling of a very powerful sort, and also movements of revenge—think of the Brixton riots. The phenomenon of the success of a novelist like V. S. Naipaul is intimately related to the problem of the colonials descending upon the core society, and threatening to disrupt it with their mindless demands and their native drums. And above all, the real animus of people like Naipaul—and here we come back to the question of representation—is the way in which these "colored people," as they are referred to, are alleged to know how to use the media to attract attention to their plight. That is endlessly the theme, that all native resistance movements, whether urban, black movements in America or London, or in the Third World, have for their root *raison d'être* never the sense of outraged injustice that they feel, but rather their desire to use the Western media, which is gullible and falls into their trap. Remember how the holders of the hostages in Iran were described as essentially using the American media; the Viet Cong did the same thing. There is always this intense fear that somehow the economy of representation is being abused by the Other, and that, I think, is a very constant motif. At the same time, we hear continual declarations about the openness and freedom of the press.

CRARY/MARIANI: Naipaul's brother, Shiva, wrote a book about Jonestown in which he infers that any Third World nationalist leader is necessarily a deranged or psychopathic egomaniac. He says, referring to Western liberals and leftists, "Those who ought to know better nourish our crazy dreams of resurrection and redemption, those safely beyond the borders of our madness underwrite our lunacies." How do we account for this identification with the forces of external domination?

SAID: In the parts of the Third World that I know, the Naipaul line is symptomatic of the development of a new class of technocrats for whom the center of the world is Silicon Valley. So there is that technocratic identification. Secondly, the first postcolonial generation has now passed. I'm speaking here of the generation from roughly World War II through the early seventies: Sékou Touré, Abdul Nasser, Sukarno.

CRARY/MARIANI: A generation whose identity was bound up with the vocabulary of national liberation.

SAID: Yes, represented in a sense by a kind of nationalist bourgeoisie. Now that period is over, and what these societies are facing is the problematic of the technocrat, which in the end boils down to imperatives like: we have to feed our people, we have to worry about oil, distribution, etc., *plus* we have to face the problem of what is called national security. Those are the issues. In other words, technical services on the one hand, and national security—which really means staying in power—on the other. The nationalist energy is over; something must be found to replace it, so you create outside enemies. Every one of the Arab countries, many of the African and Far Eastern countries as well, depend therefore on a praetorian guard. There's the notion of an outside enemy against which you must defend, imperialism, and so all the old slogans of nationalism are retained. At the same time, there is this great technocratic leap forward—or attempts at such—based on an uncritically internalized modernization model. In such a context, therefore, things tend to break down constantly and, in addition, the insurrectionary stage still has some life in it—you see it in Tunisia, Egypt, Latin America, appearing in one country or another for a time. In El Salvador, you try to have an election and the ballot boxes are stolen. So out of this unstable mix of technocracy and national security you have a nostalgia developing for colonialism or religion—atavistic in my opinion, but some people want them back. Sadat is the great example of that: he threw out the Russians, as well as everything else that represented Abdul Nasser, ascendant nationalism, and so forth—and said, "Let the Americans come." Then you have a new period of what in Arabic is called an *infitah*—in other words, an opening of the country to a new imperialism: technocratic management, not production but services—tourism, hotels, banking, etc. That's where we are right now. And Naipaul derives from that phenomenon.

CRARY/MARIANI: A significant figure right now, in terms of how his identity has been fabricated by the Western press, is Quaddafi. It seems the main reason that such a wildly distorted image of him has been produced is that he is an independent leader; that is, someone who cannot be bought or integrated into a cold war or trilateralist arrangement for global management.

SAID: There isn't much hope that he can be bought off (of course, he's quite wealthy on his own). In all the rhetoric about terrorism, Libyan hit teams, etc., much of it has nothing to do with Quaddafi, but goes back to Dostoyevski and Conrad, who imagined a whole notion of terrorism for its own sake and terrorism as an aesthetic activity, rather than as a political thing. But what is dimly perceived about Quaddafi in all his seeming craziness is that he represents the threshold of a third phase. In other words, first you have nationalism and nativism, then you have technocracy; then the system bifurcates at this point into, on the one hand, nostalgia for colonialism—"come and help us"—and on the other hand, religious revivalism—Khomeini, Quaddafi. In other words, the people who say, "Look, put your faith in the Americans or the Russians, etc.," are now forced to admit that depending on outside powers has been a sordid failure: our people are just as poor as they were, we are still indebted to the IMF or the United States. The only answer, therefore, is Islam. And that is what Quaddafi is, and as such, he is truly formidable. Because if you go through the Arab world and the Islamic world generally, there is a genuine popular sense about "Islam" which threatens every National Security State. The irony of the NSS, at least in the Arab world, is that each of them has failed completely. Not one has protected its borders, much less the security of the country. Iran, under the Shah, was an NSS, and was obviously an American client regime. The Arab regimes, nearly every one of them, has been attacked by Israel, invaded, their lands occupied: so, Islam is the answer. What gets lost in all of this is a secular alternative.

CRARY/MARIANI: The National Security State versus technocracy—this is the conflict for parts of the Third World today. What are the alternatives, what possible models could be constructed?

SAID: To go back to Fanon, what you find is insurrection, and the absence of what you might call a utopian dimension, since the ethic of violence really prevents genuine critical reflection. Ideally, what you would like is a connection between Fanon and Adorno, and that is totally missing. In other words, activism, nationalism, revolution, insurrection on the one hand, and on the other, the excessive kind of theoretical reflection and speculation of the sort one associates with the Frankfurt School—which in the end becomes resignation, as you recall. And for the Third World, the former—nationalism, etc.—becomes the National Security State. Somehow, we need another dimension which involves, in fact, thinking about the future in ways that are not simply insurrectionary or reactive.

CRARY/MARIANI: A critical process which would have to involve the figuration of alternative futures.

SAID: Exactly. The point is that I am not talking about inventing utopias or utopianism. Chomsky talks about this in reference to C. S. Pierce's notion of *abduction*, a formulation of hypotheses based upon the known facts. You posit something, take in as much as you can of the present, and out of that, and in fidelity to that—imperfect though our apprehension of the known facts may be—you *abduct* from it a possible future hypothesis. And that process, that dimension, is missing in the present situation. I think it is beginning to develop in certain kinds of critical work done in connection with representation and imperialism in particular.

Orientalism is in some ways a negative book, but at the end I do try to talk about a noncoercive, nonmanipulative view of society. You also find this alternative pursued in feminist studies, where the problems are posed really seriously. So, what are the ways of positing a hypothesis based on certain apprehensions, where you do the work of deconstruction and demystification, and yet at the same time posit a direction which is not simply incorporative, but something that deals with the future in some genuinely alternative way? Generally, this is not the kind of critical work people are doing, and in the Third World it is unlikely to develop very much because it cannot be done by one person but has to be a cooperative effort. That's the whole point. So, to go back to Foucault, he is really interested in doing his work on his own, but the collective is where I think the future lies.

CRARY/MARIANI: Do you see any possible set of circumstances under which there could be any concrete identification between certain sectors in the U.S. and what you and others have described as anti-systemic movements? What would be the common ground of that identification?

SAID: I have no doubt that the basis of it would have to be a critique of domination, or of imperialism as domination.

CRARY/MARIANI: But this critique would obviously take a very different form than it did in the sixties.

SAID: Absolutely. The sixties were enthusiastic, utopian. They represent an attempt at recovery and recuperation of certain kinds of, shall we say, primitive or immediate experiences. What I'm talking about is something much more reflective, which would include a critique of imperialism in its cultural forms, not simply as capitalist economy.

REPRINTED FROM *WEDGE*, NO 7-8 (WINTER-SPRING 1985): 4–11.

WALTER ADAMSON: Since you are interested in the strategy of reading rather than in recovering the writer's "original vision," why couldn't your approach be called a "reader response approach"? What are your reservations regarding reader response theories?

GAYATRI SPIVAK: The kind of reader response theory that is in vogue here in the United States seems to suggest that one could assume a community of readers without troubling to look at the socio-political production of these communities or questioning the notion of hegemonic communities. The question that I have to pose when people ask me to distinguish my position of "interest" from reader response is: who is the reader? My position *vis-à-vis* reader response is reactive: the political element comes out in the transaction between the reader and the texts. What I am most insistent upon is that the politics of the critic or the reader should be put on the table as scrupulously as possible. Textual criticism cannot just be a judgment on the basis of disinterested readings by a presumed community.

ADAMSON: It sounds to me as if your criticism of contemporary reader response theory is a criticism about its failure to live up to its own promise. Couldn't your own political reading incorporate reader response criticism as well as more traditional strategies of looking at the politics in the text?

SPIVAK: Yes. In fact in Eastern Germany there is a variety of reader response theory which is trying to take this into account. But when that phrase—"Reader Response Theory"—is invoked here in the U.S., we generally retreat from the question of interested political readings.

ADAMSON: Why don't we move to the question of whether or not there is an essentialism involved when we posit binary oppositions like book–author or individual–history.

SPIVAK: It seems to me that the first opposition, that between book and author, has been used to exculpate the author, saying that it is the book we are dealing with and not the author. Or the opposition can operate so as to prove the author's transcendence of history. That's the first opposition. The second opposition on the other hand, between individual and history, has been used either to assert the unquestioned shaping role of the individual as undivided consciousness or to separate that consciousness out as a text, where everything else becomes context. When I talk about those two oppositions and say that I am using them strategically, I do so knowing that in general these are essentialist problems that arise when these binary oppositions are used. But it is not possible, within discourse, to escape essentializing somewhere. The moment of essentialism or essentialization is irreducible. In deconstructive critical practice, you have to be aware that you are going to essentialize anyway. So then strategically you can look at essentialisms, not as descriptions of the way things are, but as something that one must adopt to produce a critique of anything. This gesture on the part of the critic relates to the two oppositions in two different ways.

When we operate with the opposition book-author, we want to avoid the kind of simple reversal whereby the critic's hands remain clean and the critic becomes diagnostic in a simple symptomatic reading. We keep ourselves within the book's field and see how far we can go when we respect that. In the second case, the individual and history, we want to see the individual consciousness as a crucial part of the effect of being a subject, which is itself a part of a much larger structure, one which is socio-political, politico-economic, psycho-sexual. Now all of these elements are discontinuous with each other so that you can't easily translate from the one to the other. But, nonetheless, all of these things are organized as narratives which reflect a sort of weave of presence and absence. As a result of this, you lose the confidence of *having* something which is *causing* something or *controlling* something. And from this point of view the question what is that whole thing, the whole network, no longer remains pertinent except in the context of the universalizing subject of knowledge .

In fact, Perry Anderson's recent critique of post-structuralism, *In the Tracks of Historical Materialism,* is a good example of this. He looks at the network of textuality as a continuous weave, himself tacitly assuming the position of that universalizing subject. He then proves that post-structuralism was an inevitable development from structuralism and that the two movements posited relationships between subject and structure, individual and history that entailed each other. We see this in the light of a graspable whole network and this as a kind of necessary trajectory. The pertinent chapter ends with the assertion that the question answers itself. That would in itself be symptomatic of the kind of danger that we are trying to avoid, the essentialist danger, where you translate all of the elements within that larger structure into a kind of continuous configuration which the knowing subject can control.

ADAMSON: The next obvious question, to allow you to say more about your own view of the critical process, is to ask you how to advance the process towards a feministly interested reading. Obviously there must be as many answers to that question as there are feminists. What's yours?

SPIVAK: I don't know what a feminist looks for. To an extent, my gesture towards the text is a very old-fashioned one. I think that the critic's first task is to attend to the text. So that I try, knowing that of course it's impossible to suspend myself, as it were.

Having said this, I would add that my interests now, to an extent, are to be seen as: in what way, in what contexts, under what kinds of race and class situations, gender is used as what sort of signifier to cover over what kinds of things. It really is a discovery which arises through actually attending to texts. So I'm a little wary of trying to locate a program with which one actually confronts a text. I think the preparation of the critic takes place, to an extent, before the confrontation with the text just as much as with it.

ADAMSON: It seems that your view of the critical process, at least as you've articulated it so far, is as much an education of the critic as it is the critic's education of the reader. Do you also think that literary criticism can be a kind of, let's say, feminist literary guerrilla warfare towards the readers?

SPIVAK: I suppose it can be. But then again, would one have to assume a sort of "kneecapping" position, as if women are history transcendent? Of course there is a sort of euphoria in that. But, nonetheless, I think as a long-term proposition it won't last in the wash. Guerrilla warfare takes place where guerrilla warfare takes place, and that's not academic literary criticism.

ADAMSON: Let me move on to your concept of the fractured semiotic field. In what sense is the world a semiotic field? And what do you mean by fracturing?

SPIVAK: I don't think that the world is a semiotic field. By semiotic field I had meant something as simple as this: that there are collections of axioms in the socius, depending on your position within the socius, and these axioms are by no means unified all over the globe. What I was suggesting was that when a writer writes, she doesn't just write in English or French, she also writes in these so-called sign systems, and it's in this sense that one can see the socius as a very heterogeneous collection of what I called, I think now somewhat wrongly, semiotic fields. With respect to the notion of fracture, what I am talking about is obviously the problem of cultural self-representation. The way in which semiotic fields are tapped for cultural self-representation, in fact, always covers over the dislocation between the kinds of axiomatics that are being used, and whatever it is in the "culture" that constitutes the hidden agenda of the suppression of ideological production. Let me say that, very broadly speaking, the fracture goes either in the direction of utopianism, or in the direction of a Golden Age complex. One sees the best example at festivals. And one of my favorite examples is how, at Fourth of July picnics, the United States which is, after all, a micro-electronic capitalism, represents itself as engaging in independent commodity production. That's what I would call a fractured semiotic field. But if you say something is a semiotic field, you're suggesting that it is nothing but a text, nothing but language, nothing but words and meanings. I wasn't trying to reduce hard reality to nothing but signs. I was talking about the fact that, within the practice of representation, which is defined within the enclosure named the aesthetic, this is one strategy of tracking the socio-economic; by noticing in what way and through the covering over of what fractures, semiotic fields are being tapped.

ADAMSON: You say that you don't want to identify hard reality with the production of meaning within semiotic fields. What do you fear is missed in doing so?

SPIVAK: I'm very interested in a persistently critical practice and I think that, once one has unrecognized totalizing impulses, one can end up privileging one's own disciplinary practice. I'm not suggesting that there is a necessarily hard reality out there. In fact I would argue the opposite, that it is always dredged up as a slogan. But I would also not want to identify such reality with the production of signs. Something else *might* be going on. The concept of the sign itself, after all, is something which has emerged within certain kinds of disciplinary practices.

ADAMSON: It seems that the signifier "man" does more than float. It disguises itself under an unproblematic cover, the signifier human. Can you say something about anthropomorphism and the concept of man as historically independent?

SPIVAK: When Derrida criticized Sartre's anthropomorphic rereading of Heidegger, that critique of anthropomorphism was picked up in two ways, and over the last, almost twenty years, we've seen it going in two directions within the deconstructive establishment. One has been for the critic to say, do not look in it for a *human* story, but rather for the text's constitution of its own textuality or narrativity. Another, which has been Derrida's track, has been to say: look here, it is almost as if the sign, anthropos, has no history. Perhaps that was what led him to say that one might look at the sign, woman, rather than simply say, get the human out of the way and look at the text's constitution of its own narrative. It was from that point onwards that he started worrying about the sign, woman.

ADAMSON: Could you comment on the relationship between ideology and literary criticism, or ideology and the social world, both as a battle for domination, and in relation to critical readings by literary critics?

SPIVAK: I think there's a real problem when the critic of ideology takes a diagnostic position and forgets that she is herself caught within structural production. This obviously brings us to the ghost of Althusser, because the other side of the critics taking a diagnostic position is a symptomatic reading. I think when Althusser speaks of ideology having no history, he was really writing as a philosopher and was suggesting that we think ideology before we can think history. I also think that Althusser was ill-served there by turning to Lacan in order to develop his notion of the primacy of interpellation and so on. In Lacan, what he found, after all, was still a discussion that was caught within the notions of the subject and the patronymic, the name of the father. If one looks at the current Derrida, who talks about the auto-position of the subject saying yes to itself before the possibility of discourse, I think one can use that as a lever to lift Althusser's text. One thinks ideology before one can think history as something out there, before one can, in fact, conceive of the fact that history is the narrativizations of various kinds that are in a field of contention. When, within specific readings, people universalize one or another ideology, that, I think, has very little to do with what Althusser was trying to say. Althusser was using a kind of argumentative grid which was not sufficient to the power of his insight. He did keep on saying that one must continually rethink the distinctions between ideology and history, ideology and science, ideology and philosophy, and he finally came out recommending a *pratique sauvage*, a wild practice, a wild philosophy. It seems to me that we have the task of reinscribing the Althusserian insight there, rather than throwing him away as a closet idealist.

ADAMSON: You say that we have the task of reinscribing Althusser. Does part of that project involve determining the production of the text in the last instance, in Engels' phrase?

SPIVAK: I'm very glad you mention Engels. The problem is that determination, as a critique of causality, has been transformed into determinism as the fixing of causes disguised as the final instance. In his *Science of Logic,* Hegel was trying to speak about determination as the possibility of the inauguration of discourse, as we would say today perhaps the inauguration of philosophy. It is certainly a critique of causality that Hegel is advancing. To transform that into determinism has done a great deal of harm. The way I would read Althusser is to look at the notion of relative autonomy and see how, if one really thinks it through, it is looking at discursive practices—let's call it political, economic, and ideological—which cannot be translated one into the other in a continuous way. If one looks at it like that, then one can even go beyond the notion of many determinations, political, economic, ideological—you name it, Marxist, feminist, anti-imperialist —one can even take it into the notion of over-determination as speaking of discontinuous determinations. We are in the process of throwing away that complex notion of relative autonomy, rather than using it practically, because we are being operated upon by a cultural politics of the transformation of a critique of causality into something that is the most iron-clad philosophy of causality. It seems to me that in Marx, the relationship between consciousness and materiality, or the final determining role of the economic, remain powerful moments of bafflement that one can work at. But in the context of a fundamentalist notion of reading, we're in the process of misunderstanding that, misappropriating it by virtue of the particular fracture between determination as critique of causality and determinism as a reinscription of causality.

ADAMSON: What I find confusing is the way you adeptly fuse what I have always regarded as two very different discourses, semiotics and Marxism. In the latter, of course, we're concerned with the relationship of being and consciousness, and in the former we're concerned with the relationship of language and society and those two don't necessarily fuse very easily. You were speaking of fractured semiotic fields. Is it worthy of our interest to attempt to determine the causes of the fracturing of the semiotic field or is it enough simply to locate the manner in which the semiotic field is fractured?

SPIVAK: I'm a very eclectic person. I use what comes to hand. I'm not a fundamentalist. And I'm not an Althusserian in the strict sense. I'm more interested in opening up texts than in establishing, like some medieval scholar, the authenticity of a text. Within literary criticism, quite often an interdisciplinary practice means nothing more than neutralizing the vocabulary from another discipline and taking it to describe yet once again what happens between reader and text. Psychoanalysis certainly has suffered in this way. Similarly, quite often you'll see that value production, for example, is taken as an analogy for linguistic production. One ought to remember Marx's caution in the *Grundrisse,* that it would be a mistake to make an analogy between the production of value and the production of language. From my point of view, it would be much more interesting to see what happens as literature, the literary text, is completely inserted into the circuit of the production of commodities. That's how we get our best seller lists, and what gets remaindered, what gets written, what the construction of readership is, and so on. It would be much more interesting from my point of view to see how, when that is happening, the literary artist begins to say over and over again that literature produces use value. There is a fractured semiosis if you like. The whole notion of the creative imagination comes in as literature gets into the circuit of commodity production in the most brutal sense. That, to me, is a more interesting way of using Marxism within literary criticism than constantly making analogies between literary production and the production of value.

ADAMSON: Of course, a major preoccupation for Marxists is the advancement of the proletariat. I would agree with you that we have to give up the concept of a unified subject, as Marx has it in the proletariat and other people have in patriarchy or whatever. How is it possible to speak coherently for and about marginalized groups once we give up this concept?

SPIVAK: When I criticized Foucault in my talk in Melbourne, I was not suggesting that Foucault himself had not brilliantly tried to represent the oppressed. What I was looking at in the late Foucault was the theorization of that project as letting the oppressed speak for himself. It seemed to me that theorizing in the late Foucault actually buys into the privileging of "concrete experience," which is something that is also used by the other side, by capitalism. There is an impulse among literary critics and other kinds of intellectuals to save the masses, speak for the masses, describe the masses. On the other hand, how about attempting to learn to speak in such a way that the masses will not regard as bullshit. When I think of the masses, I think of a woman belonging to that eighty-four percent of women's work in India which is unorganized peasant labour. Now if I could speak in such a way that such a person would actually listen to me and not dismiss me as yet another of those many colonial missionaries, that would embody the project of unlearning about which I've spoken recently. What can the intellectual do toward the texts of the oppressed? Represent them and analyze them, disclosing one's own positionality for other communities in power. Foucault has done this. In fact, I can't think of another person, another intellectual, who has done this in our time in the Western context. What I was objecting to was that theorization of letting Pierre Rivière speak for himself, and what the theoretical articulation does for the people who are influenced by Foucault, enthusiastic academic intellectuals, who at the same time swallow Foucault's critique of the watershed intellectual and make Foucault into a watershed intellectual!

ADAMSON: Does speaking to marginalized groups and yet not "de-skilling" oneself mean anything about the kinds of texts that one ought to speak about?

SPIVAK: When I said that one shouldn't invite people to de-skill themselves I was talking about a kind of anti-intellectualism that exists among academics and counter-academics. One ought not to patronize the oppressed. And that's where this line leaves us. Unlearning one's privileged discourse so that, in fact, one can be heard by people who are not within the academy is very different from clamoring for anti-intellectualism, a sort of complete monosyllabification of one's vocabulary within academic enclosures. And it seems to me that one's practice is very dependent upon one's positionality, one's situation. I come from a state where the illiterate, not the functionally illiterate, but the real illiterate, who can't tell the difference between one letter and another, are still possessed of a great deal of political sophistication, and are certainly not against learning a few things. I'm constantly struck by the anti-intellectualism within the most opulent university systems in the world. So that's where I was speaking about de-skilling.

ADAMSON: But the heart of my question nonetheless remains and that is, ought one to choose one's texts in the light of the interests, desires, prejudgments of marginalized groups? Or ought one to choose one's texts in light of what we suppose they ought to be interested in? Or should there be no conscious choosing of texts of this type at all?

SPIVAK: Again, I don't know. I can only speak of my working life which has been spent as a teacher of literature in the United States, in Europe, and in England. It seems to me that I cannot speak of what marginalized people ought to be interested in. In Melbourne I ended my talk with an account of the suicide of a teenage woman in Calcutta in 1926. What I was doing with the young woman who had killed herself was really trying to analyze and represent her text. She wasn't particularly trying to speak to me, I was representing her. I was re-inscribing her. To an extent, I was writing her to be read and I certainly was not claiming to give her a voice. So if I'm read as giving her a voice, there again this is a sort of transaction of the positionality between the Western feminist listener who listens to me, and myself, signified as a Third World informant. What we do toward the texts of the oppressed is very much dependent upon where we are.

ADAMSON: Let me ask you one final question. In one of your talks in Melbourne you said that the prime task of feminism should not be to retrace the figure of woman. What did you mean by that?

SPIVAK: Well, I was trying to say that although Derrida was, in some ways, retracing the figure of woman, that's not identical with the project of feminism. And I was really talking about "global feminism" since that seems always to be on the agenda these days when one speaks in the West. It seems to me that if one's talking about the prime task, since there is no discursive continuity among women, the prime task is situational anti-sexism, and the recognition of the heterogenity of the field, instead of positing some kind of woman's subject, women's figure, that kind of stuff. It seems to me, if you really want to trace the figure, then you should start looking elsewhere in the globe. Psychoanalysis and counter-psychoanalysis can easily become the gift of capitalist imperialism to the cause of feminism.

ADAMSON: So you're saying that tracing the figure of woman would be another one of those essentialisms which you think it is better to avoid.

SPIVAK: In the name of anti-essentialism, and in the hands of hegemonic feminists, it sometimes becomes that. If one can situate it geopolitically, if one can situate it within the work place, I think some excellent work can be done, is being done, and tracing what we are calling the figure of woman. But when we speak of the "prime task," my heart is elsewhere.

QUESTIONS ON BEHALF OF *THESIS ELEVEN* WERE FORMULATED BY PHILIPA ROTHFIELD AND SNEJA GUNEW, AND POSED BY WALTER ADAMSON. THIS PIECE HAS BEEN EDITED AND REVISED BY PHILIPA ROTHFIELD.

REPRINTED FROM *THESIS ELEVEN*, NO. 15 (1986): 91-97.

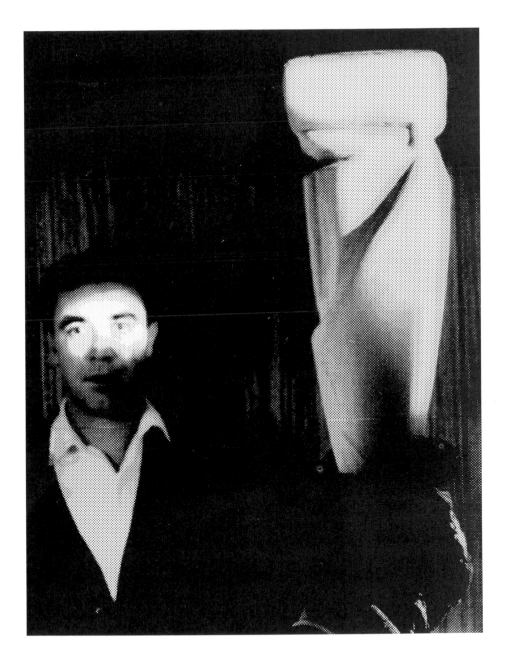

The text printed here is situated somewhere between speech and writing. It is a modified transcript of a seminar given by the Pembroke Center for teaching and research on women with guest speaker Jacques Derrida. The speaker referred to as "Response" is not the writer Jacques Derrida, but is rather our account of his responses. The category "Question" denotes edited versions of queries posed by members of the seminar and visitors... Due to the improvised nature of the seminar's dialogue and the vulnerable philosophical position M. Derrida is placed in only two sets of quotation marks appear in this edited text. We thank M. Derrida for allowing us to publish this transcript—this text, authorized but authorless.

DERRIDA:

"Subjects/Objects is a wonderful title."

The seminar began with Jacques Derrida's introductory statement. His inquiry concerned the status of "women's studies" as an institution.

INTRODUCTION: In reference to the lecture on Kafka's text, one can say that if the Law is the condition of the institution, if the institution is the Law, then the guardians of the institution are also the guardians of the Law. And as the research in women's studies gains institutional legitimacy, it also constitutes, constructs, and produces guardians of the Law. It induces men from the country who come before the Law to try to accede to it, to see it, to touch it, to penetrate it. Thus departments of women's studies in America are now becoming a relatively solid institution. It is certainly important to acknowledge the problems, limitations, and resistances to the institution met even in the United States.

Yet one can say without error that the United States is a pioneer in this aspect, that there are more women's studies programs in the United States than anywhere else in the world. And from this point of view, to criticize women's studies—from whatever aspect—is an error, a mark of ignorance, of obscurantism, since anywhere else in the world women's studies does not have the institutional power that it already has in the United States. One can only wonder: what are the risks and the stakes of the institution of women's studies? Do the women who manage these programs, do they not become, in turn, the guardians of the Law, and do they not risk constructing an institution similar to the institution against which they are fighting? In other words, the first question could be, what is the difference, if there is one, between a university institution of research and teaching called "women's studies" and any other institution of learning and teaching around it in the university or in society as a whole? It is certain that the range of work in women's studies is enormous, and that there are already considerable problems to pose, of bodies of work to study, of objects to define, and that women's studies has a great future. Nevertheless, if this future is of the same type as that of all other departments, of all other university institutions, is this not a sign of failure of the principles of women's studies?

In the universities of Western Europe and the U.S. we see an institutional model reproduced which on the whole was constructed at the beginning of the nineteenth century in Germany, in Berlin—and the U.S. is probably more faithful to this model than are most of the European countries. All the objects, all the fields which presently structure the university today were already established by the nineteenth century, whether studies of literature, philosophy, physics, mathematics, geography or social studies—nothing new, except women's studies. There was no place foreseen in the structure of the classical model of Berlin for feminist studies. Thus with women's studies, is it a question of simply filling a lack in a structure already in place, filling a gap?

Fascinating things would be done, new things discovered, knowledge advanced, and this is necessary—but one would not alter the model of the university, and in consequence, one would insidiously reproduce in the modern university, whether one knew it or not, the old model, which is fundamentally phallocentric or "phallogocentric."

As much as women's studies has not put back into question the very principles of the structure of the former model of the university, it risks being just another cell in the university beehive. If one tries to analyze, to gain an overview of the state of women's studies in the world and notably in the U.S., where the movement is the strongest, one has an ambiguous feeling. One has the feeling that on the one hand a certain positivity of research is very successful, one discovers all sorts of things, one exhumes new corpuses, one studies women's literature, one uplifts from under the repression, from out of the realm of the forbidden all sorts of feminine signatures, feminist discourses which were obscured, one brings out not only literary but anthropological, political, and social dimensions. All that is very positive, certainly. On the other hand, the effort to put back into question the structural principles which I mentioned before, which construct the university law, the academic law, that is to say, in the end, the social law in general—because the university is not a separate bloc, it represents society, society represents itself through the university—one has the impression that the questioning of this principle is unequally developed in comparison to those studies which we could call "positive." This question concerns the fundamentals of the institution. In that sense, the risk of failure of women's studies is the risk of its very own success. The more it proves its positivity, its necessity, and brings proofs to the masculine directors of the university—masculine, whether women or not—the more it legitimizes itself by this power; the more then, it risks to cover up, to forget, or to repress the fundamental question which we must pose.

Thus, the risk is not only the unequal development between positive and progressive researches, both political and scientific, which are necessary to pursue, but there is a more dangerous and adventurous question. It is that whoever asks questions by definition not coded on these principles of progress risks appearing—in the eyes of women who are activists for women's studies—reactionary, dangerous, only limiting the progress of their positive research. This would include, for example, whoever suggests that we do not need Women's Studies departments at all, and that it's not necessary to construct institutions of this sort, that it is necessary that the concern finds other routes outside the universities where departments are established on the old model. Those—whether men or women—who risk that question, also risk in one form or another being rejected by that which calls itself Women's Studies.

This is a question of the Law: are those involved in women's studies—teachers, students, researchers—the guardians of the Law or not? You will remember that in the parable of the Law of Kafka, between the guardian of the Law and the man from the country there is no essential difference: they are in oppositional but symmetric positions. We are all, as members of a university, guardians of the Law—people who assure a tradition, who maintain a heritage, who are critics and evaluators, and at the same time who are men from the country, naïve in front of the text, in front of the Law. Does that situation repeat itself for women's studies or not? Is there in the abstract or even topical idea of women's studies something which potentially has the force, if it is possible, to deconstruct the fundamental institutional structure of the university, of the Law of the university?

There seem to be two hypotheses, two responses. On one hand, there is the positive deconstruction, which consists of saying that one cannot be content with only positive research, but that one must push to the end of the radical question concerning the university Law, and do more than simply institute a department of Women's Studies. That is the optimistic deconstruction, the deconstruction which would not submit to the Law. And then there is another deconstruction, perhaps not resigned or fatalist, but more conscious of the law of the Law and of the fact that even the radical questioning, even the radical deconstruction of the institution of the university by women's studies would not be able to reproduce the Law in the face of the Law. It is not a question of transgressing the Law. In any case, if one takes again Kafka's text, if one were to radically deconstruct the old model of the university in the name of women's studies, it would not be to open a territory without Law—the theme of liberation if you like. But it would be for a new relation to the Law. It is necessary to establish the departments of Women's Studies which would resemble their brothers and sisters of literature, philosophy, anthropology, etc., but after one had done that, one would already have found the Law again. But at least one would have radically changed the situation. One would have rediscovered the Law, but at least one would not be bored any longer. That would be the pessimistic deconstruction.

It is a question of two affirmations, one which appears in classically coded language—optimistic, liberating, revolutionary—and the other which appears on the contrary more modest, more conscious of the fact that at least one radically changed things. One will have brought a better situation, again in front of the Law, which would give one time to grow old, to die like the man from the country. This is the first question—it is a question about strategy. Of course, it has been a necessary phase, strategically speaking, to build women's studies. But what should be the next step? Only this first move, this first effort? Or something totally new? And is it only a question of strategy—is not strategy itself the real risk?

QUESTION: I was just wondering to what extent one can carry your discussion of the Law last night over to this question by thinking about the practitioners of women's studies as women subjects, who can, unlike men, identify with the Law—neither with the man from the country or the keeper of the Law, but with the Law itself: the hymen, the forbidden place, and use that as some kind of strategy by subverting from within. Not through building women's studies, but through feminizing disciplines, which, in very simple terms, is tried sometimes in this country. It's called "integration" of women's studies into the curriculum. But this integration is often a simple way of subverting the curriculum. *Feminizing* the curriculum on the other hand, is trivializing it, is dismantling it, is displacing it; it is making it as trivial as women, and I wonder if it isn't our real strategy: that we work from the base of an operation such as this in order to trivialize philosophy, to trivialize history, to trivialize economics.

RESPONSE: The best choice would be to have the two gestures at the same time: to have a Women's Studies department with a solid, autonomous structure, without giving up the idea of penetrating all other fields. To remain within a department; would be a failure. On the other hand, if you give up the idea of a feminine studies program, then you will weaken the feminine cause. So, the only response to this question would be—joint appointments! Now…coming back to the first step in your question—as to the Law—you will remember, the Law in Kafka's story was neither male nor female. The doorkeeper and the man were subjects—subject to the Law, and "subjects." So a problem arises: if you keep the philosophical axiomatics, implying that women are subjects, considering women as subjects, then you keep the whole framework on which the traditional university is built. If someone tries to deconstruct the notion of subjectivity within women's studies, saying "well, woman is not a subject, we no longer consider woman as a subject"—this would have two consequences: one radically revolutionary or deconstructive, and the other dangerously reactive.

This is the risk. The effect of the Law is to build the structure of the subject, and as soon as you say, "well, the woman is a subject and this subject deserves equal rights," and so on—then you are caught in the logic of phallogocentrism and you have rebuilt the empire of the Law. So it seems that women's studies can't go very far if it does not deconstruct the philosophical framework of this situation, starting with the notion of subject, of ego, of consciousness, soul and body, and so on. The problem with this strategy is that it's difficult to make so many gestures at the same time. Doing research in classical fields—and we need such research in anthropology, in literature—under the titles of subjectivity and soul and body, and civil rights, and at the same time undermining the very structure you're trying to transform.

QUESTION: I wonder if there isn't some use in the de-naturalization of man as a universal; in making men—not "Man," but men—the specific objects of study.

RESPONSE: Yes, that's a necessary gesture. What we could call the neuterization of sexual marks, has as you know, the effect of giving power to man. When you say, "well you are in a neuter field, no difference," we all know that in this case the subject will be man. So, this is a classical ruse of man to neutralize the sexual mark. In philosophy we have such signs all the time; when we say that the ego, the "I think," is neither man nor woman, we can in fact verify that it's already a man, and not a woman. It's always the case. So, to the extent which universality implies neutralization, you can be sure that it's only a hidden way of confirming the man in his power. That's why we have to be very cautious about neutrality and neutralization, and universality as neutralization.

QUESTION: I wanted to pursue the question of subject/object. In a piece of Gayatri Spivak's,[1] a review of *La Carte Postale*,[2] she, in talking about the privileged place of woman in your work, says, "of all the names that Derrida has given to originary undecidability, woman possesses this special quality—she can occupy both positions in the subject/object oscillation, be cathected as *différence*, writing, the *pararegon*, the supplement, and the like. Other names of undecidability *cannot*, without special pleading. Derrida's arrival at the name of woman seems to be a slow assumption of the consequences of the critique of humanism as phallogocentrism..." and so forth. I want to ask you about the difference between woman and Woman, and the deconstruction of subjectivity and subject/object around woman. How does one do it?

RESPONSE: That's a difficult question. Of course, saying that woman is on the side, so to speak, of undecidability and so on, has only the meaning of a strategical phase. In a given situation, which is ours, which is the European phallogocentric structure, the side of the woman is the side from which you start to dismantle the structure. So you can put undecidability and all of the other concepts which go with it on the side of femininity, writing and so on. But as soon as you have reached the first stage of deconstruction, then the opposition between women and men stops being pertinent. Then you cannot say that woman is another name, or a good trope for writing, undecidability and so on. We need to find some way to progress strategically. Starting with deconstruction of phallogocentrism, and using the feminine force, so to speak, in this move and then—and this would be the second stage or second level—to give up the opposition between men and women. At this second stage "woman" is clearly not the best trope to refer to all those things: undecidability and so on. The same could be said for undecidability itself! Undecidability is not a point of arrival. It's also a letter, a misconceived letter, because undecidability—the theme, the motif of undecidability—has to do with a given situation in which you have an opposition or a dialectical logic.

So, the motif of undecidability is linked to a given situation in which opposition is strong. But once you have deconstructed this opposition, you do not need undecidability any more. And there are many many kinds of undecidability. There is one kind of undecidability which is a kind of calculus, a kind of logic, a kind of programming or unprogramming a program, but with a symmetrical relationship to the program. And then there is another undecidability which is totally heterogeneous to the former one, which is totally foreign to the realm of calculus, to the realm of opposition, to the realm of programming and so on. By analogy, we could say the same about "woman." There is one meaning to the word "woman" which is caught in the opposition, in the couple, and to this extent you can use the force of woman to reverse, to undermine this first stage of opposition. Once you have succeeded, the word "woman" does not have the same meaning. Perhaps we could not even speak of "woman" anymore. Of course, these two stages are not chronologically altered. Sometimes you can make the two gestures at the same time, and sometimes you cannot go from one to the other.

QUESTION: But if we use a new triad that still had an opposition of man and woman but had a homonymous yet different tropic use of "woman" as the third term, wouldn't we have the same sorts of reservations that we have with the reigning triad of man and woman with the homonym "man" as the third term? That homonym there seems to imply a synecdochal relationship in that a man can represent the higher category of "Man." Perhaps the tropic use of "woman" is so unfamiliar that we would not slide into homonymy as safely and as routinely as we do with the current use of "man." Perhaps because it's not a metaphoric use, because every one of us in the room has felt the difficulty of undertaking the responsibility to be the Capital W, "Woman." What is the difference between the two systems?

RESPONSE: First of all, the two systems carry similar danger. "Triad" has not been named, you know: triadic structure, which is a dialectical solution. There is no dialectical solution to the problem. Then: in our situation, in this cultural and historical situation, the terms "Man" and "Woman" are not at all the same. This is not an eternal and universal situation. This could change. But in the Western countries, in phallogocentric cultures and so on, the situation implies that there is a difference. In our language, when one says "Man" with a capital M and "Woman" with a capital W…it's not at all the same, not at all, because "man" with a capital M means "mankind." Woman with a capital W means… "Truth" or things like that, but doesn't mean mankind or womankind.

QUESTION: You have this question about woman's studies, that it might simply add something to the existing structure of this academic institution and not question it. I think it's a problem that's very, very important, and I don't know if we're answering it. I have no illusions about the road to freedom and liberation, but a Women's Studies program does institute some different relationship to the Law, and if women were absent before in the traditional academic institutions, maybe now women are more present. So it's a very relative progress, but I suppose it is a progress. But then with this background, how do you feel as a…I don't know if I dare call you a deconstructionist philosopher. What is the relationship of your research and pursuit, and the way that deconstruction is absorbed—I can't say absorbed, it's *swallowed*—with tremendous eagerness by American universities, even more than in France?

RESPONSE: It's more complicated, even in the United States. Of course the reception is larger in the United States than it is in France, but it's not…"swallowing." In fact, there are many signs of a very strong and growing resistance in the United States. And it seems to be exactly the same resistance—and there's nothing fortuitous in that—exactly the same resistance which is opposed to women's studies. Exactly the same people, and the same arguments and the same schemes. For instance, and this is only an anecdote—but a significant one—it has been written somewhere that deconstruction in the United States was successful among feminists and homosexuals. And there is always something sexual at stake in the resistance to deconstruction. Of course it's never simple. It's never easy to formalize, but we can be sure that the force for resisting deconstruction is the same. It's probably the reason why feminists or feminist scholars are to some extent interested in deconstruction, because the struggle is the same. Now, why is it the same? Because deconstruction has developed itself as a deconstruction of a system which is called phallogocentrism, which is a whole structure, which is a system so to speak. And it's not only a matter of concepts, of philosophical battle, but it's also a problem of how to write, how to behave in front of texts, in the institution, and of the relationship to literature and philosophy and so on. That's why it seems to me that there is a strong link between deconstruction—deconstructions and feminine studies, women's studies; but these strategic difficulties are also the same; with the same aporias, the same traps.

QUESTION: In your interview with Christie McDonald,[3] there's an implication that there are two kinds of feminism. The first is a sort of emancipatory movement that is within the tradition of progress, and in some ways very boring, but very secure also. Very necessary but also not imaginative. It works more or less within the framework. In that interview the optimistic deconstruction says that we must not be content only to enact or conduct positive research, and I think that that kind of feminism is a little bit like the women's studies that does positive research and which also exists, and which is important. And then that same optimistic deconstructionist says that we must do something more than build a supplementary. And that looks a little bit like the maverick feminist who dances. It's a way of doing things which can think almost beyond, or re-think the existing structure. I can see that, but I think that that is not really an opposition, necessarily, to the other kind of position which, as you said, is the one that is conscious of the law of the Law, in the sense that you think that you can do something different but you may not think, therefore, that you can go beyond the existence of the Law. It's one thing to say I destructure the subject, and it's another thing, I think, to say

I destructure structure or I destructure Law.

RESPONSE: We cannot be sure there is a way of destructuring Law. You see, deconstruction cannot be transgression of the Law. Deconstruction is the Law. It's an affirmation, and affirmation is on the side of the Law. This is rather difficult. Usually we represent deconstruction as a negative or de-structuring movement, which it is not. It is an affirmative movement, first; and then, as an affirmation, it is not an affirmation against the Law or going beyond the Law. What's difficult to think is that the Law is an affirmation, has the structure of an affirmation. It's not something which limits the desire or forbids the transgression. As soon as you affirm a desire, you perform something which is the Law. The Law says, "yes." That's difficult to understand. The Law is not simply negative.

That's why writing in a deconstructive mode is another way of writing Law. And this is paradoxical. That's one thing that was demonstrated last night, that when Kafka writes "Before the Law," of course he describes a powerful structure, and then he deconstructs all the systems of the Law and shows you how impossible it is to see the Law, to enter the Law, to transgress the limit past the door. But what he is doing, in the meantime, is writing a text which in turn becomes the Law itself. "Before the Law" is the Law. We are in front of it as in front of the Law. He reproduces the situation, and the Franz Kafka signature, or the signature of the text, makes the Law—in a deconstructing movement. So deconstruction affirms a new mode of Law. It becomes the Law. But the Law is guaranteed by a more powerful Law, and the process has no end. This is why deconstruction is not a movement of transgression, of liberation; of course, it has some effects of—in a given situation—effects of emancipation, of transgression, of liberation, but, in the end, it is not.

QUESTION: When we were reading "Choreographies," there was one passage we stopped over and spent a lot of time trying to deconstruct. It is precisely one where you talk about the gift; this is in your response to Christie McDonald. You say, "I am moving much too rapidly but how can I do otherwise here? From this point, which is not a point, one wonders whether this extremely difficult, perhaps impossible idea of the gift can still maintain an essential relationship to sexual difference. One wonders whether sexual difference, femininity for example, however irreducible it might be, does not remain derived from and subordinated to either the question of destination, or the thought of the gift." Do you think that you could unpack that for us?

RESPONSE: Let's begin with the idea of destination. In general, when one speaks of "man" or of "woman" one supposes, for example, that a man speaks to a woman, that a woman speaks to a man, that they are identifiable subjects, and that between them there exists an exchange. The messages, the gifts, caresses, desires, objects, etc., have a giver and a receiver, a destination between two subjects. In as much as a gift has an assignable destination, it is an exchange—therefore, it is not a gift. There is a difference here between a gift and an exchange. If there is, from the man to the woman, or from the woman to the man, a destination of whatever kind, of an object, of a discourse, of a letter, of a desire, of *jouissance*, if this thing is identifiable as passing from subject to subject—from a man to a woman, or from a woman to a woman, or a man to a man, etc., etc.—if there is a possible determination of subject—at that moment, there is no longer a gift. Consequently, there is no gift except in that all determinations— particularly sexual determination as classically defined—are absolutely unconscious and random. And this randomness is the chance of the gift—the gift must be given by chance.

If the gift is calculated, if you know what you are going to give to whom, if you know what you want to give, for what reason, to whom, in view of what, etc., there is no longer any gift. And in order for this chance to arise, it is necessary that there be no relation with consciousness, experience, or the representation of sexual determination. When we speak here of sexual difference, we must distinguish between opposition and difference. Opposition is two, opposition is man/woman. Difference on the other hand, can be an indefinite number of sexes and once there is sexual difference in its classical sense—an opposition of two—the arrangement is such that the gift is impossible. All that you can call "gift"—love, *jouissance*—is absolutely forbidden, is forbidden by the dual opposition.

In consequence, to "unpack" the ellipse, we cannot be sure that there is ever a gift. If someone says to you that there is a gift, you can be sure that that person is mistaken. But if there is the gift, it can only be on the condition—not of non-sexuality—but of sexual nondetermination, in the sense of opposition. That is, not in sexual indifference, but in a sexuality completely out of the frame, totally aleatory to what we are familiar with in the term "sexuality." There can be a heterosexual or a homosexual relation; homosexuality does not exclude itself from this situation.

This does not mean that there is the gift only beyond sexuality but that the gift is beyond sexual duality. To refer to the recently published text called *Geschlecht*, a reading of Heidegger's notion of *Dasein: Dasein* is neither man, nor spirit, nor subject, consciousness nor ego, but sexually neuter; that is, it has no sex. Heidegger did not consider this non-sexuality to be a negative attribute with regard to the opposition man/woman; in other words, it is not a term denoting asexuality. *Dasein* is not indifferent to the marks of difference. Heidegger's discourse is not simple, nor simply beyond classical thought on this subject; certainly this motif on neutralization in his discourse could also reconstruct phallocentrism. There is a certain neutralization which can reconstruct the phallocentric privilege. But there is another neutralization which can simply neutralize the sexual opposition, and not sexual difference, liberating the field of sexuality for a very *different* sexuality, a more multiple one. At that point there would be no more sexes…there would be one sex for each time. One sex for each gift. A sexual difference for each gift. That can be produced within the situation of a man and a woman, a man and a man, a woman and a woman, three men and a woman, etc. By definition, one cannot calculate the gift. We are in the order of the incalculable, of undecidability which is a strategic undecidability where one says "it is undecidable because it is not this term of the opposition or the other." This is sexual difference. It is absolutely heterogeneous.

QUESTION: I have a question about the relationship between sexuality and identity. It seemed to me that, from the analysis of the problem of the gift, in order for the system to work, when you have sexual indeterminacy in this binary way, then you have no possibility that the individual, or that the parties, be identifiable, recognizable, determinable. Sexual indeterminacy implies the indeterminacy of the people, of the subjects. However, one could say that you're sexually indeterminate, but you're not indeterminate racially, for example. Or there's the possibility of identification, and of destination, therefore, which is not bound to sexuality. Is that right?

RESPONSE: In the moment, in the core instance of gifts, it doesn't mean that we have to give up any sexual determinations, but the experience of gifts itself—if it takes place—implies such a sexual indeterminacy. The gift, effacing all determination, sexual or otherwise, produces the destination. Supposing that a gift has been given; that supposes that before it took place, the giver is not determined, and the receiver is not determined. But the gift determines; it is the determination, it produces the identity of the giver and the receiver. The gift is not simply floating in a definitive determination. It gives itself the right to determine. That is why the gift is always a strike of force, an irruption. As an example, in *La Carte Postale* there is a text which is called "Télépathie." In this text it says that such enunciations are not always addressed to anyone, but will only be determined in their destination after their answer. The one who responds, receives it, becomes the receiver. The performativity of the text produces its receiver, but in no way does it pre-exist it. It is the receiver who is the determining factor of the gift. It is not really a "message" structure, for a message presupposes that "X" sends "Y" for "Z," and in the situation of the gift there is no message. It is only the other, at the moment when it receives it, who decides the destination, and who says "it is me who answers," or, "it is mine."

Consider the Declaration of Independence. Jefferson wrote the first draft, the other representatives corrected his text—they were not at all satisfied with it—and the Declaration was signed. But the question is "Who signed the Declaration of Independence?" If one analyses the text, one can first of all say that not Jefferson, for he was the editor, and not the representative, for they spoke in the name of the "good people," but the American people signed the Declaration of Independence. And if one reads the text, one can see that the good people of the United States signed the text in the name of God. It is God who guarantees their good faith, and it is ultimately God who signs the Declaration of Independence. That means that the American people did not exist as the American people before having signed the Declaration of Independence. And it is in signing that they conferred upon themselves the right to call themselves the American people and the right to sign. It did not exist before the signature. Thus, the scriptor does not exist before the signature. The signature itself, which imposes the law, is in itself a performative act which in a certain way produces its own subject, which gives the person the right to do what he is doing. Here is an enunciation—the Declaration of Independence—which arises with a burst of force before there is even a receiver. Thus there is a gesture which, at the limit, produces the receiver, and at the same time produces the sender. When there is such a gesture, an enunciation, it speaks of indetermination but produces determination. It is by the gift that the Law is produced. It is this signature which engenders the sender, the receiver, the signer. It is a performative act—not to put great trust in this concept, but to use it only for convenience—of the gift which produces the giver and the receiver, who at that time become determined, determine themselves as such. It happens all the time, when one says "yes" in marriage for instance.

QUESTION: What is the relation between the performative function of the gift and the conception derived from Heidegger of a kind of limit-notion that might never even exist but points beyond and might also liberate into a kind of non-role-specific diversity of sexualities? It's pretty clear that *Dasein* is quite curiously neutral; I think everyone has noticed that. What is the connection between these two dimensions of the gift?

RESPONSE: The relationship between the theme of indeterminacy on the one hand and the performative on the other could be clear under the condition that one does not simply accept the opposition of performative to constative. You always arrive at a point where this opposition doesn't function any more, but if you take the concept of performative as a conventional assumption then you have to do with a way of speaking or writing—of promising—which is presupposed by any other form of language. The promise, for instance, is a fundamental assumption of any speech act. As soon as one speaks, one is promising. And this promise doesn't simply fall under the concept of performative. If you agree that a signature or everything that amounts to a signature in a statement or in a writing or even in a gesture is performative inasmuch as it doesn't rely on a ready determination, then you cannot rely on the sexual opposition.

In the classical theorization of speech acts, a performative must rely upon conventions. So that's why one cannot be confident of the category of performatives in this case, because there can be no performative if there is no law, if there is no convention which guarantees the efficiency, the pertinence of any performative. There is a performative which creates its own conventions, or if not creates, at least upsets or transforms the system of conventions. For instance, the Declaration of Independence relies on many conventions, but also creates a new framework for new conventions. To this extent it's a performative, and it is a kind of subversion of the existing situation, of the relationship with Great Britain. In that sense, every event of gift is subversive, because it doesn't rely on any given program.

Perhaps it's not even subversive because subversion is a way of relying on given conditions. A gift is something else; it's not subversive, it's not conservative. Subversion is also a program. It has to do with the programmed destruction of a certain amount of conditions. It is totally heterogeneous to subversion as well as to conservation. That is, if it takes place, which is never guaranteed.

QUESTION: As you posed the optimistic and the guarded reading of Women's Studies programs, I wondered by what standard one would read it as either the optimist or the pessimist. I'm a historian, and so I kept thinking that one could write a history of these programs either way, and yet could one try to articulate the measure or the standard by which one could say the subversion had been accomplished, or the transformation achieved, as opposed to the institution incorporating this potentially subversive force?

RESPONSE: There is no measure, not in the form of a theoretical statement, of a theoretical statement signed by a historian. If you want to write the history of women's studies in this country, you won't be able to stop the movement. Your own history can be an active interpretation and can be part of a conservative interpretation of women's studies or another part. So, there is no historical metalanguage on women's studies. But within the space of women's studies, both gestures are always possible. In the same room, in the same seminar, each one of you may sometimes make a conservative gesture and sometimes a subversive one. The history that you could write of women's studies belongs also to the movement; it is not a metalanguage, and will act either as a conservative moment or a subversive moment. Because there is no theoretically neuter interpretation of the history of women's studies. The history will have a performative part in it.

QUESTION: This then brings us to the question of political strategy. And maybe then one asks: in what terms does one understand which of the gestures—or both of the gestures—that you describe as possibilities is better. It seems to me that when you were asking the question you stood outside and posed it as the "optimistic deconstructionist." One can maintain a radical critique and open up new territory and on the other hand one that is more aware of the law of the Law.

RESPONSE: This may not answer the question, but one way of dealing with these problems, not necessarily within women's studies, but on the whole, is to try to do both things at the same time, to occupy two places, both places. That is why deconstruction is often accused of being conservative and...not conservative. And both are true! We have to negotiate. To maintain, for instance, Women's Studies as a classical program, a now classical program, and at the same time to ask radical questions which may endanger the program itself. And what is the measure? You must check everyday what is the measure. One thing may be the good measure at Brown, but perhaps it would be the worst thing at Yale for instance. There is no general device. In some situations you have to behave in a very conservative way, in tough conservative ways, to maintain, and at the same time, or the day after, to do exactly the contrary.

QUESTION: The gift: in every one of its appearances, we get a new configuration of subjects, objects, of identities. That is, with each occurrence of the gift, I suppose, one could occur as male or female in a certain configuration of subjects. In every production of this gift situation we assume that all of us could appear as something different. Even historically different, I suppose. I wonder if you take that as a positive limit, if it's a limit-case. I'm not sure it has any value, moral value, whatsoever.

RESPONSE: It has no *a priori* value. There is no value before it has taken place. Once it has taken place, one will see what is the worth. If you are the receiver of a gift which makes you "woman," you will see. You will say if it has a positive or a negative value. It will be your evaluation of the gift. One can't say ahead of time, "well, this will endanger you."

QUESTION: Then, relating it to the positivity or negativity of the situation of women's studies. If there's merely a reversal, in which men become objects of study and women become the mastering subject, you merely recapitulate the same structure you had previously. But every repetition of the gift would be a repetition not of the same, but exactly a repetition of the different. If that's possible. It seems to me that for women's studies, then, that can be taken as a positive strategy. If there's a battle of the sexes, then women can't win it, they can just end it. It seems to me that this gift implies an interesting notion, where the notion of sexuality disappears in the triumph of feminism.

RESPONSE: No one ever said that sexuality would disappear. Without a doubt, if the success of women's studies would be to constitute men as an object of study, and women as mastering subjects, nothing will have happened. It is necessary not to reproduce the same structure. And you can't say that the gift must always produce something. The gift is not a production. But there are gifts which only call upon repetition and not reproduction. To receive a gift, in the Nietzschean sense, is to say "I want it to begin again," that it happens again, not that it reproduces. And that suggests something on the order of repetition. The "yes" of the gift must be repeatable from the start. Thus it is necessary not to mix the value of production and reproduction, newness, repetition of the other.

QUESTION: This question is related to something you said earlier. You said that in Western culture, the word "man" means "mankind" and the word "woman" means "truth." But in your own writings woman seems to be theorized as a whole list of things mentioned earlier, in the quotation from Gayatri Spivak. And to use one phrase from "The Law of Genre,"[4] a "random drift" which affects the masculine genre and threatens to make it other. I guess I'm asking you to explain how woman as man's "random drift" is different from woman as man's "truth."

RESPONSE: This is an abyssal question, for there is a certain determination of truth which permits one to answer that woman as truth is that which stops the drift, that which interrupts and assures truth. But there is a way of thinking about truth which is more adventurous, risky. And at that point, truth, which is without end, abyssal, is the very movement of the drift. There is a way of thinking about truth which is not reassuring, which is not in general what we think of truth. That would bring us into a discourse about the truth of truth, and Heidegger who says that truth is non-truth; the field is open. As is the case with women's studies and any discipline, at a certain moment one can no longer improvise or hurry. You have to go slowly, look at things in detail. At a certain point it is necessary to stop; one cannot improvise on a question of truth. It would not be surprising, considering all the fields of research in women's studies, that one day, in a program of Women's Studies, there will be the question of truth, and that someone will spend three or four years researching "truth."

DERRIDA

"I think that you should change the title of your magazine."

1. Gayatri Spivak, "Love Me, Love My Ombre, Elle," *Diacritics*, Winter 1984, p. 19—36..
2. Jacques Derrida, *The Post Card* (Chicago: University of Chicago Press, 1987).
3. Interview. Jacques Derrida and Christie V. McDonald, *Diacritiocs* "Choreographies," (Summer, 1982).
4. Jacques Derrida, "The Law of Genre," *Glyph* 7 (1980).

EDITED BY JAMES ADNER, KATE DOYLE, AND GLENN HENDLER.
THIS SEMINAR WAS CONDUCTED IN BOTH FRENCH AND ENGLISH. THE FRENCH SECTIONS WERE TRANSLATED BY JAMES ADNER. REPRINTED FROM *SUBJECTS/OBJECTS* (SPRING, 1984), PP.5-19.

EXTENDED SENSIBILITIES: THE IMPACT OF HOMOSEXUAL SENSIBILITIES ON CONTEMPORARY CULTURE

Arthur Bell, Jim Fouratt, Kate Millet, Vito Russo, Jeff Weinstein, Edmund White, and Bertha Harris

BERTHA HARRIS: I suppose I am the cattle prod here, commonly known as the moderator. I don't want to get too managerial, although my instinct in these circumstances is to get rather managerial. We have more or less agreed on a format as follows: each panelist will talk for about ten minutes either from notes, or from a paper, or extemporaneously. Then there will be questions, rebuttals, manifestos, statements, hysterics, whatever, from the audience.

I thought, too, that it would be better for me to introduce each panelist now, rather than interrupt the flow of these presentations with little bits of biography.

To my left is Vito Russo, whom you all know as the author of *The Celluloid Closet,* which is, as far as I know, the only really good book on gays and film. Vito is also an actor, who is presently performing in a Derek Wilson play at the Process Theater on Church Street. He is the co-producer and director of an upcoming thirteen full hours of WNYC TV on *The Lesbian and Gay Show* on Channel A, which will address itself to the history of the movement before "Stonewall." Vito publishes regularly in a magazine called *The Moviegoer*, and he just finished a piece on Frances Farmer.

VITO RUSSO: Like everybody else in town. [audience laughter]

HARRIS: Jeff Weinstein writes for *The Village Voice* on a regular basis about food, art, books, fashion, and I suppose whatever else tempts him. He told me that he came out in California, and he has been in Gay Liberation since 1970. He also writes short stories, is one of the founding members for the National Writers' Congress, and was formerly the managing editor of *Artforum*.

Edmund White's most recent novel is *A Boy's Own Story*. You must all rush out in the morning and buy it, if you haven't already. Ed told me that he is presently working on a "straight" novel. [audience laughter] It is called *Caracole*.

I am sure I don't really have to introduce Kate Millet. She turned the world upside down and set it right many years ago, when she published *Sexual Politics,* without which, I suspect, none of us would be here tonight. You also know her as a novelist—the author of *Flying, Sita,* and an extraordinary book called *The Basement*. Her most recent book is entitled *Going to Iran*. She is also a painter and sculptor, and I remember her twenty-five years ago as a school teacher.

Jim Fouratt is an impresario, an actor and a writer for *Rolling Stone* and *New Times*. He also says that he is a social activist, which I expect he will explain in his own good time.

Arthur Bell told me that I could say anything I wished about him, so I will only say what you all know, that he writes a marvellous column for *The Village Voice,* and that he just had drinks with Elizabeth Taylor and Richard Burton. [laughter]

ARTHUR BELL: Now that is "gay sensibility."

HARRIS: Ed White will go first.

EDMUND WHITE: On the way up here, I overheard Jeff Weinstein say that "there is no gay sensibility, and it has a tremendous amount of influence." Basically, that is my position too. If gay sensibility exists, it does not exist as a mystical attribute of a mythical entity—all gays, whenever and wherever—but as a particular point of view local to the United States now. I would contend that we have nothing in common with the homosexuals of classical Greece, if it even makes sense to speak of homosexuals rather than homosexual acts at that time. Indeed, I wonder what, if anything, we have in common with homosexuals in England or the United States of the last century or, for that matter, what Quentin Crisp would have to say to gays under twenty-five, aside from recounting a few shared experiences of humiliation and oppression. My idea is that the homosexual as a composite entity that transcends historical or cultural frontiers, is a false unity. Therefore, in discussing the role of homosexual sensibility, I would deny any significance to the first term, "homosexual," other than as a momentary one, suited only to a very limited context. I have an even harder time with the word "sensibility," since it strikes me as an uncomfortable and not very useful word. Are we happy talking about a French sensibility, a black sensibility, a female sensibility? In each case, the term is limiting, chauvinist, racist, or sexist, because it suggests that there is but one sensibility inherent in a large group. Surely, you may be objecting, these groups have identities, or else we couldn't identify them as groups. I would claim, however, that the most progressive way of looking at such groups is the simplest way: blacks have their color; the French have their language; women have their identifying sex; and gays have their sexual attraction to members of the same sex. To be sure, given dominant societal conventions there are certain social consequences to coming out. Different consequences depending on when and where one comes out, and whether one is black or white, tan or yellow, old or young, male or female, beautiful or homely, rich or poor. Some of these may even inform as private and elusive an activity as making art. I would identify four elements of contemporary affluent, white, gay male taste in the United States today. They are ornamentation, the oblique angle of vision, fantasy and theatricality, and finally, in terms of content, an interest in, and an identification with the underdog. Let me address these elements one by one.

By ornamentation I mean an interest in pattern, decoration, detail—the luxurious proliferation of detail. I am thinking of the novels of Ronald Firbank, the costumes and designs of Erté or Beardsley, but also the harsher, more brutal proliferation of ornament in the novels of William Burroughs, or the strange suavities in the paintings of Mel Otum. What I am suggesting is that the dominant male heterosexual taste eschews ornament. In fiction, this masculine taste prefers narrative to description, dialogue to internal meditation, basic prose to convoluted syntax, showing to telling. Remember all those teachers of creative writing who say, "show, don't tell me." Understatement and control are vaunted as though they were eternal aesthetic verities, but I would contend that these values tend to reinforce the status quo. If a writer has a strange, new, subversive point of view, he or she must state it. Proust must state his pessimistic view of love, friendship and society, since he could never contrive to make the reader deduce such a view from any set of actions. This also, of course, works with reactionary writers that have peculiar views. If D.H. Lawrence is so preachy, it is because nobody would ever conclude the strange things he concludes from a series of actions. It is Hemingway who represents a conservative cult of virility and physical courage, and it is he who can rely on understatement and control. By contrast, Proust, who offers a radical critique of all values, burdens his page with endless details, qualifications, and explicit messages. In Hemingway, there is a high percentage of action and dialogue compared to reflection. In Proust, these proportions are reversed. Proust's explanations, his ceaseless authorial interventions, are necessary in order to impart his unique and radical point of view. Paradoxically, this explicitness can often serve an oblique or odd angle of vision. I am not only thinking of Proust, but Genet, and also the best gay writer who is active today, Toni Duvert.

I won't go on except to summarize my feelings at the moment. Over the last few years, I have changed my mind several times as to the existence of "the gay sensibility." In conclusion I will say that both terms, "gay" and "sensibility," are suspect for me but that with severe restrictions, we can isolate certain aspects of contemporary gay taste. I would attribute the subjective aspects of taste I have tried to enumerate here to the objective condition of twentieth-century Western gay life.

HARRIS: Thank you. Jim Fouratt will follow that brilliance with his own.

JIM FOURATT: I would like to say "pass" after that, but I want to straighten a few things out. First of all, I think it is important that I make an announcement. In the back row is my fiancée, Alice Stein. We are going to be married in October. I didn't tell the people who organized the panel this, but I thought it was important to let you know that although I am getting married, I am glad to be here and I think you all have a right to live.

BELL: Are you kidding?

FOURATT: Now, I would also like to say that when I first came to New York, I was told that all the good actors, all the good artists, all the good dancers, all the good writers, all the good filmmakers were gay. I can tell you today, that none of them are.

I have yet to meet a famous movie star who is gay, I have yet to meet a famous actor who is gay, I have yet to meet a famous dancer who is gay, and I have yet to meet a famous artist who is gay. At least they have never told me they are. Now, there has been some experimentation. I will tell you myself that I have experimented with people of the same sex, and I think that it has broadened my experience and theirs. [audience laughter]

The point is that the culture at large only recognizes homosexuals in an underdog, or cult, or minority way. The homosexual influence on contemporary culture, as Jeff was just quoted as saying, doesn't exist and influences greatly.

My agent and my mother wanted me to make the announcement of my pending marriage to Miss Stein who is sitting in the back row, that is, if I am ever to work again. I am joking, obviously.

I am going to leave the intellectual arguments to the people who have developed them here. I am trying to talk more about what it means to be alive in 1982 and to try to exist in the contemporary world. I will tell you that in my experience the state of affairs for any artist who comes out today is very sad. The difficulties in the commercial world are almost insurmountable. I have had friends who, in the surge of activist optimism during the late sixties and early seventies, did come out and put their sexuality on the line, and sometimes their art has suffered greatly for it. What does this mean? It means that we live in a homophobic society, although we artists, we critics, we who control culture, are predominantly gay. What does it mean when we have no real power? Why doesn't Lily Tomlin come out if she is gay? Did Rock Hudson really marry Jim Nabors? [laughter] Did James Dean sleep with...? You know, these are the questions, and we laugh about them. This is our sensibility. I don't know about you, but I always want to know the real answer. When I was seventeen and got drunk, and passed out on Montgomery Clift's doorstep, it was because I thought he was a homosexual. Yet, I don't know, for sure. I haven't seen it confirmed any place that he was. I know he was neurotic; I know that he killed himself, that he drank a lot, and that he took a lot of drugs, as do most of the people in our culture that we suspect are homosexual. I don't know if Robert Rauschenberg is gay. I know he was married and has a son. I see that written all the time. I don't know if Merce Cunningham is gay, he is not sitting up here. I could go on and on. It is not important to name the famous people who are gay. The reality is that contemporary culture does not allow these people to acknowledge it publicly. So what they have done is created a sensibility which is homosexual. I am using the word homosexual in a sense that the dominant press does, to include women: homosexual and lesbian. Many of the things that Ed spoke about, particularly the identification with ornamentation, just make my teeth chatter, yet this is the way most people perceive gay sensibility if they allow us a place in culture at all. We are sensitive, we are delicate, we have a way with words, with style, with fashion, with color, whatever. When it comes to our decisive contributions to contemporary culture, however, I would emphasize the following instead: the capacity to feel and identify with the underdog, which Ed also spoke about—it's our capacity to hide ourselves in the mass of life and show our passions behind a scrim or in the shade that has forged the sensibility—and finally, our potential to go beyond that which society sanctions our imaginations to explore.

Does this make great art? I don't know. Does it make pop art? I don't know. Mr. Warhol lives with his mother. He is another artist who is "not" gay. He goes to church on Sunday. It just goes on and on. With all due respect to everyone here, it bothers me that we all know each other. Where are some of the other names that I have mentioned? Why aren't they here? Why doesn't Lily Tomlin come out, if she is gay? The answer is in order to survive. To have any decisive effect on culture, it seems to me, sadly, that the artist stays in the closet because the artists who wish to become commercially successful are dependent upon the dominant culture to endorse them. Among people not concerned with commercial success, we can have a few legends: the Gertrude Steins, etc. We can go on about those people, those effete people we looked to when we were sixteen and said "This is gay," "that is who I can be when I grow up."

In pop music, when punk came about, I was amazed to find out that a good forty to fifty percent of the people who were involved in the scene at CBGB's were homosexual or lesbian, or asexual. They were repressing a sexuality because they couldn't identify with the dominant gay life style. They didn't identify with being a disco-diva or whatever they were supposed to be, so they hid. It was a new mask. And yet to me, not only here in New York but in that whole movement, there was a real homosexual sensibility, a whole breaking down of roles within that scene. A woman could play an instrument and be acknowledged as a musician, rather than as a woman playing a bass. These changes were very significant. In that asexual, quasi-violent world, there were a lot of lesbians and gay men who did not know how to say "I am a gay person—I am a lesbian." They were post-Stonewall and they didn't identify with the politics. I think we see this among young painters and dancers today too. They don't want to identify with what some of us at this panel fought for very hard, and yet they continue to be victimized in the same way that we were. Until the dominant culture is changed, I don't know how beneficial it is to talk about our effect on contemporary culture, except in a subversive way, in terms of tearing down and of identifying with others who are also oppressed.

I see that Alice has left the back row. I don't know what this means. I just want to say that my intimate relationships with Peter Hujar and Howard Weinraub and Robert McClans and Tom Hill were just boys getting together. They were just an exploration of things that make us better human beings, and I really wish that all the gossip and all the talk behind my back would stop because it hurts Alice and my mom. [audience laughter and applause]

HARRIS: What Jim said, and what I think we recognize as so true, is that one doesn't know whether to simply burst into tears or go and blow up the *New York Times*. Since I guess we are going to do neither, we will move on to Vito Russo.

RUSSO: Thank you, Alice. I am glad Jim framed what he said the way he did, because the things that I prepared to say to you address the fact that I don't think there is such a thing as a gay sensibility and then, what kind of impact that non-existent gay sensibility has on all of us. Jim went right to the heart of the basic problem with our topic.

I knew when I agreed to participate tonight, that the topic of the panel, "The Impact of The Gay Sensibility on Contemporary American Culture" would be completely foregone. I suspected that while we all argued whether or not there was a gay sensibility, we would never get to its impact on the culture. The fact that this is perhaps inevitable should tell us something about the nature of what we are trying to do here. All those names that Jim listed of famous movie stars and writers and painters and rock singers, who won't come out, can't come out, who would be committing suicide by coming out, are evidence that the work of gay people, in order to be commercially or even artistically accepted, must completely and utterly deny its gayness lest one became a "gay actor," just a "gay writer," only a "gay artist," nothing but a "gay performer." Arthur Bell was once referred to in the popular press as not just a gay writer, but a good writer. I always knew he was a good writer, but I was proud that he was also a gay writer. Right in there somewhere, is the crux of the gay sensibility problem. When Jim mentioned Lily Tomlin, Rock Hudson, Jim Nabors and whoever else, I was thinking: "I bet a lot of people are saying to themselves, we don't really want to know whether those people are gay or not"— and I think the truth is that we have to pretend that it is not important. In order to work, in order to be successful at what you do best, you hide. When I try to identify gay sensibility in film, I can never figure out whether it is gay sensibility because a gay person is watching it, or because a gay person made it, or both, or neither. I can think of no gay director working today whose work exhibits what anyone on this panel so far defined as gay sensibility. It's an irony that I have to sit here and tell you that there are working gay directors in Hollywood who I cannot call on today or use their work as examples. That is why the question has to be raised in such a context.

Is there a gay sensibility? I would like to explain it to you this way. I chose the title *The Celluloid Closet* because I was talking about a closeted subject. There is a phrase, coined by Claude Lévi-Strauss, called *bricolage*. There is also an excellent book, called not "Gays in Film" but *Gays and Film*, which is published by the British Film Institute and edited by Richard Dyer. In it he talks about gay people practicing in the cinema what Claude Lévi-Strauss called *bricolage*. That is playing around in our minds with the cinematic elements offered to us in order to bend their meaning to our own purpose. This is something that, because of ghettoization, because of the inexplicable sorrow of the closet, gay people have had to practice on art in order to force it to reflect their own lives. The truth that women can love each other in an emotional and sexual way, or the truth that men love each other in an emotional and sexual way is almost never presented on the screen. For instance, true lesbianism, women relating to women on their own terms, and not in male terms—not sexually for male gratification—has never been presented on the screen. So you go to the movies and as a fourteen year old lesbian or gay man, you see something up there in the dark that speaks to you and you think to yourself: "This has something to do with who I am," but at that time in your life you don't even know yet what the word is for what you are. I can think of moments in my own life when that happened to me, and I would call those moments gay sensibility. I looked at James Dean zipping Sal Mineo's jacket in *Rebel Without a Cause,* and saying: "The poor kid was always cold." And I knew this had something to do with my life. I looked at Dietrich in a top hat and tails in *Morocco* kissing another woman on the lips to make Gary Cooper jealous, Garbo in *Queen Christina* and in *Gilda,* Glenn Ford and George Macready, and I thought to myself these are gay relationships. But was I practicing on the cinema a form of *bricolage,* a form of playing around with the elements of the movie in order to bend them to my own purpose? Yes! What I was doing was saying: "I live here too." And since this image does not serve my life, I will imagine a way in which it could if the world were different. So I think that what I call gay sensibility is a product of ghettoization, a product of a world in which people have been forced to hide. Perhaps the definitive example of gay sensibility is an eighty-five year old gay man or woman who has spent a life-time giving a performance. Think about what it means to give that performance so perfectly and so completely that they die with only the knowledge that they have carried it off. A sort of perfection in a way, and yet, does anybody want to call that a positive gay sensibility? When Ed cited an "oblique angle of vision" as a characterization of gay sensibility, it made me think of how, as a gay person, one grows up with the people around you, including your parents, assuming you are straight. At some point of course you know different, and so you acquire a kind of double vision. You are able to see both the truth and the illusion. Growing up with this double vision helps you to practice it on art, on cinema, on writing. You imagine all sorts of things in order to create a world where you exist.

I remember seeing Garbo in *Queen Christina* looking out the window and talking about going out and being lost in the snow. She does go out eventually dressed as a man and ends up at a country inn, where she meets John Gilbert who plays the ambassador to the King of Spain. They talk about Spain, and she asks: "How are things in Madrid. Has Spinoza written anything new lately?" And he asks her: "When was the last time you were in Spain?" Garbo replies: "I have never been there, only in my thoughts." And Gilbert says; "Well that is interesting that you can speak of Spain so nostalgically, never having been there." And she responds: "Yes, one can feel nostalgia for a place one has never been." I think sometimes this is what gay people do, when they see themselves on the screen in places where there is no homosexuality. They see something on purpose. The German film, *Mädchen in Uniform,* directed by Leontine Sagan in 1931 from the script by Christa Winsloe, based on her play *Yesterday and Today,* was about a young girl who falls in love with her teacher, confesses this fact in a drunken moment after the school play, and is subsequently ostracized. When the film came out in America, the censors wrote, and I quote from memory: "This film will not have any public showing in the United States of America because it depicts an abnormal relationship between women in boarding school life." They cut seventeen scenes out of *Mädchen in Uniform* before they approved it for release in the United States. When it opened in New York, minus any concrete lesbianism, the critic from *The New York Daily Mirror* said: "All the mental experimentalists were at hand last night to see *Mädchen in Uniform* open, because it has been billed as the celluloid version of *The Well of Loneliness*. And boy were they surprised. It is nothing but a simple, clean, wholesome tale of schoolgirl crushes." So you see what happened; the censors removed it, the critics said it wasn't there, and anybody who still saw it was queer. What I am proposing is gay sensibility as turning hiding into an art form, as turning being in the closet into something poetic and beautiful. I don't buy all the old gay experimental films from the thirties and forties. People are always asking why I don't talk about Maya Deren in *Meshes of the Afternoon*. I think that homosexuality in those films was something rather precious. As far as I am concerned homosexuality is not poetry, it is prose. This preciousness in the way people approach homosexuality stems from the fact that we have been forced into denying our existence and at the same time trying to justify it with works of art. You can't do both. The examination of people's work based on their sexuality will not occur until people are "out." It is beside the point. And so, I guess I want to close by saying that I do not think that J. Edgar Hoover has anything in common with Oscar Wilde.

By the way, you were talking about rock stars. Somebody at RCA Records told me that Elton John's statement in *Rolling Stone* about being bisexual had disastrous ramifications for him. Thirteen year old girls were calling RCA Records up by the hundreds saying, "Tell us that it isn't true, and we promise to believe you." I think that expresses what people want to know about gay artists in this society—nothing. Everything beautiful about our experience is turned into a product of the majority. Take, for example, the way music that the gay community discovered was recycled in the form of The Village People for a heterosexual audience. That is what will happen to all gay culture and it is the fault of gay people themselves. We keep ourselves where we are by saying: "I don't want to be just a 'fag' writer, I don't want to be just a 'dyke' actress." If Lily Tomlin is gay and she doesn't want to come out, it is because she doesn't want to be known as that "dyke" actress. Until every dyke actress is out of the closet, until every gay writer is out of the closet and we don't have to have phrases in the press like "this person is good, not just gay," there isn't going to be gay sensibility. [applause]

HARRIS: I am practically rendered speechless by the statements that have come before me, and I hardly know how to make a transition between what Vito just said, and what I have to say. There is so much there that I want to respond to. But instead of actually saying what I intended to say tonight, I just wonder if anybody in this audience ever remembers an actor named Lash LaRue. [response from audience] Aha! So when I was six years old and going to the Haymound Theater in Fairdville, North Carolina to see Lash LaRue in these Western serials, it meant, I think, that I was queer. Around the age of twelve I started tuning into Milton Cross and the Metropolitan Opera every Saturday afternoon on the radio, much to my parents' displeasure. I have always been enormously in favor of perversion and much of what I have to say tonight concerns perversion. But I'll start by sort of going back to where Ed left off in the sacred grove, because very little of my own life enters me any more, unless I can turn it into the lies that we call fiction.

Nearly everything I have to say has to do basically with fiction, although much of it is so general I suppose you could take it to mean almost anything. For the purposes of brevity and because it is the announced topic, I am going to use the word "homosexual" to mean both men and women, gay and lesbian. I should say ahead of time that if I say anything about contemporary culture it will be an accident, because I basically live in the late nineteenth century where I feel very safe. I just don't know what contemporary culture is. And remember that if you are offended, I will be delighted. [audience laughter]

The homosexual sensibility is more, I think, than what a homosexual feels when she or he is making or contemplating a work of art. I think it is an objective reality which has existed in art and in our response to art since artmaking became a practice indigenous to civilization. All great art has some element of the gay sensibility in it, in that all art might be described as a refusal to leave the world alone, as a tampering with reality, a manipulation of things as they appear to be ordained until they seem to be something entirely other. The homosexual sensibility in art making, I believe, goes further than this. When in the grip of its effect, the artist has made two previous decisions: first, that reality is interesting only when it is distorted, and second, that reality lacks interest because it is controlled by usefulness which is pertinent only to the heterosexual continuum. The positive decision our hypothetical artist makes then, is to attach herself or himself to the inexpedient and the impertinent. And I am using these words in the way that the masters of culture define them.

The first thing one notices about his or her completed work is that it makes no contribution whatsoever to any concept or plan for usefulness in this world. And this is the reason why such work is often called trivial. The heterosexual appetite for usefulness drives dominant culture. Its art must somehow reinforce connections with history, inheritance, antecedents, friends, neighbors, tribes, and so forth, and in so doing give us the illusion that a future exists.

The drama of the heterosexual enactment comes about when the cycle of history and the future is somehow threatened by external factors such as war or organized bigotry, or, internally, by strife within the family. The resolution of the drama and the satisfaction of the heterosexual appetite comes with the reassurance that no matter how bad things get, we will eventually hear the door bang open and somebody will shout: "Hi honey, I'm home!" Now I should add here that nearly every homosexual I know, except really poetic types, also shares this heterosexual appetite. Faggot, fairy, dyke, pervert, invert, queen, these words are not so much evidence of our unfailing inhumanity, as they are, in their backhanded way a recognition of a human as well as an aesthetic need for risk as an alternative to safety. They are in a sense declarations of a desire for the unsafe. The hostility inherent in those words is the product of a desire to be released from the tediousness of cause and effect and to be catapulted into the surprise of pleasure. "To feast with panthers," as Oscar Wilde put it so much better than I can.

Altogether, I think this means that we find "real" life, which I guess simply means biological inevitability, just as burdensome aesthetically as it often gets in day-to-day living. When the burden becomes overwhelming, we are beset by a need for the fantastic, the fabulous, the otherworldly, the grotesque, the bizarre, the precious and the morbid. That is, we feel we will go crazy if we don't immediately get something queer into our lives! [audience applause]

Now I think I should say that if I say "we" I mean the human race. I don't just mean homosexuals, although I mean us more than them, of course. So I think the homosexual sensibility begins with the perfectly "natural" instinct to work *contra naturum*. We can't endure nature, unless we are free to do more than rearrange or abstract it, or conceptualize it, or minimalize it, or whatever the hell one does with it. We must also be free to pervert nature, and feel and see it perverted. That is, we must be free to act, or work, or respond in ways that are preeminently useless. W.H. Auden once said, "A poem is not supposed to make anything happen." The heterosexual sensibility however, is based on encouraging things to happen, particularly in ways that are socially useful. When homosexual artists cooperate with usefulness in their work, they are divesting themselves of the singular privilege of the homosexual sensibility which is to make things stop happening. Coming out in real life is an act of sanity and good citizenship. To continually reproduce the coming out process in one's work, however, is to act like a heterosexual, according to the definition I have just proposed. It is to make one's work socially useful. It is to employ correct thinking as opposed to making things queer. Since Stonewall, there has been an enormous proliferation of work which literally and graphically proposes that the homosexual scene and the homosexual dilemma are the true renditions of what we have been referring to as the homosexual sensibility. Now this kind of reasoning baffles me, and tends to make me feel that to choose to be a homosexual artist means that one is also choosing some variant of social realism as one's aesthetic implement. This bothers me again, because as I understand social realism, and I haven't had much truck with it, it is the antithesis of what I think of as the homosexual sensibility. Now we can't all, of course, live and work as *fin de siècle* dandies, although I certainly wish we would put more effort into it. [audience laughter] And furthermore, I also think that we should try to stop confusing our ideas about the homosexual sensibility with the practice of homosexuality. We can begin by saying that the sensibility has a life of its own, separate from, and independent of, the practice or practices that define the homosexual. What this would mean in actual terms is first of all freedom for the homosexual artist to use and or abuse the heterosexual sensibility when that suits his or her project. It would further, I think, free the homosexual artist from the pressure to respect certain political imperatives which have become associated with the practice of homosexuality. I believe too, that it would also free the heterosexual artist to create out of the homosexual sensibility. By making homosexuality public, as many of us in this room have done, we have also made it available to everyone's imagination. As a homosexual you can do or be whatever you can get away with, and to employ the homosexual sensibility as an artist is also to become axiomatically elitist. To choose to fabricate uselessness is to step away from accountability. Thus the single bond uniting the practice of homosexuality and the homosexual sensibility is this elitism. Eventually, however, if the work is good enough, one's perversion of the useful will come to seem aesthetically essential to the world at large. Cold comfort if you are dead, but that is how it goes. If you are alive, then, of course your "employment" must be to revise and reanimate this sensibility as it is co-opted.

I don't know how the following writers of fiction spend their free time, but I do think they are important to name here as women and men who are currently making wonderful art out of what I consider homosexual sensibility. Lois Gould's two most recent novels, *Sea Change* and *La Presidenta*, may not be familiar even to those of you who religiously read every lesbian or gay novel that comes out, because they are not marketed as gay, yet they are, I think, infused with what we are talking about. Janet Frame, the New Zealand novelist, fills the bill in all of her fiction as does James McCourt in his novel, *Mardou Gorgeous,* which is one of the most extraordinary works of contemporary fiction going. MacDonell Harris's novel *Hermes* is also terribly pertinent as is the English novelist Adam Mars Jones's *Lantern Lecture and Other Stories.* All of Angela Carter's fiction is important here but I would strongly recommend her two books, *The Bloody Chamber* and *Fireworks.*

There are more, of course, including works by members of this panel and members of this audience that belong on this list. And of course there are the great stylists who come thundering out of the past—Nabokov, Henry Green, Djuna Barnes, Ivy Compton Burnett, and finally Flannery O'Connor, because she knew how to recognize a freak when she saw one. [audience laughter] Now, of course, as you and I know, these writers may or may not have been gay, but I think that what they do in their work creates something that I would describe as a homosexual sensibility. Style, after all, is fiction entire. The homosexual sensibility is marked by eloquent postures of hyperbole, and everything else is straight. Thank you. [audience applause]

Jeff Weinstein.

JEFF WEINSTEIN: ...offend somebody? No, I am not offended, but I just wanted to say that, though social realism can be deadening sometimes, at other times it can be awfully queer, especially when it is not permitted. I know you used social realism as a point of contrast to narrow the field down, but I want to broaden the definition of what can be queer. In fact, a lot of what I have been hearing, most of which I agree with, is either an attempt to encompass everything in the world that's good as gay or homosexual, or to separate it off. But now I am beginning to respond, and maybe first I should say a little bit of what I prepared.

Sensibility, even without the word gay attached, would be very difficult to define. So we shouldn't feel discouraged if we can't define our topic today, although there have been more real attempts at doing so here than I had expected. I did want to say, though, that I was just reading Martin Duberman's diary excerpts in the homosexual issue of a journal called *Salmagundi,* and they reminded me of something. Gay sensibility in the forties and fifties in this country encompassed a lot. Things like, for men, shortened trousers or angora sweaters as well as a range of coded ways of identifying each other. But Duberman's sensibility as revealed in his diary was basically one of "aren't we neurotic, and aren't we sick, and aren't we shameful." He commented brilliantly about how this has had to change and how he hopes that it has changed. I continue to wonder how much it really has.

I want to tell you a little bit about the arguments I have heard recently about gay sensibility, gay style, and gay culture, which we seem to be conflating. And why not? Recently, some people including the curator of the "Gay Sensibility" show at The New Museum, have told me that they think we are now in a kind of "post-liberation" period. The assumption is that the gay sensibility should reflect this new state. We are now finished with the difficulties of "coming out," and presumably we can somehow take whatever is left of our gay experience and bring it to the rest of culture. I think Vito has already explained how this is impossible, but it is something younger gay artists and writers today are worried about. They think that somehow we will be limited by our need to come out. I don't think this washes. Even if it were true, it's true only in the largest of cities. Certainly "gay sensibility" (I keep putting quotes around this tag) if it exists, has to exist in the mass culture. I want to talk a little bit about mass culture and how we recognize cultural codes as a way of identifying what is gay and what isn't. We have been talking about "we" and what we know and what we don't know. One thing that interests me in this respect is the "clone" sensibility. The "male" sensibility has become a "gay sensibility." OK, we know that some gay men have invented a very interesting style of wearing clothes and the style serves many purposes, as any style does. I am not dressed that way tonight, though I expect I have the outfit at home. I could put it on. [audience laughter] I don't know who invented it; I know who first used the word. He was a journalist from San Francisco, but I want to think about what it means. You see a guy who has on his tight T-shirt, very tight button-fly Levis, tighter, in fact, than they were meant to be worn, and you can be fairly sure that he is gay. Other gay men know this, and nowadays, other straight people do too. This is a kind of *bricolage,* or rather assemblage—putting together pieces of things and changing them. There is some bravery connected with wearing these clothes, bravery because this is a "coming out" costume. I am not going to say that it is art, although I want to. I will say that it is a parcel of gay culture generations of "coming-outers" old, and some people of the next generations will conclude that men who are not dressed in this outfit can't be gay. We all know this is not true. The reason I bring this up is that, although the "we" that we talk about tends to be a "we" defined by how we deal with the world culturally, this "we" is not as homogeneous as it sometimes appears. You notice this when you go out of New York. I just got back from San Diego and the "clone" outfit there has slightly different variations. It depends on what you can buy in the shopping centers there, versus what you can buy here. Nonetheless there is a difference, and the difference will be differently interpreted. There is a kind of localism that we have to talk about in culture even when we talk about sensibility—different places, different kinds of people. We all know that blacks and non-whites of different kinds dress differently. This is one thing I would like you to remember when we are thinking about gay sensibility.

The other notion about gay sensibility I've heard discussed recently is the "ghetto theory," which we have talked about a little bit already. I want to discuss it a little more because the implications are interesting to me. The idea suggests that Jean Genet would not have written something like *Miracle of the Rose* if he were not gay and if he were not in prison. That gay sensibility would not exist were we not oppressed, were we not outsiders, or underdogs. It's another version of the starving artist theory that runs through Western culture. This theory was very much current at the time William Blake was painting, and he constantly railed against it because he knew that many artists were not poor and could not afford to be poor. Well, the poverty-artist theory is a persistent one, because we uphold it, because it does connect to the theory that if we are not oppressed, what will we have left? If we start coming out and things get better, I am not saying that they will, but if they do, what will gay art be? What will gay sensibility be? Will we lose the things that we love so dearly? Will that zippered jacket that you mentioned become less important? It probably will. What I want to propose is that the fear that I have heard from some of the people speaking that gay art or gay sensibility is permanently connected to the position of being an underdog, to gay oppression; that art is a response to a difficult life; and that gay art in particular is a response to our need to hide, to be secret, this is not the real issue—I think that what we fear is losing our own history. This is a valid fear. We should fear for our history because our history has been taken away from us. Part of what we have been doing in these last twenty, thirty, forty years at the most, is trying to rewrite history—to resurrect those who have had to fight—who may even have tried to come out but have not succeeded because they were written out. Women know this from their own experience. If you have ever looked at Janson's *History of Art*, the standard college text book, you know there isn't one woman in that book. We know now that there have been plenty of women artists, and consequently history is being rewritten. We have to do this. The fear is real. What I wanted to do a little bit, is propose a way of dealing with that fear, because there might be something positive that we have realized. We are a minority at the moment, and perhaps we will always be a minority. Though our art may be a product of our minority status, as gay people we have learned something other people have not. Like many feminists, we know better than others the arbitrary nature of sexuality, certainly of gender and of sex roles. Gay people know this. Lesbians know this. The eighty-five year old who has had to act for a lifetime knows this. They may all be able to see it in art. I don't see oppression disappearing, I don't see this as a post-liberation period, but because right now we are gay, we know the arbitrary nature of these things and can—must—utilize this knowledge. I think that we can work with the cultural legacy that people have tried to hook to a pre-liberated period, in an ongoing fight for liberation. We have spoken about coding. This has to do with all art and certainly with all good art. Masking, mirrors, secrets, closets, there have been closets in art and one wonders (I'm thinking of Vito's *bricolage* idea) if the artist intends them to be looked at in this way. Well, we will look at them this way, we have to, we will reinterpret the word "closet" every time it appears. We have done this already. We have also talked about costume as opposed to fashion. The arbitrary nature of dress is something that we can certainly take on. I think that there is something in gay sensibility that may have to do with seeing possibilities that don't yet exist and actualizing them. We have had to do this for survival in history. I think that there are some fructifying possibilities here.

HARRIS: Kate Millet will now speak. And following Kate, Arthur Bell will close this part of the evening.

KATE MILLET: Well, the business of an impact, that is one problem. The other is homosexual, still more problematic. Then there is sensibility, more problematic still, and finally contemporary culture, hm....

I am going to take the existence of homosexual sensibility for granted, and I am going to address these questions passionately, because I drove from Poughkeepsie today, and there is so little homosexual sensibility there. There are so many different Americas. In Poughkeepsie we are trying to establish a women's art colony, but most of the rest of Poughkeepsie is very removed from our intentions. Sanding walls and listening to country music is not at all infused with homosexual sensibility, however likable these chores may be.

Driving down here, it occurred to me thunderously, what if we were to rephrase this question and were to ask: What is the impact of lesbian sensibility on Contemporary Culture? I would respond right off hand without even shifting gears, that it's zilch. [audience laughter] Then I would back up and say, well, not quite. There is a little tiny subversive "give us a chance," sort-of-merest-hint of a sensibility in and through the women's movement, a movement which is accused all the time of being lesbian and is really, far more even than the critics probably know. [audience applause] There is certainly something special about the independence which lesbian sensibility represents as compared with all the other "faces" women have presented throughout history. There is something very practical too in the autonomy of the lesbian, because you see, lesbians are the first women who have had to earn their own living. Nobody is going to earn it for us. So, if we eat, we eat together, this is significant. This cohabitation is social acknowledgement. This is very important, because this independence from the family and from marriage cannot be arrived at in any other way. This probably explains why there is no history of lesbianism. Virtually no history, I mean there is Bertha Harris and Gertrude Stein, but between Sappho and Gertrude Stein you have a long blank. Perhaps something happened in the harem, but I can't find out about it any better than you can. Autonomy, economic independence, money, social status, none of these things could be achieved before the female emancipation movement in the nineteenth century. So you got your first lesbians, and very aesthetic ones at that, in Paris and the United States as it became possible to attain economic, sexual, and social independence.

There is an enormous difference between this history of female homosexuality and the history of male homosexuality. If you are going to try to identify lesbian sensibility, affecting and impacting on contemporary culture, I would look to the dyke, because she is the real threat. It's the very "outness," the way in which the dyke is greeted with hostility by hard hats and horror by mothers-in-law and ladies who cash out your groceries, that is simply wonderful. She may not represent a high culture sensibility, she is probably going to have the wrong kind of hair cut and a peacoat, but she will be what she is in a way that is terrifying. And she is not called bulldagger for nothing. It goes back to *Boadicea* and so forth. This is some kind of female warrior who is absolutely in revolt, who never can quite be quelled, and who will fight you over that alone. That is an enormous and wonderful kind of courage. It probably won't make it into the polite salon which permits a sort of a "let's taste" attitude towards various subcultural transgressions. I think that soon the market people will adopt a "let's taste" attitude towards homosexuality because there is a lot of money to be made from homosexuals, maybe not so much from lesbians. They are a little more hard up. We will see in the future (and I share a certain dubiousness with my friends here), whether or not we are "post" liberation—how free we are, how OK this is, how much has been achieved. I would say very little, but I am still going to be patriotic and stick to this topic tonight and I will address the homosexual sensibility as it is generally understood. It almost includes lesbians, but it doesn't quite. Really we mean gay men. Homosexual sensibility is a confrontational phrase from the start because the "sexual" is right there. I think any impact that homosexual sensibility has on contemporary culture concerns the forbidden. We are talking about what has been forbidden, and is now permitted. The fact that homosexuality is permitted at all is important. In terms of culture at large, which is after all patriarchal and very straight and square and dependent upon rigid sex roles, homosexuality has been forbidden except in strictly codified circumstances. It has been absolutely forbidden to women, and permitted to men only in particular circumstances—in ancient societies and in the near East at the present. But even in these cases it has been permitted only in specific ways—in terms of homosexual acts which initiate heterosexual conventions of dominance and submission, of man and boy, of boss and the one used and abused. Otherwise it has been forbidden throughout the Christian era, and the church has inflicted terrible punishments. If it exists at all, it has been just past the range of the eye, as a whiff and aroma, bare and shallow. There has been much ornament, perhaps to disguise, and there will be a lot of role switching. That which is unknown—the alien, the interdict—will always be forbidden fruit. Not only in terms of the sexual act, but in terms of the aura around it, the time, the place, the climate, the sort, and the class. All these partake of the not-to-be-known, the not-to-be-touched, and therefore constitute a world always beckoning. In as much as it becomes permissible all of this changes, and we all harbor an ambivalence about this. Do we lose our "romantic" status? You see, we have been coated in that for quite a while and it is a very integral and wonderful part of the "homosexual" experience. It's the other side of the coin of the ghetto.

Predicting the future is always very tricky, but suppose that what happens is that the "forbidden" becomes "permission," and this permission extends to everybody, not only to us, and along with fantasy, bisexuality is permitted. Finally, we may not even be a minority. This would utterly change the face of our puritanical patriarchal society.

Pleasure is a very important part of the homosexual aura—a very important part of homosexual life. Pleasure, luxury, taste. Even if it is just an empty wine bottle with a candle in it. You see, we thought to use candles! We always did buy just the right records and cared desperately. There is a tremendous urge, not just for culture, but for all kinds of refinement, grace, fashion. You could argue that American taste is really not dictated by the ruling class. Our ruling class has no taste anyway. Taste and refinement are really dictated by the homosexual sensibility which is only now rearing its ugly head and showing its beautiful smile for the future. This is a society that now even drinks wine, remember when they didn't. Our experience is part ghetto, part closet, part all that knowing-suffering and being a minority. I don't like the expression "underdog"; I don't think that it's fair even to use that term, though it is somehow central. We always hold up a kind of a mirror to the heterosexual regime: they-we, them-us. We know them a great deal better than they know us and we know the "us" that always registers in their eyes. We have always known how ridiculous gender roles are, and that is why they are so camp and such fun but "they" take them tremendously seriously. That is why they send some off to shoot and get shot and the rest go around in nurses' caps. Patriotism, the economy, their loan systems, the church, and the family, all of the underpinnings of patriarchal society depend on this coercive heterosexuality. Everybody must keep to their little place as either masculine or feminine. Whatever impact "our" sensibility might have will be in the future rather than right now. It is only beginning to be felt and we are in the middle of it, so it is very hard to understand. I think the ancient institution of patriarchy is beginning to crumble and we, the entire society, are being faced with new freedoms, and with this comes the fear of freedom. It is an enormous time of exploration and opening up. A great many more things are becoming possible, and new experiences and sensations are all affecting the mainstream sensibility. But first it is confronted with "our" sensibility that has been in this lone place, and watched the other from afar. As the two come together the entire spectrum of what culture or the human condition— whatever art records, or defines—changes enormously. We don't really quite know. We are the catalysts but not the clones. Thank you. [audience applause]

HARRIS: Arthur Bell.

BELL: When I agreed to come up here, I told the young man who put together the panel that I am not much of a speaker and I don't give speeches, but that I would be very happy to participate in the question and answer period. "Well can't you…" he didn't say anything for about ten minutes and then he asked, "what about a minute or two." I answered, sure. Now I really feel as though I have been ravished by intelligence. I cannot get over the…wow! I really have no business being here. It reminds me of when the movement was founded by a man I happened to be fucking at the time, and all that stuff was going on in my apartment. I was in the kitchen making jello, trying to make brown jello and combining the flavors, because I wasn't understanding any of the stuff that was going on in the other room. Although I think I understand a lot of it now, I also feel—and I suppose this sounds terribly presumptuous—but I feel as though I am gay sensibility and I don't know what I am and I don't know what I do, but it just is. So I wrote down one little thing on my typewriter before I left the apartment with the decorator. [audience laughter] I am not kidding. And I wrote down…(it sounds so inane). I wrote that gay sensibility is a generosity of spirit, and an ability to cut through crap like a scalpel with a wry sense of humor. And that is it. I think that if this is what we do, and I really feel that in essence, this is what a lot of us who have it do, it is something that straight people may have picked up. A lot of straight people have picked it up. A lot of straight people have it more than we have it. And I'll answer questions. [audience applause]

HARRIS: The floor is open, as they say.

AUDIENCE: We are always accused of being subversive, and of course they are right. But I think we are even more subversive than we are accused of being. In part, it has to do with the gay use of verbal and non-verbal communication to mean more than it usually does. Double meanings in verbal communication, and the whole "art" of non-verbal communication to get across messages that the straight world will not pick up on, this is something that we are always involved in. This is gay sensibility if there is one. I don't really think that there is a gay sensibility outside of that. And I doubt for example that music or abstract painting expresses a gay sensibility. It seems that if there is gay sensibility in art that it has to speak to this content, whether it is overt or suggested.

HARRIS: Thank you. If someone else doesn't speak, I'm going to call on you.

AUDIENCE: This question is directed to Bertha Harris, Kate Millet, and Ed White in particular.

It seems to me that there is something underlying what all three of you cited as an element of gay sensibility. I would like to know if this way of putting it all together makes any sense. It seems that nobody cited one of the defining characteristics of gay and lesbian experience—the fact that we do not produce families with children. It struck me that all the things you are talking about, love of ornamentation, change, theatricality, non-productivity, might have to do with people who are not tied into patriarchal vertical structures that stretch out through time to our friends and our own lives. For the most part it would seem that when you look at our lives, it is in terms of that horizontal network around us. The question for us has been how to enrich that? How do we make a beautiful life in the present for ourselves? Does that contribute in any degree to the kind of thing we are talking about as gay sensibility?

WHITE: I agree with some of the things that you are saying. There is a functional element in looking at our subject. We can ask, how do gays fit into contemporary society and what function does this interest in ornament serve? And then there is a historical way of looking at it. Twenty years ago Susan Sontag advanced the idea in her famous essay on camp that although camp sensibility is not exactly the same thing as gay sensibility, it constitutes it in part. Sontag linked camp, in turn, to a long tradition of dandyism. I imagine that there are a lot of people in this room who know more about this than I do and I'm sure some of you have interesting things to say about why gay sensibility was derived from dandyism. But I think that this relationship to dandyism is a historical given. Why dandyism continues to function today and why it is particularly appealing to us is another question. It seems to me that at least for gay men, in coming out one is released from certain rather rigid notions of virility. It seems, for instance, that American writers who are heterosexual males, feel obliged, or rather did, to write in a rather chastened style and anything else was considered "writing like a woman." Gay men having already bitten the bullet and come out, and having already renounced that kind of gender identification are free to indulge in a very widespread (there is always a danger in using the word "natural") human interest in ornament. It seems to me that it is a rather peculiar and civilized, and, I think, finally temporary, idea, to have chastened art.

MILLET: You touched on something that I meant to say more about and that is the possibilities for hedonism. As gay men and women we are not bound by this vertical structure; we have the luxury to concern ourselves with more than just existence and so to live on this horizontal plane among our peers and friends. If we carry this too far however, we run the danger of cutting ourselves off from ongoing generations. There is a possibility of really odious selfishness in people who have no responsibility for feeding and taking care of little people—who have nothing to do with their money except buy more cars. On the one hand, this real possibility for endless, stupid materialism provides the perfect market research test case. On the other, this freedom opens itself not only to the arts, but also to the art of living. One manifestation of this possibility of a more pleasure-seeking and hedonistic, a more genial existence than is typically urged on us in a tight, tribal, totally expedient society would be something like the interest in luxuriant ornament you mentioned. But this, I think, is a subset of the more general resistance to utility that you also recommend.

HARRIS: Jeff Weinstein wants to say something, and after him, Jim Fouratt. Everybody has something to say about this.

BELL: I don't.

WEINSTEIN: I just wanted to make a quick argument for thinking in more relativistic terms. We may be looking for some kind of absolutism here in terms of what constitutes gay-lesbian sensibility.

FOURATT: I think this idea about ornamentation as particular to gay sensibility, this focus on ourselves and on our peer group, is really very dangerous and old fashioned. I think that as "outsiders"—like Kate, I prefer the term to "underdog"—we have a capacity for community and for the celebration of community. Our focus on physicality may lead us to be more involved with, for lack of better word, ornamentation. But the capacity for community, and to celebrate our outlawed love, is central.

One of the biggest closets always was that we were allowed to take care of children and raise children and teach children as long as we didn't come out. I think one of the worst things for the generations before us was that we were denied the acknowledgement that we loved and cared for the generations that succeed us. For me, and I know this is true for others here too, what happens to the young gay person is very important. I think we have to get away from this marketing idea that we are rich and we are this and we are that. I don't know about you guys, but most of my friends are not rich and some of them even have children.

BELL: Well, ornamentation in journalism makes lousy journalism. And you don't see that too much in the best gay papers. I mean, you look through a *New York Native* and it is really tough journalism. A lot of those stories, particularly the stories that Brett Averill has done on murders, are as pithy and trenchant as anything that Hemingway has written. I think that ornamentation in writing, when it comes to novels, is also just junk. I truly detested that book that everyone was yelling about, *Dancer from the Dance,* because it was one of those things where the guy wrote a sentence with a hundred-seventy-six words and then followed it with a sentence with three words. It was just showing off. I don't know if this is gay or just pretention.

HARRIS: *Que sera, sera.* Vito has some more to say on this score.

RUSSO: I keep thinking of the word "community" coupled with the word "outsider," and I wonder how or if a group of people can become a community of outsiders. I wonder if a community of people who are different can come out as people who are different, and remain different? I don't know a community that remains different and visible. People, in order to come out, must join the majority. In other words, you will hear a gay person go on television and say to David Susskind: "The rest of the world should accept us because after all, we are in most ways just like you." I don't hear people going on television and saying: "We are not like you. We are different. The acceptance of our difference means changing the world. Teach people to learn to love difference, to celebrate difference." I am wondering if gay people can come out without getting swallowed up. To stress what is like everybody else about us, rather than to stress what is different and maintain that difference through the ages. I mean, is that possible?

FOURATT: We are not like everybody else, no matter how we try, come on!

RUSSO: But don't you always hear people on talk shows saying, this is not a sexual issue, this is a civil rights issue. Don't you hear Jerry Falwell say that if gay people are allowed to come out, if gay people are permitted to have legitimacy, it will change the world. And then the gay people who are on the show with Falwell reply, No, no, no, that is not true. This is simply a civil rights issue. All we want to do is protect our civil liberties and jobs.

MILLET: We should always be honest and admit that we will change the world. Heavens!

FOURATT: They know. Even if we don't tell them. Jerry Falwell knows what our threat is.

RUSSO: I think he is right, but I think that homosexuals present themselves as people who could easily fit in, if we could only forget about the sexuality.

WHITE: I must interrupt this highly vocal group, because we promised the audience room in which to speak.

AUDIENCE: I am interested in the American musical theater. When one learns that Cole Porter and Larry Hart were homosexuals, some of their most personal lyrics, which are lyrics of despair or disenchantment take on a rather different meaning. I wonder if the panel has any view.

BELL: Alright. [audience laughter] Well, if you are talking specifically about lyrics like "Glad to be Unhappy" which Larry Hart wrote for *The Boys from Syracuse*. It's a poignant love song that could fit a man or a woman or anybody in a given situation like that. I mean, what is it that you want to say? That they are different? I don't think that has anything to do with it. Who wrote "My Bill?" Was it Oscar Hammerstein? Or "Why was I Born", to which I think Hammerstein wrote the lyrics. I mean these are as poignant as anything Larry Hart wrote and Hammerstein allegedly was straight.

FOURATT: But the point is that millions have listened to those songs and identified with them without knowing who Cole Porter slept with or what the tragedies or joys of his life were. And yet it touched them. If Cole Porter was a homosexual, would he have been as successful? If he were known as a homosexual composer? I don't know. But the fact that he was successful, and that he touched people the way he did, came from his sensibility, and from the social reality around him.

MILLET: He could translate.

AUDIENCE: The point isn't that Cole Porter was homosexual, but that his audience was hearing him. I mean it doesn't matter.

PANEL MEMBERS TOGETHER: Exactly. Yes.

FOURATT: It's his humanity.

WHITE: Harvey Fierstein's *Torch Song Trilogy* is brilliant because it reaches people, not because it's gay. But it is nice to know that it is on Broadway.

WEINSTEIN: Now one wouldn't want to interpret art by looking at biography only, but it is awfully nice to know these extra facts. Some of Cole Porter's songs do sort of rise up to the surface for me and speak a little more directly to what it was like when I could not say that I was gay. In a few years, this may not be so important. I'd love it if that were the case. But the art will still be there and I'd like to know a little more about it.

AUDIENCE: What do you have to say about the recent rise in homosexual sensibility in advertising? The Marlboro ads, Winston ads, and so on? I have seen very few articles about this.

WHITE: What is fascinating to me about those ads is that anything is possible, the most extreme images are permissible, even wanted, solicited, as long as the word "homosexual" is never used. Calvin Klein put his lover's ass on Times Square with his name on it. [audience applause] I mean, that really rivals Hadrian and Antennos [laughter] in terms of its massive audacity. But of course that was perfectly acceptable. I read the other day that Bloomingdales did sixty thousand dollars worth of business on the Calvin Klein underwear. Apparently homosexual sensibility sells very well as long as the word homosexual is not used. Perhaps that is what Jim Fouratt was saying.

HARRIS: I am the one who brought up the business about elitism. There has been a good deal of discussion about being an oppressed homosexual. I didn't hear the word queer or gay or lesbian or homosexual until I was about nineteen years old, but I remember being queer from the time I was around ten. And at the same time I also began to feel possessed by a sense, not of being worse off than everybody else, but of being better than everybody else. No matter how poor, broke, or disadvantaged I have been in other areas, I have always felt extraordinarily gifted where my taste and sexuality are concerned. That is what I meant by feeling that I was part of an elite.

AUDIENCE: I want to point out that women's music is certainly out of the closet, and I think it is very different from anything that has been discussed here so far. Women are writing and singing to other women. On Friday night, there was a sellout concert in Carnegie Hall; I think that constitutes a phenomenon. Perhaps because the women's movement has given women much more courage professionally, some women musicians are willing to sacrifice money to really be honest. As Vito suggested, if everybody came out it would be OK, so I wonder if Kate, or Bertha, or someone would like to comment a little bit on why women have been able to do this, and why the oppressed male musicians have not.

MILLET: One of the things I thought about in discussing this subject was that the one place that it was hardest to find a homosexual sensibility was in popular art. How many *Personal Best*'s do you really come up with, in how many years of the cinema? The movies are very loath to depict homosexuality and obviously they are the real arbiters of mass taste, the real monitors of conformity. By and large movies are endlessly, tediously, rapturously heterosexual. Think of *Romeo and Juliet*. There are so many other forms of true romance.

There is this tendency to fall back into the conformity of the male stated and defined way of seeing and acting. It was a long time before a woman asked a question tonight. We are dealing with another minority within a minority, and with another form of unconscious predominance. I find it discouraging to hear so many people say, "You can't succeed if you come out," and so forth.

BELL: That's silly. Look at me. [audience laughter]

MILLET: Yeah. I mean, if you want to be an artist to succeed, you are worse than an idiot. You don't become an artist to get anyplace. [audience applause]

HARRIS: I want to go back for just one second to my idea about perversion. You see I don't look any longer for graphic depiction of gay or lesbian love in popular culture. What I look for is an event or book or movie that I can pervert to suit my reality. For instance, *Jaws*, I think, is a superb lesbian movie. [audience laughter]

It's the best and most direct and the most graphic expression of a lesbian sensibility I have ever seen. In the terms of its hostility towards men, its menacing character, the paradigm of the *vagina dentata,* what else do you want! [audience applause] I mean, bite it right off, and take control of the earth and the sea, that all those heterosexuals are littering with coke cans. Conversely, a movie that was incredibly successful like *La Cage aux Folles* was not to me a movie about being gay; it was about a family. That is why everybody responded to it so heart-warmingly at the box office.

RUSSO: Don't laugh. *La Cage aux Folles* was the highest grossing foreign film in American screen history.

Don't you think, Bertha, that though it is a wonderful thing to be able to claim the artifacts of mainstream culture for our sensibility it can be a trap? If we are talked into the fact that we have to make what we can of everything, we never get to see any specific concrete realization of our truth. Why is it that an openly gay screen actor cannot play a heterosexual love scene and have the whole world know that in his private life he is really gay? Because the Hollywood illusion depends on the ability of the majority of fans to fantasize about going to bed with that person, and it won't work if everybody knows that a major male star is really queer. He can never make love to a woman on the screen again, because the audiences simply will not buy it. Straight actors can play homosexuals and people are willing to suspend their disbelief, and say: "Oh he is just playing a fag." But if a real fag plays a heterosexual, nobody is ever going to buy it, and that sort of disturbs me.

HARRIS: Give credit where credit is due. Take Leonard Frey and Michael Greer for instance.

BELL: What about Leonard Frey and Michael Greer?

HARRIS: I agree that it is a terrible solution for me to treat *Jaws* as a lesbian movie, but until something better comes along....

RUSSO: We just named two openly gay actors, and the reason you have never heard of them is because they are openly gay.

FOURATT: I want to go back for just a second to the question about music. You brought up a very interesting point. Over the last ten years, I have gone to a lot of women's concerts, and there is a feeling there unlike other concerts. Even as a gay male, I could participate on a certain level and it saddens me that more men have not attended these. Though I think this musical movement serves a particular need of the women's community, I happen to know that some of the musicians want to break out of this context. I hate to say it, but success and the need to survive motivates many people, unless they have trust funds. The contradiction is that there are a lot of trust funds around, but if a record company like Olivia is to survive it will have to expand its audience. I just want to make one point which embodies this same contradiction and about which I believe each of us can do something. On the one hand, we have to be very supportive of each other in a communal sort of way. I know that whenever I see a gay art show, a gay book, a gay movie, a gay play, I go because I have a hunger for some kind of identification or union with this community. On the other hand, I think that we must move and claim our own space in mass culture. This is what I try to do. I try to bring our gay sensibility, whatever that may be, into a space where there are other sensitive people. By "sensitive people," I mean to include heterosexuals. I think this is where we can effect culture. I always worry about the groups that go off and make art for themselves or for a small community and do not interfere with the larger world. How we cooperate is another question, for another time, but I believe we must participate openly.

—November 29, 1982

RECORDED AT THE NEW SCHOOL, NEW YORK, NEW YORK. ORGANIZED BY THE NEW MUSEUM OF CONTEMPORARY ART IN CONJUNCTION WITH THE EXHIBITION *EXTENDED SENSIBILITIES*, CURATED BY DAN CAMERON.

:tant galaxy may ...

...astronomers, remote g...
...mic Rosetta stones. Be...
...glimmers of light take...
...o reach earth, these gal:...
...rations of stars, dust, ga...
...planets—offer a unique...
...nto time and provide ...
...the universe. As Physic...
...ing has observed: "Wher...
...iverse, we are seeing it...
...st." In those galactic ou...
...s hidden the answer to a...
...y: How soon after the ...
...t of the big bang, from...
...se presumably emerge...
...es form?

...team of scientists at-...
...g last week's meeting ...
...International Astro-...
...al Union in Baltimore...
...ave unearthed an im-...
...t clue to answering ...
...uestion with the an-...
...ement that it has dis-...
...d the most distant gal-...
...yet seen by man.
...nated 4C41.17, the ...
... is located some 15 ...
...light-years away (a ...
...light-year is equal to ...
...ximately 6 trillion ...
...—about 90% of the ...
...e from the earth to ...
...isible limits of the ...
...se.
...t the discovery is not ...
...n mileage record. ...
...alaxy is being seen ...

Fifteen billion light-years from home: a computer enhancement of 4C41.17

The artists and collectives represented in this section share the conviction that art can precipitate political change when individuals or groups associated with the artworld collaborate with other communities. The practices discussed here offer alternatives to modernist programs that rely on a conception of art as an autonomous enterprise divorced from the social. "Art and Community" proposes an "activist" approach to art-making distinct from what one might term "gallery socialism," the production and exhibition of art that addresses political issues but nevertheless fails to escape the ideological confinement of conventional showcase spaces.

Because of the artworld's complicitous relationship to the social class that subsidizes it, the efficacy of art as a means of remedying political and social ills is frequently discounted when compared with direct social action. The art market has an astonishing capacity to appropriate issues of an urgent political nature, transforming them into objects of consumption and passive contemplation, without calling its own existence into question.[1] If politically engaged artistic production is to function as more than a utopian substitute for politics proper, it must subvert conventional artistic forms and institutions just as its content criticizes dominant ideology. The goal of activist art is not to aestheticize politics but to politicize the realm of aesthetics.

Creative emphasis within activist practice is focused less on the production of a work of art and more on the total "process." Outreach, postering, demonstrations, coalition formation, broadcasting, educational workshops, and other traditionally "non-art" activities are the source of its subversive and transformative power. These artists and collectives acknowledge the integral role audience participation plays in the production of meaning. Recognizing that all aspects of perception are ideologically conditioned, they investigate the determining role of unequal and specialized social conditions in the formation of audience constituencies and contexts of reception.

The "aesthetics" of activism address the concerns of communities routinely deprived of dominant media exposure, as well as those of cultural producers who have been systematically excluded from the art-historical canon. As David Hammons explains in a conversation with Kellie Jones, "if your art doesn't reflect the status quo, well then you can forget it, financially and otherwise." Activist efforts aim to foster a sensitivity to cultural specificity, confronting the racial, sexual, and class marginalization imposed within and outside the artworld establishment.

Quoting Malcolm X, Hammons states that conventional artmaking "doesn't do anything...it's like novocaine;" he argues that "doing things in the street is more powerful than art." To escape the reified condition of gallery practice, Hammons installs many of his constructed objects at outside urban locations and frequently works in a performative mode, hawking wares in the city streets as a way of interacting with "new kinds of people."

The selections in this chapter are in some cases historically interrelated. Joseph Beuys' teaching at the Free International University has served as a precedent for the community based projects of Tim Rollins and K.O.S. (Kids of Survival) in their Bronx classroom, as well as for Jimmy Boyle's Gateway Exchange in Edinburgh. Responding to the fact that many of the Gateway Exchange members are now living with AIDS, Boyle recently transformed the organization (now called the Solas Center) in order to cope with these new demands. Rollins characterizes the artistic products of K.O.S. as "trophies of a very long method,"[2] maintaining that one cannot separate the group's paintings from the totality of their project. He sees this practice as a dialectical process of "learning and burning," in constant dialogue and tension with history. Both Boyle and Rollins have created interactive environments that promote the development of cultural self-determination, while at the same time emphasizing the importance of the multifarious spirit of the collective.

Video artist Dara Birnbaum provides the transcript of an interview she conducted with a group of white teenagers from Howard Beach about the racially-motivated murder of Michael Griffith, a black man, which took place in their Queens neighborhood. Birnbaum had originally deleted this material from the broadcast version of her tape *Charming Landscape*. By recovering the footage here, she questions her power as an editor and the devices she used to create the illusion of editorial closure. Birnbaum's contribution examines the impact of constant media exposure and peer pressure on a teenager's perception of his or her ability to effect social change both as an individual and as a part of a larger political movement. Similarly, Jonathan Borofsky investigates the social conditions surrounding and leading up to criminal offense. His interview with prison inmate James Pettaway at the San Quentin State Prison in California brings the issues of prison reform into focus.

Gran Fury, an artist's collective within ACT UP (AIDS Coalition to Unleash Power), initiates a range of agitprop projects including the design and distribution of posters and flyers devoted to disseminating clear, factual information on AIDS. To counteract the incomplete and often misleading information propagated by government agencies and the destructive impact of mainstream media coverage of the AIDS epidemic, ACT UP found it necessary to extend their educational campaign to subways, streets, and diverse neighborhoods. In combating AIDS, Gran Fury prescribes neither the production of great works of art which will "outlast and transcend" the epidemic, nor an activism limited to "putting up stickers in Soho." Examining artworld reaction to AIDS in conversation with David Deitcher, Gran Fury expressly challenges the status of fundraising as a solid artworld response to the epidemic. While some consider the market potential of art as one of its more operative uses, Gran Fury aligns itself with Douglas Crimp's view that fundraising endeavors are among the most facile responses to social crisis. They perpetuate "the idea that art itself has no social function (aside from being a commodity), that there is no such thing as engaged activist aesthetic practice."[3] As one Gran Fury member explains, "activism must include distributing meals, providing services, doing things that empower people."[4]

The conversations included in this section represent only a small number of individuals and collectives currently operating in the interstices between the artworld and other societal frameworks. Furthermore, many artist/activists have rejected artworld "visibility" in favor of more limited neighborhood-based commitment. Whether an individual or group operates on a local "grassroots" level or chooses to pursue artworld recognition as a part of a political agenda, their various methods of integrating art and social change offer innovative models that will hopefully encourage spectators to intervene aggressively in the historical process, thereby becoming collaborators themselves.

1.   Walter Benjamin, "The Author as Producer," *Reflections*, Peter Demetz, ed. (New York: Schocken Books, 1986), p. 229.

2.   Quoted in Rosetta Brooks, "Tim Rollins and K.O.S. (Kids of Survival)," *Artscribe*. No. 63 (May 87), p.47.

3.   Douglas Crimp, "AIDS: Cultural Analysis/Cultural Activism," *October* 43 (Winter 1987), p.6. It is important to note that neither Gran Fury nor Crimp is objecting to AIDS fundraising efforts per se, realizing on a pragmatic level that such efforts, when properly conceptualized and executed, are necessary given the criminal negligence of government agencies to provide adequate funding and services.

4.   Gran Fury, unpublished preliminary conversation for The New Museum, March 1989.

THIS SECTION TITLE HAS BEEN ADAPTED FROM A SLOGAN CREATED BY GRAN FURY FOR THE KITCHEN'S DECEMBER/JANUARY 1988–89 CALENDER THAT READ: "WITH 42,000 DEAD, ART IS NOT ENOUGH," A FIGURE THAT HAS NOW SIGNIFICANTLY INCREASED. SUBSEQUENTLY USED IN OTHER SITE-SPECIFIC WORKS BY GRAN FURY, THE SLOGAN CAUSED CONSIDERABLE CONTROVERSY REGARDING THE ROLE OF ART IN COPING WITH THE AIDS EPIDEMIC. MANY PEOPLE WERE OFFENDED BY THE STATEMENT BECAUSE THEY BELIEVED THAT IT WAS MEANT TO DISQUALIFY ART THAT DID NOT FUNCTION AS AGITATIONAL PROPAGANDA. THE FOLLOWING CONVERSATION BETWEEN DAVID DEITCHER AND MEMBERS OF GRAN FURY ADDRESSES THE VARIOUS REACTIONS TO THIS PROJECT AND ITS CONSEQUENCES.

TIM ROLLINS

Trevor Fairbrother

TREVOR FAIRBROTHER: Let's get some basic information.

TIM ROLLINS: I'm from a working class family and town in Maine. In 1977 I moved to New York, enrolling in the School of Visual Arts to study and work with Joseph Kosuth. I became involved with politically aware artists through a group called Artists' Meeting for Cultural Change that met on Sunday evenings in Soho. Being very green, I did a lot of observing and listening. Through that experience I learned that artists as a breed are practically impossible to organize—they're political only through symbols. The key revelation for me was that the artworld was not much more than a professional or business community. There's nothing more suspicious than politics without people.

In 1980 I cofounded a collective of young artists, called Group Material. Our headquarters were at a storefront gallery in the East Village. We began as a group of socially-minded art students disgruntled at the time by the so-called "alternative spaces" in the city. Group Material was far more interested in the social processes that give art objects their meaning. We created exhibitions for the largely Hispanic neighborhood around us, and the artworld as well. It was like a workshop. I think we were strongly influenced by the Russian constructivists and their idea that the design and theme of an exhibition determined the content of the artworks within. The constructivists made revolutionary art with great unity between form and content, and context, yet they failed politically. Their example is an enormous inspiration to me now.

FAIRBROTHER: Explain K.O.S.—Kids of Survival—its funding and its relationship to the school system.

ROLLINS: I developed K.O.S. and the Art and Knowledge Workshop while working for the past seven years as a full-time teacher in the Special Education department of a junior high school in the South Bronx. This is where I met practically all the members of K.O.S. My classroom was a sort of refugee camp for students with learning problems who were not doing well at all in their other classes. Yet many of these "unteachable" kids had extraordinary artistic talent, and they responded well to my understanding of their interests and to the structured freedom of my room. The classroom became a working studio, and the art the commanding authority.

More important, though, than turning the kids into artists is teaching them to become full citizens responsible for their own culture. The social purpose of the K.O.S. project is always growing and expanding, and often leaves the paintings we make in the dust.

FAIRBROTHER: How did your format of working on book pages evolve?

ROLLINS: By accident. Remember, most of my kids have learning problems, and perceived books as useless, the enemy, things that made them feel stupid and inferior. So I decided to read aloud from books considered too difficult for the kids, and have them draw what came to their minds—not illustrating the text, but relating the meaning of it to their everyday life. I would buy several beat-up, used editions of a novel, and place them around the classroom. Well, during one of these reading sessions, Carlito, who was eleven years old then, misunderstood the directions and started drawing directly on the pages of the book—which was Orwell's *1984*. At first I wanted to slug him for messing up a nice book—but I liked the way the page looked. It had two layers of meaning and history. There was an incredible struggle on the picture plane. The next day we were gluing up the entire novel *1984* to work on.

FAIRBROTHER: Why did your style of painting change over the next year or so?

ROLLINS: The first paintings were from what I call the "blood and guts" tradition of political art, using negative imagery to indict and hopefully to transform what's going on in society. Looking back, in these first works I was a victim of my own good intentions. These works presented a white outsider's view of the South Bronx, and the kids and I were representing ourselves and our neighborhood in the same way the dominant ideology represented us, with references to drugs, shoot-outs, misery, fires, lurid color, and cartoonish characters. I deeply admire the artists of this tradition: Grosz, Heartfield, Golub, Spero, and Sue Coe. But then I also love LeWitt, the Bechers, Ryman, Newman, and Reinhardt. I had to realize that the imagery coming from the kids wasn't going to meet my political expectations. As we all worked deeper, the images had more to do with fantasy, eroticism, religion, and beauty.

I think it's difficult to make a work of political art that is beautiful. It's difficult to make a work of art that's accessible, that lets people in, but then confronts them with complex and unpleasant issues. The work with K.O.S. has made me deal with artists whom I thought I had all figured out: Picasso, Cézanne, Ensor, Redon, and Kahlo. And I had to reconsider our work in the light of great African and Hispanic art, folk art, and popular culture.

With the first *Amerika* we achieved a unified method and imagery. It's funny, because people assume we were influenced in that work by Bosch or the Surrealists. But the real precedents for our *Amerika* series were the works of Dr. Seuss and William Morris. In a roll of wallpaper, William Morris created a fierce indictment of industrial capitalism, far more effective than any of his socialist political tracts.

FAIRBROTHER: Has the work of Joseph Beuys been important to you?

ROLLINS: Beuys was a great artist and a bad politician. He transformed the course of fine art, but placed too much faith in symbols. I'm inspired by his activism, but frankly, I'm far more fascinated with the quality of his objects: his materials, his touch, and his lines. Beuys provides a beginning, but this must be built upon.

FAIRBROTHER: You feel that his charisma kept his ideas too close to him and his aura, instead of pushing them out into the world?

ROLLINS: Yes. His was too private a language. And the idea that the world is a social sculpture is very dangerous, because who's doing the molding? Society is not an artwork. Art is a construct of society. Just because you've made a revolution in art doesn't mean you can ignore the problem of making social transformation as well. This idea informs our own working method. We rewrite the books with our lives, our images, to make new meaning.

FAIRBROTHER: How do you feel about all the art that ends up in museums—does that seem alive to you ?

ROLLINS: Works of art aren't alive. It's how we relate to these objects that lends them life. The kids and I look at art objects in museums to gain inspiration and courage for making something new, but we don't want to get lost in them. You can see Reinhardt and Kahlo in the *Alice* pieces; Pollock and the Surrealists, decorative and tribal arts in the *Amerikas*; Yves Klein and Anselm Kiefer in the *Fahrenheit* works.

FAIRBROTHER: How are the *Fahrenheit 451* pictures made?

ROLLINS: We made the first *Fahrenheit 451* work using the book *Fahrenheit 451* itself. We took the Bradbury book apart, as usual, and fixed the pages onto the linen. Then we burned another copy of the book in a big turkey pan, reducing the whole novel to ash. All of a sudden, the teaching machine went into action. The kids started taking the books home to read, just because they .were up for burning. It became a dialectic between learning and burning.

The compositions are technically collages. After laying down the book pages, we apply acrylic transparent varnish in small sections, and sprinkle the ashes gently over the surface of the work. Sheets of plastic, gently pressed on top of the varnish, then carefully peeled off, are used to imbed the ash.

We didn't want to make these things too beautiful, but to give them a terrible beauty, a melancholy effect, as delicate as a tear.

FAIRBROTHER: I want to stress your collaboration, and the rules that you've had to bend to make K.O.S. exist.

ROLLINS: I believe that real individualism can emerge only through collective action.

This idea comes from Emerson and his notion of self-reliance. For all its problems, America has definitely been this strange team effort. Ironically, you can see this in people who've been marginalized, people like my kids. All these different backgrounds, all these contradictions and frictions—this is the heat that keeps a project like ours going. The balance between individuality and collective effort is delicate, but it must exist.

FAIRBROTHER: Your latest project is *The Scarlet Letter* —that's a difficult book for those kids to read.

ROLLINS: Just as Hester is wrongly condemned to a life of poverty and silence, so is the South Bronx and too many of its individuals. The kids are really into signifying and identity. This is the major impetus behind graffiti—this verifying of an identity in a hostile, leveling environment. And so, our *Scarlet Letter* is about taking an unjust stigma and turning it into a transcendent emblem of pride. As in all of our works, we take our interpretations and offer them up, just like prayers. Our works are as futile and powerful as prayers.

REPRINTED FROM THE CATALOGUE FOR THE EXHIBITION *THE BINATIONAL: AMERICAN ART IN THE LATE 80S*, ORGANIZERS: DAVID A. ROSS AND JÜRGEN HARTEN, CURATORS: TREVOR FAIRBROTHER, DAVID JOSELIT, AND ELIZABETH SUSSMAN, (BOSTON: THE INSTITUTE OF CONTEMPORARY ART AND MUSEUM OF FINE ARTS, 1988), PP. 168–172.

Jimmy Boyle is an artist, writer, and the founder of the Gateway Exchange/Solas Center, a community arts project in Edinburgh. For much of his earlier life, however, Boyle was better known as "Scotland's Most Violent Man"—the most notorious fighter and gang leader ever to come out of Glasgow's infamous Gorbals slum. The epitome of the "hard man"—a type still treated by the Scots with a strange mixture of respect and fear—he remains a famous and controversial figure in Scotland.

Convicted of murder, Boyle served fifteen years of a life sentence. Much of this period was spent in solitary confinement as a result of constant violent confrontations with prison authorities, until he was eventually transferred to the Special Unit of Barlinnie Prison in Glasgow. This experimental program offered prisoners some responsibility for and control over their own lives, and it was here that Boyle discovered his talent as a sculptor, which eventually led to a complete transformation of his life. He has subsequently exhibited his work at the Demarco Gallery in Edinburgh and at the ICA in London. His autobiography, *A Sense of Freedom* (1977), became a bestseller.

Once released, Boyle and his wife Sarah founded the Gateway Exchange, a studio space, gallery, theater, and video workshop that goes beyond the traditional arts center, focusing on social issues, particularly the problems of young people with prisons, drugs, mental health, and now AIDS.

This interview is in two parts.

RUSSELL FERGUSON: I know that the Gateway Exchange does a lot of different things. Do you see the art making there as integrated with the other activities?

JIMMY BOYLE: I feel that art is anything you do in life. You take this building—an old washhouse—and you put a lot of energy and creativity into transforming it. When I came out of prison after fifteen years—a public figure and quite wealthy because of the book I wrote—I asked myself, "What am I going to do?" I thought it would be nice to go somewhere in the sunshine, and in fact I did that for three months, but I still felt deeply connected to the problems affecting people in Scotland. So my wife Sarah and I decided to go back and do something. What we did was establish the Gateway. We felt that the problems affecting our young people in particular were so serious that something had to be done there and then. The great thing is we said, "Let's do it," stuck the money into buying the Gateway, and opened the doors. The response was fantastic. We had the building to renovate, and as you've seen, it's quite large. We managed to scrape up the minimum £20,000 which our architect said we would need to start. We had people coming in who were on junk and wanted to get off it, and saying, "Look I need help." We would ask them, "Are you good with a paintbrush? Are you good with a hammer, a chisel, a saw?" and they would start working away. People came from different places: people who were unemployed, people on the verge of getting into trouble, people who came from good backgrounds, but who felt that they had to get out of that sort of prison. In many respects, looking back on it, I think one of the key components of the Gateway Exchange's success is that we didn't make it a ghetto for any one particular problem. We'd get some guy in here trying to get off a heroin habit of a hundred and fifty quid a day. He'd turn round and say to somebody else, "What was your habit?" and the guy would say "I haven't got a habit. I wouldn't touch drugs. I was just rotting away at home, unemployed, and felt I had to do something." That was all fine and well when there was physical work to do, but there came a time when that stopped. We felt—and this comes from my own experience as a sculptor and a writer—that we didn't want pool tables or a dartboard, because they don't challenge or stimulate people. Instead we thought, let's make creativity the central theme of the whole place, and that's why we started the video department, the sculpture and painting studios, woodcarving shop, drama workshop, pottery, and darkroom.

FERGUSON: You'd include fixing up the buildings, the drug programs, everything as a form of creativity?

BOYLE: Absolutely.

FERGUSON: Tell me about your relationship with Joseph Beuys. Your ideas seem to have something in common.

BOYLE: Well, Joseph and I certainly had a very close friendship. In the early days when I met him he'd done this piece called *Coyote—I Love America and America Loves Me*. When I introduced myself I said, "I am the coyote," which I was; I was the one that was shunned by society, and locked away, and kept in a cage. From that moment we hit it off. Although we'd come from different backgrounds there were affinities between our work, our beliefs, and our approaches to the world.

FERGUSON: Weren't you associated with his International University?

BOYLE: Yes. Very much so. This is it [The Gateway Exchange]. This is what it's all about. I certainly believe in it, and I believe that people who have the good fortune to be artists, to be creative, must go beyond putting paint on canvas. When you see the amount of people working, and doing things at the Gateway you think, "This is real." The Gateway works because people start to develop and open up. What we do here is very much what Beuys was about in terms of putting it into action at a grass roots level. These people are potentially violent, and you watch that violence change to creativity.

FERGUSON: Do you feel that when you were growing up you had this feeling inside you, and that just because of the way it was in the Gorbals, violence was almost the only way it could come out?

BOYLE: Yeah. There's no doubt about that. Having been brought up kind of tough, in the Gorbals, denying any creative aspect of myself—I expressed myself through violence. Besides the poverty and that, the educational system was substandard. It didn't allow you to articulate your needs, or your problems. Therefore what, in a sense, happened is that your body became the means of communication, and violence became a means of communication. Somebody in the art world might say, "There's this artist, he's fantastic. He does this, and he sells his paintings for this." In the Gorbals people would say, "There's Jimmy Boyle; he's a fantastic fighter. He does this and does that," and that's where your kudos came from.

FERGUSON: Beuys worked pretty successfully in the mainstream art world. So does Tim Rollins, for example, in New York. How do you see your relationship with the kids and the people who come in here? What is your relationship to the art market and the "artworld"?

BOYLE: In many respects it's quite loose, because I feel that a lot of what goes on in the artworld is corrupt. For me the process of art—the whole expression of creativity—is such a pure and precious thing. Am I to encourage kids from the streets who have become completely cynical, through junk, or violence, or getting in trouble, to give up these things only to move into another corrupt world? I put the work I make on sale here. A lot of people say I do it too cheaply, but that just doesn't matter for me. The thing is to participate, and that's good for me. I've made a conscious decision to keep away from that side of it. But I don't want to generalize. There's a lot of good people that I connect to in the artworld. I believe in art, and I believe in creativity, but I don't believe in the commercialization of it. I don't agree with the £7,000,000 for a Van Gogh. My God, what is this all about. Having said that, some of these kids go away and do work which is fantastic, and they'll have to negotiate their own way through that system. The main thing is that here they get off their feet and connect to creativity. I love the idea of somebody coming in and saying, "Oh, I wouldn't touch that poofy stuff," and within six weeks they're acting, or they're painting, or they're sculpting.

FERGUSON: Is that a common problem with people who come in here for one reason or another: that they think it's "poofy" or "sissy"?

BOYLE: Not so much, because we tackle so many other things. There's the renovation to do, which involves a lot of hard work. But most of them do come in with that attitude regarding art, because it is so alien to them. We're used to it. They just feel it won't happen, but I always believe in the magic of it. It will happen. It does happen.

FERGUSON: Besides getting people here to make art, doesn't part of your mission involve reaching new audiences as well?

BOYLE: Absolutely. When we do exhibitions, eighty percent of the people who come through the gallery are non-art people, and I think that's important. I've never been one to preach to the converted. They should be devoting their energies to other people, without me wasting energy on them.

FERGUSON: Have you avoided getting funding from the government?

BOYLE: Yes. Nobody gets paid. We could get money tomorrow from the government, but it would come with strings attached that would restrict us from saying what needs to be said about the issues. They would also begin to refer people to us from the courts and from elsewhere, which would, in effect, make us an extension of the system.

FERGUSON: You'd be getting off on the wrong foot if people were referred to you straight from a court or by a probation officer, because they're going to come in with the attitude that….

BOYLE: "I have to be here." Whereas the Gateway is a self-help program. People come in and we say, "This is the start of a very important journey for you. You're going to question yourself, and you're going to be questioned by others, but it's up to you whether you stay the course."

FERGUSON: What about yourself? Are you still doing a lot of your own sculpture, or is it more difficult now?

BOYLE: Well, a group of us just finished a bronze piece for the city of Hull. We've got the bronze foundry here. We'll have an exhibition in December, so we're all working for that. I'm also writing a novel at the moment.

FERGUSON: Kids come here for one reason or another and get involved in art. Are you finding that most of them stick with it, or is it just that it opens up their creativity generally, and then it can then be diverted elsewhere?

BOYLE: Well, I think both, but certainly the latter: it can be focused in other ways, but most people find themselves doing sculpture or painting or drama. The other thing, and this is what we discuss at our Wednesday meetings, is that for some people the program becomes a drug, and they don't want to leave. So we say, "We've become a substitute for smack to you. Look, you're clinging on. You won't leave this building. You'd be in this building twenty-two hours a day if you could get away with it." What we're saying is "Hold it. Take it easy." Because that's a bad thing as well. Because it's a place that's built their confidence and given them things, it's very difficult for them to let go. We put all of that on the agenda.

FERGUSON: So it's important to you to integrate creativity and life in the real world.

BOYLE: Yes. Because it is about life, isn't it?

FERGUSON: Your charismatic personality was a factor even when you were in prison. Clearly the prison authorities tried to use that against the Special Unit and against you. But even outside prison it has been a factor. You became well known, and you'll always have to deal with that. Do you find that has carried over here?

BOYLE: No. We're always very sensitive to that issue here. I'm particularly sensitive to it, because I think it diminishes the effort that other people have put into the Gateway. We put the "Jimmy Boyle factor" square on the table. How much of a distortion am I? What are we really doing here? We always try to remind people that come in that there's more than Jimmy Boyle here. My reputation has its pros and cons for the organization and we recognize that, but I don't want people to be crushed by the whole "charismatic personality" thing. At some point I want to leave the Gateway. And if I'm here under false pretenses—if it all revolves around my ego—then it's going to collapse when I go away.

—May 22, 1987

FERGUSON: What has changed since we spoke in 1987?

BOYLE: Well, the changes have been quite dramatic. The Gateway had grown so big that we were becoming bureaucrats and losing touch with our own work. The most important change however, was brought about by the AIDS and HIV epidemic that has swept into Edinburgh in a big way. A lot of our drug-using clientele was affected, so it was a natural extension of the work we'd been doing to turn the place into an AIDS resource center. The Gateway is now the Solas Center [Solas is Gaelic for light]. The very fact that we now get local government funding has changed the nature of the place completely. We now have paid staff. When we weren't getting any money, it was a way of life, it was a piece of social sculpture. It has changed into a much more mainstream sort of organization. We do have a degree of autonomy in relation to the local authorities, but whether Gateway can continue the way it did—I don't really think so, to be honest with you. The way the Gateway operated was, in my view, quite revolutionary and, for want of a better word, subversive.

What we did was enable people to come in and explore their own potential—to make very powerful statements, whether it was through sculpture, performance, or painting. I don't think that will continue to the same extent in the new Solas Center. There will be creative activity, but not as much as at the Gateway. To my mind it's quite tragic, but on the other hand we're living in a place which is devastated by AIDS, and there is very little being done about it, so maybe it's revolutionary in that sense, in that it's tackling what is still extremely taboo in Britain.

FERGUSON: Could you say some more about the impact of the AIDS crisis in Edinburgh, and how it has affected your work?

BOYLE: A lot of the kids who were using the place were street people who suddenly discovered they had HIV. To them it was all a big joke in the initial stages. They continued to share needles, and they continued to sell their bodies. We told them that this was serious, but it was difficult to convince them, even though they were the people with the virus. They would trek up to the hospital that was designated to deal with the issue, and they would all meet up there and laugh and joke and feel that it was all a load of nonsense. The only reason that they went to the hospital was that they thought they could get some drugs out of the doctors. They weren't going out of fear that they had this terrible virus. Slowly, over a period of about a year, the seriousness of the problem became apparent to them. Some of them started to develop symptoms very quickly. People became tremendously worried and strained. Many drug addicts lose their teeth, and when they went to a dentist, the dentist would be dressed up like a spaceman with black rubbish bags all round the walls. When their teeth were pulled, they were told to swallow their blood. These things are extremely harrowing. One guy who had been in prison for a drug-related offense told us that he had got a blood test for a completely different reason, an injury or something, and when the two screws took him back to prison, they told everybody—no degree of confidentiality whatsoever. This guy was devastated. He had a wife and a couple of kids outside. All the prisoners and the prison staff were calling him big Rock Hudson. This was the sort of story that was coming in to us. A lot of the people we knew who had the virus had kids, and we were watching them die, and their families fall apart. We felt we had some responsibility to try to deal with this problem. Every time the local authorities have tried to get something going, the public backlash has been incredible. When they tried to get a hospice, the local population went to real extremes, lobbying members of Parliament and getting all sorts of media coverage. They prevented the local authorities from opening the hospice. When they managed to get housing, so that people could have some degree of comfort, the Conservative politicians drummed up a lot of terrible publicity again. This goes on all the time. Everything the local authorities tried to do themselves was stonewalled, so when we came to them, they were happy to work with us. We have won a lot of support from the local people here, through the drug issue. We carry some credibility.

FERGUSON: How do you see the role of art now? Have you been depressed by the way things have gone?

BOYLE: For me, as a sculptor and a writer, working with the people in the Gateway has been absolutely inspiring. I've watched people come in and use creative means to build up their confidence. I'm not at all depressed, because I'm sure some of the most inspiring work I've ever seen is going to come out of this. I'm sure, because I've seen so much already.

—May 1, 1989, Edinburgh, Scotland

In 1985–86, my partner Gary Glassman and I traveled to San Quentin State Prison, the California Institution for Women, and the California Rehabilitation Center. We spoke to thirty-two prisoners, men and women, and asked them about their lives. The result of these interviews is a fifty-eight-minute video documentary called *Prisoners*.

Why did I do this? Why did I go to talk to prisoners? Well, we are all learning to be free. But there are people who make our lives a lot less free. They make us lock our doors, put bars on our windows, and worry about our own safety as well as the safety of the people we love. They create fear. But I know these people are human beings—not that different from myself, and I feel for them. They have to live their lives locked up in cement boxes. What a waste! Could they have been born criminals or has something happened in their lives, their minds, to make them criminals? What can I learn from these people? What does it mean to be free? The following is the transcript of a condensed interview with James Pettaway, one of fifteen two-hour video interviews conducted at San Quentin State Prison.

JONATHAN BOROFSKY: When thinking about your childhood, do you remember any specific limitations?

JAMES PETTAWAY: Well, I think as a child I wasn't really aware of limitations. It was as I began to grow that I realized that was a fantasy rather than the reality. I started to notice the difference in the kids in the classroom. Even though we were all at the same school, we had our differences. Some were dressed better, some could go to the cafeteria, others had to bring peanut butter-and-jelly and baloney sandwiches. I was in the baloney-sandwich group—the "brown bag" group. I noticed how the teacher would treat some—the ones who went to the cafeteria and dressed very well. They got treated one way, and we "brown baggers" got treated another way. I think that probably had a negative effect on me, because it kind of left me with a feeling that I was different, you know, maybe not as good as these guys.

BOROFSKY: Were you in an interracial school?

PETTAWAY: Not until the eighth grade, because I went to school in Alabama and this was in the fifties and sixties, and there just wasn't much interracial stuff. But around sixth or seventh grade that began to change because the integration thing was forced upon us. And I say "us" meaning the schools, the students, and everybody. I didn't really want it, because even though there were some differences between us blacks there seemed to be even greater differences when you start to get an interracial situation.

BOROFSKY: What did it feel like to go to a white school?

PETTAWAY: I felt even more uncomfortable. Because not only did you have the cafeteria group, now the cafeteria group is white, you know, which makes you feel even more different. Because now you're getting into an area where you are starting to develop these negative feelings about yourself: "I'm not as good." Because of that knowledge you begin to try too hard. You try to be too nice. You try to be too smart. Instead of breaking down barriers, it seems that you are creating barriers. And within that setting, frustration begins to come and anger begins to build up. You know, you don't recognize these things at twelve years old; this is a thirty-four-year-old guy looking back at when he was twelve. There's a lot of animosity that builds along with that negative feeling about yourself.

BOROFSKY: How did you relate to your mother and father?

PETTAWAY: Well, my mother and I got along very well because we were a lot alike. More so than my father and I, because he was—I guess the word you'd use these days would be "macho." He was a T-shirt-and-beer kind of guy. And I was quite the opposite. I mean, I would rather stay inside and read a book than go outside and play ball with the kids, and that kind of thing created a tension between him and me, because to him I was acting like a sissy. We just didn't understand each other, because to me he seemed stupid, and to him I seemed—whatever I was.

BOROFSKY: Did it ever come to physical blows?

PETTAWAY: Well, yeah. In the early years, it was physical because he was stronger and he had the authority because he was my father....

BOROFSKY: Did you develop a resentment from being pushed at an early age by him?

PETTAWAY: Yeah, very definitely. It was almost at the point of going beyond resentment to outright pure hate. And it wasn't until I was twenty-one or twenty-two that we got together and started to talk. And I started to understand him and he tried to understand me. But up until then, there wasn't a great deal of love between the two of us. There were some things that went on between him and my mother that I didn't understand and I didn't like, and I thought were awful. I don't think he treated her as well as he should have, as well as she deserved to be treated. Because you've got two people here: one's very beautiful, very tender, loving, and intelligent...and then you've got a brute animal. But I don't look at what's behind, or what's ahead. I'm kind of dealing with "today is the day." I've got to make it through today, and I've got to concentrate all my energy on that.

BOROFSKY: People try to assemble and focus their energy on the outside, too. Do you think it's helping you in here to do that?

PETTAWAY: Well, it's doing several things for me. One, it's helping me to keep a positive attitude. Secondly, it's helping me to hang on to sanity. And the third thing it's doing is keeping me from putting a rope around my neck or slashing my wrists. Because I think that if I didn't go through it a day at a time, if I looked at the past mistakes or what was behind and then compounded that with what lies ahead, I think that the two combined would probably be more than I can deal with.

BOROFSKY: I'd like to ask you what lies ahead.

PETTAWAY: Okay, what lies ahead is essentially uncertainty. I don't know what's going to happen. I could leave tomorrow, I could be here for the next twenty years.

BOROFSKY: Is that the maximum on your sentence?

PETTAWAY: No, I could be here from now on.

BOROFSKY: Without parole?

PETTAWAY: Oh no, there is a possibility—but here we are talking—what, I'm thirty-four, close to thirty-five. We're talking—say I get out in twenty years—I'll be fifty-five years old. Fifty-five years old is not the end of the world. There's still a few years left. But if you've spent the previous twenty years in prison, particularly in a setting like this where there is nothing productive, there is no incentive, no motivation—everything positive that you get you have to dredge up from within yourself—if you've spent the previous twenty years in an environment like that, it's difficult to even have a desire to go out there.

BOROFSKY: Would you be scared to do it, afraid you'd fail?

PETTAWAY: Well, it really isn't a matter of failure. I think it's more a feeling of What's the use? I mean, you're out of it. You're out of touch with what's going on out there. How are you going to function out there? What can you do? What can you contribute? How can you support yourself? You have no family, you have no friends, you know, because your family has died by now. Your friends left when you went to jail. So what are you going to do? You don't collect social security. You work here, but you don't get social security. Any pay you get, the most you can do is buy the essentials—soap, toothpaste, cigarettes if you smoke, coffee, and things like that. So you're not in a position where you can save anything. You can't invest in anything 'cause you don't have the money to make investments.... So you get out, and I think what they give you is $200. This is 1985—$200 buys you nothing, really. You don't have a place to stay, no clothes. What are you going to do about a job? You're fifty-five years old, and, shit, what have you done the past twenty years?—Oh, I was in prison.

BOROFSKY: What would you like to see changed within the prison system?

PETTAWAY: I would like to see opportunities presented to those who want them. I would like to see educational programs. As things are now, if you've got a high school diploma here in San Quentin, as far as education is concerned you are out of luck, there is nothing else for you.

BOROFSKY: Because the programs they have only take you through high school?

PETTAWAY: That's the maximum.

BOROFSKY: So you'd like to see college programs?

PETTAWAY: Right. I would like to see something happening where a guy could establish some kind of future for himself. He knows he's going to be here for twenty years and he knows he's going to be facing a certain situation when he gets out. Let him work. I mean you don't have to pay him $50,000 a year, but let him earn something—enough to put aside something while looking ahead. Let him feel good about himself for a change. Let him feel like, Hey, I'm somebody, I can be part of the cafeteria group....

BOROFSKY: It's possible that society out there, when presented with that idea, will say, Why should we give them any of our attention? They committed crimes, killed and robbed—just leave them behind bars! How do you react to that?

PETTAWAY: I think that's an extremely bad attitude—as well as being selfish. It probably adds to the problem because people feel that way. See, because even at fifty-five I'm going to be back out there, and if I'm out there in a totally negative situation with absolutely nothing to lose because there is nothing for me to gain, can you imagine the frame of mind that I'm in?! The frame of mind is such that I don't give a damn! I mean, I don't give a damn if I just blow your brains out! So what!? I'll go back to prison—good! Then I don't have to worry about anything anymore. See, what happens here is that society doesn't realize that you've got to pay for me one way or the other. If you don't help me while I'm in, then I come out with a negative attitude, and you've got to pay to put me back in, and you've got to support me while I'm here. It's your money. I mean, you pay taxes, I don't.

BOROFSKY: Why do people end up in here?

PETTAWAY: I think there are as many reasons as there are people...and then there are some similarities. I think there is essentially a feeling you don't fit. You always have the attitude that I'm different. I'm not like everybody else. And out of that, you try to salvage something positive. Okay, so I'm not like everybody else, so I don't have to do what everybody else does. The law says you can't do this—fuck the law! I'm not like everybody else, the law is for them! So you do things that they say are contrary to what is normal behavior. Because you really don't feel good. You are feeling bad about yourself to begin with. So you are looking for things that will provide you with some positive reinforcement, and you can't find it through mainstream things, so you become the outlaw. That's your glory. So that's one of the main reasons, I think. It's because you are different. And when you come here, that difference is reinforced by other convicts and by the people who are in charge of running the prison.

BOROFSKY: How's that reinforced?

PETTAWAY: Well, because the prisoners, people doing time, they are also looking for that positive feeling, and they glorify the violence. They glorify being an ass-kicker. They glorify being able to walk up to a guy and jab steel in him and not feel anything. They glorify not having feelings, being cold and hard. That's the ultimate experience. You don't feel nothing.

BOROFSKY: Why aren't you like that?

PETTAWAY: Because I really don't choose to be that way. It goes against my nature. I'd be caught up in the same trap I was caught up in before I came here, and that is trying to be something that I'm not. I'm a very feeling person.

BOROFSKY: What are you in here for?

PETTAWAY: I'm in here for aiding and abetting a first-degree murder. Aiding and abetting means that I didn't pull the trigger, but I didn't do anything to prevent the trigger from being pulled. In fact, it also implies that I encouraged it.

BOROFSKY: Was this in relation to a robbery?

PETTAWAY: Oh no, no, no. This wasn't a robbery. This was a friend of mine that was killed.

BOROFSKY: What gets you through the day in here?

PETTAWAY: In the morning when I wake up, it's kinda like getting ready to go out and play a very important game—a Super Bowl, or something. I've got to psych myself up. I've got to prepare myself. I've got to just lay there for a while and get ready to deal with it. I've got to tell myself good things, like, everything is gonna be all right, that I'm all right, and that I'm really not worthless or useless or whatever. And I've got to prepare myself to go outside the cell, because you can't go out unaware. Because if you do, you may not come back in. Just being able to make it through the day itself is a big thing. I work as a clerk in the education office, and I do a lot of typing and I have a chance to work with the computer. The computer is a challenge to me. To go in and write a program and run it and have it do what I want it to do—that's a sense of accomplishment. I've done something! You see, I'm looking for something that I can feel good about having done. I may type a letter—no misspelled words, everything looks absolutely fantastic—no big deal, I mean, it's only a letter, but you've got to find little things like that to feel good about, because you don't get any external reinforcement. Because most of the staff view you as not being human. You know, you are a prisoner, an animal—you're not like us. You're even below the brown-baggers!

One of the things that helps me a great deal is the Bible. I started to read it, and I started to see some absolutely dynamic things for day-to-day living. I'm taking these things in and I'm beginning to apply them, and they're having very good results for me. Because most of the bullshit, most of the hassles I'm able to avoid by simply putting these little principles into practice. You know, when I'm talking to somebody and they come out with all this foolishness, this absolute garbage about "pimpin' the hos," and robbing and "let's move on the white boys…" I separate myself from that.

BOROFSKY: Do you find a lot of prisoners here whose crime was drug-related?

PETTAWAY: I think if you could talk to people and you could get them to be truthful about it, ninety to ninety-five percent of them would say they were either on drugs when they did whatever they did or they did whatever they did to get drugs. Drugs and women are two of the main problems for men in prison.

The drugs probably came from a feeling of insecurity. You don't feel good. People who don't feel good really need drugs because everybody wants to feel good! I don't care if you're sleeping in doorways or if you've got mansions and more money than you'll ever spend in your life, you want to feel good! People who come to prison are usually people who don't feel good about themselves. So drugs are a problem.

Now, for women—most of the men that come to prison have difficulties in relationships with women. They don't know how to deal with women. They feel uncomfortable with women. They go from one extreme to the other; they either put them on a pedestal or treat them like dogs. It's very difficult for most guys in here to relate to a woman in that happy medium where she is—

BOROFSKY: Equal?

PETTAWAY: Well, not necessarily equal, because you're asking a whole lot. Even people on the outside—most men don't think of women as being equal. There is always that "You're OK but you're still just a peg lower than I am." But to treat them as though they were another human being who's just as valuable as I am.

BOROFSKY: Earlier you said that you observed your father treating your mother badly. One might assume that you would end up treating women like he did.

PETTAWAY: Partly because I hated him and hated everything he was—the way he acted, the way he treated women: that had an effect on my relationship with women. Most of this that I am saying wasn't necessarily things that I understood five years ago. These changes have happened over the years.

BOROFSKY: How do such changes happen?

PETTAWAY: Well, I don't like this. I don't like being here. I don't feel that I should be here. And I'm looking for ways not to ever come back here again. So I have to think about things that led me to coming here. I've gotta go back and from the very first memory sort of retrace the steps and see the wrong turns, see the wrong decisions, see the wrong feelings, see the wrong attitudes. Because if I don't do that, there's no way I can straighten them out. I'm not saying that everything I did in the past was wrong, because I did a lot of positive things in the past, too. What I'm doing now is sort of a sifting process. I'm getting out the things that shouldn't be there, and retaining the things that I feel to be positive. I'm trying to take the mask off. I'm trying not to have a different face for every situation. It's just that simple.

BOROFSKY: You seem to have a strong ability to feel compassion. Where did you get this? Was your mother that kind of person?

PETTAWAY: She was an extremely compassionate person. I mean, she was one of the most beautiful people I've ever met in my entire life. She encouraged me, she kind of pushed me along. When my father was going through his trips about "You should get out and play" or "Look how skinny you are," she would kind of let me know that it's all right not to be big. It's all right to not have muscles. I mean, the world needs some soft and sensitive people, too! When my father would go off into one of his things and wanted to get physical with me, there was nothing she could do about it.

But seeing the hurt that she felt made me feel stronger. It got to the point where he would beat me and I would just look at him. It hurt like hell, but I wasn't going to let him know how much it hurt. "I'm not going to cry...."

BOROFSKY: Where is you mother today?

PETTAWAY: My mother died almost twenty years ago.

BOROFSKY: How old were you then?

PETTAWAY: Seventeen.

BOROFSKY: That was, no doubt, a difficult time.

PETTAWAY: Well, I think that was an experience that just devastated me. I've never been through anything that painful in my life. I just felt alone. I was frightened. I felt bitter—why her, not him? I also felt a deep sense of guilt because I felt that I had contributed to her death—in the sense that around fifteen I started to become involved with things that really hurt her. And I think that perhaps she died of a broken heart. After she died, I think I went crazy.

BOROFSKY: If you could, for a moment, imagine me being your mother, what would you tell me?

PETTAWAY: I'm sorry.

I could say a lot of other things, but that's what it amounts to. I'm sorry. And if I could go back and undo what's been done, I certainly would, and do things totally different. But I can't do that, so the only thing I can do at this point is to take where I am and try to use that to make things better for what lies ahead. To somehow pay back—maybe that's the wrong word for it but that's what comes to mind. To help someone else's life. And to be loved, I think. I'm human. Everybody wants to be loved, whether they admit it or not, whether they are able to accept it or not.

BOROFSKY: What about helping other prisoners within the walls?

PETTAWAY: There's this kid—well he's not a kid—he's a twenty-two-year-old. When I met him, he was wild, the kind of guy you just wanna kill, ya know? At any rate, he became my cell-mate, and we started to talk. He would tell me certain things and he wouldn't hear it from anyone else. In other words, what he told me stayed with me. He started to tell me more things, and I got to understand him. I got to tell him how I felt.

He just got transferred Thursday, and the change between when I met him and what he is now is like the difference between day and night. And he told me something that made me feel so good that if we hadn't been standing in the yard there, I probably would have cried. He said, "Being in the cell with you is the best thing that ever happened to me...." I mean, I can't tell you how that made me feel—that I'd done something. Here, in this place where there is absolutely nothing good to do, I'd done some good! At first he couldn't read, I taught him how to read. I got him interested in books and learning about himself and about how to deal with people. He's grown from a wild, silly, violent, unfeeling, immature child into a man! The change was so obvious his mother wrote me and—but you see, the thing there was that he wanted it, he wanted to change. And he was presented with an opportunity, an alternative, and he took it.

That's what I'm saying that the prison system should be all about. Present a guy with an opportunity. Give him an alternative. Not everybody's gonna take it because some people will never change. You've got guys here, forty, fifty years old who have been coming to prison since they were eight or nine years old, and they don't want to change. You talk to them and they talk about going back out there, what they're gonna rip off. But you've got a lot of youngsters here, a lot of young guys. Give them a chance. Give them an opportunity. Some will take it. What if only ten percent take it? That is ten percent that can contribute something. Shit, give me a chance—to bring it down to a more personal level—give *me* a chance! Give me an alternative! That's the one message I would like to get across.

Present some alternatives, because you're gonna pay either way it goes. You're gonna pay for either constructive things or you're gonna pay for the destructive acts—which may be directed at you. Most guys don't plan things, not the guys here. You should talk to some of these guys, the kinds of crimes they have committed. It's not like you see it in the movies—they plan it, the blueprints—no, no, it's the spur of the moment.

BOROFSKY: Random?

PETTAWAY: Right, and it could be you. It could be you....

REPRINTED FROM *ARTFORUM*, VOL. 26, NO. 7 (MARCH 1988): 94–97.

JOSEPH BEUYS

Kate Horsfield & Lyn Blumenthal

KATE HORSFIELD: Were members of your family involved in any pursuit of creativity when you were a child?

JOSEPH BEUYS: No, I could never find out an interest in creativity. Perhaps there was one forefather from the Dutch roots of my family who was interested in science, but never could I find an interest in art.

HORSFIELD: When you were a small child, did you have a direct interest in art?

BEUYS: No, this idea never came to my consciousness then, but if I look back, I find that what I did as a child had a lot to do with an understanding of art, from which I later developed this so-called "enlarged understanding of art" that has to do with the theory of social sculpture, the radical transformation of the world. So, what I did as a child—what I experienced in the fields, in nature and also in the industrial part of human activity, in small factories—had a kind of character which people can now see in the Guggenheim Museum pieces, for instance; but this is only apparent through a reflection about my interests as a child and the work I did then; and surely, not only what I did as a child, but also what I felt and what I thought, what I experienced and what...yes, imagined.

HORSFIELD: Can you talk specifically about some of these particular kinds of feelings or experiences?

BEUYS: Yes—one of my most important general feelings during that time was that I felt myself, on one side, in a very beautiful environment; but from the side of social behavior, I felt that everything was in a very big debacle. I felt a dramatic contradiction in my life and when I was five years old, I felt that my life had to go to an end because I experienced already too much of this contradiction.

I had the feeling that another kind of life—perhaps in a transcendental area—would give me a better possibility to influence, or to work, or to act within this contradiction. So, this was my general feeling: on the one side, this beautiful undamaged nature from which I took a lot and had a lot of possibilities for contemplation, meditation, research, collecting things, making a kind of system; and on the other side, this social debacle that I felt already as a coming dilemma.

Yes, as a child I was aware of it, but later I could analyze the debacle. During my childhood, I was confronted with the nature of this behavior but didn't analyze the root of such a debacle; nevertheless, surely, this is an intuitive comprehension that already a child can feel; that in such a condition, the root must be in the behavior of the people.

You must see this as a very complicated thing insofar as I cannot accuse a single person to have been the cause of this debacle, this single person against me, and in no way do I intend to criticize certain people of my neighborhood in their behavior toward me; but I saw the relationship between people, I saw their thoughts, I saw their kind of expressionistic behavior in every difficult situation. I saw all the time the unclearness in the psychological condition of the people. You know, that was the time called the "Roaring Twenties" and I felt that this expressionistic behavior, this unformed quality of soul power and emotion of life...I saw it, that it would lead to a kind of catastrophe. That was my general feeling.

HORSFIELD: Before you made the decision to be an artist, you were following some early interest in science and you had made up your mind to be a scientist to a certain extent....

BEUYS: That is true.

HORSFIELD: What goals did you have as a scientist, and, then, what made you stop science and look more closely toward art?

BEUYS: Yes...I started from this positive point of the environment, where things in nature were undestroyed, relatively undestroyed, and I began already as a child to work with a sort of circus and theater, a methodology and system which were related to natural phenomena: animals, insects, plants.

When I was seven or eight, I got interested in research already done. I had teachers who were also close to this interest and I had a kind of laboratory all the time until fifteen years of age, when I developed really and factually a laboratory which was involved with physics, chemistry, zoology, botany and such things and I decided to study natural sciences. Then it was already near the time when the Second World War began and that activity was stopped by my call to military duty.

During the war, when I was a soldier, I had the privilege from my commander, when we were situated in a town where there was some academic activity, to go in my free time to the University. And since we had kind of a resting time in Poland, I had the opportunity to visit Poznan University. I think I had an event there, during a discussion with a professor of zoology about the whole theory of natural science, when I found out that this could not be my ability, to become so specialized in such a positivistic, materialistic field; these two terms came to my consciousness then, you know. It was a kind of methodology of the materialistic understanding of the world. So, I realized that the necessities of the so-called exact, natural sciences were a restriction for my specific ability and I decided to try it another way.

Then, during the rest of the war, I was pondering this problem. I had to make a decision about such an established understanding of research of the world and I had to think of a methodology to bring up my specific ability to cooperate with other people, simply to say...not to bring up very, very important things, that was not in my mind. In my mind was the question: how to cooperate with other people in a more meaningful way, to overcome not only the dilemma which I experienced in my youth already and from which the consequence was the Second World War—and this even stronger dilemma which I was mixed up in during the war. I thought about the necessity to come to a decision, to reconstruct, to renew the whole problem of life, labor, work of the people...yes, this was for me the question after the crucial point of humankind's creativity and its implications: freedom of people in their creative work and how to develop from this necessity a kind of social order, another understanding of science and to try it with art. So—then—I tried it with art.

HORSFIELD: One thing I'd like to ask is what was the art climate? What did you see about art as a field, you know, where could you attach your notions of experimentation and what kind of goals could you have?

BEUYS: Yes, sure, it's a very important question because there was almost nothing to be seen, to be hopeful for in this field. The only hope I had was when I saw one day a photograph of a sculpture which was put away during Hitler's time. It was a sculpture by Wilhelm Lehmbruck, a German sculptor of expressionistic style. This was perhaps the only example, Lehmbruck, between my sixteenth to nineteenth years in which I saw a possibility for art to be principally of interest to innovate some things, instead of writing a very boring, naturalistic repetition of what is already done by nature.

That was a time, one must know, which was very isolated, generally, in Germany, during the fascist era and even more specifically isolated in that region where nobody was interested in art. That was a kind of tradition there, not because people were uncreative, but their professions were mostly agricultural and as far as the industrial impulse of the last century also had its traces in that area, they were workers, employed in factories. Within such a population, almost nothing existed culturally.

It was simply that they didn't know how to work in this specific field and also because of their involvement in the religious tradition—a Catholic area. So, when I saw such examples, one by Lehmbruck and also then some paintings, when I searched for interesting materials, I felt a possibility for art which would be better for my ability.

HORSFIELD: At this point, were you studying art?

BEUYS: Yes.

HORSFIELD: What kind of people were your teachers and how did they influence you at this time?

BEUYS: I started to prepare myself to enter a state academy. It was difficult during that time because all these institutions had been destroyed and they were all functioning in a kind of improvised roofing and only a few students could have the possibility to study. So, immediately after the war, after my time in prison, I began to work on some examples of what I felt could be a kind of proof of my skill, my ability and with this stuff I went to the Academy of Dusseldorf and they took me, which was a wonder during that time. I, myself, was very astonished that they took me in this chaotic condition.

I started the university with a teacher who was very academic. I had nothing else to do than to copy models in a naturalistic, almost medical, way. He was pointing out to me where every muscle had to be, had to be observed, reproduced, and I made a lot of anatomic models until I felt very bored with this repetitive character of doing and again I felt that it was a kind of science rather than art. I felt the parallelism with science and the influence that a materialistic understanding of it had on art. My professor appeared to me like a surgeon in a hospital with a white coat and he had some tools in his breast pocket like a doctor, when he came for correction. I felt like in an operating room, you know, and the work was exactly the same. I felt very upset and came in difficulties with this teacher who personally I loved very much because he was a generous person, a very noble character; but I came in difficulties and left him to try with another teacher.

This teacher, Ewald Matare, was well known during that time in the area. He had a style of his own, an understanding of art which was really a kind of innovation for me during that time. He had an autonomy in the understanding of art, but with a medieval methodology. He was a believer in the "Bauhutte"[1] idea, he was an admirer of the ornament, of what we call in Germany "Masswerk,"[2] the geometrical... *"rechtfertigung was heisst rechtfertigung"*? [3]... He was convinced that geometry and ornament should be the basis for all decisions in art. Then I was surely with a very good teacher, an autonomic character, but again I came in difficulties with such a dogma—with such a strict belief in an older concept of art, coming from the Middle Ages, which brought me to a contradiction and discussion with him. He used to pay attention to my experiences with forms in different materials, and through his observation, he declared me, simply, crazy. He didn't say that I was unable, no. He was saying that perhaps I was his most able student, but at the same time he felt it his duty to inform officials about the impossibility to take me later, for instance, as a teacher, because I was crazy—in his mind, completely crazy—a mad man.

This was a time when I spoke a lot about the necessity to find a secure basis for further doings; I came to realize that it wouldn't lead to a solution of the problem to take, for instance, Buddhistic concepts, or Middle Ages "Bauhutte" concepts, or to take Tao things or other Eastern wisdom, to recreate spirituality within humankind. I was intensively involved with a kind of...yes, epistemology at that time and this was a reason for him to discard my work. He believed that an artist has to do the things, has not to speak too much, not to get so confused in such complicated stuff like historical analysis, and has not to brood upon these things. In his eyes I was a brooder, brooding on problems which humankind would never be able to solve, and from this point of view it appeared to him as a kind of madness.

It was already the beginning of my coming away from the traditional art world, getting more and more in connection with people who were interested in interdisciplinary research, and so I had more friends and more discussions with scientists again, and because I already had a scientific background and vocabulary, it was always a very intensive relationship with scientists of different fields. This is now the time from '52 until the next point in my life—this point was a kind of breakdown of everything.

HORSFIELD: Let me just insert one question before we go to that.

BEUYS: Yes, sure.

HORSFIELD: To what extent were you interested in aesthetic solutions in the actual physicality of artmaking?

BEUYS: Say it again, please.

HORSFIELD: To what extent were you interested in aesthetic solutions and in the process of making art?

BEUYS: Again, it's very important to understand the question and I didn't understand it clearly, therefore, please, say it again.

HORSFIELD: O.K., as a contrast to art as a carrier of ideas, how interested in the aesthetics of solving a problem were you?

BEUYS: That was not a point at all for me. The word "aesthetics" does not exist for me. I found out during all my time in an official institution, a state academy, that this use of the word aesthetics meant nothing, in my understanding. I couldn't locate this meaning of aesthetics, which was a very nebulous, undetermined idea. I couldn't put it in any real and concrete way in my work, my problem, my view. But later, after what I said was the next period in my life, I stated my understanding of it: human being is aesthetics. Aesthetics is the human being in itself.

HORSFIELD: You mentioned something earlier, before we started discussing your education as an artist, about being called into the war, during which period you were a pilot. I'd like to ask you about that time, and what were some of the incidents that happened to you, how they affected your concept of art as a social tool, and how it began to manifest itself in works of art?

BEUYS: Sometimes those things are looked at in a false way; these physical experiences during the war—accidents, damages on my body, wounds and such things—are overrated in regard to my later work.

HORSFIELD: How were they overrated?

BEUYS: People look at it in too simplistic a way. They say that because I was in the war with Tataric tribes, for instance, and came in contact with these families, which took me in as a kind of family member to give me perhaps the possibility to desert the army, or when I was badly wounded such tribes found me and covered my body with a kind of fat, milky stuff, and even felt, that this would be the reason why I used such materials later in my work.

HORSFIELD: Is that true?

BEUYS: True is this event during the war, but not true that that was the reason to take this stuff later for my sculpture. If this were true, then I ask why did I come so late to use such materials?

The proof of why this cannot be true, and is not true, is that before I did these things, I built up a theory to which these materials seemed the most appropriate, to make clear a theory of sculpture, a theory of social order, a theory of the action as a living sculpture and so on.

So, I came to elements, theoretical elements, of isolating materials, raw materials, organic materials. I didn't take these things just as a kind of immediately dramatical means because I was in a dramatic situation during the war, no, not at all; I wasn't interested in that; but later on, when I built up a theory and a system of sculpture and art, and also a system of wider understanding, anthropological understanding of sculpture being related to the social body, and to everyone's lives and ability, then such materials seemed to be right and effectful tools to make clear this theory and to bring impulse in the discussion during the actions and the performances. But yes, surely, I remember the period of war, surely this time was very important for my whole life, and it is a very interesting point that the same material was involved in this emergency condition, personally and for the whole world during that war. So that was later also a very useful element to make clear how to overcome, one could say, the wound of all of us, not only mine. These elements appear as a kind of secret affinity in my life, but this relationship was not the motivation for me to use them.

HORSFIELD: Would you say that these materials were chosen by you at a later time, developing out of your theory of sculpture?

BEUYS: Yes, you see they are clearly developed, and there were a lot of forerunners until I came to the simple decision to take such materials; and taking these materials, after my thoughts on the necessity of building a theory, I saw, then, the interesting relation they had to my biography.

HORSFIELD: Were you surprised?

BEUYS: No, I wasn't surprised, because I told you already that, during my childhood, I made such things instinctively, and from the creativity of a child, seeing the things in the same way as now. I worked with machines, one could say simply, that worked without fuel, without so-called physical energy, which would function with concepts. And now, I am slowly on the point to develop such machinery to work without physical energy, and as I can remember that already as a child I did the same things this made a significance in my life, that parallelism of past and future.

HORSFIELD: How do you approach deciding to do a piece of art, or in certain cases an action, what comes up to you before you start to do it? What do you know about it, and how do you proceed?

BEUYS: I know a lot before I start an action. I know a lot about the necessity of the general idea of sculpture, but I don't know anything about the process in which the action will run. When the action runs, my preparation works, because I am prepared to do a thing without knowing where it goes. You see, it would be a very uninteresting thing—it would have nothing to do with art—if it were not a new experiment for which I have no clear concept. If I had a clear concept of solving the problem, I would then speak about the concept and it wouldn't be necessary to make an action. Every action, every art work for me, every physical scene, drawing on the blackboard, performance, brings a new element in the whole, an unknown area, an unknown world.

So, I never have a clear concept for a performance; I only make a decision about tools, for instance, but I don't determine the run of the action, or the character of the action at all. I never make actions to make actions, as a kind of innovation in the art world, as a new style; but I must say that the nature of the actions as a possibility to arrive at an understanding of art, for the most part was translated into an official modern art style, and again became restricted to the enclosure of an ivory tower, reduced to a traditional view of art as a history of formal innovations without being seen as a possibility to innovate the whole social body. You see that is the dilemma in the art world—but I try to overcome that situation as much as I can; nevertheless, the problem always reappears, and I am always confronted with the temptation of the system to destroy such an impulse.

HORSFIELD: I'd like to ask you in terms of people participating in your work, the audience for example, whether you want to refer to the audience at the actions, or the audience in Europe, or at the Guggenheim. A lot has been made out of the fact that people have to rely so much on verbal or written interpretations of your work, in order to understand the symbols and the quality of the meaning behind it. This seems to me, in a way, to be a contradiction with the intention of reaching out across society.

BEUYS: If it were true, then it would be a contradiction; but you see, it isn't true. That is transported by a lot of unclear sources and unclear positions by people who are involved in this whole difficulty. Journalists, critics, and art historians, they are all building up this misunderstanding, that one must have interpretations for the phenomena of the production. It isn't true, simply it isn't true. People could work without interpretation, and they still can work without interpretation, but perhaps it is also interesting.... Let's stop on this point, so as not to blur it out.

I never preserved a tool, or a part of my laboratory, one could say, to avoid this term "artist." Because this is already an allusion to a kind of traditional understanding in a restricted way which wouldn't work on its own form, or the relationship between form, material and so on. Sometimes appears such a thing, and such a tool, which doesn't work without interpretation, but I would never give it as an example of my understanding of sculpture, or as a stimulating phenomenon to see something about the problems involved. So it is not necessary to have such an interpretation.

One of the most important statements of the enlarged understanding of art is that not only materials—formed, or in chaos if necessary—has to do with sculpture. Thought is a sculptural process, and the expression of the thinking forms in language is also art. This totality of humankind's creativity, beginning with feelings and thoughts, and their expression in a special material, the language material, for which you need your body and physical tools, your tongue, larynx, lungs, the air, the sound waves, the ear of the other person, all have to do with the idea of sculpture in the future.

There is on one side the physical consequence of the thought: the forms being realized in buildings, in architecture, in agricultural forms, in so-called sculptures because they have a special form, they imply a special imagination rather than being only a repetition of the given. It is possible for people to see those tools, the result of a process; they can see, one could say, the "hardware" character of a process. But from this point we should look at the source, where the sculptural process starts, and it is the thought, the thinking power and its consequence: information, which means for me bringing form in material conditions.

Already when I speak I need my own body, the physical, flesh; it is a kind of clay to form into; and I need my lungs, I need my tools here, existing in my anatomy, I need the physical conditions of other forms of life, in my brother or my sister. I must at once eliminate discussions, interpretations, misunderstandings, deviations of the problem. I have to put everything in this process to bring up as much as possible the germ, the point of development in a special direction, to bring up a reasonable basis where new culture in the future could spring off.

So, that is the second part of the problem; that the language, the thinking on the problem is a more important sculpture even than the end of the process existing in tools or in paintings, or in drawings, or in carvings. This transcendent character of information, in an invisible world, gives us at the same time the proof and a clear knowledge that we are not only biological beings, material beings, but first spiritual beings, not existing on this planet—that we are only partly existing on this planet—and being involved in wood, in felt, in fat, in iron, in rubber, or whatever resources of this planet.

That is for me the reason to speak, and it is the dignity of the speech. Otherwise, if this phenomenon, this reality, is not clear, then the consequence is that every speech is bla-bla, no social power exists, everything is chaos. And the other consequence is: let them do what they do, let the government do what it wants to do, I go out, I go apart and try to survive during my life time, and every language, every expression of human beings is bla-bla. If you don't find the necessity to speak, then surely the language is bla-bla. That is why I stress the necessity to find clear epistemological reasons to go on with art, which begin in humankind's thinking powers to mold, and to bring up the quality of what traditionally appears as the form of a thing, to impulse the world with a radical other understanding of culture.

In the past, it was the special spiritual authority of the high priest, the leader, or the pharaoh, or the tribal collective, the chief of the tribe, then later it was the capitalistic dependency on money power and state power, and now it has to deal with the world which is built up by people, people's creativity; but this will only be possible if people get slowly clear about the power they have, which starts in the thinking, the molding character of the thought. And the transference is in language forms, and other kinds of language, as in the art work where sculpture in its special physical form means also language—one must not have such a limited understanding of language.

That is for me the reason why I have to speak, and I have to speak more often than I do so-called art work. You see, the complication is that I have to use something...I have to use a traditional determination for ideas, so when I speak about art, I can only say that there are two kinds of art: the traditional art, which is unable to bring up art at all, or to change anything in society or in the ability and the joy for life, and then, there is another kind of art, which is related to everybody's needs and the problems existing in society. This kind of art has to be worked out at the beginning, it has to start from the molding power of the thought as a sculptural means. If this sculptural agent is not active in the beginning, it will never lead to result in any physical form, or the physical form will only be pollution for the world, and will only enrich the whole rubbish of production we already have. That is my meaning.

—January 1980

1. Guild of Gothic cathedral builders during the Middle Ages.
2. Precision, exactness of a work.
3. Justification—How do you say "justification"?

THIS TEXT IS A TRANSCRIPT FROM THE VIDEO INTERVIEW TAPE PRODUCED BY LYN BLUMENTHAL AND KATE HORSFIELD. THE INTERVIEW WAS TAPED IN NEW YORK DURING BEUYS' RETROSPECTIVE AT THE GUGGENHEIM MUSEUM IN JANUARY 1980.

REPRINTED FROM *PROFILE* VOL. 1, NO. 1, (JANUARY, 1981): 5–15.

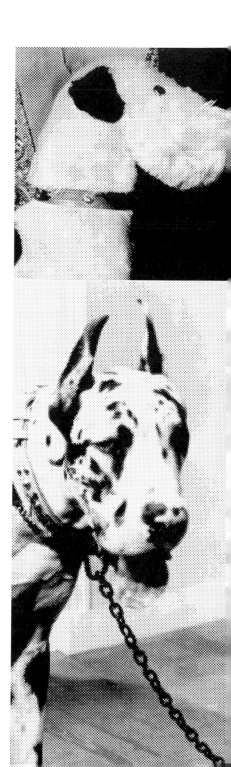

Dara Birnbaum

*By "popular"...was meant a certain range of reference, a style of delivery, and
a claim—mostly implicit, but flaunted on the right occasion—to be addressing
one kind of audience and excluding several others....*
—T.J. Clark, *The Painting of Modern Life*

Howard Beach, a predominantly white, working-class neighborhood in Queens,
dominated New York City headlines in late December 1986. A group of white
teenagers there had beaten a black man named Michael Griffith and his two
companions with sticks, baseball bats, and other weapons. Fleeing his attackers,
Griffith ran onto the Belt Parkway, where he was killed by an oncoming automobile.

Shortly after this time, in 1987, I conducted an interview for my videowork
Charming Landscape, the last section in my *Damnation of Faust* trilogy. In this
interview, while discussing their own neighborhood, two white teenagers attempt to
relate to "larger" issues, including Howard Beach and Vietnam. Howard Beach was
then a present tense. Now, at this writing, it has resurged as "headline news"—the
Turner Broadcasting System advertises "CNN Headline News" as a "habit"—and has
been "resolved" through a court decision reached December 21, 1987. Vietnam was
then—as it is now—a "recurrent" past tense. Reemergent, and repackaged as "the
Vietnam Experience," it has become almost a household cliché in the eighties.

Few comments from this interview made it to tape (the final version of which was
broadcast on WNET in 1986, reaching an estimated audience of 187,500 per night, and
on WNET and WGBH in 1987, reaching approximately 412,500 viewers per night).
How and why did other comments get away during the editing process? Were they
replaced—their space taken by other, more vital information? Or did they simply stay
hidden—perhaps remaining as the "unseen"?

I'm curious not only about how these "exclusions" and "inclusions" relate to one
another, but also about how these choices have *real* effect (*real* here meaning *larger*
and more *visible*) on the audience. Had I, on my side of the dialogue that I desired
between artist and audience, committed the same error that I feel presently prevails in
the arts: acting on the assumption that art is capable of maintaining a history divided
and separated from the "daily events" of our time and culture?

To consider the action of editing is to reemphasize *process* over *product*, or the
continuously shifting and undercertain event over the definitive object and statement.
Since the foregrounding of process still seems to provide the greater possibility for
effecting change, I find it imperative at this time to look at my own most recent

activities, my own *art-making* practice.

How does exposure to information, obtained through the interpretations of mass media, contribute to our formulating of perspectives? What mass media information had the jurors of Howard Beach been continuously exposed to prior to the time of the trial? What was the cumulative impact of the television shows they had seen? What determined their perspectives, enabling them to perform a critical function: to take actions and make decisions that could determine the life of another? A 1984 study projected that the average American child will see over 75,000 thirty-second television commercials by the age of ten. What exposure did the teenagers in my interview have to Howard Beach? How much were they able to identify with its *mass-media* representation, or with the even more distanced and dislocated representations of "the Vietnam Experience" (Time-Life's "What did you do in the war, Daddy?").

In an effort to explore these questions, I desire to reclaim the following extracted statements and images, which were originally "edited out"—which, in fact, had never been "edited in."

DARA BIRNBAUM: What about something which affects you which is larger than your own neighborhood, like Howard Beach?

GD: When I found out about How—about that *racist story*, where the white kids beat up on the blacks for supposedly no reason, I thought it was very uncalled for. Everyone knows it wasn't right. There may be a white guy sitting home and watching TV who's saying, "That's good for him!"—you know, for the black kid. But inside he knows he's wrong. Everybody *really* knows what's right and wrong—you feel it. What if it was one of theirs, if that was them or someone else, you know what I'm saying?

PH: Since I'm originally from another place, I can say that when I lived in California I went to school with a lot of black kids and there really wasn't much racism at all. Oh, there was a little bit, it's always there. There was a tension, but nowhere near what it is here in New York, in either direction. I never got beat up by blacks and blacks never beat up on the whites.

GD: The kids I grew up with in New York have never been anywhere but here. There were other kids who thought that this fight at Howard Beach was wrong—that is, for the three white guys to do it. But me and PH, we've been other places, different places. These kids haven't been anywhere, they only know the neighborhood. That's all they know, so they were brought up with what they had, it was very close-minded, just themselves with their own race. I was brought up like that too, but I went here, I went there, I explored and I talked to other people just to find out, out of curiosity, how they are. Here it's like being stranded on an island with the same people and they're all the same, 'cause that's all they know.

BIRNBAUM: Do you think there's any way either of you could change that?

PH: I think that it's, uh, oh God, no. [laughs] You have to—I understand a lot of where that attitude comes from, and so not only do *they* have to change, but the other side has to change too. Both sides have to change at the same pace. Otherwise nothing's ever going to really work out. The reason I started getting prejudiced is I went to school uptown with a lot of black kids and I saw what they saw. You're really thrown into it, you know. It's an instant battle. I got beat up. I got beat up here too, and then I didn't like guineas, I didn't like blacks, I didn't like anything. I liked myself—well, I didn't really like myself either.

GD: That's where we started judging people as *individuals*. Because we got abused from both sides, really, where everybody's wrong.

PH: I think that maybe you can change it on an individual basis but as a whole group, no. I don't think you can change the whole group.

BIRNBAUM: Do you realize that in the years in which you were born there was a movement to actively protest the war in Vietnam, that sometimes millions of people united in demonstrations in the streets? What would happen if you didn't agree with actions which this government is now committing, like continuing to engage in nuclear weaponry? As an *individual*, do you have any feelings about this—the way you seemed to express your feelings about racism? Have you brought these issues up amongst yourselves?

PH: Well, we talk about it, but my views on government are still very confused. I don't always know how I feel. I do, but I don't. Sometimes I think in certain ways but I don't always know why I feel those ways.

BIRNBAUM: Well, do you see yourself as capable of having a direct relationship to current events now that you're of an age to vote? Does it concern you what your country's policies are? Do you see a way of directly playing into and affecting the policies of this country? In the sixties there seemed to be a belief that individuals united together, for a cause they believed in, could effect change. With a *larger*, more *visible* group it seems that you can begin to see the extent of people's reactions, for example with the demonstrations against the war in Vietnam. What do you think happened in Howard Beach? Is there any relationship we can draw? It seems that when similar conflicts, clashes on issues, usually occur it's typical to try to gain power by getting a *larger* number of people around you for support, or even protection. So, as an *individual*, how do you assert yourself? Let's say that if you were in a group whose thinking was, at times, different from your own—would you feel that you could still express yourself? Could you still maintain your identity in the group?

GD: That's where you lose your identity. That's where you say to yourself, "Well, should I let them know? How should I act?" Sometimes I say, "Oh well, if they don't like it, that's all right." Sometimes you split your personality and think, "I'll just be with them and be like they are for now." You'll talk to this person that's a certain way and you'll try to be that way, and that's the way you wind up for that few minutes or however long you're there. Then when you walk away, you become yourself again. I really don't know who I am yet because of these split personalities which I've created. But I have an idea. Even though I didn't find myself yet—I didn't find my one self, me.

PH: When *I'm* with a group of people, if they're very prejudiced, I'll let them know that I'm not. And if they don't like that, I'll leave. If they don't mind, then I'll stay with them and continue talking with them, but to myself I say, "Well, that's the way they are. That's too bad for them. They're losing out and I'm not." *But I will express how I am different from them*—I can't let that go by. I can't fake it! In that way I feel comfortable. I wouldn't feel comfortable hiding my real feelings—I don't think I could.

GD: See, *I* have to. Because—they're too many of them. And there's just me. I'm one with them 'cause I grew up with them, and I can't really come out and say, "Well, I'm not prejudiced." I can't be open enough. I can be, but I don't want to, 'cause I don't want the hassle.

REPRINTED FROM *ARTFORUM*, VOL.26, NO. 7 (MARCH 1988):117–119.

DAVID DEITCHER: How did you come together as a group?

MARK SIMPSON: It started when The New Museum offered ACT UP the opportunity to use the window, and a group of people got together and did that.[1] When that project was over, the group met again. We wanted to do more and Gran Fury came out of that.

TOM KALIN: Upward of fifty people worked on the window. There were big workshop sessions, like the one where the slabs of concrete were made by cutting rubber stencils. All the labor-intensive work was being done in someone's studio with fifteen or twenty people there at a time. Various people came in for specific tasks. I came in myself because I knew how to do mural photography. Other people came with their own abilities—the person who made the neon and so on. After the window happened people didn't meet as a group for a month. Then we had a potluck dinner. Various people, many of whom are here now, called each other up and started to meet and to talk about making the posters.

SIMPSON: The people who joined together said that they wanted to work together as a group again—Gran Fury hadn't been chosen yet as a name.

DEITCHER: Are there people who join and then go away, and then come back again? And if they do go away, are they welcome back?

SIMPSON: Yes. Some people come only once in a while, and others come regularly.

DEITCHER: There are other members of ACT UP who do visual work, like the Silence=Death Project. What relationship does Gran Fury have to them?

DONALD MOFFET: There's some overlap.

AVRAM FINKELSTEIN: I'm the only one here from that project.

GRAN FURY IS REPRESENTED HERE BY TOM KALIN, MARK SIMPSON, DONALD MOFFET, AVRAM FINKELSTEIN, MICHAEL NESLINE, ROBERT VASQUEZ, LORING McALPIN, RICHARD ELOVICH, AMY HEARD, AND JOHN LINDELL.

DEITCHER: But there were others involved in the design of that initial poster, right?

FINKELSTEIN: Yes, but they only overlapped with this collective by lending the use of the Silence=Death image to The New Museum window. They preceded us by almost a year.

DEITCHER: Are there others still involved with the Silence=Death Project, including yourself, who also do other activities?

FINKELSTEIN: That's right.

DEITCHER: Consisting of what?

FINKELSTEIN: That's not something I'm really comfortable answering because that collective works differently.

DEITCHER: I'm curious because, as someone who walks around lower Manhattan a lot, I see so much work that I can variously attribute to Gran Fury, the Silence=Death Project, or ACT UP. For instance, prior to the recent demonstration at City Hall there was a proliferation of funny, scathing fact-based posters pasted to walls. Were they your work?

FINKELSTEIN: No, Ken Woddard designed those posters.

KALIN: I think it's important to disentangle who did what. But who really knows who Little Elvis is?—the people who made those stickers saying, "THE AIDS CRISIS IS NOT OVER"—and so, in terms of a history, it's really obscure and will probably stay that way.

DEITCHER: Can Gran Fury support its activities?

MICHAEL NESLINE: Financially? No.

KALIN: But we're beginning to get grants.

ROBERT VASQUEZ: We're deep in debt and we've just been winging it, or getting small contributions.

DEITCHER: So the work that has been done—with the exception I guess of The New Museum piece—was work that you had to support yourselves with your "paying" jobs?

SIMPSON: Including The New Museum piece. They gave us $200 and we spent $2000.

FINKELSTEIN: ACT UP gave us the rest. A lot of it is begged, borrowed, and stolen. That's just the way ad hoc groups function.

DEITCHER: How would you describe the function of Gran Fury?

NESLINE: I'd say that all of us are interested in creating art work—or propaganda—that addresses the AIDS crisis and that will be seen by different parts of the public and affect their understanding of this crisis. It would provoke them, cause a reaction, make them think, and hopefully educate them. Our projects should have the effect that a demonstration by ACT UP has.

VASQUEZ: I believe that the work is meant to stimulate thought and to bring a whole new vocabulary—a whole new way of looking—to bear on the AIDS health crisis, by presenting imagery that is different from the mainstream stuff that people are subjected to by the mass media. We want people to question what is out there. One of the ways that Gran Fury does this is by using imagery that's already in circulation. The project that comes to mind most recently is the Art Against AIDS project, which we are calling the Benetton ad because it looks very trendy.[2]

DEITCHER: Does that mean that you find the design of Benetton ads useful?

VASQUEZ: Exactly. We used the style.

FINKELSTEIN: Some of it has to do with putting political information into environments where people are unaccustomed to finding it. It's confrontational. By placing an image like ours alongside advertising posters, people are not in the mindset to deal with our kind of information, and it creates a whole other context—a whole other environment. People are less defensive. It's very different from being handed a leaflet where you automatically know someone's trying to tell you something and you may not be receptive to hearing it. But when you're walking down the street and you're gazing at advertising art, who knows what goes through people's minds? So it's an appropriation tactic that's somewhat confrontational and has been very effective for us.

KALIN: I think what we do is make interruptions in public information and dominant media concerning AIDS, and what we've done has made use of a variety of tactics. There's been stuff that's responded to the sex-negative advertising that's been put out by the Department of Health in New York that promotes abstinence and is unrealistic or presents information that tries to enrage people or to provoke them into demonstrating. When ACT UP was given a Bessie Award, we bought a half-page ad in the program to interrupt that space—to put a decoy into it. For a moment people took it for granted, just like "The New York Crimes" project.[3] People might think that it's true, and it might slip in and do its damage.

DEITCHER: So you insinuate yourselves into spaces and situations by appropriating particular formats. That's a bit like the tactics that Situationists used in Europe during the late fifties and sixties. Since you've already spoken about Benetton—about commercial art—how self-conscious are you about the relationship that your works have to contemporary and historical art forms?

KALIN: Name them.

DEITCHER: Well, I could begin with John Heartfield and Dada, but I suppose I'm really thinking about Hans Haacke, Barbara Kruger, Jenny Holzer, or Situationism.

LORING McALPIN: It's all up for grabs.

KALIN: Like "Futura Extra Bold"—Barbara's type of choice. We don't sit around and say, "let's do a piece like so-and-so." It happens as work is being done because it's in our lives. Some of us make art outside of this context—outside of this collective project—and some of us don't. It's just one part of the flow of information that people who live here in New York are accustomed to.

SIMPSON: Besides, all those people appropriate what they do....

NESLINE: I'm not an artist and I don't know who any of these people are, but I recognize their art and I know that this particular style, this particular tactic, or this particular technique works for this kind of message that we want to put out.

VASQUEZ: It's not as if appropriation is unique to what we do. Madison Avenue appropriates "fine art" constantly.

RICHARD ELOVICH: You're probably hearing that there's a concern, an awareness of where different things come from, but I think that that's kept in perspective. I think we're aware of where things are coming from, but we have priorities.

DEITCHER: Because there are larger issues involved?

ELOVICH: Yes. And sometimes this flares up in discussion. I think that the one consensus is that there are priorities.

DEITCHER: Another "appropriation" of yours—*The New York Crimes*—astonished a lot of *Times* readers who went to their local newspaper dispensing machines and found your work passing—with complete success—as the front section of their daily paper. Tell me how that came about.

NESLINE: We knew that the demonstration at City Hall was coming up and without very much discussion about what we could do for it, or wanted to do for it, Avram had this idea of doing a parody of *The New York Times,* and we all thought that was a really cool idea. So we approached different committees at ACT UP to submit articles about various issues, and those articles were laboriously edited and rewritten and re-edited and then it was laid out.[4]

AMY HEARD: We got access to a computer to do the word processing—surreptitiously, of course. We would have liked to do the production using the computer, but that didn't work out, so we ended up having to produce the thing using photo-typesetting.

DEITCHER: You pirated the equipment?

HEARD: The computer, yes. But we paid—a lot—for the typesetting.

NESLINE: It still accounts for about half of our debts.

DEITCHER: Any response from the *Times*?

KALIN: No. We should have been more aggressive about it. We should have found a way of forcing them to respond, but we were so anxious about the possibility of lawsuits....

FINKELSTEIN: And then there were others who didn't have anything to do with production, but were involved with distribution and could have gotten into trouble.

NESLINE: Mathilde Krim at AMFAR got a phone call from Hoffman-Laroche. They were extremely distraught and nervous, because of the back cover.[5] They assured Mathilde Krim that the gentleman who was quoted is a really good guy. They were very upset about it, and they wanted to know what could they possibly do so that they wouldn't be firebombed or something. Mathilde apparently wasn't sure what to think. She spoke to David Corkery and he said well, hey, the guy said it, and he's fair game. If they want to do something, then why don't they spend more money on AIDS or contribute money to some appropriate cause.

VASQUEZ: Mathilde Krim is not a member of Gran Fury. [Laughter]

DEITCHER: When you said you've responded to the sex-negative materials that the Department of Health has been disseminating, what projects were you referring to?

KALIN: Well, one thing that we're doing right now is the San Francisco bus project. It's jointly sponsored by Creative Time in New York and Art Against AIDS nationally. It's a photograph showing a series of six heads: one lesbian couple, a gay male couple, and a heterosexual couple of mixed color, all kissing just like in the Benetton ads. And the copy reads, "KISSING DOESN'T KILL. GREED AND INDIFFERENCE DO." And it has the Art Against AIDS logo. In New York the logo is replaced with the statement: "CORPORATE GREED, GOVERNMENT INACTION AND PUBLIC INDIFFERENCE MAKE AIDS A POLITICAL CRISIS." An earlier project might be, "READ MY LIPS," or "MEN USE CONDOMS OR BEAT IT." Speaking personally, I think that along with being enraged and wanting to engage in direct action—which can mean many things—we should also be giving ourselves something to look forward to. The media and information that we make doesn't have to be only adversarial. It can also be affirmative at a certain level and necessarily it should be that way.

FINKELSTEIN: Of course, in the given context, being affirmative about sex *is* being adversarial.

VASQUEZ: Another strategy we employed last year that we haven't talked about is the "1 in 61" poster, which was a case where we took advantage of two things that the media were putting out at the time. One was that heterosexual women didn't have to worry about HIV transmission through sex. The other was that one out of sixty-one babies being born in New York were HIV-positive. When we got together to do that piece, we had no idea that it would end up being a "racism" poster. We were able to articulate something that no one else—or very few people—were really aware of at that time, by drawing two statements together to articulate something as it hadn't been before.

KALIN: I think it's also important to talk about the translation of that poster because I remember that the voice of the Spanish translation was a very different voice. It was much more like a call to action, and it was empowering. The English was much more like a savvy, accusatory thing.

DEITCHER: Did the Spanish copy differ literally?

KALIN: The complete poster read: "AIDS: 1 in 61/ 1 in every 61 babies born in New York City is born with AIDS or born HIV-antibody positive/ So why is the media telling us that heterosexuals aren't at risk? Because these babies are black. These babies are Hispanic./ IGNORING COLOR IGNORES THE FACTS OF AIDS. STOP RACISM. FIGHT AIDS." That last line doesn't quite translate. In Spanish it reads, "EL SIDA no discrimina entre razas o nacionalidades. PARE EL RACISMO! LUCHE CONTRA EL SIDA!"

McALPIN: It's something that we did struggle with for a while because at a certain point we wanted to start reaching out to other communities. But we had to be realistic about the extent to which we could do that in the group with no Spanish speakers. It was a problem simply realizing that there was a lot of work that needed to be done for those communities and that we had to think before stepping in to do it. How could we understand what their issues really were?

VASQUEZ: At the same time that this was happening with Gran Fury, the issue of race started coming up more and more at ACT UP's weekly meetings as more and more people of color walked into the organization. So for a lot of people it was a new way of thinking—realizing that there were different people within the AIDS community that were not necessarily white homosexual men, and that you had to reach these people. The next question was: how do you reach them in the most culturally sensitive way? I very much respect Gran Fury for that "1 in 61" poster because it was clear and it wasn't condescending. It spoke about the issues, and the reaction that I got from Latino people who read it was that it was a kind of rallying call. They said, it's good that someone is saying this and that this crisis is being acknowledged.

KALIN: I work for a film production company, and we make prevention films about AIDS. It's made up of filmmakers and community-based organizers. It's so clear that these issues really require an entire process of relearning and handing over. So in this specific instance the filmmakers are actually disempowered, and it's the community-based organizations that are pointing to the messages that should be specifically tailored to Latino women, for instance. As a group I think we're realizing that, when you hammer out this copy word for word, month after month, and then you translate it into Spanish and, well, it makes no sense. The syntax of it isn't culturally specific, culturally relevant. It's all about trying to squeeze the right meaning into the wrong shape. I think, for me at least, this points up the fact that if we want to do additional projects that will reach a specific non-white and/or non-English-speaking community, instead of trying to have our ideas channeled, we have to go to the community and try to work with something that already exists in terms of concern and voice.

DEITCHER: What other posters would you think of in relation to this issue?

MOFFET: There's one that states, "When a government turns its back on its people is that civil war?" That's a billboard project that developed shortly after "1 in 61."

NESLINE: We spent a good summer hashing over the wording and the image.[6]

FINKELSTEIN: Maybe it had its best life as subway billboards in Germany which is what that odd format was designed for, because we were in this exhibition in Berlin.

SIMPSON: That's what it was made for. And so there were sixteen up total: eight each for two weeks—seven in German, one in English.

McALPIN: We had problems in New York just getting it up because we had arranged to have it on Sale Point billboard spaces last fall, but when they saw the copy they said, you can't put that up beside our other advertising. That delayed the project another few months until we finally just went out and sniped it.

DEITCHER: So you've tried to do work on billboards in the city but they weren't accepted?

FINKELSTEIN: Yes. That's where the appropriation techniques backfire because you can't get the space. Also there's a tendency, I fear—harkening back to the Silence=Death project—that when you appropriate a sort of yuppie technique or an appeal to a non-politicized audience, that people tend to embrace the commerciality of it, embrace only the look of it, and it loses its edge. In that way appropriation loses its bite and sometimes I worry about it as a long-term strategy.

DEITCHER: It seems ironic that Gran Fury has actually revitalized a strategy that—at least within the context of art world business-as-usual—has become a cliché of academic postmodernism, a non-issue. Among the "happening" artists, dealers, and critics nobody talks about appropriation any more, but in a discussion of activist work like yours it's still meaningful. Perhaps that's what happens when you return appropriation to its functional, political roots in Dada.

MOFFET: We haven't exhausted it. There were other interesting things we learned from the billboard project besides what we've mentioned. Once it went up, something I think we suspected was confirmed: it's not a very effective billboard because it has way too many words on it. It's okay in a subway where the viewer is doing nothing but standing, but it doesn't work as a billboard for the streets of New York because its function there would have to be something you can read as you approach it and pass it by, and this one is too long to do that.

DEITCHER: Yes, but there are sites where it can work. You've put one up on the side of a building at Church and White Street which is a great location because it can be seen from several vantagepoints. It's very near city government offices; for instance, the Courts on Broadway, and the Department of Social Services which is one block away. Obviously, the context is important to the success or failure of any piece.

KALIN: Now I'm thinking about "WITH 47,524 DEAD, ART IS NOT ENOUGH." That statement we made for a specific context and now we're being flogged for it.

DEITCHER: I wasn't aware that it was originally made for a calendar for the Kitchen.[7] I came upon it later, in the window of Printed Matter, and it did make me wonder. For example, are there cultural responses to the AIDS crisis that are illegitimate?

FINKELSTEIN: I don't think we are saying that any type of cultural response is illegitimate or irrelevant. What we are saying is that what, in terms of Western culture, is regarded as a "cultural" response completely disregards alternative responses. When we came up with "Art is not enough" many issues arose that we'd discussed on and off: the appropriateness of being invited into gallery spaces, what that means to the kind of work we do, where it's appropriate and where it isn't.

SIMPSON: That was stuff that came up later. The original piece was planned for the Kitchen. The people we were targeting with that information were artists and their audience. We were saying, "Art is not enough; do something more." When we did it, we were thinking, art is not enough; fundraising is not enough; memorials are not enough. You know, it was a call to people to get off their asses and do something more.

KALIN: In a sense you're both right, but it makes me anxious to carry this discussion forward. What Avram was saying is true: when you have sixteen words you can't say that direct collective action is culturally specific and depends on what you do. Not everybody has the ability or the freedom to go to daytime demonstrations, for instance. I think the problem may stem from a limitation within the format and language of advertising. When you polish everything down to this burnished sixteen word sentence it doesn't say all the other things that you may be trying to refer to.

FINKELSTEIN: I still consider this project successful, even though it's largely misunderstood. It's created a debate in the art world that previously didn't exist, at least with reference to AIDS.

KALIN: I don't agree with that. I don't want to contribute to a polarized view of this situation between artmaking and activism, or artmaking and direct political action. I guess I'm thinking about this raging debate that centered on the organization of a show called *Against Nature*, which featured art by gay men.[8] The question was, is it okay to be making work that is lyrical, or camp, or humorous? Or should art work be terse, direct and didactic? I just think that those polarizations are simplistic and unhelpful for the most part. But I also think there's merit in a lot of discussion and I think that's one of the ways in which Gran Fury gains its strength.

MOFFET: I am unwilling to back off from "Art is not enough" because it does say a lot. The art world is no more or less implicated in this mess than any other professional field in this country; it just so happens that this is where we are. In the midst of this crisis the statement still makes sense to me.

HEARD: Especially in something like the Ohio State catalogue[9] where you opened it up and smack dab in the middle there's this huge thing—"WITH 47,524 DEAD, ART IS NOT ENOUGH/Our culture gives artists permission to name oppression, a permission denied those oppressed. /Outside the pages of this catalogue, permission is being seized by many communities to save their own lives./WE URGE YOU TO TAKE COLLECTIVE DIRECT ACTION TO END THE AIDS CRISIS." People were giving us the eye and were a little bit mad—who are you to tell us what to do? But it's important that they have to confront this issue, just like *The New York Crimes* forced the Wall Street banker on his way to work to think about the sort of inequities within this society and the government's response to AIDS. I think that's why I stand by it, because we have to think about what it means.

ELOVICH: I feel more ambivalent about "Art is not enough" because I think that when we originally composed the slogan there was a context for it. We were suggesting that memorials are not enough, and that quilts are not enough. Now it has become an "art" argument. I sat through a performance last week of Tim Miller in which he basically threw a tantrum. It was so manipulative in terms of using activism for a kind of self-serving purpose. Miller staked a position by attacking Dennis Cooper's work and saying, there's no room for any kind of obsessiveness or darkness in work now, because everything has to be about getting those hospital beds. I felt much more positively about the use of "Art is not enough" in *The Village Voice*.[10] I'll give an example of how highly charged the situation has become. An artist, David Wojnarowicz, went to a presentation on AIDS issues at the School of Visual Arts, and he was in a rage because he felt like he was fighting his way out of a paper bag. He wasn't quite sure where things were going—what it was all about. His work deals explicitly with AIDS issues and he's living with AIDS. He felt that the presentation we gave suggested that there was something wrong with showing his work in galleries. He felt he'd struggled and kept at it and finally now he was able to make some kind of living by exhibiting his work in galleries. He gets his butt kicked by the FDA, by various government agencies, only to find that it's being kicked by AIDS activists. I don't want to function in that way. I came out of art school in the mid-seventies, going to galleries and seeing Flavin and Kosuth, and I know what it's like for covert rules to be operating.

HEARD: I don't think we want to be proscriptive about it. I think it's more of a provocative thing.

KALIN: One of the things I liked about the piece was the fact that we implicate ourselves when we say it. After all, we're using art to say that art is not enough.

ELOVICH: I think it worked a little better in the *Voice* because it's a call to arms, as opposed to an indictment for not doing the right thing. The *Voice* piece used an image of a demonstration more explicitly than did the Kitchen poster. There was a demonstration image at the Kitchen too, but it was on the reverse side. By putting the slogan and the image together, and by the timing of it, I think it functions more as a call to arms than an art argument.

NESLINE: I think there is an art argument to be made. I'm not so naïve about the artworld as to perceive it as one monolithic thing, but there is a major part of the artworld which takes in the latest issue and chews it up as fodder. I don't think that the AIDS crisis should be allowed to be exploited in that way by artists. And if we serve as a goad to prevent that from happening, then that's all for the best to me.

DEITCHER: I want to continue to discuss this issue, but from a slightly different perspective. What is to be gained—or lost—for you as a group of activists by using the museum/gallery/artworld setting?

NESLINE: As a nonartist who is a member of an art collective, the thing that is most interesting to me about being part of the artworld is the power that is granted to artists. Mark put it eloquently in the past when he remarked that an artist is one of the few people in our society who can say, "I want to do my piece in the middle of the airport," and actually be permitted to do it. ACT UP cannot have a demonstration in an airport, and that is why it's valuable to me to participate in this artistic endeavor. I'm perfectly willing to exploit the power of the artworld if it will allow us to do what we want to do where we want to do it. But I absolutely cringe at the idea that because AIDS is this year's hot artworld topic, that next year AIDS will be passé. If that means that Gran Fury is passé, that's fine, but AIDS is not an issue that can be disposed of because it's last year's issue. If "Art is not enough" addresses that, more power to it.

KALIN: I agree with a lot of what you're saying. Some artworld responses—and the ways that world describes the relationship between art and AIDS—can be horrifying. I'm thinking about the catalogue essay for the Art Against AIDS auction[11], or more recently, this "Blow the Whistle on AIDS" campaign which is my particular pet peeve and has attracted the participation of every major museum in the country. It consisted of selling a silver-plated designer whistle for $250 for the regular edition, and $500 for the limited edition, so that you can "blow the whistle on AIDS." Only forty percent of the money is being given to AMFAR—which itself is questionable as a conduit to people who really need money like the Community Research Initiative, or countless small community-based agencies that are dealing with people of color—and yet this is what the artworld considers to be a healthy response to AIDS. Rosalind Solomon or Nicholas Nixon's horrifying photographs of people with AIDS are other troublesome reactions often construed as positive artworld responses. We don't need more Nicholas Nixon images. We don't need "Blow the Whistle...."

MOFFET: I think we used to thumb our noses a bit at the power and the performance of that complete art system, with its journals and magazines, but that power is real.

DEITCHER: What kind of power?

MOFFET: The power of distributing the word, of telling people what some people are doing. The press has been crucial to us in a lot of ways, whether or not we want to acknowledge that, or respond to it, or just say it's okay.

DEITCHER: At first you said, if I can quote you, "We had to get out of Soho—get out of the art world."

MOFFET: But that's just what we did in our first project: the "1 in 61" piece was not only culturally explosive for us, but territorially we went to the Bronx; we went everywhere. I think it's a question of strategy. To date, the only time the work of Gran Fury that has ever appeared in a gallery was this painting, *Riot*, which intentionally reflected on a specific project by General Idea. I don't think it's a question of anyone in the group being proscriptive about operating in the museum or gallery context. I don't think that as an artists' collective we're unlike other individual artists and collectives who are involved in institutional critique. It's just that we happen to be doing it rather narrowly, in relation to issues specific to AIDS.

SIMPSON: One of the reasons we accepted The New Museum project was because it made a window on Broadway available and we wanted that opportunity to reach everyone who walked by it; not just people who go to the galleries. Since then we've considered doing projects in galleries, and we probably will, because of the potential that they offer to reach people.

JOHN LINDELL: There's a sacrifice involved in using the gallery/museum art system. We only get to talk to that world. We wanted to use billboards to speak to a broader audience but were censored by those who control billboard space because of the character of our work. We were also censored monetarily because we need thousands of dollars to rent those billboards. By choosing to use the gallery setting—it's a classic situation—we can say anything we want, but we say it to fewer people.

DEITCHER: Then it must have been satisfying to do the window at The New Museum not just because of the site's unique relationship to the street but because of the nature of The New Museum as an institution.

SIMPSON: Well, yes and no. Because The New Museum was the *only* place like that. Bill Olander, who initiated the project was really the only person that could have done what he did. We're not going to the Whitney Museum.[12]

FINKELSTEIN: Originally that project was proposed to me by David Meieran, a friend of Bill Olander's, who was contacted by him. My initial reaction was, did they understand that we are not an art collective? When I spoke to Bill, I said that the answer was yes, that we would probably want to take that window space and make it into a demonstration. After all, that is what we do at ACT UP. I asked, would there be parameters, and he said no, you can do whatever you want so long as you know what that is, and it was on those terms that the project was accepted. After that we organized into this group.

KALIN: I think you could really work yourself into a corner though, if you were to make a firm distinction between being a political collective and being an art collective. I insist on a politic that resides in a lot of different places. In addition to direct action it resides in education, in making images or making informational fact sheets, or whatever.

—April 12, 1989.

1. *Let the Record Show*, appeared in the window of The New Museum of Contemporary Art from November 20, 1986-January 24, 1987. See Douglas Crimp, "AIDS: Cultural Analysis/Cultural Activism" in Crimp, ed. *AIDS: Cultural Analysis/Cultural Activism* (Cambridge, Massachusetts: MIT Press,1988), p. 3ff.

2. Art Against Aids is an organization that raises funds for AMFAR, the American Foundation for AIDS Research. In 1988 it commissioned Gran Fury to design a project that would run on the outsides of buses in San Francisco.

3. On April 28, 1989, ACT UP staged a demonstration with civil disobedience at New York City Hall. Gran Fury produced a "fake" *New York Times* to coincide with those actions. Six thousand copies of "The New York Crimes" masquerading as the first section of the newspaper "of record," were wrapped around the latter, and placed in newspaper dispensing machines throughout Manhattan.

4. *The New York Crimes*, included a number of illuminating and equally incriminating articles, among them, "Aids and Money: Healthcare or Wealthcare?," "Thousands of New Yorkers May be Dying in the Streets: State's Highest Court Finds City Legally Responsible," "Women and AIDS: Our Government's Willful Neglect," "N.Y. Hospitals in Ruins; City Hall to Blame," "Inmates with AIDS: Inadvertent Political Prisoners."

5. On the back cover of *The New York Crimes,* Gran Fury printed a full-page mock advertisement for Hoffman-Laroche, Inc. that showed a surgical-masked scientist measuring liquids out of a pipette into pyrex discs. Across the top of this image they superimposed a block of text containing the following comments of Patrick Gage, an employee with that firm: "One Million [People with AIDS] isn't a market that's exciting. Sure, it's growing, but it's not asthma." Across the bottom of the image was the statement, "THIS IS TO ENRAGE YOU."

6. It also says: "The U.S. Government considers the 47,524 dead from AIDS expendable. Aren't the 'right' people dying? Is this medical apartheid?"

7. On one side of the December/January 1988-89 calendar for the Kitchen was a photograph of demonstrators, and on the other was the statement, "WITH 42,000 DEAD, ART IS NOT ENOUGH."

8. *Against Nature* was curated by Dennis Cooper and Richard Hawkins, and was exhibited at Los Angeles Contemporary Exhibitions from January 6-February 12, 1988.

9. Jan Zita Grover organized the exhibition, *AIDS: The Artists' Response,* for the Hoyt L. Sherman Gallery at Ohio State University in Columbus (February 24-April 16, 1989).

10. It appeared as the centerpiece of the "Voice Centerfold" (*Village Voice*, April 18, 1989), where it functioned to advertise a night of performances at P.S. 122 to benefit ACT UP. In this case the statement was superimposed on a photograph of the march on Washington for abortion rights that took place on April 9.

11. The auction, held at Christie's, New York, to benefit AMFAR in 1987, was accompanied by a catalogue with an essay by Robert Rosenblum. In it he described art's capacity to give pleasure to the senses, fortify the spirit, and raise money for AIDS research, but denied that it has the "slightest power to save a life." See Robert Rosenblum, "Life Versus Death: The Art World in Crisis," in *Art Against AIDS* (New York: American Foundation For AIDS Research, 1987), p.32. For a critique of this position see Douglas Crimp, "AIDS: Cultural Analysis/Cultural Activism," in Crimp, ed., *AIDS: Cultural Analysis/Cultural Activism* (Cambridge, Massachusetts: MIT Press, 1988), pp.3-16.

12. Shortly after this interview was conducted, Gran Fury was invited to participate in the exhibition *Image World: Art and Media Culture* at the Whitney Museum. The show's organizers turned over the wall facing the front window of the museum to Gran Fury, where they exhibited *Kissing Doesn't Kill, Greed and Indifference Do*. The Museum also rented billboard space at two locations for another work by Gran Fury.

DAVID HAMMONS
Kellie Jones

DAVID HAMMONS: I can't stand art actually. I've never, ever liked art, ever. I never took it in school.

KELLIE JONES: Then how come you do it if you can't stand it?

HAMMONS: I was born into it. That's why I didn't even take it in school, because I was born into it. All of these liberal arts schools kicked me out, they told me I had to go to a trade school. One day I said, "Well, I'm getting too old to run away from this gift," so I decided to go on and deal with it. But I've always been enraged with art because it was never that important to me. When I was in California, artists would work for years and never have a show. So showing has never been that important to me. We used to cuss people out: people who bought our work, dealers, etc., because that part of being an artist was always a joke to us.

But like someone told me, "Art is an old man's game, it's not a young man's profession." He said it was a very lonely, lonely, lonely profession. Most people can't deal with all the loneliness of it. That's what I loved about California though. These cats would be in their sixties, hadn't had a show in twenty years, didn't want a show, paint everyday, outrageous stamina. They were like poets, you know, hated everything walking, mad, evil; wouldn't talk to people because they didn't like the way they looked. Outrageously rude to anybody, they didn't care how much money that person had. Those are the kind of people I was influenced by as a young artist. Cats like Noah Purifoy and Roland Welton. When I came to New York, I didn't see any of that. Everybody was just groveling and tomming, anything to be in the room with somebody with some money. There were no bad guys here; so I said, "Let me be a bad guy," or attempt to be a bad guy, or play with the bad areas and see what happens.

In Los Angeles, Senga Nengudi and I shared a studio. Her work was so conceptual and I was working in frames then. So by us sharing a studio, she got more figurative and I got more conceptual. That's when she started doing the pantyhose; those pieces are all anatomy. Before, she used to put colored water in plastic bags and sit them on pedestals. This was the sixties. No one would even speak to her because we were all doing political art. She couldn't relate. She wouldn't even show around other Black artists her work was so "outrageously" abstract. Senga came to New York and still no one would deal with her because she wasn't doing "Black Art." She was living in Harlem. So she had to leave here and go back to L.A. and regroup. Then I came in after her, I said, "I'll try it, I'll try it with my shit."

It was a totally different thing when I came here in 1974. It was a painter's town exclusively. If you weren't painting you could forget it. And I was doing body prints then and was moving into conceptual art. I had to get out of the body prints because they were doing so well. I was making money hand-over-fist. But I had run out of ideas, and the pieces were just becoming very ordinary, and getting very boring. I tried my best to hold on to it. It took me about two years to find something else to do.

I came here with my art in a tube. I had a whole exhibition in two tubes. I laid that on the people here and they couldn't handle it, nothing in it was for sale. This was after the body prints. This was after I had taken off for a couple of years and come up with an abstract art that wasn't salable. These things were brown paper bags with hair, barbecue bones, and grease thrown on them. But nothing was for sale. Other Black artists here couldn't understand why you would do it if you couldn't sell it.

I was influenced in a way by Mel Edwards' work. He had a show at the Whitney in 1970 where he used a lot of chains and wires. That was the first abstract piece of art that I saw that had cultural value in it for Black people. I couldn't believe that piece when I saw it because I didn't think you could make abstract art with a message. I saw the symbols in Mel's work. Then I met Mel's brother and we talked all day about symbols, Egypt and stuff. How a symbol, a shape has a meaning. After that, I started using the symbol of the spade; that was before I did the grease bags. I was trying to figure out why Black people were called spades, as opposed to clubs. Because I remember being called a spade once, and I didn't know what it meant; nigger I knew but spade I still don't. So I just took the shape, and started painting it. I started dealing with the spade the way Jim Dine was using the heart. I sold some of them. Stevie Wonder bought one in fact. Then I started getting shovels (spades); I got all of these shovels and made masks out of them. It was just like a chain reaction. A lot of magical things happen in art. Outrageously magical things happen when you mess around with a symbol. I was running my car over these spades and then photographing them. I was hanging them from trees. Some were made out of leather (they were skins). I would take that symbol and just do dumb stuff with it, tons of dumb, ignorant, corny things. But you do them, and after you do all the corny things, and all the ignorant things, then a little bit of brilliance starts happening. There's a process to get to brilliancy: you do all the corny things, and you might have to go through five hundred ideas. Any corny thought that comes into your head, do a sketch of it. You're constantly emptying the brain of the ignorant and the dumb and the silly things and there's nothing left but the brilliant ideas. The brilliant ideas are hatched through this process. Pretty soon you get ideas that no one else could have thought of because you didn't think of them, you went through this process to get them. These thoughts are the ones that are used, the last of the hundred or five hundred, however many it takes. Those last thoughts are the ones that are used to make the image and the rest of them are thrown away. Hopefully you ride on that last good thought and you start thinking like that and you don't have to go through all these silly things.

It was just like a chain reaction. I started doing body prints in the shape of spades. So when I moved into using just the spade image it flowed. Then I started painting watercolors of spades. After that, I stopped using the framed format entirely; I had chains hanging off the spades. I went to Chicago to a museum and saw this piece of African art with hair on it. I couldn't believe it. Then I started using hair.

JONES: So where did you get the hair from, barber shops? People didn't want to give it up, did they? They thought you were going to do some serious magic on them using that hair.

HAMMONS: No they didn't mind it. Except there was a place in Harlem that said no they wouldn't give it to us, this Haitian place.

In L.A. I had one place that I got hair from, this one shop, because it was so hard to ask people. I'd wait until everyone left the shop, I'd sit out front until the shop closed. I would always ask this one guy. Eventually, I got used to him and he got used to me. In New York, I wouldn't get the hair. I had this friend get it for me. He was very outgoing, you know, sold you insurance and all that kind of stuff, a gallery dealer, he'd talk to anybody. He'd talk to the barber and I'd just pick up the hair.

There's so much stuff that I want to do with the hair that I didn't get a chance to do, because I just can't stay with any one thing. Plus I got really bad lice. Everyone kept telling me I was going to get lice. I shrugged it off as just a possible occupational hazard. But I did get a really bad case of head lice. Hair's like the filthiest material. It's a filter. When the wind blows through it the dirt stays on the hair. You could wash your hair every single hour and it would still be dirty. But I have information on Black people's hair that no one else in the world has. It's the most unbelievable fiber I've ever run across.

I was actually going insane working with that hair so I had to stop. That's just how potent it is. You've got tons of peoples' spirits in your hands when you work with that stuff. The same with the wine bottles. A Black person's lips have touched each one of those bottles, so you have to be very, very careful. I've been working with bottles for three years and I've only exhibited them a couple of times. Most of my things I can't exhibit because the situation isn't right. The reason for that is that no one is taking the shit seriously anymore. And the rooms are almost always wrong, too much plasterboard, overlit, too shiny and too neat. Painting these rooms doesn't really help, that takes the sheen off but there's no spirit, they're still gallery spaces.

I think the worst thing about galleries is, for instance, that there's an exhibition opening from 8-10 p.m. The worst thing in the world is to say, "Well I'm going to see this exhibition." The work should instead be somewhere in between your house and where you're going to see it, it shouldn't be at the gallery. Because when you get there you're already prepared, your eyes are ready, your glands, your whole body is ready to receive this art. By that time, you've probably seen more art getting to the spot than you do when you get there. That's why I like doing stuff better on the street, because the art becomes just one of the objects that's in the path of your everyday existence. It's what you move through, and it doesn't have any seniority over anything else.

Everybody knows about *Higher Goals*—the telephone pole piece—up there in Harlem. If I'm on the street up there I say, "I'm the guy who put that pole up there." I'll be on 116th or 110th and Amsterdam and talk to anybody and they'll say, "You're the one who did that. Yeah, I know where that is, I know you. Brother, come here, this is the cat who did the pole, yeah." So sometimes I'll just say that to talk to somebody on the street, at three or four in the morning or something, it's like a calling card. I've been trying to put it in the Guiness book of records as the highest basketball pole in the world but I don't know who to call.

I like playing with any material and testing it out. After about a year, I understand the principles of the material. I try to be one step ahead of my audience. Some artists are predictable. You've seen their patterns over the last ten years. They're staying within these frameworks because it's financially successful. I look at these cats and this is what I never ever want to be or never ever want to do. Why should I stay safe? It takes a long time to analyze a form—whether it be metal, oil paint, whatever—it may take them their whole lifetime to analyze this material. But who gives a fuck? There are so many things to play with. And I question if what these artists are doing is art or not. I don't think it is. An artist should always be searching and searching for things. Never liking anything he finds, in a total rage with everything, never settling or sacrificing for anything. That's what I enjoy anyway.

I always try to use materials that are not easy to obtain. Like now I have all this elephant dung that I'm working with.

JONES: How did you get that?

HAMMONS: It was for a garden. Angela [Valerio] was getting some for her plants. I was there with her and saw some of this elephant manure. It was interesting. It's about the size of a coconut. So I'm painting on it now. I've been working with it since about April 1985.

JONES: You did pieces for a while that had dowels with hair and pieces of records on them. Like the piece you did for the Atlanta Airport.

HAMMONS: Those pieces were all about making sure that the Black viewer had a reflection of himself in the work. White viewers have to look at someone else's culture in those pieces and see very little of themselves in it. Like looking at American Indian art or Egyptian art, you can try to fit yourself in it but it really doesn't work. And that's the beauty of looking at art from other cultures, that they're not mirror reflections of your art. But in this country, if your art doesn't reflect the status quo, well then you can forget it, financially and otherwise. I've always thought artists should concentrate on going against any kind of order, never accepting any order not even their own, but here in New York, more than anywhere else, I don't see any of that gut. Because it's so hard to live in this city. The rent is so high, your shelter and eating, those necessities are so difficult, that's what keeps the artist from being that maverick.

JONES: It's funny though, because people always think that the starving artist is the most important one. That all that angst and starvation is what makes your art good.

HAMMONS: It does make the work good if you understand the starvation. Like Van Gogh said, he who lives in poverty and loves that poverty that he lives in will always be in the heartbeat of the universe. But you have to love the poverty, and there are very few people who love poverty; they want to get rid of it. So if you are in poverty and dislike it, well then you have a real problem and it's going to reflect in the work. But if you're in poverty and enjoy it and can laugh at it, then you have no allegiance to anything and you're pretty much free.

Anyone who decides to be an artist should realize that it's a poverty trip. To go into this profession is like going into the monastery or something; it's a vow of poverty I always thought. To be an artist and not even to deal with that poverty thing, that's a waste of time; or to be around people complaining about that. Money is going to come, you can't keep money away in a city like this. It comes but it just doesn't come as often as we want.

My key is to take as much money home as possible. Abandon any art form that costs too much. Insist that it's as cheap as possible is number one and also that it's aesthetically correct. After that anything goes. And that keeps everything interesting for me.

JONES: Would you say that your work has any political element in it? Because of not running after the status quo or being more free to do what you want and not really worrying about the money thing like so many people are doing? In other words, by abandoning running after the money, does the work become more political in a certain sense?

HAMMONS: I don't know. I don't know what my work is. I have to wait to hear that from someone.

JONES: Like who, regular people on the street?

HAMMONS: They call my art what it is. A lot of times I don't know what it is because I'm so close to it. I'm just in the process of trying to complete it. I think someone said all work is political the moment that last brushstroke is put on it. Then it's political, but before that it's alive and its being made. You don't know what it is until it's arrived, then you can make all these political decisions about it.

Sometimes I do say, "This is going to be a political piece," Like *Soweto Marketplace* that was at Kenkelaba House (*Dimensions in Dissent*, December 1985). Then trying to make it is so difficult, because I want it political and I want it conceptual and I want it visually interesting. I want it gloomy, I want it hidden away from the crowd. All of these kinds of things come into play. So I'm dealing with about five different levels.

I'm learning a lot from Fellini, watching his movies over and over again. I think the movie people are much more advanced than other visual artists. They can make you cry, they can make you laugh, they can scare you. Paintings don't do that, they used to but not any more because the audience knows the game too well. But it's the artist's fault because the artist isn't researching and making the game more real. We've let filmmakers take the game from us because of our nonchalance.

If you know who you are then it's easy to make art. Most people are really concerned about their image. Artists have allowed themselves to be boxed in by saying "yes" all the time because they want to be seen, and they should be saying "no." I do my street art mainly to keep rooted in that "who I am." Because the only thing that's really going on is in the street; that's where something is really happening. It isn't happening in these galleries. Lately I've been trying to meet a new kind of people in this city and not the art scene. Otherwise you end up with, "Man, your shit's baaad, your shit's happening, you're the man," all this absurd praise. You start flying and thinking that your shit don't stink. I've invented a rule book for myself, that's gotten me over all of this stuff. If an artist doesn't have his own rules then he's playing with those of the art world, and you know those are stacked against you.

I have all these safety valves that I use. Like if it's on the ground, I pick it up and put it on a branch. It's still outside of me, I just found it. One artist accused me of "showing a bad image of Harlem." And I said: "I'm not showing anything. I'm just putting stuff that's on the ground onto a tree. I'm not responsible for that wine bottle getting there. All I'm doing is playing with it, activating it in some form."

Selling the shoes and other things on the street I think is my personal best; those little shoes, that's my best shot. I do it whenever I need a fix, I guess; when I know I need attention and want to make someone laugh. It's like having an opening for me when I do that piece, because I interact with the people. And I don't have to wait for these galleries. It's a way for me to show people how I see the world. I get a chance to watch people interact. It's interesting...if you have an item between you and other people, then they can relate to you. If you don't have an item you're enemy number one. But if you have an item between you then it cools them out and they can deal with you. It's amazing how something like a little shoe can just turn someone's head around.

JONES: Have you ever talked to people on the street—like when you had that bottle tree piece in the vacant lot next door to Studio Museum, did you ever stand around there and listen to what ordinary people said about it?

HAMMONS: I was in there one time and some people asked me what I was doing and somebody said, "He ain't got nothing better to do." And I thought, I didn't have anything else to do, that was the reason I was doing that. So they ask the questions and answer them themselves. If you're quiet or don't have anything to say, they say it all for you.

JONES: Do you think everyday people have a greater grasp of what you're doing than....

HAMMONS: Than I do?

JONES: Than you do or than other people who are politically astute, or versed in art?

HAMMONS: They're the number one, because they're already at that place that I'm trying to get to. Sometimes I carry a whole arch of wine bottles around in the neighborhood. I walk from 125th up to 145th street and people follow me, ask me questions, give me answers, tell me what I can do. They just give me tons of information and I don't give them any. I'm just carrying this piece around like it's a log or something. Once a woman said to me, "Mister, excuse me, but could you please tell me what that is?" I said, "What are you speaking of?" Then I said, "Oh, it's just some wine bottles." I play off it. I do this every once in a while to cleanse myself. It's putting myself out there on the street to be made fun of. I think it's important to be laughed at.

Black people, we have more problems with being made fun of then any people I've ever met. That's why it's so important for us to be cool, cool, cool. If you're not cool then you're something else and no one wants to be that other thing. But that other thing is what I'm interested in, because you have to really work at getting to that other space. Black artists, we are so conservative that it's hard to get there, you have to work at it, really, really work to be nonconservative. We've come up under this Christian, puritanical, European form of thinking and it's there, deep-rooted. It can be worked at, loosened up some, but it's very difficult. What happens with my work is like I'll be working on piece A but I'll do some little aside things on my way across the studio to get to piece A and these aside things will be more important because they are coming out of my subconscious. These aside pieces will become more interesting and haphazardly loose and piece A, that I've been working on for months, will be real tight.

Doing the things in the street is more powerful than art I think. Because art has gotten so...I don't know what the fuck art is about now. It doesn't do anything. Like Malcolm X said, it's like novocaine. It used to wake you up but now it puts you to sleep. I think that art now is putting people to sleep. There's so much of it around in this town that it doesn't mean anything. That's why the artist has to be very careful what he shows and when he shows now. Because the people aren't really looking at art, they're looking at each other and each other's clothes and each other's haircuts. In other sections of the country I think they're into seriously looking at art. This is the garbage can of it all. Maybe people shouldn't look at art too seriously here because there's so much.

The art audience is the worst audience in the world. It's overly educated, it's conservative, it's out to criticize not to understand, and it never has any fun. Why should I spend my time playing to that audience? That's like going into a lion's den. So I refuse to deal with that audience and I'll play with the street audience. That audience is much more human and their opinion is from the heart. They don't have any reason to play games, there's nothing gained or lost.

JONES: The piece that was at Art on the Beach, does it have a name?

HAMMONS: I called it *Delta Spirit* because it was about that kind of spirit that's in the South. I just love the houses in the South, the way they built them. That Negritude architecture. I really love to watch the way Black people make things, houses, or magazine stands in Harlem, for instance. Just the way we use carpentry. Nothing fits, but everything works. The door closes, it keeps things from coming through. But it doesn't have that neatness about it, the way white people put things together; everything is a thirty-second of an inch off.

So working with the architect was fun because our shit was outrageous. You had to have an architect on this project. So I hired Jerry Barr, we did *Higher Goals* together in 1983. He came up with the structure of *Delta Spirit*, he designed it. It was very puritanical. You know he's a big-time architect, all over the world. He's designed houses in Paris, Cuba, and Africa and places. So this was one of his concepts. What I had to do was take that concept and put Negritude in it, which was a porch. He wanted to buy brand new wood; he wanted to spend about one thousand dollars on wood. But I had found all this lumber in Harlem and had stacked it up in these piles on various corners. So we just went around with a truck and picked up all the lumber, took it downtown, and started making the house. It was built in the shape of a hexagon, a six-sided figure, using six-foot poles, everything is six feet long.

JONES: Was that your idea?

HAMMONS: No, that was all Jerry's. I don't know how to stack wood, to keep wood from falling down. That's why he was important to the project. He knew how to stack wood and he knew how to get the best out of a piece of wood. I was just going to build a lean-to, a little shed, and take all the money and go home.

JONES: Do you think by doing a piece as cheaply as possible, that puts you on the same footing with a lot of people who are just trying to survive? Like you said, these newspaper stands in Harlem, I mean obviously these people don't have, they're not going to spend three thousand dollars on wood....

HAMMONS: Exactly. But these stands serve the same functions and they do the same things. They just aesthetically different.

JONES: When you were doing *Delta Spirit* did you go down South and look at houses, or did you make the piece from memory?

HAMMONS: It's based on memories of the South. It also had a lot to do with Simon Rodia's *Watts Towers*. I love his work, it's one of the best. When I was in L.A., these towers just really influenced me. I would like to work on one piece for the rest of my life; just one piece, like him. As opposed to toying around with all these other little things. Just make one piece. Most artists want at least one piece to be immortalized. So one piece would do it. Because we're making one piece anyway, I guess, fragments of it.

JONES: So what ever happened to *Delta Spirit?*

HAMMONS: It's still there. Yeah, I go out there all the time.

JONES: Really, I thought it was taken down. I thought it was going to be moved to Harlem.

HAMMONS: All of that got too boring to deal with. I got tired of thinking about it. So it might be there for a couple of years. But I didn't get the five hundred dollars that they paid the artists to dismantle their work. I'm waiting for the snow because I wanted to photograph it in the winter and document it under all seasons. I just see it as a piece of public sculpture. That's the other reason why I haven't taken it down.

I would like to burn the piece. I think that would be nice visually. Videotape the burning of it. And shoot some slides. The slides would then be a piece in itself. I'm getting into that now: the slides are the art pieces and the art pieces don't exist. [*Delta Spirit* was vandalized before Hammons could realize his concept of burning and videotaping the piece.—Eds.]

I have a video of *Delta Spirit* now, taken in the summer [1985]. It's also on this Fat Boys video; they showed it for about sixty seconds. Their managers thought it would be good to have as a stage prop.

I have no idea if there was any real connection between the Fat Boys and *Delta Spirit*. My position is, that it's just irrelevant to me. I was working on the house, if someone wanted to use it, I stay away from that thing because it doesn't relate to what I was doing. But if anybody can relate to it, good. Let them weave themselves in it and through it.

The Fat Boys were like big heifer cows who waddled out of a limousine, who are going to die within three years if they don't take care of their physical situation. These young boys, three hundred pounds each, waddling down to the house and out of breath before they get there. And everyone else making all the money around them. So their whole thing is out to lunch.

JONES: But I wonder if a lot of people see the Fat Boys video and see that house and are affected by that image.

HAMMONS: It's not on long enough. There's a close-up and they're on the porch and they come off. You'd only know about it if you knew about the house. I told my kids in California to watch for it.

JONES: To me, that house, *Delta Spirit*, was a conglomerate of Black people's living. The way they put things together. It's not exactly the way a white or European person would do it.

HAMMONS: But it transcended that and went on into another level. Its significance changed as it got more ornamented; as it got more detailed, it went universal. People started seeing it who were from places like Tibet and Vietnam, for instance, and told us about houses they've seen like that in all corners of the world. Getting this type of feedback also affected the piece.

JONES: That's why I thought the connection with the Fat Boys might be kind of interesting. Kind of bringing it back to city kids, and maybe giving them a chance to identify with it.

HAMMONS: It was really funny working on *Delta Spirit* because the other artists were so embarrassed by us or for us. They didn't know what we were going to do. They just saw this huge junk pile and everybody wanted to get rid of the wood, they thought it was an eyesore. We were the last ones to get the structure up, and we had a ball. We never got it finished, even though we worked on it every day.

JONES: It's still not finished, and it might not ever be finished. Like you said, it's that same piece that you work on and work on, and even when you die it's not finished.

HAMMONS: The way I see it, I have two pieces of public sculpture up on the island of Manhattan now. And looking for a third.

JONES: The pieces that you are doing now with bottles, your standard wine bottle with things like crosses and the Georgia clay inside of them. Are they related at all to the Thunderbird bottle pieces that you were doing before?

HAMMONS: With these bottles I'm using now, I got the inspiration from the book *Flash of the Spirit* [by Robert Farris Thompson]. On one page I saw this little juju man sitting up there with a cross in a bottle. The thing about these bottles I love is that people have to ask how you got those things in there. It's like a trick. It's like they're saying, "How'd you do that trick?" Or I get this from people, "Oh, I know how you did it, you took the bottom off the bottle and glued it back on." And I say, "Yeah, that's how I did the trick." But visually it's hard now to mess with people because everybody is so hip on what's happening. I like when people ask how I do things because that means they don't know. Whereas in a painting everybody knows, or everybody thinks they know: "It's an extension of such and such that's coming out of Picasso, or that's a collage from the such and such school." That kind of stuff. So I'm trying to find these holes or these gaps to play in.

I just finished a piece with a voodoo doll in the bottle. That was fun. And then there's the bottle caps. I love bottle caps. Because I can get trillions and billions and zillions of those things. Whatever you see a lot of, you can use, you can build something off of. So I want to work with them forever. I also want to come back to the hair. All of these things I want to come back to at another time. Now I'm just laying down some kind of foundation; these pieces are like visual notes, like how you put notes in your notebook. These are all notes to come back to at another time, elements to reconnect in the future. The hair, the bottle caps, the bottles, they'll all represent themselves in another salad on up the road somewhere.

—January 20, 1986.

REPRINTED FROM *REAL LIFE*, NO. 16 (AUTUMN 1986):2-9.

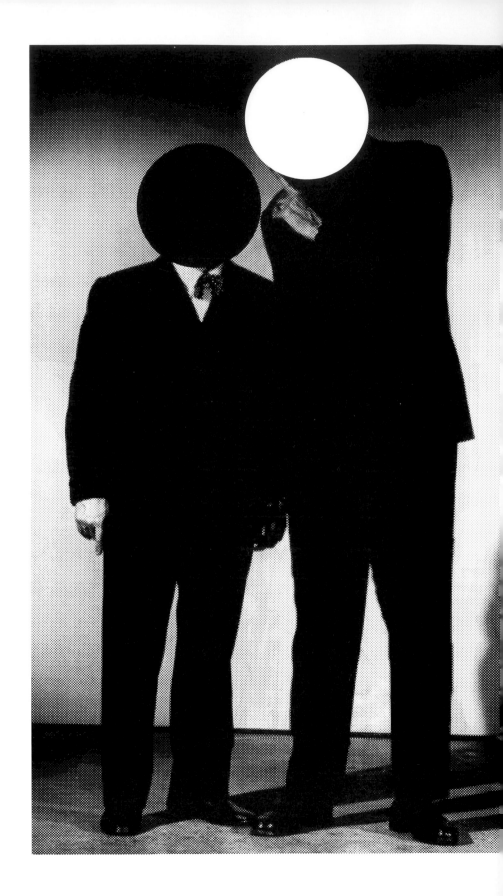

Popular culture has been the subject of growing scholarly attention in recent years, and inevitably this new specialty has provoked a backlash from defenders of traditional cultural hierarchies. Hilton Kramer's assertion that "all forms of popular culture should be banned from courses in the arts and the humanities,"[1] reflects an awareness that the pieties of "high" culture are now widely challenged. Yet those who pursue the study of "low" culture often continue to do so in the specialized language of academia. Wrenched from its context and presented as a series of texts for analysis, popular culture is frequently drained of its vitality. Too often the real voices of its producers go unheard in this debate. The encounters that follow offer instead something of the spontaneity and directness characteristic of the speakers. With their internal inconsistencies and sudden shifts of ground, these conversations resist easy assimilation. In this very instability, sometimes fueled by outright anger and hostility, we can hear the voices of people trying to retain some real control over their work in frequently difficult circumstances.

At the heart of the punk movement lay the tremendous unleashed desire of the participants simply to make themselves heard in a society which had written them off. The whole ethic of punk favored action over passivity. Punk challenged the hierarchy of star and audience, and its rejection of traditional musicianship let everyone onto the stage. "You can't even play your instruments," someone in the crowd shouted at the Sex Pistols. "So what?" was the sneering response. The move from reception to creation constitutes the basis of a profound revolt and accounts for the bitter resistance such movements in popular culture inevitably meet from those in authority. Members of a consumer society are supposed to consume their entertainment, not to create it.

For Malcolm McLaren, the cultivation and manipulation of an utterly self-conscious "badness" led to his greatest success, the Sex Pistols. With every excess the Sex Pistols gained popularity, tapping directly into the deep well of youthful hostility and resentment. Like Elvis Presley twenty years earlier, the Sex Pistols made it glamorous to be "bad." Where Presley's manager, Colonel Tom Parker, a true cynic, devoted his energies to making Elvis safe for corporate America, McLaren hid a rebel idealism beneath a veil of amorality. As he says now, he "lit the fuse" and an alienated generation responded with exultation.

As the Sex Pistols completed their rebellious arc, the record business regained control, and for McLaren badness entered a stage of entropy. When the energy stopped flowing back from a mass audience, his scandalous gestures began to seem more like clever commercial gimmicks than magnificent blows against a complacent society. In McLaren's words, "It is very, very difficult to decide now what is bad."

As with the punks, the desire for control and the need to create an identity are evident in the comments of the women rappers speaking with Jill Pearlman. Faced with resistance in the intensely macho world of rap music, Roxanne Shante reveals a pragmatic cynicism which makes Malcolm McLaren's opportunism look mannered in comparison. When Sparky D says that if the two of them were to do a show at Madison Square Garden, it would sell out, Shante replies: "only 'cause they want to hear us call each other bitches." Though Shante bluntly accepts the need to make some "wack" commercial product, because radio stations "like it wack," this cynicism only fuels her obvious drive to do what she wants: to keep talking back, directly and publicly, to the people who try to put her down.

A double interview with the drag performers Ethyl Eichelberger and Lily Savage highlights their affinities as well as their differences. Similarities range from the apparently trivial (both were raised on farms) to the clearly significant (both are ambivalent about the term "drag queen," but both ultimately accept it). Their differences, though, are equally important. Ethyl Eichelberger is self-consciously part of a theatrical tradition. She draws on the semi-underground tradition of burlesque, drag, and Yiddish theatre as well as the "high" tradition of Shakespeare and Greek tragedy. Where Eichelberger's sources are all theatrical and entail a rejection of mundane reality, Lily Savage, despite her claim to "never get political," draws her deeply class-conscious material from exactly the specificities of daily life which Eichelberger seeks to transcend. Eichelberger identifies with Nefertiti and Clytemnestra, and aspires to the Metropolitan opera. Savage models herself on her relatives and aspires to *Brookside*, a working class TV soap opera.

In the conversation between Scott Johnson, Laurie Anderson, Anthony Davis, and Steve Reich, these composers, all of whom have engaged popular forms, address the ambivalences generated by that process. Anthony Davis is forthright in declaring racism to be a central issue: "...The reason that we have trouble embracing the concept of popular culture as the real root of our art is the fact that popular culture, particularly in music, is mainly Afro-American." In the wide-ranging debate which follows, Davis calls the adoption of black and non-Western musical forms "a new kind of colonialist impulse." He in turn is challenged by Steve Reich for using the European bel canto tradition in his opera *X*, a choice which Davis forcefully defends. This conversation moves back and forth between the participants' respect for cultural and musical traditions and their desire to engage with those traditions as individuals. Perhaps Scott Johnson sums it up best when he says, "What I want to do is to be a traditional composer in a tradition that doesn't exist yet."

There are more questions than answers here. Unlike the relatively seamless flow of academic discourse, these discussions rarely arrive at neat conclusions. The desire for stability and tradition is played out alongside the parallel urge to rebel and disrupt. The terrain of mass consumption is a treacherous one, full of opportunities for surrender and compromise. Rigorous consistency is not always the best strategy to deal with a harsh reality, but in boldly using whatever material comes to hand, these performers succeed in making their distinct voices heard, and thus they shape both their own lives and the culture of which they are a part.

1. "Studying the Arts and the Humanities," *New Criterion*, (February 1989): 4.

MALCOLM McLAREN

There's no point in me talking about all the things I've done; I need to explain the method behind the madness. I think the best way I can do this is to give you an account of myself from a very early age.

I think that I can sum up by telling you that I was a very bad boy, and that's no lie. I'd say that the fact that I was bad goes back to childhood when I cut a tail off a rocking horse in the nursery, exploded fireworks in my house, or tore up all the school's exercise books and was thrown out at the age of five.

I went back to school, more or less, at the age of nine. I was never on time, and I kicked everyone when I played soccer. I was a very bad pupil. I was constantly punished, but the punishment for me was a sincere form of flattery. I could never date a girl; no one could get that close, and I would never be kind enough. In order to coerce others, I forced everybody else to play truant. At the age of nine, I formed a box gang. They hid in a box outside the school making sure that they would not be seen, so the teachers couldn't make them attend. I liked that. I adored people calling me bad 'cause it felt good. I think that I felt it important because when things were good, I seemed to feel terrible. I felt absolutely nothing and was only concerned with who I could upset next?

I first heard rock & roll—I think it was "Rock Around the Clock"—back in the mid-fifties in England. The first time I saw a teddy boy, it provoked in me sheer menace, so much so that I crossed the road to get out of his way. The badness that this chap managed to promote made me love the clothes that he wore and helped make me understand that you could *look* bad—not just be bad. I realized fashion could make you look completely out of step with everything else that people were terming good. In other words, you became an outsider. That made me fit in, and I tried to look sexy doing that and became almost a male seductress who would only get near in order to run away. It was a bit like a T-shirt I later created in my shop during the Sex Pistols era, with the slogan "Fuck your mother and run away." I was a great pretender 'cause I never did that, but the posture—the posture was good.

The Sex Pistols was me when it was bad and something else when it was good. The color black, if it could be defined as a color, meant to me something very warm and very beautiful. All the drawings I made when I finally entered art school were the absolute opposite of what teachers suggested when they would tell you that white came forward and black went back. Black for me came forward and white just disappeared. So upon making self-portraits, I would often draw my head with so much graphite that they just ended up as big blocks. The eyes became so dark that they literally burnt holes in the paper. My figures continued to be black because I felt that the blackness had a kind of disappearing quality which you couldn't really determine or control. I drew a series of those figures set against a landscape that was just a series of lines I'd often been made to write as a child—"I will not be bad." I just changed the "not" to "I will *so* be bad." That amused me no end, but, in art school it was somewhat of a loss.

You see, the establishment notion of "bad" finally needed to be redefined. The notion of "good" meant to me things that I felt I just absolutely wanted to destroy. At the beginning of the seventies, when I left art school, to me "good" meant Bryan Ferry; it meant green velvet loon pants, hippies, bright young things, social realism, the American flag, and television. If I were to wake up one morning and find which side of the bed I'd been lying on, I knew that there would be a list of either good names or bad names. That list was the beginnings of me deciding how to use bad and make it work in a way that ultimately might change popular culture itself. The list of names supported the slogan "Wake up one morning and find out what side of the bed you've been lying on," which was the first T-shirt sold in my shop SEX in 1974.

In that list there was a name: the Sex Pistols. That name meant for me all sorts of things. It came about from the idea of a pistol, a pin-up, a young thing, a better-looking assassin, a Sex Pistol. I launched the idea in the form of a band of kids who could be perceived as being bad. When I discovered the kids had the same anger—that they could wear black—it was perfect. I thought they could never stop me dreaming, and help me never return to what I was terrified of, normality. In that dream world which lasted maybe two years, I tried to be very bad. Whenever I was being good, I realized I was doing no good at all. As soon as something became good—a shirt, a dress, a design, a shop, the group—I'd destroy it immediately and start something else.. It's extraordinary when I think about it now, these things only occur to you in retrospect. I only felt good when those people said it was bad. The characters Johnny Rotten and Sid Vicious exposed that anger and kept me in step with everything that I felt from a very early age and allowed me to continue to stay horrible.

Fashion for me was really looking bad, looking sometimes poor, looking always the opposite of what was in. And I kept busy constantly defining that hole in the fashion industry and the music industry, until they decided suddenly that it was cool to use the same notions to sell their philosophy too. That's when things got very confused.

I suppose that was the start of this decade which for me has been one of great confusion and perhaps one that will lead us to begin to think about the world as becoming totally in love with its past and completely bored with its future. That doesn't put you in a very good place. I've got to admit that. Cynicism, one of the most fashionable words in America today, is about "it's cool not to look cool anymore," because fashion seems definitely out. And America begins to be something you could describe as antique. Sort of a tarnished spectacle, one that is still selling rock & roll. What does that mean now? Marilyn Monroe, what does she mean now? And Levis, what do they mean now? And Coca-Cola, how does that taste now?

Well, the Japanese find America fabulous and tend to be buying it like there's no tomorrow. It reminds them of the golden age when America (after the war) thought itself important enough to mean something in the world of popular culture. Our culture reminds the Japanese that they have probably more to say and basically teach us—that our culture was something of a museum. They were right, only now thirty years on, since '55, our culture has become something that is completely and utterly in love with its parent. It's become a notion of boredom that is bought and sold, where nothing will happen except that people will become more and more terrified of tomorrow, because the new continues to look old, and the old will always look cute. Now American culture begins to place everyone in a position where it is very, very difficult to decide what is bad because Michael Jackson seems to be that. So maybe it has to be redefined; maybe it's been redefined for us. Certainly for me. So perhaps you'd better not look bad anymore. Perhaps to look good is subversive. I don't know.

We do live in confused times, and I want to maybe delve into what I've done in this decade. Now artists have problems deciding whether they're entrepreneurs, whether they're impresarios, mercenaries, public relations officers, corporate investors, stock brokers, or painters and decorators. It's difficult for everyone to want to be any of those things today, simply because an artist is uncertain of whether he's being honest—whether he has credibility. The word "street" has been redefined and talked about and applied, in *Vogue* ads, television commercials, Hollywood spectacles, television series, and so on, to the point that we don't know what "street" is, other than trying to look back and find some things that might expose an idea that those in the establishment haven't been aware of. I say that because rock & roll doesn't necessarily mean a band. It doesn't mean a singer, and it doesn't mean a lyric, really. It means that indefinable attitude that allows you to go bump in the night and, I think, not return to normality. It's that question of trying to be immortal.

When I made an album four years ago using opera, it wasn't for the purpose of feeling chic. It was because opera and its characters seem so mythic and so much more irresponsible than any characters or rock & roll gods were. There is not a worse or badder or sexier character than Carmen. Madonna pales in comparison. There is no more evil and sexier guy than Don Giovanni in rock & roll. Mick Jagger pales in comparison. To see those opera enthusiasts struggle in their jobs and then go immediately to the opera house to see *Carmen* for the thousandth time bewildered me no end. It was clear that they were going to some pagan ritual. That the operatic spectacle was like some Dionysian rite. It was another kind of religion, and it meant that us mere mortals who couldn't live our lives like Cho Cho San, or Carmen, or Tosca, or Don Giovanni, could exalt in their paradise of emotion. That for ninety minutes we could get a glimpse of the emotion, love, and death, that they had lived. There was something so fantastic for me in that spectacle. I realized that instead of sculpting characters out of the street like the Sex Pistols, Adam and the Ants, Boy George, or Bow Wow Wow, that you didn't need these characters. There is no way that they could ever be as powerful or as potently intriguing and lasting and spellbinding and mythic and godlike as Carmen or Tosca. It drove me to create a rock & roll record by taking the characters out of these librettos.

That for me was another way of being bad, and another way of trying to retain whatever passion I must have felt when I pulled the plug on the Sex Pistols when they were beginning to play too good.

AUDIENCE: What was your childhood like?

MALCOLM McLAREN: Very Victorian. I was brought up by my grandmother and she taught me to read and write. I read most of the novels by Brontë and all those other dark, gothic characters by the age of nine. By age thirteen I couldn't read anymore. It was a background that was full of theatrics. I was brought up to have absolutely no fear of anyone, because I was to feel ultimately superior. Very fascistic upbringing, I would say.

AUDIENCE: What went wrong with the Sex Pistols?

McLAREN: The Sex Pistols and their lyrics and content didn't provide you with any way of reconstructing anything. They were just talking about the death of everything. It was an acknowledgement of the fact that rock & roll as a popular culture had finally ceased to be, as it developed its own aristocracy. I think the Sex Pistols were part of breaking it down and saying that there was no point any longer in playing well. Who'd give a shit? It's boring. I mean, that was my interpretation and I probably sold that better than anyone, often to the detriment of those working with me, who ultimately really did want to be good. This was particularly the case with John Lydon. It was a philosophical point we couldn't agree on.

AUDIENCE: But there were other punk bands who did want to be constructive.

McLAREN: Yeah, you are probably talking about The Clash. They were much more professorial; I was always anti-that. I was concerned with purely bad entertainment. This is not to be facile; I just never believed in the professorial nature of rock & roll. For me it was far too overblown. When a band plays more than thirty minutes, I don't care who they are, I'm absolutely bored to death. And The Clash could lecture you for hours.

AUDIENCE: How did you come to work with Bootsy Collins?

McLAREN: Well I never knew Bootsy until the earlier part of this year. I don't know, really. I think he just…. Being white and coming from London and a Victorian upbringing, he reminded me of a witch doctor. I was thrilled. I was only looking for his badness but he tried to feed me health food and he'd go bicycling in the morning before he recorded. That was alright. I felt that was his art of disguise.

AUDIENCE: What do you think of the fact that punk has persisted?

McLAREN: It has to do with people wanting to relive something that they missed out on. It's a game that is probably played in Kuala Lumpur. It's something that probably exists in Brasilia. It's an attitude that if you didn't get it the first time 'round, you might be able to glean it from a few journalistic articles and a couple of odd bootlegs. And if everybody is happy doing that, I ain't one to stop them really.

AUDIENCE: What is your relationship with the music industry?

McLAREN: I have never read a contract, to be honest. I couldn't; it's just not in me. The industry? Well, I think of "them" as providing hot dinners and a few plane tickets. I can't consider them consequential. I am sure many people make splendid careers in the record industry through empire building and gangsterism, but—if you have been drawing trees all your life and reading Emily Brontë—you just really don't get into it on this level. It is another sensibility, that I just wasn't…. Sometimes I feel saddened a little that I am not able to do that stuff. But there you go.

AUDIENCE: Where are you sourcing your creativity?…

McLAREN: Well I…. That is kind of hard to answer.

SAME: …You have a wonderful mind….

McLAREN: Well, I'm not brilliant, otherwise I wouldn't be standing here.

AUDIENCE: Could you tell us something about your experience in art school?

McLAREN: Art school in 1968 was about getting rid of the easel. It was about ransacking the churches. It was about the politics of boredom. It was about suggesting to you in a certain way that you might be out to change things, but not by going through the committees and the socialist cult movements that existed in art school at the time. You could change things by—dare I say—sloganing a wall, throwing a brick through a hamburger bar. It seems trite now, but at the time we were delighting in it.

AUDIENCE: Were you influenced by Situationism?

McLAREN: It was this very profound idea, I got to tell you. It was hard to read. I think Situationism is such a convoluted idea. It is very difficult to actually manage to do.

AUDIENCE: If you were going to be bad now, what would you do?

McLAREN: I don't know. I think that the words are being redefined hourly. As I said to you earlier, I don't have any answers in that arena. We live in confused times, and I think that there is a lot of reading to be done. I think that people involved with pop culture including perhaps myself are somewhat responsible for the visual side taking preference over the word. Now I think that the word is slowly beginning to take over from the visual side of things. Somewhere in there, somebody will learn something, maybe.

AUDIENCE: Why have you been living in Hollywood?

McLAREN: It's just one big hell of a factory and one giant hotel, but for us Europeans it tends to represent America a lot more than anyplace else. We are fed movies that only show us Hollywood's landscape; you know, the guy munching papayas, living in a palm tree, listening to the Beach Boys. So, like any other sucker, I went there to take a look. I got involved, got my ass bitten a couple of times, thought about it a bit, and tried to figure out if there was anything there one could work with. One is always looking for some other medium, some other situation to find a method of working within. I didn't think I wanted to continue working in fashion, or necessarily even music, but I found, on the whole, L.A. is a place where you can live and die in about two weeks. It is not a place where you can learn very much. That is what I mean. It's hard to spread and build upon. You find that Hollywood is a town built on very malevolent thinking.

AUDIENCE: What did you think of the film *Sid and Nancy?*

McLAREN: I think there was a great deal of truth in it. I liked it. It would have been better if it had been made like an opera. I think it would also have been better if it would have portrayed John Rotten and Sid Vicious and Nancy as a fantastic human triangle, highlighting Sid's struggle between staying with John or dying with Nancy. I think that the story of the Sex Pistols in the first act was difficult to understand, only because there have been so many contradictory accounts of that period. No director could have figured it out. When you finally arrived at the Chelsea Hotel in the second act, you could see that the director was more comfortable with the characters of Sid and Nancy, and that to me was the film.

AUDIENCE: Do you like rap groups like Public Enemy?

McLAREN: Yeah, they are fantastic. I think that rap music is the only thing that is really exiting now. There are no two ways about it. They are like a kind of black Sex Pistols in a way.

PAUL TAYLOR: For the second part of today's Mac-Attack, I am introducing four panelists. The first speaker is Greil Marcus, who I am very pleased to have here from California. He is a well-known rock critic, and the author of *Mystery Train*. A new book is forthcoming in April, from Harvard University Press, called *Lipstick Traces*. This is, I believe, a secret history of negation in the twentieth century.

After Greil Marcus, we are going to hear from Richard Hell, whose music is well-known to all of us. Less well-known is the fact that he is now associated with the Poetry Project here in New York City, where he edits the new literary magazine, *CUZ*. An expanded edition of his recently published book of poems *I was a Spiral on the Floor* will appear in 1989. His bands, over the last decade and more, have been: The Neon Boys, Television, The Heartbreakers, and The Voidoids.

Jon Savage, who is sitting to my right, assisted me with the show at The New Museum. He is from London, and is the author of *England's Dreaming,* which is a book about England and the Sex Pistols that focuses on the years 1975 to 1979. Jon writes for television, newspapers, and magazines in Britain, and he has the dubious honor of having been on the barge on the Thames at the time when the Sex Pistols and everybody else were dragged off.

Finally, Stephen Sprouse is one of my favorite fashion designers. He has been working since 1983, and currently has a shop in Soho. His styles synthesize techniques and imagery from both pop art and punk, which I think makes him a very relevant speaker today. So, let us hear from Greil.

GREIL MARCUS: I'm going to start off by reading a few quotes, and then talk about them a bit. The first is from Denis Browne, a close friend of Sid Vicious. This is simply something he said to me a few years ago. He was talking about what it was like to be in London when the Sex Pistols were first noticed.

> The week they were all assaulted, beaten, razored, when they truly could not go out, except in clandestinity, that was the week the polarization in England was beyond belief. It was a crunch. There was an enormous support all over England for the Sex Pistols. Not just among teenagers, but

also among very young kids, ten, twelve, and from all sorts of people who were definitely not kids, such as myself, and as well from people who were a good bit older than myself—people who somehow really seemed to think that Johnny Rotten was the Anti-Christ. That out of all this chaos and destruction, would come the last days—the millennium.

Then Johnny Rotten talking in 1986 about that same period:

It was good at the time. It could have gone anywhere at one point. It kept people on edge. It kept me on edge, I know that. I was scared to walk down the street half the time. At the end there was a pointless rerunning of a B movie, packed with the obvious. It shouldn't have been. It could have been something very courageous, and an absolute change. And yes, we could have won.

And then Joe Strummer of The Clash, talking just a couple of months ago:

I wish we hadn't taken it so seriously. It said, let's sweep away everything and start again. But after a few years, when all the old buzzards came back, it obviously hadn't swept away anything. It was a hiccup rather than a complete change.

And the interviewer says to him: "Didn't you realize that was inevitable all along?" And Strummer says:

Well, I should have. I had seen all that before when I was taking my "O" Levels, all that Vietnam protest stuff and Paris raging in 1968, but then again, we wouldn't have even gotten into it if we hadn't been fanatical.

Now, I've read these quotes because what I think of when I think of punk today is free speech. Punk to me was a form of free speech. It was a moment when suddenly all kinds of strange voices that no reasonable person could have ever expected to hear in public were being heard all over the place. When the kind of people you would want to look away from when you walked down the street—I am not talking about people dressed up in costumes—were suddenly making demands on you as public speakers. I mean people singing on records. There was a brief but very intense time when absolutely anything could be said. I think it was the Sex Pistols who gave people permission to say anything—I mean, if this ugly, hunched-over kid could stand up and say, "I am the Anti-Christ" and make it believable, then anything was possible. People went around trying to figure out what it was they wanted to say. That is a very difficult question, and they began to come up with marvelous answers, answers of incredible humor. You began to hear about things in songs you could never have expected to hear. I think of "Holidays in the Sun." Here is a song with words in it that had never appeared in pop songs before—words like "Communist" and "the Berlin Wall." And yet the whole song is organized around some odd critique of the idea of a vacation. Very complex little song. Also terrifying, just in the way it sounded. Out of that anything could have happened. Well, this didn't come out of nowhere. In many ways I think of punk, particularly in England around 1976-1978, as a restaging or a recapitulation of something that happened in a very different and more focused form in May 1968 in Paris, when there was a rebellion or revolt—no one ever knew what to call it. In France they call it "the events," a nice neutral term. It could be a lot of traffic accidents from that description. What happened was that based on an incident that was fundamentally trivial and should have remained localized by any rational standard, thousands of students began to leave their schools and then go back to reoccupy them, take them over. Thousands and then millions of workers began to do the same thing, in factories, in offices, in theaters, wherever they happened to work. It was a wildcat general strike. The country came to a stop. It ceased to function. And in a bizarre way there weren't any issues. There weren't any concrete demands. Although there were people running around saying, "Hey, let's demand a two percent wage increase, let's have Pass-Fail grades," that is not really what it was about. What happened was, the country stopped, and suddenly everybody began to talk. My favorite description of May 1968 in Paris, which is really May-June—it lasted about forty days—was somebody saying, "It was a month of talking." For a month, everybody spoke to everybody else. You could talk about anything. People who had never stood up in front of more than two people, were standing up in front of thousands; fifteen-year-old girls, seventy-year-old men were trying to talk, haltingly, but in sometimes very eloquent ways, about how they wanted to live. Well, this was a terrifying moment for a lot of people; and it ended. It ended formally. I think punk recapitulated that. I think that those kinds of events were coded in the songs, in the attitudes, in the stances, in the sound in various people's voices, in the act of speaking freely. What has come of that is a very strange cultural phenomenon, and that is that punk—a few songs, a few ideas, a few slogans—has become a kind of...I don't quite know the word...but a kind of seed, and you can plant it almost anywhere and it will recapitulate itself. I am thinking of an article called "Punk in a Small Spanish Town" by a friend of mine, Robin Cembalest, which appeared in *The Village Voice* a couple of months ago. She lived for a year in a little town in Andalusia. And there were "punkies" in that little town. That is what they called themselves. She first ran into them when they were sitting in a cafe listening to "God Save the Queen," and they realized she spoke English; so they asked her to translate the song for them, and she did. And this little punky culture began to develop among a small group of kids in this town over the next year or so. As those kids began to try and find out what they wanted to say, and began to define themselves against the life that they had been raised to lead and had always taken for granted, they began to discover incidents in their own history as Spanish people, incidents of anarchism, incidents of rebellion. They began to construct a whole new past for themselves, which is the same thing that I think happened with punk. When punk arrived, lots of people, people like me, said, this is familiar somehow. But it wasn't familiar. I hadn't seen anyone like Johnny Rotten before. But I was responding—we were responding—because yes, we had seen it before. We had seen it in May '68, where it was noise, not music. Which is what a lot of people said about punk. And if you look back farther, you can see the same kind of incidents and events of free speech being played out in other moments and places. I am not going to trace for you a whole historical thesis. I am just going to offer this idea: punk is free speech. And free speech is something that is not obvious. You have by some cultural magic been given the opportunity, been given permission to say what you think. Or someone demands that you say what you think by forcing you to take sides, which in a lot of ways the Sex Pistols did. That is what Denis Browne was talking about, the "polarization," the "crunch." He was saying that suddenly in England you had to be for or against the Sex Pistols. That is something that certainly hadn't happened in rock & roll since Elvis Presley. As I recall, when I was in fourth grade, that was the only question: were you for or against Elvis Presley. And a lot of people, mostly boys, said they were against him, but secretly they were for him. They didn't have the nerve to say it. And I think probably the same thing happened with the Sex Pistols. That kind of crunch, that kind of polarization, that demand on you, to say where you stood, and why you stood there, that's one of the main reasons that I am here. I could talk about other things. I could talk about how Malcolm to the contrary...about how so much of the music that was made in London in that period is great music, the Sex Pistols particularly. But I leave that for now. Thank you. [applause]

TAYLOR: We are going to hear from Richard Hell, who was an originator of so much of what we now call punk.

RICHARD HELL: I kind of postponed and avoided taking part in this. I wasn't originally going to do it because I didn't think there was anything new and interesting to say about it. There's been so much coverage of the subject in the last ten or twelve years and it's all blown out of proportion. It has even reached academia. It's a dead subject. It is easy to study, because it's a corpse. You know punk, the way we are discussing it here, was a kind of a blip in a cultural cycle. Like the beatniks in the fifties, or being a Parisian emigré in the twenties. That offers youth an opportunity to feel free, to express themselves, as Greil was saying. And I don't think there is anything too fascinating about that. I was kind of disappointed in Malcolm's show. I thought it was thin, but the records are great. And I don't mean just the Sex Pistols, but the scratch stuff, the African stuff, the Madame Butterfly. The show I think—and that side of Malcolm's work—is kind of empty and vulgar and false, but the music is terrific. The music is what has life in it. I tried originally to turn down participating in this discussion, and then I was called again a week or two ago, and the rent was due. So I agreed to do it, but I wanted to do it with some kind of integrity. It would be easy and obvious to just get up here and be a punk but you guys are paying, so I am going to try to give you some information. And the only kind of information I can think to give...I have covered the subject in print. I wrote an article for *Spin* about the Sid and Nancy movie; I am on record elsewhere. It is funny, when I heard Malcolm begin, he was going to talk about himself, so that is what I am going to do too. We took the same route. Small world. So I realized there would probably be a lot of kids, students from F.I.T. and not just strictly cultural historians, sociologists, and shit like that. So I thought I would describe a little bit about what I was thinking and doing in 1970-74, which is when I contributed to what is known as punk.

I was a high school dropout. I always hated school. I came to New York to become a writer in 1967—the tail end of the flower children—but I never felt comfortable with that mentality, that kind of consciousness, though I took my share of acid as all the punks did. Acid and speed chased with beer. But I felt very much an outsider, and as a teenager is likely to, I also felt like I was neglected—that I wasn't getting enough attention. I felt like I could see how the world operated and everybody else was pretending that things were running smoothly when they really weren't. I also had a history of interest in poetry. I was always a sort of literary type. I really liked to read. I kind of kept it a secret because I didn't want to have anybody walk over me because of that. I still wanted to hold my own on the street. I was really influenced by the twisted French aestheticism of the poets of the late nineteenth century like Rimbaud, Verlaine, Huysmans, Baudelaire, etc. Moving up into the twentieth century I also admired the surrealists Breton and Vallejo. Breton was a real favorite. And a lot of my view of the world came from that. As a matter of fact, the hair cut that got associated with punk was something I developed very consciously from two different directions. Around 1973 I was here with my friend, Tom Verlaine, whose name was Tom Miller at the time. We both liked the same writers. We would stay up all night writing poetry together. We really thought we didn't belong anywhere. In fact, we really didn't like each other [Richard and audience laughter] but there was no one else that shared the same kind of warps, so that drew us together. I was publishing books; I had a little printing press. I was twenty at the time and it felt very futile. I wanted to shake up the world. I wanted to make noise, but nobody reads. I could identify with that, I wanted to be true to my heros, but I could see reading could be very boring if you weren't conditioned to enjoy it, so we would stay up all night writing, and I got to feel that was a dead end. About 1972-73 we decided we were going to make a band. I was real inspired by the attitude of the New York Dolls and the Stooges. We were both big fans of the Velvet Underground. Tom was a real musician; he actually had a guitar [audience laughter]. I thought it was time to make some noise in some other way besides sending out these little slips of paper that people utterly ignored. And yeah, what I was talking about was the haircut. So it came from two directions. I don't know whether you can see this, but this is the last issue of the magazine that I was publishing at the time. It came out in 1971. You see it has Rimbaud and Artaud on the cover. Does that haircut look familiar? And the other angle about the haircut was: I looked at the Beatles and thought, what made their haircuts so appealing? Why did people fall in love with the Beatles for those haircuts? And my conclusion was that they looked like the haircuts of children of their generation, like a bowl haircut, where you just put a bowl over your head and clip around the edges. My generation grew up with crew cuts. They got all grown out because—what eight year old likes to go to the barber? So that's how the punk cut originated. We wore ripped up clothes that we wrote and drew on, because the whole thing we were doing at the time, the whole intention was to deliver on stage your core self without any filters—to be the same off stage as on stage—because rock & roll at that time was all pretentious stadium glitter. There were bands playing, like Yes and Emerson, Lake and Palmer [audience laughter]. They were the dregs of the sixties with this revolting new development—imitating classical music. So we wanted to destroy that and bring the music back to the real kids. We were living in New York City and I always thought of rock as genuine urban kids' folk music. When I was a teenager in the sixties, there was a period for a couple of years where the music was really the network of news for teenagers, where you defied the lives and conventions of the grown-ups and talked to each other over the airways about what life was really like and what it felt like to be alive. We wanted to bring that back, so part of the principle was, that we were going to reinvent ourselves to be our own ideal picture of what we were like on the inside. We wanted our insides to be outside—to be made visible. And we were really angry and we were really laughing too. The group I am talking about, was the Neon Boys (Television before we added a second guitar player). I left that group shortly thereafter, and Television became something entirely different. The hatred between Tom and myself overcame the affection [audience laughter]. Where was I, Malcolm? He is ignoring me. What was I getting at? Oh, yeah, I was talking about the final idea which was "I don't care!" [audience laughter, applause] That was one of the first songs we wrote, and that was really the root of the idea of the blank generation, because in trying to be honest, in trying to look at what our position was, that was it—"I don't care!"—with a lot of principles behind it. [applause]

TAYLOR: And now Jon Savage is going to talk about the English milieu at around the same time.

JON SAVAGE: It struck me that what I could easily talk about is the fact that I wasn't a practitioner at the time, I was somebody who was moved by what was going on in England at that particular moment. But I was, and still am, a journalist; I was outside looking in, but I certainly felt affected by what was going on. One of the things that I can easily do is to talk about certain aspects of what England is like and what it does to American pop culture because I primarily see punk as being an American idea transplanted to England with inevitably different consequences. First I want to talk about a man called Larry Parnes, who you may not have even heard of. He was called an impresario. He was a Jewish guy from Brondesbury in North London which is a very nice suburb. He was in the rag trade or something like that, and he was scuffling around the music industry, and he was gay, and he had the bright idea of packaging this funny new music that was coming over from the States, which was called rock & roll. He was basically the first English manager; he started the modern English music industry. He saw these kids coming over from the States, and they were obviously sexy in a particular way, with their haircuts and various types of clothes, and he thought, this is a little bit like a tail fin on a Cadillac. So what I should do is package this stuff. I should take all the signs of what this stuff is—the haircuts and the sex—and transplant it to England. So what he did, is he picked up these English singing stars like Tommy Steele, who was England's first rock & roller. He had this stable of boys. Some people said they were named after how they were in bed. I don't know if that is true or not, but they had names like Duffy Power, Vince Eager, Marty Wilde, and Johnny Gentle, and they were the first English rock & roll stars. The great thing about them is that they were really tragic, and they were really bad. The English did not understand what was happening in America at all because it was too new; it was something that came over like a Martian space ship. But they started packaging it and synthesizing it straight away, and that is what English pop culture is. It is not necessarily a pop culture of origination; it's a pop culture of synthesis. If you like, it is a new kind of imperialism. Whatever you want to call it, it is pop culture that puts a whole mixture of stuff together—puts it together with a look, sometimes an ideology, certainly an idea—then repromotes it. That is the first thing I want to say about English pop culture.

The second thing is, that because of the particular nature of England, the emotional experience of living in England day-to-day is one of intense claustrophobia. Now it may not be the same claustrophobia one experiences living in New York, but it is certainly pretty intense and maybe a bit more depressing. You don't get the highs, but you certainly get the lows. English people don't talk to each other on trains. If you talk to them on the street, and they don't know you, they just look at you and think that you must be very weird and rush on. It is a static country with a very rigid class structure. It's a very oligarchic country, in that only a few people have access to the stuff of life including riches, education, etc.. England is also a country that is very urban-dominated. New York is a very big city, and there are various other metropolitan areas in the United States, but in England there is much more city (I include in the city the suburbs) than there is country. So you have a vast reservoir of youthful energy, kids, people who are older like myself and are still youthful, who don't necessarily have access. They don't have access to politics; they don't have access to a good lifestyle; and the way that they hurl all their energy, their resentments, and ambitions into the world, is through pop culture. This is why in England we have this very peculiar pop culture which is a mixture of total blatant shameless packaging and ripping off, but which is also loaded with politics and all sorts of ideas about fashion and aesthetics. It's pretty complicated, and it is often quite hard to understand. It took me a long time to understand the records that I really liked when I was growing up. It was the Who and the Kinks and the Stones in the mid-sixties. It took me a long time to realize what those records were saying. I understood them emotionally; I didn't understand them intellectually.

The other thing about England which is very different from America—and, I am sorry if you know all this, but I think it is worth repeating—is that as far as the music and the fashion industry is concerned, England is a very centralized culture. Basically, you can have a good idea, you can have a weird bit of clothing, you can be sweet, or you can put penises on your satin clothing, and the next week you will be on *Top of the Pops*. You will be seen by eleven million viewers, which is about a fifth of the country. So you have instantaneous mass access to pop culture and pop culture ideas. I think that is relevant in talking about punk. I don't want to talk about punk a great deal, but I don't agree with Richard that there is nothing more to say about it. None of the accounts that I have ever read tell it like it was for me, which is why I am writing one now. I have seen some that come close. To me it was a time in London of very rapid transits, of a lot of people shooting around like pinballs. It had to do with claustrophobia—to do with things happening very quickly. You have groups who would form; they would play their second gig; they would get a write-up; and within three weeks they would have a record. Within two months they would have a hit. Groups like the Adverts couldn't play, but they made terrific records, which still stand out. The other thing I have never heard explained is the emotional sense that anything was possible. This is to some extent what Greil was talking about, and to some extent what Richard also suggested, and it is an extraordinary sensation to feel. It's like a flame (this sounds very romantic, but I am very romantic about it and I don't see what's wrong with that), a flame that never quite goes out. It had to do with the fact that nobody really knew what was going on (my apologies to Malcolm), and that for some reason this group, the Sex Pistols, managed to crash through all these barriers. They suddenly made a record and then everything started coming down like a pack of dominoes. That feeling is something that I still retain, and I always want to retain. So when we are talking about accounts of punk, I see lots of things called punk nowadays. To me it isn't a satisfactory term at all. It is a very sloppy term, and like all definitions, it actually means less than it originally did. I think of the phenomenon we call punk paradoxically, not so much as a nihilistic one, although there was a lot of nihilism involved, but as one of great optimism; less a manifestation of cynicism, but on the contrary one of idealism. And that is something I would always wish to see in popular culture. Thank you. [applause]

TAYLOR: One of the things we might address at question time is the descent of the "ideals" of the punk era into cynicism at present. This may or may not have occurred. Certainly we have seen a lot of the styles redefined in the mainstream fashion world. One of the prime-movers in this respect is Stephen Sprouse, who is going to show a video and talk about his work. It is interesting to keep in mind the way in which, although many people say that punk is absolutely over—we can see that it is still alive, a prime force in design and fashion, particularly, as conjoined with pop art—in Stephen Sprouse's work. [applause]

STEPHEN SPROUSE: I don't really know what to say. It was nice to be asked to do this, because I have always been a big fan of Malcolm and the Sex Pistols and Richard, but I'm no authority on punk. I just think it's cool. I like the way it looks; I like the music. When you were doing it, I was living in the Bowery with friends, and we had a band. I would go to CBGB's every night and hang out. I was just a fan. I ripped off all his ideas, and I still do; so it was nice to meet him as well as Richard. Let's see, what else did I write down? Oh, metal. Heavy metal. Metal is kind of like punk in America, all these wasted kids going to concerts; it's not the same but it's similar. I still think that Hardcore is the heavy metal of the nineties. Even though it looks so American, with the plaid shirts and crew cuts, it's still threatening for the masses. Other than that, I don't have much to say; so I decided to use this as an ad, and I got a video. That's about it.

[VIDEO IS SCREENED] [applause]

SPROUSE: Thanks Eileen for making the video real fast.

TAYLOR: Any questions?

AUDIENCE: It's insulting to come here and be shown an ad.

TAYLOR: I think this is a little more than an advertisement. It's quite self-effacing on Stephen's part to call it an advertisement.

SPROUSE: That upsets me that you think it's insulting. Malcolm really inspired me, Richard inspired me. I screened it because I've been inspired by rock; I have a big company behind me now, which is great.

AUDIENCE: How did punk come about?

MARCUS: There are moments in history and culture that nobody can predict, when things come together, and things suddenly break open. Those moments can be very valuable to pay attention to and remember because they don't last. It is important to be able to recognize them when they come again.

HELL: You create them; you don't sit back and recognize them. You take things into your own hands and make them happen.

MARCUS: Well, I don't know that it's that simple.

HELL: Look, if you take a little initiative and do it yourself and not just sit back and be passive, you can change everything, at least for a few minutes—at least long enough to show that it is possible. That is what punk really demonstrates.

MARCUS: Absolutely, but you can do that again, and again, and again.

HELL: It has to happen again every generation. That is why it is so trivial really to talk about "punk."

MARCUS: It doesn't just happen once every generation. There are people doing it every day, thousands of times a day, in this city, all over the world, right this minute. Sometimes it connects and spreads, and sometimes it doesn't. That is what I was talking about.

[applause]

HELL: Yeah, the point is to make it happen. To have enough faith in your own stance and the way you see things at your best.

MARCUS: Richard was saying that you have to take a step forward, you have to try to create something; so that if only for a few minutes you can show that anything you want to do is possible. That is what I was saying people are doing every minute of every day—not just punks, but people of every description. I wasn't talking about 462 bands writing new songs. There are countless ways of trying to break through, to do something you have never done before, to find out what it is you are wasting your time on this planet, rather than sitting back and saying: I wish someone would come along and tell me what to do tonight.

Let me tell you a story which I think you will recognize a hundred percent. This is another story of the recreating of punk that my nephew told me.

He was in a band called Minimal Man in the late seventies and early eighties in San Francisco. I asked him what being in that band was like, why he was in it and what it meant for him because I didn't know him at the time. And he said: all of his life, from the time he could remember—back to when he was five years old—he had always been a spectator; he had always stood a few paces back and watched. He had watched what had gone on in his family and at school; he had watched what other people did. He had always felt like a watcher—impotent, unable to make a contribution—even to interrupt a conversation that someone was having. Even if he had an idea, he would suppress that idea. That was how he lived his life, and that was how he understood himself. In the midst of the punk scene, which recreated itself in San Francisco just as it did in cities all over the country and all over the world (he was going to the San Francisco Art Institute and once again he was taking a few steps back and watching what the interesting people were doing and working on his own stuff in private), he became friends with a guy named Patrick Miller, who wanted to start a band. Now Patrick didn't know anything about music; he didn't even play any instruments. What he knew was silkscreen, and he liked to make faces with flesh rotting off them and silkscreen them all over the city. His most famous face is on the Berlin Wall; he made it to Berlin, stuck it up, left and went somewhere else. Patrick said, this is what I have to say to the world but it's not getting through (a story very much like the one Richard was telling); "So I think we have to form a band." My nephew said, "This is ridiculous. I can't play anything." And Patrick said, "Didn't you ever take music lessons?" My nephew said, "Yeah, but I played stand-up bass; you can't play that in a rock & roll band." Patrick laughed, and so for the first time in his life, my nephew became not a spectator. The reason he became not a spectator—this is something I don't quite understand about what Richard said—is that being on stage was not like being off stage. It was scary. It was dangerous. He didn't know what was going to happen next. Anybody who has had to speak in public has probably had a dream the night before about what happens when you get up to speak. Usually you forgot to get dressed. For my nephew getting up on stage was living out this dream every night. Then there would come the moment when that fear would break away, and something new would happen. Now, what I am saying, is that that was an experience lived out by an unbelievable number of people all over the world. Now I am talking specifically about a few people getting up on stage and trying to get something across—no longer living as spectators. I'm talking about something that comes together and happens. People are trying to make it happen all the time; it rarely turns into culture—into a moment that we can come together and talk about and understand what we mean. All I am saying is that I think it is important to know just for your own sense of satisfaction and delight in life, that those incidents come again. Take advantage of them when they come because they are rare. [applause]

AUDIENCE: I never saw you at CBGB's.

MARCUS: I live in Berkeley, and I don't come out to CBGB's to catch a band. Things happen all over the place; you don't have to be in New York to seize the moment. [applause]

AUDIENCE: *(to Malcolm McLaren)*   Didn't you just tap into something that was already there?

MALCOLM McLAREN: It was a real gift, because I didn't sell anything. You pretend there was a group, but there wasn't really. It was just an attitude. People were surprised that the attitude was much bigger than the group, and that ultimately sold itself. I just lit the fuse, that is all. I was an agent provocateur.

AUDIENCE: There's a difference between real involvement and exploitation?

SAVAGE: Yes, of course. I think that in every moment of pop culture there are opportunists, and there are the people who really want to make things happen. I think there is always a much lower percentage of people who want to make things happen, than who are opportunistic. So in fact what you are saying is right, but I would say that Malcolm was someone who wanted to make things happen. It doesn't have to do with the money.

AUDIENCE: *(to Greil Marcus)* Doesn't the quote you read by Joe Strummer suggest that he thinks it's all pointless?

MARCUS: In his quote, as I read it, that is not what he meant at all. The interviewer is saying, "Oh come on, didn't you know how ridiculous that idealistic crap was?" And Strummer starts off by saying, "Yeah, I guess I should have," and then he comes back within two sentences and says "But without being fanatical, nothing would have happened"—meaning, "I wouldn't have anything ever to say. 'Hey, I was here.'" That is how I read it.

SAVAGE: Whether they are idealistic or opportunistic, people who were punks probably still remember it as a high spot in their life. Now I think that is a good thing. If you want to disagree with that, do! [applause]

AUDIENCE: Aren't we killing off punk by talking about it? Isn't all this just about selling something?

TAYLOR: That is similar to the remarks we have heard from the floor and from the panel about us being theoreticians. Richard called all of you academics, even though I find it hard to believe. It's a similar thing. It is all terribly commercial, and there is a loss of idealism. I wonder if Richard could talk about...did you make a lot of money, Richard?

HELL: I wouldn't be here if I made money.

AUDIENCE: Wasn't punk really just about fashion?

HELL: When we were first coming out—the way we looked and everything—the message was, "Look the way you feel." It wasn't, "Look like me." Belief in yourself against the forces of convention and repression and dishonesty—it's there in the music. If you try to turn it into an abstract theoretical description, it sounds clichéd. You can't even hear it, because words are too amorphous.

AUDIENCE: How does "marketing" relate to the claims of authenticity and self-expression that are made for punk?

SAVAGE: You have this very peculiar packaging on one side and this inauthenticity. As a pop culture principle, I have to say that I really like inauthenticity. I don't like authenticity in popular music; I don't think it works. I think Bruce Springsteen is possibly the most inauthentic person I have ever seen because I don't believe him. And what I was trying to say was that on one side, or all mixed together (however you want to look at it), you have this real shameless exploitation, and on the other, you have this really quite fundamental energy that has to do with a wish for change, with politics, with a small "p." If you are talking about squatting, for example, if you want to go into the social history of it—one of the things that fueled punk rock in 1976 was the availability of a lot of squatting land in the center of London where kids could live very cheaply. One of the reasons punk rock is not happening in London now is that people cannot live anywhere in central London. They can't move around like pinballs on a pin table. It's the same thing that is happening here—Yuppification. The places where people used to squat have turned into flats selling for seventy thousand pounds. So, yeah, of course it is important, and I wouldn't wish to sell anybody short. I think it is all mixed up.

HELL: Once you start taking into account the expectations of the audience, it gets very awkward. That is part of the reason why I stopped playing, because I found myself having to take into account what they expected of me, and I didn't know how to deal with that. It's really confusing. You don't want to let it influence you, but you know that you are speaking from that history, and you've got to modify what you do in order to make what you mean really clear, especially when it is a pop cultural thing—when half of your messages are being warped by the way they are presented anyway. Whether it is by stupid interviewers or stupid advertisements by the record company, you don't have any control over those things. The points that are being picked up aren't really the significant ones, so I kind of withdrew from that arena. I also saw that the Sex Pistols were doing what I wanted to do—what I sort of initiated—better than I could have. I don't want to be put in a position of disappointing people's expectations. That is part of what is difficult about rock & roll if you have a mission, instead of going out and trying to be stylish and popular. You are working in a medium that is really contrary to your intentions. Maybe when you are brand new it can work for a minute.

TAYLOR: Richard, is this to say that as an artist you should aim to be more in control of the means of your work's distribution and presentation?

HELL: Absolutely. Anybody wants that.

TAYLOR: So the artist has to be more of an entrepreneur?

HELL: No, that doesn't follow, but I thought it was kind of a challenge to figure out a way to send out the message that I wanted via those channels, like the haircuts I was talking about—the influence. I think that is what Malcolm does. He looks at how the media operates and takes advantage of it. I have mixed feelings about Malcolm and his operation, but I do think it's fascinating.

TAYLOR: So we come to the area of merchandizing. Stephen Sprouse was being criticized for presenting an advertisement, but in fact, maybe this is the way to control your image.

AUDIENCE: What about Vincent Van Gogh? He wasn't an entrepreneur.

TAYLOR: Today, Vincent Van Gogh is just a little germ of an idea in the corporate world.

SAVAGE: I don't think that Vincent Van Gogh is just a little blip in the corporate world, I have to say. I just disagree with that statement.

MARCUS: I would love to say something about newness and novelty. I think that one of the most wonderful things that can happen in life is a shared moment when things seem absolutely new, when you say to yourself, "nothing like this has ever happened before." That is the basic feeling of falling in love, right? There have never been feelings like this before! No one has ever felt the way I feel. Of course, you know people have. This doesn't convince you for a second. There are moments when you know you are witnessing something that never happened before; it's amazing, so marvelous, you will never be able to explain it to somebody who wasn't there. Well, in scientific terms there is no such moment. You find out after that moment has passed that it has a rich and convoluted history. If you want to go back and find that history, you are going to find out a lot about who you are, how you came to be, and where you may end up. Richard went on a different path. He began in the past and moved forward. History was clear to him in advance. But those moments of newness —it's a fallacy on the one hand, on the other hand it's what you live for. And that is a very different kind of thing than, "What is the band this week?" That is not newness; that is not even novelty. That is an assembly line, and once a week the bell is supposed to ring. Newness and novelty have to do with shock. "My God, what's going on!" I mean, it's an old metaphor. It will never wear out. Like the metaphor that Jon used about rock & roll in England in 1955, it was as if some Martian spaceship landed. That is a great metaphor about what it felt like when rock & roll arrived, whenever and wherever it arrived. It felt like it came from Mars. It was that strange and that weird. Nothing angers me more than reading musicological studies where someone has traced the genesis of rock & roll back to the blues and country and whatever, and as you are reading the chronology, there is no moment when there was a breach, when something happened. When everybody suddenly turned around and said, "Wow, the world seems different today." Instead, A - B - C - D. And that isn't what life feels like. You can prove it, but it is not going to be true. That is all I want to say about novelty. Those moments are rare. I keep saying the same thing, but that is because I go back, I listen to the records that were made in London in '77 and '78, and my mouth drops open every time, and I wonder why is it so hard just to make that happen? It's complicated.

AUDIENCE: Did you enjoy yourself at the time?

HELL: I had a great time, and I'm having a good time now. Of course, I am always very suspicious of good times....

MARCUS: I had a great time. I think I might have a great time next year, but this year is something else.

SAVAGE: I am the same as Greil. I had a great time. I might have a great time next year.

McLAREN: I think it's always been dreadful. From the day I've been born it's been a dreadful life, and I am still looking for somewhere to go, everyday, and it gets harder. Unlike most artists, I decided that it wasn't cool to care because it's all too dreadful. As far as I am concerned, the more hell I can create, the happier I will be. [applause]

But you have to realize that the terminology of "good" and "bad".... We are constantly rewriting what these words actually mean. I mean, the word "anarchy" crept into a child's dictionary in 1976. It probably didn't exist before then, except in clouds of books, a long, long time ago. The notion of "bad" is affixed to Michael Jackson today. But if you don't want to be like Michael Jackson, you've got to look "good" and make that sound subversive. In England, we have a very simple work ethic. You are brought up by your parents to listen to them. Then you go to school, and you listen to your teachers. Then you go to work and you listen to your employer. If you didn't want to work from the day you were born you don't want to fucking listen to anyone—my criterion was to do that and do it well.

I am constantly having to reinvent those terms for myself. Harboring under the clouds of opera allows me perhaps to be more passionate than otherwise.

I haven't really been to an opera, to be quite honest. I do think that Carmen is an excellent character. She's an icon, and I think she is probably more interesting, where I am coming from, than perhaps Madonna or Annabella or John Lydon.

This fantasy that everybody has, that they have to go out and start revolutions. You don't. Let it start and join it. I don't think you go out often to start it yourself. Sometimes you can join in. I'm joining the opera crowd. They may not like me. [applause]

The thing that nobody understands in this audience is this idea of stealing things. Stealing things is a glorious occupation, particularly in the artworld. To be able to steal Jesse Jackson's speech and turn that into something else—I think that is as admirable a kind of thinking today as it was yesterday. If you turned Jesse Jackson's speech into a fantastic rap record, I think it would probably have a great deal of value, maybe even more than Public Enemy.

AUDIENCE: How does The New Museum Show fit into your project?

McLAREN: The exhibition is not my exhibition. That is a museum deciding to put on an exhibition about the things that I have done—I am not the designer of the show, and I am not the curator of the museum—for you and others to look at and gain some opinion. In terms of your question about what I have done—I was there. I think that is sufficient.

TAYLOR: We were all here. I thank you. One lesson that we all might have learned is that despite the fact that this symposium is all taking place within the context of the fashion and art industries, ideas and issues are being contemplated. It is up to the rest of you to decide whether ultimately that is academic. Thank you.

—September 24, 1988

TRANSCRIPT OF DISCUSSION WITH SPEAKERS AND AUDIENCE MODERATED BY PAUL TAYLOR, SEPTEMBER 24, 1988 AT THE FASHION INSTITUTE OF TECHNOLOGY, NEW YORK. CO-SPONSORED BY THE NEW MUSEUM OF CONTEMPORARY ART AND THE FASHION INSTITUTE OF TECHNOLOGY.

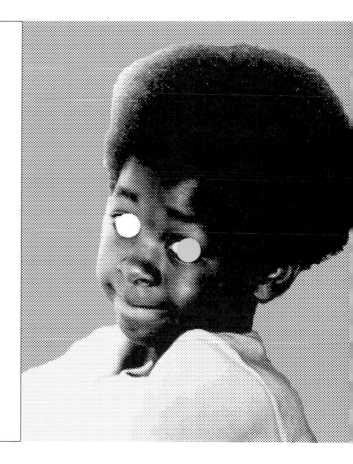

GIRLS RAPPIN' ROUND TABLE

Roxanne Shante, Millie Jackson, Sweet T, Sparky D,
Yvette Money, Ms. Melodie, Peaches, Synquis,
and Jill Pearlman

JILL PEARLMAN: Why did it take women until now to break through as rap artists?

MS. MELODIE: It wasn't that the male started rap, the male was just the first to be put on wax. Females were always into rap, had their little crews and were known for rocking parties, schoolyards, whatever it was. Females rocked just as hard as males rocked.

M.C. LYTE: We have a lot of obligations, right? Like, uh, help me out, girls...children...because just like in business....

MILLIE JACKSON: You've got to prove yourself double.

LYTE: There you go.

JACKSON: Rap has been conceived as a male thing, like it's unladylike to be dissin' somebody. So that's a natural turnoff for males, who are usually in charge of the money.

PEARLMAN: So there hasn't been much change in the generations, is that what you're saying?

LYTE: That sums it up.

SWEET T: They'll say something like, "Hey, you good for a girl." [Pandemonium]

SYNQUIS: Like all the guys are dope. [Laughter]

JACKSON: Hey, you punch good for a girl, too.[Laughter] I was talking about the people who have to promote you, the people holding the purse strings. You see more money going towards the male groups than the female groups.

EVERYBODY: Yup, yeah, yeah.

SWEET T: Guys always had the upper hand.

JACKSON: In my time they said, okay, that's a good group, but hey, they gonna get pregnant, and then you have to redo all of that.

EVERYBODY: Yeah, yeah.

JACKSON: It's a bad investment.

ROXANNE SHANTE: That's what I went through, 'cause I have a vulgar show. Yeah, I use very vulgar language and my stage show is quite different from my regular personality, and everyone always says, "the things you say, my God!..." [Pandemonium] So usually I go through a lot of that, "My God, why you talking like that?" And I say, "Well, those are things you say to get paid."

JACKSON: Right.

SHANTE: 'Cause if I get up there and I be nice, they be like, that's Shante? They expect me to get up there and just go off, so I go off.

JACKSON: The whole idea is you have to do something different, or you're just another ordinary singer, just another ordinary rapper. You've got to give them what they expect.

PEARLMAN: Did record companies not take you seriously as rappers, just think it was a gimmick?

SYNQUIS: That's what they always do to girls. They down with the males.

JACKSON: That's the same thing they said about me: it's a gimmick.

SYNQUIS: You've got to prove yourself. It's hard on girls when it comes to record companies. You've got to prove yourself first before the record company be one hundred percent behind you, before you record.

SHANTE: I don't know, I didn't go through that.

JACKSON: But I think rappers had to prove themselves in general, male or female. First you have to prove yourself as a rapper, then as a rapping female.

PEARLMAN: Is there group spirit among females or is there more competition?

SHANTE: Me and Sparky, as far as shows, we're like the super super rivals, okay, and I mean, we have said things to each other...[laughter]...I mean, that Millie wouldn't even say.

SPARKY D: I want to tell you that I have called myself the Millie Jackson of rap. I shouldn't tell you, but that's true. I have to shake your hand. [Gets up to shake Millie's hand.]

JACKSON: Well, thank you darlin'.

SHANTE: We wind up realizing we're in this to win, we're in this to make money, so we figured we'd team up together rather than she be in Texas one night and I in Colorado. Instead we say fuck it, we both get together and go to Texas. Stay together, get on the same bus, go some place else, do it again.

SPARKY: Exactly.

SHANTE: And as far as having babies, it doesn't hold back anything. It doesn't. Because I have a son.

SPARKY: And I just had a brand newborn child.

JACKSON: And I got two.

SPARKY: I have a beautiful daughter.

LYTE: Aahhh. Everybody together now, oooooaaaaah .

EVERYBODY: Ooooaaaah.

SHANTE: It makes your job; it makes you strive that much harder, to know that you have to succeed so they won't say, "See, I told you she was just a girl, she got pregnant, she had a baby and it's over." As to where they can say, "Well damn, she's really doing a lot, she's a mother, she does shows, she makes records, and got time to show her face in the place." You know what I'm sayin'?

PEARLMAN: Do you take your son on tour?

SHANTE: Everywhere. He's a strict hip-hopper. It's in the blood. He sleeps all day, stays up....

SPARKY: ...all night, so does mine. I'm starting on tour July 1st. My daughter's coming with me everywhere. When she's one year old, I'm gonna put her little voice in an Emulator. Her name's Little Sparky. Okay, like Shante said, she and I got a little rival thing that will always be like that, but if she needs help, she can always dial my telephone number, I will help her. But other girl rappers, I speak to all of them. Most of them say, "Sparky, how you do this, how you do that?" And I will explain, give them the inspiration. For example, Sweet T. I did that for her ever since she made her record. Okay, Salt 'n Pepa, "Sparky, come to my dressing room, show me how to do this, how to do that." Now they're the number one female rappers, who knows if they're gonna say hi to Sparky. There's animosity here, it's like, we gotta beat Sparky D, I have to beat Sweet T. Because they're only a few girls...girls are bitches and that's just how it is. You just got to put it down to the bottom line, to sum the whole thing up. But that doesn't mean I'm not gonna wish everybody luck.

SWEET T: I haven't done shows with you guys, but we just did a show with Finesse and Synquis and Lyte. When we go on the road, there's no problem. We get off the plane, to the hotel, hit the shopping area, you know what I'm sayin', all of us together.

LYTE: Get bombed after the show.

SHANTE: Some people keep it hidden.

SPARKY: I was gettin' ready to say that, Shante.

SHANTE: They be frontin' each other. It's there.

SPARKY: It's just women, period. I come in, okay, you dressed up, you with your man, okay, and I'm goin' out with mine. Okay, we're friends, and I go, what you wearin'? You say, "I'm wearin' my Louis Vuitton suit." You think I'm not gonna put on my Gucci suit? You know, it's gonna be like that. We're all women. Who got long hair, who got extensions, who got more jewelry, who got the Gucci suit? Oh, she got them phony shoes on. [Laughter]

JACKSON: But men do the same thing. We just talk about people in general. When you're on the road, and you have nothing to do, you get bored, you gossip.

PEACHES: It seems like the guys don't act like that, it seems like they get along.

SHANTE: Yes they do. I'm gonna tell you, I was on tour with Def Jam, and it's more envious between guys than it is with anyone else.

PEACHES: But the guys, if the guys don't like each other, they're still hanging together. The girls, they don't like you, they ain't gonna be with you.

SPARKY: It's just like basketball. After the game, we all drink Bud.

PEARLMAN: Who's the queen of rap? On your records, you've probably each claimed it. [Pandemonium]

SPARKY: There's no queen. On everybody's record, they be queen.

PEACHES: I guess everybody's their own queen.

LYTE: That's what rappin' is. You top bill yourself.

JACKSON: Queen is in the eye of the beholder.

SPARKY: Run-DMC's got the money. So do LL. So do Whodini. There's enough money to be made, I feel nobody's the queen. Whoever's the queen, speak up. [Laughter]

JACKSON: I'm queen. I'm queen. I don't rhyme when I rap. My rap is not rap rap. It's talk rap.

SPARKY: And that's where I learned my rap, from talkin'. And listenin' to your records, Millie. "Love of Life" and "Search for Tomorrow."

SHANTE: I've mocked her maybe once or twice. When I started out rapping, right, by me being so young, so little, everybody always used to say, "she's so cute [Shante pinches her cheek], she's so this," then when they hear me talk, they'd be like....

LYTE: What a mouth.

SHANTE: You know, that's the reason why my show's the way it is. I don't have to prove that no more, I've grown up now. But before it was to get rid of that cute little girl act. Finally, I just broke out of the shell.

JACKSON: She must be on drugs, that's what I get, she gotta be high.

SHANTE: It's a different part of me that gets up there and does all that.

PEARLMAN: How do you feel about anti-female raps, which are sometimes violent? They're calling girls skeezers, always on guys' jocks?

SHANTE: Those are those women, these are these women.

PEACHES: We got rhymes talkin' about guys.

SWEET T: You don't take it personally. You talkin' about somebody else.

PEARLMAN: Do you ever want to respond as women?

LYTE: I do my stuff, they do theirs.

JACKSON: They're probably referring to the band bandits, that's the name I have for the groupies.

SWEET T: They're something else, let me tell you. After the shows, at the hotel, the police come lookin' with pictures, knock on the guys' hotel door, is this girl with you?

LYTE: They almost beat my DJ up 'cause one of these guys' sister was in his room and the guy was standing in front of my DJ's door waiting for his sister to come out.

PEARLMAN: How about the reverse?

SWEET T: It's girls that come, and they want to ask you this and ask you that.

SPARKY: The guys just look at you, and they know better not to knock at your door.

PEARLMAN: Are they afraid of you?

SPARKY: I guess so.

LYTE: 'Cause girls are bitches and we'll tell you, get the hell out of here.

JACKSON: Not only that, I think it's what you do. Back to that non-feminine act. Because in my case, it used to be like that. When I was pregnant, a guy came up to me and said, "Oh, you're pregnant. I thought a man would have to knock you down to knock you up." [Silence. OOOHHHHH. Laughter]

LYTE: I think I would have hit him.

JACKSON: Well, I was pregnant, you know. See you when I drop it, fella.

SHANTE: I know, 'cause it's different for girls. You know you can't go out there skeezin'. And there'll be some cutie pies, oh, my God. The guy from out of town, with the big chain that you never even seen before, it look like a turtleneck. And he just be on yours because he seen you on stage and he want to make an impression on his friends. And he comes backstage, you know, and he just...sits there, and oh, my god, you just be....

LYTE: Pulls out his money, countin' it and stuff.

SHANTE: You be sittin' there and you be like—No...No...I can't...I can't. Whereas if it was the other, vice versa, the guy would be like, Yo, I am gonna skeeze.

SPARKY: The guys that you are traveling with are watching too. Like, seen him coming a mile away.

PEARLMAN: Why can't you?

SHANTE: Because it's not ladylike. And they just dying to say something.

LYTE: You can't give the public that chance.

SPARKY: Sometimes the other guys on the tour, the other people on the show, they be watching who comes out your door, they be saying, "Oh, LL came out of Shante's room."

SHANTE: What an example, right?

SPARKY: That's no hype, right?

MELODIE: Could I interject? Guys don't approach a female rapper like a girl would do a male, because they look at you on a different level. They look at you as being a homegirl, that's my homegirl, that girl is bad, they just really want to give you a compliment.

SWEET T: Sometimes they be too scared.

SYNQUIS: If you're gonna go to that party like Shante was saying—if you go there, the drug dealer is sittin' there lookin' all fly. If you fucked him, [nervous laughter] when you got back to New York, oh, she went with so and so.

PEARLMAN: So it's gossip that stops you.

JACKSON: No, it's AIDS.

PEACHES: Guys do it, anyway, though, in or out the business. Guys just do it, girls don't.

PEARLMAN: Doesn't it make you angry?

EVERYBODY: Yes, yeah.

SYNQUIS: Sometimes you wish you was a guy.

SPARKY: My husband [Spyder D] is a rapper, and it's rough. I go and he goes on the road, 'cause he has his own career. The shit is just hard. He just did a video, okay? You know what I'm doing at home? Where's my video? I want a video, too. You did a video, I want a video. He took beautiful pictures at the Seaport. Why I don't take pictures? You get jealous. It's just too hard.

JACKSON: You got nerve. You got nerve, because if you and him don't make it, now what? You done fucked up your bedroom, your career and everything all in one fuckin'. Not me, I got to separate my apples.

SWEET T: My boyfriend [Joeski Love] is also a rapper. And I went on the road with him when he was touring, you know, and I stood there and I watched him, the girls come up and I stand back and watch him take thirty, forty, fifty pictures, they're huggin' him, and they're this and they're that, and I stand back. But now that I'm doing shows, he can't come. You know, because he can't stand back like I can do. Like, people want to come, ask questions, whatever. He won't accept the same thing that people are gonna want to talk to me. He's like, oh I saw you do that on stage, what's up with that, your pants are too tight, what are you doing?

SPARKY: I can't shake. I can't use that record when I say, "Sparky D has a big butt." That's my show.

PEARLMAN: And you took it out?

SPARKY: No. It's my world. He got to live in Sparky D's world.

SWEET T: And it's the same thing. He don't go, so he doesn't know what happens.

SPARKY: But I must admit he put his career in front of mine. But there's the argument everyday, you really think this is your fuckin' world.

JACKSON: Good luck.

MELODIE: I just wanted to say, girl fans are more emotional....

SYNQUIS: They want to scream and cry.

MELODIE: Girls want to be down more than guys want to be down. They want to have that sense of belonging. I am married to a male rapper [Chris Parker, KRS-1 of Boogie Down Productions]. My experience of being on the road with Chris, I'm like, a female can come up to you, can hug you, do what you want to do, sign whatever you want to sign. My gripe is I don't want a female to kiss you. I mean, who is she?

SHANTE: Melodie stands at the hotel door and say, listen, the fans stop here. You can give all the autographs you want, coming up in the elevator, but the fans stop right here.

MELODIE: Yeah, they have to. I mean, the females can do what you want to do, but as long as I'm here, don't disrespect me. Because when you disrespect me, then I have to act like a street person, get ignorant, you know what I'm saying? We have our limits, and he knows what to do and he knows what not to do, you know.

PEARLMAN: Do you care about being ladylike, or do you feel that you're carving a different image for women?

JACKSON: I don't give a shit about image.

SPARKY: I gonna tell you, I'm not all woman on stage.

PEARLMAN: What are you? [Laughter]

SPARKY: I'm all woman, physically.

JACKSON: Not feminine.

SPARKY: Exactly. I don't want to deal with female. Female is soft. Female is a fruit.

MELODIE: Let's define that, Sparky. What a woman is and what a lady is. Now you can be a woman, and be yourself like you are all the time. A lady is when you have the door opened for you.

SPARKY: A lady is a Gold Lucky Smile Rapper. What are you smilin' for? I don't smile at all.

JACKSON: It's entertainment, so whatever you're talking about, you're supposed to be demonstrating what you're saying. So how you goin' be saying, (through a smile) "You ain't shit, I don't like you." [Laughter]

SPARKY: I can't, I don't sound soft at all. I'm hard. I wake up and I go, [hard] hello. I never talked soft in my life.

YVETTE MONEY: I just recently did a show in Philly for an after-prom, and I haven't heard the last of it yet. This guy, he was in front of the stage and he called me a b....

JACKSON: ...A bitch?

LYTE: [laughing] I was about to say the same thing.

YVETTE: So I took his head and put it between my legs and told him to suck it.

LYTE: Oh, no you didn't.

YVETTE: People was like, and my manager was like, wait a minute, you can't be doing that kind of stuff. But when people do things like that to you, you don't know how to react.

SHANTE: I get that all the time.

SYNQUIS: You just do what you gotta do.

JACKSON: Suppose he had done it for real?

YVETTE: He didn't want to take his head out of there, really.

SHANTE: As far as I'm concerned, I am the most dogged female rapper there is. And I think so because I've had records and records made about me and everyone of them is on a negative slant. I have not heard one positive. [Pandemonium]

PEACHES: Nuh uh. Steady B said I like you. I be following you to school, this and that, and you said, yo, who are you, you dissed him.

SHANTE: Listen to this, though, I get dogged. I get everything from Roxanne Shante ain't nothing but a project ho. Shante is only good for steady fucking, Shante this, Shante that....

SPARKY D: You'd be mad if nobody was talking about you. When somebody's talking about you, don't worry, they making you money. When they not talking about you, then you worry.

JACKSON: Do you know you were the first woman rapper I ever know of, because they were talking about you?

SHANTE: I mean, but man, it's like, then to have my mother hear stuff like that, you know what I mean.

PEACHES: That's hard.

SHANTE: That's what really makes it hard, otherwise I don't care. I mean, every show I go to I'm usually called, yo fuck that bitch, and then they expect me to reply because that's what they want me to do, you know? They come to my shows for me to dis someone, and if my show goes too smoothly, then someone will make sure things get a bumpy ride. And then when my mother starts hearing things like that....

YVETTE: My father hasn't heard the X-rated side of "Yvette's Revenge" yet, and it's been four years.

JACKSON: My stepmom, not my real mom, is a born-again Christian.

EVERYBODY: Hummmmm.

JACKSON: She'd say, "You are doing this and you are doing that." I said, "You're just as guilty as I am, do you know this is paying for that. If I was you, I couldn't live in that house. You know who's paying that mortgage?" And all of a sudden it's a whole different outlook.

PEARLMAN: Like in male rap, is there the same kind of tension about being soft for you?

SPARKY D: Yes, you have to come hard.

SWEET T: You get stepped on.

SPARKY D: You come soft, you get booed off the stage, okay. You have to start hard, okay, like I said again, you can't smile anymore.

PEARLMAN: Does everybody feel femininity is soft?

OTHERS: No, no.

SHANTE: It depends on your show. If I was to get up there in a pair of shoes and a dress, I'd be over.

SPARKY D: So would I.

SHANTE: First time I get up there get ready to do this and my dress split and I fall on my shoes, you know what I'm sayin', I'd be over.

LYTE: Sometimes you have to draw a line on how hard you get, 'cause I seen a couple girls perform and it's like, Yo! and they be like beboppin' on the stage, and I was like, whoo. I think that sort of turns off the guys a little bit.

SPARKY D: Exactly. In your show you have to know how to deal with the women and the men. Women like me more than the men.

LYTE: That's a bit of a problem, isn't it?

SPARKY D: You know why? Men like me the way I come out, okay, and women like me cause I tell the men, you ain't shit, okay. You dress like a woman, you wear tight clothes and show your body. You get the men by the way you dress, you get the women by telling the women the men ain't shit.

PEARLMAN: Do some men think the tough act is sexy?

EVERYONE: Yes, yeah, yup.

LYTE: Gives them a challenge.

JACKSON: They get that mother image way back in the subconscious mind.

SYNQUIS: But some men don't like girls acting harder than they are. They think if we go out she probably beat me down.

JACKSON: The men can handle that, sweetheart. It's the boys who don't know how to deal with that.

SWEET T: There's so many different things you've got to look at, try to draw a fine line on all of them to come across as—yourself.

PEARLMAN: Where do you think female rappers are going?

SHANTE: We're all going to hell, we curse too much....

SPARKY D: To the top.

SWEET T: No place else to go.

SHANTE: They got a dope shoe store called Puss 'n Boots about five blocks from here, that's where I'm heading after I leave here. I'm out of Soho and I'm going in that direction.

YVETTE: I think everybody should stick together now.

SHANTE: I'm glad you said that. You want to know why most female rappers don't stick together? My concept of it is because nobody really wants to see anybody be better than them. You know, you don't want to see where you've been rappin' and all of a sudden somebody comes out, like this, Kaya! It hits you hard.

PEARLMAN: Do you feel Salt 'n Pepa took your place?

SHANTE: Okay, as far as my place, I'm a solo rapper, they in a totally different category. I'm not one for talking about anybody, it's in my blood 'cause I'm a girl, girls gossip. But still, um, I'm not one for talking about anybody, but as far as Salt 'n Pepa, they're not rap artists now, they're pop artists. There's a big difference. Ever go to Latin Quarter and want to, ah, push it, come on, it wouldn't come off. But the only reason it come off is because the radio station made it grow on you.

EVERYBODY: Right, yeah.

SHANTE: When you listen to the album, you skipped that record. Now you have to think, damn, you got to start thinkin' like them. If they like wack shit, then we all gotta get wack. Just for a moment, just to get one cut per album, and that would be the cut to make everything go platinum, because they like it wack.

SPARKY D: Just like Sweet T and Lyte and everybody said, oh boy, Salt 'n Pepa again. It was hard for me to go back from the rock bottom, then see Salt 'n Pepa, everybody constantly talking about Salt 'n Pepa. But then again it wasn't, because those girls asked me to help them, and I feel I helped them a helluva lot. They kept asking, "Could you help me, could you help me?"

JACKSON: Do you think they're gonna admit that?

SPARKY D: No, okay, it's my world and they're living in it, and you can tell them Sparky D said that. [Pandemonium]

SHANTE: Everybody needs stepping stones.

SPARKY D: Everybody keep talkin' about Salt 'n Pepa as the queens. Only reason why is nobody had a record out when they were out. And they was at the right place at the right time.

MELODIE: Thank you for saying that, they took advantage....

LYTE: ...of the situation, that's what you gotta do.

SYNQUIS: It was the time.

SHANTE: During the time Salt 'n Pepa came out, I was pregnant.

SPARKY D: During the time Salt 'n Pepa came out, my mother died, and I went rock bottom.

SYNQUIS: When they came out, I was just startin', I was like on studio time.

LYTE: When they came out, I wasn't even listening to rap.

SPARKY D: Everybody's Salt 'n Pepa, Salt 'n Pepa, Salt 'n Pepa, that's kind of upsetting to my nerves, I'm not gonna lie, they're very beautiful girls, but when it's time to come on stage....

SYNQUIS: Everybody's on their own.

MELODIE: When they came out with "I'll Take Your Man," I was gonna come out with an answer record, "I'll Kick Your Ass," it just never, I was like, fuck that, I ain't with that, you know, my style is basically rockin' the party.

YVETTE: I think we should stick together as well as the guys, too, to make rap grow because people keep knockin' rap.

LYTE: I'm sick of constantly being reminded, "I opened up these doors for everybody." I'm sick of hearing that, the doors would have been opened sooner or later.

SYNQUIS: Yo, it's gonna be like that every day. Me and Finesse, it's harder on us because we're the next like, female team. They're callin' us like ketchup and mustard. I was like, we're sugar and spice, how's that? They were like ooohhh, why don't we have them battle? They just want to see you battle, they want to see you knock the competition down. Ain't gonna be no battles, you know what I'm sayin', they good, we good.

YVETTE: You have a show with another female, people assume you're gonna battle, and you gonna hate each other and try to pull each other's hair out, and that kind of stuff.

SYNQUIS: And they want to see it.

LYTE: Yo, the first thing I said when I found out Sparky and Shante were comin', I was like, wait a minute, in the same room?

SPARKY D: People always see it like that, this is how it started.

SHANTE: We could do a show together today, and it would be packed just because of the old rivalry.

SPARKY D: Old rivalry, when we first met, it was May 4th.

SHANTE: Um, hum, I was scared to death, I thought she was gonna stomp me, I said, she's mad, y'all, she's mad.

SPARKY D: It was in Raleigh-Durham, there were about 8,000 people, and I tell you, I came on stage, okay, dissin' about everything. I cried, I couldn't get off stage, I couldn't move, nothin'. She came on stage screaming, crying at the same time. Everywhere we go, Sparky D and Shante, we even had shirts, with boxing gloves, okay. Even though we didn't like each other, okay, the same day we did that, in the studio, this girl asked me for $100 and I gave it to her.

SHANTE: And this bitch made me give it back.

SPARKY D: We been through hell. We been through hell, we scared of each other, and I tell you one thing, she taught me how to come on off the top of my head. I'll repeat it, there's no one better, she can come off the top of her head and talk about all of us at the same time. Okay, she taught me that, and I used to tell her, you have to get more into the audience. Like she helped me, I helped her.

SHANTE: Yeah, we did progress a lot together.

SPARKY D: Right to this day, if we go out and say, Shante and Sparky D is doing a show in Madison Square Garden, it will be jam packed.

SHANTE: Only 'cause they want to hear us get on stage and call each other bitches.

YVETTE: I'm just talking about us sticking together as far as, like, black people, as far as the ladies and the men, all of us should stick together, instead of always trying to knock each other out of the way.

SHANTE: I bet you this is one thing I can say, if we all went on a show out of town, and some Columbus, Ohio type bitches tried to roll on us, I think we all would be in there together. But as far as the industry, there's always competition.

SWEET T: If there's no competition, why isn't there one record label and everybody's on it? Record labels compete, everything is competition.

SHANTE: Word up, they talk about, she was so black she was marked absent at night.

SPARKY D: [to Yvette] Are you from Philly? See, that's why.

LYTE: You from brotherly love.

SPARKY D: New York is different. Rap was born here.

—Summer, 1988

REPRINTED FROM *PAPER* (SUMMER, 1988): 25-26.

Neil Bartlett went to New York and talked to the legendary drag queen Ethyl Eichelberger, and then he came back to London and repeated the questions he'd put to Ethyl to Lily Savage, current queen of the London drag scene. He invited the artists to speak by asking them very simple questions, making as few assumptions as possible about their relation to the usual terms of reference of *Performance*. Their acts have many points of coincidence; but they are artists working in completely different traditions and different cultures, and they know nothing of each other's work.

Ethyl Eichelberger is a character actor whose work is informed by an encyclopaedic knowledge of the early history of American vaudeville, burlesque, drag, and Yiddish Broadway. He plays both men and women, and has been a longstanding member of Charles Ludlum's Core. He is best known for a series of monologues in which drag drives head-on into radical performance entitled *Great Women of History.* The flamboyant but much maligned women (Nefertiti, Clytemnestra, Elizabeth I, Lucrezia Borgia) crash around on tiny painted stages, accompanying themselves on the accordion, shedding pounds of jewelry and giving us the dirt on their respective sexual politics and philosophies.

Lily Savage has been voted Entertainer of the Year two years running by readers of *Capital Gay*. She always plays the same character, and almost always wears a different frock. Accompanied by a stuffed fox called Skippy, Lily appears in towering wigs, thigh-length boots and the sort of rags that give Petticoat Lane a bad name. Her act is a semi-improvised barrage of chat, news items and plain filth, all delivered in a heavy Liverpudlian accent. She plays in gay pubs and clubs all over the country.

NEIL BARTLETT: Where do you come from?

ETHYL EICHELBERGER: Midwest, Illinois. I grew up on a farm.

BARTLETT: How did you start doing this?

EICHELBERGER: In the fifth grade. I played the witch in *Hansel and Gretel,* my mother made me a black crepe paper dress and a big black pointed hat and she put pink yarn on it for hair and I've never recovered. No actually it goes back even further than that. I believe that in a past life I was a man who played women's parts—in Ancient Greece, or I'm not sure if it was Greece, I have a feeling that it was that place that Phaedra was from, you know, Crete. Phaedra was the first character I played. I was in a repertory company, a very good company called Circle in the Square in Rhode Island,

and in the summers we would have time off and I would get very depressed; I need to work, and if I'm not working I just get very depressed and so in the summer I started doing *Phaedra* in the Robert Lowell translation, and I'm still doing it. I play all the parts and that's twenty-seven years that I've been doing that now. I love it.

BARTLETT: Do you think of yourself as working in a particular tradition?

EICHELBERGER: There's a whole group of things that have contributed to my work.... I think of myself as a tragedienne. If I have to wear a label then that's the label I would choose. I'm an American performer, and I say that to you not just because you're British, but I have to say it even louder here, because so little respect is paid by Americans to the American tradition—you know if you want a performing job you have to be able to work in a good British accent, they really prefer the British. What I come out of is, well, I was part of a song and dance team, where I grew up in the Midwest; when I was a kid I was a tapdancer, and I used to see (God this is showing my age) I used to see the travelling minstrel shows. I come out of a really grassroots performing tradition, and it is a living tradition, it's only the academics that give us trouble.

It's vaudeville, it's burlesque and it's Yiddish theater—those actors are especially important to me, you know that down here was Yiddish Broadway, especially their tragedy, that was an important tradition here in the East Village, on Seventh Avenue. People do view me more now as comedy, well if people think of me like that then that's fine, I've found that if they laugh then that gives me a chance to go on and perform. Let them laugh, it's fine.

Look, I don't say this to everybody, but I know you're sympathetic. I am a drag queen. You can put that down in quotes. I am a drag queen, that's who I am. So.

Of course I'm a drag queen working in the theater. Julian Eltinge, he was a great performer here, his theater still exists, it's a movie house now on Forty-Second Street; and then there's Burt Savage, who was his friend, he worked there in this theater [The interview took place in Charles Ludlum's Theatre of the Ridiculous. Billie Holliday also played there], he was in the Greenwich Follies, that wasn't a drag revue, but he was in it as a Follies girl. Who else do I think about?... Charles Renault, he was another Broadway performer. But you know I'm not just working in drag, I don't do just women, but you know if you look at any of the great burlesque clowns, the vaudeville clowns, many of our best comics, they've all done drag. You know there's a church here called the actors' church, a little Episcopalian church between Madison and Fifth, on Thirteenth Street. They call it the actor's church because in the early days of this country there was a famous actor, and no one would bury him, they couldn't find anyone to bury him. It was like Molière, nobody would have him, there was no consecrated ground that would accept him. And then this church accepted him, they buried him, and so it became the actors' church. Well I recently researched this story, and I found out that this man, this actor, the reason why they wouldn't bury him was that not only was he a blackface performer, he was a "black-faced wench," which means he played women's roles. There are ties everywhere. But you know this country has strange moral problems; it was created by Puritans, and because of that they've always tried to sweep the drag queens under the carpet, and to find them and to use all that in your work you really have to dig. Renault's picture, I have it in a picture book that shows the history of Broadway, and it shows this very beautiful woman and it doesn't even say it's a man, it doesn't mention that this was a man. But there are enough people always to keep the tradition alive. Drag performers have been more accepted into the artworld and in the worlds of rock & roll than in the theater. But that's not traditional drag like you get in the bars, it's Art, as opposed to just female impersonation.

BARTLETT: So where does your material come from?

EICHELBERGER: I'm a poet. I use this tradition and these historical characters to write my poetry; I'm a storyteller and in the telling of the story I invariably get my own work in, I make the work my own. If I'm telling the story of King Lear then I set it in this country, he owns a mountain, and I make it like Jimmy Carter, those terrible families, they own entire states and become Presidents and all the time they're saying "Oh I'm just a simple country boy." I'm not setting out to talk about who's running for the Senate. My material is dealing with politics in the terms of our lives, the lives of people I know.

BARTLETT: Why do you choose to play strong women?

EICHELBERGER: Your persona does change when you cross the sex barrier or whatever it is, but with me it's the opposite, even though the women I'm playing are strong, as a man I'm very hard, but the minute I become a woman…what works for me is something very soft and quiet. What I do best is become very vulnerable. Even though I'm over six foot tall.

I'm a character actress, so when I choose these women I choose them because they interest me historically. Nefertiti I chose because she wasn't Cleopatra you see, I'm not the leading lady, I'm a character actress. I choose to be the other woman. When I do the *Oresteia* I do it from Clytemnestra's viewpoint, not Electra's. Lucrezia I chose because she was so maligned, there was this woman who everyone says was so beautiful and her father was the Pope for God's sake and her brother was Cesare, who they wrote *The Prince* about, and they say she was such a lovely woman, so nice, and yet she was just used by her family, married off. Lucrezia was a pawn; I relate to women politically because they are second-class citizens. Nefertiti, I believe she didn't actually exist, I have this theory that it was just Aknhaten in drag, she didn't have to look like that statue at all, she was paying the artist, she just said make me beautiful.

BARTLETT: Do people ever tell you that your work insults women?

EICHELBERGER: Not any more. That was the seventies. The stupidity of that remark stands on its own. You say it and it bounces right back up and hits you—that someone who desperately wants to be part of that world is being insulting...you're saying I worship and I adore you and I would like to be like you—so. It's a very silly statement that I can put into one word: bigotry. It speaks for itself; say it and you stand there looking like a bigot.

BARTLETT: Are you playing a woman, or are you a drag queen, or an actress?

EICHELBERGER: I'm playing the parts. I don't think about anything else. I'm an actor, basically. I do the character on stage the best I can. It's no different for me if I play men or women, it's no different. You just go do it.

BARTLETT: Do people treat you as a woman?

EICHELBERGER: Sometimes. Yeah. When I'm lucky. People are very *nice* to me. I like it either way but I find that with me, the way that it happens to me is that when I'm dressed as a man no one ever kisses me, and the minute I put on drag people kiss me on the cheek, they kiss me on the chin—don't ever kiss me on the mouth because you'll smudge my makeup—they come up and kiss me and hug me and they never do that when I'm not in drag. I'm a hairdresser too, a theatrical hairdresser, and that opens doors for me, because then women really do open up for me. American women are taught to give attitude to a drag queen, they think it's competition or something silly. They open up to me more as a hairdresser, they'll open up to me, confide in me. They're more relaxed with that than with drag.

BARTLETT: Is she you?

EICHELBERGER: Do I change? No. No. Ethyl's my real name. And this tattoo is me. It's forever. (When Ethyl performs in backless classical robes, she displays a back entirely covered with a magnificent tattoo).

BARTLETT: Do you have a sexual relationship with your audience?

EICHELBERGER: It gets very confused. That is how some people see drag. If I see that coming then I always try to stop it; I've learned to do that. My drag is not sexual, it's political, if one has to label it. I've never had sex in drag. I'm not that interested, it doesn't make sense to me. Puh-leeze.

But people do relate to you sexually when you do drag. The other night, this man comes into my dressing room, we'd just got a standing ovation, I felt like a million dollars, and then he walks in and says to this other guy in my dressing room I bet you're glad you don't have to look like that, so I turned round and confronted him, I mean the fact that he would come backstage, at the Lincoln Center, to an actor who has just worked his ass off, and he thinks that I'm out there trying to pick up men. What did he think? Well he didn't think, he's just seen a woman and so he thinks I'm after their genitalia, oh please, get out of my dressing room and don't come back. Or get out there and buy a ticket and pay to see me act.

BARTLETT: Does playing in drag ever feel like an act of revenge?

EICHELBERGER: No. I've been lucky. I don't feel the need for revenge in my life. For me, stepping out on stage in drag is a way to get an audience, a way of setting myself up as an artist, of finding my own voice. When I was performing as a man people didn't really want to know but as soon as I put a frock on I had a packed house. And I just love feeling beautiful. It's not revenge, it's a fulfillment to know that I look so beautiful. Oh yes, I know I'm not a classic, I mean I'm not going to play Elizabeth Taylor. But when I play Nefertiti I do it in a real Fortuny gown, it's a real one. You feel beautiful even though you know you aren't.

BARTLETT: Who are your idols?

EICHELBERGER: Charles Ludlum is the great genius of my life. He has influenced more people in this city, more artists, more theater than anybody else.

I love Margaret Rutherford. She is one of my idols. I have millions of her movies. Well, I have several. Margaret Rutherford's son is a transsexual, that just happened a year or two before she died, and I read this quote, because you see I knew that she just had to be a wonderful woman, and she said, they asked her what she thought and she said, "We loved him as a man and now we'll love her as a woman." And she was a great actress.

Zasu Pitts, she was a silent movie actress, a great beauty, she was in Stroheim's *Greed*, and then when the talkies came she had this funny voice. But she didn't just drop down dead and die, she became a comedienne, playing these dotty crazy women. She did that in order to continue being an artist.

The drag performer I emulate is Lynn Carter, a great American drag, he did all the classic acts, Mae West, Marlene all of that; and he owned his own club in Provincetown and another club in the winter in Puerto Rico, and he did the Jewel Box review which toured all over this country. Besides being a great performer he was smart enough to keep his life together, he owned these clubs and put together this review and toured it. That's why I respect your Bette Bourne. She's not only a great actress, she keeps that company together, she creates work for people.

BARTLETT: Does your mother know what you do for a living?

EICHELBERGER: Oh yes. My parents are wonderful. I'm very lucky. I'm one hundred percent Amish Mennonite; they came from Germany via Alsace-Lorraine to this country, and they don't go to the theater at all. My parents left that community, they wanted to live in the world. And they wanted an artist in the family, so they've always supported me, they've seen me work in drag. They're glad that I'm happy and healthy.

BARTLETT: Do you work differently if you're in a theater instead of a club?

EICHELBERGER: I try to be universal—that's why I use historical characters. But you've got to be in both worlds, to keep on changing. You can't turn your back on either of them if you take your art seriously. Drag performers are always at the bottom of the totempole, but I choose to work with great performers, and the great artists aren't just downtown or uptown…you work in some fabulous, tacky, dismal bar, the next day you have to air your costumes because of the smoke, but you work with magnificent performers, and then you go uptown and you feel like you're at the Holiday Inn; but there are wonderful artists there too.

BARTLETT: Does it piss you off that the theater makes your work as a drag respectable?

EICHELBERGER: I'm a missionary. I do what I know I was born to do. I do it because it's what I am. I work with a lot of young people in the different places I work, different kinds of theaters and bars, young people who are chosen to be drags or whatever, anyone who is outside the normal world of the theater, and they'll come and find people like me, and I do not smoke, I do not drink, I try to show that you are responsible for what you do and say when you are on stage, it doesn't matter if somebody else wrote the words, and it's by virtue of all that the fact that I'm doing drag up at the Lincoln Center thrills me. I can turn to a young person and say, look, I'm up there, it can be done, if this is what you want to do. I'm there. They're not ashamed of me.

BARTLETT: Where would you like to play?

EICHELBERGER: I always said the Metropolitan Opera, and now here I am, right next door. The Met. Doing one of my own works. They're operas anyway. Actually I already have what I want. I have an audience. I've made that happen.

BARTLETT: Where do you come from?

LILY SAVAGE: From the docks. Birkenhead. I was brought up in Ireland though. My mother couldn't afford to give up working in the summer holidays and so I was packed off to me Aunties out in the west of Ireland. Milking a cow's fuck all to me, oh no. I didn't know what a toilet was, it was just up behind the hedge, and we didn't have no bath or nothing like that. I developed a hatred of dairy produce. I still can't eat butter, no way, I saw where it comes from, oh no, this bloody great tit covered in warts and dragging the milk out of it, I just can't touch the stuff. Oh it made me a bit delicate being brought up on the farm.

BARTLETT: How did you start doing this?

SAVAGE: Oh Christ. They used to have these things in the Black Cap, like talent nights, and they said why don't you get up one morning and have a go, so I did, and then somebody behind the bar said do you want to do a double act, and I thought, oh well I'll have a go, I thought it was just a doddle to get up there and give it a bit, you know, but it's not, I soon found that out. The whole thing of being Lily Savage started by mistake, because you know I never used to go on the mike, oh no, and I was in the Elephant and Castle on their amateur night thing and they said to me we haven't got a compère, please will you do it, so I got rat-arsed drunk and I just sat there, and like two hours later there was no sign of an act, nothing, it was just me up there going on about well first this happened and then that happened. I thought, well I prefer this to miming. I just went home and worked on it a bit. Everytime I work I say well you've done it again, you've got away with it; no really, I just stand there and waffle on about nothing. I think the thing about it was that no one else ever mentioned drugs, or talked frankly on stage about unemployment, or sex, and there I was on about oh we're busy tonight, must be Giro week and all this shit, and people actually come up to you and say to you I don't feel ashamed signing on now, and if you can do that then it's very nice, you're not just some snotty drag queen miming away or whatever, you're approachable, they can get hold of you and identify with you.

Of course I'd done about two hundred other jobs before that. I was the clerk of the court in a magistrate's court, and I tried to be a social worker. That was with Camden, I did that for three years, did me three year stint. I've always got me mother in mind you see, this is a Liverpool Catholic upbringing for you, saying now you've got a good job, you know, it's drummed into you, do you know what I mean, I remember when I was seventeen I went to the Civil Service and they told me its a marvellous job, bloody good pension, and I thought fucking hell I'm sixteen, I'm just not interested in being sixty-five, but anyway, I've always got that under my belt, I can always go back to being a social worker. It's nice to have something. I don't really want to be doing drag when I'm fifty.

BARTLETT: Do you think of yourself as working in a particular tradition?

SAVAGE: Well, there's a London style, and then there's a Northern style, you know, all off down the Oxfam and then fucking hell out comes the dildo and the pregnancy routines, all this hairy old stuff. It's Northern humor, Liverpool humor. I suppose what I do is just Liverpool. They say it's universal but it's not, Liverpool style, not at all. If I'm in the wrong environment then it doesn't go at all, if I'm at the Garden or at some place where they're all very posh and hooray they all go eh, what is this person on about, because they've never had to deal with things like that before, the type of things I'm talking about. I just change the act quick and I do it like I was somebody's cleaning lady, because they can relate to that. But it's not so much of a big act what I do, it's just this same character, people say it's like a relation that you never got to know but wish you had, I'm just on all the time about the family, the kids, having a drink, it's all low-key, it's all very school of hard knocks, just talking about how things are these days. Sometimes I come on a bit of the wicked witch, but I'm certainly not glam drag at all. If I'm wearing something stupid or outrageous then that's all the better for me. I only get embarrassed if I'm trying to wear some smart dress, do you know what I mean, if I've thought oh well I'll try on a bit of glam here, then I'm not happy at all. This is going to sound dead grand, but when I try and be the glam drag queen, forget it, complete wash out, I can't handle it, I just can't do all the posing and that, I just think get this fucking thing off me and give me me boots. I just don't feel right. Mutton dressed as lamb.

BARTLETT: So where does your material come from?

SAVAGE: All what I do when I do Lily is just do me mother and me Auntie. Like you know I was brought up in Liverpool and there's me Auntie lying on the couch, and I say what's up with you, and she says, oh I've just had me coil out, and it's so funny I was howling, and she says, what's so funny, and she's on about this coil, this part of her body that's been removed, and her doctor won't give her valium so she goes to another one that will, and so there you are talking about these seventy-year-old women doling out the vallies like hardened drug addicts, "how many have you got off yours?"—like everything I do is just the Liverpool thing, but blown up completely. That's where all the Catholic stuff comes from. Someone brought me one of these holy water fonts, hideous, it played "Ave Maria," and I went all to pieces, got it up on the mantelpiece and all that, and I went on about the Pope for a while, and then out comes the stopper and I started using it as scent, splash it on, do you know what I mean. Religion's a very heavy subject, but in Liverpool it's fucking murder. I was brought up in it. Don't talk to him he's Orange Lodge and all that crap. That's why Lily's kids [Bunty and Jason—Ed.] go to this Catholic school. She only goes to church to nick the candles—last time Lily was in church was when the electricity strike was on. And the reason she's always slagging off nuns is 'cause I was brought up by nuns. What a wicked breed of bitches they are I can tell you. Scarred me for life.

BARTLETT: Why do you choose to play strong women?

SAVAGE: Lily has to be a strong woman because she's surviving with her kids and the husband in nick and the alcoholic mother and all and this, that and the other, and like she is never miserable, she'll lose her temper and have a bit of a drink but she's a survivor basically. And that way I can kick off—I get frightened to talk about politics because I'm too ignorant when it comes to politics, but I'm constantly kicking off on Maggie and the lot of them. I get on my high horse and kick off if I think something's wrong, but I always do it as Lily, she's always onto the Giro, and how the heck am I expected to live on eighteen pounds a week and all this caper. I'd never do it myself, not as me. I never get political. I suppose I do kick off on the AIDS thing, and I do have a go at people's attitudes. I had a gang of straights in one night, it was a stag do, and they were saying "Come on sing us a song, he's getting married in the morning," and I said, "If I was in the straight pub tomorrow and my boyfriend and I said we've been together ten years would you sing us a song please, would you have a smiling compère saying of course love, of course lads, would you fuck, there'd be a mass fucking lynching," I said, "There's the door, fuck off, this is a gay pub." That's Lily coming out.

BARTLETT: Do people ever tell you that your work insults women?

SAVAGE: No. Funny enough I've had a couple of people but it was the men not the women. I'm not a misogynist, no way, like up in Liverpool you never say oh she's a dyke, she's a lesbian, you don't give a fuck, they're just there in the club with you. Down here I know it's totally different, "fucking dykes" and all that, but I can think of fifty gay men who I'd like to push under a bus and fifty dykes who are smashing. You do see some acts that go on about fish and all that kind of caper, it's fucking disgusting that kind of attitude, I mean to say that when you're dressed up as a woman, you're trying to emulate them. I know I go on about me coil and the PMS but I'm not doing it in an insulting way. I say "Do you take Feminax" but even when I do their heads in I'm not taking the piss, I'm trying to include them. Some acts are but I don't want to be tarred with that brush, I'm not misogynist, fuck off…if you say to straight men right we're having fancy dress on they come with great big balloons and the wife's skirt and it's fucking vile, but with gay men it'll be a bit more stylized, you know, smart. With a hat.

BARTLETT: Are you playing a woman, or are you a drag queen, or an actress?

SAVAGE :   I don't know. It's weird. I don't change when I get the gear on. The things I talk about aren't the things a fella would talk about, but they're not really the things a drag queen would talk about, 'cause I'm on about me PMS and me coil, women's complaints, but they're blown up out of all proportion…. I'm a professional, but what's a professional anyway, turning up on time or getting on a bit late and going down a storm. Some drag queens call themselves actors, and I know I've done a bit of Fringe stuff but if you've sold fruit and veg four times you don't call yourself a fruit and veg merchant. Drag queen I suppose I am. There's no way of getting round it, I'm just a drag queen. I don't set myself up to be a bird. I want to be a character, a cartoon character.

BARTLETT: Do people treat you as a woman?

SAVAGE: Oh yes, they come up and tell me everything, they come up with all sorts, I know more about broken affairs, who got this and who got that. It's nice, because people trust you, and they're very protective as well; if there's some trouble, if there's some straight who's pissed and who's starting, my god they get them out quick. And if I start the violence, a bit of verbal, you know if I kick off on somebody they love it, they go mental and the same people, if I'm dressed as a man, they won't talk to me, that's the weird thing. I get so many people come up for a little chat because they feel they can talk to her, and I listen to it all and then hit them over the head and tell them to fuck off, and off they go, nothing maudlin about it. Lily says "Can't pay your leccy bill? Oh fuck, I'll come round and make a hole in your meter and shove a pin in," and I would and all. Shove the needle in and don't get caught. That's Liverpool for you. I was brought up with a needle in the meter. I could never open the door in case it was the telly man or the Prudential. It's a joke. It's disgusting. All those pensioners who can only afford to have one bar on.

BARTLETT: Is she you?

SAVAGE: Lily is just me tarted up a bit. Tarted up a lot. If I get a bit stoned, out she comes with all the good advice, have a drink love and all that, that's just Lily. Basically it's just me being mental. Three years with Camden Council did me head in. Of course Lily Savage isn't gay. She's got two kids. She did have lesbian tendencies years ago, I mean she's tried it. I never take me wig off. Never go into the pub unless I'm in the full regalia, I can't stand all that take the makeup off and you're one of the boys.

BARTLETT: Do you have a sexual relationship with your audience?

SAVAGE: No way…those queens that can pass as women and all that they get straight fellas after them and all that. But the thought of going with a fella in drag…I mean when you get in bed and take the frock off, you've got two dirty great tits which is cottonwool, a pair of boots, eight pairs of tights and this enormous wig, I'm sure you're not going to have sex in all that. The only type of fellas I attract in drag is heavy masochists, they really want to be kicked around. I suppose it's the boots and riding crop. I just tell them to fuck off. No way. I don't think Lily Savage is sexy. She thinks she is. But no way. No chance. Shame isn't it really. Tragic.

BARTLETT: Does playing in drag ever feel like an act of revenge?

SAVAGE: Yeah, it's delicious. Sitting up there and slating off what you hate, in a packed pub, saying things, *bliss*, and they're all cheering, and they all feel the same way, and you can feel it, and they just need somebody to say it, yeah, lovely, when you're on about some wally like that James Anderton, just pulling him down, and you've got like two-hundred people full of scorn and derision for this man, and you're at the helm, it's lovely. Being a drag queen you've got so much shit to face. Fucking hell.

BARTLETT: Who are your idols?

SAVAGE: I love Jazz, me. George Melly. Nina Simone, people like that. I like Dame Edna, she makes me die, love her. I hate Cilla Black. Can't stand her. Can't bear her. I saw Dave Allen do Captain Hook in a panto, he got this kid down the front, this little boy and he says put out your hand, and he flicks his ciggy ash in it, and then he says you can sit down now, and I thought, oh god that's ace, that's really villainous doing that to a little child. I'll remember that. But I can't see Lily doing panto. All those ugly sister gags on Boxing Day in Wigan in front of a bunch of people you don't really like.

BARTLETT: Does your mother know what you do for a living?

SAVAGE: Oh God, they don't even know of Lily's existence thank you very much, they're all Irish Catholics, it'd put them in hospital if they found out. I think she'd think I was humiliating myself by dragging up. She hates Danny La Rue on the telly. She likes Dame Edna but that's because she thinks she's a woman. I've told her it's all a pisstake but she won't have it. "Do you hear our Paul's dressing up as a woman in London." Oh heck, there'd be a posse of them straight down here on the coach.

BARTLETT: Do you work differently if you're in a theater instead of a club?

SAVAGE: Well, I'm going to do this bit at the National Theatre and, well, it's a play. That to me is a totally different thing. I feel totally safe, whatever happens, if the NF come in I think I'm safe because it's a play. It's a childish attitude. No one mentions drag at all, the character thing is asexual, also it's such a weird play. You can get away with murder in those places can't you?

BARTLETT: Does it piss you off that the theater makes your work as a drag respectable?

SAVAGE: Well, I went to see this play and I just went mental for it, it was so off the wall and so I thought, oh fuck it I'll have a go. It's something different, a break from the drag scene. I play a woman, but they just accept me as a character. If you got up and did your act you wouldn't be acceptable, do you know what I mean, that pisses me off slightly, they're sitting there watching you but they wouldn't dream of going down to a gay pub. Because it's called Fringe Theater it's alright, you're legit and they say, oh it's all acting, and then ten minutes later you're in a taxi haring off down the road to do some pub in exactly the same outfit and you're a drag queen. It all confuses me, I can't understand it.

BARTLETT: Where would you like to play?

SAVAGE: I want to do a part on *Brookside*. I've got a friend in that. I'd be off like a shot.

REPRINTED FROM *PERFORMANCE*, NO. 48 (JULY/AUGUST 1988): 21–27.

NEW MUSIC:

Scott Johnson, Laurie Anderson, Anthony Davis, and Steve Reich.

SCOTT JOHNSON: OK, to begin with, even the most hermetic artists bump into larger social concerns through their training or the politics of getting work, but beyond those peripheral relationships, I think that it's difficult for music to say anything clear and unambiguous about the world. It's an abstract art form. It doesn't make pictures of anything except through titles and shifting referential conventions.

LAURIE ANDERSON: I don't get what you mean by abstract.

JOHNSON: What I mean by abstract is that there is no necessary one-to-one representational relation between a musical act and an act in the world. People can use visual art to make specific comments about the world—to make pictures, stories, analogies....

ANDERSON: I couldn't disagree more. Music to me is the most physical art form; period. It's the most emotional and physical and bound to the world. It makes you move, and it's heard in groups. People cry when they hear it. You don't hear people cry in front of paintings when you go to a museum. That's abstract to me. Stuff to do with your eyes—that's really abstract.

ANTHONY DAVIS: Music is collective and social.

STEVE REICH: I think what he has in mind is music without words—chamber music. What did Beethoven mean with his late quartets?

JOHNSON: We are flipping our definitions of abstract. I do agree with you, in the sense that music is extremely emotional and direct, but it's emotional about the act of listening to the music or being there when it's played. It's a picture of its own effects.

REICH: That's true if it doesn't have words, but if it does, then all of a sudden it is talking about something and it is very much about a particular time and place.

DAVIS: Music always suggests time and place just by its tradition and by how we define ourselves in relation to a tradition. Music is a social act. Music is performed by people and it is created in a social context. It is hard, though, because if you look at our tradition in music in terms of, say, the blues—to what extent can you say that is a social comment?

JOHNSON: It is, but through the words and the social context.

ANDERSON: Not just through the words; all those blue notes make you sad.

JOHNSON: Because there is a convention derived from speech about what it means to have a pitch that is a half a semi-tone lower than such and such....

REICH: That's right. Beethoven is a good indication of what was going on in Germany at that period of time, and so is Schoenberg. Just in the music, forget about the words. A real criticism of certain pieces is that they don't sound like *where* they are coming from. Right now, for instance, rock & roll is our folk music, and other kinds of music may well reflect that.

JOHNSON: Or reflect on someone's reflection.

REICH: And that's a musical thing, not a verbal thing.

DAVIS: It's rhythmic forms as well as melodic. I think that dealing with pitch first rather than with the idea of rhythmic structures is a Western European prejudice. In Mozart's operas the rhythmic structures were identifiable; they were dance forms. I think that's important. The music was physically suggestive to people. Those dances had meaning.

JOHNSON: Actually, dance is really the key thing. I talk a lot about the connection to folk music, and to a great extent that means a connection to dance music. What Laurie was saying about the physicality—it's a social thing, but it's a social thing that is tautological. It's about itself; it's about being there right now. And dance is the perfect example of that. Social dancing, I mean, not art dance. It's this process—this emotional thing that happens to people in a room at a certain time—and it is not necessarily about what happened to anybody else at any other time. It's a very self-contained thing, and a lot of what is peculiar and a little bit neurotic about the twentieth century is the disappearance or masking of dance forms in concert music. As you say, that is what happens if you are making something now about something that happened in Italy in the eighteenth century. In this century, tradition became this kite attached to a string. Somewhere down the line there was a folk tradition where it connected.

REICH: Well, it does seem like everybody here today has been very aware of how people have danced and what kind of music they have danced to from, let's say, the forties until the present. This has influenced everybody here in various ways, and maybe that is reflected in the fact that a lot of our music has been danced to by art dancers who may also be aware of what's going on in social dancing. So, I think you're right, but I think that you are talking about people who are more associated with universities.

DAVIS: Schoenberg was very aware of dance forms.

REICH: And *Pierrot Lunaire,* of Cabaret songs as well.

DAVIS: We make icons of these figures, but in Berg's music you hear all kinds of dance influences, particularly jazz and ragtime. You hear this when you listen to *Lulu* or anything like that.

JOHNSON: Not to mention Bartok.

DAVIS: Of course. But I think it's an American phenomenon to perceive these European forms as icons completely set apart from our culture; the irony is that Europe has been influenced by us so deeply. That's what European music has really been about in the twentieth century—a reconciliation of this American influence.

JOHNSON: It's a kind of sacred and profane opposition, like the medieval situation in which church music could not include a drum, or even earlier, when you couldn't bring in an instrument of any kind, because there was something profane about everything but the human voice. I am suggesting that, psychologically, what has happened in this culture is that America has taken the classical tradition, and in its desire to mimic what it perceives as a higher historical or class position, it has turned the European tradition into a sacred cow and thought of its own homegrown music as profane.

REICH: Again you are talking about all the people that you would rather not listen to. You are talking about Horatio Parker instead of Charles Ives. You are not talking about Gershwin or even Copland. You are not talking about Laurie or me or Anthony or yourself. There has been a lot of this, but it seems to me it is very much on the wane. We are kind of beating a straw man.

ANDERSON: Let's talk about something else. What is next?

REICH: Before I came in the door, I was walking down the street, just free-associating about music theater and what it was or wasn't, and I came to the conclusion that what it wasn't was opera. What I am working on right now is leading toward music theater in a very different way; so I really have this subject very much on the brain. Some of us are involved in opera and some of us clearly aren't.

ANDERSON: I think of myself as doing opera in a kind of stretched-out sense of the term.

REICH: Well you may, if you want to call everything an opera.

ANDERSON: No, only if it is based on the voice.

REICH: ...A certain kind of voice. It is a voice that was conceived in Italy and Germany, to fill a room of about a thousand folks with no amplification and to be heard over an orchestra. To do that, the apparatus of the voice had to be very large, and that created a vocal style—bel canto and the German development thereof.

ANDERSON: You are saying that opera has to be bel canto?

REICH: Well let's just start with what we know opera was.

JOHNSON: "Opera" is musical theater in its most sophisticated form. But let us start instead with what happens in our own evolving culture when people do a theatrical performance with singing. Now we have microphones, and we have microphone voice, which is a whole different thing. What I am saying is that, yes, you can say that academically speaking this is not opera, opera as we would hear it at the Met, but doesn't it perhaps amount to an equivalent—a developing contemporary equivalent?

REICH: Well, if you want to make a distinction as I would, between music theater, which is anything that happens in a theater with music, and opera, which is a special case of that; then Kurt Weill for me is like a signpost that says: Stop! A new kind of band, a new kind of voice. He is like a turn in the road. Not *Lulu*, not Berg—that's the old stuff.

JOHNSON: Where did he get that voice? He got it from the popular tradition.

REICH: He got it from what was around him at the time in Germany. He got it from the cabaret theater, from bands, from popular music, right?

DAVIS: I don't see the division.

REICH: You don't want to see the division.

DAVIS: No, I don't. I like the operatic voice. I like the vibrato. Basically, I am attached to the emotion—the emotion of a line. I'm attached to the idea of the melody having a certain charged quality. I remember doing *X*, and we had these arguments and discussions about vocal style all along. I was very adamant about the fact that I wanted to write for the operatic voice, but I thought *X* was a special case, particularly because of the myriad traditions that black singers have to deal with just for their survival. So there are opera singers who can scat sing, who can sing jazz, who can do all these things. And that interests me, because in a way this opens up the possibility of developing a different standard for vocal technique and for what can be done in the opera house. I love Kurt Weill's stuff. I think it is great. But I was more interested in stretching the range, the tessitura, and exploiting the visceral and emotional quality of the voice.

ANDERSON: And where is that coming from, Church or opera?

DAVIS: I think from a gospel tradition.

REICH: But you don't hear that in *X*. What you hear in *X* is Italian opera.

DAVIS: I don't think that is true at all.

REICH: I was shocked at the lack of black vocal style.

DAVIS: Black music is a far broader concept than you would have us believe. I can't allow my music to be defined by stereotype, by what you think black music should be. I also feel there is a tradition from Leontyne Price, etc.—the tradition of great black singers who have mastered opera—and I believe in the power of that kind of singing. It is also a question of rhythm. I would have to say, as far as my music goes, that it was rhythmically informed by the Afro-American tradition. We all come to different solutions. I came to a completely different solution, and it was a real response to what I feel is a phenomenon: the abandonment of music. I think that what is happening in opera is actually a retreat from the notion of the music really being the centerpiece of work. That is what I rejected in postmodernism.

ANDERSON: What do you think the centerpiece is?

DAVIS: It has become the director's work as opposed to the composer's work.

JOHNSON: But back to the initial question about opera and musical theater. You have a "voice," which is a technology, in a way. You have a way of training, and that is the operatic voice as an acoustic phenomenon, a solution to a problem: how do you fill a hall—how do you compete with an orchestra with one voice?

REICH: Put a mic on it, man!

JOHNSON: And now you can put a mic on it. You can whisper. Laurie runs herself through machines, whispers, makes the tiniest sounds, and they can fill the hall; now we are talking about an utterly different technology of voice and an utterly different way of producing sounds.

REICH: Here is a story closer to home. My wife and I used to sing "Summertime" around the house, and my son asked what it was. So I told him, George Gershwin's *Porgy and Bess*. We asked his aunt to get him a record of it but we didn't specify what recording. So she got him the Houston Grand Opera's version, and we put it on and someone sang: "Summertime..." [mimics operatic voice], I saw his face fall. I just took the tape, smashed it with a hammer, and said, "That's all right, we'll get another one." [laughter]

JOHNSON: It's interesting if you look at American children, one of the things that they will do when making fun is to take a Wagnerian stance and make a child's mockery of a Wagnerian voice. Whereas, thinking about opera and when it occurred, it was a fairly popular entertainment. I mean, not at the level of a sitcom....

REICH: Verdi and Puccini were enormously popular in their time. No question about that.

JOHNSON: Yes, but they weren't pop music in the sense that the music hall stuff was. There were other things going on.

REICH: I am not criticizing opera as it grew up in Italy in the seventeenth and eighteenth centuries, or in Germany in the eighteenth and nineteenth centuries. I am wondering what it is doing in New York City in 1988. What I am saying about Gershwin is that it is not elevating his music to have Leontyne Price sing the title role; it is debasing it by taking it out of character. The result is embarrassing. The same thing for Bernstein's *West Side Story* when it was sung by opera singers.

JOHNSON: This is a case in point of a very interesting problem which is this: we have this semi-static "technology" which is the acoustic voice. It is not defunct in the sense that people can't do it, but it is socially and culturally a museum piece.

DAVIS: I don't believe that. I find body mics debasing and alienating.

JOHNSON: But over the course of the twentieth century, the opera has become smaller and more specialized—more and more of a museum piece. Now Anthony finds the operatic voice beautiful, and wants to use it. If he uses it, he immediately calls a question to the listener's mind, "Why that classical voice, why not a gospel voice?" Since you are a black American composer writing about Malcolm X. In other words, here is a situation in which your intentions as a creator of music are getting hemmed in by a lot of sociological associations which have very little to do with....

REICH: ...With Malcolm X....

DAVIS: A Gospel representation of Malcolm X would be totally inappropriate. It would employ a musical form that would signify everything antithetical to Islam, to Malcolm's spiritual heritage.

JOHNSON: Steve, what I am saying is that your objection here is an example of what I'm talking about. You hear the opera voice and you say, "Why isn't there a gospel voice?" To get to the general principle here, the whole umbrella that this discussion about *X* comes under is that of personal choices versus cultural precedents. If you choose to use the older technique, it appears almost as a statement of content, not just a choice to use a certain sound—to exercise a certain personal fascination with sound.

DAVIS: Sure. There is violent opposition on my part to what I thought was the emptiness of postmodernist music.

REICH: What kind of music is that?

DAVIS: Well, what I mean is that not everything has been explored with the acoustic voice. I think that I was very interested in the emotional immediacy of the voice, with the idea of using the extremes of the voice—using line, etc. It was very personal. Also, there are all kinds of things in *X* that I think stem from the "Afro-American" jazz tradition, bebop, etc., but I wanted the immediacy of the voice and the physicality of sound because I found dealing with body mics very alienating. The story that I was telling in my work was not about alienation; it was not that kind of story.

JOHNSON: But once again, we are only talking about one piece.

DAVIS: If he wants to talk about it I have to take him on.

JOHNSON: When I saw *Gospel at Colonnus* in Paris, there was one really striking moment—a disconcerting moment—where a soloist who was a wonderful singer used a real Gospel voice, and right in the middle of a sort of cadenza she flew into a very brief bit of bel canto trilling. It stuck out so incredibly. The point being that we are taught to hear these things as separate because right now they are. There is no in-between voice yet. We can talk about this business of high art and European classical academism, and how we have all grown beyond that, but we can't really grow beyond that until we have materials which allow us to make work wherein those questions of conflict don't even arise.

DAVIS: I pretend in my work that those conflicts don't exist.

REICH: I am not attacking Anthony's opera alone; I am attacking all opera written recently in America. They all sound very artificial and unbelievable.

ANDERSON: It doesn't sound like an American voice.

REICH: It just doesn't feel like it is coming out normally. When I hear someone sing a Gershwin song, or when I hear someone sing any kind of jazz or rock & roll, whether or not I like the music, at least it's here and now. I know where I am and what era we're in. You cannot recreate a voice from another period.

ANDERSON: I hear it when I hear Ronald Reagan talk.

REICH: That's interesting, what do you hear?

ANDERSON: Well, I have been completely obsessed lately with studying these political speeches and the old fascist language and speeches.

REICH: Who else have you been listening to?

ANDERSON: Hitler for one.

REICH: You too?

ANDERSON: Hitler as a drummer. He starts off with this kick-snare thing going, with dum di dum.

REICH: But it's very Germanic, isn't it. It's like *Triumph of the Will* music.

ANDERSON: Oh yeah. It's all rhythm and no pitch. He starts the audience going. They are grooving to this thing that he is laying down, and pretty soon they are marching and they got to go somewhere...like Poland. Then you look at Mussolini, listen to his speeches. He is singing bel canto: *"Frontiere, frontiere..."* [sings]. And off they go across the border. When Ronald Reagan is talking to you, he is singing, "When you Wish Upon a Star," and it pushes every single American button.

JOHNSON: It pushes the Walt Disney button.

ANDERSON: Americans can relate to this kind of blue fairy stuff, because that is American music. It is real mild and it tricks you.

REICH: You are getting down to the real thing, which is the tone of voice.

ANDERSON: And it is a cracked voice, and it has a lot of pauses, and it's old granddad talking to you.

JOHNSON: Walter Brennon.

ANDERSON: Yes, all these guys. They are masters. You can't avoid listening to this voice because it's on the news, it's everywhere. And his pauses....

JOHNSON: The well-placed chuckle.

ANDERSON: Yeah, the little chuckle. As if he is trying to remember something that happened a long time ago but can't quite pin it down. These are beautiful pauses.

REICH: When I hear this voice, I sometimes say, "False, give me the real thing."

ANDERSON: Yeah, where do you find the real thing, though....

REICH: You find it in the street, you find it in good popular music, you find it in good "serious" music.

JOHNSON: You find it in blues, the first place I was really struck by it was in blues. It is homegrown *sprechstimme*. The subtlety of a good blues singer blending what is clearly a musical tone into something that is speech. It has an integrity and a naturalness to it that I have never heard in any Schoenberg performance.

ANDERSON: You could really do an opera with that. It would really be breathtaking.

JOHNSON: But to then break into true singing and then break into speaking.

DAVIS: I guess I am very much apart in terms of this discussion because I am really fascinated by learning about voice in the classical tradition. I was interested in the emotional power that I could get, and I felt that was as immediate as anything else. I really do feel that to say that was artificial is wrong.

JOHNSON: Only in context. I think that is what Steve is saying. In the context of America right now....

DAVIS: I think that is really wrong because America right now is many different things. America right now is not one thing.

JOHNSON: That is true.

DAVIS: We still have these visions of Americana that I find....

ANDERSON: Grotesque, I bet. [laughter]

DAVIS: Yeah, of course. I was interested in emotional power coming from the music. That gets to me—the kind of power you get from Coltrane.

ANDERSON: Why do you feel you have to explain that? I mean, everybody would agree with what you are saying.

JOHNSON: The point is that here we have been talking about documentary, about speech and less finished voices. Let's take opera and blues; opera is a very finished voice. It is the product of training; it was perfected according to a certain methodology.

REICH: And so is Bessie Smith.

JOHNSON: Exactly. And what you get with a finished tradition or a finished way of making sound, is a polished opportunity for the kind of emotional power you are talking about. But nothing is free. You trade off; you lose a certain spontaneity. Maybe Bessie Smith loses less spontaneity than bel canto, because hers is a less formalized tradition.

Back to what Laurie is saying about speech. One of my favorite things to listen to is the pedal point of a newscaster. When these people speak, they go: "And today dada*Da* [low note]. And dadada*Da*." You can find where the *Da* is; some people have F-sharp, and you can play an F-sharp pedal tone, and you can almost hear modes; they are singing glissy modal melodies over a pedal.

REICH: I have been spending the last few months doing nothing but transcribing speakers.

ANDERSON: Which speakers?

REICH: Well, they are people you don't know. They are anonymous people. One of them is the governess who took me across the country when I was three and four—an Irish woman who is now in her seventies and living in Queens. Another is a retired black Pullman porter who used to work on train lines between New York and Los Angeles that I would ride in those days. Another is a Dutch woman who spent some time in a concentration camp and who speaks English with a Dutch accent; she is now living in Seattle. Another one is a Hungarian man who lives in Boston who spent most of the war wandering around the woods in Hungary and never got caught. Another one is a Belgian woman who was basically a French speaker, living in this country, and who just recently died. Those are the voices that are in this piece. What I had to do was figure out what to use from a couple hours of tape and then play it until I could write it down.

DAVIS: That is something that Strauss did. He employed speech rhythms.

JOHNSON: Not quite the same thing!

REICH: Strauss didn't do it because Strauss didn't have a tape recorder! Janácek, however, actually thought about it.

JOHNSON: This is very different from composing on paper. I mean, I collected tapes. When I worked on *John Somebody,* for instance, to get people to speak naturally, I would put a microphone in front of them and have them call somebody on the telephone, because that is the one situation where people relax in front of a microphone every day.

ANDERSON: Do you think people relax in front of a telephone? Don't they have a telephone voice?

JOHNSON: Well, they have telephone voices, but they are as habitual as face-to-face speech. At least you get something that is normal, everyday behavior. But the point is that once you sit down with a tempered instrument—a keyboard—in front of you and you try to transcribe a tape, you cannot do it exactly. The difference between an F-sharp and a G gets vague.

DAVIS: What are the rhythms? That interests me more than pitch.

JOHNSON: The rhythms are another whole job. They operate in exactly the same way.

REICH: You can codify them but they're not exact.

DAVIS: When I was writing the opera, I was writing in speech rhythms, using Malcolm X—the way he spoke, the way speech rhythms work—but I felt freer with the pitch because, in a way, that stems from what *sprechstimme* originally was supposed to be. What Richard Strauss did was use speech rhythms as a basis for melodic writing. I was finding in myself a reason for why I use repeating rhythms, and I found it was a funny merger with the idea of rap.

ANDERSON: This really should be a tape, because everybody is a perfect example of what they are talking about. It is really kind of creepy.

REICH: We are all as we speak.

JOHNSON: In other words we associate things that we get through this less important sense with emotions, not with intellect. We associate them with funny memories, déjà vus. In other words, the less important the sense is, biologically, the more an art form based on that sense has a clearly emotional aura. But the nose is so low on the scale that we don't have an art form for it.

ANDERSON: Those smell movies never got off the ground. In Tokyo you can buy cans of homecooking and spray it around your house, or freshly brewed coffee. Who's making bacon pie?

JOHNSON: But what I was proposing, was that since the ear is a less important organ, every time that music bumps into visual art, it loses, unless it is opera or a rock video where the whole thing is set up specifically for the musician.

ANDERSON: It loses what?

JOHNSON: It loses its preeminence. In other words, dancers get music to go *behind* their dance; when you see the concert of a choreographer and a composer, it's the dancer's concert. We assume that as a rule, and it is the same thing for music, for theater, or for film, which is a really extreme example.

REICH: But not music theater.

JOHNSON: Not music theater, where the work is conceived by the composer. But it always takes a backseat unless you set up a safe-house, a concert hall, where everybody is coming just to see that music.

ANDERSON: "Just to see that music."

JOHNSON: Precisely. I am also thinking about what it looks like when you see music being performed. What does a classical concert hall look like? Performers become as blank as they possibly can. Nobody wears anything funny except soloists. Nobody does anything with the lights. They try to utterly neutralize vision so that the music can take priority over that dominant sense of sight.

ANDERSON: I saw Cab Calloway a couple of nights ago. He is pretty vivid. They showed a bunch of his old films during the concert. When he is on the train and the porter is...oh, you would like this thing....

REICH: Fill me in!

ANDERSON: The whole band is sleeping and he gets this telegram: "Producer says you have to change the first number." So they all get their horns and start playing in the aisles while the train is rocking around. It is really wonderful, but they had only the skinniest pretext for doing visual stuff with music.

JOHNSON: The pretext is Cab Calloway; the pretext is the guy. In music theater, the plots are often so flimsy that you couldn't make a non-musical theater piece out of it. I mean, sometimes the acting in opera is ok, but it isn't Dustin Hoffman.

DAVIS: Because it is not naturalistic? Are we trying to embrace naturalism? I am not sure if that is necessarily good.

JOHNSON: I am saying that I don't think it is possible in music. It is not natural to run around singing—not in conversation.

REICH: You have been taking singing lessons?

ANDERSON: Yeah. I was humiliated into it by these backup singers.

REICH: I hope you don't lose whatever you had before you took lessons.

ANDERSON: No, I wanted to be able to sing if I wanted to. But the point was that all of these lessons have been about where that crack is between talking and singing. And it is just a very important point....

REICH: I'm really curious; I have never heard anybody describe them that way.

ANDERSON: Hmm. Yeah, we do a lot of stuff—throw balls, visualize things.

REICH: She is aware of that area.

ANDERSON: Oh yeah.

JOHNSON: Thinking about your musical structures in a way, a lot of your pieces strike me as being songs even if you don't sing—the form, the length. Songs or poems, I would say.

ANDERSON: They are conversational as well—lyric poems. They don't have choruses. They are generally real linear, especially the stuff that I have been doing on this record or at least on one of the sides. This is turning into a two-record set. One side is just all talking with no pretense of doing anything else.

REICH: What's going on in the background?

ANDERSON: Nothing—paper rustling. No attempt whatsoever to make it musical in any way. That is my favorite side so far.

REICH: Your text?

ANDERSON: It's just talking.

JOHNSON: Does it happen on a continuous side or a series of sections?

ANDERSON: Yeah, fifteen minutes or somewhere around there. You kind of think, "Why was this committed to vinyl? To what end?" You know, I like stuff like that. All the songs are monster forty-eight track productions; so I wanted the flip side to be completely simple.

JOHNSON: The thing that always struck me about your work is that it suggests song, structure, form, length, topic, and then does something peculiar with these elements.

ANDERSON: It never takes the bait.

JOHNSON: It's a tease.

ANDERSON: Yes, I can't get behind that song structure.

JOHNSON: But you use it.

ANDERSON: Yeah, sure, but only to mess it up.

JOHNSON: What I like about it is that it can somehow be recognized by audiences that don't know about Art. It is appropriation, almost, of a way of listening, of a habit of listening that everybody shares. I mean every culture has songs.

ANDERSON: I wish there were more work songs.

JOHNSON: Yeah, what would a work song for a clerk typist be, or a business executive? [laughter]

ANDERSON: Some good PC work songs would really be nice, because so many people are into that now. They are lost in their separate little brains. It would really be nice to make music for them to work by.

[Intermission]

JOHNSON: If we are all so enlightened and beyond this modernist set of "no-nos...."

ANDERSON: Yeah, what are our "no-nos?"

DAVIS: Artists' expression of class. There is no getting past that, and postmodernism doesn't make you immune to that.

JOHNSON: So what class is this? What is our interest group, or our various interest groups, then?

DAVIS: One thing about America is the rejection of popular culture. It has real heavy overtones of racism. The reason that we have trouble embracing the concept of popular culture as the real root of our art is the fact that popular culture, particularly in music, is mainly Afro-American. The "High Art" world has basically been this protected sphere. I always look at it as the last vestiges of making the world safe for white European art.

REICH: I would think that, at this point, it is completely the opposite, with many composers searching out popular traditions. We have all done work that obviously comes out of the popular culture.

DAVIS: But the problem is....

REICH: Like it or not, your problem is really that you are the object of the interest and not knocking on locked doors. What is the attitude of those who control the New York Philharmonic, the Metropolitan Opera, or the Brooklyn Academy of Music? The war over the use of popular sources has been won.

DAVIS: That is not true; the war has not been won. Talk to any black artist. To me the downtown orthodoxy is as bad as the uptown orthodoxy. There is no difference.

JOHNSON: There has been progress, but the situation is still bad. I agree that both scenes reflect the racial attitudes of the parent society of which they are a part.

DAVIS: In a sense both groups distinguish themselves by being exclusive—exclusive racially. And that is part of the design.

JOHNSON: You are attributing intentionality, the idea that somebody is designing things.

DAVIS: But of course there is intent. Racism in America involves intent; it is not   an accident.

JOHNSON: In a way it is an accident; it is basically something that gets dumped in the lap of people who are born and trained into it before they are self-aware because *their* parents were trained into it, as were their parents before them. Nobody stops the cycle because nobody is fully conscious as an individual until it's too late.

ANDERSON: It is just what they think the world is like. It is just habit.

JOHNSON: It is a habit of perception. It takes intent to break it. It takes no intent at all to continue it.

DAVIS: Oppression is intent. I think it has to do with a sense of responsibility.

ANDERSON: That's it—power and money, and people who have power and money.

DAVIS: And it is basically to preserve status—your position.

JOHNSON: That is where the intent comes in. When someone gets threatened and defends their interests.

DAVIS: I think that is very true. That is an overriding concern to me in terms of cultural issues in America.

JOHNSON: Anybody in their right mind would have to say that eighty percent of American popular music in the twentieth century has come from fifteen percent of the population or whatever percentage of the overall population the black population accounts for. From jazz to rock, each successive style has been initiated in the black community. That is perfectly clear, but it hasn't been reflected in an improved status for black artists.

DAVIS: The issue is the appropriation issue.

JOHNSON: You have jazz, a folk music which grows into an art music. There is still jazz music which is clearly popular music around, but the tradition grew an art music offshoot which has outlasted the dance bands.

DAVIS: Since the fifties, really, or even earlier than that—since the forties.

JOHNSON: I see it starting to happen with Ellington in the thirties; and finally, with Charlie Parker and bop, you had this flowering. An interesting problem is that American embarrassment in wanting to match European "High Art"—the fact that American jazz continues not to have the cachet of classical music in the culture at large, at least in America. I think it is different in Europe. To what extent is that a by-product of American post-colonial self-hatred, and to what extent is that pure racism?

REICH: …Rock & roll has taken over. Jazz was displaced by rock, remember.

JOHNSON: As popular music, not as art music.

REICH: No, wrong. I saw it happen around the time of Coltrane's death. The same audience that would have gone to Birdland in the fifties when I went, was going to hear a rock concert at the time of the Beatles.

JOHNSON: But that's audience. What about complexity?

REICH: James Brown attracted more interest than Cecil Taylor.

JOHNSON: But there is a big difference here. You are talking about audience, but there is the musical issue of complexity. Where in the sixties was the rock player who could play what a bop player played in the fifties? The chops weren't there. Culturally, there was an audience moving away from jazz toward rock, but rock is the younger form. Rock just didn't have the kind of complexity and the opportunity for avant-gardism that it has since developed. It's in the stage that jazz was in the forties.

DAVIS: A stage of colonialism, that is all. Elvis Presley signaled the end of that wave of appropriation. When white American culture gets bored with a particular movement in black culture it appropriates another strain. We see it right now with the interest in South African music. I sense a new kind of neocolonialist impulse to appropriation.

JOHNSON: To what extent does this have to be viewed as a negative or colonialist appropriation, and to what extent is it simply a case of people hearing music that they like and wanting to hear more of it?

DAVIS: It takes Paul Simon to get it here, doesn't it?

ANDERSON: But did it get here with Paul Simon?

[unison] Not really.

DAVIS: It didn't really get here with Elvis Presley, either.

REICH: But there is another question: What is happening in Africa? I went to Ghana in 1970. I went to Accra and from Accra I went out to the university where I studied with The Ghana Dance Ensemble. The Ghana Dance Ensemble was three years old then, because in 1967 they started having a modern country. Before that, these musicians played locally for the chief in their home towns. The chief had money so they were employed; they had a full-time gig. By 1967 the chiefs were still there, but their money was gone; so if you wanted to be a professional musician and get paid for your playing, you had to—either by musical ability, political connections, or the usual combination of both—get a gig with The Ghana Dance Ensemble, which at that time would tour internationally. The ensemble was made up of musicians from different tribes, and a musical event that would have taken three days in the village now took twenty minutes and was put on a proscenium stage, because that way you could play in a house when you were travelling. Now what happened was that an economic and social change created a change in the form of the music. What has happened in the eighteen years since 1970? What I hear is a lot of rock & roll-influenced music coming out of West Africa because rock & roll is where the money is. It probably seems boring and irrelevant to play the basically "classical" pieces that arose out of a life form that is pretty much kaput. Now the opportunity to travel and to succeed in the world comes with a ticket that says "rock & roll." So you get these various hybrid forms. You can say this is the way of the world; you can say this is great; or you can say something has been lost. I think all three are true.

JOHNSON: Exactly. The point is that folk music, the nature of what a folk music is, has changed for many reasons, but mostly because of technology.

REICH: And the economic organization of a country.

JOHNSON: Yes, folk music is not done on the back porch anymore. Somebody else does it and you buy it. So you caught the tail end of the actual village music?

REICH: There are times when something will go like that [snaps fingers] because of something drastic that happens of a political/economic nature. The way people live changes—the way they survive and feed their family changes—and music changes too. Money and how you live and survive has a lot to do with the kind of music you make, the kind of instrument you play, the kind of hall you play in, the kind of sound system, etc. All these things come out of folk considerations—how you live, what is around you.

JOHNSON: And then the *nature* of folk music changes. What I am saying, in terms of rock & roll taking over the African music scene.…

DAVIS: Reggae and Brazilian-influenced music also greatly affected African popular music.

JOHNSON: Right, but it was a homegrown, voluntary phenomenon. Nobody came in and said you have to play rock & roll. People played rock & roll because they liked it, because they heard this reflection of African music bounced back off of America and it made sense. I don't see that as a case of appropriation. I see it as a natural interaction of influences. Now if you start talking about Paul Simon and tour organizers and PR, then you are getting into the area of appropriation. But you don't even get to this area until somebody has first made the music. First you have to have the thing itself.

DAVIS: But Simon took much of the political content out of it, too.

ANDERSON: Yeah, but this situation is a little bit different. Ladysmith Black Mambazo has titles that are thirty-five words long, and the song itself is just two. "Your brother-in-law fucked my daughter and I am going to get a big brick and come over to your hut tonight and clobber you." [Everyone laughs]

REICH: —Refrain!

ANDERSON: But on the other hand, a lot of musicians who have played with him learned stuff from Chubby Checker. They love Chubby Checker. They love Fats Domino. They learned to play guitar like that. So if you listen to their guitar styles.…

REICH: You get a time warp—another kind of appropriation going the other way.

ANDERSON: Yeah. They are masters of that guitar style. You can't find anyone in New York who plays like that; I've tried. When Paul was doing that benefit, there were about a hundred musicians and about eight people rehearsing them. It was so great. That is actually the way one should do a record: book three floors of a hotel and really great musicians.

JOHNSON: Wire every room.

ANDERSON: I have to go over to London now to find one of those guys because I can't find a single player in New York City who can play like that—so back, so tight, so loose. One guy I met through Paul left South Africa because there aren't a lot of studios, there aren't opportunities. Some of those guys really appreciate the chance to tour and to record. Also, Paul pays everyone so well and gives them a chance to go places and meet people. When they were in town, everyone was going crazy hiring them for their sessions. "You got the Africans this afternoon? Oh good, how about tomorrow morning." And then these guys—great percussion players, great guitar players—would come by these sessions and have a great time. They made a lot of connections and seemed to really appreciate learning other kinds of styles. I met most of them because they came to my rehearsals. They couldn't count the music and they said, "That is real interesting, let me try to play that." It was really cool. I know what you are saying, but I met a lot of people who were in what you would think could be an exploitive situation, and they were using it to their own advantage, which is wonderful.

JOHNSON: There is a difference between being aware of those sorts of socio-political-racial-class influences and having your perception of music ruled by them, and taking a political party line about sound. I mean it is ultimately about people making music and about all the accidental and unpredictable ways in which people get together and music occurs. This doesn't happen by the rule book. After the fact you can say that this is why that happened or this is an example of this or that cultural force, but when you sit down to do it, you are not doing it to illustrate a cultural force. For an artist, the intellectual considerations are pretty much after the fact, I think.

ANDERSON: Well, unfortunately, a lot of the time it all comes down to concrete things like money. One thing that I admire is the way Paul has worked with these people. He says, O.K., we share publishing, we share the money. Not many people would do that. "This is partly your music. You did that; I did this. And this is how we split it, and we draw up a contract. You sign it, and then I'll sign it." There are horrible things that can happen in this kind of situation, but there are also things that everybody can do when they are working with somebody outside of their usual world, or when they are collaborating in general, to make it fair. It's not a matter of just tipping your hat to the issue but of saying, "I am going to share the money with you."

DAVIS: But there are so many other examples that are not fair, especially with the sampling technology. There is a case in a dance piece, where they used a Louis Armstrong solo and put it through an emulator. That starts to bother me. There are a lot of issues of rights abuses here. The history of music in America has been so much about that. It is really naïve to say, "Well look, we can't really talk about that. Let's just talk about music in a pure sense." Those problems are very real.

ANDERSON: It comes down to personal politics and what you as a composer are willing to say about your own sources. Everybody can try to be clear about that, and try to open up the issue. The tradition says don't do that. You are an artist, and an artist is supposed to be original. It is also about style. [everyone talks at once]

DAVIS: That is buying into that whole Western European myth.

JOHNSON: Avant-gardism as a twentieth-century phenomenon is the most extreme example of this extreme worship of individuality, as if somebody had sprung from Zeus's forehead or something. Lately I haven't heard so much of this. In the seventies, there was this incessant bickering about who did what first. I don't know, maybe I am not hanging out with the same crowd....

REICH: That will never stop as long as the earth continues to revolve. That is human nature.

JOHNSON: But there is the flow of influences that you can't deny. It's like a language. We all speak a language, we invent sentences, but we do not invent the individual words.

ANDERSON: We didn't invent most of the sentences either. [laughter]

JOHNSON: You think the thoughts that your language and your training allow you to think. Avant-gardism places this value on pretending that it is otherwise. We are embedded in a culture. Maybe radical individualism is a Western European thing. I don't really know; I haven't been any place else.

REICH: When you had a common practice in the West, for example when everybody played the same kind of music in figured bass—Bach, Handel, that period of time—it was a question of how you did something that everybody did. The situation was the same in Africa when I was there in 1970. Now we have players who are able to do a certain style, and others who simply aren't because there is no common agreement when you sit down to play. That is a twentieth-century Western problem, and it is spreading.

JOHNSON: It is spreading the way recordings and communication spread. All of a sudden, we have to carry hundreds of years of Europe around in our brains plus all of the non-Western cultures that have been previously inaccessible simply because they were far away.

ANDERSON: Geez, melting pot. Come on!

JOHNSON: Yes, but that is a lot of information to process, and that is why we don't have a common practice.

ANDERSON: That's great!

REICH: That began a long time ago. Certainly it had already started early in this century.

JOHNSON: But now it has reached a point of acuteness, where there is just so much information, and it is so contradictory. Back to the topic of an operatic voice and a microphone voice. I fully expect that at some point, some new tradition is going to develop; somebody is going to solve this problem. Either someone will come up with a solution, or we will stop hearing it as a problem.

ANDERSON: I don't hear it as a problem now, I don't think.

JOHNSON: But a lot of people do. They hear it as a conflict.

REICH: I hear it as something grating, as something organically grating. I hear bel canto voice and I leave the room.

JOHNSON: But are they intrinsically incompatible, or do we just hear these things as opposite because of our underlying cultural assumptions. What I am saying is that we hear an improvising rhythm section as something that should not be in the same room as a string quartet.

DAVIS: Depends on the string quartet.

JOHNSON: Yeah. Depends on what they are playing. The point is that it is the composer's job to write music where these things comfortably coexist.

DAVIS: They can violently interact. That is interesting too.

ANDERSON: We are not looking for comfort. Violent interaction!

REICH: Successful interaction is what I'm talking about, because you are going to see mixtures. The individual forms in various countries, including ours, are definitely going to recede and African-Asian-American influences are all going to roll more and more into one ball of wax. The question is, "who handles it best?" It's the same old story as it's always been.

JOHNSON: There is going to be a death of pure traditions. [unison response]

DAVIS: I disagree with the whole melting pot thing. There is a lot of separatism in our society and culture, there is a kind of apartheid in our culture. As we've seen, there are always new Afro-American traditions emerging. I see a plurality of tradition; I don't see a merging of traditions.

ANDERSON: I have to say that I really do.

REICH: What is jazz and rock & roll, for that matter, if they are not a merging of African and European music? I am lost. Once you introduce harmony, which doesn't exist in our form in Africa, and once you introduce the kind of rhythms that clearly didn't exist in Europe, then you have the kind of American combination which is so organic that, for a while, it was a real common practice. Now you have all kinds of offshoots.

DAVIS: Sure, but I still don't see this as the end of separate traditions. I see this as a plurality of traditions.

JOHNSON: There will always be separate traditions, but there will also always be that merging going on. It's a dialectic. We have been involved for some years in a melting trend, after a period of glacial separation and hierarchy in music. It's a big mess right now, and I think it is a good idea to continue to make a great big goddamn mess for the next ten years and then sort it out later.

DAVIS: I see this as a kind of violent upheaval. This is not a thing where you see the melding of traditions. I see this as a violent interplay of traditions where there is constant appropriation, constant borrowing, constant stealing, back and forth, in all directions.

JOHNSON: And then there are periods of consolidation.

ANDERSON: Television is the great equalizer. That is what is great.

REICH: I think she's right, but I don't know if it's a happy ending.

ANDERSON: You know, I have this class that I teach a couple times a week to these kids— mostly Chinese kids, seven years old. They are really really great writers. We are working on stories and writing, and they know nothing about China, although most of them speak mostly Chinese. The people they want to write about are all the superheroes, and people from outer space—people they find out about from television. They are not singing fake opera when they are trying to make fun of people; they are singing songs from the Saturday morning characters. Most of these characters I have never even heard of. That is how they are learning about American culture; this school doesn't even have a map up of China. They are Americans, and they are reminded about it all the time.

REICH: My grandfather didn't talk about Europe. He didn't want to talk about it.

DAVIS: But the thing is in different stages. The idea of coming here in order to belong, the immediate rejection you have to make....

ANDERSON: How much of it is a veneer? I don't know that.

REICH: I think that for a child it's not.

DAVIS: But then I think when you are a teenager, at a certain age you say, "Who am I?"

REICH: What did I sell my birthright for?

DAVIS: And then you go into it. That happened to me, and it happened to other people. That kind of self-discovery is very important. I think it is a natural thing—the idea of belonging as a kid at that age. It is very strong. [everyone speaks at once]

REICH: Take the case of the African musicians who played with Paul Simon. At a certain point they feel it's really great, but if they want to go back and recreate their original music, it's gone. You can't go back and say, "Hey kids, let's have that older world," and it's the older world that made that music possible. The sad thing is that they can only go back and create a nostalgic remembrance of it, or something that conjures that up in our minds, because it's gone.

DAVIS: But then that becomes a different thing. Your memory creates a new reality, and that is the way tradition changes. In black music in America, the idea of trying to reclaim identity after it has been appropriated...if you look at the Swing era, which was essentially appropriated, or the bebop period, how can you reclaim this as your music, as opposed to that other imitative shit? We can look at the blues again, really getting back to it, but now it is a different thing. It becomes a different thing.

JOHNSON: Exactly. I think the most interesting thing to do, and what I want to do, is to be a traditional composer in a tradition that doesn't exist yet. [laughter] Is that a happy ending?

—1988

THIS CONVERSATION WAS ORGANIZED BY SCOTT JOHNSON.

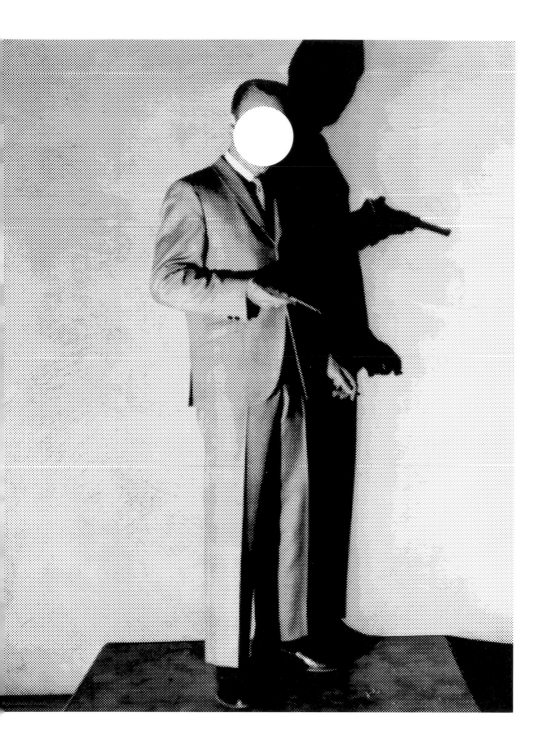

RESISTANCE TO INTERPRETATION: AUTHORITY AND INSTITUTIONS

Marcia Tucker

Let's call it the "authority effect".... This "authoritative" language speaks as though the other person weren't there. Or perhaps more accurately, it doesn't bother to imagine who, as Hawthorne said, is listening to our talk.[1]   —Jane Tompkins

To be regarded as an authority in any discipline, profession or field of endeavor is generally thought of not just as a positive distinction, but as one to be actively sought after. In recent years, however, the question of specialized authority has moved to the center of a debate in which theorists have addressed the issue of how one acquires and maintains it, and at what (or whose) cost. In the field of art history, where the expert discriminations of the connoisseur determine and sustain the traditional canon, the central modernist judgments of "quality" and "genius" have been the subject of an especially thorough-going critique. Rather than disinterested and autonomous representations of fixed truths, these valuations can be seen to reflect biased agendas constructed from a field of potential alternatives.

In an interview that originally appeared in *October* magazine, the Polish-born artist Krzysztof Wodiczko discusses his public projections with Douglas Crimp, Rosalyn Deutsche, and the Polish art critic Ewa Lajer-Burcharth. Wodiczko explains that by projecting large-scale images directly onto the facades of public buildings and monuments, he intends to render the ideological function of architecture transparent, thus challenging the regimes it supports and celebrates. Having emigrated to the United States by way of Canada, Wodiczko compares the position of artists working in the Soviet Bloc, Canada and the US, vis-à-vis the question of censorship, from a privileged perspective. He concludes that repression from one country to another varies only in degree, reminding us of Marx's definition of censorship as "centralized criticism."

Agendas and attitudes clash in a heated, often cantankerous, debate among a roster of contemporary architecture's most prominent figures. In this rare colloquium of giants, Philip Johnson, Leon Krier, Tadao Ando, Kevin Roche, Michael Graves, Robert Stern, et al., address such issues as financial gain, popularity, and the balancing of academic and aesthetic concerns in relationship to both practical restrictions and the desire to make buildings that respond to the needs and feelings of their users. The spirited exchange falls apart when Krier ridicules Ando's proposal for housing that incorporates traditional Japanese spatial concepts. Striking is the extent to which some of the participants are unable to consider, much less accept, any practice that challenges the authority of their own tradition.

In a lengthy and equally impassioned exchange between Museum of Modern Art curators William Rubin and Kirk Varnedoe and critic Thomas McEvilley that originally appeared in several consecutive issues of *Artforum*, we are privy to a battle between two divergent points of view concerning the contextualization of the art and artifacts of "tribal" cultures. Here, the authority of the modernist aesthetic, which informs the removal of the art of other peoples from its original site and function in order to highlight superficial stylistic affinities, is fundamentally challenged. The decontextualization of so-called "primitive" artifacts and the denial or glossing over of their original functions are seen by McEvilley as co-optive, colonizing acts serving the agenda of mainstream Western culture. Rubin and Varnedoe defend their exhibition as a recontextualization which admits the makers of these "neglected" objects to the global community of artistic genius.

A chapter from James Clifford's book, *The Predicament of Culture,* broadens the arena of debate to include considerations of how non-Western objects are treated by anthropological institutions like The Museum of Natural History. According to Clifford, cultural anthropology and modernist art both presume "a primitive world in need of preservation, redemption, and representation," thereby suppressing the reality of tribal cultures and artists. Clifford calls for a move beyond what he terms the traditional taxonomic system, suggesting exhibitions of "truly indigestible 'outside' artifacts" and a transformation of the situation "whereby one portion of humanity can select, value, and collect the pure products of others."

A 1977 interview with Roland Barthes provides an unusually informal look at this extraordinarily influential thinker. What comes across is Barthes' modesty and his resistance to institutionalized academic and intellectual conventions. He admits, in various moments, to not reading, or reading too late; to finding his inability to understand a foreign language "relaxing"; to finding intellectuals useless; and to taking a "minimal position" with regard to politics. Barthes finds his basis in anarchism in the word's "most etymological sense"—not necessarily as the refusal of power but an "extreme sensitivity to its ubiquitousness." In his own work, Barthes searches for a way of writing which doesn't paralyze or intimidate the reader, and a style of teaching in which the speaker is not always privileged over the listener.

In her book *Reading Lacan,* Jane Gallop examines the French psychoanalyst's re-reading of Freud with emphasis on those aspects of Lacan's writing which unsettle accepted theoretical assumptions in the field. The "Prefatory Material" excerpted here takes the form of an internal dialogue with the criticisms of an anonymous reader and provides an alternative to the requisite posture of "mastery" over one's subject. Having come to believe that Lacan is "impossible to understand fully, impossible to master," Gallop is determined to undo the "oppressive mystification of the Lacanian institution," not by renouncing her authority as a critic, but by using it with an end to deconstructing the position of authority itself. Mirroring Gayatri Spivak's interest in "unlearning privilege," Gallop proposes a feminist practice that would "relinquish authority from a position of authority." In her refusal to authorize a single point of view, Gallop provides a text that opens out onto the reader, suggesting the infinite extensions of that "great surface...[that] unstable, shifting terrain of mediation"[2] that is discourse itself.

1. Jane Tompkins, "Me and My Shadow," in *Gender and Theory* no.1, *Dialogues on Feminist Criticism,* ed. Linda Kauffman (UK: Basil Blackwell, 1989,) p.129.

2. Michel Foucault, *The Archaeology of Knowledge & The Discourse on Language* (New York: Harper Torchbooks, 1972), p.117.

A CONVERSATION WITH KRZYSZTOF WODICZKO
Douglas Crimp, Rosalyn Deutsche & Ewa Lajer-Burcharth

ROSALYN DEUTSCHE: Last winter you showed *The Homeless Projection* as a proposal in a New York gallery. What procedures would be required to execute the work in its proposed site of Union Square?

KRZYSZTOF WODICZKO: I can only recall for you the procedures required for a work proposed for Washington Square in 1984. It was explained to 49th Parallel, the gallery that helped organize the project, that permission was needed from the New York City Department of Parks and Recreation and from the community board of the area. In that case, the Parks Department had no objections, but the community board, which was asked for approval on short notice, said no. A single individual, the head of the community board, was responsible for the refusal, because the decision had to be made in an interval between board meetings. He explained that the board had refused many other proposals, apparently because they are not interested in organized public events, which they feel would disturb the normal activities of the park. As you know, Washington Square has a very rich life, students, people exercising, drug traffic. I haven't attempted yet to realize *The Homeless Projection*, but I assume the procedures would be the same for Union Square.

Prospect Park, which administers Grand Army Plaza, where I did a projection in 1985, also has an agreement with the local community board. I was told that the agreement states that any cultural or artistic event that would bring politics to the park should be excluded. I was given the impression that my *Grand Army Plaza Projection* should not be politically explicit.

DEUTSCHE: What do you suppose they think public art is?

WODICZKO: I think they want public art to consist of undisturbing but spectacular events or objects that will satisfy the community in an easy and immediate way, which I do not wish to oppose initially. It is essential to be able to take advantage of any administrative desire for art in public places, to "collaborate" in such events and infiltrate them with an unexpected critical element. In this case the main event was the annual Brooklyn New Year's Eve gala with a fireworks display by the Grucci family, music, and hot cider. My projection was intended as an integral part of the event.

EWA LAJER-BURCHARTH: What was the reaction of the authorities who contracted you to do the event?

WODICZKO: I was invited to participate by Mariella Bisson, a special officer in the Prospect Park administration for organizing an art-in-the-park program. She is an artist herself and is very knowledgeable about the park's history, a committed "patriot" of the park, devoted to the notion of the park as a space of both historical and contemporary aesthetic experience. She has created a sculpture gallery in the interior—monstrous in its scale—of the Soldiers and Sailors Memorial Arch, and another art gallery in the boathouse in the park. She thought that one of my projections, regardless of its subject, would create an added attraction for the gala, differentiating this year's event from previous ones. But her supervisor was not informed about what I intended to project, even though it was known some two weeks in advance, since we had to do trial runs. Instead the supervisor learned of the projection from the *New York Times,* whose section on what to do on New Year's Eve mentioned that U.S. and Soviet missiles would be projected on the arch. That must have smelled of politics to the supervisor. Not knowing how my projections function, how they illuminate the relation between image and architecture, the park administration evidently feared they had condoned a work of political propaganda. But once the projection was in place, it didn't have the shock of propaganda; the missiles looked very natural there. The projection lasted for only one hour, from 11:30 to 12:30 the next year, and when the supervisor arrived it was all over. But she still wanted to see it, so even though I was packing up my equipment, I set it up again for her. She was amazed by her own positive reaction to it, seduced by the brightness and glamour of the image, "pleasantly surprised," she said, by the integration of image and architecture. "The customer must be satisfied. Misunderstandings are out of the question!" as Witkiewicz wrote in the epigraph for his "Rules of the Portrait Firm" in the 1930s.[1] I heard that the threatened reputation of the art officer was restored immediately.

DOUGLAS CRIMP: What about the people who came to see the fireworks?

WODICZKO: That's a different story. Part of the public was disappointed that the slides didn't change. Slide projections mean, for most people, a "slide show," a multi-image spectacle. Because the public had to look for other aspects of the image than those of relationships between different images, they had to try to see the relation between the image and the architectural form. At first, people don't see architectural structures as images in themselves; they see them as physical surfaces, as screens for the projection. But keeping the image static helps to integrate it with the architecture.

DEUTSCHE: How many people saw the projection?

WODICZKO: I was told that fourteen hundred people attended the event, but since the Grand Army Plaza is Brooklyn's major vehicular traffic circle and the red lights forced cars to stop exactly in front of the projection, many more hundreds of people must have seen it. Many cars stopped or slowed down despite the green light, and some circled around for a second look. Most of the people who came to the event were from the black and Hispanic community in Brooklyn, many of whom were school children. They were people who had no place else to go to celebrate New Year's Eve. Some members of the cultural intelligentsia, as well as some junior-high-school students who had seen photographs of my projections shown at The New Museum at that time, made an effort to be there. The projection was on the north side of the arch and therefore could be seen, not from Prospect Park, but from the small adjacent park in front of which the arch stands. Cars drive all around that park, making it a very circumscribed and intimate viewing area. There are no sculptures or reliefs on the north side of the arch. This is a monument to the Northern army, so the south side of the arch is very busy with representations of the army marching south to liberate the South from "wrongdoing." The monument has absolutely nothing to say about the North, because if it did, it would have to reflect on itself. So despite the fact that the arch is symmetrically designed to carry sculptures on both sides, there is no sculpture on the north side.

LAJER-BURCHARTH: So you were interested in completing the monument symmetrically with images that ironically echoed the structure and the elements on the southern side. For example, you projected a padlock, a sign of constraint and limitation, on the keystone of the arch as a dissonant equivalent of the figure of Liberation, the winged Victory.

CRIMP: It also reinscribes the North/South conflict with an East/West orientation.

WODICZKO: After growing up in the East, it certainly helps to arrive in the West from the north—by which I mean Canada—in order better to see all sides of the arch, especially the repressed, northern side. Ironically, this arch, which is conceived as receiving the victorious Northern army and which uses a classicizing beaux-arts style, is challenged by two small realist bas-relief sculptures by Eakins placed inside the arch. They are the only two figures actually walking north, coming back from the war, extremely tired. One of the horses is limping. As far as I know, this is the only monument in the world that contains such an internal debate, aesthetically and historically. The fact that a realist was allowed to enter the beaux-arts domain in reverse direction is extraordinary.

Anyway, my reorientation of the arch to an East/West conflict converts the reading of the arch from its commentary on the South to one of left and right, to the weight of the arch's two bases. The people viewing the projection offered their own interpretations. What I liked was that everyone was trying to impose his or her reading upon others. It turned into a political debate based on reading the symbols and referring to the contemporary political situation. It was a time when the public was being prepared for impending peace talks between the U.S. and Soviet governments. There were great expectations about coming back to the conference table and perhaps for a reduction of the arms race. I wanted to respond to this, but, of course, it's impossible today to be optimistic and intelligent at the same time. So I wanted the people to see various possibilities. But since everyone was interested in convincing others of his or her own reading, only a few seemed to realize that the various readings were all simultaneously possible. One reading was that the missiles were two phallic symbols. Another was that the projection was about disarmament, the nuclear freeze, the liberal position. And a third group spoke of the interdependence of the superpowers, the fact that they are locked together, that they cannot exist without each other, and that there is a frightening similarity between them. Because the debate was open and easily heard, all the readings were most likely received by everyone, and hopefully this social and auditory interaction helped the visual projection survive in the public's memory as a complex experience. For a moment at least, this "necro-ideological" monument became alive.

Halfway through the projection, behind and above the arch, there was another audiovisual experience for eight minutes that gave the projection a new, enhanced context. The fireworks—detonations, explosions, aerial illuminations—this display would have had a double meaning for anyone who had experienced bombings of cities or who, growing up in the ruins of cities, had seen films of those bombings. This was certainly the case for the Polish intellectuals among the spectators, among them the critic Szymon Bojko.

Bojko, who lives in Poland, wrote a popular book on Soviet constructivist graphic design.[2] He is able to address, both popularly and historically, the relation between art and propaganda. Through his connections in the Soviet Union, he knows a lot about Vkhutemas,[3] the Soviet predecessor of the Bauhaus.

Working in the sixties in the cultural department of the central committee of the Polish United Workers Party,[4] Bojko managed to influence the committee with very clear ideas on the organization of industrial design education, research, and practice. He came to see my *Grand Army Plaza Projection* with a group of Polish and American friends from New York, so I was very interested to see how they would respond. They were relieved to see that there were both Soviet and U.S. missiles, because they had heard that one of my projections in Stuttgart consisted of only a Pershing II missile and that one in Canada was of only a U.S.-built Cruise missile. So there was probably some talk of my not acknowledging both sides of the problem, which is a very sensitive issue in Poland. They also suggested the reading of the interdependence between the superpowers, and some of them mentioned the ironic relationship between the heroic monumentality of the arch and the new "heroism" and "monumentality" of intercontinental ballistic missiles. Poles are very well-educated about public monuments. As the Polish playwright Slawomir Mrozek put it, "Somewhere between the monuments and the memorials lies Poland."

LAJER-BURCHARTH: Your projections also remind me of an important aspect of Polish May Day parades. The focal point of the parades, the pompous facades of the socialist-realist buildings on the main street in Warsaw, used to be adorned with huge, four-story-high portraits of contemporary Polish heads of state hung side by side with those of Marx and Lenin. This display was obviously a kind of wish fulfillment of the Polish rulers anxious to secure symbolic continuity between themselves and the unquestioned heroes of the communist past. The socialist-realist architecture was made to reinforce this continuity with the authority of its classicizing forms. And the portraits reciprocated as an endorsement by the current leadership of the excessive grandeur of this postwar architecture. Obviously, the effect of your projections is very different. Far from this reciprocal completion, the clashing of image and architecture calls into question the authority of both. But wouldn't you say that the Polish context is relevant to your attitude toward images of authority?

WODICZKO: Yes, to the extent that the architecture of the sixties, and even more so that of the seventies, the Gierek era, embodied a new style, a fetishism of progress, a Westernized, technocratic version of progress (echoing Lenin's New Economic Policy), a "state productivism," if I may put it that way. In this period the acquired capitalist, "scientifically exploitative" organization of production was wedded to the state socialist, centrally planned, bureaucratic exploitation of workers' labor, all in the name of achieving a higher, which is to say, closer to Western, standard of living. The environmental evidence of Gierek's new New Economic Policy was painfully visible in the form of the rapid development of office towers, gigantic hotels, shopping centers, automobiles, super highways, and urban vehicular arterials. In this context, the grand official manifestations of the seventies provided an opportunity to see very clearly the propaganda effects of both the earlier, Stalinist architecture, which now looked "romantic," and the new Western-style, abstract, technocratic architecture.

LAJER-BURCHARTH: With the advent of Gierek an important change was introduced into the official symbolic practices in order to take account of the new economic order. In the May Day parades, portraits of contemporary Polish leaders were no longer used. Gierek's leadership was represented instead by such signs of technocratic progress as the new Forum hotel, built by a Swedish contractor, at the site where the parade ends. This building and others built in the seventies became the backdrops for portraits of Marx and Lenin. The architecture itself was intended to testify to the successful continuation of their ideals.

CRIMP: Are you saying, then, that this kind of political manifestation was central to your own understanding of the relationship between image and architecture?

WODICZKO: It did help to be able to see the impact of a grand but temporary political decoration on the public's perception of buildings, of the cityscape as a whole. It also helped me to understand the effect of the absence of such decorations after they were taken down, to remember the architectural "after-image" of a political slogan or icon, its lasting but illusive integration with the building. Such an experience suggests, of course, the possibility of a temporary, *unofficial, critical* "decoration," difficult to imagine in Poland, where censorship of the public domain is total, but a little easier to imagine here, where censorship is also strong but less centralized. Generally, Poland was a great laboratory of environmental ideology. But the imagery of official Polish propaganda is so architectural itself, perfect to the point of its own death. The obvious, sloganistic character, the lifeless appearance makes Polish imagery less subversive, less seductive, appearing to be less "natural" than American propaganda imagery, such as advertising or even an official event like the "Liberty Celebration." But Polish propaganda does have a powerful architectural quality which integrates well with the ideological/architectural environment. So I did learn much in Poland, but my education needed to be completed in the context of capitalist consumer culture. It was an advantage that I went first to Canada, where cultural studies of media and communications are very strong. My teaching affiliation with the Cultural Studies Program in Peterborough, Ontario, was important in this regard. Only after several years outside Poland was I able fully to comprehend the degree to which artists and designers in Poland were ideologically trapped by the Westernized, "liberal" state socialism of the seventies. Artists earned their freedom to work with what were called "various means of expression," that is, to exclude official politics from their art, by including those very politics in the work they did on commission for the state propaganda apparatus. So one was political as a collaborator-artist in the morning and apolitical as a "pure" artist in the evening in the confines of one's studio. Only a few artists and designers realized that in such a situation they were really acting as collaborators with the system not in the morning but in the evening.

CRIMP: Was this your experience?

WODICZKO: Not really. I was an industrial designer working full time in the design office of the Polish Optical Works in Warsaw, so I was not working freelance, not vulnerable to the changing desires of the ideological design market, and not needing to work for the propaganda apparatus as most painters, sculptors, and graphic designers did. I worked in a factory designing professional instruments such as microscopes, measuring devices, electronic systems for quality control, scientific research, laboratory, and medical purposes. At one point I was on a design team that was asked to design a geological compass....

LAJER-BURCHARTH: An ideological compass?!

WODICZKO: You almost spoiled my story, because you understand too quickly. There were all sorts of demands coming from the industrial brass to come up with a less professional, more popular tool in response to Gierek's program for an increase in the production of consumer goods. That was, of course, an idiotic demand for a professional instruments company. So I said publicly, in the design office, that we would design this compass only if there were no member of the Communist Party on the design team, because north is north, not east or west. A compass can only show magnetic north. Somehow, nothing happened to me, perhaps because as an industrial designer, a member of a still-young profession, I was treated as an eccentric in the industrial world. As a graduate of the Academy of Fine Arts, I was also treated as an "artist," even though I did everything I could to counteract that view. This experience taught me how thoroughly design is submerged in politics. I learned a lot about politics even regarding the most innocent measuring instrument, something that can be done only in the most technical manner. Imagine what my designer friends were going through when designing refrigerators!

DEUTSCHE: What was your background before you worked as an industrial designer? Can you tell us something about your education?

WODICZKO: In the Soviet Union in the twenties the educational path lead from fine art to design, from analytical constructivism to productivism. For me, in the sixties and seventies, the situation was, of course, different. The period of Gomulka's de-Stalinization in Poland provided an opening for contact with Western design circles, such as the school in Ulm,[5] and with those of prewar avant-garde design, such as BLOK, Praesens, a.r.,[6] and the Koluszki school.[7] I studied at the Academy of Fine Arts in Warsaw in the sixties. The graduate program in industrial design, in which I was a student, was directed by Jerzy Soltan, a former assistant of Le Corbusier. At that time Soltan was directing a similar program at Harvard, teaching the fall term in Warsaw and the spring term in Cambridge. I'm sure that Szymon Bojko's support was crucial to Soltan's success in Poland. Soltan, his assistant Andrzej Wróblewski, now president of the academy, and Bojko had devised a post-avant-garde strategy for post-Stalinist Poland. The special education of designers was a key point of their strategy. The program emphasized the development of the students' individual and collective skills for infiltrating the institutional structure while working as common industrial designers, organizers of design offices in all branches of industry, teachers, researchers, and so on. It was a neoproductivist model. This was the period of the creation of the Industrial Design Council, whose head is vice-premier of the government and whose members are vice-ministers. So industrial design was very highly bureaucratized, much better organized than in the West or in Lenin's Soviet Union. I was trained to be a member of the elite unit of designers, skillful infiltrators who were supposed to transform existing state socialism into an intelligent, complex, and human design project. This positive social program for industrial design, indebted historically to the program of Vkhutemas, unfortunately shifted in the Gierek era to a technocratic, consumerist phase and thus adopted the international constructivist tradition in place of constructivism proper, the latter being the constructivism that developed in the Soviet Union as a means of building a society rather than decorating bourgeois society with objects. The depoliticization of constructivism's history was a very unfortunate part of our experience as artists. There is a famous museum of constructivism in Lódz.[8] In the seventies it was already quite clear that the effect, and perhaps even the mission of this museum was to depoliticize the entire constructivist tradition, intellectual and artistic, affiliating it more and more with international, Western constructivism, the de Stijl movement, and neoconstructivism such as op and kinetic art.

LAJER-BURCHARTH: This tendency to depoliticize Polish constructivism by playing down its links with the Soviet experiment should be situated historically within the liberalization associated with Gierek. The reinterpretation of Polish artistic traditions as independent from Soviet art paralleled the reorientation of the Polish economy toward the West. This view of constructivism was also part of the defensive reaction to the postwar imposition of Soviet art policies in Poland, that is, to socialist realism. The imposition of Zhdanovist orthodoxy stalled any discussion of the alternative forms of culture for the new socialist society until the late fifties.

WODICZKO: Quite openly so. As part of the six-year plan of 1949, the guidelines of the council of architects specifically declared socialist realism a critique of constructivism. This "critique" collapsed the complex history of constructivism into one international bourgeois movement, excoriated as "cosmopolitanism, constructivism, and formalism," whose "abstract forms" were said to be "always foreign to the people." But the Stalinist position, for all its regressive effect, was at least conducted in the name of social responsibility, socialist content, the national cultural heritage, a human form for the environment, and so on. The Stalinist era represented a total politicization of art and design, including a politicization of the war against constructivism. The Gierek era, by contrast, represented a total depoliticization of art and design, including a war on constructivism carried out through its depoliticization. This most recent perversion of constructivism, then, resulted in what I call socialist technocratism.

DEUTSCHE: So there was a depoliticization of constructivism in the East that is directly parallel to that in the West.

LAJER-BURCHARTH: Except that in Poland this process took place in a more overtly political context. In the West the depoliticization of constructivism was effected by the art-historical discourse, while in Poland it was an element of national cultural policy. The attempt to restore to constructivism its real history that is now taking place in the West has also begun in Poland, especially in the work of Andrzej Turowski. His *Polish Constructivism* appeared as late as 1981,[9] but Turowski wrote an earlier, popular analysis of constructivism in a book series devoted to twentieth-century avant-garde movements.

WODICZKO: His title for the earlier book was *The Constructivist Revolution,* which suggests the interplay between aesthetic and political revolution. The editors changed it to *In the Circle of Constructivism*.[10] It is against editorial policy to acknowledge openly anything as political, including constructivism. Turowski's repoliticization and rehistoricization of constructivism was a crucial experience for me. The Foksal Gallery, of which Turowski and Wieslaw Borowski were the codirectors, had established itself as a center of criticism of artistic culture. It is a type of alternative gallery not really known here in that it was run collectively by critics, and not by artists. Through the presentation of works of art, critical texts, and debates, the gallery wished to affect the larger context. They applied the avant-garde style of manifestos and interventions, but "post-avant-garde" to the extent that they accepted the limitation of utopia, dealing as they were with a reality that was already organized in the name of utopia.

When Turowski entered the gallery as a young scholar of constructivism, he contributed a Marxist methodology to the gallery's tactics and strategies, which was a very significant change, because at that time the gallery critics and artists were operating with surrealist ideas. Turowski's presence resulted in a fusion of a moral critique of established artistic culture with a social critique, and self-critique, of that culture's institutions. Turowski wrote a very important short text entitled "Gallery against Gallery." It was the beginning of the concept of the gallery as a self-critical institution, an institution questioning its own place in society in relation to other institutions, and doing so to the extent of putting into question the entire institutional system of culture. Foksal also published texts called "What We Don't Like about Foksal Gallery" and "Documentation," which called for the destruction of all the art documents. The "Living Archive" created the exaggerated idea of an archive that would protect documents by preventing their further circulation and cultural manipulation.

LAJER-BURCHARTH: This occurred in response to censorship. In Poland, unlike other Soviet bloc countries, a certain independence is granted within the domain of culture so long as culture is willing to contain itself and refrain from interaction with other social activity. Foksal Gallery was one such island of cultural criticism that was allowed to exist. But even this self-imposed marginalization did not guarantee complete freedom of operation. When I was involved with another alternative gallery, founded after Foksal, we managed to publish several issues of a journal about critical aesthetic practices without asking for party approval for our editorial staff. We did this by using the paper allotted us for the publication of exhibition catalogues. Soon, though, we were forced to discontinue publication, not because of any specific contents, but because it is prohibited to put out a serial publication, something that can be distributed and read regularly, without the consent of the centralized apparatus of the state. Seriality itself threatened to spill culture outside its prescribed limits.

WODICZKO: The experience with censorship, with official culture, and with the entire institutional system, the changing meaning of each form of cultural activity in changing political circumstances, was a central part of my experience in Poland, especially because of my affiliation with Foksal Gallery but also because of my father.

Throughout the period of Stalinism and the Gomulka and Gierek eras, my father was involved with serious cultural politics as a conductor and artistic director of city and state orchestras and opera companies. He was famous for introducing the Polish public to the contemporary, artistically ambitious repertoire.[11] People such as my father and those associated with Foksal Gallery, just as the people like Soltan and Bojko, whom we have already discussed, learned to cope with the system of restrictions and liberties in order consciously to infiltrate and manipulate the system while also recognizing the extent to which they were being manipulated by the system. So, having close contacts with the mechanisms of censorship and self-censorship and with the politics of official artistic culture and of industry and education (I was teaching at Warsaw's Polytechnique), and having my father's example, I learned very quickly that we must adopt some kind of post-avant-garde strategy in Poland.

LAJER-BURCHARTH: Since you are speaking of the strategy of manipulating the system from within, of interfering with the codes, so to speak, were you familiar with the writings of Roland Barthes?

WODICZKO: Barthes was not unknown to me and my generation. Most of the French theoreticians, especially those working in the field of culture, were translated into Polish, possibly earlier than into English. Writings, films, plays, and art critical of contemporary bourgeois culture were always welcomed by the Polish censorship apparatus. It was, however, difficult to learn from writers like Barthes how to operate critically within the Polish situation. Once one realized the best strategies for one's own place, though, it was easier to understand what Barthes was suggesting for the West. But we should not forget that the situation during the late sixties and early seventies was in some respects similar in France and Poland. We lost our student battles in 1968, too. We lost faith in our utopian revolutionary approach, and we needed new strategies. Polish students' demands differed from those of the French students, but there were many similarities. Poland and Czechoslovakia were part of the overall movement in the sixties. So after the failure of all of our revolutions, we found ourselves in similar situations, whether we happened to be reading Barthes or not. I wonder, by the way, whether Barthes would have understood the strategies of Foksal Gallery in the context of French cultural politics of the same period. But you know very well that Poland and France have been very closely connected. Many Polish students witnessed what happened in France in 1968. Turowski was one of them. The work of Daniel Buren and the Support-Surface group would not have been clear to me without the conversations with Turowski and some of his friends from Poznan....

LAJER-BURCHARTH: In Poznan there is a dynamic Marxist intellectual milieu, a rarity in Polish academic life.

WODICZKO: I realized that what the Polish constructivists Katarzyna Kobro and Wladyslaw Strzeminski were dreaming about, "the organization of the rhythms of life" as the ultimate aesthetic project, was already organized all around us. So, learning from the constructivists the relationship between society and form, among politics, art, and everyday life, by combining this with the knowledge of futurist, dada, and surrealist interventions, we could begin to understand that our aim was not to contribute to the further organization of the "rhythms of life," but to interrupt, interfere, and intervene in the already highly organized "rhythms of life."

CRIMP: So this strategy of interruption or interference, which might be said to characterize your work now, is something that you had already developed in the Polish context.

WODICZKO: Yes, seeds of my critical activity here in the public sphere can be found in my early works in Warsaw, especially in the two "deconstructivist" technical "inventions." The first of these was *Instrument,* presented to the public in Warsaw in 1971. I designed it with the help of technicians from the Experimental Music Studio. It was an electro-acoustic instrument/costume that transformed, through my hand gestures, the accidental noise of city traffic into modulated sounds that only I could hear. The second was *Vehicle,* constructed with the help of Foksal Gallery, and shown publicly in Warsaw in 1972. Through a system of gears and cables, the vehicle was propelled forward by perpetually walking back and forth on its tilting top surface. It thus transformed the conventional back-and-forth pacing associated with intellectual reflection or with being stymied into the forward movement associated with the official notion of progress. You can see that my metaphoric vehicle was an ironic reconsideration of such an optimistic, techno-socialist project as Tatlin's *Letatlin.*[12]

DEUTSCHE: If, to some degree, your work still involves the interruption of the official organization of society, how does such a strategy function here, in a different context? In Poland, as you've explained, you had to work within a social organization that includes official and overt censorship, while here censorship functions very differently; the entire organization of the social is much less apparent, much less obvious. How do you transfer the ideas which had formed your strategies in Poland to a different context?

WODICZKO: By trying to intervene in the public sphere as close as possible to the legal and technical limits that are imposed. Acting in the public sphere in the West, I have confronted not only a different category of censorship, but a different level. There is a greater general possibility for working in public, but this creates a need for more complicated strategies to deal with a complex set of institutional, corporate, state, and community restrictions. But the "transfer of ideas" to the West must be discussed in relation not only to forms and categories of censorship, to different kinds of artistic unfreedom, but also to the applicability of the ideas to the new situation. It is safe to say, however, that, despite all the differences, there are great similarities in our everyday lives in relation to our physical environment, whether in Poland, Canada, the U.S., or the Soviet Union. There are similarities in the ways that architecture functions as an ideological medium, a psychological partner, in the way it educates, orders, participates in the process of socialization, in the way it integrates its "body" with our bodies, in the ways it rapidly changes or even destroys our lives. My public projections developed first in Canada, because in Poland I could not even consider such an art form simply because of technical limitations, and obviously because of the censorship of the public sphere. Even to use images from the press for my gallery projections, which I had done in an exhibition called *References*, I needed to have permission, because individuals don't own images; the state does. The result is that it is impossible to change the context of images, because the state is perfectly aware of the semiotics of the image. In order to use images, one must resort to metaphor rather than direct statement.

CRIMP: Do people learn to read metaphors better in such a situation than they do here, to perform a hermeneutic operation on every image?

LAJER-BURCHARTH: This is, in fact, how culture survives. Filmmakers, writers, and artists who want to comment on social reality usually employ metaphor. Otherwise their possibilities of affecting public opinion are very restricted.

DEUTSCHE: But can't the censors also read those metaphors?

LAJER-BURCHARTH: Yes, they can, but they are also embarrassed to admit that they can recognize them, because that would imply that they are aware of the shortcomings or problems that the metaphors address. They are afraid to admit to the pertinence of the criticism. This is why the books of the journalist Ryszard Kapuscinski, which expose the corruption of such regimes as those in Ethiopia and Iran,[13] are permitted to be published. Otherwise, the censors would implicitly acknowledge their recognition of the analogies of those regimes with the regimes of Eastern bloc countries, of Poland itself.

WODICZKO: One must read Dostoevski's *Crime and Punishment* to understand the relationship between censor and censored. You learn the language of the censor in order to communicate, and, to some degree the censor must also learn your language. There is a final episode to the narrative of *The Grand Army Plaza Projection* that is relevant here. Several months ago I went to Poland and presented Foksal Gallery with a proposal to show a reconstruction of the project in the gallery. The idea was submitted to the censorship board and the woman in charge explained that it would be impossible to present the work because it would violate article number eight hundred and something or other of the censorship code, which says that under no circumstances are weapons of the U.S. and Soviet Union to be visually depicted as of equal weight, volume, or quantity. An exhibition of documents of my public projections is opening at Foksal Gallery in September this year with *The Grand Army Plaza Projection* and a few others excluded. A catalogue with reproductions of the projections and my theoretical texts is being published. The texts, both in English and in Polish translation, are of course censored. "Public Projection," originally published in the *Canadian Journal of Political and Social Theory* in 1983, attempts to situate my work in the relations among body, architecture, power, and ideology. This was accepted for publication with only one "criticism"; the words "power" and "ideology" must be omitted entirely.

DEUTSCHE: But presumably you knew what would not pass the censorship when you submitted your proposals.

WODICZKO: No, because the laws of censorship have changed. But also the very essence of authoritarian existence is that you never really know what is allowed and what is not. There used to be a "black book" of censorship, a general list of rules and regulations. That has now been replaced by a code of specific regulations, which is changed regularly in response to changing circumstances, so the situation is much worse now. It is much more difficult to fool the system when there are very highly qualified censors immediately interpreting changing conditions and implementing regulations. Some of these people have Ph.D.s; they are "intellectuals." It is a perfect illustration of Marx's definition of censorship, which is that it is centralized criticism. So in Poland there is a kind of centralized art criticism. No one in Poland can complain of the lack of "critical response" to his or her work. Art criticism is democratically guaranteed!

CRIMP: Apart from the contents of the images, what is the response in Poland, not only of the censors, but of the intellectuals, to the production mode of your work? Is there any problem of their reading this as aesthetic activity? Are they sufficiently aware of recent developments, albeit marginalized, in the West to understand your mode of working?

WODICZKO: I don't think there is a general problem with understanding my working methods in Poland, nor is there a problem of information about art developments in the West. Information about the West is temporarily limited today, but in the seventies it was quite accessible, and is beginning to improve again. Hans Haacke's and Daniel Buren's work, for example, is well known to Foksal Gallery, Akumulatory 2, Studio, and many other galleries. Foksal showed Lawrence Weiner, Art and Language, Victor Burgin, European and American Fluxus, and so on. Poland is marginalized less by lack of information about art in the West than by the lack of information about art in Poland available in the West.

LAJER-BURCHARTH: I don't think the political nature of Krzysztof's work would prevent people in Poland from accepting it as aesthetic practice. After all, they are used to looking for political messages coded in art rather than in the political discourse itself, which is considered totally corrupt.

WODICZKO: My work receives an informed response in Poland. If there is any problem, it is related to different perspectives on global politics, between my perspective, which developed just across the border from the U.S., and theirs, which develops across the border from the monstrous presence of the Soviet Union. Polish censorship and Polish intellectuals have similar but opposite doubts about my position with regard, for example, to the question of the equivalence of Soviet and U.S. weapons.

CRIMP: What were the circumstances of your leaving Poland?

WODICZKO: I did not really leave Poland in 1977, in the sense that I had the idea of not returning. It's only that I didn't want to lose contact with the outside world. It was extremely crucial for me to see Poland from the outside. Each time I returned to Poland I was more aware of the extent to which social questions were neglected, how thoroughly we were locked into the prison of an Eastern European perspective. My position was never met with much understanding, even within Foksal Gallery. As long as questions were limited to the politics of culture, things were fine, but when I went beyond that domain, my views were treated as irrelevant. So I wanted to continue to travel back and forth. How naïve I was! Obviously there is no such possibility. You might not get your exit visa; then again you might also not get your entry visa to a country in the West. I had to face the typical dilemma. It was set up for me by the Polish police, who began to blackmail my friends, reading all of our correspondence and sometimes quoting telephone conversations verbatim in order to terrorize friends, who also needed to get exit visas. This particularly involved a woman whom the authorities discovered had previously been secretly traveling with me. In the eyes of both the Polish police and the immigration authorities of the Western states, this should never be done, because two people, especially couples, might not return. When one person leaves and the other stays, it's less suspicious to the bureaucracies in both East and West. The result was that my friend was psychologically assaulted by the police, and after a year was warned that she could leave only if I came back. The only answer to this was not to go back, because one should under no circumstances make a deal with the police. Such a deal often means to them that one is weak and frightened enough to accept other deals. I didn't want to lose my critical perspective about both socio-economic systems, I wanted to learn more from being here, but I never planned consciously to stay. But finally a decision was, in effect, made for me, because one cannot stay anywhere indefinitely without papers. This is the sort of story that later gets collapsed into the "decision to emigrate."

CRIMP: You were then in Canada?

WODICZKO: Yes. I had a number of part-time teaching positions there. The longest was at the Nova Scotia College of Art and Design in Halifax, where I taught for three-and-a-half-years. I began teaching in the design program but later moved to the intermedia program, for which I acted as coordinator for one year. It was a very fortunate opportunity, because that program is connected to the visiting artists program, so I was able to meet and work with people such as Martha Rosler, Mary Kelly, Dan Graham, Dara Birnbaum, Allan Sekula, Connie Hatch, Judith Barry. I also co-organized the Cultural Workers Alliance, a short-lived project, first in Toronto, then in Halifax. It was an unaffiliated, umbrella organization of the left for members of the cultural intelligentsia, a forum for political and artistic discussion, particularly focused on the labor situation in the cultural sector. I managed to involve a number of the more radical students from the college, which provided them with an opportunity to discuss the relationship between the college and the community, the politics of the province, and of Canada generally, something which could not easily be discussed within the college. Certain people at the college considered it a conflict of interest to give any such support to the radical students, but I thought it my obligation to involve them, to help them to see critically their place not only within the college but within the entire cultural system. It was during this period that I began working with public projections.

DEUTSCHE: Were you invited to do a projection on The New Museum of Contemporary Art in New York, or did you apply for the opportunity? And what was your projection's relationship to the exhibition *Difference: On Representation and Sexuality?*

WODICZKO: I was asked to participate in the "On View" series, smaller exhibitions held in conjunction with major shows, such as the *Difference* exhibition. It was not my primary focus to relate my projection to that exhibition. If there was a relation to the *Difference* show, it was mediated through the relation of my projection to the architecture and to the politics of the entire building. The situation at that time was very dramatic. It was winter and I was living very close to the main shelter for homeless men and quite close to a shelter for women. I saw many people living on the street, trying to survive the bitter-cold temperatures by burning tires. It was therefore shocking to me to see one of the largest buildings in the entire neighborhood empty. It was very evident that the building that houses The New Museum was completely dark. People speaking to me at the time of the projection had no doubts whatsoever about the meaning of it. I learned that the upper floors of the building were awaiting new tenants at a price of nearly one million dollars each and at the same time The New Museum received the basement and ground floor spaces for free, or at least for a very cheap rent. The very fact that the museum moved into the building creates a certain myth for the building. There are, in fact, two exhibition spaces there. One is for The New Museum exhibitions, and next door there is an exhibition of the former state of the building and how it will look after renovation, a real estate exhibition. There is obviously a connection between the presence of the museum and the subsequent conversion of the entire surrounding area into one of art galleries and other art-related institutions and businesses. I'm not saying that there is direct responsibility on anyone's part, but this is a mechanism and it's important to recognize and reveal our place within that mechanism, even if we cannot change it at this point.

CRIMP: Is it not a part of your working methods, as it is of Haacke's, for example, to investigate the particulars of such a situation?

WODICZKO: If I were to project information onto the building about its operations I would certainly undertake systematic research, but what was immediately striking here was the emptiness of this huge structure when all around it people were living on the street. The bottom padlock was decided upon later, when I learned more about the connections between the museum and this art/real estate operation. So this was, first, *The Astor Building Projection,* and then, second, *The New Museum Projection.*

CRIMP: Since we're on the subject of The New Museum, I wonder if you want to comment on the *Sots Art* exhibition shown there recently, insofar as it is a show of artists from the Eastern bloc, specifically the Soviet Union, working, with one exception, in the American context.

DEUTSCHE: You've already made an interesting comment to me about the exhibition, noting that the museum relegated the critique of bourgeois culture—Connie Hatch's *Serving the Status Quo,* the Group Material work—to the small, back space while giving much greater prominence to the art which purports to be a critique of Soviet society.

WODICZKO: Without in any way taking back that comment, I have to express my enthusiasm for the fact that The New Museum provides so much space and time in its program for critical work, and I'm sure there are many reasons for a political stratification of that space. In order to survive, that institution must deal with a very complex situation, responding to the conflicting demands of its sponsors and supporters, as well as its various curators. If there had been a reversal of critical priorities in this particular case, it would have created a far greater impact on the community, which I obviously would have preferred, but it is impossible for me to judge the organizers' intentions. So, in spite of many reasons for dissatisfaction, this last season at The New Museum consisted of a fair number of critical exhibitions, including, for example, *The Art of Memory, the Loss of History.*

CRIMP: Perhaps I can refocus my question regarding a so-called dissident art by Eastern bloc artists showing in the American context by referring to the event organized for May Day at the Palladium by Komar and Melamid, two of the central figures in the *Sots Art* exhibition. They staged a mock May Day celebration in the discotheque which is partially owned by Roy Cohn, who, as you well know, is one of the most repulsive reactionaries in recent American political history and has recently been disbarred in New York State. Another of the owners, Steve Rubell, was quoted in the newspapers as saying that one of the things he liked about the Palladium was that it was a place where young people could forget about the problems of Nicaragua. The Palladium is also the discotheque that uses artworld celebrity events as the drawing card for its clientele.

DEUTSCHE: In such a context, I don't see how Komar and Melamid's May Day celebration can be seen as anything but cynical.

WODICZKO: Not everything is to be seen from the perspective of the New Yorker. From the vantage point of global relations, I would like to try to see their point, which is not to say that I would support it. Though they have organized this event here, it is possible to imagine that they would prefer a double event, to stage simultaneously a discotheque in Red Square, for example. Perhaps they would like to be able to show the degradation of the Soviet May Day celebration by juxtaposing it with something equally degraded in this context, such as an art-world disco.

LAJER-BURCHARTH: But what is the purpose of staging this mockery of a Soviet political manifestation in New York in 1986? If Komar and Melamid want to criticize the atrophy of this particular symbolic practice, doing so in New York only diverts our attention from the historically specific factors responsible for this atrophy in the Soviet Union. And, when suggesting that these once spontaneous workers' celebrations ossified into their opposite in the East, do these artists wish to imply that the May Day parade has also lost its meaning in the West? One of the reasons for the loss of meaning of the May Day parades in the Eastern bloc is constraint: people are *forced* to participate. But in the West participation is, of course, still voluntary. It was a great surprise to me to see masses of people joyfully celebrating May Day in Denmark, where I lived after leaving Poland. It is Komar and Melamid's glib implication of the cultural and political equivalence of the two that I find problematic.

WODICZKO: It would be interesting if such an event could be extended—not for balance, not to adopt the liberal position—to show the disco as equally ideologically determined, as equally a part of official life as the political manifestations in the Soviet Union. But, in fact, Komar and Melamid are not clearly critical of either system. They submerge themselves with perverse pleasure in the repressive realities of both Soviet and American existence, wallowing in what they see as the equivalent decadence of both empires. They perform art-historical manipulations to support their political nihilism, creating, for example, pop-art versions of socialist realism. I question the political clarity and social effectiveness of adopting pop-art strategies for the critique of Soviet culture. Even though they developed a powerful humor, which would have been a liberating experience in intellectual circles, it would hardly have been so liberating for anyone who did not enjoy the privileges granted to artists in the Soviet Union. There is a similar problem in the reception of their work here in the United

States, where people only have the most general notions of socialist realism and of the Soviet reality.

DEUTSCHE: In discussing *The Grand Army Plaza Projection* you mentioned various possible readings of the work. But there are other works, such as the projection of the swastika onto the pediment of the South African embassy in Trafalgar Square, that have very unambiguous meanings. Does the necessity of responding to specific political events suggest a different kind of projection?

WODICZKO: That was a very short-lived dilemma for me because I had to make a decision very quickly. I already had permission for the projection on Nelson's Column, permission to project hands onto the column. I had therefore already committed one violation in not projecting hands but rather a huge intercontinental ballistic missile wrapped in barbed wire, and tank treads underneath the lions, at the column's base. But I knew they wouldn't be able to stop me. For one thing bureaucracy doesn't work at night, even if the media does; BBC televised the projection nationally. I also knew that I had six xenon arc slide projectors concentrated in Trafalgar Square. No one knows when such an opportunity might happen again and it certainly never happened to me before. Many people would have liked the opportunity to affect this building, for example those who were demonstrating in front of it just at that time. The projection on Nelson's Column was to take place on two consecutive evenings. So the first evening, I came prepared with slides with spots of different sizes to test the proper focal length of the projection on the South African embassy. I had a very short negotiation with myself. Artists are so trapped in their own so-called histories. I thought, "Wait a minute, this is not the type of work you do. You do not project swastikas." But the other side of me answered, "So what? Just because you haven't done this sort of thing before doesn't mean that there isn't a reason to do it now. What do you know of your so-called artistic development?" I agree with you, Rosalyn, that this might open up new possibilities for a more specific contextual type of intervention. It's public art, and one must respond to changing circumstances. It was just at this time that a delegation had come from South Africa to ask the British government for more money, which Thatcher actually gave them, a very shameful act. So my little negotiation was quickly resolved and I reproduced the swastika slides of different sizes. All I had to do was to use one of the projectors from *The Nelson's Column Projection* and turn its 400mm lens ninety degrees. It was projected over the sign in the pediment, which many people knew. There is a relief of a boat, underneath which it says "Good Hope." This building is the most illuminated of all buildings in central London, obsessively illuminated, as if it were afraid to wake up in the morning and not find itself. The projection lasted for two hours. Of course I consulted a lawyer. The only charge on which they would be able to arrest me was for being a public nuisance, and those were the grounds on which they stopped the projection. After two hours I saw the police sergeant coming. I switched off the projector and removed the slide, so he could do nothing. But he told me that if I were to resume the projection I would be arrested, and he also said, very pompously, "If I might offer my personal opinion, I find your projection in very bad taste." Photographs of the projection appeared in the press the following day in conjunction with condemnations of apartheid, so the South African embassy sent an official letter of protest to the Canadian embassy, which is just across Trafalgar Square, and which was exhibiting documents of my work. The Canadian embassy responded with a letter saying that the views of individual Canadian citizens are not the responsibility of the Canadian government.

CRIMP: I'm curious to know more about the legalities of such a situation. Can a slide projection, which is after all immaterial, be considered a means of defacement?

WODICZKO: We should be precise. This is not a clear legal question but a paralegal response of the police based on their own interpretation of regulations. That doesn't mean that what I am doing is illegal, but neither does it mean that I cannot be arrested.

CRIMP: Was it especially difficult to get permission from the Swiss government for the projection on the Swiss national parliament building?

WODICZKO: It was a bit difficult, especially for Jean-Hubert Martin, then director of the Kunsthalle in Bern, who was negotiating the permission for me, since my projection was done for a show he was coorganizing called *Alles und noch viel mehr*. I knew that I would have to use an image that would be acceptable to the bureaucracy, and here I think my Polish experience helped. One has to know the psychology of officialdom, which is in many ways similar wherever I work, because it involves the very concept of modern bureaucracy, the kind of bureaucracy which is supposed to be objective, objective in the sense of helping people take advantage of "democracy." I knew I wanted to project onto the pediment, since it was the only free surface on the building. It was a question of what would be acceptable, and then, when accepted, what would make a point. I figured no one would object to the image of an eye, and at the same time they wouldn't have to know that the eye would change the direction of its gaze, looking first in the direction of the national bank, and then at the canton bank, then the city bank of Bern, then down to the ground of Bundesplatz, under which is the national vault containing the Swiss gold, and finally up to the mountains and the sky, the clear, pure, Calvinist sky. It was difficult for them to refuse to cooperate because the work was part of the Kunsthalle show, which had already received the support of the city. Of course, the parliament building belongs not to the city but to the federal government, which would not want to create tension between itself and the city. I had spent a certain amount of time in bars in Bern and I learned there about the Swiss gold below the parking area in front of the parliament, a fact which most people in Switzerland take for granted. It's not, after all, so bad to be a tourist. Sometimes you learn things that local residents take for granted and are then able to expose the obvious in a critical manner. But of course tourism cannot simply be treated as an individual experience. It is becoming an ever-more complex political phenomenon which requires its own analysis. I intend to focus my projectors on this phenomenon in my work for the Venice Biennale this summer.

1. S.I. Witkiewitz (1885–1939), painter, photographer, playwright, theoretician, created The Portrait Firm in 1925 as an ironic response to bourgeois conditions of art in Poland. "The Rules of the Portrait Firm" were first published in 1928. A translation into French appears in *Présences Polonaises* (Paris: Centre Georges Pompidou, 1983), p.73.

2. Szymon Bojko, *New Graphic Design in Revolutionary Russia* (New York: Praeger, 1972).

3. Vkhutemas, an acronym for the Russian for Higher Art and Technical Workshops, was founded in the Soviet Union in 1920. In 1927 it was re-formed and renamed Vkhutein (State Higher Art and Technical Workshops); it was dissolved in 1930. For a brief history, cf. Szymon Bojko, "Vkhutemas," in *The 1920s in Eastern Europe* (Cologne: Galerie Gmurzynska, 1975), pp.19–26.

4. *Polska Zjednoczona Partia Robotnicza*, the official name of the Communist Party in Poland, which was created during World War II from a merger of the Polish Socialist Party and the Polish Workers Party.

5. The *Hochschule für Gestaltung* was founded in Ulm, West Germany, in 1955. Walter Gropius delivered the inaugural address, saying, "The work once begun in the Bauhaus and the principles formulated there have found a new German home and an opportunity for wider organic development here in Ulm." The school was closed in 1968.

6. BLOK (founded 1924), Praesens (founded 1926), and a.r. (Revolutionary Artists, founded 1929) were the major Polish constructivist groups as well as the names of their publications.

7. Katarzyna Kobro and Wladyslaw Strzeminski taught at the industrial school in Koluszki in 1930-31 using a curriculum based on the educational principles of Vkhutemas and the Bauhaus.

8. At the instigation of Strzeminski and the a.r. group, an international collection of modern art was formed in 1931 at the museum of Lódz, now the Museum Sztuki.

9. Andrzej Turowski, *Konstruktywizm polski* (Warsaw: Polish Academy of Science, Institute of Art, 1981).

10. Andrzej Turowski, *W kregu konstruktywizmu* (Warsaw: Wydawnictwa Artystyczne i Filmowe, 1979).

11. Bohdan Wodiczko (1911-1985) was conductor and artistic director of the Baltic Symphony, Lódz Symphony, Cracow Symphony, Polish National Orchestra, Polish Radio Orchestra, Lódz Opera, and Polish National Opera. He was responsible for introducing postwar Polish audiences to Stravinsky, Berg, Nono, and other modern composers, as well as for engaging such avant-garde figures as Tadeusz Kantor as directors of opera productions.

12. Vladimir Tatlin worked on his flying machine *Letatlin* between 1929 and 1932, at which time he attempted to launch it. He called his glider "an everyday object for the Soviet masses, an ordinary object of use."

13. Ryszard Kapuscinski, *The Emperor: Downfall of an Autocrat*, trans. William R. Brand and Katarzyna Mroczkowska-Brand (San Diego: Harcourt, Brace, Jovanovich, 1983) and *Shah of Shahs*, trans. William R. Brand and Katarzyna Mroczkowska-Brand (San Diego: Harcourt, Brace, Jovanovich, 1985).

REPRINTED FROM *OCTOBER*, NO. 38 (FALL, 1986): 22–51.

JOHN BURGEE: This project is for a site in Boston. It is an office building; the program called for two million square feet. The site is a strange shape, and the surrounding streets are curved and irregular. Other new buildings have been placed awkwardly into these surroundings, so we attempted to find a way to fit our building better to the site and to shape it in an unusual way. In a city like Boston the older scale is a tremendous problem. We tried to reduce the scale of our building by breaking it down into separate volumes—two high glass towers overlaid with a grid of granite, and smaller rectangular volumes with punched windows and a Palladian motif like some other buildings around Boston. The window treatment also serves to break down the scale. There is a sub-grid of reflective glass underneath the grid of granite, with the light that actually allows vision in the center.

PHILIP JOHNSON: It is perfectly obvious that this is a break with our historicist trend. Basically there are two platonic solids, a cylinder and a parallelepiped, jammed together in a most unpleasant way to make a "village." You notice the "medieval" overtones, perhaps, in the top slits and the "eighteenth century" overtones in the Palladian window motif.

ROBERT STERN: I would like to hear a little more from the architects about their attitude toward the building's top, and the difference between a high-rise building and a skyscraper—if there is such a difference.

JOHNSON: You will have to explain what you mean by the difference between a high-rise building and a skyscraper. I do not know the difference.

STERN: In my lexicon a skyscraper is one that has a positive conclusion in the sky, a pinnacle—something like the AT&T or Pennzoil buildings in your own work—whereas this building just seems cut off, with a rather small cornice.

JOHNSON: If you are working with platonic solids, you do not have tops and bottoms.

KEVIN ROCHE: My question is, how does this building relate to the surrounding buildings?

JOHNSON: The surrounding buildings that already exist are four stories high. This site is within a low-rise part of Boston. We do not know who is going to buy the other available lots; we only know that they will be told they have to go along with our decisions. We are the people who are setting the style here. But they will face the same problem we do: how do you develop something of this large a scale in a little old town?

ROCHE: When you speak about the building as a "village," you seem to be suggesting that the people of the village are simply the occupants of the building. However, this village does not contribute to the city of Boston.

JOHNSON: [Nodding] Does not contribute to the city. It is a problem of isolation again.

ROCHE: It is a problem of isolation and how to design two million goddamn square feet that should not be in this part of Boston.

CESAR PELLI: I would like to pursue Bob's question. How do you decide sometimes to make a building that looks like AT&T and sometimes like this one? Two buildings that express two very different, maybe mutually exclusive, ideas of what a very tall building should be?

JOHNSON: How do you decide? Just by the difference in the circumstances. AT&T required a building that stood up vertically.

BURGEE: The shape of the site primarily. AT&T required a more rectangular building because of its rectangular site.

PELLI: The point is not the shape in plan. The point is what the building says. These two buildings say two very different things about what architecture is, what tall buildings are, where architecture is today. You do not note the difference. It is time to do so.

JOHNSON: I do not believe in principles, in case you haven't noticed.

ROBERT SIEGEL: How do you decide, in a plan where there are separate volumes, how to distribute the square footage? Speaking as someone who would want to rent space in the building, or as a person who builds speculative buildings, I would like to know if you are concerned much with the plan configuration. Is there any economic rationale to the plan?

JOHNSON: The rationale was denied.

JACQUELIN ROBERTSON: John and Philip can get their developer clients to do almost anything, even if it contradicts the developers' rules or rationale.

HENRY COBB: There are no such rules—I agree with Philip. Office buildings are the most malleable things you can build.

JOHNSON: Much more malleable than the clients will tell you. The most absurd building in the world is Pennzoil. I was told that they would never rent the smaller spaces, but they rented them for two dollars more per square foot than those in the rest of the building—

FRANK GEHRY: On the street level, there seems to be some ambiguity about the plaza, where you have the large monumental entrances....

JOHNSON: Those are not real entrances. There is always a front door that you do not use and a back door that you really enter—the building we are in is a prime example [Thomas Jefferson's Rotunda—Ed.]. Besides, everybody really comes in through the parking lot; they go underneath and take the shuttle elevator.

GEHRY: Why have it then?

JOHNSON: Oh, for effect.

REM KOOLHAAS: You have given a very impressive display of indifference and also an impressive display of how to create your own freedom and your own awareness. But once having conquered these things, or created them for yourself, you then make a composition of extremely stiff and awkward elements that does not seem to explore your freedom in any visible way. What baffles me is the contradiction between your casualness and the extreme uptightness, the awkward elements.

JOHNSON: Good point. I just choose the elements.

KOOLHAAS: OK, then, but I would like to know on what basis.

JOHNSON: Oh, there isn't any.

PETER EISENMAN: Philip, Rem's point is well taken, and I was hoping we would get to it very early in the day. You abhor the term "pastiche." The fact is that with all these contradictions and your so-called indifference you are making a pastiche of a complex rather than a genuine complex: a plaza in which people do not enter, corners in which intersections are articulated inconsistently, a base that has four different string-course heights and really four different scales. You use the term "platonic solids" and then make a Palladian arched entry. There are so many questions that remain unresolved that I have to raise the question of pastiche.

JOHNSON: I do not mind the word "pastiche."

EISENMAN: You don't?

JOHNSON: No, of course not. You are quite right. You are making very good points, both of you. The sacrifice of some of those values that you mention is deliberate. The only analogy I can think of is the Welsh castles, all of which were built because Edward the Sixth liked to look at castles. Ed made them any old way he pleased. And you couldn't figure out the rationale if your life depended on it. There is no more pastiche here than in a Welsh castle.

ROB KRIER: I have one major problem—it does not have anything to do with the details. It has to do with the idea of a high-rise building. I would never design a building that is higher than the number of floors I can climb with my own legs. In designing high-rise buildings we solve some immediate problems of the client, but these buildings always remain a problem for the city—from traffic to many other concerns. We do not need high-rise buildings anywhere in the world. Not in America or anywhere else. The principal problem in my view is articulating urban space and developing the urban structure.

JOHNSON: No answer to that—

ROBERTSON: A friendly argument.

JOHNSON: I have read your book and I agree with it completely, but I am a whore and I am paid very well for building high-rise buildings. I think that going into an elevator is one of the most unpleasant experiences a man can have, and I do not see why we need them. We have all the room in the world. If you fly over this country, you wonder where all the people are.

PELLI: This is too good an opportunity not to pursue this point. You described your building in terms of givens on the one hand and options on the other; then every time a principle was put on the table you said you do not give a damn about it. What do you give a damn about?

JOHNSON: We give a damn, I think John described it very well, about making a citadel, a village, an irregular place.

PELLI: That is circumstance, not architecture. Not something that you really believe in. What do you think makes these buildings legitimate architecturally?

BURGEE: It is a reduction of the scale so as to relate to the scale of surrounding buildings—

PELLI: All circumstance. What makes these buildings architectural in your mind?

JOHNSON: I think it is something else. I am not a philosopher.

PELLI: You are evading the issue.

JOHNSON: You are bringing up a false issue. What is anybody doing when he is building a building? Figuring out the shapes that fit the site.

SIEGEL: All the building volumes are articulated as if they were separate pieces standing on their own, which then were attached. When attached they do not have any effect on each other. There is no tension between neighboring elements; you have a completely undisturbed building. How is this different from making facades on detached buildings and just jamming them together?

JOHNSON: It isn't different. We smashed them together. That is the way they got all mixed up.

RAFAEL MONEO: I think that in this underlying indifference toward technology, toward function, toward details, there is something almost new in the treatment of skyscrapers. In your approach to building the citadel, the only remaining task for the architect is to develop a strategy toward the land, toward landscaping the city. You do not have any nostalgia for ideal theories of architecture in the Albertian sense. Perhaps this is your job, to do something that in the end can only be understood in one way. This lack of nostalgia probably affects not just your project, but many of the projects in this room.

LEON KRIER: Gentlemen, I am glad that we are so quickly into the midst of the subject. Our problem is really that of critical judgment. In fact, critical judgment is the most important tool of the artist. It is not enough to produce an object and have it criticized by somebody else. As artist or architect, you are the one and only person to judge it; you hold sole responsibility for it. Many of you here at this eminent gathering are capable of getting a very large commission, maybe to build a city of fifty skyscrapers, each as high as the Empire State Building, but perhaps only two people at this table would choose to refuse that commission. Of course, after accepting it and coming up with your solution, you would say, "It is not our fault. We didn't make the zoning. We did not do our own plans." To you I say, you will burn in hell for what you are doing, because it is wrong and you know it is wrong! The problem is that today's zoning not only forces you to build monstrosities, but it promotes a ruthlessness that is characteristic of most modern developments. Zoning projects the future; it describes exactly what our cities will be like in twenty years; it is not just an abstract idea.

Military strategy teaches you that when you have reached a point where you are no longer in command of events, you are losing the battle. There was a time when wars were won not just through total destruction, but by measuring one's forces and then moving them in the best possible way. Today we fight to the end, and that is a very bad strategy for victory. Now, as you may know, both my brother and I have rather grand ambitions to redesign the whole universe to our liking. I am now going to explain very briefly one of these ambitious conceptions, which I applied to the district of Tegel in Berlin, but before doing that I would just like to describe something that dawned on me recently concerning what happened to modern architecture. Modern architecture was not really an invention but a confusion, an end of development. Motor cars, airplanes, petrochemical plants, billboards—this is quite literally the whole gamut of the modern vocabulary. What we thought were innovations were in fact just confusions of forms and types of construction.

What will be happening in the next few years is that buildings—your buildings—are going to ape buildings, villages, and citadels, but only to ape them; they will not be real work. For that reason, and so as not to become a victim of events, I refuse to build until I can build a city, or a piece of a city, in a way that I believe to be correct. For a while I was obsessed with defining the maximum size of any given design problem. What is the maximum size of the city? In the present instance, a competition project for a site in the north of Tegel, the site was too small to solve the real problem. Most of you would say, "My work is not to look beyond the site but just to work within it," but I say that attitude is wrong and you are going to burn in hell for it. Therefore, what I tried to do in this project was to define the whole city and not just one quarter, not just one small site. The site, as given, was divided into two zones: one for housing and one for culture and sports. Through the efforts of Richard Meier, a jury member for this competition, the existing zoning regulations were waived, so that one could mix buildings of different functions. Nonetheless, all the competitors respected the zoning automatically, without having been asked to do so, because that is the way they are accustomed to working. Houston, Texas, has no zoning laws, yet it is developed exactly like any other American city because it is part of the system.

The area that I chose to consider in my project is as big as the whole of medieval Florence. I divided it into four quarters. This was logical—four quarters make one city. My "city" is exactly the size of an *arrondissement* in Paris, which also has four quarters. This works well for pedestrians: the surface area of one quarter corresponds to what one pedestrian can cover to perform his duties in one day—with comfort and style, let us say. I then traced a number of streets, squares, and alleys. The public buildings, instead of being crammed into one culture and sports zone, were broken down programmatically into the smallest shapes possible and then placed in the most important locations in the quarter—on the squares, not the streets, because the squares are the focal points of any city. At the intersection of the main streets I placed a grand, central square. Three-story-high buildings allow me to house 150 people per acre.

These would be done in very simple vernacular, with good stucco facades and fine windows. The public buildings would be built in the best possible materials—stone, granite. The master plan establishes an order for the future. My idea is to invite the few architects that I respect to design the public buildings because their work is predictable; when they build, one knows what the result will be. The rest of the urban fabric is designed according to a very simple set of rules, of heights, of use, of different styles and proportions, so that one can predict what the place will be like in twenty years.

I lost this competition to Mr. Charles Moore, who obviously is more in tune with the profound nature of our times than I am. But I have continued to work on this scheme since then. And I am still working on it. It will be completed soon, and then it will be made public. For every move I have made I will take responsibility. I have talked to developers. The most beautiful cities have always been built by developers who made a lot of money; yet very often they left marvelous cities. That is what I have tried to accomplish here. Every move is a basic idea—which has nothing to do with the site, but is universal. Platonic. There is a universal law that rules it all, but that also creates a very specific place, a completely unreproducible place.

PELLI: It is interesting to hear you talk not about architecture, but really about theology. This theology is not Christian theology, but more Greek mythology. You talk about our burning in hell, but the worst possible sin is for one to compete with, or pretend to be, God—and you are really trying to be God. I find that a fundamental flaw that vitiates your position. For myself I have no fear of burning in hell, but I only think of myself as a person.

KOOLHAAS: When Philip Johnson spoke I was thinking that maybe we were witnessing a definitive bifurcation between European and American architecture, whereby American architecture would quite deliberately reach a kind of degree zero for articulation and argument, while European architecture would be obsessed with it. What baffles and intrigues me, and might be a subject for this meeting, is how it is that the kind of nonarticulation of Johnson on the one hand and the moral earnestness, the religious dimension—uh, you name it—of Leo Krier on the other tend toward conclusions that are very often interchangeable.

ROCHE: Leo, you will probably burn in hell yourself for your arrogance in assuming that the role of the architect is that of dictator—that he dictates everything in our life, everything in our environment. The arrogance that Philip showed, the disregard for people, for use, is many times less than your arrogance, for you take on the whole city. The very idea that an architect will undertake a project like that without the participation of other people, without the involvement of people, is a madness that ultimately will destroy us all.

KRIER: Yes, I find it interesting that I should be accused of arrogance by Kevin Roche. I just write and draw and take responsibility for it. If you draw a plan of a city, if you make decisions about zoning, whether you like it or not, you decide how the people in that city are going to live and move around for the next fifty years.

BURGEE: But you too would assume responsibility for all that. It amounts to the same....

ROCHE: You would do it without the involvement of people?

KRIER: Yes, absolutely, because the architect is supposed to be the one mind that plans and oversees all parts of the city.

ROCHE: What gives us the right to make those decisions?

KRIER: We take it....

PAUL RUDOLPH: I find this project of the utmost interest because it is a scheme to which many people can contribute. It outlines the relationship of building types to each other. You are obviously very interested in the hierarchy of building types, something we no longer have in this country, where public buildings are often physically small in comparison to private housing or corporate buildings. For us it is entirely the opposite of what you have suggested. Saint Patrick's Cathedral in New York started out as a very large building, but now it is small in relationship to everything else. I don't find what you say abominable, but our problems are so different from what you outline that it is difficult for us to relate to it.

EISENMAN: I don't like to get into the issue of arrogance, but there have been arrogant poets and painters, people who "just write and draw." What I find most difficult is your reference to the winning scheme being more in tune with the profound nature of our time. This sounds very much like the modernist idea that architecture can express the will of the people, or that architecture is the expression of the Zeitgeist. Just as modernism had a preferred aesthetic, it seems that you also have one. As Rem was saying, the fact that you come to the same conclusions as Johnson is absolutely understandable. Your preferred aesthetic simply uses a different sets of judgments, a different set of values. If we do have a Zeitgeist today, it has nothing to do with turning our heads back to the nineteenth century, but rather with dealing with a problematic future. You don't seem to address that at all. Your unwillingness to address a very real and imminent hell, the one that biologists, psychologists, and philosophers are talking about, is very strange. It seems to me an abrogation of responsibility.

JOHNSON: Leo hasn't talked about what he is greatest at—he's one of the finest artists in the world. Besides going to hell or heaven—I couldn't care less myself, I won't be there to watch it—we should talk about whether someone is a good artist or not. Leon Krier doesn't have principles any more than I have, only he's a better architect. That temple-like building in the plan, which he didn't discuss, is an extraordinary tour de force of his direction in architecture. The fact that he wants to leave all the buildings to others is something I'll never understand because he himself is such a goddamn good architect.

PELLI: He did not present his work in terms of art at all. I think he has the right to set the tone of the discussion....

JOHNSON: He can talk about what he pleases—I really want to praise him as an artist. I don't care what he says.

STERN: Leo has enumerated a principle other than an ecclesiastical one, an architectural principle that is very clear: that the subject of architecture may once again become architecture, as opposed to things external to architecture, whether they be steamships, factories, or whatever. His buildings very convincingly reveal the continuity of many architectural ideas from the past. The big split, of course, comes when Leo has to confront the kinds of problems that many say are the problems of our day, problems that have grown up in an American culture as opposed to a European one. The dilemma for me, Leo, is how you jet-plane to Charlottesville, yet refuse to design an airport. That is the troublesome part of the argument, not the work.

KRIER: I would love to design an airport, there is nothing wrong with airports. I love airplanes. I am not against machines, but they must serve you; obviously the present ones do not.

STERN: I want to ask if anyone has a cultural problem with the thousand-year evolution of the classical Greek temple. It seems that nobody here does. Today we need some of those values to redefine our new order.

KRIER: Because we live in problematic times artists believe they have to create problematic works of art and listen to problematic music, but this has nothing whatsoever to do with the purpose of the fine arts. The fine arts are interested in solutions, not in problems, and the project of classicism is to find the most elegant solution to a problem.

TADAO ANDO (Translator): This is a house in the downtown area of Osaka, the second largest city in Japan. The area is densely populated and physically a very chaotic environment full of lower-middle-class houses and small factories. The project consists of three units, one measuring six by nine meters, one six by six meters, and one seven by seven meters, grouped around a courtyard. The basic questions were how to introduce nature into limited living spaces and how to make such spaces seem larger. The answer was through simplicity.

From early in history the Japanese have lived crowded together in very restricted areas, but they have overcome the limitations of the size of their shelters through spiritual awareness. This is most apparent in the tea ceremony room, a narrow room in which an infinite extension of space can be sensed. Even in a room that is only two tatami mats in floor area, a very deep spiritual understanding can be reached. I believe that this Japanese tradition of spatial consciousness needs to be maintained today, and that it is vital to an aesthetic of simplicity.

Creating a relationship between human beings and nature is one way of expressing infinity in a limited space. Nature will always be essential to dwellings, no matter how modern our lifestyle becomes. Architecture plays an important role as a medium for bringing back into the city aspects of nature such as sunlight, wind, and rain with which we are in danger of losing contact.

This is a private house for five people. It is divided in two: one side is devoted to the living spaces and has three stories; the other side is left empty. I believe it is important to have such an empty space, even if it is small, in a tightly designed house. This is the traditional way in which houses have been built in Japan.

Modern architecture has been built using the same materials, technology, and methods throughout the world. However, we all have spiritual roots to the places and cultures to which we belong, and these we must take care not to sever. Unless architecture is true to national character and the spirit and aesthetic sense nurtured by tradition, there can be no authentic dwelling.

The spatial organization in this house is typical of traditional houses. When one enters it one must go through the empty space; one then goes upstairs to enter the living spaces. A connection is thus created between these inside living spaces and the street, and by extension between the private house and society. The living spaces may appear to be ordered very geometrically, but people can in fact move around in them freely.

Natural materials have been used for all parts of the house with which the human body comes into direct contact, including floors, doors, and furniture. Such materials age with time and repeated use, and they constitute a record of the life led in the house. This house represents my own expression of the traditional Japanese attachment to materials that age naturally. In designing I always consider human beings together with nature, and materials together with the dimensions they will have.

I would like to find the true character of houses and an authentic way of life by overcoming physical limitations of size and by establishing—through complex spatial compositions—a close relationship between architecture and daily life, and between human beings, nature, and natural materials.

KRIER: [Ironical] Clap, clap. clap, clap. clap, clap.

STANLEY TIGERMAN: I have seen many of Ando's projects. I went through this house last September. His work is very tough, but it is very traditional Japanese architecture, very powerful.

ROCHE: I think that it learns from tradition in a way that we in the West do not; we tend to borrow forms and this doesn't. In that sense, it is a true traditional Japanese house, and we can learn a great deal from it.

KRIER: I want to know why you treat the house in this way. Nothing about it reminds me of anything I associate with houses. I can't bear to touch the concrete walls; just looking at them kills people—Japanese people and all other people in the world. Isn't that so? Why didn't you make any windows looking out into the street?

ARATA ISOZAKI: Because of the terrible mess outside, which he believes is quite disturbing. I almost agree. He built the concrete walls across the courtyard to make the space create its own beauty. He divided the house exactly in half, then gave the living area several windows to look over its own outside space. In this way he introduced nature into the living area. This is the typical Japanese method.

ROCHE: The character of the Japanese house, which is similar to that of the Chinese, resides in the contemplative nature of the interior. It's the difference between the house and the home. When I said "traditional" before, I meant this in the sense of the contemplative interior. It has nothing to do with where you put the television set or where the children put their toys or books. It carries on the essence of a form of living, of a culture.

SIEGEL: I wonder about the implication of a house like this as a prototype. Has Ando done any larger-scale housing projects, and if so, does he approach their planning in a similar way?

ANDO (translator):   I don't always follow the same approach. When I create a house like this I follow my own sense of how to do it.

ROCHE: It is an unfair question because obviously it entails another problem.

SIEGEL: I don't agree. This building is evidently designed to fit into a narrow lot.

BURGEE: Leon, did you want to speak?

KRIER: Yes. I wonder how much we can take here. I am sure that if I had gone on applauding for half an hour you people wouldn't have understood why—confusion is so rampant. You don't know what things mean. We dare to meet here, to talk about this miserable hole in which I am sure none of us would want to spend more than five hours. It is a prison. Now we are going to spend another ten hours here perhaps looking at similar things. Imagine that a person like—not Jefferson, but someone like Tom Wolfe was here; you would give him material for ten more books. The level of discourse is such a miserable intellectual ruin that I feel like leaving. On the other hand, there are about twenty people here who are responsible for the architectural scene nowadays—that is, not only for how houses and buildings look, but how cities are going to be built and shaped. So for God's sake, I plead with you to talk about the real problems—we have not come here to listen to ways of relating inside to outside space. We all know how to do that. We are all architects. We also know that our cities are in ruins, that the legislation now in use is destructive. Why can't we talk about that? Why don't we talk about these problems? I am not making them up. As architects you are making the problems, and now you are being punished—not by God, but by a society that despises you. You know this. A man like Tom Wolfe writes a book about the profession, a book totally ridiculous in its argument, totally unscientific, unartistic, absolutely the bottom of the bottom of arguing, and here we are. How can we listen to somebody describe this miserable hole and take him seriously? How is it possible? Answer, someone ….

ROCHE: I can answer that. Because Ando designed this house for his client; if his client chooses to live in this cell, we shouldn't deny him that choice. The question of whether Ando considers this building to be prototypical is unimportant; anyway, he does not consider it to be. I agree with what you say about the level of conversation here. I tried to raise that point at the very outset. What is it we are talking about here; what is our responsibility, why are we disregarded by society?

KRIER: I beg you to talk about that.

MICHAEL GRAVES: I would like to talk about it through architecture, Leo, only through architecture. If the level of discourse is not high enough for you, or for anybody else, then it is your responsibility to raise it, but not to admonish anybody else for asking the questions they want to about architecture at any level.

KRIER: This has nothing to do with architecture. It is a miserable hole.

GRAVES: He obviously doesn't think it is a miserable hole.

KRIER: It is not a matter of what he thinks. Architecture has a tradition of thousands of years, and we are the inheritors of it.

GRAVES: Well, he is just an architect, as you are, and we are all members of this society; we do not separate ourselves from that society. I disagree with you about this house. I think that there is something here. I am sorry to shift the conversation, Leo, because I know you want to continue, but there is, in both Ito's and Ando's buildings, an idea that seems to reflect a new Japanese sensibility. It is not the former Japanese sensibility; that is exemplified by the old temples, by the idea of the way the landscape enters a room. It is also not the artifact culture that we Westerners now understand or have understood. There is a separation between us perhaps, between those of us who understand the building as an artifact that has significance to society in a collective sense—the table as an artifact, the chair as an artifact—and those of us who see the building as an abstraction of space and light. Those two presentations called "Eastern" that we've seen are devoid of this interest in artifacts. This interest has been supplanted by light and space, by a void that has a shape and quality about it that are interesting to us in an abstract sense. I will leave it at that because I do not think that this is a specifically Japanese sense—especially as we see Japanese culture now becoming so completely Westernized.

EISENMAN: I would like to respond to Leo because I think we could sit here all day and debate theology. In the end, the people here, all of us, in one way or another are trying to build buildings that are not merely buildings, but contain ideas about society. Insofar as the buildings we have seen reflect an incapacity to concern themselves with these ideas, that is part of the current situation. But you can't scream to us that we must be in a different situation. It is your prerogative to interject your own point of view and say that you don't feel that these buildings are in fact raising the level of discourse; that is fine. But I could sit here and clap all day when you present your buildings because for me they also represent a paucity of discourse. It is presumptuous for you to proclaim to us what the appropriate level of discourse should be. It shows a certain arrogance toward everyone else. We are trying to learn how to communicate rather than to stifle communication.

REPRINTED FROM *THE CHARLOTTESVILLE TAPES: TRANSCRIPT OF THE CONFERENCE AT THE UNIVERSITY OF VIRGINIA SCHOOL OF ARCHITECTURE* (NEW YORK: RIZZOLI, 1985): 14–29, 118–127.

DOCTOR LAWYER INDIAN CHIEF
'PRIMITIVISM' IN TWENTIETH CENTURY ART
AT THE MUSEUM OF MODERN ART

Thomas McEvilley, William Rubin & Kirk Varnedoe

THOMAS McEVILLEY:

Something, clearly, is afoot. Richard Oldenburg, director of the institution here, describes one of its publications and the exhibition it accompanies, both titled *'Primitivism' in Twentieth Century Art: Affinity of the Tribal and the Modern,* as "among the most ambitious ever prepared by The Museum of Modern Art." "Over the years," he continues, "this Museum has produced several exhibitions and catalogues which have proved historically important and influential, changing the ways we view the works presented, answering some prior questions and posing new ones."[1] Indeed, this is an important event. It focuses on materials that bring with them the most deeply consequential issues of our time. And it illustrates, without consciously intending to, the parochial limitations of our world view and the almost autistic reflexivity of Western civilization's modes of relating to the culturally Other.

The exhibition, displaying 150 or so Modern artworks with over 200 tribal objects is thrilling in a number of ways. It is a tour de force of connoisseurship. Some say it is the best primitive show they have seen, some the best Eskimo show, the best Zairean show, the best Gauguin show, even in a sense the best Picasso show. The brilliant installation makes the vast display seem almost intimate and cozy, like a series of early Modernist galleries: it feels curiously and deceptively unlike the blockbuster it is. Still the museum's claim that the exhibition is "the first ever to juxtapose modern and tribal objects in the light of informed art history"[2] is strangely strident. Only the ambiguous word "informed" keeps it from being ahistorical. It is true that the original research associated with this exhibition has come up with enormous amounts of detailed information, yet since at least 1938, when Robert Goldwater published his seminal book *Primitivism in Modern Painting,* the interested public has been "informed" on the general ideas involved.[3] For a generation at least, many sophisticated collectors of Modern art have bought primitive works too, and have displayed them together. For five or so years after its opening in 1977, the Centre Pompidou in Paris exhibited, in the vicinity of its Modern collections, about 100 tribal objects from the Musée de l'Homme. Though not actually intermingled with Modern works, these were intended to illustrate relationships with them, and included, as does the present show, primitive objects owned by Picasso, Braque, and other early Modernists. More recently, the exhibition of the Menil Collections in Paris' Grand Palais, in April, 1984, juxtaposed primitive and Modern works (a Max Ernst with an African piece, Cézanne with Cycladic), and sometimes, as in the present exhibition, showed a Modern artist's work in conjunction with primitive objects in his collection. The premise of this show, then, is not new or startling in the least. That is why we must ask why MoMA gives us primitivism now—and with such intense promotion and overwhelming mass of information. For the answer one must introduce the director of the exhibition, and, incidentally, of the museum's Department of Painting and Sculpture, William Rubin.

One suspects that for Rubin the Museum of Modern Art has something of the appeal of church and country. It is a temple to be promoted and defended with a passionate devotion—the temple of formalist Modernism. Rubin's great shows of Cézanne, in 1977, and Picasso, in 1980, were loving and brilliant paeans to a Modernism that was like a transcendent Platonic ideal, self-validating, and in turn validating and invalidating other things. But like a lover who becomes overbearing or possessive, Rubin's love has a darker side. Consider what he did to Giorgio de Chirico: a major retrospective of the artist's work, in 1982, included virtually no works made after 1917—though the artist lived and worked for another half century. Only through 1917, in his earliest years as an artist, did de Chirico practice what Rubin regards as worth looking at. This was a case of the curator's will absolutely overriding the will of the artist and the found nature of the oeuvre. (It sure made the late work chic.) A less obvious but similar exercise occurs in Rubin's massive book *Dada and Surrealist Art* [4] —a book not so much about Dada and Surrealism as against them. The Dadaists of course, and following them the Surrealists, rejected any idea of objective aesthetic value and of formally self-validating art. They understood themselves as parts of another tradition which emphasized content, intellect, and social criticism. Yet Rubin treats the Dada and Surrealist works primarily as aesthetic objects, and uses them to demonstrate the opposite of what their makers intended. While trying to make anti-art, he argues, they made art. Writing in 1968, at a time when the residual influence of the two movements was threatening formalist hegemony, Rubin attempted to demonstrate the universality of aesthetic values by showing that you can't get away from them even if you try. Dada and Surrealism were, in effect, tamed.

By the late seventies the dogma of universal aesthetic feeling was again threatened. Under the influence of the Frankfurt thinkers, and of postmodern relativism, the absolutist view of formalist Modernism was losing ground. Whereas its aesthetics had been seen as higher criteria by which other styles were to be judged, now, in quite respectable quarters, they began to appear as just another style. For a while, like Pre-Raphaelitism or the Ashcan School, they had served certain needs and exercised hegemony; those needs passing, their hegemony was passing also. But the collection of the Museum of Modern Art is predominantly based on the idea that formalist Modernism will never pass, will never lose its self-validating power. Not a relative, conditioned thing, subject to transient causes and effects, it is to be above the web of natural and cultural change; this is its supposed essence. After several years of sustained attack, such a credo needs a defender and a new defense. How brilliant to attempt to revalidate classical Modernist aesthetics by stepping outside their usual realm of discourse and bringing to bear upon them a vast, foreign sector of the world. By demonstrating that the "innocent" creativity of primitives naturally expresses a Modernist aesthetic feeling, one may seem to have demonstrated once again that Modernism itself is both innocent and universal.

'Primitivism' in Twentieth Century Art is accompanied by a two-volume, 700-page catalogue, edited by Rubin, containing over 1,000 illustrations and nineteen essays by fifteen eminent scholars.[5] It is here that the immense ideological web is woven. On the whole, Goldwater's book still reads better, but many of the essays here are beautiful scholarship, worked out in exquisite detail, Jack Flam's essay on the Fauves and Rubin's own one-hundred-page chapter on Picasso exemplify this strength. The investigation and reconstruction of events in the years from 1905 to 1908 recur in several of the essays: these years constitute a classic chronological problem for our culture, like the dating of the Linear B tablets. At the least, the catalogue refines and extends Goldwater's research (which clearly it is intended to supplant), while tilling the soil for a generation of doctoral theses on who saw what when. Its research has the value that all properly conducted scientific research has, and will be with us for a long time. In addition to this factual level, however, the catalogue has an ideological, value-saturated, and interpretive aspect. The long introductory essay by Rubin establishes a framework within which the other texts are all seen, perhaps unfortunately. (Some do take, at moments, an independent line.) Other ideologically activated areas are Rubin's preface, and the preface and closing chapter ("Contemporary Explorations") by Kirk Varnedoe, listed as "codirector" of the exhibition after "director" Rubin.

A quick way into the problems of the exhibition is in fact through Varnedoe's "Contemporary Explorations" section. The question of what is really contemporary is the least of the possible points of contention here, but the inclusion of great artists long dead, like Robert Smithson and Eva Hesse, does suggest inadequate sensitivity to the fact that art-making is going on right now. One cannot help noting that none of the types of work that have emerged into the light during the last eight years or so is represented. Even the marvelous pieces included from the eighties, such as Richard Long's *River Avon Mud Circle*, are characteristic of late sixties and seventies work.

A more significant question is the unusual attention to women artists—Hesse, Jackie Winsor, Michelle Stuart, and above all Nancy Graves. Though welcome and justified, this focus accords oddly with the very low proportion of women in the show that preceded *'Primitivism'* at the new MoMA, *An International Survey of Recent Painting and Sculpture*. That show had a different curator, yet in general it seems that curators need a special reason to include a lot of women in a show—here, perhaps the association of women with primitivism, unconsciousness, and the earth, a gender cliché which may have seemed liberating ten years ago but may seem constricting ten years hence.

In the context of Modern art, "primitivism" is a specific technical term: the word, placed in quotation marks in the show's title, designates Modern work that alludes to tribal objects or in some way incorporates or expresses their influence. Primitivism, in other words, is a quality of some Modern artworks, not a quality of primitive works themselves. "Primitive," in turn, designates the actual tribal objects, and can also be used of any work sharing the intentionality proper to those objects, which is not that of art but of shamanic vocation and its attendant psychology. Some contemporary primitivist work may also be called primitive; yet the works selected by Varnedoe are conspicuously nonprimitive primitivism. The works of Smithson and Hesse, for example, may involve allusion to primitive information, but they express a consciousness highly attuned to each move of Western civilization. Rubin and Varnedoe make it clear that they are concerned not with the primitive but with the primitivist—which is to say they ask only half the question.

There are in fact contemporary artists whose intentionalities involve falling away from Western civilization and literally forgetting its values. These are the primitive primitivists; they are edited out of the show and the book altogether. The farthest the museum is willing to go is Joseph Beuys. Varnedoe explicitly expresses a dread of the primitive, referring darkly to a certain body of recent primitivist work as "sinister," and noting that "the ideal of regression closer to nature is dangerously loaded," that such works bring up "uncomfortable questions about the ultimate content of all ideals that propose escape from the Western tradition into a Primitive state."[6] The primitive, in other words, is to be censored out for the sake of Western civilization. The museum has evidently taken up a subject that it lacks the stomach to present in its raw realness or its real rawness. Where is the balance that would have been achieved by some attention to work like Eric Orr's quasi-shamanic objects involving human blood, hair, bone, and tooth, or Michael Tracy's fetishes of blood, hair, semen, and other taboo materials? The same exorcising spirit dominates the schedule of live performances associated with the exhibition: Meredith Monk, Joan Jonas, and Steve Reich, for all their excellences, have little to do with the primitivist, and less with the primitive. Where are the performances of Hermann Nitsch, Paul McCarthy, Kim Jones, and Gina Pane? Varnedoe's dread of the primitive, of the dangerous beauty that attracted Matisse and Picasso and that continues to attract some contemporary artists today, results in an attempt to exorcise them, and to deny the presence, or anyway the appropriateness, of such feelings in Western humans.

Our closeness to the so-called contemporary work renders the incompleteness of the selection obvious. Is it possible that the classical Modern works are chosen with a similarly sterilizing eye? Was primitive primitivist work made in the first third of this century, and might it have entered this exhibition if the Western dread of the primitive had not already excluded it from the art-history books? Georges Bataille, who was on the scene when primitive styles were being incorporated into European art as Modern, described this trend already in 1928, as Rosalind Krauss points out in the catalogue's chapter on Giacometti. He saw the aestheticizing of primitive religious objects as a way for "the civilized Westerner...to maintain himself in a state of ignorance about the presence of violence within ancient religious practice."[7] Such a resistance, still dominant in this exhibition almost sixty years later, has led not only to a timid selection of contemporary works but to the exorcising of the primitive works themselves, which, isolated from one another in the vitrines and under the great lights, seem tame and harmless. The blood is wiped off them. The darkness of the unconscious has fled. Their power, which is threatening and untamed when it is present, is far away. This in turn affects the more radical Modern and contemporary works. If the primitive works are not seen in their full primitiveness, then any primitive feeling in Modernist allusions to them is bleached out also. The reason for this difficulty with the truly contemporary and the truly primitive is that this exhibition is not concerned with either: the show is about classical Modernism.

The fact that the primitive "looks like" the Modern is interpreted as validating the Modern by showing that its values are universal, while at the same time projecting it—and with it MoMA—into the future as a permanent canon. A counterview is possible: that primitivism on the contrary invalidates Modernism by showing it to be derivative and subject to external causation. At one level this show undertakes precisely to co-opt that question by answering it before it has really been asked, and by burying it under a mass of information. The first task Rubin and his colleagues attempt, then, is a chronological one. They devote obsessive attention to the rhetorical question, Did primitive influence precede the birth of Modernism, or did it ingress afterward, as a confirmatory witness? It is hard to avoid the impression that this research was undertaken with the conclusion already in mind. The question is already begged in the title of the exhibition, which states not a hypothesis but a conclusion: *'Primitivism' in Twentieth Century Art: Affinity of the Tribal and the Modern.*

The central chronological argument, stated repeatedly in the book, is that although the Trocadero Museum (later the Musée de l'Homme) opened in Paris in 1878, primitive influences did not appear in Parisian art till some time in the period 1905 to 1908. This thirty-year lag is held to show that the process of diffusion was not random or mechanical, but was based on a quasi-deliberate exercise of will or spirit on the part of early Modern artists—in Rubin's words, an "elective affinity."[8] It was not enough, in other words, for the primitive images to be available; the European receptacle had to be ready to receive them. As far as chronology goes the argument is sound, but there is more involved than that. What is in question is the idea of what constitutes readiness. Rubin suggests that the European artists were on the verge of producing forms similar to primitive ones on their own account—so positively ready to do so, in fact, that the influx of primitive objects was redundant. For obvious reasons Rubin does not spell this claim out in so many words, yet he implies it continually. For example, he writes that "the changes in modern art at issue were already under way when vanguard artists first became aware of tribal art."[9] The changes at issue were of course the appearance of primitive-like forms. The claim is strangely improbable. If one thinks of Greco-Roman art, Renaissance art, and European art through the nineteenth-century, there is nowhere any indication that this tradition could spawn such forms; at least, it never came close in its thousands of years. A countermodel to Rubin's might see readiness as comprising no more than a weariness with Western canons of representation and aesthetics, combined with the gradual advance, since the eighteenth-century, of awareness of Oceanic and African culture. The phenomena of art nouveau (with its Egyptianizing tendencies) and *japonisme* filled the thirty-year gap and demonstrate the eagerness for non-Western input that was finally fulfilled with the primitive works. Readiness, in other words, may have been more passive than active.

Clearly the organizers of this exhibition want to present Modernism not as an appropriative act but as a creative one. They reasonably fear that their powerful show may have demonstrated the opposite—which is why the viewer's responses are so closely controlled, both by the book and, in the show itself, by the wall plaques. The ultimate reason behind the exhibition is to revalidate Modernist aesthetic canons by suggesting that their freedom, innocence, universality, and objective value are proven by their "affinity" to the primitive. This theme has become a standard in dealing with primitivism; Goldwater also featured the terms "affinities," rather than a more neutral one like "similarities."

A wall plaque within the exhibition informs us that there are three kinds of relations between modern and primitive objects: first, "direct influence"; second, "coincidental resemblances"; third, "basic shared characteristics." This last category, referred to throughout the book as "affinities," is particularly presumptuous. In general, proofs of affinity are based on the argument that the kind of primitive work that seems to be echoed in the Modern work is not recorded to have been in Europe at the time, Ernst's *Bird Head*, for example, bears a striking resemblance to a type of Tusyan mask from the upper Volta. But the resemblance, writes Rubin, "striking as it is, is fortuitous, and must therefore be accounted a simple affinity. *Bird Head* was sculpted in 1934, and no Tusyan masks appear to have arrived in Europe (nor were any reproduced) prior to World War II."[10] The fact that the resemblance is "fortuitous" would seem to put it in the category of coincidental resemblances. It is not evidence but desire that puts it in the "affinities" class, which is governed as a whole by selection through similarly wishful thinking. In fact, the Ernst piece cannot with certainty be excluded from the "direct influences" category either. The argument that no Tusyan masks were seen in Europe in 1934 has serious weaknesses. First of all, it is an attempt to prove a negative; it is what is called, among logical fallacies, an *argumentum ex silentio,* or argument from silence. All it establishes is that Rubin's researchers have not heard of any Tusyan masks in Europe at that time. The reverse argument, that the Ernst piece shows there were probably some around, is about as strong.

A similar argument attempts to establish "affinity" between Picasso and Kwakiutl craftspeople on the basis of a Kwakiutl split mask and the vertically divided face in *Girl Before a Mirror*, 1932. For, says Rubin, "Picasso could almost certainly never have seen a 'sliced' mask like the one we reproduce, but it nonetheless points up the affinity of his poetic thought to the mythic universals that the tribal objects illustrate."[11] The argument is weak on many grounds. First, Picasso had long been familiar with primitive art by 1932, and that general familiarity, more than any "universals," may account for his coming up with a primitive-like thing on his own. The same is true for Ernst and the *Bird Head.* Modern artists don't necessarily have to have seen an object exactly similar to one of their own for influence to exist. Anyway, the similarity between *Girl Before a Mirror* and the "sliced" Kwakiutl mask is not really that strong. The mask shows a half head; the girl has a whole head with a line down the middle and different colors on each side. Rubin attempts to correct this weakness in the argument by noting that "Northwest Coast and Eskimo masks often divide integrally frontal faces more conventionally into dark and light halves."[12] But most of the world's mythological iconographies have the image of the face with the dark and light halves. Picasso had surely encountered this common motif in a variety of forms—as the alchemical Androgyne, for example. There is, in other words, no particular reason to connect his *Girl Before a Mirror* with Kwakiutl masks, except for the sake of the exhibition.

In addition to Rubin's reliance on the notoriously weak argument from silence, his "affinities" approach breaches the Principle of Economy, on which all science is based: that explanatory principles are to be kept to the smallest possible number (*entia non multiplicanda sunt praeter necessitatem*). The Principle of Economy does not of course mean keeping information to a minimum, but keeping to a minimum the number of interpretive ideas that one brings to bear on information. The point is that unnecessary principles will usually reflect the wishful thinking of the speaker, and amount to deceptive persuasive mechanisms. In the present case, ideas like "elective affinity," "mythic universals," and "affinity of poetic thought" are all *entia praeter necessitatem*, unnecessary explanatory principles. They enter the discourse from the wishful thinking of the speaker. An account lacking the ghost in the machine would be preferred. The question of influence or affinity involves much broader questions, such as the nature of diffusion processes and the relationship of Modernist aesthetics to the Greco-Roman and Renaissance tradition. In cultural history in general, diffusion processes are random and impersonal semiotic transactions. Images flow sideways, backwards, upside down. Cultural elements are appropriated from one context to another not only through spiritual affinities and creative selections, but through any kind of connection at all, no matter how left-handed or trivial.

The museum's decision to give us virtually no information about the tribal objects on display, to wrench them out of context, calling them to heel in the defense of formalist Modernism, reflects the exclusion of the anthropological point of view. Unfortunately, art historians and anthropologists have not often worked well together; MoMA handles this problem by simply neglecting the anthropological side of things. No attempt is made to recover an emic, or inside, sense of what primitive aesthetics really were or are. The problem of the difference between the emic viewpoint—that of the tribal participant—and the etic one—that of the outside observer—is never really faced by these art historians, engrossed as they seem to be in the exercise of their particular expertise, the tracing of stylistic relationships and chronologies. The anthropologist Marvin Harris explains the distinction:

Emic operations have as their hallmark the elevation of the native informant to the status of ultimate judge of the adequacy of the observer's descriptions and analyses. The test of the adequacy of emic analyses is their ability to generate statements the native accepts as real, meaningful, or appropriate.... Etic operations have as their hallmark the elevation of observers to the status of ultimate judges of the categories and concepts used in descriptions and analyses. The test of the adequacy of etic accounts is simply their ability to generate scientifically productive theories about the causes of sociocultural differences and similarities. Rather than employ concepts that are necessarily real, meaningful, and appropriate from the native point of view, the observer is free to use alien categories and rules derived from the data language of science.[13]

The point is that accurate or objective accounts can be given from either an emic or an etic point of view, but the distinction must be kept clear. If etic pretends to be emic, or emic to be etic, the account becomes confused, troubled, and misleading.

MoMA makes a plain and simple declaration that their approach will be etic. Materials in the press kit which paraphrase a passage of Rubin's introduction argue, "As our focus is on the Modernists' experience of tribal art, and not on ethnological study, we have not included anthropological hypotheses regarding the religious or social purposes that originally surrounded these objects." Rubin similarly argues in his own voice that "the ethnologists' primary concern—the specific function and significance of each of these objects—is irrelevant to my topic, except insofar as these facts might have been known to the modern artists in question."[14] The point of view of Picasso and others, then, is to stand as an etic point of view, and is to be the only focus of MoMA's interest; emic information, such as attributions of motives to the tribal artists, is to be irrelevant.

This position is consistent in itself, but is not consistently acted on. In fact, it is violated constantly. It must be stressed that if the emic/etic question is to be neglected, then the intentions of the tribal craftsmen must be left neutral and undefined. But Rubin's argument constantly attributes intentions to the tribal craftsmen, intentions associated with Modernist types of aesthetic feeling and problem-solving attitudes. The very concept of "affinity" rather than mere "similarity" attributes to the tribal craftsmen feelings like those of the Modernist artists, for what else does the distinction between affinities and accidental similarities mean? The claim that there is an "affinity of poetic spirit" between Picasso and the Kwakiutl who made the "sliced" mask attributes to the Kwakiutl poetic feelings like those of Picasso. The assertion that their use of "parallelisms and symmetries" demonstrates a "propinquity in spirit"[15] between Jacques Lipchitz and a Dogon sculptor attributes to the Dogon a sensibility in general like that of Lipchitz. And so on. Rubin says that the "specific function and significance of each of these objects" is irrelevant—for example, what ceremony the object was used in, how it was used in the ceremony, and so on. The use of the word "each" here is tricky. It is true that Rubin ignores the specific function of each object, but it is also true that he attributes a general function to all the objects together, namely, the aesthetic function, the function of giving aesthetic satisfaction. In other words, the function of the Modernist works is tacitly but constantly attributed to the primitive works. It is easy to see why no anthropologist was included in the team. Rubin has made highly inappropriate claims about the intentions of tribal cultures without letting them have their say, except through the mute presence of their unexplained religious objects, which are misleadingly presented as art objects. This attitude toward primitive objects is so habitual in our culture that one hardly notices the hidden assumptions until they are pointed out. Rubin follows Goldwater in holding that the objects themselves are proof of the formal decisions made, and that the formal decisions made are proof of the aesthetic sensibility involved. That this argument seems plausible, even attractive, to us is because we have the same emic view as Rubin and MoMA. But connections based merely on form can lead to skewed perceptions indeed. Consider from the following anthropological example what absurdities one can be led into by assuming that the look of things, without their meaning, is enough to go on:

In New Guinea, in a remote native school taught by a local teacher. I watched a class carefully copy an arithmetic lesson from the blackboard. The teacher had written:

$$4 + 1 = 7$$
$$3 - 5 = 6$$
$$2 + 5 = 9$$

The students copied both his beautifully formed numerals and his errors.[16]

The idea that tribal craftsmen had aesthetic problem-solving ambitions comparable to those of Modernist artists involves an attribution to them of a value like that which we put on individual creative originality. An anthropologist would warn us away from this presumption: "in preliterate cultures…culture is presented to its members as clichés, repeated over and over with only slight variation." "Such art isn't personal. It doesn't reflect the private point of view of an innovator. It's a corporate statement by a group."[17] Yet Rubin declares, again relying only on his sense of the objects, without ethnological support, that "the surviving works themselves attest that individual carvers had far more freedom in varying and developing these types than many commentators have assumed."[18] Surely Rubin knows that the lack of a history of primitive cultures rules out any judgment about how quickly they have changed or how long they took to develop their diversity. The inventiveness Rubin attributes to primitive craftsmen was probably a slow, communal inventiveness, not a matter of individual innovation. In prehistoric traditions, for example, several thousand years may be needed for the degree of innovation and change seen in a single decade of Modernism. Rubin asserts formalist concerns for the tribal craftspeople "even though they had no concept for what such words mean."[19] Consider the particular value judgment underlying the conviction that the only thing primitives were doing that is worth our attention, their proof of "propinquity in spirit" with the white man, was something they weren't even aware of doing.

From a purely academic point of view Rubin's project would be acceptable if its declared etic stance had been honestly and consistently acted out. What is at issue here, however, is more than a set of academic flaws in an argument, for in other than academic senses the etic stance is unacceptable anyway. Goldwater had made the formalist argument for tribal objects in the thirties; it was a reasonable enough case to make at the time. But why should it be replayed fifty years later, only with more information? The sacrifice of the wholeness of things to the cult of pure form is a dangerous habit of our culture. It amounts to a rejection of the wholeness of life. After fifty years of living with the dynamic relationship between primitive and Modern objects, are we not ready yet to begin to understand the real intentions of the native traditions, to let those silenced cultures speak to us at last? An investigation that really did so would show us immensely more about the possibilities of life that Picasso and others vaguely sensed and were attracted to than does this endless discussion of the spiritual propinquity of usages of parallel lines. It would show us more about the "world-historical" importance of the relationship between primitive and modern and their ability to relate to one another without autistic self-absorption.

The complete omission of dates from the primitive works is perhaps one of the most troubling decisions. Are we looking at works from the fifties? (If so, are they modern art?) How do we know that some of these artists have not seen works by Picasso? One can foresee a doctoral thesis on Picasso postcards seen by Zairean artists before 1930. The museum dates the Western works, but leaves the primitive works childlike and Edenic in their lack of history. It is true that many of these objects cannot be dated precisely, but even knowing the century would help. I have no doubt that those responsible for this exhibition and book feel that it is a radical act to show how equal are the primitives to us, how civilized, how sensitive, how "inventive." Indeed, both Rubin and Varnedoe passionately declare this. But by their absolute repression of primitive context, meaning, content, and intention (the dates of the works, their functions, their religious or mythological connections, their environments), they have treated the primitives as less than human, less than cultural—as shadows of a culture, their selfhood, their Otherness, wrung out of them. All the curators want us to know about these tribal objects is where they came from, what they look like, who owns them, and how they fit the needs of the exhibition.

In their native contexts these objects were invested with feelings of awe and dread, not of aesthetic ennoblement. They were seen usually in motion, at night, in closed dark spaces, by flickering torchlight. Their viewers were under the influence of ritual, communal identification feelings, and often alcohol or drugs; above all, they were activated by the presence within or among the objects themselves of the shaman, acting out the usually terrifying power represented by the mask or icon. What was at stake for the viewer was not aesthetic appreciation but loss of self in identification with and support of the shamanic performance. The Modernist works in the show serve completely different functions, and were made to be perceived from a completely different stance. If you or I were a native tribal artisan or spectator walking through the halls of MoMA we would see an entirely different show from the one we see as twentieth century New Yorkers. We would see primarily not form, but content, and not art, but religion or magic.

Consider a reverse example, in which Western cultural objects were systematically assimilated by primitives into quite a new functional role. In New Guinea in the thirties, Western food containers were highly prized as clothing ornaments—a Kellogg's cereal box became a hat, a tin can ornamented a belt, and so on. Passed down to us in photographs, the practice looks not only absurd but pathetic. We know that the tribal people have done something so inappropriate as to be absurd, and without even beginning to realize it. Our sense of the smallness and quirkiness of their world view encourages our sense of the larger scope and greater clarity of ours. Yet the way Westerners have related to the primitive objects that have floated through their consciousness would look to the tribal peoples much the way their use of our food containers looks to us: they would perceive at once that we had done something childishly inappropriate and ignorant, and without even realizing it. Many primitive groups, when they have used an object ritually (sometimes only once), desacralize it and discard it as garbage. We then show it in our museums. In other words: our garbage is their art, their garbage is our art. Need I say more about the emic/etic distinction?

The need to co-opt difference into one's own dream of order, in which one reigns supreme, is a tragic failing. Only fear of the Other forces one to deny its Otherness. What we are talking about is a tribal superstition of Western civilization: the Hegel-based conviction that one's own culture is riding the crucial time-line of history's self-realization. Rubin declares that tribal masterpieces "transcend the particular lives and times of their makers";[20] Varnedoe similarly refers to "the capacity of tribal art to transcend the intentions and conditions that first shaped it."[21] The phrase might be restated: "the capacity of tribal art to be appropriated out of its own intentionality into mine."

As the crowning element of this misappropriation of other values comes the subject of representation. Rubin distinguishes between European canons of representation, which are held to represent by actual objective resemblance, and the various primitive canons of representation, which are held to represent not by resemblance but by ideographic convention. Our representation, in other words, corresponds to external reality, theirs is only in their minds. But the belief that an objective representational system can be defined (and that that system happens to be ours) is naïve and inherently contradictory. It is worth noting that tribal peoples tend to feel that it is they who depict and we who symbolize. Representation involves a beholder and thus has a subjective element. If someone says that A doesn't look like B to him or her, no counterargument can prove that it does. All conventions of representation are acculturated and relative; what a certain culture regards as representation is, for that culture, representation.

Rubin's love of Modernism is based on the fact that it at last took Western art beyond mere illustration. When he says that the tribal artisans are not illustrating but conceptualizing, he evidently feels he is praising them for their modernity. In doing so, however, he altogether undercuts their reality system. By denying that tribal canons of representation actually represent anything, he is in effect denying that their view of the world is real. By doing them the favor of making them into Modern artists, Rubin cuts reality from under their feet.

The myth of the continuity of Western art history is constructed out of acts of appropriation like those Rubin duplicates. The rediscovery of Greco-Roman works in the Renaissance is an important instance of this, for the way we relate to such art is also in a sense like wearing a cereal-box hat. The charioteer of Delphi, ca. 470 B.C., for example, was seen totally differently in classical Greece from the way we now see him. He was not alone in that noble, self-sufficient serenity of transcendental angelic whiteness that we see. He was part of what to us would appear a grotesquely large sculptural group—the chariot, the four horses before it, the god Apollo in the chariot box, and whatever other attendants were around. All was painted realistically and must have looked more like a still from a movie than like what we call sculpture. Both Greco-Roman and primitive works, though fragmented and misunderstood, have been appropriated into our art history in order to validate the myth of its continuity and make it seem inevitable.

It is a belief in the linear continuity of the Western tradition that necessitates the claim that Western artists would have come up with primitive-like forms on their own, as a natural development. The purpose of such theorizing is to preclude major breaks in Western art history; its tradition is to remain intact, not pierced and violated by influence from outside the West. The desire to believe in the wholeness, integrity, and independence of the Western tradition has at its root the Hegelian art-historical myth (constructed by the critical historians like Karl Schnaase, Alois Riegl, and Heinrich Wolfflin) that Western art history expresses the self-realizing tendency of Universal Spirit. (This is Rubin's vocabulary. He once declared, for example, that Pollock's paintings were "'world-historical' in the Hegelian sense."[22]) When brought down to earth—that is, to recorded history—this view involves not only the conclusion that the shape and direction of Modern art were not really affected by the discovery of primitive objects, but another conclusion equally unlikely, that the shape and direction of European art were not really influenced by the discovery of Greco-Roman works in the Renaissance.

In fact, Western art history shows three great breaks: one when the population of Europe was changed by the so-called barbarian invasions in the late Roman Empire, which led to the transition from Greco-Roman to Christian art; the second with the Renaissance, the transition from Christian art to European art; the third at the beginning of the twentieth century, with the transition from European to Modern art. Each of these breaks in tradition was associated with a deep infusion of foreign influence—respectively Germanic, Byzantine, and African/Oceanic. To minimize these influences is to hold the Western tradition to be a kind of absolute, isolated in its purity. From that point of view, the adoption of primitive elements by early Modernists is seen as a natural, indeed inevitable, inner development of the Western tradition. But the context of the time suggests otherwise. In the nineteenth century the Western tradition in the arts (including literature) seemed to many to be inwardly exhausted. In 1873 Arthur Rimbaud proclaimed his barbarous Gallic ancestors who buttered their hair,[23] and called for a disorientation of the patterns of sensibility. The feeling was not uncommon; many artists awaited a way of seeing that would amount simultaneously to an escape from habit and a discovery of fresh, vitalizing content. For there is no question that the turn-of-the-century fascination with archaic and primitive cultures was laden with content: Baudelaire, Rimbaud, Picasso, and Matisse were attracted, for example, by the open acknowledgment of the natural status of sex and death in these cultures. By repressing the aspect of content, the Other is tamed into mere pretty stuff to dress us up.

Of course, you can find lots of little things wrong with any big project if you just feel argumentative. But I am motivated by the feeling that something important is at issue here, something deeply, even tragically wrong. In depressing starkness, 'Primitivism' lays bare the way our cultural institutions relate to foreign cultures, revealing it as an ethnocentric subjectivity inflated to co-opt such cultures and their objects into itself. I am not complaining, as the Zuni Indians have, about having tribal objects in our museums. Nor am I complaining about the performing of valuable and impressive art-historical research on the travels of those objects through ateliers (though I am worried that it buries the real issues in an ocean of information). My real concern is that this exhibition shows Western egotism still as unbridled as in the centuries of colonialism and souvenirism. The Museum pretends to confront the Third World while really co-opting it and using it to consolidate Western notions of quality and feelings of superiority.

Hamish Maxwell, chairman of Philip Morris, one of the sponsors of the exhibition, writes in the catalogue that his company operates in 170 "countries and territories," suggesting a purview comparable to that of the show. He continues, "We at Philip Morris have benefited from the contemporary art we have acquired and the exhibitions we have sponsored over the past quarter-century…. They have stirred creative approaches throughout our company."[24] In the advertisement in the Sunday *New York Times* preceding the *'Primitivism'* opening, the Philip Morris logo is accompanied by the words, "It takes art to make a company great."

Well, it takes more than connoisseurship to make an exhibition great.

1. Richard E. Oldenburg, "Foreword," in William Rubin ed., *'Primitivism' in Twentieth Century Art: Affinity of the Tribal and the Modern*, (New York: The Museum of Modern Art, 1984), p.viii.

2. The Museum of Modem Art, New York, press release no.17, August, 1984, for the exhibition *'Primitivism' in Twentieth Centuny Art: Affinity of the Tribal and the Modern*, p.1.

3. Revised and republished as Robert Goldwater, *Primitivism in Modern Art* (New York: Vintage Books, 1967). In 1933, 1935, 1941, and 1946, the Modern itself had exhibitions of archaic and primitive objects separately from its modern collections. René D'Harnancourt, director of the Museum for nineteen years, was an author on the subject.

4. Willlam Rubin, *Dada and Surrealist Art* (New York: Harry N. Abrams, 1965).

5. Two by Rubin, two by Kirk Varnedoe, two by Alan G. Wilkinson, and one each by Ezio Bassani, Christian F. Feest, Jack Flam, Sidney Geist, Donald E. Gordon, Rosalind Krauss, Jean Laude, Gail Levin, Evan Maurer, Jean-Louis Paudrat, Philippe Peltlier, and Laura Rosenstock.

6. Kirk Varnedoe, "Contemporany Explorations," in Rubin, *'Primitivism,'* pp.662, 681, 679.

7. Rosalind Krauss, "Giacometti," in Rubin, *'Primitivism,'* p.510.

8. William Rubin, "Modernist Primitivism: An Introduction" in Rubin, *'Primitivism,'* p.11.

9. Ibid.

10. Ibid., p.25.

11. Rubin, "Picasso" in Rubin, *'Primitivism,'* pp.328–330.

12. Ibid. p.328.

13 Marvin Harris, *Cultural Materialism: The Struggle for a Science of Culture* (New York: Vintage Books,1980), p.32.

14. Rubin, "Modernist Primitivism," in Rubin, *'Primitivism,'* p.x.

15. Ibid., p.51.

16. Edmund Carpenter, *Oh, What a Blow That Phantom Gave Me!* (New York: Holt, Rinehart and Winston, 1973), p.54.

17. Ibid., pp.53,56.

18. Rubin, "Modernist Primitivism," in Rubin, *'Primitivism,'* p.5.

19. Ibid. p.19.

20. Ibid. p.13.

21. Kirk Varnedoe, preface in Rubin, *'Primitivism,'* p.x.

22. Cited in Peter Fuller, *Beyond the Crisis in Art* (London: Writers and Readers Publishing Cooperative Ltd., 1980), p.98.

23. Arthur Rimbaud, *Une Saison en enfer* [A season in hell], trans. Louise Varèse (New York: New Directions,1961), p.7.

24. Hamish Maxwell, in Rubin, *'Primitivism,'* p.vi.

REPRINTED FROM *ARTFORUM* (NOVEMBER, 1984):.54–60.

WILLIAM RUBIN:

After years of work on an exhibition, a curator derives a certain satisfaction from a review that attempts to engage the basic issues of his show in a fair-minded way and on a high level of discourse. This is true even when the review is largely negative, as in the case of Thomas McEvilley's article on The Museum of Modern Art's *'Primitivism'*. Most analyses of exhibitions and their books fall away and are soon forgotten. McEvilley's could be one that becomes part of the history of the event it addresses. I hope, therefore, that he will take this extended commentary on his text at least somewhat as a compliment—an attempt to further thrash out and clarify some ideas and attitudes that mean much to both of us—and not as an exercise in logomachy. The questions McEvilley raises go far beyond the exhibition to the nature and motives of The Museum of Modern Art itself, and I appreciate the opportunity *Artforum* has given me to air some of these matters.

No project on the order of *'Primitivism' in Twentieth Century Art* can work out entirely satisfactorily and wholly free of inconsistencies. Had we to do the book and show over again, there are some things I would surely do differently (I do not necessarily speak here for my colleague, Kirk Varnedoe, whose comments follow). My auto-critique revolves largely around the definitions of "affinities," some of which, I think, could and should have been more sharply etched. I am, however, largely satisfied with the presentation of the main body of the show, the sections called "Concepts" and "History," both of which McEvilley attacked from a variety of angles. A few of his criticisms of these sections are well-taken. I find, however, that notwithstanding his evidently good intentions, his review is interwoven with sufficient misconceptions, internal inconsistencies, and simple errors of fact that—given its seriousness—it should not go unchallenged.

At the outset, McEvilley has some very kind things to say about our show, among them that it was "thrilling" and "a tour de force of connoisseurship." As he proceeds, however, he describes the exhibition as operating in a kind of psychological, social, and historical void resulting from my supposed commitment to what he calls "Formalist Modernism." He concludes his text with the put-down that "it takes more than connoisseurship to make an exhibition great."

There is some kind of contradiction here. I'm not sure what McEvilley means by "connoisseurship," which—etymologically at least—implies far more than he presumably would wish to grant me. If I were wearing "formalist" blinders, could I really have chosen a great group of tribal works? Is their greatness not a function of their profound affectiveness on spiritual, poetic, and psychological—as well as on formal—levels? And do they not express, implicitly at least, societal values? Surely McEvilley does not believe that these qualities can be wholly separated from the objects' phenomenological (or plastic) configurations. Were not these affective factors necessarily, therefore, dimensions of my choices? While such components of the sculptures' expressiveness can be isolated for the purposes of discussion—indeed, the linear character of criticism virtually requires this—they cannot be separated from one another in the actual experience of the art.

McEvilley's repeated reproach that our show had no anthropological underpinning (of which more below) comes perilously close to suggesting that the tribal works, presented just in themselves, propose but a set of forms that communicate no "meaning" or "content." Picasso's remark, "all I need to know about Africa is in those [tribal] objects," was characteristic for him in its hyperbole; it was also flip. But it nevertheless embodied a crucial point, namely that Picasso felt (quite rightly, I believe) he could apprehend aspects of the spirit, values, and nature of African civilizations through their art. Indeed, while some of the observations he put into words were anthropologically wrong (e.g., his notion of "freedom" in relation to tribal art—as I pointed out in our book), the sense of Africa he intuited through its sculpture rings truer today than does most anthropological writing of his day.

By reducing the virtues of our show to "connoisseurship," McEvilley also diminishes—if he does not entirely dismiss—what I hope art historians will consider a significant contribution to our discipline, one that revises many basic received ideas about primitivism. For McEvilley, our art history is largely an "overwhelming mass of information" and he concludes that "on the whole, [Robert] Goldwater's book [*Primitivism in Modern Painting*] still reads better." McEvilley suggests that the "general ideas" of our exhibition have been around since 1938 (the date of Goldwater's book) and points to instances in which other institutions (Centre Pompidou, Grand Palais) have purportedly provided at least limited prototypes for our project.

No one, I think, admires my late friend and colleague Robert Goldwater more than I. The preface to *'Primitivism' in Twentieth Century Art* is devoted to expressing this admiration. The fact is, however, that the premises of our exhibition are very much at odds with many of his conclusions. If by "reads better" McEvilley is referring to Goldwater's lapidary literary style, I would be the first to cede the point. But in terms of substance, our conclusions are at odds with Goldwater's as regards a host of basic questions about which only one or the other of us can be right. Hence, if we have not simply fallen on our faces as historians, we have done more than merely, as McEvilley would have it, "refine and extend" Goldwater's research.

Most of the reproductions in Goldwater's book were of Modern works. Even in the revised and enlarged edition of 1967, only eight tribal works were illustrated, four of them paired visually with Modern objects. None of the eight had belonged to Modern artists and, so far as we know, only one of them was even in Europe in the days of the pioneer Modernists. Our multiplication of juxtapositions illustrating proposed (and often provable) relationships between Modern works and tribal objects in the artists' collections (or visible in museums they are known to have frequented) overturns one of Goldwater's basic principles, an insistence on the "extreme scarcity of the direct influence of primitive art forms" on twentieth century art. Moreover, Goldwater made no allowance for what we have called "invisible" influences (as documented by the pairings of Picasso's *Guitar* and his Grebo mask, [Henry] Moore's "Upright Internal and External Forms" and the British Museum's Malanggan, and [Marius] de Zayas' *Alfred Stieglitz* and the Pukapuka Soul-catcher). Nor did he connect the invention of collage, assemblage, and mixed media to the experience (Picasso's especially) of tribal art—or, indeed, treat most of the other topics taken up in the "Concepts" section of our exhibition. Finally, the artist's own words have undermined Goldwater's key assumption that Picasso's interest in tribal art was primarily formal. We are obliged to assign to Picasso's rediscovery of the "magical" roots and powers of art a more critical place in his development than we do any plastic or technical ideas he derived from tribal objects.

Contesting the Museum's assertion that our exhibition is the "first ever to juxtapose modern and tribal objects in the light of informed art history," McEvilley cites two purported precedents: the Menil Collections exhibition last spring at the Grand Palais, which "juxtaposed primitive and Modern works (a Max Ernst with an African piece, Cézanne with Cycladic) and sometimes, as in the [MoMA] exhibition, showed a Modern artist's work in conjunction with primitive objects in his collection"; and the Centre Pompidou, which "exhibited, in the vicinity of its Modern collections, about one-hundred tribal objects from the Musée de l'Homme." "Though not actually intermingled with Modern works," McEvilley says of the hundred objects, they "were intended to illustrate relationships with them and included, as does the [MoMA] show, primitive objects owned by Picasso, Braque, and other early Modernists."

McEvilley's recollections here certainly don't jibe with mine or, as it turns out, with the facts. A rapid check reveals that 1) two vitrines at the Centre Pompidou together never contained more than twenty or so objects; 2) none of them ever belonged to Picasso or Braque; 3) objects in the Beaubourg vitrines could hardly have been intended to "illustrate relations" with Modern art since they were chosen by Jean-Hubert Martin "without respect" as he says, "to historical or formal questions" from a group proposed by Francine Ndiaye of the Musée de l'Homme, who has only a glancing acquaintance with Modern art, and whose mandate was to select such objects as would constitute an overview of African art; 4) the choice of African sculptures included many of types—and from tribal areas—totally unknown in France in the days of the "early Modernists." As for the fascinating Menil show—which, in any case, took place after the writing of our book—my recollections (as confirmed by Dominique de Menil herself) are that 1) the tribal material was shown almost entirely in its own separate areas; 2) contrary to McEvilley, no Modern works were "shown in conjunction with primitive objects from [the artists'] own collection[s]"; indeed, no tribal works from the collections of important Modernist artists were included anywhere in the Menil collections show; 3) the juxtaposition of the Cézanne with a Cycladic sculpture and the Ernst with an African work were determined by Mrs. de Menil's "pleasure in seeing them together," and were *not* the demonstration of any historical connection. Thus, the two supposedly precedent primitivist events posed by McEvilley were not instances of "informed art history"; they were not, strictly speaking, instances of art history at all.

Why this determined effort on McEvilley's part to demonstrate that the premises and content of our show were "not new"? The answer may be found in one of the most remarkable rhetorical twists I have ever encountered. By convincing his reader that our efforts are "not new," McEvilley feels licensed to ask "why MoMA gives us primitivism now." The answer to this turns out to be his real point, namely that the "temple of formalist Modernism" is using the primitive to "revalidate" the Modernist movement in the face of "several years of sustained attack" which supposedly led us to need a "new defense." "The ultimate reason behind the exhibition," McEvilley insists, "is to revalidate Modernist aesthetic canons"—whatever *they* are. "How brilliant," he opines, "to attempt to revalidate classical Modernist aesthetics by stepping outside their usual realm of discourse and bringing to bear upon them a vast, foreign sector of the world."

How brilliant, indeed. Brushed aside here is the real history of our show, and the fact that it was an attempt to render explicit some art historical concerns that were implicit in MoMA exhibitions going back almost fifty years (*African Negro Art*, 1936; *Indian Art of the United States*, 1941; *Arts of the South Seas*, 1946). No apparent consideration was given to my conversations with Picasso of fifteen years ago which led me to conclude that the received art history of primitivism was profoundly distorted and that the whole topic would have to be restudied, or to the almost five years of the exhibition's actual integration (nor to the fact that if we hadn't rebuilt the Museum, the show would have taken place some years ago). By sweeping aside both the real motivations for, and the chronology of, this show (most of which is spelled out in our book), McEvilley could transform the nature of the event, and with it the actually fortuitous fact that it takes place "now" rather than some years ago, into an act of contemporary art politics.

For a man who, elsewhere in his text, shows a tremendous concern for the logic of argumentation, McEvilley's motivating of me is astonishing. Putting himself inside my mind, he confidently discovers and asserts agendas of which I had never thought. Anyone who knows me will consider laughable the idea that I would think Modernist art needs "revalidation." As I stroll through the galleries of the collection, the last thing in the world I imagine is that Cézanne, Picasso, Pollock *et alia* need to be authenticated by "primitives" or anyone else. It is not Rubin but McEvilley who thinks they need "revalidation," and he conveniently projects onto me the strategies of his own art-political ways of thinking.

Perhaps the most persistent criticism in McEvilley's long article was directed to our omission of anthropological matter in relation to the tribal objects. He decries the fact that "no anthropologist was included in the team" with the result that the "wholeness" of the tribal objects is sacrificed to "the cult of pure form"; thus the show constitutes an act of "ethnocentric subjectivity inflated to co-opt [tribal] cultures and their objects... [showing that] Western egotism [is] still as unbridled as in the centuries of colonialism and souvenirism." "The museum pretends to confront the Third World while really co-opting it and using it to consolidate Western notions of quality and feelings of superiority." (Needless to say, had I really been concerned with Western "feelings of superiority," I would hardly have mounted a show the very terms of which guaranteed that the tribal works would on average be superior to the Modern ones.[1])

The Museum, of course, had no intention of confronting tribal cultures, or even tribal objects as such (i.e., in their own terms), no less the whole Third World. To have done so would have hopelessly confused what the Museum was in fact doing—namely, studying the reception of tribal objects by Western artists, the ethnocentricity of which history we ourselves described as manifest and accepted as given. But McEvilley won't let us have a show about that reception, which is, of course, precisely what "primitivism"—as opposed to "the primitive"—signifies. He wants the tribal objects presented in a wholly integral way (never spelled out) in which not even anthropological museums show them.

It isn't that McEvilley cannot understand our aims. Indeed, he quotes us saying: "As our focus is on the Modernists' experience of tribal art...we have not included anthropological hypotheses regarding the religious or social purposes that originally surrounded these objects." And also that "the ethnologists' primary concern—the specific function and significance of each of these objects—is irrelevant to [our] topic, except insofar as these facts might have been known to the modern artists in question." He might also have added our observations that primitivism "refers not to the tribal arts in themselves, but to the Western interest in and reaction to them," and that it was "an aspect of the history of Western art, not of tribal art."

"This position," McEvilley admits, "is consistent in itself." But he insists we are not entitled to it because we have "not consistently acted" on it. (What would have been more inconsistent with our position than the inclusion of precisely the anthropological information McEvilley calls for, about which the artists knew nothing?) Now, I don't doubt that given the breadth of our project, we have been guilty of some inconsistencies, although I do not agree that most of the examples McEvilley adduces—which have to do with the modes of functioning of tribal artists—are, in fact, inconsistencies (as we shall see below). But McEvilley seems not to understand the fact that *whatever the inconsistencies in execution* (and those he signals are in the book rather than the exhibition), *they do not by any twist of logic nullify the admitted consistency of our original perspective.* Even if we hadn't made those observations about tribal artists to which McEvilley objects, would he not still have wanted anthropological input? Wouldn't he still have objected that the tribal objects were decontextualized, that "the blood is wiped off them?"

Of course, the tribal objects in our show are decontextualized (as they are in the Metropolitan Museum of Art, or, even more relevantly, in anthropological museums as well). In fact they are more than that; they are *recontextualized*, within the framework of Western art and culture. *And that is what our particular story is all about.* McEvilley simply refuses to accept the fact that our story is not about "the Other" but about ourselves. As I observed in my introductory chapter, "prior to the 1920s...at which time some Surrealists became *amateurs* of ethnology, artists did not generally know—nor evidently much care—about such [anthropological] matters." But as I also observed, the artists' lack of interest in or knowledge of the objects' religious purposes and functions did not mean that they were uninterested in "meanings." It was rather that "the meanings which concerned them were the ones that could be apprehended through the objects themselves." *This* is the real rub for, as we shall see, McEvilley refuses to accept that such meanings exist; indeed, that the tribal sculptures are, *in fact,* art.

Suppose we were to have taken McEvilley's advice and given an anthropological dimension to our show. What anthropology, whose anthropology should it have been? Should we have proposed the views of anthropologists of the Trocadéro itself in Picasso's time, such as Maurice Delafosse, who interpreted African tribal art as an Egyptian derivation? Not only is the work of such anthropologists irrelevant to our subject because unknown to the Modern artists, but it is wrong.[2] Even in our own day, there are an immense number of fundamental disagreements among anthropologists themselves, some of whom still credit the view, as does McEvilley, that there is no such thing as tribal art—only religious artifacts.

McEvilley appropriates the mantle and the voice of anthropology with far more certainty than is possessed by any professional anthropologist I have met. He constantly presumes to know and speak for the "intentionality" of long-dead tribal artists when, in fact, anthropology knows virtually nothing about them. He confidently puts himself into their minds in the same way he did into mine—and possibly with as little accuracy. Having granted the consistency of our perspective (at least in theory), he nevertheless states that by "their absolute repression of primitive context, meaning, content, and intention (the dates of the [tribal] works, their functions, their religious or mythological connections, their environments)," MoMA has "treated the primitives as less than human, less than cultural—as shadows of a culture, their selfhood, their Otherness, wrung out of them." Does McEvilley himself know how little is known about most of these tribal objects? Even had they been relevant, we would have had to face the fact that the specific functions and the religious or mythological significance of many if not most of the tribal objects in our show are unknown (and will probably never be known). And many of the meanings attributed to some of them by previous generations of anthropologists are being dismissed left and right.

Consider the question of dates, which McEvilley seems to think we have suppressed: "The complete omission of dates from the primitive works is perhaps one of the most troubling decisions," he writes, though he admits that "many of these objects cannot be dated precisely." In fact, *not a single one of them* in our show can be dated precisely, and precious few can be dated approximately. Even the small minority that were field-collected by anthropologists have only a *terminus ad quem;* one can only speculate as to how long they existed before collection. Most of the tribal objects in the show have little history, or dubious ones. Even the decision as to whether most of them are nineteenth or twentieth century objects is speculative, and usually made by historians of primitive art on a subjective rather than scientific basis. Far from being suppressed, the question of dates is not only discussed in the book, but is summarized on a panel that is repeated three times in various places in the exhibition. I excerpt from our panel: "Since accurate dates are not known for most tribal art, no dates appear on the labels for tribal objects in this exhibition. These objects are often short-lived, in part because of their largely perishable materials, in part because they were not preserved after being desacralized. Hence, most of the fine tribal art preserved in the West dates from no earlier than the later nineteenth and early twentieth centuries, and represents the later phases of long-standing traditions."

Where dates of tribal objects are relevant to the history of primitivism, they are the dates at which artists could have seen them in museums (what Picasso, for example, could have seen in the Trocadéro in 1907) and at which they purchased the pieces in their collections. We have spent hundreds of hours researching these dates and, where discoverable and relevant, have given them.

As one who has probably spent far more time haunting anthropological museums than has McEvilley, I can assure him that in virtually no cases do their labels give more information on "context, meaning, content, and intention" than we do. Will McEvilley please tell me how he learns anything about the "religious or mythological connections" of the objects in the vitrines of Tervuren, the Musée de l'Homme, or the Völkerkunde museum in Berlin (whose "fine arts"-oriented installation surpasses that of the Metropolitan)? Do these objects have more "blood on them" than those at MoMA? To be sure, some anthropological museums provide short general text panels at the beginning of sections, but provide little or nothing on individual objects. Even these introductory panels are only possible because the material in their vitrines is geographically homogeous. Suppose—as demanded by McEvilley—we had wanted to provide "environments" for objects that came from over a hundred different cultures and societies, how could we have done it?

Does the presentation of tribal sculptures by themselves—the way great museums present all other cultures' sculpture from the Egyptian to the present—really imply treating their makers as "less than human, less than cultural"? Perhaps only if, like McEvilley, you consider the objects "not art, but religion or magic"—as if most of the world's sculpture *is not both art and religion at the same time.* Though this crucial fact gets lost in his fulminations against "formalist Modernism," McEvilley *never accepts tribal sculptures as art*, nor their carvers as "artists"—or even "sculptors"; the latter remain relegated to the caste of "craftspeople." For McEvilley, the mere assertion that these "craftspeople" were artists, not to say great artists, smacks of "co-option." I wonder how many of his readers who saw our show and stood before the monumental Nukuoro Island carving of the goddess Kave that introduces it, share McEvilley's conviction that what they were looking at was "not art."

Generations ago, anthropologists considered tribal sculptures only artifacts, and even Franz Boas held that their sculptors' function never exceeded the role of copying and the problems of craftsmanship. This assumption was partly based on the absence of a word for art in most tribal languages. But the same is true for the ancient Egyptians; yet that culture's painting and sculpture is not denied the status of art. Of course, the tribal sculptor, living in a religiocentric society made (the majority of) his objects in the spirit and to the purposes of religious practice and expression—which was also true of Egyptian and Christian Medieval artists, among others. He also considered himself a craftsman—as did his Egyptian and Christian counterparts (the medieval painters were enrolled in the saddlers' guild for the simple reason that painting saddles was one of their primary duties). But no less than his Egyptian or Christian counterparts, the tribal sculptor was *also* an artist, and we have presented him as such—"misleadingly," according to McEvilley. In any event, the nineteenth century prejudice that tribal peoples produced no art has today been given up by most anthropologists.

Underlining certain similarities in the work of tribal and Modern artists does not mean, as McEvilley claims, that we have presented the tribal artist as a Modern one; we present him as an artist *tout court*. According to McEvilley, "Rubin's argument constantly attributes intentions to the tribal craftsmen, intentions associated with Modernist types of aesthetic feeling and problem-solving attitudes." This is simply not so. I did, of course, attribute to tribal sculptors the need to make aesthetic decisions, but that is because they functioned—among other things—as artists. The kind of questions I saw them confronting in terms of their ideographic language (which, McEvilley notwithstanding, did not invent itself)—a problem such as "how to make a nose"—could only be described as "Modernist...problem-solving" by someone with McEvilley's skewed perspective. All art involves some sort of problem-solving, whether it happens self-consciously or not. And in attributing to tribal sculptors an aesthetic instinct, which the anthropologist Robert Lowie (and, since him, many other anthropologists) have considered a common denominator of all mankind, I have simply chosen to believe those anthropologists whose views seem to me to accord with my experience of the sculptural objects themselves. McEvilley has chosen others, and we will have to agree to disagree. In terms of primitivism, however, it doesn't matter one whit which anthropologists you follow inasmuch as the Modern artists understood and acted upon the tribal objects as *art*.

I believe that it is McEvilley, not MoMA, who treats the tribal peoples as "less than human, less than cultural" by denying their cultures the fact of their art and their great artists. (He attributes the diversity and range of tribal art, which is considerable even within certain individual tribal units, to something he calls "communal inventiveness"—a process I leave the reader to try imagining.) He has a lot to say about MoMA's presumed inability to appreciate the otherness of the Other (which was more than evident to me *in tribal objects* long before I began reading anthropologists on primitive art). It is, indeed, exceedingly difficult to dissociate ourselves from Western values and ways of thinking sufficiently to truly appreciate the otherness of Third World peoples, as contemporary anthropologists are trying especially hard to do. But this was not what our show was about. Nor, in regard to this otherness, does McEvilley have any monopoly on virtue, since many leading anthropologists disagree sharply with his ideas.

It should also be remembered that there is another, negative "otherness" that is at issue for us in the West. This is the view that the Other is lazy, unintelligent, fit only for *travail de nègre* and, above all, uncultured. Most early anthropology is shot through with such prejudices, and the respect and admiration we find for tribal peoples on the part of Picasso and Matisse in the first decade of the century were not—with rare exceptions—to characterize anthropology until after World War II. If the peoples of the world are to get along with each other, they will not only have to appreciate their respective "otherness," they will have to recognize their common humanity. Some of us still do not think Schiller's hope that *"alle Menschen werden Brüder"* is tainted by co-option. By denying the manifest genius of tribal artists, McEvilley excludes whole peoples from this cultural commonality.

1. Many critics and visitors to the exhibition noted that the quality of the tribal works was, taken as a whole, higher than that of the Modern works. This was accepted in advance as an inevitable result of the premises of the exhibition. Except for those tribal works that were in artists' collections, or those museum objects which had had a direct historical relation to the work of individual Modern artists (and the two together constituted a minority), the tribal works I chose were all—by my lights—the best of their types I could find during many years of study in public and private collections all over the world. Unlike the Modern art, these profited from unfamiliarity. The Modern works were by definition limited to artists involved with primitivism: hence, not only were many great Modern artists not represented, but others who were in the exhibition (Brancusi, for example) were, for historical reasons, represented by objects that were not necessarily their very best. (Some artists were not as well represented as they should have been because loans were unobtainable: Matisse's great and highly relevant *Blue Nude* and *Madame Matisse*, could not, for example, be borrowed.)

   Not surprisingly, only the greatest of Modern artists, such as Picasso and Brancusi, could hold their own against the best tribal artists. Nobody, I think, considers that Picasso or Brancusi suffered in the comparison. That some other artists did was inevitable. Needless to say, I did not look upon the exhibition as a contest of quality, a *mano a mano* between tribal and Modern artists, and I could have easily stacked the cards in either direction. I knew that our public was far more familiar with great Modern art than with great tribal art, and was at pains to emphasize the latter. The only review of the show that came to grips with this particular issue, analyzed it, and understood it properly, was "Rubin's Primitives" by Allen Wardwell, which appeared in the November *Art World*.

2. I do not mean here to imply that everything Delafosse and his early twentieth-century colleagues wrote about African art was wrong—although to read the critiques of them by contemporary anthropologists one could conclude that very little of what they said was right. There was, however, one anthropologist writing early in the century whose work, as Lydia Gasman has insisted, is interesting to consider in connection with Picasso's ideas about tribal art, and that is Marcel Mauss. Though Gasman is wrong in thinking that Picasso might have read Mauss' 1903-1904 essay on magic (Picasso did not read anthropological texts, and his French in 1907 would not have been up to it in any case), Mauss's ideas parallel those of Picasso, participate in the same zeitgeist. It is interesting to consider this in the light of McEvilley's view of Goldwater's book, a great part of which is devoted to a review of anthropologists' ideas: ironically, the one group of anthropologists Goldwater does not deal with is precisely, as Gasman observes, the French school of Mauss and his followers.

In his criticisms of my contributions to the *'Primitivism'* exhibition, Thomas McEvilley is occasionally sloppy (he thinks I wrote two chapters in the book; I wrote three). He is also selectively forgetful, as when he chidingly suggests that an outdated "earth-mother" notion motivated my selection of contemporary women artists. This ignores the part of my essay that explicitly denounces this very cliché at length (pp. 680–81); yet McEvilley must know the passage, for he elsewhere quotes from it as evidence of my censorship of primitivism's deeper truths! Also, he generally overestimates my contributions, by supposing my handling of the contemporary sections in both show and book can be taken as centrally representative of the exhibition's conception; whereas in fact these contemporary sections were later add-ons, organized (as should be expected, given their content) on significantly differing premises. But let all this pass—I'm glad to be associated with the show, and to confront the substantive issues McEvilley raises in his serious and impassioned review.

McEvilley accuses me of writing on primitivism in a "value-saturated, interpretive" way. He is absolutely right: my essays, and particularly the contemporary essay with which he takes special issue, do have this character, and were intended to make those values and interpretations very evident. His opposing views also have this character—what he would term an "ideological" aspect—but I am afraid he is less forthright in declaring, or perhaps less clear in understanding, their implications. Often, in fact, it seems to me that he is more deeply guilty of the very mistakes he attributes to William Rubin and to me.

He holds that the artists I selected, and the issues I raised, did not confront primitivism's "raw realness, or its real rawness." He admires instead contemporary artists "whose intentionalities [a word he favors as a substitute for the simpler 'intentions'] involve falling away from Western civilization and literally forgetting its values." Their work is not just better primitivism, but fully *primitive*, he says, because it shares "the intentionality proper to [tribal] objects." Yet these attitudes McEvilley admires are quintessentially modern and Western, involving goals that obviously could never have been held by tribal artists—who by definition never had civilized Western values to forget. McEvilley's semantic abuse of the already beleaguered term "primitive" is the least of his confusions here. He blames Rubin and me for supposedly attributing modern Western intentions to tribal artists, and opines that "The need to co-opt difference into one's own dream of order...is a tragic failing. Only fear of the Other forces one to deny its Otherness." Yet when he attributes *tribal* intentions to *Modern* artists, Otherness vanishes in a more global identity of purpose than we would ever suggest, or believe possible, between creators in vastly different cultures. McEvilley thus seems unwittingly to reinforce the very prejudice of Western superiority he claims to reject. In his account, contemporary artists can know all about Primitive motives, and subsume them within their more complex projects; but the Primitive may not be credited with harboring any analogue of modern ways of thinking.

What, one should ask, constitutes this global notion of tribal purposes about which McEvilley seems so clairvoyant—this idea of an essential "intentionality" that for him embraces Senufo and Sepik, Polynesian and Punu alike? The definition is never fully spelled out, but the traces can be found in a constellation of effects he evokes. Primitive creation involves for him "violence" in religious practice, "awe and dread," objects drenched in blood, seen in "closed dark spaces, by flickering torchlight," and a "terrifying power" of the "darkness of the unconscious." In short his is a deeply Romantic vision—latently more than a little racist—whose rather limited terms seem more appropriate to the generation of Joseph Conrad, or to a particularly unreconstructed Freudian, than to a 1980s understanding of the variety and complexity of social and mental life in tribal societies.

Imagining the power of tribal art exclusively in these terms, McEvilley seems to see only one legitimate avenue for its contact with Modern art: the domain of psychodrama and the expression of the dark unconscious. He accuses me by contrast of a "dread of the primitive, of the dangerous beauty that attracted Matisse and Picasso and that continues to attract some contemporary artists today." As instances of this ongoing tradition, he cites Hermann Nitsch, Paul McCarthy, Kim Jones, and Gina Pane. It would seem that the pairing of Matisse and Picasso might already suggest that there is a wide range of Modern primitivist responses that matches the wide range of tribal art. And no matter how deep one's respect for Nitsch, et al, it is peculiar praise to hold them up as the true legatees of Matisse. If "dread" is what keeps me from constructing this kind of genealogy for primitivism, may I continue to live in fear.

McEvilley claims that I timidly avoid facing up to the kind of primitivism he prefers, and even "deny [its] presence." This is false, and misinforms his readers. My "Contemporary Explorations" chapter explicitly and pointedly considers views such as those he holds, and primitivizing art of the kind he admires. I don't deny these notions of the primitive exist, or that numerous contemporary artists believe in them sincerely. I do argue, however (in ways better examined in the essay itself), that there are other valid ways of thinking about the primitive that inspire other serious artists, and I explain why in the end I find these latter more rewarding and stimulating. I try to explain, moreover, that the strain of romantic, expressionist primitivism McEvilley favors, with its fantasies of total escape and forgetting, has disturbing undercurrents that are ultimately authoritarian in their implications.

My essay examines different ways interchanges between Modern and tribal art have worked, and stresses that the two spheres have points of contact in the mind as well as in the gut—Minimalism and Cubism are points of departure, or zones of affinity, as valid as angst-torn expressionism. Tribal art in my view can inspire not only violence and dark dread (a response which, as Rubin explains at length in the book, is often based on misconceptions of tribal life and misunderstandings of tribal forms), but also wit, fantasy, and sophisticated complexity—many tribal objects project, in fact, a classic sense of dignity and serene repose. Modern culture in turn provides not simply encumbering values which need forgetting, but also powerful new ways of insight into the variety of tribal creation. This view is indeed "value-saturated and interpretive"; it's intended to be so, and declares itself as such. McEvilley, on the other hand, who believes that Modern artists can willfully acquire the "intentionality" of their tribal counterparts, may similarly dream that there is some other way—presumably his own—in which a reading of primitivism and of the primitive can involve no such shaping premises.

One panacea he recommends is scrupulous attention to intention and context. Berating Rubin and me for excluding anthropological data from the exhibition labels for tribal objects, he seems to be arguing that proper awareness of original intentions will save us from the imperialist sin of misreading primitive art in our own terms. As I believe he demonstrates, however, construals of intention are every bit as problematic and value-laden as other forms of "appropriation" from tribal sources. But I do not mean by this to damn appropriation per se—only to ask McEvilley to rethink some false divisions he's setting up. He suggests that my extolling "the capacity of tribal art to transcend the intentions and conditions that first shaped it" should be restated as "the capacity of tribal art to be appropriated out of its own intentionality into mine." I would be happy enough with the paraphrase, if I thought McEvilley understood what he was saying. For someone so committed to an idea of the power of the unconscious, and its communication across the barriers of time and culture, a nostalgic devotion to the notion of an inviolate, ultimately controlling intention seems curious and inconsistent. In fact, even without appeal to unconscious factors, it is plain to see that no act or object, by Shakespeare or a Yoruba carver, would have any broad or long cultural impact if its meaning or potential consequence were totally constrained by its founding motivations (which are finally unknowable in any event). As modern literary theory has driven home repeatedly, there is no validity in a model of knowledge based on the ideal of a privileged reading of an original determining intention. All art, culture, and communication functions by "appropriations" from one context to another. McEvilley and the artists he admires appropriate the Primitive to their purposes just as certainly as I do. Between our two appropriations, the question is not which is pure—neither is or can be—but which is barren and which fertile, which is liberal and open-ended and which, in McEvilley's own terms, is a "rejection of the wholeness of life."

Unhappy with the exhibition's decontextualization of tribal objects, McEvilley offers what he seems to think is an ultimately damning image in riposte: a parallel but reverse decontextualization, where the Western object (in this case a food container) is adopted by New Guinea tribesmen as a clothing ornament. McEvilley concludes that our museum showing tribal objects is as ludicrous as the natives wearing Kellogg's boxes. On the contrary, though, the ability to see art value where others see only garbage (as for example in cubist collage, or [Robert] Rauschenberg) is to my mind a kind of receptivity, and creative intelligence, that is well worth respecting and thinking about. Specifically, the tribal use of Western discards is a potentially fascinating phenomenon, of which McEvilley has chosen a relatively uninteresting instance. He ignores the more telling examples of this kind of bricolage that we included in the exhibition: a striking Guere mask made from bullet casings, or an exceptional fetish fashioned around a bottle of Suze liqueur. By acts of appropriation, disregarding the functions the Western objects originally fulfilled, the tribesmen saw new possibilities for the discards and gave them new life and meaning. I agree with McEvilley that it's fair to draw a parallel between this activity and the modern Western attention to the formerly neglected power of tribal objects. But his reading of the situation ascribes naïve stupidity to the natives and deluded venality to the Westerner, while mine would stress the common potential for invention, for expansion of cultural limitations, and for communication, that makes both actions compellingly and positively human.

THOMAS McEVILLEY:

I'm the one who barked these grouchy bears out of the woods, so I guess I have to listen to their howling and gnashing of teeth. In a sense it's a chance in a lifetime. We rarely see these bears out in the open—especially the big one. The angry bears, rising from what they must have thought was a well-deserved sleep, are after me. But they are shoddy arguers. Helpless in the face of issues which their replies indicate they barely understand—and then only in a nineteenth-century kind of way—they have adopted the courtroom strategy of discrediting the witness rather than responding to his testimony. They have attempted to undermine the readers' confidence in me by claiming inaccuracies in my text.

Let's consider this charge of inaccuracies. Varnedoe leads off with a daring revelation of a typographical error—how feeble, to attempt to discredit me on the grounds that a sprite of the typesetting or proofreading realms, after the finished, correct text had left my hands, didn't pick up the fact that three had been changed to two—a common sort of scribal error—deep in a footnote. The thing to notice is not that there is a typo—because that happens—but that this scholar and curator, with a month to comb the text, could find nothing more important to criticize in the introduction of his reply than a typographical error in a footnote. Rubin shows a more ambitious version of the discrediting strategy: he wants to bury my readers' faith and my criticisms deep in an atmosphere of manufactured doubt. He begins his reply, understandably, by distancing himself from Varnedoe's "Contemporary Explorations" section of the show; he specifies the parts of the show that he is pleased with (the "Concepts" and "History" sections) and makes no mention of Varnedoe's unfortunate venture into the contemporary. He goes on to expressions of his familiar Picassoism, then defends the two-volume book that accompanies the exhibition from my statement that it merely refines and extends the research of Robert Goldwater. "But in terms of substance, our conclusions," he says, "are at odds with Goldwater's as regards a host of basic questions." Those familiar with Goldwater's book will recognize that this is a gross overstatement. The lines and themes of research are Goldwater's, the terminology is Goldwater's; what is at issue where they differ, as in Rubin's insistence that Goldwater did not recognize as many examples of direct influence as does Rubin's team, is just the gathering of more information.

The strategy underlying Rubin's approach, I suspect, is both to weaken the readers' confidence in me and to attempt to bog me down in answering petty disagreements, in the hopes that I will never fight through to the issues themselves—since those are the challenges Rubin wishes to avoid. I must drag the reader through a certain amount of this petty bickering about details, both in order to clear the reader's mind of manufactured doubt about the integrity of my article, and to illustrate Rubin's method of debate. Here's the sentence that is meant to lean the readers back in their chairs, distancing them from me once and for all: "His review," Rubin writes, "is interwoven with sufficient misconceptions, internal inconsistencies, and simple errors of fact that—given its seriousness—it should not go unchallenged." The charge of these supposed factual errors centers around a paragraph in which I demonstrated with a few obvious examples—and I could have used others—that the practice of regarding and exhibiting primitive and Modern works together was not really new to this show, as one might be led to believe by the claims and promotion around the show, despite its qualifier, "in the light of informed art history." Rubin professes to find my statements about recent earlier exhibitions to be nests of inaccuracies. First is my statement that the Centre Pompidou, for several years beginning in the late seventies, "exhibited, in the vicinity of its Modern collections, about one hundred tribal objects from the Musée de l'Homme," some of them owned by early Modernist artists including Braque and Picasso, with the intention of illustrating relationships with the Modern works in the Beaubourg collection. In reply Rubin attacks first my number, one hundred. Citing the authority of Jean-Hubert Martin, who was at the time a Beaubourg curator and in charge of the loans from the Musée de l'Homme, he declares: "1) the two vitrines at the Centre Pompidou together never contained more than twenty or so objects." But in conversation with me subsequent to his conversation with Rubin, Martin stated that each vitrine—not both together—held twenty or twenty-five objects, bringing the total to forty or fifty at any one time. And there is more than meets the eye hidden in Rubin's unobtrusive little word "never." Why doesn't he just say (however mistakenly) that the vitrines did not hold more than twenty objects? Because he is repressing the fact or doesn't know that the objects in these vitrines were changed, since more objects had been borrowed from the Musée de l'Homme than the vitrines would hold. "Never" means not at any one time, and has nothing whatever to do with the total over a period of time. No listing of the total number of objects has been located, but Beaubourg curator Jean-Yves Mock, whose memory provided my original estimate of one hundred, still says that figure is not unreasonable.

Next, Rubin denies that any of the objects in the Beaubourg vitrines had ever been owned by Braque or Picasso. In fact, at the writing of my article one of the authorities on this subject had ventured the opposite opinion, yet finally it seems this point must remain moot, in light of the fact, acknowledged by Rubin, that no exact listing of the objects has been found. Still, the fact that some of the objects there belonged to early Modernist artists is acknowledged by all. Rubin goes on to say that these objects "could hardly have been intended to 'illustrate relations' with Modern art since they were chosen by Jean-Hubert Martin 'without respect,' as he says, 'to historical or formal questions….' " In clarifying this point to me, Martin said otherwise: the primary purpose of the installation was to open viewers' eyes to non-Western ways of seeing, he remarked, but added, "Of course it was also to remind people, without specific historical scholarship, that the painters in Paris at that time [early in the century] were aware of primitive art." Indeed, unless one were trying to point out a relation of some type, why else would one exhibit primitive works in a museum specifically dedicated to *l'art moderne?*

Rubin's second set of claims of inaccuracies focuses on my remark that the exhibition of the Menil collections, *La Rime et la Raison* at Paris' Grand Palais in the spring of 1984 "juxtaposed primitive and Modern works (a Max Ernst with an African piece, Cézanne with Cycladic) and sometimes, as in the [MoMA] exhibition, showed a Modern artist's work in conjunction with primitive objects in his collection." I am going to quote Rubin on this point, minor as it is, in order to demonstrate the more clearly his method. Again he numbers his points as if stacking up an inexorable case against me. He writes: "1) the tribal material was shown almost entirely in its own separate areas." Again, note the unobtrusive little word, in this case "almost." The fact Rubin can neither growl away nor live with is that the tribal objects were not shown *entirely* in their own separate area. That was my point, and he concedes it while pretending to deny it. Yes, the Ernst *was* shown with an African piece; yes, the Cézanne was shown with a Cycladic piece; and so on, through examples I have not mentioned. Rubin goes on: "2) contrary to McEvilley, no Modern works were 'shown in conjunction with primitive objects from [the artists'] own collection[s].'" Yet there is a plain statement in the catalogue, by Walter Hopps, curator of the exhibition, discussing the mixing of primitive and Modern objects, in which he notes, *"Ainsi, dans la section des surréalistes, on trouve, à côté de leurs oeuvres, des objets leur ayant appartenus"* (thus, in the section on the Surrealists, beside their own works one finds objects that belonged to them). These include, for example, Eskimo masks, of which *"plusieurs furent acquisés…par des surréalistes français établis à New York"* (several were bought…by French Surrealists living in New York).

His next point is no stronger: "3) the juxtaposition of the Cézanne with a Cycladic sculpture and the Ernst with an African mask were determined by Mrs. de Menil's 'pleasure in seeing them together,' and were *not* the demonstration of any historical connection." Here again the unobtrusive little element, in this case the italicizing of "not," directs the reader away from the point. The point is that Rubin has acceded completely to my statement, while again pretending to reject it. He has had to agree that the Cézanne was shown with the Cycladic piece, the Ernst with an African, and so on. To distract attention from that fact he attempts to shift the readers' attention to the last part of the sentence through the emphasis. Of course, the works were "*not* the demonstration of any historical connection." I never for a moment said they were. I am being corrected on statements I never made. Here again is the key catalogue passage from that show, on which my statements were in part based.

> *Ici l'art primitif est représenté à égalité avec l'art occidental; l'art*
> *occidental le plus ancien est juxtaposé avec l'art le plus moderne. Les*

affinités ne sont pas chronologiques, elles sont conceptuelles, iconographiques et formelles, destinées à suggérer les correspondances profondes entre les valeurs esthétiques et spirituelles de peuples et de temps fort divers. Ainsi, dans la section des surréalistes, on trouve, à côté de leurs oeuvres, des objets leur ayant appartenus. Dans la même esprit, quelques oeuvres modernes sont exposées au milieu d'objets archaïques ou traditionnels.

(Here, primitive art is represented equally with Western art; the oldest Western art is juxtaposed with the most modern. The affinities are not chronological but conceptual, iconographic, and formal; they are intended to suggest the deep correspondences between the aesthetic and spiritual values of very different peoples and times. Thus, in the section on the Surrealists, beside their own works one finds objects that belonged to them. In the same spirit, several Modern works are shown among ancient or traditional objects.)

Hopps goes on to mention the Ernst with the African piece, and so on. Rubin attempts to reduce the importance of the Menil show, along with the Beaubourg installation, saying they are "not instances of 'informed art history'"; he even goes so intemperately far as to say, "they were not, strictly speaking, instances of art history at all." And why not, in the case of the Menil show? His reason is that the juxtapositions under discussion "were determined by Mrs. de Menil's 'pleasure in seeing them together.'" Now, to say that the pleasure of the eye of a sensitive and long-trained collector is not automatically an exercise of informed art history is already somewhat questionable. The collection itself is an act of "informed art history," and the Menil show was the quintessential demonstration of collectorly connoisseurship's long habit of mingling the Modern and the primitive. When Rubin declares that because objects were juxtaposed merely for the pleasure of seeing them together the show is disqualified as informed art history, doesn't he realize that he is damning his own show too? Why, for example, was Picasso's *Girl before a Mirror* shown with the Kwakiutl mask—even on the cover of the catalogue and a poster for the show, as if this juxtaposition were the essence of it all? As I demonstrated in the article, there was absolutely no reason whatever to show these particular two pieces together except Rubin's pleasure in seeing them together. Indeed, the greater part of his show was made up of that pleasure and his indulgence in it.

The careful way Rubin's and Varnedoe's letters are constructed is to give the impression that many factual inaccuracies have been found in my text. Rubin, for example, makes his remark about inaccuracies, then goes on for several paragraphs about matters of critical dispute that have nothing to do with claims of factual error. This blurring of the distinction between factual error and critical dispute is a basic method in both letters. If we pause and count up the inaccuracies they have found, we see that Rubin has found none, and Varnedoe has come up with a typographical error in a footnote. That is all. Enough with the distracting fog of these tactics. Rubin's achievement was not, surely, in originating the idea of juxtaposing primitive and Modern objects, nor in being the first to act it out, but in doing it more extensively than his predecessors had—in fact too extensively, considering that certain of his juxtapositions are meaningless.

It is in their treatment of the real issues that these men reveal, I think, a poverty of intellect. I am serious when I say that they seem to have brought only nineteenth-century ways of thinking, nineteenth-century minds, to bear on the discussion. Very near the beginning of his statement Rubin takes refuge in references to "my conversations with Picasso," a tactic that amounts, throughout his text, to the fallacy called the Appeal to Authority. In an obvious Appeal to Authority Rubin defends himself from my belief that more information should have been given about the primitive works by quoting Picasso's remark, "all I need to know about Africa is in those [tribal] objects." Rubin comments, "Picasso felt (quite rightly, I believe) he could apprehend aspects of the spirit, values, and nature of African civilizations through their art." But Picasso's remark could just as clearly mean, "all I need to know about Africa is how these objects look," for that is indeed all you get from just looking at them: how they look. Later, Rubin, quoting himself, says that the meanings that concerned Modern primitivists "'were the ones that could be apprehended through the objects themselves.' *This*," he goes on, "is the real rub for, as we shall see, McEvilley refuses to accept that such meanings exist." Here Rubin is relying on an implied claim to universal sameness of aesthetic feeling, an out-of-date piece of Platonic lore that has no ground in evidence whatever. The surprising thing is that Rubin evidently has no inkling of cultural conditioning and what it does to one's eyes. The meanings that we read directly from tribal objects are highly unlikely to be the ones the tribal image-makers intended; they will predominantly be the ones that our own cultural conditioning has ingrained in us. To say, as he does, that one can derive the intended emic content merely by looking at the tribal works is to say that we need no study of ethnology at all, no struggle with the emic-etic problem—in short, no attempt to understand the tribal images and image-makers on their own terms; our own terms, he is saying, must be universal, evidently just because they are ours. This is in fact the principle on which his show and book are based. That, after reading my article, he fails to perceive the simple and basic point of cultural relativity indicates how deep is his resistance to it and how unquestioning is his commitment to the claim of the universal supremacy of Western cultural values.

In another defense against my charge that the realities of the tribal works were actually repressed in both the '*Primitivism*' show and, above all, the book, Rubin says that the museum was "studying the reception of tribal objects by Western artists." "But," he laments, "McEvilley won't let us have a show about that reception, which is, of course, precisely what 'primitivism'—as opposed to 'the primitive'—signifies." This is of course not strictly true. I said that I would be far happier with the show (and book) than I am if they had truly limited themselves to the reception; the problem is that both the show and the book (especially Rubin's introductory essay) attribute motives to the primitive as well as to the primitivist—in fact, the same motives—making them (what else?) like us. It is primarily in his category of "affinities" that he attributes to the tribal image-makers this and that Modern Western aesthetic feeling and ambition, ignoring their own expressions of their feelings and ambitions. Rubin shows a strange immunity to criticism here. He refers to his "auto-critique," which would feature improvements in his "affinities" category; yet his categories were one of the leading subjects of my article and he has nowhere replied to my criticism of them, except vaguely to imply that he is privately improving them.

Throughout Rubin's letter he resorts to the childish tactic of throwing my accusations back at me ("*You* are"—"No, *you* are"—this is Varnedoe's reflex too) rather than answering them. He says, for example, that McEvilley "constantly presumes to know and speak for the 'intentionality' of long-dead tribal artists.... He confidently puts himself into their minds...." In fact, I have attributed no motives to the tribal image-makers, except to deny, on the soundest of anthropological, linguistic, and psychological grounds, that the motives he attributes to them apply. When Rubin claims that "many leading anthropologists disagree sharply with [McEvilley's] ideas," he is suggesting again that I presented some definition of tribal Otherness. Of course I did not; I criticized Rubin's definition, since his idea of Otherness is simply to make it look like oneself. And for his part Varnedoe writes, "[McEvilley] seems to be arguing that proper awareness of original intentions will save us from the imperialist sin of misreading primitive art in our own terms." Yes, that is to an extent what I mean, and I direct the readers' attention to the somewhat mocking tone of the phrase "imperialist sin." Like a Westerner of the nineteenth-century, Varnedoe cannot take the question of an imperialistic sin at all seriously, though to many it virtually leaps off the walls of the exhibition. A prominent non-Western artist, for example, hearing the show praised, said, "No; we don't want to be their mascots."

Both Rubin and Varnedoe claim that the absence, in both the show and the book, of information about the attitudes of the people who made, used, and understood these objects is justified by our lack of knowledge of such attitudes. "Construals of intention are every bit as problematic and value-laden as other forms of 'appropriation' from tribal sources," says Varnedoe; and Rubin asks, "Does McEvilley himself know how little is known about most of these tribal objects?" They suggest, in other words, that since we cannot know what these things were made for, we are justified in projecting our own fantasies onto them. Rubin asks, "Will McEvilley please tell me how he learns anything about the 'religious or mythological connections' of the objects in the vitrines of Tervuren, the Musée de l'Homme, or the Völkerkunde museum in Berlin...?" Why, I'd be glad to. I would suggest first of all more attention to the relevant ethnologic literature (yes, it is there) and, above all, to the history of religion. Of course there are many problems in the anthropological literature and many blind places in our knowledge of tribal attitudes, but in fact the one area where there is rather abundant knowledge is that of ritual practices, which is the major area relevant to the works in the exhibition. To illustrate the sometimes difficult types of content that primitive images might have, I might even be so bold as to suggest my own monograph on some Indus Valley icons, published in *RES*, journal of the Peabody Museum of Harvard University and of the Laboratoire d'Ethnologie of the University of Paris. I would be glad to provide further reading lists.

Both Rubin and Varnedoe seem determinedly innocent of serious attention to the question of how primitive cultures develop and change. In prehistoric art, for example, thousands of years may be needed for a small development in image-making. The situation is very likely the same in more recent tribal cultures. This I referred to as "communal inventiveness," which Rubin describes as "a process I [Rubin] leave the reader to try imagining." Well, one might for example try imagining the American automobile industry, where stylistic change arises through a communal development, or again look at a shelf full of books and contemplate the changes in book design over the last hundred years, or, again, the design changes of utilitarian objects like household goods and cigarette lighters, all of which change in essentially communal ways. The evidence is that tribal images were regarded as utilitarian objects by their makers and users, and that their design changes would better be compared with those of our utilitarian objects than with the originality-obsessed Western practice of art.

When Rubin says that I want "the tribal objects presented in a wholly integral way (never spelled out) in which not even anthropological museums show them," he is being disingenuous. Rubin claims that I "demanded" "'environments'" in the installation; no such demand occurs in my article. I want the objects written about without attributing our motives to their makers. I want writing and exhibiting that are as clean as possible of ego projections. That is all. In response to my request for more information about the tribal objects, Rubin and Varnedoe claim that they cannot be dated and, somehow, need not be dated. Yet anyone who opens a scholarly book on primitive objects, or who visits anthropological museums (and by the way, I'll put my hours in them against Rubin's any day), will see that at least approximate dates are usually given for the works. The fact that these dates are reconstructed by scholars does not in the least invalidate them, as Rubin claims; *all* dates are reconstructed by scholars. The fact that these reconstructions will change as the available evidence changes does not mean we should ignore them; it means that at any time we must use the best possible scholarly approximation, with an understanding that it is less than absolute. Without dates how do we know that we are dealing with what Rubin calls "long-dead tribal artists"? One very good reason for including dates in this show—one brought up in my article and conveniently ignored by both Rubin and Varnedoe—is that it is absolutely certain that tribal image-making since the nineteenth century has been increasingly influenced by Western arts and crafts. The distinction between ethnic and tourist arts is all-important.[1] As soon as a market began to exist for tribal objects their character changed. If the objects in the show are all genuine, that is, premarket, or pretourist works, then they were used in ritual ways as I described in the article; if they were not so used, then they are the products of tourist industries. In other words, the omission of dates amounts to another hidden tactic for avoiding the confrontation with the actual uses of these objects in their tribal settings. One could almost believe that Rubin would rather show tourist works, since they were never used in ways that Western eyes have trouble facing.

Let's consider the tribal object that Rubin uses in an attempt to suggest that my approach is opposed to aesthetic feeling and appreciation—the large Nukuoro Island figure that introduces the exhibition. Rubin identifies this figure as "the goddess Kave," and says no more. By mentioning the mythological title Rubin gets one foot into the ethnology of the piece, but never puts the other in. And why not? Brian Brake, James McNeish, and David Simmons, in their book *Art of the Pacific,* show the same icon of Kave and note that she was a goddess to whom human sacrifices were offered.[2] Rubin has, in other words, invoked the very positive feelings that Greek mythology and related traditions have instilled in us toward the idea of a "goddess," in connection with a figure that should have very different associations. If he was going to name her at all he should have told us not only who but *what* she is. The other way would have been simply to present the icon as an object, with no references to goddesses and myth-names at all. Let me put the point clearly: *if* the Kave icon is authentic, then it was used in its own culture for human sacrifices rather than for aesthetic enjoyment; if, on the other hand, it was never bloodied by human sacrifice, then it is probably not authentic but a tourist work.

Rubin focuses very extensively on the fact that I raised questions about calling tribal objects artworks plain and simple. He says that to me the tribal objects are "not art, but religion or magic." This fragment of a quotation from my article eliminates context and attributes to me a point I made about a hypothetical tribal observer. What I actually wrote was this: "If you or I were a native tribal artisan or spectator walking through the halls of MoMA we would see an entirely different show from the one we see as twentieth-century New Yorkers. We would see primarily not form but content, and not art, but religion or magic." The statement, by the way, is correct beyond a doubt. I have not, in other words, denied these objects any status by questioning the way their wholeness is fragmented and repressed as they are appropriated into Rubin's art realm. The question ultimately is not whether these things are or are not art (an essentially barren question of linguistic usage), or whether they should or should not be regarded as art; the real issue is how these men regard art and its relationship to the world, to history, to culture, to civilization. This is not exclusively a question about so-called civilized versus so-called primitive cultures. It is a question about the critic's or curator's willful ego-projections onto the objects. (How Rubin represented the works of the Dadaists and Surrealists in an earlier book is a similar case.) The problem with calling the tribal objects art merely through their design similarity to Modern art is precisely that this tactic amounts to a rejection of the intentions of the makers and an imposition on them of foreign intentions that would not have made sense to them.

Varnedoe replies to my desire that the tribal image-makers' intentionality be attended to by claiming that "modern literary theory has driven home repeatedly [the idea that] there is no validity in a model of knowledge based on the ideal of a privileged reading of an original determining intention." By "modern literary theory" he seems to mean the formulation by W.K. Wimsatt and Monroe Beardsley, in the forties, of the idea of the intentional fallacy. Of course, an artist's statements cannot be allowed utterly to control the interpretation of his or her work, but neither can they be ignored. In any case the idea of the intentional fallacy is wrongly brought up by Varnedoe here; it does not apply to my argument. I am talking about the fact that cultural objects arise in cultural contexts, and that within that larger context—in which the particular maker's personal and specific intentions are merely a detail within a larger whole—they are communally understood in certain ways which, for that culture, constitute the reality of the object. Varnedoe's invocation of the intentional fallacy springs from his misunderstanding of the difference between the word intention, which refers to an individual's intention and is what the intentional fallacy is about, and intentionality, which is a larger world-constituting type of understanding having always communal resonances. The whole-cloth nineteenth centuryism of Varnedoe's thought is revealed in a display of comedic ignorance. He quotes me as using the term "intentionalities" and notes parenthetically that this is "a word [McEvilley] favors as a substitute for the simpler 'intentions.'" He evidently doesn't recognize that "intentionality" is a technical term in the philosophy of Edmund Husserl and in the whole phenomenological movement. I used the word "intentionalities" rather than the very different word "intentions" to indicate that, like linguistic philosophy, phenomenology also would give us insight into the problems at issue here—to indicate that I was discussing the way that one's cultural horizon, like one's language, both shapes the mind and constitutes the world it relates to. Twentieth-century ways of thinking like linguistic philosophy and phenomenology have tried precisely to pry us loose from the unremitting colonialistic egotism of our nineteenth-century ways. Varnedoe remains silent in the face of such arguments, evidently not recognizing the terminologies. Both he and Rubin even use quotation marks around "intentionality" as if to suggest that it is some monstrous, affected coinage of mine. The anthropological linguists Edward Sapir and Benjamin Lee Whorf have argued very influentially that if a people's language does not permit the expression of a certain concept, then there can be no reason at all for saying that that people have that concept. This fact has been experimentally confirmed in a number of ways.[3] Now, in light of that, can there be any justification for ignoring the fact that the languages of the tribal cultures whose objects were seen at MoMA utterly lacked words or even circumlocutions that could express what we mean by art? It is a simple fact, both on linguistic and on ethnological grounds, that the makers and users of the tribal objects in the MoMA show did not regard them at all as we regard our art. Why then should our concept prevail over theirs in discussions of their objects? Is it not merely arrogance to bring in our term from outside, on all the tribal objects we like, as if we knew what they were? Is it not in fact a dead end to show no curiosity about attitudes different from our own?

The making of objects whose only or primary function is pure contemplation and aesthetic appreciation is, in Western cultural history, peculiar to ancient Greek culture and its descendants and offshoots, including us. Something similar, but by no means identical, arose in T'ang dynasty China. Most of the world's cultures did not know of this activity until they came into contact with the European stream of influence. What we call art, in other words, as opposed to functional types of image-making and craftsmanship, is not an etic or objective and universal phenomenon.

Rubin, noting that tribal peoples lack a word for art, remarks, "But the same is true for the ancient Egyptians; yet that culture's painting and sculpture is not denied the status of art."

The fact is that most of what we regard as Egyptian artworks the Egyptians themselves understood as functional objects within the very practical activity of funerary magic. To us, the activity of making something art prominently involves the act of displaying it or reporting on it to others. But virtually every object in the great Egyptian Museum at Cairo was made to be buried underground and hidden from human eyes and from human knowledge forever; nor is there anywhere in the abundant Egyptian literature any hint that ghosts or gods or anyone else were intended to take aesthetic pleasure in these objects in the way we do. The reasons why they were so gorgeously designed and crafted, then, remain a mystery which it should be our concern to penetrate rather than to avoid with an easy term. We could honestly say that these things are funerary objects, and then go on to say that we like to look at our artworks next to their funerary objects. But instead we co-opt the whole cultural reality of these objects into our language game, so that we can use a word we feel at home with, regardless of the fact that it has a very limited and partial application to them. Rubin and Varnedoe are implicitly declaring that everything native to these non-Western cultures is unimportant next to our mania for calling their spoons and things art. The tribal person, in other words, has no dignity in terms of his or her own aspirations and concepts. Our conviction that we understand these things properly by calling them art, even that we elevate them by giving them that name, necessarily implies that the people who made them and the people for whom they were made did not understand them properly—a bizarrely skewed claim. It is to avoid such atrocities of thinking that I suggest we begin to loosen up our habit of believing that we honor those objects by conferring on them our revered concept "art."

"McEvilley," says Rubin, "simply refuses to accept the fact that our story is not about 'the Other,' but about ourselves." In fact my point is the opposite. What is at issue is not simply a matter of attempting to understand other cultures; it is a matter of attempting to understand ourselves. By forcing other cultures into our own familiar modes of naming and feeling we rob them of the power to reveal ourselves by our otherness from them, we rob them of the power to show us our limitations and to suggest possible ways to grow beyond those limits.

Rubin shows no awareness of the complexity of the question, "Is it art?" In a very important sense that question is meaningless until completed with some such phrase as "Is it art to you, or to me, or to that person there?" This phenomenological aspect relates, again, to the linguistic. The rule of usage as the arbiter of meaning was the fundamental insight of twentieth-century linguistic thought, the center of the work of both Ferdinand de Saussure and Ludwig Wittgenstein—the insight that there was no necessary relation between word and thing. As Saussure said, the connection between the signifier and the signified is arbitrary, governed merely by usage. In Wittgensteinian terms, to be art simply means to be called art. The question is not, "Is it art?," but, "Is it called art?" In this sense, for the figure of the goddess Kave, for example, the answer is double: no, for its makers and the people of the culture in which it was made, it is not art; and yes, for us who call it art, it is art. It is art by our redesignation of it as such; it is art in the same way that unhewn stones brought into a gallery by Robert Smithson were made art by the act of so designating them.

Finally, I think it is clear that Rubin's emphasis on the question, "Is it art?" involves a serious misreading of my article. I did not say the tribal objects were not art, but that there were several senses in which something might be called art, and that some of these clearly don't apply to the tribal objects. Neglecting the complexities of the question altogether, Rubin asks, in effect, why did McEvilley question the practice of calling these things art and nothing more, and the only answer he can imagine is this: McEvilley must think it's not good enough to be art!

He then, most regrettably, takes this drastic misreading to the limit. "Most early anthropology," says Rubin, "is shot through with such prejudices" as "the view that the Other is lazy, unintelligent, fit only for *travail de nègre* and, above all, uncultured." How easy this blatant reversal of my argument makes it to deal with me. But it gets even worse than that. "I wonder," Rubin asks gravely, "how many of his readers who saw our show and stood before the monumental Nukuoro Island carving of the goddess Kave that introduces it, share McEvilley's conviction that what they were looking at was 'not art.'" He has, in other words, simply struck up the national anthem of the kingdom of aesthetic feeling, as if I alone were saying that these objects are not noble, spiritual, and great. In fact, I am saying something quite different—that these objects fall outside the categories of our language, that this is the great freedom they offer us, and that a vast opportunity is lost when we force them into one of the categories of our known language with its familiar and limited horizon or intentionality. But note that along with me Rubin has excluded, without a glance at them or a feeling for them, the Nukuoro Islanders themselves, who, supposedly "like McEvilley," think that the Kave figure is "not art"—not because it is of insufficient formal beauty to be called art, but because, for all its magnificent formal beauty, like a mountain or an automobile it happens to be something else. Rubin thinks he is doing the Nukuoro Islanders a favor because he is saying that they are like him; but what if they don't want to be like him? He should face the facts of what the Nukuoro Islanders themselves did before that figure of Kave to which he sings the anthem of aesthetic feeling.

In terms of the affirmation or denial of the art identity of tribal works, three periods of history must be distinguished. There was the period prior to the scholarship of Franz Boas, when primitive objects were denied the status of art as if it were an honor that they did not deserve, as if they were just not good enough to be called art. Then came a second phase in which tribal objects such as those in the show were thought to be formally and intellectually "good enough" to be called art and the habit arose of so calling them. More recently the possibility has arisen of a third phase, which anthropologists are finding the way into now, when one may begin to look at the tribal objects from the point of view of their own culture and to realize that, whatever they are, they fall in between the categories on our grid. In other words, it is not the objects that are inadequate but our conceptual grasp of them. My skepticism about the act of bestowing the word art in these and certain other contexts is a phase three rather than phase one attitude. I think this is obvious to anyone who reads the article. I must not, of course, be misconstrued as meaning that there should be no museums of primitive art, or courses in primitive art, or studies of the relationships between these objects and ours, and so on. The objects in question are of such great interest that one delights in studying and regarding them, and in so doing the temptation to relate them to things that look like them from our own culture is easily submitted to. But I suggest that the phase three act must be different from the phase two act of aesthetic appreciation that we are all so good at and comfortable with. What we must learn is to see a doubleness, the two aspects at once, simultaneously feeling these objects as art, which is our way of appreciation, and maintaining a sharp and constant awareness of the fact that the people of their own culture did not so feel them. This keen awareness of cultural relativity and of the arbitrariness of one's own horizon is simply the necessary step in maturation for our culture—and a step necessary for the safety of the whole world.

Finally I must deal with the cheapest of Rubin's and Varnedoe's tactics against me, their presentation of me as an ideologue because I speak of subjects besides formal similarities. Rubin says I have transformed the event into "an act of contemporary art politics," and refers to my "art-political ways of thinking." He is practicing the familiar tactic of dismissing criticism by calling it "political"; what I performed was an act of criticism, not an act of politics. Rubin's accusations of political motivation are paralleled by Varnedoe's claim that I am a person interested in violence and the darkness of the unconscious, echoed by Rubin's repeated quotation of a phrase in which, thinking, for example, of the human sacrifices to Kave, I used the word "blood." This is really low argumentation. They have attributed to my personal tastes the qualities of primitive religious practices that I denounced them for ignoring and censoring. There is no doubt whatever that primitive religious practices were characterized by what we would call violence, and that many of the objects in the show, if they are genuine, were used in conjunction with sacrifices and ritual bloodshed. I asserted that these men, by editing out the facts, misrepresent the objects. Their replies suggest that because I would not edit out the real qualities of primitive religious rites, I must have a ghoulish attraction to blood and violence. In their view, it seems, an accurate and realistic description of primitive ritual practices would be unhealthy; a totally misleading and censored version like theirs, on the other hand, is supposedly the product of a healthier mind. This is what I meant by saying that they shouldn't have dealt with the topic at all: if they feel that the realities of the topic have to be censored out on moralizing grounds, then they manifestly are not the right people to have treated the topic in the first place. Their assumption that to face the topic squarely would somehow show bad character reveals an appalling lack of scholarly integrity. They are forgetting that scholarship (including art history) is a type of science. I felt that the context of blood was necessary to confront because *it was factually there.* Rubin's and Varnedoe's belief that Western civilization and its ethic are served by ignoring the realities of the topic shows an absolute lack of understanding of the difficult responsibility of science to face up to all the facts, not just the pleasant ones.

But these letters, of course, get even worse than that, for example the part where Rubin slops Mom, country, apple pie, and German slogans all over me. It's his grand peroration, where he goes for nothing less than a destruction of the idea of my humanity. You remember: "If the peoples of the world," he intones somberly, "are to get along with each other, they will not only have to appreciate their respective 'otherness'"—note the quotation marks: here again is something he doesn't really think exists—"they will have to recognize their common humanity." (Wow!) "Some of us," he says, "still do not think Schiller's hope that *alle Menschen werden Brüder* is tainted by co-option. By denying the manifest genius of tribal artists, McEvilley excludes whole peoples from this cultural commonality." But I have not of course for a moment denied the genius of tribal peoples; I have suggested that it might be saner and more interesting to try to appreciate their genius in as many of its own terms as we can, and that it is to an extent possible to find those terms out. So why don't we try to do it? As far as excluding people from "this cultural commonality," I seriously question whether what the peoples of the Third World need is the kind of Western-imposed "commonality" implied by a German slogan that is more about forcing people to be one's brothers than about becoming theirs. I, and I think they too, want out of that sick dream. It sounds too much like a Leni Riefenstahl film to me, all the peoples of the world trudging along together hollering out the *Ode to Joy*. That Rubin would introduce such a completely gratuitous and sophistic argumentum *ad hominem*, one so ungrounded in argumentation, is disgraceful, and a disgrace that our readers will have seen he shares with his collaborator, whose only tactics are sophistic reversals, ad hominem arguments, and empty denials. In response, for example, to my claim that his "Contemporary Explorations" section was dominated by the earth mother view of the female, he asserts that he denied that association in his essay; well, deny it he might, but the fact remains that that is what he did in the exhibition. Both men in effect say, "don't watch what I actually do, just listen to my claims about what I do."

I gave the *'Primitivism' in Twentieth Century Art* exhibition reasoned criticism, and Rubin and Varnedoe gave me back rhetorical tricks. I gave them historical and philosophical arguments and they met not one of them, not one, dear reader, because they *could* not. They are bad bears indeed, and I am going to bark them back into the forest now as I barked them out some months ago so we could look at them. I did not think they would look as bad as they do. I expected worthier adversaries.

1. See, for example, Nelson H.H. Graburn, ed., *Ethnic and Tourist Arts* (Berkeley: University of California Press, 1976.)

2. Brian Brake, James McNeish, and David Simmons, *Art of the Pacific* (New York: Harry N. Abrams,1980), p.132.

3. See, for example, B. Berlin and P. Kay, *Basic Color Terms* (Berkeley and Los Angeles: University of California Press, 1970); A. Capell, *Studies in Socio-Linguistics* (Hawthorne, N.Y.: Mouton, 1966), and R. Brown and E. Lenneberg, "A Study in Language and Cognition," in S. Saporta, ed., *Psycholinguistics* (New York: Holt, Rinehart & Winston, 1961).

REPRINTED FROM *ARTFORUM* (FEBRUARY, 1985): 42–51.

WILLIAM RUBIN:

Under normal circumstances I would not trouble *Artforum*'s readers with a continuation of the exchange between myself and Thomas McEvilley on the *'Primitivism' in Twentieth Century Art* exhibition at the Museum of Modern Art. However, there are important issues which have been obscured in this fray and these need clarifying. Thus I ask the reader to rise above the intemperate tone of McEvilley's "final word" and to—dare I say?—please bear with me.

In places, McEvilley and I argue past each other, creating differences where I hope we might in time agree. But there is no mistaking the huge gap in opinion that separates us. McEvilley's disgust with the history of Western colonialism—a history I deplore as much as he does—unfortunately leads him to the kind of indiscriminate extremism where Schiller becomes a sloganeer comparable to Hitler's pet filmmaker, and where we are asked to admire most those contemporary artists who somehow have the gift of "literally forgetting [Western civilization's] values." McEvilley is surely not alone in his anti-Western position—but he is surely right if he senses that these are not the positions of the organizers of the exhibition. It is no wonder that he finds so much to criticize in the show and, as I took the trouble to suggest at the beginning of this exchange, anyone interested in these issues can only be impressed by the sincerity and intensity of his response.

But there is obviously one tradition of Western thought that McEvilley admires—at least, so one would gather from his eagerness to cite experimental evidence and his appeal to scientific method in art history—and that is the Western practice of scholarly and scientific inquiry, which rests ultimately on the tradition of critical dialogue. I more than share McEvilley's enthusiasm for this tradition, and, as any student of my writings will know, I have in the past found such exchanges—many of them stemming from disagreements at least as great as that between McEvilley and myself—to be immensely profitable and stimulating.

I had hoped that the exchange between McEvilley and myself would continue that tradition. But in order for such exchanges to be productive it is necessary that the intellectual basis of critical discussion not be undermined. In the history of rational inquiry, it has generally been thought unproductive to attack what you take to be your opponent's motives rather than his arguments—and particularly unproductive to attribute to him sinister or conspiratorial motives. Nor does it advance the discussion to appeal to discredited or, worse, unnamed authorities. And it is fatally destructive to the nature of discourse—however much it may appeal in the heat of intellectual contest, and even on what may seem to be a minor point—to fabricate evidence rather than admit error.

Anyone who has taken the trouble to read my writings or attend my lectures will be as unable as I am to recognize McEvilley's portrait of me as a kind of high priest who insures the mysterious "canons" of what McEvilley calls "formalist Modernism" and who dwells in "the temple of formalist Modernism" on Fifty-third Street where the "cult of pure form" is unashamedly practiced according to the "dogma of universal aesthetic feeling." I suppose that I should be flattered to be mistaken for this Druid, since he is obviously quite a guy. (He will do *anything*—including mounting exhibitions that co-opt entirely unrelated art—in order to "revalidate Modernist aesthetic canons.") But then (I surmise) he has some unattractive traits, too: according to McEvilley, he is always ready to abandon a colleague when it seems convenient. Thus, McEvilley writes that Rubin "begins his reply, understandably, by distancing himself from [Kirk] Varnedoe's 'Contemporary Explorations' section of the show." My remark about not speaking for my colleague did no more, of course, than recognize that, as Varnedoe was appending his own letter, I considered him more than able to speak for himself. Lest there be any doubt whatever in McEvilley's mind, I very much like Varnedoe's selections for "Contemporary Explorations" as I did his entirely persuasive letter outlining the principles behind them. Above and beyond inevitable differences in judgment—indeed, in part because of them—Varnedoe's particular contributions to all parts of the show were critical to its success.

Alas, all those who will now haunt the galleries of the Museum hoping for a glimpse of the Dark Lord of Modernism will be sadly disappointed. My own ambitions are much more modest than those McEvilley imagines for me. In all my work I have never thought to "validate" Modernism; I am only trying to understand it. Nor can I fathom what McEvilley means when he says, citing our show of the late work of Cézanne, that Modernism is "self-validating." Is it that it doesn't have to be approved by the party or the church? Or McEvilley? And how does Cézanne's art go on "validating and invalidating other things?" What does it "invalidate?" What has been suppressed from MoMA's twentieth century collection because "invalidated" by Cézanne? And is Modernism "above the web of...cultural change" as McEvilley claims? What better example of the way it is not than primitivism itself? The very year of Cézanne's memorial exhibition, artists presumably "validated" by him, Picasso and Braque, began to study tribal art, which Cézanne would surely never have considered "valid."[1]

It is my supposed fixation with something called "pure form" (a meaningless phrase I have never used nor would think of using[2]) that, according to McEvilley, has left me entirely uninterested in the historical context of any art. I, on the other hand, would never have become an art historian were I not committed to the belief that the fullest understanding of art objects requires that we know as much as we possibly can about the cultures from which they came. It is precisely because I am concerned with historical context that I virtually omitted anthropological information from the exhibition, richly stimulating though I find it—where it could only have misled the viewer about the actual intellectual context and content of Modernist primitivism, which, after all, was the subject of our show. It is simply a fact that (with but rare exceptions, beginning only around 1930) the cultural and historical context of twentieth-century primitivism did not include anthropological information; it was totally irrelevant to the pioneer Modernists' reaction to tribal objects.

The rare instances when Modernist artists possessed some ethnological information were noted in our book. However, the problem with even these anthropological "facts" is that they usually turned out to be fictions—i.e., theories discredited by later anthropologists. Let me give a classic example. Michel Leiris was one of many ethnologists I consulted several times in preparing our show. A member of the Dakar-Djibouti mission of 1931-33, he is an expert on the collection of the Musée de l'Homme, a great writer, and was long a close friend of Picasso. He told me that, by the thirties, Picasso would certainly have heard that the big-nose Baga (Guinea) Nimba figures and masks were a sort of "goddess of fertility"—the way many collectors and dealers in African art still refer to them.[3] This merited being brought into the discussion because Picasso owned two such figures and a giant mask (which stood in the entrance of his chateau), and the big nose busts of Marie-Thérèse Walter he sculpted at that time (and her image in *Girl before a Mirror*) associate *her* with a kind of fertility goddess.

Today, however, the anthropologist Leon Siroto, a specialist in West African art, will tell you that the Baga figures have nothing demonstrable to do with a "goddess of fertility" and that, even for the mask, such an interpretation is inadequate ("fertility" is only one of its possible aspects) and misleading (because the very word "goddess" is Eurocentric and wrongly applied in the case at hand to African cult symbols). So had we presented these tribal objects from the perspective of today's anthropology we would have had to explain that on this rare occasion when a Modern artist actually knew something about "primitive context, meaning, [or] content," what he knew was essentially a fiction. I can imagine the visitors reeling out of the galleries after attempting to digest such dual-track information. That the operative fictions of Modernist primitivism were in fact Eurocentric, was, of course, something we had accepted, indeed, insisted upon from the start. The whole history of Modernist primitivism, at least until very recently, took place within the context of Eurocentric assumptions, and it cannot be recounted or understood outside those terms—certainly not within the ex post facto framework of today's advanced anthropology.

Similar strictures apply to the problem of providing dates for tribal works. Our omission of individual dates for the tribal objects, which we had described as mostly from the later nineteenth and early twentieth centuries, was seen by McEvilley as "another hidden tactic for avoiding the confrontation with the actual uses of these objects in their tribal settings"—as if the latter ethnological concerns were relevant, or had ever been our purpose. Moreover, not a single tribal object in our show can be dated "precisely," and precious few can even be dated approximately. Where tribal objects are given dates by scholars, such dates are almost always of the exceedingly elastic order of those attributed to a handful of objects in the Menil family collection catalogue (where many of the African objects are totally undated and only six of the forty-four Oceanic objects are given even approximate dates). As in this catalogue, the most focused dates scholars normally proffer for these objects are of the order of "nineteenth century," "nineteenth-twentieth centuries," and "twentieth century." As "twentieth century" could apply equally to objects made yesterday and those that predate the Modernists discovery of tribal art, it is obvious that this or other vague dates are useless for the study of primitivism. Far more important—indeed, crucial—for the study of primitivism was the question of the dates at which objects could have been seen in the West, a subject to which we devoted an immense and unprecedented scholarly effort. (McEvilley's claim that in "anthropological museums...at least approximate dates are usually given for the works" is simply untrue. In the African section of the Musée de l'Homme in Paris—as I took the trouble to reconfirm on a recent visit—not one of the labels for any of the hundreds of objects contains even an approximate date. The same thing is true for the tribal objects in the African and Oceanic galleries of the American Museum of Natural History, among other ethnological museums.)

Of course, in the largest sense, there *are* "anthropological" issues at stake throughout the show, in that it deals with human artifacts and was always intended to raise larger questions about the nature of human creativity. Here there is room for rich and profitable debate between McEvilley and myself, as there is, indeed, room for such debate between art historians and anthropologists, as well as, of course, among anthropologists themselves. (It was precisely in order to welcome and further such debate that we invited a group of distinguished anthropologists and historians of primitive art to join us in a day of intellectual exchange about the exhibition, in early November.) It is, of course, a basic assumption of the exhibition that when we talk about the tribal objects as art or sculpture we are saying something perfectly sensible and meaningful. McEvilley refuses to accept this position, and embraces instead a radical form of cultural relativism. In support of this position, he dogmatically cites various kinds of evidence from art history, anthropology, and anthropological linguistics.

Now, I do not pretend to be anything of an expert on either anthropological or linguistic issues. Nor do I imagine that such immensely rich and complicated issues can be sorted out in this kind of exchange (though I would think it not impossible that some real progress might still be made). I can only envy McEvilley's authority in art history, anthropology, linguistics, phenomenology, and literary theory, and sympathize with his need to mock the comedic ignorance of those less accomplished than he. Alas, as but a poor art historian, I can only hope that after a professional lifetime in this field I know something about it, at least. And yet when I come to consider McEvilley's art-historical citations, I am often really startled. For example, in order to cut through a supposed "myth of the continuity of Western art history" (another sacred dogma of mine which somehow I had previously been unaware I held), McEvilley asks us to consider that "the charioteer of Delphi, ca. 470 B.C., for example, was seen totally [sic] differently in classical Greece from the way we see him now. He was not alone in that noble, self-sufficient serenity of transcendental angelic whiteness that we see." Perhaps I should take it less amiss to find my own ideas being transformed beyond recognition by McEvilley, when I discover that he can also somehow transform this familiar monument of introductory art history from a bronze into a marble.

I am afraid that almost all of McEvilley's art-historical assertions come from the same quarry as the marble charioteer. I had pointed out that the Egyptians produced art, although they had no word for it. McEvilley counters this by saying that "what we regard as Egyptian artworks the Egyptians themselves understood as functional objects within the very practical activity of funerary magic...virtually every object in the great Egyptian Museum at Cairo was made to be buried underground and hidden from human eyes and human knowledge forever...the reasons why their [painting, sculpture and decorated objects] were so gorgeously designed and crafted, then, remains a mystery...." Only to McEvilley. McEvilley seems to be crossing his fingers and hoping that none of his readers has been to the Egyptian Museum, where, contrary to his assertion, there are a great many objects not intended "to be buried underground."[4] Some of the objects in royal tombs were, in fact, the very ones previously used in palaces. Moreover, anyone who visits Karnak or a variety of other sites can still see a great deal of Egyptian painting and sculpture that was intended to be seen in the light of day. Indeed, the tomb paintings, sculptures, and objects were not (as Leo Steinberg said to me of this passage in McEvilley's reply) put underground to be hidden from human eyes forever. "They were designed," he observed, "to be enjoyed, both functionally and aesthetically by human eyes in an assured afterlife precisely forever. McEvilley is simply projecting his own skepticism about the afterlife upon the ancient Egyptians." Or—may I add?—"appropriating their intentionality into his."

In defense of his astonishing concept of "communal inventiveness" as a description of the process of change in tribal art, McEvilley cites "the American automobile industry, where stylistic change arises through a communal development...or, again, the design changes of utilitarian objects like household goods and cigarette lighters...." Yet, as any beginning student in the history of industrial design knows, the development of design objects—including automobiles and cigarette lighters—has been very much the consequence of individual inspirations by gifted designers. At the same time, all Western art might be considered "communal" insofar as its development depends on the sharing of ideas within artists' communities.

McEvilley's record in art-historical citation, therefore, makes me a little uneasy about the unassailable truth of the anthropological and linguistic evidence he calls on so confidently. And, indeed, a little digging in the library suggests that these assertions are not, shall we say, unproblematic. In his attempt to demonstrate that objects in the show were used for human sacrifice and ritual bloodshed, McEvilley claims to quote a secondary text on the Nukuoro Island Kave figure to the effect that "she was a goddess to whom human sacrifices were offered." In fact, the authors had said only that she is "reputed to have had human sacrifices offered to her."[5] Going back to the primary scholarly source on the Kave,[6] we discover that this story of human sacrifice derives entirely from nineteenth-century travelers' tales, a genre known for its Grand Guignol exaggerations. As Susan Vogel, director of The Center for African Art, New

York, observes, "hardly any of the African objects in the show ever had blood on them, and, in those few exceptions, it was always chicken blood, not human blood."[7] McEvilley tries to qualify his statement by saying that the objects in the show "were used in conjunction with" sacrifices, but this is equally true of classical Greek art, which also functioned "in conjunction with sacrifices and ritual bloodshed" as when animals were sacrificed on the altar-derived triple steps of the Parthenon. This is not to suggest, of course, that Greek and African rites were the same; but it does demonstrate that McEvilley's attempt to show that tribal objects cannot be considered "art" in the Western sense because they were sometimes used in conjunction with sacrificial activities is simply unfounded.

Then we come to McEvilley's claim that the "point of cultural relativism" can be upheld by the work of the linguists Edward Sapir and Benjamin Lee Whorf, whose theories of linguistic relativism have "been experimentally confirmed in a number of ways," I was puzzled to read that this was so, since the thesis, as I understood it—that people don't have something if they don't have a word for it—seemed to be falsified many times in my own modest experience as a multilingual. The French, for instance, have no word for design (in recent years they have taken to using the English word, pronounced in the English manner)—and yet who would claim that there was no design in France? I have since been pleased to learn that my own commonsense argument was in fact a key point in a famous debunking article about the Whorfian hypothesis by the eminent linguist Joshua Fishman.[8] (That is, Fishman pointed out that the claim that we have to have a single word for a thing in order to have the concept is absurd; some languages may need many words to make the same point that in others can be made with one, but that does not mean that the language determines the conceptual structures.) Moreover, McEvilley's assertion that the tribal peoples "lacked...even circumlocutions that could express what we mean by art" is simply false. The Africans can and do use numerous "circumlocutions," for they possess many words—such as "balance," "evenness," "to make beautiful"—that they use to describe the character of their art, and there is a notable literature on this subject.[9]

On the whole question of whether or not primitive objects can be called art, the simplest position seems to be this: no culture's art is similar to another's in every sense; all art is something Other. But since it is made by human beings its Otherness is a matter of degree. If we are to call an object art, it must involve some aesthetic ordering of its materials to nonpractical, expressive purposes—whatever magic or religious ends it may also have. This either is the case with tribal sculpture or it is not; and if it is—as seems to me painfully obvious[10]—then it is perfectly appropriate to call it art, though we may choose to call it many other things as well.

We now come to the question of the truth of McEvilley's claims about various other exhibitions that were supposed to have made ours old hat. I have very little appetite for this debate, since such questions of priority normally hold no interest for me at all.[11] But McEvilley insisted, and presumably continues to insist, that our show was mounted not for its stated purpose but rather in order to "revalidate classical

Modernist aesthetics." This theory, in turn, rested syllogistically on a set of "facts" purportedly proving that our exhibition was "not new" and that, therefore, it must have some other, secret agenda. The necessity of contesting McEvilley's "facts," therefore, lay less in their intrinsic importance than in their role in his reasoning—though it is worth getting the record straight in any event.

Rather than concede mistakes in the face of my critique, McEvilley returned with "proofs" designed to show the errors were mine. ("If we pause and count up the inaccuracies they have found, we see that Rubin has found none....") The slippery nature of his reply, however, has shifted the issue to the more significant and telling area of scholarly honesty. Take the question of the content of the Beaubourg vitrines. "Rubin," he writes,

> denies that any of the objects in the Beaubourg vitrines had ever been owned by Braque or Picasso. In fact, at the writing of my article one of the authorities on this subject had ventured the opposite opinion, yet finally it seems this point must remain moot, in the light of the fact, acknowledged by Rubin, that no exact listing of the objects has been found. Still, the fact that some of the objects there belonged to early Modernist artists is acknowledged by all.

For a man who accuses me of "the fallacy called the Appeal to Authority" because I cite Picasso on Picasso's own views about primitive objects, the reference to an unnamed "authority" in the above passage is extraordinary. I wonder if this "authority" is not an invention of McEvilley for, so far as I know, I am alone in having made a study of Picasso's and Braque's tribal objects and their various locations. Let McEvilley refute me by naming his "authority" and describing the bona fides that entitle him or her to an opinion on this specialized subject.[12] More importantly, however, there is nothing at all "moot" about this question. There cannot have been any of Braque's or Picasso's tribal sculptures in the Beaubourg vitrines since there are none in the collection of the Musée de l'Homme, which provided Beaubourg with the objects. Thus the issue of a supposedly lost "listing" is irrelevant. Nor did I ever "acknowledge," as McEvilley claims, that no such list had been found. I never mentioned any list. Moreover, I always assumed that the Musée de l'Homme had such a list; they do, and I now have a copy of it.[13] Finally, "the fact that some of the objects [in the Beaubourg vitrines] belonged to early Modernist artists" is not "acknowledged by all" as McEvilley claims. It was not "acknowledged" by me, nor has it been, so far as I know, by anyone except McEvilley. And with good reason, for none of the objects lent by the Musée de l'Homme ever belonged to a Modern artist.[14]

Now let us turn to the Menil family show, where McEvilley attempts to prove he is right about its role as a precedent for our exhibition by pointing to

> a plain statement in the catalogue by Walter Hopps, curator of the exhibition, discussing the mixing of primitive and Modern objects, in which [Hopps] notes, *"Ainsi, dans la section des surréalistes, on trouve, à côté de leurs oeuvres, des objets leur ayant appartenus"*

(thus, in the section on the Surrealists, beside their own works one finds objects that belonged to them). These include, for example, Eskimo masks, of which *"plusieurs furent acquises...par des surréalistes français établis à New York"* (several were bought...by French Surrealists living in New York). [Ellipses McEvilley's.]

All of this would seem pretty convincing...unless you had seen the Menil show (which McEvilley, to judge from what he says, evidently did not), or unless you had at hand the catalogue, *La rîme et la raison,* from which McEvilley has misappropriated his "facts." In the latter case you would see that Hopps' sentence about "objects that belonged to (the Surrealists)," though slightly ambiguous because poorly translated, is not located, as McEvilley claims, in a discussion about the "mixing of primitive and Modern objects." And if you had seen the show, you would have known that the "objects" to which Hopps was, in fact, referring were not tribal sculptures at all but bibelots, exotica, and memorabilia; the few tribal sculptures in those areas were not from artists' collections, nor did Walter Hopps ever say they were.[15] But that's not all. The last part of McEvilley's paragraph cites Eskimo masks in the Menil show as examples of tribal objects supposedly owned by Surrealists, an assertion elaborated with a quotation seemingly continued from Hopps' text. But this passage ("several were bought...") is by another author, occurs 339 pages later in the Menil catalogue, and does not refer to the Eskimo masks in the show.[16] Is this the scholarship that "is a type of science"?

1. Cézanne was so deeply attached to the tradition of Renaissance and post-Renaissance painting, with its emphasis on visual perception and on sculptural plasticity, that he derisively dismissed Gauguin's mature style as "Chinese painting." One can hardly imagine his having accepted the far more conceptual and ideographic stylizations of tribal art.

2. I have of course, used the term "pure painting," but only and always as a translation of French terms, as in *Dada and Surrealist Art* (New York: Harry N. Abrams, 1968), p. 15: "...Its less absolutist explorations led indeed to a revival of poetic 'painting' (*peinture-poésie* as opposed to *peinture-peinture,* or 'pure painting': as it is spoken of in the modern French tradition)," and p. 150: "...thus the collective appellation *peinture-poésie,* or poetic painting, as opposed to *peinture-pure,* or *peinture-peinture* (by which advanced abstraction was sometimes known in France)."

3. This is not meant to imply that Leiris himself subscribes to such a description, only that he said it was common coin in the thirties among amateurs of what was then universally called *art nègre,* and that Picasso would have heard of it.

4. Remembering a good deal of large sculpture from my visit to that museum, I checked with the Egyptologists at the Metropolitan Museum of Art who suggested that something less than one-fourth of what is visible of this immense and as yet not fully catalogued collection would be material not taken from tombs. Thus tomb material could hardly be said to comprise "virtually every object" there.

5. Brian Brake (photographs), James McNeish (conversations), and David Simmons (commentary) *Art of the Pacific* (New York: Harry N. Abrams, 1980). See Simmons note for catalogue no.78.

6. Janet Davidson, "A Wooden Image from Nukuoro in the Auckland Museum," *Journal of the Polynesian Society* (March, 1966). There we discover that the suggestion of human sacrifice was hearsay reported by traders, among them the donor Mr. Cousens, whose statement was published in an Auckland newspaper in 1878. The newspaper says that it "cannot say" if the statement was "well founded," and it observes; "It (the sculpture) is very rude but it is for this reason a proof of the barbarous and primitive worship in the islands" (Cf. also note 7).

7. As the making of sculptures was, for the African artist, a primarily religious function, he often—as Vogel notes—sacrificed a chicken before beginning a piece.

In Africa, human sacrifice, except in the kingdom of Dahomey and Benin, was always very rare, reserved for major ritual occasions. "Human sacrifice is a difficult subject on which to find unbiased information," writes Vogel. "Early visitors to Africa—missionaries or representatives of the colonial powers—had every reason to make their constituents in Europe believe that the Africans whom they encountered were benighted savages, badly in need of conversion or policing. They tended to exaggerate the prevalence of human sacrifice." ["Rapacious Birds and Severed Heads: Early Nigerian Bronze Rings," Art Institute of Chicago Centennial Lectures, *Museum Studies X* [1983] pp. 330–57).

8. Joshua Fishman, "A Systematization of the Whorfian Hypothesis," *Behavioral Science,* vol. 5, (1960-61): 323; cf. also Elizabeth Rosche, "Linguistic Relativity," in Alben Silverstein ed., *Human Communication: Theoretical Explorations* (New York: Halsted Press, 1974).

9. As, for example, Robert Farris Thompson, "Yoruba Artist Criticism," *The Traditional Arts in African Societies,* ed. Warren L. d'Azevedo (Bloomington: Indiana University Press, 1973) and Susan M. Vogel, "Baule and Yoruba Art Criticism: A Comparison," *The Visual Arts: Plastic and Graphic,* ed. Justine M. Cordwell (Hawthorne, NY: Mouton Pubs., 1979).

10. How else explain—among other stylistic variations—the obvious changes within established types made by single sculptors, such as the innovations of the Buli Master or the Master of Ogol? Such differences alter the aesthetic expressiveness of the objects but cannot be explained by practical cult necessities; nor do they reflect any change in iconography.

11. MoMA had never claimed that *'Primitivism'* was the first show anywhere in which tribal objects from artists' collections had been juxtaposed with their work, only that it was the first to deal with the subject in depth and "in the light of informed art history." A small exhibition had taken place in Berlin many years ago, in which some objects belonging to German Expressionist artists were shown with their work. Our show was the first to do this with tribal art belonging to all major European and American primitivists.

12. McEvilley cites two curators, Jean-Yves Mock and Jean-Hubert Martin, on other aspects of the Beaubourg vitrines. Neither, I am certain, would claim the slightest expertise on the subject of tribal art in general, nor the tribal art collections of Modern artists in particular.

13. This list and the accompanying information for both of which I am indebted to Francine Ndiaye, confirms my statement that a number of the tribal objects at Beaubourg were from regions and were of types—as well as accessioned at dates—that would have made it impossible for them to be seen by Paris Modernists. The list shows both McEvilley and me to have been in error about the number of objects involved. Beaubourg received sixty-five not one-hundred objects, of which thirteen were returned almost immediately. There is no record of how many of the remaining fifty-two objects were shown at any one time, although it is clearly more than I had remembered.

14. The only possible exception to what I have been saying about the Beaubourg vitrines, and a very unlikely one, concerns a Fang mask bequeathed to the Centre Pompidou by the widow of André Derain, which may have been shown for a short time after its arrival at Beaubourg in the African vitrine. Jean-Hubert Martin thinks this is possible, but is not sure. The *fiche* for the object indicates that it was not shown at all, and was an object we searched for during a period of years, never coming upon it at Beaubourg. Through an agent for the late Mme. Derain's estate, we finally discovered that it had been given to Beaubourg. Even in the unlikely event that this Derain-owned object were to have been shown for a short time it would fall far short of confirming that some of the objects there belonged to early Modern artists.

15. See *La rîme et la raison,* (Paris: Editions de la Réunion des Musées Nationaux, 1984), p. 16 and *passim.*

16. The quotation in the second part of McEvilley's paragraph is from the catalogue notes on the Kuskokwim masks of the nineteenth century. None of the catalogue notes is individually signed, but all were by the experts who wrote the introductory texts on the geographical area involved, as McEvilley should well have been aware. On page 355, Edmund Carpenter, writing of the Menil family Eskimo masks says that they come from a group of thirty-two pieces purchased at the beginning of the century by George Heye. *Of this group,* he notes, many were later acquired by French Surrealists established in New York. He does not refer in the quoted phrase to the Menil masks, which—as he has reconfirmed to me—never belonged to Surrealist artists.

Boy, is the big bear mad at me. Swatting at facts that pester him like bee stings, once again William Rubin has dropped the honey into the department of fact-checking to make a really exciting afternoon of it. Once again his charges of factual inaccuracy are empty. It's all strangely familiar.

Eighteen years ago in the pages of *Artforum* Rubin published a series of articles on Jackson Pollock. In April, 1967, after the second piece came out, Harold Rosenberg wrote to the editors objecting to what he felt was Rubin's misrepresentation of his famous article on Action Painting. Rubin, of course, responded to Rosenberg—the correspondence ran two rounds—and began his answer with the phrase, "Looking beyond the disputatious tone of Mr. Rosenberg's letter...." Now he begins by asking the reader "to rise above the intemperate tone of McEvilley's 'final word.'" (I don't believe in the concept of a "final word," by the way.) In the second round of the exchange Rosenberg noted that Rubin "dislikes myth but doesn't mind basing his argument on gossip." To this day Rubin relies on private conversations more than on published authority. "Every paragraph in his reply," wrote Rosenberg then, "...contains misstatements of fact. I haven't the patience (nor will the reader) to deal with more than a few examples." There is a certain graciousness in Rosenberg's refusal to tax the readers' patience by slogging through the mud of Rubin's factual claims. I am going to make the other choice, however, and walk with the reader into the woods of those claims in order to show their emptiness. (Anyway, I am developing patience at bear-hunting.)

Back then, interestingly, Rosenberg noted, before dealing with "something nasty" from Rubin, that he was not going to go into Rubin's "weird manners." This question of "weird manners" is important in the present case because a certain type of so-called gentlemanly manners is in fact nothing but a sanctimonious method for dismissing anyone or anything (such as primitive objects, or me, or any other conscientious objector) that has not been tamed and sterilized to the point of displaying similar weird manners. In the introduction to his current reply to me Rubin calls my tone toward him and the little bear "intemperate." Yet the reader of our first exchange of letters has seen that Kirk Varnedoe, Rubin's colleague and apparently also one of these old-school gentlemen, indulging his respect for "manners" and rhetorical twists, labeled me a "racist" for not liking his and Rubin's treatment of primitive objects. And the other gentleman, Rubin, described me in terms that amount to calling me an enemy of mankind. This it was that elicited my "intemperate" response.

In the present letter Rubin berates me for "the kind of indiscriminate extremism where Schiller becomes a sloganeer comparable to Hitler's pet filmmaker...." But I didn't say that Schiller was like Leni Riefenstahl—I said that Rubin's application of Schiller's words to a discussion of the Third World sounded too much like a Riefenstahl film. Schiller was a fundamental part of German high school education in the nineteenth and early twentieth centuries—the educational system that so prominently produced genocide. (Riefenstahl's progression from celebrating Hitlerism in *Triumph of the Will* to photographing tribal Africans as decorative objects out of their social and cultural context is not uninteresting in this regard.) For this reason I regarded it as insensitive to look to Schiller for a model and a motto on how to relate to the Third World. Rubin calls my raw nerve on this subject "indiscriminate extremism." "McEvilley is surely not alone," he says, "in his anti-Western position—but he is surely right if he senses that these are not the positions of the organizers of the exhibition. It is no wonder he finds so much to criticize...." To dislike his show is anti-Western: what nonsense. We've heard that tone before. Rubin thinks that to oppose his will is to oppose Western civilization.

In fact, my whole point is to oppose the ossification and sterilization of Western civilization. This debate is about art. Objects are powerful transitional devices within and between cultures. The way one culture's objects are treated in the context of another culture is a kind of conduct of foreign affairs. Rubin treated the primitive objects as if they had nothing to do with any living societies except ours, as if they were pretty objects and no more, there for us to do with as we like. It's time to go beyond. Art has; why haven't the curators of this show?

"It is precisely *because* I am concerned with historical context," Rubin writes to me, "that I virtually omitted anthropological information from the exhibition—richly stimulating though I find it—where it could only have misled the viewer about the actual intellectual context and content of Modernist primitivism, which, after all, was the subject of our show. It is simply a fact that (with but rare exceptions, beginning only around 1930) the cultural and historical context of twentieth-century primitivism did not include anthropological information; it was totally irrelevant to the pioneer Modernists' reaction to tribal objects." Rubin in essence insists that Modernist primitivism is something that applies only to the "pioneer Modernists"; in other words, that the subject of the show was limited to pioneer Modernist primitivism. On purely scholarly grounds the show would have been more coherent if he had in fact limited it to pioneer Modernism; or, rather, to pioneer Modernist primitivism. His argument for the irrelevance of ethnology would then be more defensible, though it would still raise unpleasant questions. But really the exhibition went far beyond this, as his appetite for a blockbuster show engorged more and more of the art of our century into its vitrines. Without even counting Varnedoe's "Contemporary Explorations" section, about a third of the Modern works in the show were made after 1930, the date at which Rubin says conceptual awareness of ethnology began among Western artists. If Varnedoe's section is included the figure rises to about forty percent. Many of the important works in Rubin's section of the show are from the period between 1940 and 1979, a time in which we learned an increasing amount about primitive culture. Lucas Samaras is represented with a work from 1962, Arman with a work from 1973, Italo Scanga with a work from 1979. Rubin's argument for the irrelevance of anthropological information is directly contradicted by the way he went beyond the stated premise of his show—perhaps dimly sensing the hidden countermessage that underlay it, which is that this exhibition is not about 1906 but about an attitude in 1984, the moment in which it opened. If he'd given these more contemporary works the same loving attention he gave to the pioneer Modernists, Rubin would have had to realize how relevant anthropological information is to the question of influence and affinity in the more recent works. But the truth of the matter is that these contemporary artists are subsumed as appendages to the pioneer Modernists, much as the primitive works are subsumed as their footnotes. This does not speak optimistically for the life of contemporary painting and sculpture in the Museum of Modern Art.

When Rubin and I began corresponding he asked me to realize that the show was "not about 'the Other,' but about ourselves." He meant, I suppose, that it was about Picasso, André Derain, and others, who are, if not us, in our past. To really be about us, the show would have to be about the evolution in our relationship to the Other. And it is, but only in a negative way. A century or so ago Western societies generally regarded people of primitive societies as less than human. In cultural terms this meant anyone outside the Greco-Roman diffusion stream; we could not recognize as civilization, or in fact as culture, anything that lacked that imprint. Then, early in this century, we entered a phase in which instead of dreading the non-Greco-Roman as absolutely Other we tamed it by assimilating such parts of it as we could believe to be really like ourselves in deep, underlying ways more fundamental than the Greco-Roman imprint. The easiest assimilation, since it was based on immediately perceivable similarities in design, was to move objects from ethnological to art museums. This was a great and necessary step: from regarding the Other as having no self, we came to regard it as having a relationship to our most advanced creative selves. But at this point the projections—cognitive, interpretive, evaluative—still seemed to go exclusively from us to them.

Unfortunately this is where Rubin's show stops—yet his exhibition encompasses the twentieth century up until the seventies. And although the Museum has stood still on this question, the world around it has changed. Intellectual investigation has entered a third phase in which it has become increasingly clear that the distinction between learning about oneself and learning about the Other is false: the self cannot be known without reference to an Other, and vice versa. This project of civilization could have unfolded in *'Primitivism' in Twentieth Century Art* in many ways. Robert Farris Thompson, for example, in research recently begun, has taken Picasso and Amedeo Modigliani reproductions to Africa and recorded the impressions of them given by priests and priestesses of traditional religions of Africa. This may be one way to learn what kinds of "affinities," in a deeper sense, exist between our art and theirs; this may be one way we can extend the project beyond the limits of design similarities; this may be one way we can even begin—dare I say it—to think about influence in reverse. The great thing to realize, the great necessity, is that we are at a moment when distinctions between "us" and "them" are rapidly wasting away. There are no untouched tribal cultures anymore, even ours—or perhaps this show indicated that we are the most untouched of all.

Isn't it time to remind ourselves that more is at issue here than passageways detouring off passageways and seeming always to be avoiding something? At the beginning of this debate I raised certain questions about the primitive objects included in the show. I asked, were they intended as art by their makers? Were they called art? Were they treated as art by the people for whom they were made? What was it about them that made our early Modernist artists go for them in such a big way? And why did other early Modernists, like Duchamp, receive an opposite message from them? When I asked such questions the bears replied that I was denying to these works and to their makers a status that they were supposedly seeking. This was indeed the point: I suggested they were seeking something quite different, which might also be what people like Picasso were seeking in them. As I contemplated the way they had been ripped from their meanings and hung in mix 'n match on our walls in New York, resonances came up of an ancient violence far worse than the ritual violence in the history of the objects themselves. Pliny the Younger tells of Carthaginian sailors who entered sub-Saharan Africa by way of a river which after a while went by an island. On the island they saw dark hairy things which moved like people. Going ashore they chased them and captured three wild women. But the women were untamable so they killed them, skinned them, and took the skins back to Carthage, where they were exhibited in the temple, hanging on the wall—like the objects in the show under discussion.

But as lifeless and helpless as these objects lay upon the Modern's walls, still they mutely questioned all who saw them about what they were doing there and how they fit into our designs, and, in a really quiet way, how we fit into theirs. They were, you might say, early ambassadors from the Third World. They held us in a mutual gaze in their questioning. Why, they asked, did we think we knew them? What was it about ourselves that made us want them? They asked us to think again about all these things.

In terms of the twentieth-century discourse on art, the question whether or not a thing is art can appear in several different forms. (1) There is the formalist mode: does it look like the things that we are used to calling art? This mode emphasizes the element of design above all others. One problem with this form of the question is that it can lead only to the identification of more of the same. (2) Then there is the linguistic mode of the question, most prominently in a Wittgensteinian form: is it called art? This form relates to the practical matter of what you would do to find out what art was if you didn't already think you knew—that is, ask someone whom you thought likely to know to show you or tell you which things are called art. You would find that there was no common "look" to the range of things so called, which means that this mode and the first are already in conflict. (3) The linguistic form of the question verges into an intentional form: is it intended as art; that is, is it regarded as art by its maker and by the people he or she made it for? Minimalism made this mode very common: on entering a gallery one might find an ambiguity about which objects in the room were artworks and which were construction materials. In usage this mode is probably as common as the looks-like-it mode, though they also are in conflict; that is, they designate sets which may overlap but are different. (4) Closely related to this is a functionalist mode: is it contextualized as art, that is, treated like art in the context of its society? For example, is it exhibited, is it overtly appreciated for formal values, and so on? (5) A social-functionalist mode—was it made by an artist—is also common in the discourse of the last generation or so: Andy Warhol and others answered the question, why is it art, by saying, well, it was made by an artist, and that would make it art. Since the conventions of usage are arbitrary, we can agree among ourselves to call things art on the basis of any one or more of these criteria. But we should be careful always to know on just what basis we are using the word, and also to know how many of the modes of definition do and do not apply in a certain case.

In his current letter Rubin offers the following definition of art: "if we are to call an object art, it must involve some aesthetic ordering of its materials to nonpractical, expressive purposes...." In this definition the first mode, design similarity, which appears as "aesthetic ordering," is combined with the third mode, artistic intention, which appears as "nonpractical expressive purposes." Yet primitive objects qualify as "art" only on the first of the five points, similarity of design. This elementary clumsiness about the most basic of art questions is the source of the problems in Rubin's show. For the primitive objects might look like art, but were not intended as art. Having made his decision, Rubin was forced either to abandon expressive intent as a necessary part of his definition or to falsely insist that primitive art arises from intentions that we would recognize as "nonpractical expressive purposes." Hence the necessity for the "affinities" category, and the rejection of "communal inventiveness."

He has been so easily led into this problem by his primary emphasis on design similarity as the criterion of art. Yet in terms of twentieth-century art history this is the least useful of all the modes of definition. Duchamp's Ready-mades would not qualify. Nor would a conceptual art piece employing only language, which clearly does not look like art; yet it is called art, it was intended as art, it is treated as art, and it was made by an artist. Quotational art is a direct mockery of the looks-like-it formula. Furthermore, the criterion of "look" does not allow for innovation. If that criterion had retained its hold on the late nineteenth-century mind as firmly as it has on Rubin's and Varnedoe's, Modern art would never have happened. Modern art arose primarily out of the other four modes of the question.

Roy Sieber, writing on "The Aesthetics of Traditional African Art," describes what I think happened in the MoMA primitivism show. "Admiration in isolation," he wrote,

> easily leads to misunderstanding, and African art, its functions only vaguely apprehended, has fallen prey to the taste of the twentieth century. While noting the vitality and strength of purpose that pervade it, its admirers misread conservatism for spontaneity and commitment to style for freedom.... Such adulation springs from a Western aesthetic rooted in a romantic love for exotic precocity, and, perhaps inevitably, has developed into fashionable cliché taste.

Sieber describes the function of object and image-making in African societies as "intensely practical," having to do with the magical obtaining of "wealth, prestige, health, children, wives," and so on.

In my last letter I suggested that it was relevant in terms of the intentionality of the "primitive" works that the languages of their makers lacked a word for "art." I cited the idea advocated by Benjamin Lee Whorf that the semantic structure of a language, that is, the system of concepts enunciated in its dictionary, is partly formative of cognitive and behavioral patterns. In reply Rubin says he is "pleased to learn that my own common-sense argument was in fact a key point in a famous debunking article about the Whorfian hypothesis by the eminent linguist Joshua Fishman." Well, I know the article and I have an incredible report for the reader. Fishman is not, in the first place, "debunking" the Whorfian hypothesis; he conceives himself to be among the many people constructively working on it. Secondly, he affirms that the presence or absence of a word in a language's lexicon is cognitively significant, and thirdly, he cites some of the same research on color perception I cited.

I had gone so far as to say that the languages of Africa and Oceania even lacked circumlocutions which could express what we mean by the word "art." What I meant essentially was that these cultures—by definition—are those that have not been swept up in the diffusion stream of Greco-Roman culture and hence do not have the specialized concepts peculiar to that stream. Rubin replies that African tribal peoples do have terms to discuss art. But in fact, as the anthropologist Daniel J. Crowley remarks in the essay "An African Aesthetic," these terms discuss only craftsmanship. As others have pointed out, for example, terms meaning "smoothing of the surface" are very prominent in African tribal object discourse, but there are none for compositional factors, or for such Western aesthetic concepts as disinterested contemplation or functionlessness. "New masks were preferred to old because they have the stronger power that comes with youth," Crowley says. What's at issue in such decision-making is magical power, not aesthetic power.

"Each artist," Crowley goes on, "considers (or says he considers) his own work superior to all others except that of his own teacher." This is the custom of the magician, or shaman, whose own magic must be claimed the best, except that it depends on his or her master's magic, which therefore must be even better. Finally, Crowley remarks that in African attitudes toward art, "the stress on technical skill rather than on personal expression parallels the value systems of Western craftsmen such as carpenters and joiners." One anthropologist seeking to find the names of makers of masks found it very difficult even when the maker was local, because no one ever thought of who made them, just of who owned them. This is the way we relate to goods like automobiles or hand-knit sweaters. It is of course true that there is a degree of personal variation in African sculpture and that investigators like William Fagg and Robert Farris Thompson have managed to distinguish works of individual artists. "But the marks of identity," as Edmund Carpenter writes, "turn out to be details of craftsmanship or minor stylistic innovations. This is not self-expression. Carvers merely interpret traditional designs the way actors interpret parts." "Questions of 'creativity' and 'self-expression,'" Carpenter notes, "...belong to literate traditions. The labels just do not apply to preliteracy." The point that Rubin finds difficult to confront, but which we must, is that although purely in the design sense primitive objects are obviously like our Modern art, still they were not made in anything like the mind-set that we call self-expression. The point is that the production of beautiful objects can be carried out without any of the high-art feelings that we associate with it. This should hint to us vastly different available understandings of our own activity.

My purpose is not, of course, to deprecate the non-Western works—it could only seem that way to one who took our values as absolute—but to reassert their selfhood, and let them be themselves. Our cultural mindset associates art so strongly with concepts like self-expression that it is difficult for us to confront cultural objects that conform to our sense of beauty but do not arise from anything like our mood of self-expression. What Rubin did was work the material as he would, which, as it turned out, was in his own likeness. What he and countless others have found in the primitive objects is the type of aesthetic decisions they are familiar with; they find an account of the type they would give—because of course they are giving it. They find themselves. The question that we must face is whether our so-called etic, international, quasi-objective, scientific point of view is not just another emic or tribal point of view—just our own tribal attitudes and values inflatedly projected into an absolute (an etic norm), much as any tribal member does with the myth of his or her tribe. What awaits us if we take this step may be an experience of ourselves so far gone in mystery as to be unimaginable now.

In an interview in *The New York Times* of February 20, ostensibly about a new position at the Museum for a contemporary curator, Rubin discussed the criticism *'Primitivism' in Twentieth Century Art* has received. "A lot of people are grinding their own political axes," he said, "and while I'm not blaming them for that—gung ho, let them do it!—I ask only that they get their facts straight." I think most of us did. Significant critiques were offered by a number of critics, among them Arthur Danto, who focused on the show's philosophical presuppositions, *The Nation*, and Cynthia Nadelman, who dismantled some of its art-historical connections for *Artnews*. Both these authors regarded substantial numbers of Rubin's juxtapositions of Modern and primitive works as "meaningless." Michael Peppiatt attacked several of Rubin's assertions of influence. According to a story in the January 1985 *Art & Auction*, *Connaissance des Arts*, the magazine Peppiatt wrote for, refused to publish Rubin's and Varnedoe's replies on various grounds, including content, length, and the inclusion of color photographs. The situation, judging from the *Art & Auction* story, became deeply embroiled, with strong feelings on both sides. "Here I spent five years on the exhibition," Rubin is quoted as saying, "I broke my back to make observations in scholarly ways, and some fellow used the show as an excuse to say we presented suppositions as facts." Rubin, according to *Art & Auction*, threatened a lawsuit against *Connaissance* and the president of the company that publishes the French magazine, Dimitry Jodidio, complained that "...Rubin has commanded his side to sue, if required.... We can't work with Rubin now—a pity." In the end, no lawsuit was brought, and the main points of Rubin's and Varnedoe's letters were published by another French magazine, *Art Press*, in December. Later *Connaissance des Arts* agreed to publish another letter by Rubin, with no illustrations, in their March issue. There's a lot riding on this, you see. In the *New York Times* interview Rubin said that Hilton Kramer and I were "firing at each other, through the medium of the exhibition. My attitude about it is, a pox on both your houses." In fact neither Kramer nor I mentioned each other. Rubin seems to feel that he is invisible in the center.

Rubin refers to the "success" of the exhibition that Danto called "stupendously misconceived." One is forced to wonder what success means to him. Is it the turnstile? The blockbuster? The approval of a nonspecialized press? The problem with this is that the Museum should have its sights set much higher than entertainment. It should be an institution that would lead the way into a serious cultural future, yet its idea of success seems to have more to do with resisting change, and with a hobbyist enthusiasm for the past. Rubin presented a value system that had been firmly in place for sixty years as if it were a terrific new discovery. This is a holding action against the future, and against art's tendency to make a living advance into it rather than ride in on a morgue table surrounded by the scent of formaldehyde.

In Rubin's latest letter the claim of the show's success is framed as an endorsement of Varnedoe. "Lest there be any doubt whatever in McEvilley's mind, I very much like Varnedoe's selections for 'Contemporary Explorations'…. Varnedoe's particular contributions to *all* parts of the show were critical to its success." I would say it another way: Varnedoe's failure was critical to the failure of the show, to its failure to address the real issue, which is the present—and the contemporary was specifically his job. The Modern's failure to confront the primitive is directly connected to its failure to confront the contemporary. This linkage seemed implicit in the *Times* article, where criticism of the museum's hibernation through contemporary painting and sculpture was edited together with the criticisms the primitivism show received. Varnedoe's input was both antiprimitive and anticontemporary. About a third of the works included were by dead artists. The truly contemporary, like the truly primitive, wasn't clean enough for Varnedoe. It has the unpredictability of life upon it, and this exhibition, in the grip of a cliché of the classic, veered with an unstoppable impetus toward the cult of permanence, eternity, and the past. Like a gentleman of the old guard, Varnedoe edited out of the contemporary section anything that too conspicuously lacked "weird manners." In his catalogue essay he even wrote about his selections as ethically motivated toward sustaining Western institutions, as if Western civilization were so weak and nonadaptive that it would not have a chance in a confrontation. But this is ossification. Cultures do not grow by resisting changes.

A vision very much like Varnedoe's in his choices for his section of the show was seen ten years ago in a show called *Primitive Presence in the Seventies,* at the Vassar College Art Gallery, which Carter Ratcliff wrote about in the November 1975 *Artforum* in an article called "On Contemporary Primitivism." These were conceptually the same shows: both emphasized women, especially Nancy Graves, and the ranges of types of work were similar—Ree Morton's pieces of wood on the floor in the earlier show, Richard Long's stones at the Modern; Salvatore Scarpitta's *Fish Sled* instead of Michael

Singer's *First Gate*, and so on. I am not saying that these artworks are alike in themselves or in their makers' intentions, but I am discussing the curatorial use that can be made of them by exploiting design. Faced with the whole challenge of the present and the future, the shock is that Varnedoe came up with a conception no fresher than one curated by undergraduates at Vassar ten years ago. His approach to art—and Rubin's, too—is similar to that of Australian aboriginal shamans who would bury power objects in the ground, or hide them in caves; as long as they remained buried, the aborigines believed, the end of the world was postponed. The ritual functioned as reassurance about the endurance of their traditions. If we look at ourselves the way we look at them we can see something similar. We segregate artworks away in places dedicated to maintaining a sense of permanence on every level. The older works that have survived into the present through being buried in museums reassure us that our traditions are intact. The younger works more recently buried derive from the example of the older ones the assurance that they too will survive into a distant future—and with them, it is implied, the traditions that produced them. The primitivism show was a kind of ritual which transpired in a magical atmosphere of complete control. Viewers were bullied through by an exceptionally manipulative and interfering system of wall plaques. As with the canned tours at places like Disneyland or Graceland, the viewer's mind was not offered an inch of space to move in.

The Museum of Modern Art has given us a nineteenth-century model on the most pressing issues of the about-to-dawn twenty-first century. In this generation, tribal points of view are being shed: Roland Kirk plays the didgeridoo in Texas while Mozart's Susanna sings from a radio in the outback. Today any artist can be stylistically primitive or stylistically Modern. To perpetuate, on the basis of differences in look, the distinction that obtained a century ago is to commit a blindness worse than that of the eye. There is no longer much justification for the distinction; today primitive and Modern are elements in a single vocabulary. In the emerging global information moment, classical Yoruba tradition will take its place beside classical Greek tradition, primitivist Modernism beside Modernist primitivism. This is the great and epochal subject that Rubin and Varnedoe so willfully missed. We no longer live in a separate world. Our tribal view of art history as primarily or exclusively European or Eurocentric will become increasingly harmful as it cuts us off from the emerging Third World and isolates us from the global culture which already is in its early stages. We must have values that can include the rest of the world when the moment comes—and the moment is upon us. Civilization transcends geography, and if history holds one person in this global village, it holds another. In fact, if one of us is privileged over the other in art-historical terms it is the so-called primitive object-makers, through whose legacy we got our last big ride outside our own point of view, and called it Modern art.

The debater who will relate only to facts is not unlike the formalist who will relate only to shapes and colors. Rubin says he argues with my statements of fact because my conclusions are based on them; yet he never touches a point with significant content, but only numbers and details that cannot alter the outcome one way or the other. I am confident of my facts, but Rubin's attitude goes beyond them; it is symptomatic of the whole lost opportunity of this exhibition, which commissioned a team of scholars to seek out details of fact without ever using the information to address larger questions about the subject. Facts need a surrounding framework of ideas to make them meaningful, and their situations are never static. The frameworks have to be constantly revised as social needs change, and the facts have to be constantly revised as the state of the evidence changes. These remarks are not in reference to Rubin's letters to me but to his larger confusion between facts and growing knowledge. He notes, for example, that the pioneer Modernists sometimes held mistaken ethnological views about the objects they were relating to, and he condescendingly contemplates "the visitors reeling out of the galleries after attempting to digest such dual-track information." But it would not be very hard to explain, say, that the Modernist artist thought such and such an object was used in a fertility rite when in fact it was used in a healing rite. The visitor might have considered with interest whether that view did or did not appear in the work, and how different or the same the primitive object looked under the different interpretations, and so on. Some actual thought and questioning might have gone on. Rubin's apparent assumption of the visitor's lack of intelligence precludes this.

Hibernation can be a productive method—one can go into solitude and come back with understanding—or it can cloud the mind with dreams of scrambled facts, of fabricated evidence and marble charioteers. "The charioteer of Delphi," I wrote, "ca. 470 B.C., for example, was seen totally differently in classical Greece from the way we now see him. He was not alone in that noble, self-sufficient serenity of transcendental angelic whiteness that we see." The word "marble" is Rubin's, not mine, and comes up in his claim that I misreported the classical bronze as a marble work—after which he exercises his wit against me by referring to "the marble charioteer." Rubin never deals with the question of why I brought the charioteer up in the first place. My point was about the manipulation of the object through its context; we now see the work alone on a pedestal in a white room in the Delphi archaeological museum, in the typical kind of installation with which we relate to works from other cultures or times by isolating them so that they are available to receive our projections. The charioteer is decontextualized in this artificial white atmosphere and made meaningless in terms of his native context, function, and intention. I drew the analogy in my initial article as a criticism of the installation of the primitive works at MoMA, where, similarly, fragments of complex pieces were isolated in such a way as to render them meaningless in their own terms, as if indeed they had no terms of their own. Rubin chose to ignore this issue, as well as others that related to the example of the charioteer, and instead to argue a point of physical detail that would not have affected the argument in any way even if he had gotten it right.

Rubin's dispute over the goddess Kave is on no higher a level. I said the goddess had human sacrifices offered to her; no, he says, she was only *reputed* to have had human sacrifices offered to her. But the practice of human sacrifice is always known by report, which is to say, repute. This is a tactic Rubin employs repeatedly: he checks out one of my statements, finds that I was right, then pretends to have found otherwise by focusing on something like the word "reputed," which does not materially change the evidence in the case in question. The reports of human sacrifice in Oceanic religious practice go far beyond empty travelers' tales. Any study of ritual practices in the area in the nineteenth century (and for that matter well into the twentieth) will confirm it.

At this point in his argument Rubin makes an interesting transition. He appeals to the authority of Susan Vogel, of The Center for African [not Oceanic] Art, who observes, "hardly any of the African [not Oceanic] objects in the show ever had blood on them, and, in those few exceptions, it was always chicken blood, not human blood." To begin with, I did not claim that human sacrifices had been offered to any African pieces. Rubin's calling in of an Africa authority on a question in Oceanic art, his not even addressing the question at hand, is indicative of his unconscious politics toward these objects, which he makes use of as he will. He goes on to say that "McEvilley tries to qualify his statement by saying that the objects in the show 'were used in conjunction with' sacrifices." The locution "tries to qualify" is odd here: I *did* qualify the statement. Does he suppose that I meant that the statues were used to club victims to death, the masks used to smother them? I wrote, "Many of the objects in the show, if they are genuine, were used in conjunction with sacrifices and ritual bloodshed." Vogel clearly confirms this for the African works. Rubin has hidden in a footnote the crucial statement: "As the making of sculptures was, for the African artist, a primarily religious function, he often—as Vogel notes—sacrificed a chicken before beginning a piece." In other words, the pieces were involved in bloodletting from their very beginning as a matter of course; their later careers would add to it. In the same footnote Rubin goes on to acknowledge that human sacrifice was performed in Africa on major ritual occasions and more frequently "in the kingdoms of Dahomey and Benin." His authority, though having nothing to do with the Kave question at all, has inadvertently confirmed my larger point.

Farther up in his text Rubin notes that "classical Greek art…also functioned 'in conjunction with' sacrifices and ritual bloodshed.…McEvilley's attempt to show that tribal objects cannot be considered 'art' in the Western sense because they were sometimes used in conjunction with sacrificial activities is simply unfounded." But he has missed the point. The ancient Greek and tribal African situations were not the same in this respect. Many of the objects from Bronze Age Greece that are now in our museums were anonymously made ritual and tomb objects, as in traditional societies around the world, including Africa and Oceania. But around 600B.C. this situation was visibly changed. Greek artists began self-consciously to sign their works and to use them for nonritual display; soon picture galleries came into existence. This is really when art in our full sense of the word began. In the classical period of Greek culture to which Rubin is referring, there were residual sacrificial rites in connection with sacred architecture, but there was also a self-conscious practice of making artworks intended for self-expression and aesthetic appreciation and nothing else. The ritual environment in which some classical Greek artworks found themselves was not their *raison d'être*, as it was in traditional African and Oceanic societies. (Today some self-conscious artworks are sited in ritual locations—the Roman Catholic mass, for example, with its symbolic sacrifice of flesh and blood, is sometimes performed in the Rothko Chapel—but this does not make them primarily ritual objects.)

The general obsession with numbers in these replies from MoMA is getting comic. Varnedoe was after me about a number in a footnote, Rubin about a number in the text. Can't they read words? Rubin, in the current letter, refers to the forty-four Oceanic objects in the Menil show when really it seems to be forty-five. Isn't it dumb of me to even bother bringing it up? The jackpot number that really set this debate cooking is one-hundred, a figure I mentioned in the original article. In addressing "McEvilley's claims about various other exhibitions that were supposed to have made ours old hat," Rubin insists, "I have very little appetite for this debate, since such questions of priority normally hold no interest for me at all." The body language of that sentence as well as all the PR around his show—not to speak of his effort to deny the importance of the many other exhibitions—say the opposite.

In my article in November, in an effort to pick a fairly recent example of these earlier exhibitions, I wrote: "For five years or so after its opening in 1977, the Centre Pompidou in Paris exhibited, in the vicinity of its Modern collections, about one-hundred tribal objects from the Musée de l'Homme. Though not actually intermingled with Modern works, these were intended to illustrate relations with them...." Rubin replied, citing Jean-Hubert Martin, that "the two vitrines at the Centre Pompidou together never contained more than twenty or so objects." I then replied, "But in conversation with me subsequent to his conversation with Rubin, Martin stated that each vitrine—not both together—held twenty or twenty-five objects, bringing the total to forty or fifty at any one time.... No listing of the total number of objects has been located, but Beaubourg curator Jean-Yves Mock, whose memory provided my original estimate of one hundred, still says that figure is not unreasonable." Now, in his latest letter, Rubin mentions that he has nudged the Musée de l'Homme into finding the list and, in the usually unread footnotes, that the number was actually sixty-five. (Rubin remarks in his footnote that thirteen pieces were returned to the Musée de l'Homme "almost immediately"; in my original inquiry I was told that the vitrines, immediately after the installation, looked over-crowded, resulting in the removal of some pieces. I assume that these were the objects returned.) I am glad Rubin had the power to unearth the original list; I didn't. But I could have said the vitrines contained "a number" of primitive objects and made the point. My number was the number given in our checking and it is still closer to the mark than Rubin's original twenty.

In the article I went on to say, because this is what I had heard in my fact-checking, that some of the objects in the vitrines had belonged to early Modernist artists including Picasso and Braque. Three months later, on the same subject, I wrote in my reply to Rubin's first letter: "Next, Rubin denies that any of the objects in the Beaubourg vitrines had ever been owned by Braque or Picasso. In fact, at the writing of my article one of the authorities on this subject [i.e., the vitrines] had ventured the opposite opinion, yet finally it seems this point must remain moot, in light of the fact, acknowledged by Rubin, that no exact listing of the objects has been found." In his current letter Rubin places great emphasis on my use of an unnamed authority and on my statement about the list. He naïvely equates my reference to an unnamed source with the logical fallacy *argumentum ad auctoritatem*, the Appeal to Authority, though the two rhetorical moments have nothing to do with one another. In fact they are opposite: the point of the Appeal to Authority is that the name of the source is what carries the power to convince; I repressed the name of my source to protect him from the underlying power situation of this debate.

As for the list, Jean-Hubert Martin, then of the Beaubourg, told me that though it was probably extant its whereabouts were uncertain. Rubin declares, with odd, hysterical emphasis, *"I never mentioned any list."* But the fact that he had not seen a list was tacitly acknowledged by several elements in his argument. He spoke for example, of his recollections, then referred to a "rapid check" of the facts. Now the question is, a rapid check of what? If he was checking the list, then he had it and was being misleading about the number twenty, which I knew from Martin and Mock to be definitely too low. If he was checking the memories of informants, then he did not have the list. I was giving him the benefit of the doubt; perhaps I was being too generous. Now that he says he has the list Rubin makes a bald denial ("none of the objects lent by the Musée de l'Homme ever belonged to a Modern artist"), and then, in a footnote, takes it back and acknowledges that there may have been at least one such case as I claimed. Someone with lots of spare time and no hobbies might undertake to analyze and publish the list and clear the matter up.

Of course, I brought up the vitrines in the first place to illustrate the point that the practice of exhibiting primitive works either with Modern works or in their milieu was nothing new or unusual. The case was sound, and Rubin hid among the numbers to evade it. But it should be emphasized that there is no ambiguity whatever about this. Rubin's primitivist hat is indeed an old one; it's the amount of surrounding research that's new, what they call the "light of informed art history." One could go on naming earlier shows that exhibited primitive art in the milieu of Modern art till the bears come out of the caves and say they're sorry. Rubin's essayists in the catalogue are well-aware that the practice began early in Modernist primitivism itself. (Even Rubin, nudged by my article, acknowledged some of them in his first letter.) Alfred Stieglitz showed African wood carvings at the Gallery 291 in 1914. In 1915 Modern and primitive works were shown together at the Modern Gallery in New York. In 1933 the Museum of Modern Art showed *American Sources of Modern Art (Aztec, Maya, Inca);* in 1935 *African Negro Art;* and in 1941, *Indian Art of the United States,* curated by René d'Harnoncourt. A key precursor, one that had special status in the background of Rubin's show but that he chose not to mention in his letter—occurred in 1967. In that year the Musée de l'Homme held a major exhibition called *Arts primitifs dans les ateliers d'artistes*. Here, according to the Musée de l'Homme catalogue (I did not see the exhibition), were exhibited primitive art objects that had been in the collections of Braque, Picasso, Derain, Matisse, Max Ernst, Jacques Lipchitz, Vlaminck, Henry Moore, and dozens of other Modern artists. Here were the fantastic photographs that moved so many at MoMA of Picasso in his studio with a variety of primitive objects in 1909, and above all of Braque in 1911, playing an accordion in front of a wall with a Fang mask on it. And on and on.

Ultimately Rubin is so obsessed with the idea that his exhibition had no precedents that he makes my comments in regard to the Menil collection exhibition, *La Rîme et la Raison* the linchpin or rhetorical climax of his letter. I did not see the show. I was not writing about artworks in themselves but only about the record of what had been exhibited, and this record is available through the extensive catalogue. There is of course no requirement of firsthand viewing for scholars who are writing about the record of things. I have written about Plato without ever having seen him. Astronomers write about the stars without visiting them; physicists write about things too little or too big to see. Present-day writers on the Armory show write about it from the published record, not from having seen it. The press release on the Menil-collection show clearly suggests that it paralleled the MoMA project in its main lines. It said, for example, that "the show tracks the ideas early twentieth-century artists found in primitive art, and the relation of these works to successive, linked waves of European and American art movements: Cubism, Surrealism, Abstract Expressionism, and Minimalism." In addition, I saw in the catalogue several references to the mixing of primitive and Modern objects. This is what I wrote about it in my initial article: "More recently, the exhibition of the Menil Collections in Paris' Grand Palais, in April, 1984, juxtaposed primitive and Modern works (a Max Ernst with an African piece, Cézanne with Cycladic), and sometimes, as in the present exhibition, showed a Modern artist's work in conjunction with primitive objects in his collection. The premise of this show, then, is not new or startling in the least."

I want to remind the reader that in his first letter Rubin listed three objections to those remarks. I replied. In the current letter he has abandoned two of his objections and focused everything on the statement that the exhibition "sometimes showed a Modern artist's work in conjunction with primitive objects in his collection." In that regard I depended on certain indications in the catalogue. There was, for example, a statement by Walter Hopps in the introductory essay that "in the section on the Surrealists, beside their own works one finds objects that belonged to them." The question now is, what kind of objects? The statement appears among sentences on the mixing of primitive art and Modern art, and I understood, on the basis of context and of the inference contained in the word "*ainsi,*" or "thus," that this sentence was on the same topic. Rubin first objects that "Hopps' sentence about 'objects that belonged to [the Surrealists],' though slightly ambiguous because poorly translated, is not located, as McEvilley claims, in a discussion about the 'mixing of primitive and Modern objects.'" The reader will have to read the Hopps passage to see what I see:

> *Ici l'art primitif est représenté à égalité avec l'art occidental; l'art*
> *occidental le plus ancien est juxtaposé avec l'art le plus moderne. Les*

affinités ne sont pas chronologiques, elles sont conceptuelles, iconographiques et formelles, destinées à suggérer les correspondances profondes entre les valeurs esthétiques et spirtuelles de peuples et de temps fort divers. Ainsi, dans la section des surréalistes, on trouve, à côté de leurs oeuvres, des objets leur ayant appartenus. Dans le même esprit, quelques oeuvres modernes sont exposées au milieu d'objets archaïques ou traditionnels.

(Here, primitive art is presented equally with Western art; the oldest Western art is juxtaposed with the most modern. The affinities are not chronological but conceptual, iconographic, and formal; they are intended to suggest the deep correspondences between the aesthetic and spiritual values of very different peoples and times. Thus, *in the section on the Surrealists, beside their own works one finds objects that belonged to them*. In the same spirit, several Modern works are shown among ancient or traditional objects.) [My italics on the English.]

Perusing the catalogue in search of more information on those objects I found, in the "Catalogue" section proper, after several hundred pages of pictures with occasional introductory paragraphs, pictures of some Kuskokwim Eskimo masks, with the following passage introducing them:

Ces masques étaient portés à l'occasion de danses et de cérémonies liées à l'invocation du monde des esprits. L'artiste qui réalisa les pièces 232 à 294 les vit d'abord "apparues en rêve." Il exécuta ensuite seize paires d'objets. La série complète, trente-deux pièces, fut achetée au début du siècle par un Américain, George Heye, et plusieurs furent acquisés ultérieurement par des surréalistes français établis à New York.

(These masks were worn on the occasion of dances and ceremonies linked to the invocation of the spirit world. The artist who made pieces 292 to 294 first saw them "appearing in dream." He then executed sixteen pairs of objects. The complete series, thirty-two pieces, was bought at the start of the century by an American, George Heye, and several were later bought by French Surrealists living in New York).

At this point I had found two references in the catalogue to things owned by Surrealist artists (a third, more general statement was consistent with these): one statement said that they were in the show, the other that they were Kuskokwim masks. The first statement was by Walter Hopps; the second was unsigned. Compressing for space, I wrote the following: *"Ainsi, dans la section des surréalistes on trouve, à côté de leurs oeuvres, des objets leur ayant appartenus'* (thus, in the section on the Surrealists, beside their own works one finds objects that belonged to them). These include, for example, Eskimo masks, of which '*plusieurs furent acquises...par des surréalistes français établis à New York*' (several were bought...by French Surrealists living in New York)."

Rubin says in reply, at the very end of his second letter, that if you held the Menil catalogue in your hands

> you would see that Hopps' sentence about "objects that belonged to [the Surrealists]," though slightly ambiguous because poorly translated, is *not* located, as McEvilley claims, in a discussion about the "mixing of primitive and Modern objects." And if you had seen the show, you would have known that the "objects" to which Hopps was, in fact, referring were not tribal sculptures at all but bibelots, exotica, and memorabilia; the few tribal sculptures in those areas were not from artists' collections, *nor did Walter Hopps ever say they were*. But that's not all. The last part of McEvilley's paragraph cites Eskimo masks in the Menil show as examples of tribal objects supposedly owned by Surrealists, an assertion elaborated with a quotation seemingly continued from Hopps' text. But this passage ("several were bought...") is by another author, occurs 339 pages later in the Menil catalogue, and *does not refer to the Eskimo masks in the show*. Is this the scholarship that is a type of science?

There are six objections here. The first, about the context speaking of mixing, I have discussed, and the second, about the appearance in the show of objects belonging to Surrealists, too. The third point—that the second quote seems to continue the first—is empty, and suggests that the bear has a punctuation problem. The two French quotations are enclosed in separate sets of quotation marks, indicating that they are not continuous. Fourth point: the second quote was unattributed: as Rubin agrees, in the catalogue it was unsigned. Fifth point: the 339 pages that intervened between the two passages were almost entirely filled with pictures; in any case, if the same subject is discussed in separated passages, one must quote separated passages. Rubin's sixth and crowning point, the culmination of his letter, is that the passage about masks owned by Surrealists "does not refer to the Eskimo masks in the show." There he has a footnote, and the footnote refers to a private conversation as his proof. I relied on the published record and believe that in my method there was no error.

This question of whether the dates of the non-Western works should have been included either in the show or the catalogue or both may seem at first glance as sterile and merely factual as the old tattered hat, but I think it is not: it points to hidden presuppositions of great moment. In the article that began this debate I objected that by omitting dates from the non-Western works in both the show and the book Rubin was presenting their makers and their cultures as really "primitive," that is, outside of history—as, really, less than human. He was acting out a presupposition that had a great deal in common with the Conquistador's belief that Amerindians did not have souls, and he was doing so ultimately for the same purpose—to justify taking over in the one case their bodies and in the other their cultural objects. I wrote, "Anyone who opens a scholarly book on primitive objects, or who visits anthropological museums…will see that at least approximate dates are usually given for the works." In his citation of this passage Rubin conveniently omits my reference to books and deals only with the question of whether museums put dates on their vitrines. Earlier on in his current letter he says that "we had described [the tribal objects in the show] as mostly from the later nineteenth and early twentieth centuries…." He is evidently referring to a wall plaque in the exhibition. But the checklist of the exhibition says nothing about the dates of the primitive objects, though of course it dates all the Modern objects. Clearly the information belongs there, for starters. Wherever it is in the book (if indeed it is anywhere) it hasn't jumped out at me. In any case it is inadequate. Rubin's unconscious politics toward the primitive objects are coming out again; lumping them all together is not something he would do for the museum's Picassos.

In my claim that the policy of most museums is to give such dates as are available I granted that precise dates are usually not available. Rubin in reply acts as if I had demanded precise dates for everything, and states that often only centuries are known, as if to show me that my request was ridiculous; yet I had specifically written: "even knowing the century would help." "Not one of the labels for any of the hundreds of objects [in the African section of the Musée de l'Homme], Rubin insists, "contains even an approximate date. The same thing is true for the tribal objects in the African and Oceanic galleries of the American Museum of Natural History—among other ethnological museums."

Well, the story certainly does not end there. Is Rubin really unaware that the Musée de l'Homme *does* in fact give such dates as are available in its most widely distributed catalogue, *Chefs d'oeuvre de Musée de l'homme* (Paris: Musée de l'Homme, 1965)? Is he really unaware that the Metropolitan Museum of Art in New York gives available dates in its primitive collection? And that the Field Museum of Natural History in Chicago does also? He refers lightly to "other ethnological museums"—too lightly, I'm afraid. The general catalogue of the Museum für Völkerkunde in Vienna gives dates such as *"vor 1879"* (before 1879) or *"Frühes 19. Jahrhundert"* (early nineteenth century) when they are available. The Berlin Museum für Völkerkunde, in a catalogue of West African masks, gives available dates. The Linden-Museum in Stuttgart, in a catalogue of objects from Cameroon, gives dates such as "collected…in Bali, 1905." The catalogue of Indonesian and Melanesian works in the Collection Barbier Müller (Geneva, 1977) gives dates. The catalogue *Exotische Kunst im Rautenstrauch-Joest Museum* (Cologne, 1967) provides such dates as are available. The Museum of Primitive Art in Rimini, in its general catalogue, edited by Delfino Rialto, gives available dates. The Museum of Primitive Art in New York, in a catalogue of the primitive works in the John and Dominique de Menil collection edited by Robert Goldwater himself in 1962, gave available dates such as "before 1896" Douglas Newton, when director of this museum, gave dates in their general catalogue, *Primitive Art Masterpieces,* 1974. As chairman of the department of primitive art at the Metropolitan Museum, Newton included dates "when known" in the catalogue *The Nelson A. Rockefeller Collection: Masterpieces of Primitive Art,* 1978. The catalogue *Traditional Art of Africa, Oceania, and the Americas,* published by the Fine Arts Museum of San Francisco in 1973 gives dates such as "collected before 1900" when they are available. The catalogue of *The George G. Frelinghuysen Collection at UCLA,* 1968, gives, when they are known, such dates as "made in the nineteenth-century." Cottie Burland, in *Gods and Demons in Primitive Art,* 1973, gives dates such as, "Collected by Dr. Emil Holub c. 1860," "Possibly mid-nineteenth century Tsimshian work," and "Made by Tlingit Indians in the mid-nineteenth century"; and Henry John Drewal, in the catalogue *African Artistry: Technique and Aesthetics in Yoruba Sculpture,* 1980, gives dates such as "probably by Akiode (died 1936)" and "possibly by Oniyide (died 1947)." A recent book by Werner Gillon titled *A Short History of African Art,* 1984, proposes correctly that it is time to begin regarding non-Western objects within the context of history.

Rubin employs a reverse form of argument when he writes of the Menil catalogue, as if disproving me, that "many of the African objects are totally undated and only six of the forty-four [sic] Oceanic objects are given even approximate dates." But the point is the opposite of what he implies: it is that the catalogue in question does give available dates. I could go on. Rubin claimed there was a general practice not to give dates; clearly he is wrong. But it is not difficult to guess why Rubin did not want individual dates in his show. Consider the pink Sulka mask that adorned the cover of *Artforum* in which my initial article appeared, and which was one of the really prepossessing objects in the show. In the 1975 edition of Helen Gardner's *Art Through The Ages* it is dated "1900-1910." Picasso's *Les Demoiselles d'Avignon,* in the Museum's collection, is dated 1907. The fact the exhibition was at pains to conceal from the nonexpert public is that "the primitive and the modern," as anthropologist Remo Guidieri wrote, "are contemporaries." And yet this contemporaneity is, finally, the most interesting fact of all. Is 1910 in Africa or Oceania a different year from 1910 in Europe? Is history only for us? Why are the object-makers of Africa and Oceania invisible to us except in this degraded, anonymous, dateless, timeless, childish, ahistorical role as pedestals for—guess what—our art? To push them into the nursery of childish timelessness while researching every tiniest detail of the chronology of the grand Europeans is grotesque.

There is an inner contradiction to this attitude that recontextualizes primitive ritual objects as art in the Museum of Modern Art and then leaves them anonymous and dateless: our Western idea of art is premised both on the maker as a self and on the historical progression of the works. I suggested that Rubin had enunciated no clear criteria for using the primitive objects the way we use our artworks, and that he did not want to think about the complexities of their transpositions. I had claimed that "virtually every object" in the Egyptian Museum in Cairo had been intentionally buried underground away from all human eyes, and that this showed something fundamentally different in intention from our intentions about art. Rubin attempts to rebut me, saying, "contrary to [McEvilley's] assertion, there are [in the Egyptian Museum] a great many objects not intended to be buried underground." He has a footnote number on this, and the footnote says the following: "I checked with the Egyptologists at the Metropolitan Museum of Art, who suggested that something less than one-fourth of what is visible of this immense and as yet not fully catalogued collection would be material not taken from tombs. Thus, tomb material could hardly be said to comprise 'virtually every object' there." The information itself is hidden in those sentences. Less than one-fourth of the objects, Rubin learned, were not taken from tombs; it follows then that more than three-fourths were taken from tombs. More than three-fourths, of course, means something between three-fourths and all of the objects. The range is conservative and an actual count, I think, would come in at around ninety percent. In any case, saying more than three-fourths is very much the same as saying virtually all. Again Rubin has confirmed my original statement. He found that I was right, pretended that he had found otherwise, and hid the real information in a footnote. (Rubin treats the footnotes like a burial area away from all human eyes.)

The red herring of whether some temple sculpture and painting was meant to be seen in the light of day is of course true, but makes no significant difference in the issue; in ancient Egypt both temple and palace were hieratic settings in which the works in question functioned magically, as they did in tombs. It is known that the Egyptians themselves regarded their sculpture and painting (as for that matter their architecture in durable materials) as functional magical objects, and expressed no consciously articulated aesthetic propositions about them. I trust it's clear that I'm not saying that they're not pretty to me, as to many Western Moderns, they have a powerful, even an uncanny, aesthetic appeal. Indirectly, by way of the Greeks the Egyptian canon of proportion and harmony trained our eyes, and can still be felt resonating behind Renaissance and Modern European art.

The second element in Rubin's Egyptian reply is his report of a personal conversation with Leo Steinberg. My quarrel is not with Steinberg, and one wonders why Rubin does not cite a published authority on Egyptology. In any case, the speaker of these remarks acknowledges that the Egyptian works were mostly buried underground—this really is an undeniable fact—but goes on to say about the buried objects that "they were designed to be enjoyed both functionally and aesthetically by human eyes in an assured afterlife precisely forever." The words "and aesthetically" are without a basis in evidence. To begin with, I hope it is clear that the speaker is referring to dead human eyes. The speaker means that after the works were deliberately buried behind the most elaborate obstacles, they were meant to be enjoyed "both functionally and aesthetically" by corpses or ghosts. I wonder if the speaker would care to cite documents for the aesthetic pleasures of the dead. I repeat that as far as I know there is not a scrap of evidence in extant Egyptian literature for the idea that ghosts or gods in the tomb were meant to take an explicitly aesthetic pleasure from these objects. In fact, there is no more articulation of aesthetic propositions in ancient Egyptian literature than in African and Oceanic tribal discourse; the category of aesthetics as we know it had not yet dawned and cannot be called a part of the intention behind the work, except in the same unconscious way that Rubin and others attributed to the African and Oceanic works in the show—that is, by the same Eurocentric projection of our feelings and intentions into their works, despite the fact that all the evidence shows their work to have arisen from quite different intentions. One wonders why Rubin doesn't tell us what the Egyptologists he consulted (and whom he does not name) had to say on this point, rather than suddenly ignoring them and going to a Western-art historian for opinions about Egyptian questions. For the absence of evidence in the literature is not the worst of it: anyone who had reviewed the material from the tombs themselves in detail would know better. Some of the highly ornamented objects, for example, were found in animal cemeteries. Were they meant to be enjoyed aesthetically by dead crocodiles, vultures, and jackals? Furthermore, the only important tomb whose original contents we know in detail is Tutankhamen's, and the speaker should note that it contained far more stuff than it could hold in exhibition. The magnificent objects that we admired in the museum show were not originally arranged for aesthetic appreciation: they were stacked on top of one another as in a closet or a storeroom. (The partial ancient robbery does not alter this fact.) They were there, in other words, because their magical presence was necessary, not because anyone would be looking at them.

Finally, the speaker chides me for supposedly ignoring the fact that the Egyptians believed in an afterlife, and that therefore the idea of aesthetic appreciation in the afterlife would have seemed less than comical to them. But the speaker seems to feel that the Egyptian view of the afterlife involved the mummy living forever in the tomb, enjoying its goods. There are traces in the Egyptian literature of such a rudimentary belief system, but in the historical period—the period in which virtually all the objects that are known to us as Egyptian art were made—this form of the afterlife myth had been subsumed within and largely replaced by a more complex myth in which the selfhood of the deceased breaks up into fragments which go various ways. Most of the tomb objects have magical functions involved in the reconstitution of the fragmented self for wanderings beyond the tomb. The self, when ritually reconstituted, does not continue to inhabit the tomb and enjoy the grave goods, but goes on to the Field of Reeds and the Court of Osiris, and finally, converted into Re, achieves an eternal life among the circumpolar stars. The tomb objects, meanwhile, lie in the tomb as a kind of magical support system. There are various forms of this myth, and none of them provides a whole self living on in the tomb and enjoying its furnishings. Rubin's views here are like those of the anonymous Greek tourist who entered an Egyptian tomb in about 600 B.C., and wrote on the wall, "I have seen these things and I understand none of them."

Well, big bear, that about wraps up the news from here. It's getting late. You might feel that I have abstracted this topic from a more concrete array. But the force and power of your show, its scale, its time and place—all these things have made it historic, because it raised questions. It made us ask exactly how and why it was deficient. I thought it was above all inadequate because the relationship was all one way.

I'd like to read you some choruses of Aeschylus and show you my favorite poems. We could both bring a friend. We could explain to our friends that we have shared something special together, you and I. Take care of kitty. I don't think I'll be writing to you much anymore, but I want to say that I hope the future profits from what we have done. And that we do not drink the black milk of morning, you and I, for doing it.

REPRINTED FROM *ARTFORUM* (MAY, 1985): 63–71.

You do not stand in one place to watch a masquerade. —an Igbo saying

During the winter of 1984-85 one could encounter tribal objects in an unusual number of locations around New York City. This essay surveys a half-dozen, focusing on the most controversial: the major exhibition held at the Museum of Modern Art (MoMA), *'Primitivism' in 20th Century Art: Affinity of the Tribal and the Modern.* The essay's "ethnographic present" is late December 1984.

Pablo Picasso,
Girl Before a Mirror (de
1932, oil on canvas,
64 x 51.25".
Collection of the
Museum of Modern Art, Ne
gift of Mrs. Simon Guggenh

The "tribal" objects gathered on West Fifty-third Street have been around. They are travelers—some arriving from folklore and ethnographic museums in Europe, others from art galleries and private collections. They have traveled first class to the Museum of Modern Art, elaborately crated and insured for important sums. Previous accommodations have been less luxurious: some were stolen, others "purchased" for a song by colonial administrators, travelers, anthropologists, missionaries, sailors in African ports. These non-Western objects have been by turns curiosities, ethnographic specimens, major art creations. After 1900 they began to turn up in European flea markets, thereafter moving between avant-garde studios and collectors' apartments. Some came to rest in the unheated basements or "laboratories" of anthropology museums, surrounded by objects made in the same region of the world. Others encountered odd fellow travelers, lighted and labeled in strange display cases. Now on West Fifty-third Street they intermingle with works by European masters—Picasso, Giacometti, Brancusi, and others. A three-dimensional Eskimo mask with twelve arms and a number of holes hangs beside a canvas on which Joan Miró has painted colored shapes. The people in New York look at the two objects and see that they are alike.

Travelers tell different stories in different places, and on West Fifty-third Street an origin story of Modernism is featured. Around 1910 Picasso and his cohort suddenly, intuitively recognize that "primitive" objects are in fact powerful "art." They collect, imitate, and are affected by these objects. Their own work, even when not directly influenced, seems oddly reminiscent of non-Western forms. The modern and the primitive converse across the centuries and continents. At the Museum of Modern Art an exact history is told featuring individual artists and objects, their encounters in specific studios at precise moments. Photographs document the crucial influences of non-Western artifacts on the pioneer Modernists. This focused story is surrounded and infused with another—a loose allegory of relationship centering on the word *affinity*. The word is a kinship term, suggesting a deeper or more natural relationship than mere resemblance or juxtaposition. It connotes a common quality or essence joining the tribal to the modern. A Family of Art is brought together, global, diverse, richly inventive, and miraculously unified, for every object displayed on West Fifty-third Street looks modern.

The exhibition at MoMA is historical and didactic. It is complemented by a comprehensive, scholarly catalogue, which includes divergent views of its topic and in which the show's organizers, William Rubin and Kirk Varnedoe, argue at length its underlying premises (Rubin 1984).[1] One of the virtues of an exhibition that blatantly makes a case or tells a story is that it encourages debate and makes possible the suggestion of other stories. Thus in what follows different histories of the tribal and the modern will be

proposed in response to the sharply focused history on display at the Museum of Modern Art. But before that history can be seen for what it is, however—a specific story that excludes other stories—the universalizing allegory of affinity must be cleared away.

This allegory, the story of the Modernist Family of Art, is not rigorously argued at MoMA. (That would require some explicit form of either an archetypal or structural analysis.) The allegory is, rather, built into the exhibition's form, featured suggestively in its publicity, left uncontradicted, repetitiously asserted—"Affinity of the Tribal and the Modern." The allegory has a hero, whose virtuoso work, an exhibit caption tells us, contains more affinities with the tribal than that of any other pioneer Modernist. These affinities "measure the depth of Picasso's grasp of the informing principles of tribal sculpture, and reflect his profound identity of spirit with the tribal peoples." Modernism is thus presented as a search for "informing principles" that transcend culture, politics, and history. Beneath this generous umbrella the tribal is modern and the modern more richly, more diversely human.

The power of the affinity idea is such (it becomes almost self-evident in the MoMA juxtapositions) that it is worth reviewing the major objections to it. Anthropologists, long familiar with the issue of cultural diffusion versus independent invention, are not likely to find anything special in the similarities between selected tribal and modern objects. An established principle of anthropological comparative method asserts that the greater the range of cultures, the more likely one is to find similar traits. MoMA's sample is very large, embracing African, Oceanic, North American, and Arctic "tribal" groups.[2] A second principle, that of the "limitation of possibilities," recognizes that invention, while highly diverse, is not infinite. The human body, for example, with its two eyes, four limbs, bilateral arrangement of features, front and back, and so on, will be represented and stylized in a limited number of ways.3 There is thus a priori no reason to claim evidence for affinity (rather than mere resemblance or coincidence) because an exhibition of tribal works that seem impressively "modern" in style can be gathered. An equally striking collection could be made demonstrating sharp dissimilarities between tribal and modern objects.

The qualities most often said to link these objects are their "conceptualism" and "abstraction" (but a very long and ultimately incoherent list of shared traits, including "magic," "ritualism," "environmentalism," use of "natural" materials, and so on, can be derived from the show and especially from its catalogue). Actually the tribal and modern artifacts are similar only in that they do not feature the pictorial illusionism or sculptural naturalism that came to dominate Western European art after the Renaissance. Abstraction and conceptualism are, of course, pervasive in the arts of the non-Western World. To say that they share with Modernism a rejection of certain naturalist projects is not to show anything like an affinity.4 Indeed the "tribalism" selected in the exhibition to resemble Modernism is itself a construction designed to accomplish the task of resemblance. Ife and Benin sculptures, highly naturalistic in style, are excluded from the "tribal" and placed in a somewhat arbitrary category of "court" society (which does not, however, include large chieftanships). Moreover, pre-Columbian works, though they have a place in the catalogue, are largely omitted from the exhibition. One can question other selections and exclusions that result in a collection of only "modern"-looking tribal objects. Why, for example, are there relatively few "impure" objects constructed from the debris of colonial culture contacts? And is there not an overall bias toward clean, abstract forms as against rough or crude work?

The "Affinities" room of the exhibition is an intriguing but entirely problematic exercise in formal mix-and-match. The short introductory text begins well: "AFFINITIES presents a group of tribal objects notable for their appeal to modern taste." Indeed this is all that can rigorously be said of the objects in this room. The text continues, however, "Selected pairings of modern and tribal objects demonstrate common denominators of these arts that are independent of direct influence." The phrase *common denominators* implies something more systematic than intriguing resemblance. What can it possibly mean? This introductory text, cited in its entirety, is emblematic of the MoMA undertaking as a whole. Statements carefully limiting its purview (specifying a concern only with Modernist primitivism and not with tribal life) coexist with frequent implications of something more. The affinity idea itself is wide-ranging and promiscuous, as are allusions to universal human capacities retrieved in the encounter between modern and tribal or invocations of the expansive human mind—the healthy capacity of Modernist consciousness to question its limits and engage otherness.5

Nowhere, however, does the exhibition or catalogue underline a more disquieting quality of Modernism: its taste for appropriating or redeeming otherness, for constituting non-Western arts in its own image, for discovering universal, ahistorical "human" capacities. The search for similarity itself requires justification, for even if one accepts the limited task of exploring "Modernist primitivism," why could one not learn as much about Picasso's or Ernst's creative processes by analyzing the differences separating their art from tribal models or by tracing the ways their art moved away from, gave new twists to, non-Western forms?[6] This side of the process is unexplored in the exhibition. The prevailing viewpoint is made all too clear in one of the "affinities" featured on the catalogue's cover, a juxtaposition of Picasso's *Girl Before a Mirror* (1932) with a Kwakiutl half-mask, a type quite rare among Northwest Coast creations. Its task here is simply to produce an effect of resemblance (an effect actually created by the camera angle). In this exhibition a universal message, "Affinity of the Tribal and the Modern," is produced by careful selection and the maintenance of a specific angle of vision.

The notion of affinity, an allegory of kinship, has an expansive, celebratory task to perform. The affinities shown at MoMA are all on Modernist terms. The great Modernist "pioneers" (and their museum) are shown promoting formerly despised tribal "fetishes" or mere ethnographic "specimens" to the status of high art and in the process discovering new dimensions of their ("our") creative potential. The capacity of art to transcend its cultural and historical context is asserted repeatedly (Rubin, 1984: x, 73). In the catalogue Rubin tends to be more interested in a recovery of elemental expressive modes, whereas Varnedoe stresses the rational, forward-looking intellect (which he opposes to an unhealthy primitivism, irrational and escapist). Both celebrate the generous spirit of Modernism, pitched now at a global scale but excluding—as we shall see—Third World modernisms.

At West Fifty-third Street Modernist primitivism is a going Western concern. It is, Varnedoe tells us, summing up in the last sentence of the catalogue's second volume, "a process of revolution that begins and ends in modern culture, and because of that—not in spite of it—can continually expand and deepen our contact with that which is remote and different from us, and continually threaten, challenge, and reform our sense of self" (Rubin, 1984: 682). A skeptic may doubt the ability of the Modernist primitivism exhibited at MoMA to threaten or challenge what is by now a thoroughly institutionalized system of aesthetic (and market) value; but it is appropriate, and in a sense rigorous, that this massive collection spanning the globe should end with the word *self*.

Indeed an unintended effect of the exhibition's comprehensive catalogue is to show once and for all the incoherence of the modern Rorschach of "the primitive." From Robert Goldwater's formalism to the transforming "magic" of Picasso (according to Rubin); from Levy-Bruhl's mystical *mentalité primitive* (influencing a generation of modern artists and writers) to Lévi-Strauss's *pensée sauvage* (resonating with "systems art" and the cybernetic binarism of the minimalists); from Dubuffet's fascination with insanity and the childish to the enlightened rational sense of a Gauguin, the playful experimentalism of a Picasso or the new "scientific" spirit of a James Turrell (the last three approved by Varnedoe but challenged by Rosalind Krauss, who is more attached to Bataille's decapitation, *bassesse,* and bodily deformations[7]); from fetish to icon and back again; from aboriginal bark paintings (Klee) to massive pre-Columbian monuments (Henry Moore); from weightless Eskimo masks to Stonehenge—the catalogue succeeds in demonstrating not any essential affinity between tribal and modern or even a coherent Modernist attitude toward the primitive but rather the restless desire and power of the modern West to collect the world.

Setting aside the allegory of affinity, we are left with a "factual," narrowly focused history—that of the "discovery" of primitive art by Picasso and his generation. It is tempting to say that the "History" section of the exhibition is, after all, the rigorous part and the rest merely suggestive association. Undeniably a great deal of scholarly research in the best *Kunstgeschichte* tradition has been brought to bear on this specific history. Numerous myths are usefully questioned; important facts are specified (what mask was in whose studio when); and the pervasiveness of tribal influences on early Modernist art—European, English, and American—is shown more amply than ever before. The catalogue has the merit of including a number of articles that dampen the celebratory mood of the exhibition: notably the essay by Krauss and useful contributions by Christian Feest, Philippe Peltier, and Jean-Louis Paudrat detailing the arrival of non-Western artifacts in Europe. These historical articles illuminate the less edifying imperialist contexts that surrounded the "discovery" of tribal objects by Modernist artists at the moment of high colonialism.

Josephine Baker in a famous pose, Paris, ca. 1929

If we ignore the "Affinities" room at MoMA, however, and focus on the "serious" historical part of the exhibition, new critical questions emerge. What is excluded by the specific focus of the history? Isn't this factual narration still infused with the affinity allegory, since it is cast as a story of creative genius recognizing the greatness of tribal works, discovering common artistic "informing principles"? Could the story of this intercultural encounter be told differently? It is worth making the effort to extract another story from the materials in the exhibition—a history not of redemption or of discovery but of reclassification. This other history assumes that "art" is not universal but is a changing Western cultural category. The fact that rather abruptly, in the space of a few decades, a large class of non-Western artifacts came to be redefined as art is a taxonomic shift that requires critical historical discussion, not celebration. That this construction of a generous category of art pitched at a global scale occurred just as the planet's tribal peoples came massively under European political, economic, and evangelical dominion cannot be irrelevant. But there is no room for such complexities at the MoMA show. Obviously the Modernist appropriation of tribal productions as art is not simply imperialist. The project involves too many strong critiques of colonialist, evolutionist assumptions. As we shall see, though, the scope and underlying logic of the "discovery" of tribal art reproduces hegemonic Western assumptions rooted in the colonial and neocolonial epoch.

Picasso, Léger, Apollinaire, and many others came to recognize the elemental, "magical" power of African sculptures in a period of growing *négrophilie,* a context that would see the eruption onto the European scene of other evocative black figures: the jazzman, the boxer (Al Brown), the *sauvage* Josephine Baker. To tell the history of Modernism's recognition of African "art" in this broader context would raise ambiguous and disturbing questions about aesthetic appropriation of non-Western others, issues of race, gender, and power. This other story is largely invisible at MoMA, given the exhibition's narrow focus. It can be glimpsed only in the small section devoted to "*La création du monde,*" the African cosmogony staged in 1923 by Léger, Cendrars, and Milhaud, and in the broadly pitched if still largely uncritical catalogue article by Laura Rosenstock devoted to it. Overall one would be hard pressed to deduce from the exhibition that all the enthusiasm for things *nègre,* for the "magic" of African art, had anything to do with race. Art in this focused history has no essential link with coded perceptions of black bodies—their vitalism, rhythm, magic, erotic power, etc.—as seen by whites. The Modernism represented here is concerned only with artistic invention, a

positive category separable from a negative primitivism of the irrational, the savage, the base, the flight from civilization.

A different historical focus might bring a photograph of Josephine Baker into the vicinity of the African statues that were exciting the Parisian avant-garde in the 1910s and 1920s; but such a juxtaposition would be unthinkable in the MoMA history, for it evokes different affinities from those contributing to the category of great art. The black body in Paris of the twenties was an ideological artifact. Archaic Africa (which came to Paris by way of the future—that is, America) was sexed, gendered, and invested with "magic" in specific ways. Standard poses adopted by "La Bakaire," like Léger's designs and costumes, evoked a recognizable "Africanity"—the naked form emphasizing pelvis and buttocks, a segmented stylization suggesting a strangely mechanical vitality. The inclusion of so ideologically loaded a form as the body of Josephine Baker among the figures classified as art on West Fifty-third Street would suggest a different account of Modernist primitivism, a different analysis of the category *nègre* in *l'art nègre,* and an exploration of the "taste" that was something more than just a backdrop for the discovery of tribal art in the opening decades of this century.[8]

Such a focus would treat art as a category defined and redefined in specific historical contexts and relations of power. Seen from this angle and read somewhat against the grain, the MoMA exhibition documents a taxonomic moment: the status of non-Western objects and "high" art are importantly redefined, but there is nothing permanent or transcendent about the categories at stake. The appreciation and interpretation of tribal objects takes place within a modern "system of objects" which confers value on certain things and withholds it from others.[9] Modernist primitivism, with its claims to deeper humanist sympathies and a wider aesthetic sense, goes hand-in-hand with a developed market in tribal art and with definitions of artistic and cultural authenticity that are now widely contested.

Since 1900 non-Western objects have generally been classified as either primitive art or ethnographic specimens. Before the Modernist revolution associated with Picasso and the simultaneous rise of cultural anthropology associated with Boas and Malinowski, these objects were differently sorted—as antiquities, exotic curiosities, orientalia, the remains of early man, and so on. With the emergence of twentieth-century Modernism and anthropology figures formerly called "fetishes" (to take just one class of object) became works either of "sculpture" or of "material culture." The distinction between the aesthetic and the anthropological was soon institutionally reinforced. In art galleries non-Western objects were displayed for their formal and aesthetic qualities; in ethnographic museums they were represented in a "cultural" context. In the latter an African statue was a ritual object belonging to a distinct group; it was displayed in ways that elucidated its use, symbolism, and function. The institutionalized distinction between aesthetic and anthropological discourses took form during the years documented at MoMA, years that saw the complementary discovery of primitive "art" and of an anthropological concept of "culture" (Williams 1966).[10] Though there was from the start (and continues to be) a regular traffic between the two domains, this distinction is unchallenged in the exhibition. At MoMA treating tribal objects as art means excluding the original cultural context. Consideration of context, we are firmly told at the exhibition's entrance, is the business of anthropologists. Cultural background is not essential to correct aesthetic appreciation and analysis: good art, the masterpiece, is universally recognizable.[11] The pioneer Modernists themselves knew little or nothing of these objects' ethnographic meaning. What was good enough for Picasso is good enough for MoMA. Indeed an ignorance of cultural context seems almost a precondition for artistic appreciation. In this object system a tribal piece is detached from one milieu in order to circulate freely in another, a world of art—of museums, markets, and connoisseurship.

Since the early years of Modernism and cultural anthropology non-Western objects have found a "home" either within the discourses and institutions of art or within those of anthropology. The two domains have excluded and confirmed each other, inventively disputing the right to contextualize, to represent these objects. As we shall see, the aesthetic-anthropological opposition is systematic, presupposing an underlying set of attitudes toward the "tribal." Both discourses assume a primitive world in need of preservation, redemption, and representation. The concrete, inventive existence of tribal cultures and artists is suppressed in the process of either constituting authentic, "traditional" worlds or appreciating their products in the timeless category of "art."

Nothing on West Fifty-third Street suggests that good tribal art is being produced in the 1980s. The non-Western artifacts on display are located either in a vague past (reminiscent of the label "nineteenth–twentieth century" that accompanies African and Oceanian pieces in the Metropolitan Museum's Rockefeller Wing) or in a purely conceptual space defined by "primitive" qualities: magic, ritualism, closeness to nature, mythic or cosmological aims (see Rubin 1984: 10, 661-689). In this relegation of the tribal or primitive to either a vanishing past or an ahistorical, conceptual present, Modernist appreciation reproduces common ethnographic categories.

The same structure can be seen in the Hall of Pacific Peoples, dedicated to Margaret Mead, at the American Museum of Natural History. This new permanent hall is a superbly refurbished anthropological stopping place for non-Western objects. In *Rotunda* (December 1984), the museum's publication, an article announcing the installation contains the following paragraph:

> Margaret Mead once referred to the cultures of Pacific peoples as "a world that once was and now is no more." Prior to her death in 1978 she approved the basic plans for the new Hall of Pacific Peoples. (p. 1)

We are offered treasures saved from a destructive history, relics of a vanishing world. Visitors to the installation (and especially members of *present* Pacific cultures) may find a "world that is no more" more appropriately evoked in two charming display cases just outside the hall. It is the world of a dated anthropology. Here one finds a neatly typed page of notes from Mead's much-disputed Samoan research, a picture of the fieldworker interacting "closely" with Melanesians (she is carrying a child on her back), a box of brightly colored discs and triangles once used for psychological testing, a copy of Mead's column in *Redbook*. In the Hall of Pacific Peoples artifacts suggesting change and syncretism are set apart in a small display entitled "Culture Contact." It is noted that Western influence and indigenous response have been active in the Pacific since the eighteenth century. Yet few signs of this involvement appear anywhere else in the large hall, despite the fact that many of the objects were made in the past 150 years in situations of contact, and despite the fact that the museum's ethnographic explanations reflect quite recent research on the cultures of the Pacific. The historical contacts and impurities that are part of ethnographic work—and that may signal the life, not the death, of societies—are systematically excluded.

The tenses of the hall's explanatory captions are revealing. A recent color photograph of a Samoan *kava* ceremony is accompanied by the words: "STATUS and RANK were [sic] important features of Samoan society," a statement that will seem strange to anyone who knows how important they remain in Samoa today. Elsewhere in the hall a black-and-white photograph of an Australian Arunta woman and child, taken around 1900 by the pioneer ethnographers Spencer and Gillen, is captioned in the *present* tense. Aboriginals apparently must always inhabit a mythic time. Many other examples of temporal incoherence could be cited—old Sepik objects described in the present, recent Trobriand photos labeled in the past, and so forth.

The point is not simply that the image of Samoan *kava* drinking and status society presented here is a distortion or that in most of the Hall of Pacific Peoples history has been airbrushed out. (No Samoan men at the *kava* ceremony are wearing wristwatches; Trobriand face-painting is shown without noting that it is worn at cricket matches.) Beyond such questions of accuracy is an issue of systematic ideological coding. To locate "tribal" peoples in a nonhistorical time and ourselves in a different, historical time is clearly tendentious and no longer credible (Fabian 1983). This recognition throws doubt on the perception of a vanishing tribal world, rescued, made valuable and meaningful, either as ethnographic "culture" or as primitive/modern "art." For in this temporal ordering the real or genuine life of tribal works always precedes their collection, an act of salvage that repeats an all-too-familiar story of death and redemption. In this pervasive allegory the non-Western world is always vanishing and modernizing—as in Walter Benjamin's allegory of modernity, the tribal world is conceived as a ruin.[12] At the Hall of Pacific Peoples or the Rockefeller Wing the actual ongoing life and "impure" inventions of tribal peoples are erased in the name of cultural or artistic "authenticity." Similarly at MoMA the production of tribal "art" is entirely in the past. Turning up in the flea markets and museums of late nineteenth-century Europe, these objects are destined to be aesthetically redeemed, given new value in the object system of a generous Modernism.

The story retold at MoMA, the struggle to gain recognition for tribal art, for its capacity "like all great art...to show images of man that transcend the particular lives and times of their creators" (Rubin 1984: 73), is taken for granted at another stopping place for tribal travelers in Manhattan, the Center for African Art on East Sixty-eighth Street. Susan Vogel, the executive director, proclaims in her introduction to the catalogue of its inaugural exhibition, *African Masterpieces from the Musée de l'Homme,* that the "aesthetic-anthropological debate" has been resolved. It is now widely accepted that "ethnographic specimens" can be distinguished from

Interior of
Chief Shake's House,
Wrangel, Alaska, 1909.

"works of art" and that within the latter category a limited number of "masterpieces" are to be found. Vogel correctly notes that the aesthetic recognition of tribal objects depends on changes in Western taste. For example it took the work of Francis Bacon, Lucas Samaras, and others to make it possible to exhibit as art "rough and horrifying [African] works as well as refined and lyrical ones."[13] Once recognized, though, art is apparently art. Thus the selection at the Center is made on aesthetic criteria alone. A prominent placard affirms that the ability of these objects "to transcend the limitations of time and place, to speak to us across time and culture...places them among the highest points of human achievement. It is as works of art that we regard them here and as a testament to the greatness of their creators."

There could be no clearer statement of one side of the aesthetic anthropological "debate" (or better, *system*). On the other (anthropological) side, across town, the Hall of Pacific Peoples presents collective rather than individual productions—the work of "cultures." But within an institutionalized polarity interpenetration of discourses becomes possible. Science can be aestheticized, art made anthropological. At the American Museum of Natural History ethnographic exhibits have come increasingly to resemble art shows. Indeed the Hall of Pacific Peoples represents the latest in aestheticized scientism. Objects are displayed in ways that highlight their formal properties. They are suspended in light, held in space by the ingenious use of Plexiglas. (One is suddenly astonished by the sheer weirdness of a small Oceanic figurine perched atop a three-foot-tall transparent rod.) While these artistically displayed artifacts are scientifically explained, an older, functionalist attempt to present an integrated picture of specific societies or culture areas is no longer seriously pursued. There is an almost dadaist quality to the labels on eight cases devoted to Australian aboriginal society (I cite the complete series in order): "CEREMONY, SPIRIT FIGURE, MAGICIANS AND SORCERERS, SACRED ART, SPEAR THROWERS, STONE AXES AND KNIVES, WOMEN, BOOMERANGS." Elsewhere the hall's pieces of culture have been recontextualized within a new cybernetic, anthropological discourse. For instance flutes and stringed instruments are captioned: "MUSIC is a system of organized sound in man's [sic] aural environment" or nearby: "COMMUNICATION is an important function of organized sound."

In the anthropological Hall of Pacific Peoples non-Western objects still have primarily scientific value. They are in addition beautiful.[14] Conversely, at the Center for African Art artifacts are essentially defined as "masterpieces," their makers as great artists. The discourse of connoisseurship reigns. Yet once the story of art told at MoMA becomes dogma, it is possible to reintroduce and co-opt the discourse of ethnography. At the Center tribal contexts and functions are described along with individual histories of the objects on display. Now firmly classified as masterpieces, African objects escape the vague, ahistorical location of the "tribal" or the "primitive." The catalogue, a sort of *catalogue raisonné*, discusses each work intensively. The category of the masterpiece individuates: the pieces on display are not typical; some are one of a kind. The famous Fon god of war or the Abomey shark-man lend themselves to precise histories of individual creation and appropriation in visible colonial situations. Captions specify *which* Griaule expedition to West Africa in the 1930s acquired each Dogon statue.[15] We learn in the catalogue that a superb Bamileke mother and child was carved by an artist named Kwayep, that the statue was bought by the colonial administrator and anthropologist Henri Labouret from King N'Jike. While tribal names predominate at MoMA, the Rockefeller Wing, and the American Museum of Natural History, here personal names make their appearance.

In the "African Masterpieces" catalogue we learn of an ethnographer's excitement on finding a Dogon hermaphrodite figure that would later become famous. The letter recording this excitement, written by Denise Paulme in 1935, serves as evidence of the aesthetic concerns of many early ethnographic collectors.[16] These individuals, we are told, could intuitively distinguish masterpieces from mere art or ethnographic specimens. (Actually many of the individual ethnographers behind the Musée de l'Homme collection, such as Paulme, Michel Leiris, Marcel Griaule, and André Schaeffner, were friends and collaborators of the same "pioneer Modernist" artists who, in the story told at MoMA, constructed the category of primitive art. Thus the intuitive aesthetic sense in question is the product of a historically specific milieu.[17] The "African Masterpieces" catalogue insists that the founders of the Musée de l'Homme were art connoisseurs, that this great anthropological museum never treated all its contents as "ethnographic specimens." The Musée de l'Homme was and is secretly an art museum.[18] The taxonomic split between art and artifact is thus healed, at least for self-evident "masterpieces," entirely in terms of the aesthetic code. Art is art in any museum.

The Earth Deity, Ala, with her "children" in her mbari house. Obube Ulakwo, southeast Nigeria, 1966.

In this exhibition, as opposed to the others in New York, information can be provided about each individual masterpiece's history. We learn that a Kiwarani antelope mask studded with mirrors was acquired at a dance given for the colonial administration in Mali on Bastille Day, 1931. A rabbit mask was purchased from Dogon dancers at a gala soirée in Paris during the Colonial Exhibition of the same year. These are no longer the dateless "authentic" tribal forms seen at MoMA. At the Center for African Art a different history documents both the artwork's uniqueness and the achievement of the discerning collector. By featuring rarity, genius, and connoisseurship the Center confirms the existence of autonomous artworks able to circulate, to be bought and sold, in the same way as works by Picasso or Giacometti. The Center traces its lineage, appropriately, to the former Rockefeller Museum of Primitive Art, with its close ties to collectors and the art market.

In its inaugural exhibition the Center confirms the predominant aesthetic-ethnographic view of tribal art as something located in the past, good for being collected and given aesthetic value. Its second show (March 12-June 16, 1985) is devoted to *Igbo Arts: Community and Cosmos*. It tells another story, locating art forms, ritual life, and cosmology in a specific, changing African society—a past *and* present heritage. Photographs show "traditional" masks worn in danced masquerades around 1983. (These include satiric figures of white colonists.) A detailed history of cultural change, struggle, and revival is provided. In the catalogue Chike C. Aniakor, an Igbo scholar, writes along with co-editor Herbert M. Cole of "the continually evolving Igbo aesthetic":

It is illusory to think that which we comfortably label "traditional" art was in an earlier time immune to changes in style and form; it is thus unproductive to lament changes that reflect current realities. Continuity with earlier forms will always be found; the present-day persistence of family and community values ensures that the arts will thrive. And as always, the Igbo will create new art forms out of their inventive spirit, reflecting their dynamic interactions with the environment and their neighbors and expressing cultural ideals.[19]

Cole and Aniakor provide a quite different history of "the tribal" and "the modern" from that told at the Museum of Modern Art—a story of invention, not of redemption. In his foreword to the catalogue Chinua Achebe offers a vision of culture and of objects that sharply challenges the ideology of the art collection and the masterpiece. Igbo, he tells us, do not like collections.

The purposeful neglect of the painstakingly and devoutly accomplished *mbari* houses with all the art objects in them as soon as the primary mandate of their creation has been served, provides a significant insight into the Igbo aesthetic value as *process* rather than *product*. Process is motion while product is rest. When the product is preserved or venerated, the impulse to repeat the process is compromised. Therefore the Igbo choose to eliminate the product and retain the process so that every occasion and every generation will receive its own impulse and experience of creation. Interestingly this aesthetic disposition receives powerful endorsement from the tropical climate which provides an abundance of materials for making art, such as wood, as well as formidable agencies of dissolution, such as humidity and the termite. Visitors to Igboland are shocked to see that artifacts are rarely accorded any particular value on the basis of age alone.[20]

Achebe's image of a "ruin" suggests not the Modernist allegory of redemption (a yearning to make things whole, to think archaeologically) but an acceptance of endless seriality, a desire to keep things apart, dynamic, and historical.

The aesthetic-anthropological object systems of the West are currently under challenge, and the politics of collecting and exhibiting occasionally become visible.

Even at MoMA evidence of living tribal peoples has not been entirely excluded. One small text breaks the spell. A special label explains the absence of a Zuni war god figure currently housed in the Berlin Museum für Völkerunde. We learn that late in its preparations for the show MoMA "was informed by knowledgeable authorities that Zuni people consider any public exhibition of their war gods to be sacrilegious." Thus, the label continues, although such figures are routinely displayed elsewhere, the museum decided not to bring the war god (an influence on Paul Klee) from Berlin. The terse note raises more questions than it answers, but it does at least establish that the objects on display may in fact "belong" somewhere other than in an art or an ethnographic museum. Living traditions have claims on them, contesting (with a distant but increasingly palpable power) their present home in the institutional systems of the modern West.[21]

Elsewhere in New York this power has been made even more visible. *Te Maori*, a show visiting the Metropolitan, clearly establishes that the "art" on display is still sacred, on loan not merely from certain New Zealand museums but also from the Maori people. Indeed tribal art is political through and through. The Maori have allowed their tradition to be exploited as "art" by major Western cultural institutions and their corporate sponsors in order to enhance their own international prestige and thus contribute to their current resurgence in New Zealand society.[22] Tribal authorities gave permission for the exhibition to travel, and they participated in its opening ceremonies in a visible, distinctive manner. So did Asante leaders at the exhibition of their art and culture at the Museum of Natural History (October 16, 1984-March 17, 1985). Although the Asante display centers on eighteenth and nineteenth-century artifacts, evidence of the twentieth-century colonial suppression and recent renewal of Asante culture is included, along with color photos of modern ceremonies and newly made "traditional" objects brought to New York as gifts for the museum. In this exhibition the *location* of the art on display—the sense of where, to whom, and in what time(s) it belongs—is quite different from the location of the African objects at MoMA or in the Rockefeller Wing. The tribal is fully historical.

Still another representation of tribal life and art can be encountered at the Northwest Coast collection at the IBM Gallery (October 10-December 29, 1984), whose objects have traveled downtown from the Museum of the American Indian. They are displayed in pools of intense light (the beautifying "boutique" decor that seems to be Modernism's gift to museum displays, both ethnographic and artistic). But this exhibition of traditional masterpieces ends with works by living Northwest Coast artists. Outside the gallery in the IBM atrium two large totem poles have been installed. One is a weathered specimen from the Museum of the American Indian, and the other has been carved for the show by the Kwakiutl Calvin Hunt. The artist put the finishing touches on his creation where it stands in the atrium; fresh wood chips are left scattered around the base. Nothing like this is possible or even thinkable at West Fifty-third Street.

The organizers of the MoMA exhibition have been clear about its limitations, and they have repeatedly specified what they do not claim to show. It is thus in a sense unfair to ask why they did not construct a differently focused history of relations between "the tribal" and "the modern." Yet the exclusions built into any collection or narration are legitimate objects of critique, and the insistent, didactic tone of the MoMA show only makes its focus more debatable. If the non-Western objects on West Fifty-third Street never really question but continually confirm established aesthetic values, this raises questions about "Modernist primitivism's" purportedly revolutionary potential. The absence of any examples of Third World Modernism or of recent tribal work reflects a pervasive "self-evident" allegory of redemption.

The final room of the MoMA exhibition, "Contemporary Explorations," which might have been used to refocus the historical story of Modernism and the tribal, instead strains to find contemporary Western artists whose work has a "primitive feel."[23] Diverse criteria are asserted: a use of rough or "natural" materials, a ritualistic attitude, ecological concern, archaeological inspiration, certain techniques of assemblage, a conception of the artist as shaman, or some familiarity with "the mind of primitive man in his [sic] science and mythology"

New Guinea girl with photographer's flash bulbs.

(derived perhaps from reading Lévi-Strauss). Such criteria, added to all the other "primitivist" qualities invoked in the exhibition and its catalogue, unravel for good the category of the primitive, exposing it as an incoherent cluster of qualities that at different times have been used to construct a source, origin, or alter ego confirming some new "discovery" within the territory of the Western self. The exhibition is at best a historical account of a certain moment in this relentless process. By the end the feeling created is one of claustrophobia.

The non-Western objects that excited Picasso, Derain, and Léger broke into the realm of official Western art from outside. They were quickly integrated, recognized as masterpieces, given homes within an anthropological-aesthetic object system. By now this process has been sufficiently celebrated. We need exhibitions that question the boundaries of art and of the art world, an influx of truly indigestible "outside" artifacts. The relations of power whereby one portion of humanity can select, value, and collect the pure products of others need to be criticized and transformed. This is no small task. In the meantime one can at least imagine shows that feature the impure, "inauthentic" productions of past and present tribal life; exhibitions radically heterogeneous in their global mix of styles; exhibitions that locate themselves in specific multicultural junctures; exhibitions in which nature remains "unnatural"; exhibitions whose principles of incorporation are openly questionable. The following would be my contribution to a different show on "affinities of the tribal and the postmodern." I offer just the first paragraph from Barbara Tedlock's superb description of the Zuni Shalako ceremony, a festival that is only part of a complex, living tradition[24]:

> Imagine a small western New Mexican village, its snow-lit streets
> lined with white Mercedes, quarter-ton pickups and Dodge vans.
> Villagers wrapped in black blankets and flowered shawls are

standing next to visitors in blue velveteen blouses with rows of dime buttons and voluminous satin skirts. Their men are in black Stetson silver-banded hats, pressed jeans, Tony Lama boots and multicolored Pendleton blankets. Strangers dressed in dayglo orange, pink and green ski jackets, stocking caps, hiking boots and mittens. All crowded together they are looking into newly constructed houses illuminated by bare light bulbs dangling from raw rafters edged with Woolworth's red fabric and flowered blue print calico. Cinderblock and plasterboard white walls are layered with striped serapes, Chimayó blankets, Navajo rugs, flowered fringed embroidered shawls, black silk from Mexico and purple, red and blue rayon from Czechoslovakia. Rows of Hopi cotton dance kilts and rain sashes; Isleta woven red and green belts; Navajo and Zuni silver concha belts and black mantas covered with silver brooches set with carved lapidary, rainbow mosaic, channel inlay, turquoise needlepoint, pink agate, alabaster, black cannel coal and bakelite from old '78s, coral, abalone shell, mother-of-pearl and horned oyster hang from poles suspended from the ceiling. Mule and white-tailed deer trophy-heads wearing squash-blossom, coral and chunk-turquoise necklaces are hammered up around the room over rearing buckskins above Arabian tapestries of Martin Luther King and the Kennedy brothers. The Last Supper, a herd of sheep with a haloed herder, horses, peacocks.

1. Parenthetical references are cited in the Bibliography.

2. The term *tribal* is used here with considerable reluctance. It denotes a kind of society (and art) that cannot be coherently specified. A catchall, the concept of the tribe has its source in Western projection and administrative necessity rather than in any essential quality or group of traits. The term is now commonly used instead of *primitive* in phrases such as *tribal art*. The category thus denoted, as this essay argues, is a product of historically limited Western taxonomies. While the term was originally an imposition, however, certain non-Western groups have embraced it. Tribal status is in many cases a crucial strategic ground for identity. In this essay my use of *tribe* and *tribal* reflects common usage while suggesting ways in which the concept is systematically distorting. See Morton Fried, *The Notion of Tribe* (Menlo Park, CA: Cummings, 1975), and William Sturtevant, "Tribe and State in the Sixteenth and Twentieth Centuries," in *The Development of Political Organizations in Native North America*, ed. Elizabeth Tooker (Washington, DC: The American Ethnological Society, 1983), pp. 3-15.

3. These points were made by William Sturtevant at the symposium of anthropologists and art historians held at the Museum of Modern Art in New York on November 3, 1984.

4. A more rigorous formulation than that of affinity is suggested by Michel Leiris in "The African Negroes and the Arts of Carving and Sculpture," in *Interrelations of Cultures* (Westport, CT: UNESCO, 1953), pp. 316-351. How, Leiris asks, can we speak of African sculpture as a single category? He warns of "a danger that we may underestimate the variety of African sculpture; as we are less able to appreciate the respects in which cultures or things unfamiliar to us differ from one another than the respects in which they differ from those to which we are used, we tend to see a certain resemblance between them, which lies, in point of fact, merely in their common differentness" (p.35). Thus, to speak of African sculpture one inevitably shuts one's eyes "to the rich diversity actually to be found in this sculpture in order to concentrate on the respects in which it is *not* what our own sculpture generally is." The affinity of the tribal and modern is, in this logic, an important optical illusion–the measure of a *common differentness* from artistic modes that dominated in the West from the Renaissance to the late nineteenth century.

5. See, for example, Rubin's discussion of the mythic universals shared by a Picasso painting and a Northwest Coast half-mask (Rubin 1984: 328330). See also Kirk Varnedoe's association of modernist primitivism with rational, scientific exploration (Rubin 1984: 201-203, 652-653).

6. This point was made by Clifford Geertz at the November 3, 1984, symposium at the Museum of Modern Art (see n. 2).

7. The clash between Krauss's and Varnedoe's dark and light versions of primitivism is the most striking incongruity within the catalogue. For Krauss the crucial task is to shatter predominant European forms of power and subjectivity; for Varnedoe the task is to expand their purview, to question, and to innovate.

8. On *négrophilie* see Jean Laude, *La peintre français* (1905-1914) et "l'art negre" (Paris: Editions Klincksieck, 1968); for parallel trends in literature see Jean-Claude Blachere, *Le modele nègre: Aspects littéraires du mythe primitiviste au XXe siècle chez Apollinaire, Cendrars, Tsara* (Dakar: Nouvelles Editions Africaines, 1981), and Gail Levin, "'Primitivism' in American Art: Some Literary Parallels of the l910s and 1920s." *Arts* (November 1984): 101-105. The discovery of things "negre" by the European avant-garde was mediated by an imaginary America, a land of noble savages simultaneously standing for the past and future of humanity--a perfect affinity of primitive and modern. For example, jazz was, associated with primal sources (wild, erotic passions) and with technology (the mechanical rhythm of brushed drums, the gleaming saxophone). Le Corbusier's reaction was characteristic: "In a stupid variety show, Josephine Baker sang 'Baby' with such an intense and dramatic sensibility that I was moved to tears. There is in this American Negro music a lyrical 'contemporary' mass so invincible that I could see the foundation of a new sentiment of music capable of being the expression of the new epoch and also capable of classifying its European origins as stone age--just as has happened with the new architecture (quoted in Charles Jencks, *Le Corbusier and the Tragic View of Architecture* [London: Penguin, 1973], p. 102) . As a source of modernist inspiration for Le Corbusier, the figure of Josephine Baker was matched by monumental, almost Egyptian, concrete grain elevators, rising from the American plains and built by nameless "primitive" engineers (Reyner Banham, *A Concrete Atlantis: US Industrial Building and European Modern Architecture* [Cambridge: MIT Press, 1986], p. 16) . The historical narrative implicit here has been a feature of twentieth-century literary and artistic innovation, as a redemptive modernism persistently "discovers" the primitive that can justify its own sense of emergence.

9. Jean Baudrillard, *Le système dea objects* (Paris: Gallimard, 1968).

10. The twentieth-century developments traced here redeploy these ideas in an intercultural domain while preserving their older ethical and political charge (see Clifford 1988: 230-236).

11. On the recognition of masterpieces see Rubin's confident claims (1984: 20-21) He is given to statements such as the following on tribal and modern art: "The solutions of genius in the plastic arts are all essentially instinctual" (p. 78, no. 80). A stubborn rejection of the supposed views of anthropologists (who believe in the collective production of works of tribal art) characterizes Rubins' attempts to clear out an autonomous space for aesthetic judgment. Suggestions that he may be projecting Western aesthetic categories onto traditions with different definitions of art are made to seem simplistic (for example p. 28).

12. Walter Benjamin, *The Origins of German Tragic Drama* (London: New Left Books, 1977).

13. Susan Vogel, "Introduction," in *African Masterpieces from the Musée de l'Homme*, eds., S. Vogel and Francine N'Diaye (New York: Abrams, 1985), p. 11.

14. At the November 3, 1984 symposium (see no. 3) Christian Feest pointed out that the tendency to reclassify objects in ethnographic collections as "art" is in part a response to the much greater amount of funding available for art (rather than anthropological) exhibitions.

15. See Michel Leiris, *L'Afrique fantôme* (1934), reprint (Paris: Gallimard, 1950), and Clifford 1988: 55-91.

16. Vogel and N'Diaye, eds., *African Masterpieces from the Musée de l'Homme*, p. 122.

17. Clifford 1988: 117-151.

18. Vogel, *African Masterpieces from the Musée de l'Homme.* p. 11.

19. Herbert Cole, and Chike Aniakor, eds., *Igbo Arts: Community and Cosmos* (Los Angeles: Museum of Cultural History, UCLA, 1984), p. 14.

20. Chinua Achebe, "Foreword," in ibid, pp. vii-xi.

21. The shifting balance of power is evident in the case of the Zuni war gods, or Ahauuta. Zuni vehemently object to the display of these figures (terrifying and of great sacred force) as "art." They are the only traditional objects singled out for this objection. After passage of the Native American Freedom of Religion Act of 1978 Zuni initiated three formal legal actions claiming return of the Ahauuta (which as communal property are, in Zuni eyes, by definition stolen goods). A sale at Sotheby Parke-Bernet in 1978 was interrupted, and the figure was eventually returned to the Zuni. The Denver Art Museum was forced to repatriate its Ahauutas in 1981. A claim against the Smithsonian remains unresolved as of this writing. Other pressures have been applied elsewhere in an ongoing campaign. In these new conditions Zuni Ahauuta can no longer be routinely displayed. Indeed the figure Paul Klee saw in Berlin would have run the risk of being seized as contraband had it been shipped to New York for the MoMA show. For general background see Steven Talbot, "Desecration and American Indian Religious Freedom," *Journal of Ethnic Studies* 12, no. 4 (1985): 1-18.

22. Sidney Moka Mead, ed., *Te Maori: Maori Art from New Zealand Collections* (New York: Harry Abrams, 1984). An article on corporate funding of the arts in the *New York Times*, February 5, 1985, p. 27, reported that Mobil Oil sponsored the Maori show in large part to please the New Zealand government, with which it was collaborating on the construction of a natural gas conversion plant.

23. In places the search becomes self-parodic, as in the caption for the works by Jackie Winsor: "Winsor's work has a primitivist feel, not only in the raw physical presence of her materials, but also in the way she fabricates. Her labor—driving nails, binding twine—moves beyond simple systematic repetition to take on the expressive character of ritualized action."

24. Barbara Tedlock, "The Beautiful and the Dangerous: Zuni Ritual and Cosmology as an Aesthetic System," *Conjunctions* 6 (1984): 246-265.

REPRINTED FROM JAMES CLIFFORD, *THE PREDICAMENT OF CULTURE: TWENTIETH-CENTURY ETHNOGRAPHY, LITERATURE, AND ART* (CAMBRIDGE: HARVARD UNIVERSITY PRESS, 1988), PP. 189–214.

ROLAND BARTHES
Bernard-Henri Lévy

BERNARD-HENRI LÉVY: Roland Barthes, you are scarcely seen and rarely heard. Outside of your books, more or less nothing is known about you.

ROLAND BARTHES: Even if this were true, it would be because I don't like interviews very much. I feel myself caught between two dangers: either that of holding forth points of view in an impersonal way thus allowing people to believe that one is a "thinker"; or that of always saying "I" which then allows one to be accused of egoism.

LÉVY: You speak about you, however, in *Roland Barthes by Roland Barthes*. But while you are expansive on your childhood and adolescence you remain strangely silent on the rest, the Barthes of maturity who had arrived at *"écriture"* and notoriety....

BARTHES: It's that, like everyone I think, I remember my childhood and my adolescence very well. I know its dates and am familiar with its landmarks. And afterwards this contrary and curious thing happens: I don't remember anymore, I can't manage to date anymore, to date myself. As if I only had a memory of the origin, as if adolescence constituted the exemplary and unique time of memory. Yes, that is it: with adolescence gone, I see my life as an immense present which is impossible to break up, to put into perspective.

LÉVY: Which means that you literally have no "biography"....

BARTHES: I have no biography. Or, more exactly, starting from the first line which I wrote, I don't see myself anymore, I am no longer an image for myself. I don't manage to imagine myself anymore, to fix myself in images.

LÉVY: Hence the absence, in *Roland Barthes by Roland Barthes*, of photographs of you as an adult?

BARTHES: Not only, in a manner of speaking, are there not any, but I scarcely possess any myself. The book you speak of is in any case divided by an inflexible line. I say nothing about my youth; I have placed this youth in photographs because this is the appropriate age, the time of memory, of images. And in the following part, on the contrary, I say no more images, because I no longer have any, and everything passes through the writing.

LÉVY: This break is also that of illness. They are in any case contemporaneous.

BARTHES: You shouldn't say "illness" in my case, you should say "tuberculosis." Because at that time, before chemotherapy, tuberculosis was a real way of life, a mode of existence, I would almost say a choice. One could even imagine, in an extreme case, a conversion to this life a little like Hans Castorp, you know, in *The Magic Mountain* of Thomas Mann... A man with tuberculosis who could quite seriously envisage, and I have done myself, the idea of a whole life spent at the sanatorium or in a parasanatorial profession.

LÉVY: A life outside of time? Substracted from the hazards of life?

BARTHES: Let's say anyway a type of life which is not without a relationship to the monastic idea. The taste of a regulated life, of strict regularity in the daily programs as in a monastery. A troubling phenomenon which pursues me even today and on which I intend to work again this year in my course at the Collège.

LÉVY: Illness is always spoken of as something which mutilates, shackles or amputates; rarely in terms of what it brings positively, even to the practice of writing....

BARTHES: Indeed. In my case, it wasn't very difficult for me to endure those five or six years outside of the world: no doubt I had a personal leaning towards "interiority," to the solitary activity of reading. What did they bring me? A kind of culture, no doubt. The experience of a "lived togetherness" which was characterized by an intense excitement of friendships, the assurance of always having one's friends at one's side, and never being separated from them. And also, much later, the strange feeling of perpetually being five or six years younger than I am in reality.

LÉVY: Did you write?

BARTHES: Well I read an enormous amount, since after all it was during my second stay at the sanatorium that I read the works of Michelet for example. To make up for that I wrote little. A total of two articles, one on Gide's *Journal* and the other on Camus' *The Outsider* which was the germ of *Writing Degree Zero*.

LÉVY: Did you know Gide?

BARTHES: No, I didn't know him. I picked him out once, far away, in the *Lutétia* café: he was reading a book and eating a pear. No, I didn't know him; but, as for many young people of the time, there were a million reasons why I should have been interested in him.

LÉVY: For example?

BARTHES: He was a Protestant. He played the piano. He spoke about desire. He wrote.

LÉVY: What does it mean, for you, to be Protestant?

BARTHES: It's hard to reply. Because, when one is empty of faith, there only remains the imprint, the image. And the image is what the others have. It is for them to say if I have the Protestant "look."

LÉVY: I mean in your apprenticeship, what did you get out of this particular thing?

BARTHES: I could say that strictly speaking, and with the greatest prudence, that a Protestant adolescence can give a certain taste for, or perverse inclination for, interiority, for an interior language, that which the subject holds constantly to itself. And then, to be Protestant, don't forget, is to have not the slightest idea what a priest is, or the liturgy.... But that must be left to the sociologists of character, that is if French Protestantism still interests them.

LÉVY: You are frequently called "hedonist." Is this due to a misunderstanding?

BARTHES: Hedonism is "bad." Unrespectable. Misunderstood. It is amazing how this can be pejorative! No one, no one in the world, no philosophy, no doctrine dares to take it on board. It is an "obscene" word.

LÉVY: But do you accept it?

BARTHES: Perhaps it would be better to find a new word. Because, if hedonism is a philosophy, then the texts which are base for it are exceptionally fragile. There are no texts. Scarcely a tradition. So it is very difficult to locate oneself when the texts are so inconsistent and the tradition so slight.

LÉVY: There is still epicurism.

BARTHES: Yes, but it's been censored for a long time.

LÉVY: You have a "morale," I suppose.

BARTHES: Let's say a morale of the affective relation. But there is so much I would have say about it that I have nothing to say about it. As the Chinese proverb says "The most obscure spot is always the one underneath the lamp."

LÉVY: One thing you say nothing about: sexuality.

BARTHES: I speak, rather, of sensuality.

LÉVY: In fact, you speak sometimes about sexuality but to minimize its importance; for instance, this sentence taken from one of your books: "A formative problem for me was more that of money than sex...."

BARTHES: What I wanted to say there was that I have never really suffered from prohibition, although it did weigh much heavier forty years ago than it did today. I admit frankly that sometimes I am astonished by the indignation of certain people against the ascendancy of normality. I don't deny this ascendancy of course, but there are interstices.

LÉVY: By what miracle did you escape?

BARTHES: I didn't escape. Simply, I have always had in myself the primacy of the state of being in love. And the consequence of this was the notion of the "prohibited," of what is prohibited, was always substituted for that of the "refused," of what is refused. What made me suffer was not to be prohibited, but to be refused, which is completely different.

LÉVY: Let's stay with this "sensuality." You speak of literature, of music or of opera, of a meal, a voyage or a language with an equal delight, as if they were equal pleasures.

BARTHES: Not always. Music and opera, for instance, are nonetheless very different. I like listening to music and I listen to a lot of it. But the real investment, for me, is to make it: once it was singing, now it is working things out on the piano. The opera is something else again. It is, shall we say, a celebration, a celebration of the voice: I am sensitive to it, but I'm not a fanatic about it.

LÉVY: Is it also a "total spectacle?"

BARTHES: Yes. But I must say that it is not along these lines that I'm personally a consumer. Without doubt there are two types of opera lovers: either one loves opera beginning with the music, or beginning with the opera itself, and I am one of the former. There are two moments for me in which I savor it and these moments are distinct: firstly the immediate surprise of the mise-en-scène which makes a kind of voyeur of me; and then, the interiorized pleasure of the voice and the music: it is there, on this second occasion alone, that I can close my eyes and complete my pleasure in the music.

LÉVY: At the bottom of this you seem to be saying at the same time that opera is not music and that it is the music in fact which you enjoy at the opera?

BARTHES: Yes, and that is even the reason why I don't believe myself to be a lover of the opera... This summer, for instance, I went to Bayreuth for the first time and I spent eight days there. It was fantastic, but during these eight days I was bored with music because there weren't any concerts outside of the opera.

LÉVY: Do you like traveling, independently of any particular attraction?

BARTHES: Once I did a lot, now less so. There was a time when if I had a few days and a few bucks I left. Towards elected countries which varied according to the years. I liked Holland, then Italy, afterwards it was Morocco. Recently, Japan.

LÉVY: The whim also, I imagine, of whatever you found there....

BARTHES: No doubt. But I never had a passion for monuments, the traces and witnesses of culture, except for painting in Holland. When I travel, what interests me the most are those fragments of the art of living which I can grasp as I pass. The sensation of falling into an easy and opaque world (for the tourist, everything is easy). Not slumming, but the voluptuous immersion in a language, for example, in which I can only perceive the sounds. Not understanding a language is an enormously relaxing thing. That eliminates any vulgarity, any stupidity, any aggression.

LÉVY: In the end, you conceive of travels in the manner of an inspired and displaced ethnography....

BARTHES: In a way. A city like Tokyo, for example, is by itself an enormous ethnographic project. I went there with the passion of the ethnographer.

LÉVY: This attitude becomes transformed, I suppose, in human relationships?

BARTHES: I will reply clearly: traveling is also an adventure for me, a series of possible adventures, and of adventures of a great intensity. It is obviously linked to a kind of lover's alert.

LÉVY: There is a trip about which...which you don't speak about, and yet one of the more recent....

BARTHES: Yes, I know, China. I spent three weeks there. In an organized manner, as always, and according to the classical pattern. Even if we had slightly special sidetracks.

LÉVY: And on your return you wrote almost nothing. Why?

BARTHES: I wrote little but I looked and listened with the greatest attention and the greatest intensity. Once that's done writing becomes another thing; some sort of salt needs to be added to the listening and looking and I didn't find it.

LÉVY: Still, China doesn't lack in "signs."

BARTHES: It's true, of course. But your joke is not useless: it points out that signs only carry me away if they seduce or annoy me. They never carry me away by themselves, I must have the desire to read them. I don't practice hermeneutics.

LÉVY: All told, you could only bring back from Peking an article on the "neuter"....

BARTHES: In fact, I couldn't find any possibilities over there for investment of the erotic, sensual or romantic orders. For contingent reasons, I agree. And structural perhaps: I am mostly thinking of the moralism of the government.

LÉVY: You speak of "fragments of the art of living," the art of living is also a way of nourishing oneself, food as a cultural fact.

BARTHES: As a cultural fact, food signifies at least three things for me. First, the prestige or the taste of the maternal model, a mother's food in the way that she conceives it and makes it: this is the food which I love. Secondly, from there, I appreciate excursions, digressions towards the new, the unique: I never resist the attraction of a dish which is presented to me as new. And then thirdly, there is an aspect towards which I am particularly sensitive, it is conviviality, linked to the act of existing together, but on condition that this conviviality is very reduced: as soon as it grows to excess, the meal bores me and I don't like to eat any more, or, on the contrary, I eat a lot in order to distract myself.

LÉVY: You didn't fully answer my previous question. What do you mean exactly when you write that money, more than sex, was a formative problem of your existence?

BARTHES: Simply this: that I had a poor childhood and adolescence. That frequently we were in a situation in which we didn't have enough to eat. That it was necessary, for example, to go for three days to buy a little pâté or some potatoes in an *épicerie* of the rue de Seine. Life really took on the rhythm of the account days, when we had to pay the rent. And I had the daily spectacle of my mother who worked hard, doing bookbinding when she was not at all suited to that sort of thing. Poverty, at that time, had an existential contour which it no longer has, in France, to the same degree....

LÉVY: While at the same time you belonged to a bourgeois family, at least in its origins...

BARTHES: A bourgeois family which was impoverished and totally without money. Hence a symbolic effect which accentuated the poverty. The awareness of a material slump, even if the familiar environment could preserve an art of living—I can remember for instance that every time I had to go back to school there were minor dramas. I didn't have the right clothes. No money when the collection went around. Nothing to buy the text books. These are small incidents, you see, which leave a strong impression, and make one a spendthrift afterwards.

LÉVY: Can this be related to your aversion for the "petite-bourgeoisie," as you often say in your books?

BARTHES: It is true, I have often employed this word; I use it less now because it comes about that one becomes tired of one's own language. In any case, it's undeniable: there is in the petite-bourgeoisie a sort of ethical and/or aesthetic element which fascinates and displeases me. Could this be original? It's already in Flaubert. Who would dare admit to being petit bourgeois? Historically and politically, the petit-bourgeois is the key to the century. This is the class which is on the rise, or at any rate, it is the class which can see itself. The bourgeois and proletariat classes have become abstractions: the petite-bourgeoisie, in contrast, is everywhere, you can see it everywhere, even in the areas of the bourgeois and the proletariat, what's left of them.

LÉVY: Don't you believe in the proletariat anymore, in its historical mission, and everything that follows from this?

BARTHES: I maintain that there was an epoch in which the proletariat could see itself, but that this epoch has run its course. In France it was a time when it was run by anarcho-syndicalism and the tradition of Proudhon; but today, Marxism and ordinary trade-unionism have replaced this tradition.

LÉVY: Have you ever been a Marxist?

BARTHES: "To be a Marxist": what does the verb "to be" mean in this expression? I said it once before: I "came" to Marxism fairly late, thanks to a dear friend who has since died and was a Trotskyist. So I became involved without ever having been militant and via a dissident strand which had nothing to do with what they were already calling Stalinism. Let's say that I read Marx, Lenin, Trotsky. Not all of course, but I read some of it. And for some time now I have not reread any, except the occasional text by Marx.

LÉVY: Do you read one of Marx's texts as if it were a text by Michelet, De Sade, or Flaubert? As a pure system of signs, generating pure *jouissance?*

BARTHES: Marx could be read in this way, but not Lenin, or even Trotsky. At the same time I don't think that one can have the kind of relationship one has with a writer like Marx. One cannot remove oneself from the political effects, the ultimate inscriptions through which a text exists concretely.

LÉVY: This is the approach of people like Lardreau, Jambet or Glucksmann....

BARTHES: I know Glucksmann, we have worked together and I like what he does. As for *L'Ange,*[1] I haven't read it but people speak to me about it. You must understand, I spend a lot of time feeling very close to these positions and then separating myself by an incalculable distance. I suppose for reasons of style, not writing style, but style in general....

LÉVY: What I mean is that unlike so many others you don't have behind you a "political itinerary"....

BARTHES: It is true that, in my written discourse, there is no political discourse in the thematic sense of the word. I don't work on directly political themes or on political "positions." And that is because I don't manage to get excited over politics, and at the present time a discourse which is not excited doesn't extend very far. Quite simply, there is a decibel level to be reached, a threshold to be stepped over in order to be heard. I can't attain this threshold.

LÉVY: You seem to be sorry.

BARTHES: Politics is not only speaking, it can also be listening. And maybe we're in need of a practice of political listening.

LÉVY: In the end, if one had to define you, the label of "Left intellectual" would attach itself quite readily for once.

BARTHES: It would be for the Left to say if it included me among its intellectuals. I've got no objections, on condition of understanding the Left not so much as an idea but as an obstinate sensitivity. In my case an inalterable basis in anarchism, in the most etymological sense of the word.

LÉVY: A refusal of power?

BARTHES: Let's say an extreme sensitivity to its ubiquitousness—it is everywhere—and in its endurance, it is perpetual. It never gets tired, it turns, like a calendar. Power is plural. Also, I have a sense of my own personal war, which is not about power, but about powers wherever they may be. It is in this way that perhaps I am more "leftist" than "left"; what mixes everything up is that I didn't derive any "style" from leftism.

LÉVY: Do you believe that a "style" or a refusal of "style" is a sufficient basis for politics?

BARTHES: At the level of the subject, politics is founded existentially. For example, power. It is not only that which oppresses or what is oppressive, it is also that which is stifling. Wherever I am stifled it means that power is operating somewhere.

LÉVY: Today, in 1977 are you not stifled?

BARTHES: I am stifled, but not very indignant. Up until now, the sentiment of the Left was determined in relation to crystalizations which weren't programs but major themes: pre-1914 anticlericalism, between-the-wars pacifism, then the resistance, then the Algerian war.... Today, for the first time, there is more of this sort of thing: there is Giscard, who is after all a small crystalizer, and there is no "common program" which I can see mobilizing any feeling, even if it is good. This is what I see as new in the present situation: I can't see the touchstone any more.

LÉVY: So this is what made you accept Giscard's invitation to lunch?

BARTHES: Now that's another thing again. I did it through curiosity, through a taste for listening a little like a myth-hunter on the scent. And a myth-hunter, as you know, has to go everywhere.

LÉVY: What did you expect from this lunch?

BARTHES: To find out if Giscard possibly had another language than that of statesman. For that, obviously, it had to be necessary to listen to him as a private man. And I did have the impression of someone who knew how to create a second discourse on his experience, a reflexive discourse. What was interesting for me was to grasp a "loosening up" of language. As for the contents, it was obviously that of a political philosophy articulated on a quite different culture than that of a left intellectual.

LÉVY: Did he seduce you, as a person?

BARTHES: Yes, to the extent that I have the impression of seeing a highly successful "grand-bourgeois" at work.

LÉVY: What did you speak about?

BARTHES: It was he who spoke most of the time. Perhaps he was disappointed—or on the contrary pleased—to have to color his image a little: but we made him talk a lot more than we ourselves spoke.

LÉVY: On the Left, this lunch has often been badly spoken about....

BARTHES: I know. There are, even on the Left, people who replace a difficult analysis by facile indignation: it was *shocking*,[2] incorrect; it's not done to touch one's enemy, to eat with him; one has to stay pure. This is part of the Left's "correct" behavior.

LÉVY: Have you ever been tempted to rework your *Mythologies* of twenty years ago in extending it to work on the Left, on the new mythologies of the Left?

BARTHES: It is clear that in twenty years the situation has changed. There was May '68 which liberated and opened the language of the Left, risking giving it a certain arrogance. Above all, in a country in which forty-nine percent of the people voted for the Left, it would be surprising if there were not a sliding or a travesty of the social mythology: myths follow the majority. So, why am I hesitating in describing this mythology? I would never do it unless the Left itself supported the project. *Le Nouvel Observateur*, for example....

LÉVY: One mythology among others: is it obvious to you that Giscard is "the enemy"?

BARTHES: Those who he represents, the men who are behind him and pushed him to where he is now, yes. But there is a dialectic of history which works such that one day, perhaps, he will be less our enemy than someone else....

LÉVY: In the end, if you were to have a political line it would be a little like the provisionary principle of Descartes, a constantly provisionary politics which is minimal, minimalist....

BARTHES: The notion of minimal position interests me and often seems the least unjust. For me the political minimal, which absolutely cannot be worked on, is the problem of fascism. I belong to a generation which knew what it was and remembers. On that my engagement would be immediate and total.

LÉVY: Does that mean that below this line, which must be pretty high, things are equivalent, and political choices indifferent?

BARTHES: The line is not as high as all that. First because fascism includes lots of things. To make things clearer, for me any regime is fascist if it not only stops people from speaking but *obliges* them to speak. And then because the natural, constant temptation of power is to spring quickly back after it's been pushed away. The line is easily crossed

LÉVY: Can a minimalist politics still desire or want revolution?

BARTHES: This is curious, that for everybody revolution is a pleasant image, and yet it is certainly a terrible reality. Though of course revolution could stay an image, one could desire or militate for an image. But it is not just one image, there are different incarnations of revolution. And it is this, you see, which complicates the problem.... I would willingly call societies in which revolution has triumphed "deceiving" societies. They are the places of major deception which a great number of us are suffering. These societies are deceiving because the State did not dwindle.... In my case, it would be demagogic to speak of revolution, but I would willingly speak of subversion. For me it is a clearer word than that of revolution. It signifies: to come through underneath to, trick things, to displace them, to carry them to another place where they are not expected.

LÉVY: Isn't "liberalism" also a minimal position which is quite suitable in the end?

BARTHES: There are two liberalisms. A liberalism which is always, subterraineously authoritative and paternalistic, on the side of one's good conscience. And then there is a liberalism which is more ethical than political; one would have to find another name for this. Something like a profound suspension of judgment. An integrated nonracism which is applicable to any type of object or subject. An integrated nonracism which would approach, let us say, the direction of Zen.

LÉVY: Is it an intellectual idea?

BARTHES: It is certainly an intellectual idea.

LÉVY: There was a time when intellectuals imagined themselves, thought themselves to be the "salt of the earth"....

BARTHES: For my own part I would say that they are more like the rejects of society. Rejects in the strict sense, that is to say that which has no use, at least unless it is recuperated. There are precisely regimes where one has the task of recuperating the rejects that we are. But, fundamentally, a reject is useless. In a certain sense, intellectuals are useless.

LÉVY: What do you mean by "reject"?

BARTHES: Organic rejection proves the passage of the material in which it results. Human rejects, for example, prove the nutritive process. Well, the intellectual proves an historical process of which he is in some way the reject. He crystalizes, in the form of a reject, the drives, the desires, the complications, the blockages which probably belong to the whole society. Optimists say that the intellectual is a "witness." I would rather say that he is only a "trace."

LÉVY: According to you he is therefore completely useless.

BARTHES: Useless, but dangerous: any strong regime wants to make him toe the line. His danger is of a symbolic order; he is treated like a patient in intensive care, an excessive who is a nuisance, but is kept in order to pin-point in a controlled space the fantasies and exuberances of language.

LÉVY: And you, you are the reject of which process?

BARTHES: Let's say that I'm simply without doubt the trace of an historical interest in language; and also the trace of multiple blockages, fashions, new terms.

LÉVY: You speak of fashion: does this mean the present atmosphere? In other words, do you read your contemporaries?

BARTHES: In fact, in a general manner, I read little. This is not a secret: it can't help striking the reader of my texts. I have three ways of reading, three sorts of reading. The first consists of looking at a book: I receive a book, someone talks to me about it, so I look at it; this is a type of reading which is very important and is never spoken about. Like Jules Romains who went on and on about the para-optical vision of the blind, I could easily speak for this first type of reading of para-acoustic information, a vague and scarcely rigorous information which functions all the same. My second way of reading is when I have work to do, a course, an article, a book, well then yes, I read books, I read from cover to cover taking notes, but I'm only reading them as a function of my work, they go into my work. Then the third reading is the one I do at night when I go home. There I generally read the classics....

LÉVY: You haven't answered my question....

BARTHES: My "contemporaries"? I put nearly all of them in the first category: I "look at" them—why? It's difficult to say. No doubt because I'm worried about being seduced by material which is too close, so close that I could no longer transform it. I can't see myself transforming Foucault, Deleuze or Sollers.... It's too close. It comes in a language which is absolutely too contemporary.

LÉVY: Are there exceptions?

BARTHES: Some. A book here and there, which has really impressed me and has gone into my work. But, on the other hand, it always depends a little on chance. And, on the other hand, when I really read a contemporary book, I always read it very late, never at the time that people are speaking to me about it. When they are talking there is too much noise and so I don't want to read. I have read Deleuze's *Nietzsche*[3] and his *Anti-Oedipus*[4] but always well after their publication.

LÉVY: And then, there is Lacan to whom you refer quite often.

BARTHES: Often? I don't know. Above all, in effect, at the time I was working on *Le Discours amoureux*. Because I had need of a "psychology" and only psychoanalysis is capable of providing one. So it was there, in this precise area, that I often met Lacan.

LÉVY: Lacanism or the Lacanian "text"?

BARTHES: Both. The Lacanian text interests me as such. It is a text which mobilizes.

LÉVY: Because of the word-play?

BARTHES: No, for that very reason. I am the least sensitive to that. I can easily see what it relates to, but at that point my attention drifts. The rest, in contrast, I often like a lot. Lacan is, in the final analysis, and to pick up again the Nietzschian typology, a fairly rare marriage of the "priest" and the "artist."

LÉVY: Is there a relation between the theme of the imaginary, which is central to your work, and the Lacanian imaginary?

BARTHES: Yes, it is the same thing but no doubt I deform the theme because I isolate it. I have the impression that the imaginary is in a sense the poor relation of psychoanalysis.

Stuck between the real and the symbolic, one could say that it loses its value, at least by the psychoanalytic *vulgate*. My next book is on the contrary presented as an affirmation of the imaginary.[5]

LÉVY: And do you read your own work? I should say: do you reread yourself?

BARTHES: Never. I'm too scared, either of finding it good and then telling myself that I'll never do it again or, on the contrary, bad, and regretting doing it.

LÉVY: Do you know, then, who reads you, for whom you write?

BARTHES: I think one always knows to whom, for whom one speaks. There is always, in the case of speaking a finite number of listeners, even if it is heterogeneous. So what makes the absolute singularity of writing is that it is really the degree zero of allocution.

The place exists, but it is empty. One never knows who is going to fill this place, for whom one is in the process of writing.

LÉVY: Have you ever had the feeling of writing for posterity?

BARTHES: Frankly, no. I can't imagine that my work or my works will be read after my death. Literally, I can't *imagine* it.

LÉVY: You say "oeuvre." Are you conscious of writing a "collected works"?

BARTHES: No. And anyway I spontaneously corrected "oeuvre" in the singular to "oeuvres" in the plural: I have no consciousness of an oeuvre. I write blow-by-blow, through a mixture of obsessions, continuities, tactical detours.

LÉVY: Are there any "oeuvres" which would be constituted in any other way?

BARTHES: Maybe not, I don't know.

LÉVY: In any case, what is sure is that you, like Valéry, often write *"à la commande."*

BARTHES: Often, yes; but, if truth be told, less and less. When it's a contract to write, the system works pretty well, whether it's the preface to a book, the presentation of a painter, the writing of an article.... Briefly, an object works well enough if it's my writing they are after. When, in contrast, it's a matter of a contract for a dissertation, treating a particular subject for instance, then it doesn't work at all. And when I allow myself to accept, then I become very unhappy.

LÉVY: Hence the frightfully fragmented nature of whatever you write....

BARTHES: It's like a slope. I am going more and more towards the fragment. Anyway I like its sensation and I believe in its theoretical importance. I was getting to the point, anyway, where I was having trouble writing full-blown texts.

LÉVY: Even if it's fragmented and subjected to the contingencies of the contract, your work is in any case traversed and unified by a few major themes....

BARTHES: There are themes. The imaginary, for example. The indirect. The *doxa*. Also the theme of antihysteria, even if it evolved recently. But I certainly say that these are themes.

LÉVY: Do you mean to say that they are not "concepts," in the philosophical sense?

BARTHES: No. They are concepts. But they are concept-metaphors, which function as metaphors. If Nietzsche's expression is correct, if concepts have, as he put it, a metaphorical origin, then it is at this origin that I replace myself. And my concepts, all of a sudden, don't have all the rigor which philosophers normally give them.

LÉVY: What is most striking in your books is less the absence of rigor than the wild character of your conceptual imports.

BARTHES: You say "wild." It's correct. I follow a kind of pirate law which has difficulty recognizing the propriety of origins. This has got nothing to do with a spirit of contestation, but with an immediacy of desire, with a kind of avidity. It is through avidity that I sometimes make off with the themes and the words of others. Also, I never complain myself when someone "takes" something from me.

LÉVY: So that the unity is less in the themes than in the area of the operations of the type about which you have been speaking?

BARTHES: Exactly. More movements and operations than themes or concepts. For example, "slippage." Slippage of images. Slippage in the meanings of words. Or then again the recourse to etymology. Or deformation, the anamorphosis of concepts. A whole series of tactics, of procedures of which in *Roland Barthes by Roland Barthes,* I should perhaps have tried to present a glossary.

LÉVY: What are these procedures aiming at? Do they even envisage a particular effect independently of their simple activation?

BARTHES: I am looking for a writing which doesn't paralyze the other. And which at the same time is not familiar. It is there one finds all the difficulty. I would like to attain a writing which is not paralyzing and which is not for all that a "matey" writing.

LÉVY: Once before you said that you were looking for "grids" through which one could apprehend or appropriate the real....

BARTHES: I don't believe that I spoke about a grid. In any case, if I have a grid, it would only be that of literature, a grid which I carry more or less everywhere with me. But I think that effects of appropriation of the real, as a friend tells me, are possible without any "grid." If I say that, it is because it is the whole problem of semiology: it was first of all a grid, and I myself tried to make a grid out of it. But when it became one, it couldn't appropriate anything anymore. And I have been obliged to go elsewhere, without discovering it of course.

LÉVY: People who don't like you speak, in relation to your books, of a superstition, a sanctification of literature....

BARTHES: I'm not against sanctification. Lacan said recently that true atheists are very rare. There is always something sacred somewhere.... So let's say that for me it fell on literature. I repeat: it is very difficult not to sanctify anything. Sollers is the only one I know of to get there. And even then it is not sure. Maybe he has his secret, like Saint-Ford in Sade. In any case, as far as I'm concerned, I certainly sanctify. I sanctify a *jouissance*, a *jouissance* of writing.

LÉVY: Language, having said that, is also spoken language. The language of the theater for example.

BARTHES: I have a complicated relationship with the theater. As a metaphorical energy it retains an extreme importance for me: I see the theater everywhere, in writing, in images, etc. But, as for going to the theater, going to see theater, it scarcely interests me anymore, I very rarely go. Let's say that I remain sensitive to theatricalization, and that this is an operation, in the sense that I was saying before.

LÉVY: Which is relevant to pedagogical speech.

BARTHES: The relation teacher-pupil is another thing again. It is a contractual relation which is a relation of desire. A relation of reciprocal desire which implies the possibility of reception and therefore of realization. I could put it in a provocative way: a contract of prostitution.

LÉVY: This year you enter the Collège de France. Do you think this will change anything in the nature of this pedagogical link?

BARTHES: I don't think so. I hope not. In any case I have always had, in the context of my seminar an "idyllic" relation to teaching. I only address myself to subjects who chose me, who come there to listen to me, and on whom I am not imposing myself. There are privileged conditions which are also, by definition, those of a course at the Collège.

LÉVY: With the one reservation that the seminar supposes a dialogue and the course a soliloquy....

BARTHES: That doesn't necessarily have all the importance usually attributed to it. There is a nasty prejudice which says that, in a pedagogical relation, everything is in the one speaking and nothing in the one listening. Let things go on, in my opinion, let as much go on in the one as in the other. Listening doesn't have to be censored in the name of speech. Listening can be an active *jouissance*.

LÉVY: In other words, no necessary or obligatory relationship of power?

BARTHES: There is the question, of course, of a power internal to the discourse, to any discourse, which I speak of in my inaugural lecture. In addition, I don't think there is any urgent necessity to suppress the principle of the course to give way to false dialogues which often end up as psychodramas. And one could well think of the soliloquy as a sort of theater, bordering on the fraudulent, fuzzy or uncertain, where a subtle game is played out between speech and listening. The soliloquy is not necessarily that of the master, it could be of the "lover."

1.   *L'Ange* by Christian Jambet and Guy Lardreau (Paris: Editions Bernard Grasset, 1976).
2.   English in the original.
3.   *Nietzsche and Philosophy* by Gilles Deleuze, translated by Hugh Tomlinson (New York: Columbia Unversity Press, 1983).
4.   *Anti-Oedipus: Capitalism and Schizophrenia* by Gilles Deleuze and Félix Guattari, translated by Robert Hurley, Mark Seem, and Helen R. Lane (Minneapolis: University of Minnesota Press, 1983).
5.   *La Chambre claire* (Paris: Editions du Seuil, 1980), translated as *Camera Lucida*, (New York: Hill and Wang, 1981).

ORIGINALLY PUBLISHED IN *LE NOUVEL OBSERVATEUR*. REPRINTED FROM *ART & TEXT* 8 (1977)
TRANSLATED BY STEPHEN MUECKE.

READING LACAN

Jane Gallop

> The pedagogical question crucial to Lacan's own teaching will...be:
> *Where does it resist?* Where does a text precisely make no sense, that
> is *resist interpretation?* Where does what I...read resist my
> understanding? Where is the *ignorance*—the resistance to
> knowledge—located? And what can I thus *learn* from the locus of
> that ignorance? How can I interpret *out* of the dynamic ignorance I
> analytically encounter, both in others and in myself?
> —Shoshana Felman, "Psychoanalysis and Education"

It is generally assumed, in practice if not in theory, that the expression "women's studies" means the study of women, women as the object of study. If unquestioned, however, this assumption creates a problem. In an open letter in *Signs* called "A Problem in Naming," Susan Groag Bell and Mollie Schwartz Rosenhan write: "'Women's studies' is a misnomer. Moreover the phrase is grammatically incorrect."[1] Yet it would seem that obedience to grammatical rules is not their principal criterion for, in proposing "women studies" as a "viable alternative," they write: "Alas, it too is grammatically incorrect since it uses a noun as an adjective."

The problem with "women's studies," as it turns out, may be that it is a grammatical construction, which is to say that it is already inscribed within the bounds of language and has a history. According to Bell and Rosenhan, "'Women's studies' used grammatically means the study of any topic whatever...as long as the study itself is performed by women.... In its literal meaning, 'women's studies' are subjects studied by women." "Used grammatically" is here synonymous with "in its literal meaning." Perhaps the objection to grammatical impropriety is actually or also an objection to something like nonliteral language, figurative or, we might even say, ambiguous language, in which a signifier could mean more than one thing, something other than what was intended.

Bell and Rosenhan close their open letter thus: "We know there is much in naming. Let us choose ours with accuracy and purpose." Naming has indeed been recognized as a central feminist concern. Not only is it a case of rejecting our subsumption under a husband's name, but questioning what will be our children's last names, and finally, most radically, questioning our own names, and our mothers' names, and so on in generational regress, as always patronyms: identity in our culture being so linked up with patriarchy. And although in theory it has been quite clear that we must reject patriarchal identity as it is manifested in the patronym, in practice the "problem in naming," in terms of our children's and our own names, has remained a big problem, with no clear solution being generally put into practice, however clever some seem in theory.

I would suggest that the discrepancy between the theoretical rejection of patriarchal identity and the practical confusion on the issue of naming is the sign not of some lack of nerve on the part of feminists but of our actually inhabiting a relation to language that makes a tremendous irony of the assertion: "Let us choose our names with accuracy and purpose." I will in this context merely comment that the view of language as a tool—reflected in the words "let us choose," "accuracy," and "purpose"—has been widely called into question, and one of the most brutal of these interrogations—Jacques Lacan's—has linked this language, which inevitably eludes our attempt to use it for our ends, to something Lacan names the Name-of-the-Father.

The problem with "women's studies," what makes Bell and Rosenhan want to lop off its "apostrophe s," is that it is ambiguous. The user cannot keep what they refer to as the "literal" or the "grammatical" meaning, that is, the user cannot keep a certain meaning, embedded in the language but not intended, from returning. The "apostrophe s" is always potentially ambiguous because it can function as either objective or subjective genitive, in other words, studies of women and studies by women.

This formulation of the problem is itself rather suggestive. The word "genitive"—which means "indicative of possession" and which etymologically traces back to *gignere*, to beget—may itself be pregnant with the history of the Name-of-the-Father as the attempt to legislate begetting under a name indicative of possession. The inevitable ambiguity of the genitive (subjective or objective) may resonate not only with the mother as bound up with the infant prior to the latter's ability to distinguish subject and object but also with women's traditional place in culture as neither object nor subject but disturbingly both. Woman's ambiguous cultural place may be precisely the standpoint from which it is possible to muddle the subject/object distinction, that distinction necessary for a certain epistemological relation to the world. Lévi-Strauss says woman is both a sign *and* an exchanger of signs, thus hers is the place in organized culture that evokes another "more primitive" epistemology in which all objects were also considered endowed with subjective status.[2] Might not one of the goals of what we so ambiguously call "women's studies" be to call into question the oppressive effects of an epistemology based on the principle of a clear and nonambiguous distinction of subject and object of knowledge?

Rather than attempt to banish it, I would like to take advantage of the ambiguity of "women's studies," in that it retains woman's traditional peculiar vantage point as neither quite subject nor object, but in a framework which sees that vantage as an advantage and not a shortcoming.

Although Bell and Rosenhan complain of the unintended and vaguer implications of the "study of any topic whatever…performed by women," there are those who have affirmed this very connotation, embracing this shamelessly loose definition of our endeavor. The present work assumes that posture: not a prudish correction of the loose and improper but an immodest celebration of the broad.

In her article "Ideological Structure and How Women Are Excluded," Dorothy E. Smith wrote: "We are confronted virtually with the problem of reinventing the world of knowledge, of thought, of symbols and images. Not of course by repudiating everything that has been done but by subjecting it to exacting scrutiny and criticism from the position of women as subject...or knower."[3] In "Breaking the Bread," Elaine Marks takes up Smith's position: "'Women as knower' is the center of our concern. Of all the many exclusions that have, until now, defined women's relation to culture, the most serious are the exclusions that keep us outside the desire for theory and the theory of desire. To be a knower at this point in the history of women's studies means to push thought as far as it will go."[4]

Accepting the "literal," "grammatical" sense of "women's studies," Marks asserts "women as knower" as the "center of our concern." The phrase "women as knower," used by Smith, repeated by Marks, is grammatically incorrect: women is plural; knower is singular. This grammatical transgression evokes an entire field of associations. Most immediately, Marks, in this article, characterizes women's studies as "collaborative." More speculatively, certain theorists such as Luce Irigaray have identified the feminine with the plural as opposed to the phallomorphic singular.[5] But finally, might we not say that "women as knower" counteracts the more grammatical and more assimilable "woman as knower"? If the center of women's studies were what any individual woman might know, our new interdiscipline would be just a heteroclite collection. Unless we were to accept an essentialistic definition of women's interests as based in their anatomy, we could not assume that the composite of what all women study would make a coherent whole. That is the absurdity Bell and Rosenhan would guard against. Yet the agrammatical "women as knower" constitutes a new subject of knowledge that is not only female but is also not a single monadic individual. If what a woman knows is different from what a man knows, the feminist understanding of that difference would emphasize not the woman's individual peculiarity but her place in a sexual class, her psychological place in a division of labor. It is the common denominators of the studies done by women—mathematically speaking, it is their intersections and not their unions—which constitute women's studies.

In "Breaking the Bread," Marks not only defines women's studies as studies by women but links this revolution in knowledge to what is going on in the *sciences humaines* in France. In seeing a conjunction between the two, Marks is able to imagine a Women's Studies that would no longer be a mere region of knowledge supplementing traditional disciplines, but—by altering not the object but the subject of knowledge, the knower— would call into question what is considered knowledge in any discipline.

Extremely attracted to the notion of women's studies as a force that could revolutionize the very structures of knowledge, I wish to pose the question of what a feminist practice of study might be, beyond the recognizable themes: women and sexual difference. For example, what would be a feminist criticism that neither read women's texts nor read for the representation of women? If women's studies involves an epistemological revolution, how would it effect realms other than those in which women are already the object of knowledge? I have no answers, but rather would like to present the first glimmerings of an idea. In truth, the notion of feminist practice I will entertain was imposed upon me by an unexpected response to my work. My theorizing was stimulated by an event, and the theory remains in the primitive state where it cannot yet abstract itself from the material conditions of its birth.

I was at work on the present book, a book on Lacan. Not a recognizably feminist project, since Lacan is not a woman, nor have I been concerned in this book explicitly to address Lacan's relation to feminism or women, which I have already done in another book.[6] Perhaps naively, I had not considered this a feminist project but had thought of it as a "straight" book on Lacan, a study that addressed the general question of how one could possibly read Lacan's text.

An early, partial version of the manuscript was submitted by the press to a reader, and the reader returned a report that made a great impression on me. It began with the point that the text was not worthy of publication because it demonstrated inadequate command of the subject matter, adding that I even admitted as much. Returning to this issue at the report's end, the reader suggested that I did not sufficiently grasp the Lacanian theory of sexual identification (again acknowledging that I admitted this) and that I should wait to write about Lacan's theory until I was no longer confused.

The major objection was thus that I was not in command of the material, not in a certain epistemological relation that maintains the proper, unambiguous distance between subject and object of knowledge. More precisely, the main objection was that I was not in command of the material and I admitted it. One other objection was tacked on at the very end of the report: that I used the pronoun "she" where the antecedent was not identified as female. The reader found this agrammatical, irritating, and confusing, and considered it an act of aggression on my part.

I am convinced that there is some intrinsic connection between the objection to avowing an inadequate grasp of the material and the objection to the use of a generic "she." The rejection of the automatic generic "he" is, of course, an important topos of feminist writing praxis. But the other gesture was not intended as feminist, but rather simply in the spirit of a Lacanian reading, that is, in keeping with the French revolution in discourse to which Marks refers. Thanks to their joint appearance in my reader's report, I have come to consider that they are, theoretically, the same gesture.

The reader was assuming my reading to be not something other, an alternative approach, but a failure at the only correct sort of reading, one that speaks from a position of mastery over a text. I was and am trying to write in a different relation to the material, from a more unsettling confrontation with its contradictory plurivocity, a sort of encounter I believe is possible only if one relinquishes the usual position of command, and thus writes from a more subjective, vulnerable position. Though I have worked long and hard at Lacan's text and with the various commentaries upon it, rather than present my mastery I am interested in getting at those places where someone who generally knows the text well still finds herself in a position of difficulty. My various mentions of insufficient command of the material are a very central part of my project.

That the reader located my inadequacy particularly in the theory of sexual identification is interesting, since Lacan's theory of sexual identification is precisely a theory of inadequacy, a theory of castration. Lacan's major statement of ethical purpose and therapeutic goal, as far as I am concerned, is that one must assume one's castration. Women have always been considered "castrated" in psychoanalytic thinking. But castration for Lacan is not only sexual; more important, it is also linguistic: we are inevitably bereft of any masterful understanding of language, and can only signify ourselves in a symbolic system that we do not command, that, rather, commands us. For women, Lacan's message that everyone, regardless of his or her organs, is "castrated," represents not a loss but a gain. Only this realization, I believe, can release us from "phallocentrism," one of the effects of which is that one must constantly cover one's inevitable inadequacy in order to have the right to speak. My assumption of my inadequacy and my attempt to read from that position are thus, to my mind, both Lacanian and feminist.

After years of study, I have come to believe Lacan's text impossible to understand fully, impossible to master—and thus a particularly good illustration of everyone's inevitable "castration" in language. The attempt to cover up one's inadequate command of Lacan's text necessitates a violent reduction of the contradictory plurality and ambiguity of that text, just as the assembling of a coherent self necessitates repression. I believe that the pretense of a masterful grasp of Lacan serves only to consolidate the oppressive mystification of the Lacanian institution. Lacan talks insightfully about the analyst as the illusion of the "subject presumed to know." I am trying to undo that illusion rather than shore it up and therefore wish to write from some other position. This project is profoundly feminist. It involves calling into question the phallic illusions of authority.

It is apparent to me now that in my response to the reader's report I was justifying my giving up the position of authority by invoking an authoritative version, an unambiguous sense of Lacan. What does it mean to invoke authority in order to legitimate an attack on authority? This ambiguity, I believe, is what promises the most. To speak without authority is nothing new; the disenfranchised have always so spoken. Simply to refuse authority does not challenge the category distinction between phallic authority and castrated other, between "subject presumed to know" and subject not in command. One can effectively undo authority only from the position of authority, in a way that exposes the illusions of that position *without renouncing it,* so as to permeate the position itself with the connotations of its illusoriness, so as to show that *everyone,* including the "subject presumed to know," is castrated.

Perhaps this ambiguous position—at once assuming and not assuming authority—is finally to be understood through its resemblance to another gesture. I do not simply use the generic "she" in this book, but alternate between "she" and "he," in the hopes of resexualizing the neuter "he," of contaminating it with the sexual difference that seems to reside in the "she." Lacan has said "the phallus can play its role only when veiled."[7] The supposed universality of the pronoun "he" depends on its not connoting the penis, on the veiling of its male sexual attributes. When any possible pronoun for the epistemological subject cannot help but connote sexual difference, then the phallic authority of universal man will have more difficulty pronouncing itself.

1. Susan Groag Bell and Mollie Schwartz Rosenhan, "A Problem in Naming: Women Studies—Women's Studies?" *Signs: Journal of Women in Culture and Society* 6, 3 (1981): 540–42 .

2. Claude Lévi-Strauss, *The Elementary Structures of Kinship,* trans. James Harle Bell, John Richard von Sturmer, and Rodney Needham (Boston: Beacon Press, 1969), p. 496.

3. Dorothy E. Smith, "Ideological Structure and How Women Are Excluded," *Canadian Review of Sociology and Anthropology* 12, 4 (1975), p. 367, quoted in Elaine Marks, "Breaking the Bread: Gestures Toward Other Structures, Other Discourses," *Bulletin of the Midwest Modern Language Association*, 13 (Spring 1980: 55. Ellipsis Marks's.

4. Marks, "Breaking the Bread," p. 55.

5. See for example, Luce Irigaray, "Ce sexe qui n'en est pas un" in Irigaray, *Ce sexe qui n'en est pas un* (Paris: Seuil, 1977), pp. 23-32; pp. 23-33 in *This Sex Which Is Not One*, trans. Catherine Porter with Carolyn Burke (Ithaca: Cornell University Press, 1985). Translated as "That Sex which is not One" by Randall Albury and Paul Foss in Paul Foss and Meaghan Morris, eds., *Language, Sexuality, and Subversion* (Darlington, Australia: Feral Publications, 1978), pp. 161–171. Also translated as "This Sex Whlch Is Not One" by Claudia Reeder in Elaine Marks and Isabelle de Courtivron, eds., *New French Feminisms: An Anthology* (Amherst: University of Massachusetts Press, 1980), pp. 99-106.

6. *The Daughter's Seduction: Feminism and Psychoanalysis* (Ithaca: Cornell University Press, 1982).

7. Jacques Lacan, "La Signification du phallus," in Lacan, *Ecrits* (Paris: Seuil, 1966), p. 692. Translated as "The Signification of the Phallus" by Alan Sheridan in Lacan, *Ecrits: A Selection* (New York, Norton, 1977), p.288. Also translated as "The Meaning of the Phallus" by Jacqueline Rose in Juliet Mitchell and Jacqueline Rose, eds., *Feminine Sexuality: Jacques Lacan and the école freudienne* (New York: Norton, 1982). p.82.

CONTRIBUTORS

WALTER ADAMSON teaches at Emory University's Institute for Liberal Arts in Atlanta, Georgia. He is the author of *Marx and the Disillusionment of Marxism.*

LAURIE ANDERSON is an artist and performer. Her multi-media works include *United States* and *Natural History.* Her latest album is *Strange Angels.*

TADAO ANDO is an architect based in Osaka, Japan.

ROLAND BARTHES (1915-1980), scholar, critic, and teacher, was Professor of Literary Semiology at the Collège de France. Among his many books are *Mythologies, Image-Music-Text,* and *Camera Lucida.*

NEIL BARTLETT is a writer based in London and a member of the editorial team of *Performance* magazine.

ARTHUR BELL was a staff writer for *The Village Voice* from 1969 until his death in 1984. He is the author of *Kings Don't Mean a Thing* and *Dancing the Gay Lib Blues.*

JOSEPH BEUYS (1921-1986) was an artist and teacher.

DARA BIRNBAUM is an artist whose works include the video *Technology/Transformation: Wonder Woman* and the book *Rough Edits.*

BLACK AUDIO FILM COLLECTIVE is based in London, England. Its members, John Akomfrah, Reece Auguiste, Eddie George, Lina Gopaul, Avril Johnson, and Trevor Mathison, have most recently collaborated on *Testament,* directed by Akomfrah, and *Twilight City,* directed by Auguiste. They are currently working on a film about Michael X.

LYN BLUMENTHAL (1948-1988) was an artist, educator and co-founder of The Video Data Bank.

JONATHAN BOROFSKY is an artist.

JIMMY BOYLE is a writer and sculptor. His autobiography is entitled *A Sense of Freedom* and he is currently working on a novel.

JOHN BURGEE is an architect.

JAMES CLIFFORD is the author of *The Predicament of Culture* and co-editor of *Writing Culture: The Poetics and Politics of Ethnography.* He teaches in the History of Consciousness Program at the University of California, Santa Cruz.

JONATHAN CRARY is a founding editor of the journal *Zone.* He teaches art history at Barnard College and Columbia University.

DOUGLAS CRIMP is an art critic, a co-editor of *October* magazine, and an AIDS activist.

SPARKY D's hits include "Roxanne, Roxanne," "Sparky D's Train," and "Throwdown." Her debut album is *This is Sparky D's World.*

ANTHONY DAVIS is a composer. His works include the operas *X* and *Under the Double Moon.*

DAVID DEITCHER is an art historian and writer. He contributes frequently to *Artforum, Art in America,* and *The Village Voice.*

GILLES DELEUZE, Professor of Philosophy at The University of Paris VIII, is the author of *Cinema 1: The Movement-Image, Foucault,* and, with Félix Guattari, *Anti-Oedipus, Kafka: Toward a Minor Literature,* and *A Thousand Plateaus.*

JACQUES DERRIDA teaches philosophy at the École Normale Superieure in Paris. He is the author of numerous books including *Writing and Difference, Dissemination, Of Grammatology,* and *The Ear of the Other.*

ROSALYN DEUTSCHE teaches art history and theory at the Cooper Union in New York City. She has written extensively about art and urban redevelopment.

ETHYL EICHELBERGER (1945-1990) was a character actor and drag performer. He was best known for his series of monologues and performances entitled *Great Women of History.*

TREVOR FAIRBROTHER is Associate Curator of Contemporary Art at The Museum of Fine Arts in Boston.

MICHEL FOUCAULT (1926-1984) taught at the Collège de France in Paris. His books include *The Order of Things, Discipline and Punish, The Archaeology of Knowledge,* and *The History of Sexuality.*

JIM FOURATT is a "cultural instigator" and member of Art Positive.

COCO FUSCO is a writer and curator.

JANE GALLOP is a professor of humanities at Rice University and the author of *The Daughter's Seduction: Feminism and Psychoanalysis* and *Reading Lacan.*

DEE DEE GLASS is a television documentary producer and director.

GRAN FURY is a group of ACT UP (AIDS Coalition to Unleash Power), members who work collaboratively in the visual arts.

DAVID HAMMONS is an artist.

BERTHA HARRIS's novels include *Confessions of Cherubino, Catching Saradove,* and *Lover.*

RICHARD HELL, a.k.a. Richard Meyers, was a member of the bands The Neon Boys, Television, and Richard Hell and the Voidoids. He is an editor of the journal *Cuz,* which is sponsored by The Poetry Project in New York City.

KATE HORSFIELD is co-founder of The Video Data Bank.

MILLIE JACKSON's albums include *Live and Uncensored, For Men Only, Tide is Turning,* and her latest, *Back to the S—t!.*

ALICE JARDINE, Associate Professor of Romance Languages and Literature at Harvard, is the author of *Gynesis: Configurations of Women and Modernity,* co-editor of *Men in Feminism,* and an editor of the journal *copyright.*

LALEEN JAYAMANNE is a filmmaker whose works include *A Song of Ceylon* and *Rehearsing.* She teaches film and drama at the University of Wollongong in Australia.

PHILIP JOHNSON is an architect. He was Director of the Department of Architecture and Design at the Museum of Modern Art in New York from 1932-1934 and 1947-1954.

SCOTT JOHNSON is a composer whose works include *Patty Hearst, Bird in the Domes* (for the Kronos Quartet), *Before Winter* (for the Boston Ballet), and *John Somebody.*

KELLIE JONES, U.S. Commissioner of the 1989 Sao Paolo Bienal in Brazil, is a writer and independent curator.

LEON KRIER is an architect, educator, and theorist on architecture and urbanism.

JULIA KRISTEVA is Professor of Linguistics at the University of Paris VIII. Her books include *Revolution in Poetic Language, Desire in Language, Powers of Horror* and *Tales of Love.*

EWA LAJER-BURCHARTH is an art historian. She is the author of *Counter Monuments.*

BERNARD-HENRI LÉVY is a philosopher and writer. He is the author of *Barbarism with a Human Face* and *The Testament of God.*

M.C. LYTE is a singer-rapper from Queens, New York. Her albums include *Lyte as a Rock* and *Eyes on This.*

THOMAS McEVILLEY is a contributing editor of *Artforum* and a professor in the Institute for the Arts at Rice University.

MALCOLM McLAREN is an impresario and recording artist. He was the manager of The New York Dolls, the Sex Pistols and Bow Wow Wow.

GREIL MARCUS is a music columnist for *The Village Voice* and author of *Mystery Train* and *Lipstick Traces.*

PHIL MARIANI is co-editor with Barbara Kruger of *Remaking History* and editor of the forthcoming *Critical Fictions.*

MS. MELODIE has been rapping since 1982, sometimes in collaboration with her husband Chris Parker, KRS-1 of Boogie Down Productions. Her latest album is *Diva.*

KATE MILLETT's books include *Sexual Politics, Sita, The Basement, Flying,* and *Going to Iran.*

YVETTE MONEY is a rap singer. Her most recent singles are "I'm Gonna Get Mine" and "The Other Side of Me."

LAURA MULVEY is the author of *Visual and Other Pleasures* and co-director with Peter Wollen of the films *Riddles of the Sphinx, Crystal Gazing,* and *The Bad Sister.*

PEACHES is a Brooklyn-based singer. Her latest single is a rap version of the Temptations' "Treat Her Like a Lady."

JILL PEARLMAN is a writer specializing in music. She is the author of *Elvis for Beginners.*

JAMES PETTAWAY, as of 1987, was an inmate at San Quentin State Prison.

GRISELDA POLLOCK, Senior Lecturer in the History of Art and Film Department at the University of Leeds, is the author of *Vision and Difference.* With Roszika Parker, she has written *Old Mistresses: Women, Art and Ideology,* and edited *Framing Feminism.*

STEVE REICH is a composer. He is currently at work on a music/video/theater project entitled *The Cave.*

TIM ROLLINS is an artist and art instructor who founded The Art and Knowledge Workshop in the South Bronx, New York. He works collaboratively with a group of his students, the Kids of Survival.

WILLIAM RUBIN is Director Emeritus of the Department of Painting and Sculpture at the Museum of Modern Art in New York. Among his many publications are monographs on Frank Stella, Anthony Caro, Cézanne, and Picasso.

VITO RUSSO is the author of *Celluloid Closet.*

EDWARD SAID is Parr Professor of English and Comparative Literature at Columbia University. His books include *Orientalism, The Question of Palestine,* and *The World, the Text and the Critic.*

SANKOFA FILM/VIDEO COLLECTIVE's most recent projects are *Perfect Image,* directed by Maureen Blackwood, and *Looking for Langston,* directed by Isaac Julien.

JON SAVAGE is a journalist and writer working in London. He is the author of *England's Dreaming* (forthcoming).

LILY SAVAGE is a drag performer based in London. His act is popular in gay pubs and clubs around England.

ROXANNE SHANTE entered the world of rap music with "Roxanne's Revenge." She has since released an album entitled *Bad Sister.*

GAYATRI SPIVAK, author of *In Other Worlds: Essays in Cultural Politics* and the forthcoming *Master Discourse Native Informant,* is Andrew W. Mellon Professor in the Department of English at the University of Pittsburgh.

STEPHEN SPROUSE is a fashion designer.

SYNQUIS, with Finesse, is part of a rap duo from Queens, New York. Their debut album is *Soul Sisters.*

PAUL TAYLOR was guest curator of the exhibition "Impresario: Malcolm McLaren and the British New Wave" at The New Museum. He is a founding editor of the journal *Art & Text,* and writes about art for the *New York Times, Vogue,* and other magazines.

SWEET T is a singer and rapper from Queens, New York. Among her hits are "It's My Beat" and "I Got Da Feeling."

LESLIE THORNTON is a film and video artist living in New York. She teaches filmmaking at Brown University.

TRINH T MINH-HA is a writer, filmmaker and composer. Her works include the book *Woman, Native, Other,* and the films *Reassemblage, Naked Spaces—Living is Round,* and *Surname Viet, Given Name Nam.*

KIRK VARNEDOE is Director of the Department of Painting and Sculpture at the Museum of Modern Art in New York.

JEFF WEINSTEIN is a columnist and Senior Editor in charge of art criticism for *The Village Voice.* His latest book is *Learning to Eat.*

EDMUND WHITE is a writer. His novels include *A Boy's Own Story* and *The Beautiful Room is Empty.*

JUDITH WILLIAMSON is a journalist, filmmaker and lecturer. She is the author of *Decoding Advertisements* and *Consuming Passions.*

KRZYSZTOF WODICZKO is an artist and teacher. His *Homeless Vehicle Project* was shown at The Clocktower in New York City in January 1989.

Adamson, Walter L. *Hegemony and Revolution: A Study of Antonio Gramsci's Political and Cultural Theory.* Berkeley: University of California Press, 1980.

Adamson, Walter L. *Marx and the Disillusionment of Marxism.* Berkeley: University of California Press, 1985.

Adriani, Gotz, Winifred Konnertz, and Karin Thomas. *Joseph Beuys, Life and Works.* Translated by Patricia Lech. Woodbury: Barron's Educational Series, 1979.

Akomfrah, John, and Pervais Khan, eds. *Third Scenario: Theory and the Politics of Location.* Special issue, *Framework*, no. 36 (1989).

Anderson, Laurie. *Notebook/Laurie Anderson.* New York: Collation Center, 1977.

Anderson, Laurie. *United States.* New York: Harper & Row, 1984.

Ando, Tadao. *Buildings, Projects, Writings.* Edited by Kenneth Frampton. New York: Rizzoli, 1984.

Ando, Tadao. *The Yale Studio & Current Works.* New York: Rizzoli, 1989.

Appignanesi, Lisa, ed. *The Real Me: Post-Modernism and the Question of Identity. ICA Documents* 6. London: Institute of Contemporary Arts, 1987.

Appignanesi, Lisa, and Jane Attala, eds. *Ideas From France: The Legacy of French Theory. ICA Documents* 3. London: Institute of Contemporary Arts, 1985.

Appignanesi, Lisa, and Geoff Bennington, eds. *Postmodernism. ICA Documents* 4/5. London: Institute of Contemporary Arts, 1986.

Armes, Roy. *Third World Filmmaking and the West.* Berkeley: University of California Press, 1987.

Artists Space, New York. *Witnesses: Against Our Vanishing.* Statements by Nan Goldin, David Wojnarowicz, Linda Yablonski, and Cookie Mueller. Exhibition November 16, 1989–January 6, 1990.

Barrish, Phil. "Rehearsing a Reading." *Diacritics*, no. 4 (Winter 1986): 15-30.

Barthes, Roland. *A Barthes Reader.* Edited by Susan Sontag. New York: Hill and Wang, 1982.

Barthes, Roland. *Camera Lucida.* Translated by Richard Howard. New York: Farrar, Straus and Giroux, 1981.

Barthes, Roland. *Criticism and Truth.* Translated by Katrine Pilcher Keuneman. London: Athlone Press, 1987.

Barthes, Roland. *Empire of Signs.* Translated by Richard Howard. New York: Hill and Wang, 1982.

Barthes, Roland. *The Fashion System.* Translated by Matthew Ward and Richard Howard. New York: Farrar, Straus and Giroux, 1983.

Barthes, Roland. *The Grain of the Voice: Interviews 1962–1980.* Translated by Linda Coverdale. New York: Hill and Wang, 1984.

Barthes, Roland. *Image Music Text.* Translated by Stephen Heath. New York: Hill and Wang, 1977.

Barthes, Roland. *A Lover's Discourse: Fragments.* Translated by Richard Howard. New York: Hill and Wang, 1978.

Barthes, Roland. *Mythologies.* Translated by Annette Lavers. London: Jonathan Cape, 1972.

Barthes, Roland. *The Pleasure of the Text.* Translated by Richard Miller. New York: Hill and Wang, 1975.

Barthes, Roland. *The Responsibility of Forms: New Critical Essays on Music, Art, and Representation.* Translated by Richard Howard. New York: Hill and Wang, 1984.

Barthes, Roland. *Roland Barthes by Roland Barthes*. Translated by Richard Howard. New York: Farrar, Straus, and Giroux, 1977.

Barthes, Roland. *Writing Degree Zero and Elements of Semiology*. Translated by Annette Lavers and Colin Smith. London: Jonathan Cape, 1984.

Bastian, Heiner. *Joseph Beuys: Blitzschlag Mit Lichtschein auf Hirsch 1958–1985 (Lightning with Stag in its Glare, 1958–1985)*. Bern: Benteli, 1986.

Baudrillard, Jean. *America*. Translated by Chris Tower. London: Verso, 1988.

Baudrillard, Jean. *For a Critique of the Political Economy of the Sign*. Translated by Charles Levin. St. Louis: Telos Press, 1981.

Baudrillard, Jean. *Forget Foucault*. Translated by Phil Beitchman, Lee Hildreth and Mark Polizzotti. New York: Semiotext(e), 1987.

Benhabib, Seyla, and Drucilla Cornell, eds. *Feminism as Critique: On the Politics of Gender*. Minneapolis: University of Minnesota Press, 1987.

Bell, Arthur. *Dancing the Gay Lib Blues: A Year in the Homosexual Liberation Movement*. New York: Simon and Schuster, 1971.

Beuys, Joseph. *Joseph Beuys: The Secret Block for a Secret Person in Ireland*. Oxford: Museum of Modern Art, 1974.

Birnbaum, Dara. "Playground (The Damnation of Faust)." *Zone* 1/2 (1986): 70–79.

Birnbaum, Dara. *Rough Edits*. Halifax: Press of the Nova Scotia College of Art and Design, 1987.

Bogue, Ronald. *Deleuze and Guattari*. London: Routledge, 1989.

Boyle, Jimmy, and Tom McGrath. *The Hard Man: A Play*. Edinburgh: Canongate, 1977.

Boyle, Jimmy. *A Sense of Freedom*. Edinburgh: Canongate, 1977.

Bromberg, Craig. *The Wicked Ways of Malcolm McLaren*. New York: Harper & Row, 1989.

Bronski, Michael. *Culture Clash: The Making of Gay Sensibility*. Boston: South End Press, 1984.

Brooks, Rosetta. "Tim Rollins + K.O.S." *Artscribe*, no. 63 (May 1987): 40-47.

Buchbinder, Howard, et al. *Who's On Top?: The Politics of Heterosexuality*. Toronto: Garamond, 1987.

Burchill, Julie. *Damaged Gods: Cults and Heros Reappraised*. London: Century, 1986.

Burchill, Julie, and Tony Parsons. *"The Boy Looked at Johnny": The Obituary of Rock and Roll*. London: Pluto Press, 1978.

Bürger, Peter. *Theory of the Avant Garde*. Translated by Michael Shaw. Minneapolis: University of Minnesota Press, 1984.

Cameron, Dan. "The Art of Survival: A Conversation with Tim Rollins and K.O.S." *Arts Magazine*, (June 1988): 80-83.

Carroll, David. *Paraesthetics: Foucault, Lyotard, Derrida*. New York: Methuen, 1987.

Carter, Erica, and Simon Watney, eds. *Taking Liberties: AIDS and Cultural Politics*. London: Serpent's Tail Press, 1989.

Chambers, Ian. *Popular Culture*. London: SEFT Publications, 1987.

Charbonnier, G. *Conversations with Claude Lévi-Strauss*. Translated by John and Doreen Weightman. London: Jonathan Cape, 1969.

The Charlottesville Tapes: Transcripts of the Conference at the University of Virginia School of Architecture. New York: Rizzoli, 1985.

The Chicago Tapes: Transcripts of the Conference at the University of Illinois at Chicago. New York: Rizzoli, 1987.

Chodorow, Nancy. *The Reproduction of Mothering: Psychoanalysis and the Sociology of Gender*. Berkeley: University of California Press, 1978.

Clifford, James. *The Predicament of Culture: Twentieth-Century Ethnography, Literature, and Art*. Cambridge: Harvard University Press, 1988.

Clifford, James, and George E. Marcus, eds. *Writing Culture: The Poetics and Politics of Ethnography*. Berkeley: University of California Press, 1986.

Collins, Jim. *Uncommon Cultures: Popular Culture and Post Modernism*. New York: Routledge, 1989.

Crary, Jonathan. *Techniques of the Observer.* Cambridge: MIT Press, (forthcoming).

Crimp, Douglas. "The Art of Exhibition." *October* 30 (Fall 1984): 49–81.

Crimp, Douglas. "The End of Art and the Origin of the Museum." *Art Journal*, vol. 46, no. 4 (Winter 1987): 261–266.

Crimp, Douglas, ed. *AIDS: Cultural Analysis Cultural Activism.* Cambridge: MIT Press, 1988.

Culture and State. ICA Documents 2. London: Institute of Contemporary Arts, 1984.

Danzig, Alexis. "Acting Up: Independent Video and the AIDS Crisis." *Afterimage*, no. 10 (May 1989): 5-7.

Debord, Guy. *Society of the Spectacle.* Detroit: Black and Red, 1977.

Deitcher, David. "Ideas and Emotions," *Artforum*, (May 1989): 122-127.

De Lauretis, Teresa. *Alice Doesn't: Feminism, Semiotics, Cinema.* Bloomington: Indiana University Press, 1984.

De Lauretis, Teresa. *Technologies of Gender: Essays on Theory, Film, and Fiction.* Bloomington: Indiana University Press, 1987.

De Lauretis, Teresa, ed. *Feminist Studies, Critical Studies.* Bloomington: Indiana University Press, 1986.

De Lauretis, Teresa, and Stephen Heath, eds. *The Cinematic Apparatus.* London: Macmillan Press, 1980.

Deleuze, Gilles. *Bergsonism.* Translated by Hugh Tomlinson and Barbara Habberjam. New York: Zone Books, 1988.

Deleuze, Gilles. *Cinema 1: The Movement–Image.* Translated by Hugh Tomlinson and Barbara Habberjam. Minneapolis: University of Minnesota Press, 1986.

Deleuze, Gilles. *Foucault.* Translated and edited by Sean Hand. Minneapolis: University of Minnesota Press, 1988.

Deleuze, Gilles. *Nietzsche and Philosophy.* Translated by Hugh Tomlinson. New York: Columbia University Press, 1983.

Deleuze, Gilles, and Claire Parnet. *Dialogues.* Translated by Hugh Tomlinson and Barbara Habberjam. New York: Columbia University Press, 1987.

Deleuze, Gilles, and Félix Guattari. *Anti-Oedipus: Capitalism and Schizophrenia.* Translated by Robert Hurley, Mark Seem and Helen R. Lane. Minneapolis: University of Minnesota Press, 1983.

Deleuze, Gilles, and Félix Guattari. *Kafka: Toward a Minor Literature.* Translated by Dana Polan. Minneapolis: University of Minnesota Press, 1986.

Deleuze, Gilles, and Félix Guattari. *On the Line.* Translated by John Johnston. New York: Semiotext(e), 1983.

Deleuze, Gilles, and Félix Guattari. *A Thousand Plateaus: Capitalism and Schizophrenia.* Translated by Brian Massumi. Minneapolis: University of Minnesota Press, 1987.

D'Emilio, John, and Estelle B. Freedman. *Intimate Matters: A History of Sexuality in America.* New York: Harper & Row, 1988.

Derrida, Jacques. *Dissemination.* Translated by Barbara Johnson. Chicago: University of Chicago Press, 1981.

Derrida, Jacques. *The Ear of the Other: Otobiography, Transference, Translation.* Edited by Christie V. McDonald. Translated by Peggy Kamuf. New York: Schocken Books, 1985.

Derrida, Jacques. *Glas.* Translated by John P. Leavey, Jr. and Richard Rand. Lincoln: University of Nebraska Press, 1986.

Derrida, Jacques. *Margins of Philosophy.* Translated by Alan Bass. Chicago: University of Chicago Press, 1982.

Derrida, Jacques. *Memoires: For Paul de Man.* Translated by Cecile Lindsay, Johnathan Culler and Eduardo Cadava. New York: Columbia University Press, 1989.

Derrida, Jacques. *Of Grammatology.* Translated by Gayatri Chakravorty Spivak. Baltimore: Johns Hopkins University Press, 1976.

Derrida, Jacques. *Positions.* Translated by Alan Bass. Chicago: University of Chicago Press, 1981.

Derrida, Jacques. *The Postcard: from Socrates to Freud and Beyond.* Translated by Alan Bass. Chicago: University of Chicago Press, 1987.

Derrida, Jacques. *Signéponge Signsponge.*
Translated by Richard Rand.
New York: Columbia University Press, 1984.

Derrida, Jacques. *The Truth in Painting.*
Translated by Geoff Bennington and Ian McLeod.
Chicago: University of Chicago Press, 1987.

Derrida, Jacques. *Writing and Difference.*
Translated by Alan Bass.
Chicago: University of Chicago Press, 1978.

Derrida, Jacques, and Mustapha Tlili, eds. *For Nelson Mandela.* New York: Seaver Books, 1987.

Deutsche, Rosalyn. "Krzysztof Wodiczko's Homeless Projection and the Site of Urban 'Revitalization.'" *October,* no. 38 (Fall 1986): 63-98.

Deutsche, Rosalyn. "Property Values: Hans Haacke, Real Estate, and the Museum." In *Hans Haacke: Unfinished Business.* Edited by Brian Wallis. New York: The New Museum of Contemporary Art and Cambridge: MIT Press, 1986.

Deutsche, Rosalyn. "Uneven Development: Public Art in New York City." *October,* no. 47 (Winter 1988): 3-52.

Dia Art Foundation, New York. *Amerika/Tim Rollins and K.O.S.* Essays by Michele Wallace and Arthur C. Danto. Exhibition October 13, 1989–June 17, 1990.

Dinnerstein, Dorothy. *The Mermaid and the Minotaur: Sexual Arrangements and Human Malaise.* New York: Harper and Row, 1976.

Doane, Mary Ann. "The Retreat of Signs and the Failure of Words: Leslie Thornton's *Adynata,*" *Millenium Film Journal,* nos. 16/17/18 (Fall/Winter 1986–1987).

Doane, Mary Ann. "Woman's Stake: Filming the Female Body." *October,* no. 17 (Summer 1981): 23–36.

Doane, Mary Ann, Patricia Mellencamp, and Linda Williams. *Re-vision: Essays in Feminist Film Criticism.* Los Angeles: The American Film Institute and University Publications of America, 1984.

Drefus, Hubert L., and Paul Rabinow. *Michel Foucault: Beyond Structuralism and Hermeneutics.* Chicago: University of Chicago Press, 1983.

Drexler, Arthur. *Ricardo Bofill and Leon Krier: Architecture, Urbanism and History.*
New York: Museum of Modern Art, 1985.

Duberman, Martin Bauml, Martha Vicinus, and George Chauncey, Jr., eds. *Reclaiming the Past: The New Social History of Homosexuality.*
New York: New American Library, 1989.

Dynes, Wayne. *Homosexuality: A Research Guide.*
New York: Garland, 1987.

Eagleton, Terry. *Against the Grain: Essays 1975–1985.* New York: Verso, 1986.

Eagleton, Terry. *Literary Theory: An Introduction.*
Minneapolis: University of Minnesota Press, 1983.

Eisenstein, Hester, and Alice Jardine, eds. *The Future of Difference.* New Brunswick: Rutgers University Press, 1985.

Fabian, Johannes. *Time and the Other: How Anthropology Makes Its Object.* New York: Columbia University Press, 1983.

Farris, John, and Robert Farris Thompson. *David Hammons.* New York: Exit Art, 1990.

Fee, Elizabeth, and Daniel M. Fox, eds. *AIDS: The Burdens of History.*
Berkeley: University of California Press, 1988.

Felman, Shoshana, ed. *Literature and Psychoanalyis.* Baltimore: Johns Hopkins University Press, 1982.

Formations of Pleasure. London: Routledge & Kegan Paul, 1983.

Foster, Hal. *Recodings: Art, Spectacle, Cultural Politics.* Port Townsend: Bay Press, 1985.

Foster, Hal, ed. *The Anti-Aesthetic: Essays on Postmodern Culture.* Port Townsend: Bay Press, 1983.

Foster, Hal, ed. *Discussions in Contemporary Culture.* Seattle: Bay Press, 1987.

Foster, Hal, ed. *Vision and Visuality.*
Seattle: Bay Press, 1988.

Foucault, Michel. *The Archaeology of Knowledge.*
Translated by A. M. Sheridan Smith.
New York: Pantheon, 1972.

Foucault, Michel. *The Birth of the Clinic: An Archaeology of Medical Perception.* Translated by A. M. Sheridan Smith.
New York: Pantheon Books, 1973.

Foucault, Michel. *Discipline and Punish: The Birth of the Prison*. Translated by Alan Sheridan. New York: Pantheon Books, 1977.

Foucault, Michel. *The Final Foucault*. Edited by James Bernauer and David Rasmussen. Cambridge: MIT Press, 1988.

Foucault, Michel, and Maurice Blanchot. *Foucault/Blanchot*. Translated by Brian Massumi and Jeffrey Mehlman. New York: Zone Books, 1987.

Foucault, Michel. *Foucault Live (Interviews, 1966-84)*. Edited by Sylvère Lotringer. Translated by John Johnston. New York: Semiotext(e), 1989.

Foucault, Michel. *The History of Sexuality*. Translated by Robert Hurley. New York: Pantheon Books, 1978.

Foucault, Michel. *Language, Counter-Memory, Practice: Selected Essays and Interviews*. Translated by Donald F. Bouchard and Sherry Simon. Ithaca: Cornell University Press, 1977.

Foucault, Michel. *The Order of Things: An Archaeology of the Human Sciences*. New York: Random House, 1970.

Foucault, Michel. *Politics Philosophy Culture: Interviews and Other Writings 1977–1984*. Edited by Lawrence D. Kritzman. Translated by Alan Sheridan et al. New York: Routledge, Chapman and Hall, 1988.

Foucault, Michel. *Power/Knowledge: Selected Interviews and Other Writings, 1972–1977*. Translated by Colin Gordon, Leo Marshall, John Mepham and Kate Soper. New York: Pantheon, 1980.

Foucault, Michel. *This Is Not A Pipe*. Edited and translated by James Harkness. Berkeley, Los Angeles and London: University of California Press, 1982.

Fox, Marisa. "From the Belly of the Blues to the Cradle of Rap." *Details*, (August 1989): 118-124.

Frampton, Kenneth, and Sylvia Kolbowski. *Idea As Model*. New York: Institute for Architecture and Urban Studies and Rizzoli, 1981.

Frampton, Kenneth. *Modern Architecture: A Critical History*. London: Thames and Hudson, 1985.

Fraser, Nancy. "The French Derrideans: Politicizing Deconstruction or Deconstructing the Political?" *New German Critique* 33 (Fall 1984).

Freedman, Estelle B., et al., eds. *The Lesbian Issue: Essays from Signs*. Chicago: University of Chicago Press, 1985.

Frith, Simon. *Music For Pleasure: Essays in the Sociology of Pop*. New York: Routledge, 1988.

Frith, Simon, and Howard Horne. *Art into Pop*. New York: Methuen, 1987.

Frith, Simon, ed. *Facing the Music*. New York: Pantheon, 1988.

Fruitmarket Gallery, Edinburgh, Scotland. *Mary Kelly: Interim*. Essay by Laura Mulvey. Exhibition November 30, 1985–February 8, 1986.

Fusco, Coco. "Black Filmmaking in Britain's Workshop Sector." *Afterimage*, (February 1988).

Fusco, Coco. "Fantasies of Oppositionality: Reflections on Recent Conferences in Boston and New York." *Screen*, vol. 29 (Autumn 1988): 80-93.

Fusco, Coco, and Robert Knafo. "Interviews with Cuban Artists." *Social Text* 15, vol. 5, no. 3 (Fall 1986): 4–53.

Fusco, Coco, ed. *Reviewing Histories: Selections From New Latin American Cinema*. Buffalo: Hallwalls, 1987.

Gallop, Jane. *The Daughter's Seduction: Feminism and Psychoanalysis*. Ithaca: Cornell University Press, 1982.

Gallop, Jane. *Intersections, a Reading of Sade with Bataille, Blanchot, and Klossowski*. Lincoln: University of Nebraska Press, 1981.

Gallop, Jane. "Psychoanalytic Criticism: Some Intimate Questions." *Art in America* (November, 1984): 9–15.

Gallop, Jane. *Reading Lacan*. Ithaca and London: Cornell University Press, 1985.

Gallop, Jane. *Thinking Through the Body*. New York: Columbia University Press, 1988.

Gautherot, Franck, and David Ross. *Dara Birnbaum*. Dijon: Le Coin du Miroir, 1986.

Geelhaar, Christian. *Jonathon Borofsky, Zeichnugen 1960–1983*. Basel: Kunstmuseum Basel, 1983.

George, Nelson. *The Death of Rhythm and Blues*. New York: Pantheon, 1988.

Gilligan, Carol. *In A Different Voice*. Cambridge: Harvard University Press, 1982.

Gilroy, Paul, and Jim Pines. "Handsworth Songs: Audiences/Aesthetics/Independence. Interview with the Black Audio Film Collective." *Framework*, no. 35 (1988): 9–18.

Gitlin, Todd, ed. *Watching Television*. New York: Pantheon, 1988.

Goffman, Irving. *Gender Advertisments*. Cambridge: Harvard University Press, 1978.

Goodwin, Michael, and Greil Marcus. *Double Feature: Movies and Politics*. New York: Outerbridge and Lazard, 1972.

Graham, Dan, ed. *Video, Architecture, Television: Writings on Video Works, 1970–1978*. Halifax: Press of the Nova Scotia College of Art and Design and New York: New York University Press, 1979.

Gran Fury. "Control. A Project for *Artforum*." *Artforum* (October 1989): 129–30, 167–68.

Grossberg, Lawrence. "On Postmodernism and Articulation: An Interview with Stuart Hall." *Critical Inquiry*, vol. 10, no. 2 (Summer, 1986): 45–60.

Guha, Ranajit, and Gayatri C. Spivak, eds. *Selected Subaltern Studies*. New York: Oxford University Press, 1988.

"*Handsworth Songs*: Some Background Notes and Interviews." *Framework*, no. 35 (1988): 4–18.

Harris, Bertha. *Confessions of Cherubino*. New York: Harcourt Brace Jovanovich, 1972.

Harris, Bertha. *Lover*. Plainfield: Daughters, 1976.

Heath, Stephen. *Questions of Cinema*. London: Macmillan, 1981.

Heath, Stephen. *The Sexual Fix*. London: Macmillan, 1982.

Heath, Stephen, and Patricia Mellencamp, eds. *Cinema and Language*. Frederick: University Publications of America, 1983.

Hebdige, Dick. *Cut 'N' Mix: Culture, Identity and Carribean Music*. New York: Methuen, 1987.

Hebdige, Dick. *Hiding in the Light: On Images and Things*. New York: Routledge, 1988.

Hebdige, Dick. *Subculture, the Meaning of Style*. London: Methuen, 1979.

Henry, Tricia. *Break All Rules! Punk Rock and the Making of a Style*. Ann Arbor: U.M.I. Research Press, 1989.

Heyward, Carl. "Anthony Davis and Episteme: Xcerpts From *X*: The Life and Times of Malcolm X." *High Performance*, no. 39 (1987): 78-9.

Hirsh, Jr., E. D., Jack Hitt, John Kalinski, John Pareles, Roger Shattuck, and Gayatri Chakravorty Spivak. "Who Needs the Great Works?" *Harper's*, vol. 279, no. 1672 (September, 1989): 43–52.

Hirshhorn, Harriet. "Interview with Trinh T. Minh-ha," *Heresies*, no. 19 (Fall/Winter, 1987-8): 14–17.

Horrigan, Bill, "Adolescent Junglebook overschrijdt Scenic Paradise: A Note on *Peggy and Fred in Hell*." *Mediamatic*, vol. 4, no. 1/2 (Fall 1989): 65–68.

Huyssen, Andreas. *After the Great Divide*. Bloomington: Indiana University Press, 1986.

Institute of Contemporary Art, Boston. *Endgame*. Essays by Thomas Crow, Yves-Alain Bois, Elizabeth Sussman, David Joselit, Hal Foster, and Bob Riley. Exhibition September 25–November 30, 1986.

Institute of Contemporary Art, Boston. *Utopia Post Utopia: Configurations of Nature and Culture in Recent Sculpture and Photography*. Essays by Frederic Jameson, et al. Exhibition January 29–March 27, 1988.

Irigaray, Luce. *This Sex Which is Not One*. Ithaca: Cornell University Press, 1985.

Jameson, Fredric. *The Ideologies of Theory: Essays 1971–1986*. 2 vols. Minneapolis: University of Minnesota Press, 1988.

Jameson, Fredric. *The Prison-House of Language: A Critical Account of Structuralism and Russian Formalism*. Princeton: Princeton University Press, 1972.

Jardine, Alice. "Deleuze and His (Br)others." *Sub-Stance* 13, no. 3/4 (1984): 46–60.

Jardine, Alice. *Gynesis: Configurations of Woman and Modernity*. Ithaca: Cornell University Press, 1985.

Jardine, Alice, and Paul Smith, eds. *Men in Feminism*. New York: Methuen, 1987.

Jayamanne, Laleen, Geeta Kapur, and Yvonne Rainer. "Discussing Modernity, 'Third World,' and *The Man Who Envied Women.*" *Art & Text*, vol. 23, no. 4 (March–May, 1987): 41-51.

Jayamanne, Laleen. "Image in the Heart (1)." *Framework*, no. 36 (1989): 33-41.

Jayamanne, Laleen. "Passive Competence." *Screen*, no. 28 (Autumn, 1987): 107-120.

Jencks, Charles. *What is Post-Modernism?* London: Academy Editions, 1986.

Johnson, Philip, and Mark Wigley. *Deconstructivist Architecture.* New York: Museum of Modern Art, 1988.

Johnson, Philip. *Writings.* New York: Oxford University Press, 1979.

Johnson, Philip, and John Burgee. *Architecture 1979–1985.* New York: Rizzoli, 1985.

Johnson, Tom. *The Voice of New Music.* Eindhoven, The Netherlands: Colophon, 1989.

Julien, Isaac, and Kobena Mercer, eds. *The Last 'Special Issue' on Race?* Special issue, *Screen*, vol. 29, no. 4 (Autumn, 1988).

Kaplan, E. Anne., ed. *Postmodernism and Its Discontents: Theories, Practices.* London: Verso, 1988.

Kaplan, E. Anne., ed. *Regarding Television: Critical Approaches.* Frederick: University Publications of America, 1983.

Kaplan, E. Anne. *Rocking Around the Clock.* New York and London: Methuen, 1989.

Kardon, Janet. *Laurie Anderson: Works From 1969 to 1983.* Philadelphia: Institute of Contemporary Art, 1983.

Kardon, Janet, Lawrence Alloway, Nancy Foote, and Ian McHaig. *Urban Encounters: Art, Architecture, Audience.* Philadelphia: Institute of Contemporary Art, 1981.

Kenny, Lorraine. "Dreams and Economies: An Interview with Judith Williamson." *Afterimage*, vol. 15, no. 1 (Summer, 1987): 18–21.

Keohane, N. M. Rosaldo, and B. Gelpi, eds. *Feminist Theory: A Critique of Ideology.* Chicago: University of Chicago Press, 1982.

Kimmel, Michael S. *Gender and Desire.* New York: Basic Books, 1989.

Kolbowski, Silvia, ed. *Sexuality: Re/Positions.* Special issue, *Wedge*, no. 6 (Winter, 1984).

Krauss, Rosalind. *The Originality of the Avant-Garde and Other Modernist Myths.* Cambridge: MIT Press, 1985.

Krier, Leon. *Houses, Palaces, Cities.* London: Architectural Design AD Editions, 1984.

Kristeva, Julia. *About Chinese Women.* Translated by Anita Barrows. New York and London: M. Boyars, 1986.

Kristeva, Julia. *Desire in Language: A Semiotic Approach to Literature and Art.* Edited by Leon S. Roudiez. Translated by Thomas Gara and Alice Jardine. New York: Columbia University Press, 1980.

Kristeva, Julia. *In the Beginning Was Love: Psychoanalysis and Faith.* Translated by Arthur Goldhammer. New York: Columbia University Press, 1987.

Kristeva, Julia. *The Kristeva Reader.* Edited by Toril Moi. New York: Columbia University Press, 1986.

Kristeva, Julia. *Powers of Horror: An Essay on Abjection.* Translated by Leon S. Roudiez. New York: Columbia University Press, 1982.

Kristeva, Julia. *Revolution in Poetic Language.* Translated by Margaret Waller. New York: Columbia University Press, 1984.

Kristeva, Julia. *Tales of Love.* Translated by Leon S. Roudiez. New York: Columbia University Press, 1987.

Kruger, Barbara. "*The Passion of Remembrance* and *Handsworth Songs.*" *Artforum*, no. 27 (September, 1988): 143-4.

Kruger, Barbara, and Phil Mariani, eds. *Remaking History.* Seattle: Bay Press, 1989.

Krupnick, Mark, ed. *Displacements: Derrida and After.* Bloomington: Indiana University Press, 1983.

Lajer-Burcharth, Ewa. *Counter Monuments: Krzysztof Wodiczko's Public Projections.* Cambridge: MIT Press, 1987.

Lajer-Burcharth, Ewa. "Urban Disturbances." *Art in America*, (November, 1987): 146-53, 197.

Lazere, Donald, ed. *American Media and Mass Culture.* Berkeley and Los Angeles: University of California Press, 1987.

Lefebvre, Henri. *Everyday Life in the Modern World*. Translated by Sacha Rabinovitch. New York: Harper & Row, 1971.

Leffingwell, Edward, and Karen Marta, eds. *Modern Dreams: the Rise and Fall of Pop*. New York: Institute for Contemporary Art, 1988.

Lemert, Charles C., and Garth Gillan. *Michel Foucault: Social Theory as Transgression*. New York: Columbia University Press, 1982.

Lippard, Lucy R. *Get the Message? A Decade of Art for Social Change*. New York: E. P. Dutton, 1984.

Los Angeles Contemporary Exhibitions, *Against Nature: A Group Show of Work by Homosexual Men*. Statements by Dennis Cooper, Richard Hawkins, John Greyson, Hudson, Gary Indiana, Kevin Killian, Boyd McDonald, and Matias Viegener. Exhibition January 6–February 12, 1988.

Lurie, David V., and Krzysztof Wodiczko. "Homeless Vehicle Project" and "Conversations About a Project for a Homeless Vehicle." *October*, no. 47 (Winter, 1988): 53-67.

Lyotard, Jean-François. *The Postmodern Condition: A Report on Knowledge*. Translated by Geoff Bennington and Brian Massumi. Minneapolis: University of Minnesota Press, 1984.

MacDonald, Scott. *A Critical Cinema: Interviews with Independent Filmmakers*. Berkeley and Los Angeles: University of California Press, 1988.

McRobbie, Angela. "Strategies of Vigilance: An Interview with Gayatri Chakravorty Spivak." *Block* 10 (1985): 9.

Marcus, Greil. *Lipstick Traces*. Cambridge: Harvard University Press, 1989.

Marcus, Greil. *Mystery Train: Images of America in Rock 'n' Roll Music*. New York: Dutton, 1982.

Mariani, Phil, and Brian Wallis, eds. *Partial Texts: Essays and Fiction*. Special issue, *Wedge*, nos. 3/4/5 (1983).

Marks, Elaine, and Isabelle de Courtivron, eds. *New French Feminisms*. New York: Schocken Books, 1981.

Mars-Jones, Adams, and Edmund White. *The Darker Proof: Stories From a Crisis*. London and Boston: Faber and Faber, 1987.

Mercer, Kobena, ed. *Black Film/British Cinema*. *ICA Documents* 7. London: Institute of Contemporary Arts, 1988.

Millett, Kate. *The Basement: Meditations on a Human Sacrifice*. New York: Simon and Schuster, 1979.

Millett, Kate. *Going to Iran*. New York: Coward, McCann & Geoghegan, 1982.

Millett, Kate. *Sexual Politics*. Garden City: Doubleday, 1970.

Millett, Kate. *Sita*. New York: Farrar, Strauss and Giroux, 1977.

Mitchell, W. J. T., ed. *The Politics of Interpretation*. Chicago: University of Chicago Press, 1984.

Modleski, Tania, ed. *Studies in Entertainment: Critical Approaches to Mass Culture*. Bloomington: Indiana University Press, 1986.

Morse, Margaret. "The Architecture of Representation: Video Works by Judith Barry." *Afterimage*, (October, 1987): 8-11.

Mulvey, Laura. "Melodrama Inside and Outside the Home." In *High Theory/Low Culture*. ed. Colin MacCabe. Manchester, UK: Manchester University Press, 1986.

Mulvey, Laura. *Visual and Other Pleasures*. Bloomington: Indiana University Press, 1989.

Museum of Modern Art, New York. *Committed to Print*. Essay by Deborah Wye. Exhibition January 31–April 19, 1988.

The New Museum of Contemporary Art, New York. *Art and Ideology*. Essays by Benjamin H. D. Buchloh, Donald Kuspit, Lucy Lippard, Nilda Peraza, and Lowery Sims. Exhibition February 4–March 18, 1984.

The New Museum of Contemporary Art, New York. *Damaged Goods: Desire and the Economy of the Object*. Essays by Gretchen Bender, Allan McCollum, Hal Foster, et al. Exhibition June 21–August 10, 1986.

The New Museum of Contemporary Art, New York. *Extended Sensibilities*. Essay by Daniel J. Cameron. Exhibition October 16–December 30, 1982.

The New Museum of Contemporary Art, New York. *Impresario: Malcolm McLaren & the British New Wave*. Essays by Paul Taylor, Jane Withers, Jon Savage, and Dan Graham. Exhibition September 16–November 20, 1988.

The New Museum of Contemporary Art, New York. *John Baldessari: Work 1966–1980*. Essays by Marcia Tucker, and Robert Pincus-Witten. Interview by Nancy Drew. Exhibition March 14–April 28, 1981.

Norris, Christopher. *Derrida*. Cambridge: Harvard University Press, 1987.

Olander, William. "The Window on Broadway by Act Up." *On View* (handout), New York: The New Museum of Contemporary Art, 1987.

Parker, Rozsika, and Griselda Pollock, eds. *Framing Feminism: Art and the Women's Movement 1970–85*. New York: Routledge & Kegan Paul, 1987.

Parker, Rozsika, and Griselda Pollock. *Old Mistresses: Women, Art and Ideology*. New York: Pantheon, 1981.

Penley, Constance, and Andrew Ross. "An Interview with Trinh T. Minh-ha." *Camera Obscura* 13/14 (1985): 87–103.

Pines, Jim. *Blacks in Films: A Survey of Racial Themes and Images in the American Film*. London: Studio Vista, 1975.

Pines, Jim. *Blacks in the Cinema: The Changing Image*. London: British Film Institute (Education Department), 1971.

Pines, Jim. "The Passion of Remembrance: Interview." *Framework*, no. 32/33 (1986): 92–99.

Podesta, Patti, ed. *Resolution: A Critique of Video Art*. Los Angeles: Los Angeles Contemporary Exhibitions, 1986.

Poggioli, Renato. *Theory of the Avant Garde*. Cambridge: Harvard University Press, 1968.

Polan, Dana B. *The Political Language of Film and the Avant-Garde*. Ann Arbor and London: UMI Research, 1985.

Pollock, Griselda. "Agency and the Avant-Guarde." *Block* (Spring, 1989): 5–15.

Pollock, Griselda. *Vision and Difference: Femininity, Feminism and the Histories of Art*. London: Routledge, 1988.

Poster, Mark. *Foucault, Marxism and History*. Cambridge: Polity Press, 1984.

Preziosi, Donald. *Rethinking Art History*. New Haven: Yale University Press, 1989.

Raven, Arlene. *Crossing Over: Feminism and Art of Social Concern*. Ann Arbor: UMI Research Press, 1988.

Reich, Steve. *Writings About Music*. Halifax: Press of Nova Scotia College of Art and Design and New York: New York University Press, 1974.

Reid, Calvin. "Chasing the Blue Train." *Art in America*, (September 1989): 196-7.

Reid, Jamie. *Up They Rise*. London: Faber, 1987.

Riverside Studios, London. *Tim Rollins + K.O.S.* Essays by Jean Fisher and Mardo Daniel. Exhibition July 27–August 21, 1988.

Rodman, Seldon. *Conversations With Artists*. New York: Capricorn Books, 1961.

Rollins, Tim. "Art as Social Action: An Interview with Conrad Atkinson." *Art in America*, no. 2 (February, 1980): 118-123.

Rollins, Tim, and K.O.S. *Collaboration Tim Rollins and K.O.S.* Special Issue, *Parkett*, no. 20 (1989).

Rose, Jacqueline. *Sexuality in the Field of Vision*. London: Verso, 1986.

Rosenthal, Mark, and Richard Marshall. *Jonathan Borofsky*. Philadelphia: Philadelphia Museum of Art, 1984.

Ross, Andrew. *No Respect: Intellectuals and Popular Culture*. London: Routledge, 1989.

Rowbotham, Sheila. *Women's Consciousness, Man's World*. Harmondsworth: Penguin, 1973.

Rubin, William. *Dada, Surrealism, and Their Heritage*. New York: Museum of Modern Art, 1967.

Rubin, William, ed. *"Primitivism" in 20th Century Art: Affinity of the Tribal and Modern*. 2 vols. New York: The Museum of Modern Art, 1984.

Ruskin, Cindy. *The Quilt: Stories for the Names Project*. New York: Pocket Books, 1988.

Russo, Vito. *The Celluloid Closet: Homosexuality in the Movies*. New York: Harper & Row, 1981.

Said, Edward W. *After the Last Sky: Palestinian Lives*. New York: Pantheon Books, 1986.

Said, Edward W. *Beginnings: Intention and Method*. New York: Columbia University Press, 1985.

Said, Edward W., *Covering Islam: How the Media and the Experts Determine How We See the Rest of the World*. New York: Pantheon Books, 1981.

Said, Edward W. *Orientalism*. New York: Pantheon, 1978.

Said, Edward W. *The Question of Palestine*. New York: Times Books, 1979.

Said, Edward W. *The World, the Text and the Critic*. Cambridge: Harvard University Press, 1983.

Said, Edward W., and Christopher Hitchens, eds. *Blaming the Victims: Spurious Scholarship and the Palestinian Question*. New York: Verso, 1988

Salusinszky, Imre. *Criticism in Society*. New York: Methuen, 1987.

Schneider, Cynthia, and Brian Wallis, eds. *Global Television*. New York: Wedge Press and Cambridge: MIT Press, 1988.

Sennett, Richard. *Authority*. New York: Vintage Books, 1980.

Sidran, Ben. *Black Talk*. New York: Da Capo Press, 1983.

Simon, Joan. "An Interview with Jonathan Borofsky." *Art in America* (November, 1981): 156–167.

Smart, Barry. *Foucault, Marxism and Critique*. London: Routledge & Kegan Paul, 1983.

Smith, Joe. *Off the Record: An Oral History of Popular Music*. Edited by Mitchell Fink. New York: Unison Productions, 1988.

Smith-Rubenzahl, Ian. "Krzysztof Wodiczko: An Interview." *C Magazine*, no. 12 (Winter, 1987): 58-63.

Sontag, Susan. *AIDS and Its Metaphors*. New York: Farrar, Strauss, and Giroux, 1989.

Sontag, Susan. *Illness as Metaphor*. New York: Farrar, Strauss, and Giroux, 1978.

Spivak, Gayatri, and Ellen Rooney. "In a Word." *differences*, vol. 1, no.2 (Summer, 1989): 124–156.

Spivak, Gayatri. *In Other Worlds: Essays in Cultural Politics*. New York: Methuen, 1987.

Spivak, Gayatri. *Master Discourse Native Informant*. New York, Columbia University Press, (forthcoming).

Stephanson, Anders. "An Interview with Fredric Jameson." *Flash Art*, no. 131 (December, 1986/January 1987): 69–73.

Stern, Simon. "Lesbian and Gay Studies: A Selective Bibliography." *Yale Journal of Criticism*, vol. 3, no.1 (1989): 253–260.

Suleiman, Susan Rubin, ed. *The Female Body in Western Civilization: Contemporary Perspectives*. Cambridge: Harvard University Press, 1985.

Taylor, Paul, ed. *Post-Pop Art*. Cambridge: MIT Press, 1989.

Thornton, Leslie. "We Ground Things Now, on a Moving Ground." *Motion Picture*, vol. 3, no. 1/2 (Winter, 1989–90): 13–15.

Tisdall, Caroline. *Joseph Beuys*. London: Thames and Hudson, 1979.

Toop, David. *Rap Attack: African Jive to New York Hip Hop*. Boston: South End Press, 1984.

Trinh T. Minh-ha. *Woman, Native, Other*. Bloomington: Indiana University Press, 1989.

Trinh T. Minh-ha, ed. *She, The Inappropriate/d Other*. Special Issue, *Discourse*, no. 8 (Fall/Winter, 1986–1987).

Trinh T. Minh-ha, ed. *(Un)Naming Cultures*. Special Issue, *Discourse*, no. 11.2 (Spring/Summer, 1989).

Venturi, Robert. *Complexity and Contradiction in Architecture*. New York: Museum of Modern Art, 1977.

Vermorel, Fred and Judy. *Sex Pistols: The Inside Story*. London: Omnibus, 1987.

Wallis, Brian, ed. *Art After Modernism: Rethinking Representation*. New York: The New Museum of Contemporary Art and Boston: David R. Godine, 1984.

Wallis, Brian, ed. *Blasted Allegories*. New York: The New Museum of Contemporary Art and Cambridge: MIT Press, 1987.

Watney, Simon. *Policing Desire: Pornography, AIDS, and the Media*. Minneapolis: University of Minnesota Press, 1987.

Weinstein, Jeff. *Learning to Eat*. Los Angeles: Sun & Moon Press, 1988.

Weiss, Andrea. *Before Stonewall: The Making of a Gay and Lesbian Community.* Tallahasee: Naiad, 1988.

White Edmund. "The Art of Fiction CV." *The Paris Review,* no. 108 (Fall, 1988): 46–80.

White, Edmund. *A Boy's Own Story.* New York: Dutton, 1982.

White, Edmund. *Nocturnes for the King of Naples.* New York: St. Martin's Press, 1978.

White, Edmund. *States of Desire: Travels in Gay America.* New York: Dutton, 1980.

Whitney Museum of American Art, New York. *Image World.* Essays by John G. Hanhart, Marvin Heiferman, and Lisa Phillips. Exhibition November 8, 1989–February 18, 1990.

Williams, Raymond. *Culture and Society, 1780–1950.* New York: Harper and Row, 1966.

Williams, Raymond. *Keywords: A Vocabulary of Culture and Society.* New York: Oxford University Press, 1976.

Williams, Raymond. *The Politics of Modernism: Against the New Conformists.* London: Verso, 1989.

Williams, Raymond. *Resources of Hope.* London: Verso, 1989.

Williams, Raymond. *Writing in Society.* London: Verso, 1983.

Williamson, Judith. *Consuming Passions: The Dynamics of Popular Culture.* New York: Marion Boyars, 1986.

Williamson, Judith. *Decoding Advertisments: Ideology and Meaning in Advertising.* New York: Marion Boyars, 1978.

Williamson, Judith. "Two Kinds of Otherness: Black Film and the Avant-garde." *Screen,* vol. 29, no. 4 (Autumn, 1988): 106–112.

Wodiczko, Krzysztof. "Design and Interviews for the Homeless Vehicle Project," *White Walls 19* (Spring, 1988): 65-79.

Wodiczko, Krzysztof, and Rudolph Luria. "The Homeless Vehicle Project," *Sites 20,* (Spring, 1988): 58-59.

Wodiczko, Krzysztof. "Questionnaire 16." *Zone 1/2* (1986): 456 -459.

Wollen, Peter, Greil Marcus, Tom Levin, et al. *On The Passage of a Few People Through a Rather Brief Moment in Time: Situationists 1957–1972.* Cambridge: MIT Press, 1989.

Wollen, Peter. *Readings and Writings.* London: Verso, 1982.

Wollen, Peter. *Signs and Meaning in the Cinema.* Bloomington and London: Indiana University Press, 1969

Young, Robert, ed. *Sexual Difference.* Special Issue, *Oxford Literary Review,* Volume 8 (1986).